# General, Organic, and Biochemistry

## NINTH EDITION

### Katherine J. Denniston

Towson University

### Joseph J. Topping

Towson University

### Danaè R. Quirk Dorr

Minnesota State University, Mankato

### Robert L. Caret

University System of Maryland

## Volume 1

MINNESOTA STATE UNIVERSITY MANKATO

3 4 5 6 7 8 9 0 BKM BKM 19 18 17 16

ISBN-13: 978-1-259-95035-3
ISBN-10: 1-259-95035-2

*Solutions Program Manager: Mark Bodensteiner*
*Project Manager: Lisa Haverland*
*Cover Photo Credits: ©ioshertz/Getty Images*

# Preface

## To Our Students

Just as some researchers study chemical change, others study learning. The two are related: there are measurable changes in the brain as learning occurs. While the research on brain chemistry and learning continues, the research on learning has taught us some very successful strategies for teaching and learning chemistry. For instance, we now know that building long-term memory requires "repetitions." When you exercise to build muscle strength, you perform some number of "reps" of each exercise for each muscle that you wish to build. That is exactly what you need to do to build your long-term memory and understanding. The Center for Academic Success at the Louisiana State University has devised study tools that have allowed students to improve their performance by a full letter grade, or higher. The following is the Study Cycle with five stages that provide the "reps" needed to perform well in any course:

1. *Preview* the chapter *before* class. Either the evening before or the day of class, skim the material; pay attention to the end-of-chapter summary with boldfaced key terms, chapter map, the learning goals, and headings. Think of questions you would like the instructor to answer. Think of this 10 minutes as your "warm up."

2. *Attend* class! Be an active participant in the class, asking and answering questions and taking thoughtful, meaningful notes. Class time is much more meaningful if you have already familiarized yourself with the organization and key concepts to be discussed.

3. *Review* your notes as soon as possible after class. Fill in any gaps that exist and note any additional questions that arise. This also takes about 10 minutes; think of it as your "cool down" period.

4. *Study.* Since repetition is the key to success, The Center for Academic Success recommends 3–5 short, but intense, study sessions each day. These intense study sessions should have a very structured organization. In the first 2–5 minutes, establish your goal for the session. Spend the next 30–50 minutes studying with focus and action. Organize the material, make flash cards to help you review, draw concept maps to define the relationship among ideas, and practice problem solving. Then reward yourself with a 5–10 minute break. Call a friend, play Angry Birds, or do anything you find enjoyable. Then take 5 minutes to review the material. Finally, about once a week, perhaps on the weekend, review all of the material that you have been studying throughout the week.

5. *Assess* your progress. Are you able to solve the questions and problems at the end of the chapter? Can you explain the concepts to others? The assessment will affirm what you know well and reveal what you need to study further.

The Center for Academic Success has many other suggestions to help students learn how to learn. You can find their online tutorials and workshops at www.cas.lsu.edu.

## To the Instructor

The ninth edition of *General, Organic, and Biochemistry*, like our earlier editions, has been designed to help undergraduate majors in health-related fields understand key concepts and appreciate significant connections among chemistry, health, and the treatment of disease. We have tried to strike a balance between theoretical and practical chemistry, while emphasizing material that is unique to health-related studies. We have written at a level intended for students whose professional goals do not include a mastery of chemistry, but for whom an understanding of the principles and practice of chemistry is a necessity.

Although our emphasis is the importance of chemistry to the health-related professions, we wanted this book to be appropriate for all students who need a one- or two-semester introduction to chemistry. Students learn best when they are engaged. One way to foster that engagement is to help them see clear relationships between the subject and real life. For these reasons, we have included perspectives and essays that focus on medicine and the function of the human body, as well as the environment, forensic science, and even culinary arts.

We begin that engagement with the book cover. Students may wonder why the cover has a photo of the Caucasian snowdrop (*Galanthus caucasicus*). What does this flower have to do with the study of chemistry or the practice of medicine? They will learn that Russian scientists extracted the drug galantamine from this plant in the early 1950s and others found that it was useful in treating nerve pain and poliomyelitis. More recently, it has been discovered that the drug is a reversible, competitive inhibitor of the enzyme acetylcholinesterase and that it can cross the blood-brain barrier. These characteristics have made it a useful drug for the treatment of mild to moderate Alzheimer's Disease. By inhibiting the enzyme, galantamine increases the amount of acetylcholine in the brain; this, in turn, enhances brain function, memory, and the ability to think more clearly.

The cover sets the theme for the book: chemistry is not an abstract study, but one that has an immediate impact on our lives. We try to spark student interest with an art program that uses relevant photography, clear and focused figures, and perspectives and essays that bring life to abstract ideas. We reinforce key concepts by explaining them in a clear and concise way and encouraging students to apply the concept to solve problems. We provide guidance through the inclusion of a large number of in-chapter examples that are solved in a stepwise fashion and that provide students the opportunity to test their understanding through the practice problems that follow and the suggested end-of-chapter questions and problems that apply the same concepts.

# Green Chemistry

# Kitchen Chemistry

# Chemistry at the Crime Scene

# Perspectives

# Contents

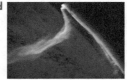

# Brief Contents

## GENERAL CHEMISTRY

## Foundations for Our Revisions

In the preparation of each edition, we have been guided by the collective wisdom of reviewers who are expert chemists and excellent teachers. They represent experience in community colleges, liberal arts colleges, comprehensive institutions, and research universities. We have followed their recommendations, while remaining true to our overriding goal of writing a readable, student-centered text. This edition has also been designed to be amenable to a variety of teaching styles. Each feature incorporated into this edition has been carefully considered with regard to how it may be used to support student learning in both the traditional classroom and the flipped learning environment.

Also for this edition, we are very pleased to have been able to incorporate real student data points and input, derived from thousands of our LearnSmart users, to help guide our revision. LearnSmart Heat Maps provided a quick visual snapshot of usage of portions of the text and the relative difficulty students experienced in mastering the content. With these data, we were able to hone not only our text content but also the LearnSmart probes.

- If the data indicated that the subject covered was more difficult than other parts of the book, as evidenced by a high proportion of students responding incorrectly, we substantively revised or reorganized the content to be as clear and illustrative as possible.
- In some sections, the data showed that a smaller percentage of the students had difficulty learning the material. In those cases, we revised the *text* to provide a clearer presentation by rewriting the section, providing additional examples to strengthen student problem-solving skills, designing new text art or figures to assist visual learners, etc.
- In other cases, one or more of the LearnSmart probes for a section was not as clear as it might be or did not appropriately reflect the content. In these cases, the *probe*, rather than the text, was edited.

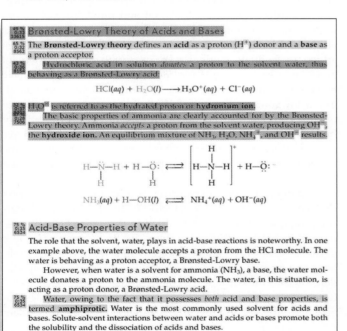

The previous image is an example of one of the heat maps from Chapter 8 that was particularly useful in guiding our revisions. The highlighted sections indicate the various levels of difficulty students experienced in learning the material. This evidence informed all of the revisions described in the "New in This Edition" section of this preface.

The following is a summary of the additions and refinements that we have included in this edition.

## New in This Edition

- Chapters 4 and 8 were completely reorganized for better integration and discussion of acid-base and oxidation-reduction reactions.
- **Two new Kitchen Chemistry boxes and eight new Perspective boxes** have been added to the ninth edition to help students see the connections between chemistry and their daily lives and future careers.
- **Each of the following sections was either rewritten or significantly revised for enhanced clarity and student understanding:** 1.1, 1.2, 1.4, and 1.5; 2.1, 2.2, and 2.3; 4.4 and 4.5–4.8 (new to the chapter and revised); 5.1; 6.4; 7.4; 8.1; 9.7; 10.1, 10.2, 10.4, and 10.5; 11.5; 12.1 and 12.3–12.5; 13.1, 13.2, and 13.4; 14.1–14.4; 15.1 and 15.3; 16.2–16.4; 17.3; 18.4–18.5 and 18.7; 19.3, 19.4, and 19.6–19.8; 20.2, 20.8, and 20.10; 21.1–21.5; 23.1, 23.4, and 23.6.

**Chapter 1** We have revised or added eight new learning goals to help the student identify the key concepts in the chapter. As with the last edition, each goal is used to label relevant sections and examples. Recognizing the importance of visual learning, we have revised six figures and introduced four new photos. Each of the tables, important devices for summarizing information, has also been revised. We recognize that students learn by doing and, to that end, we have paid special attention to the worked examples, with thirteen new or revised examples included. We challenge the student with in-chapter and end-of-chapter problems, forty-one of which are new or revised. The first chapter of the textbook develops fundamental skills that will be needed throughout the book, and we have revised or rewritten four of these critical sections, 1.1, 1.2, 1.4, and 1.5. Organizing and summarizing concepts is an important aspect of learning; for this reason, we have revised both the Summary and Chapter Map.

**Chapter 2** We continued our focus on helping students identify key concepts by adding or revising nine learning goals focusing on the structure of the atom and the periodic table. In addition, all ten of the examples are either new or modified with reworked solutions to enhance clarity. Three of the new examples, *Determining Ion Proton and Electron Composition*, *Writing Shorthand Electron Configurations for Ions*, and *Determining Isoelectronic Ions and Atoms* help students understand the octet rule and ion formation. The introduction and sections featuring isotopes and electromagnetic radiation have been rewritten. Six figures and two tables are new or revised.

**Chapter 3** We have introduced three new learning goals and revised four others. Figure 3.2 has been revised in order to help clarify the concept of covalent bonding. Bonding is fundamentally important to gaining a real understanding of chemistry; for that reason, we have paid special attention to Section 3.1,

Chemical Bonding, rewriting and revising where necessary, to provide a strong foundation for subsequent topics. Students must also learn to apply the concepts of bonding, structure, and the properties of ions and molecules. For that reason, we have added 30 new or revised in-chapter or end-of-chapter problems and questions. Both the Chapter Map and Summary have been revised to reflect changes in the chapter material.

**Chapter 4** Chemical changes have been further developed in this chapter in conjunction with calculations and the chemical equation. Significant emphasis has been placed on problem solving beginning with the introduction of nine new and two revised learning goals, nineteen new or revised examples and forty-six new or revised questions and problems. Section 4.4, Balancing Chemical Equations, has been revised, and Sections 4.5–4.8 are new to this chapter. These sections include precipitation reactions, net-ionic equations, acid-base reactions, and oxidation-reduction reactions. Four new pictures and five figures have been added or modified, including Figure 4.10, an illustration supporting the limiting reactant concept. The Summary and Chapter Map have been revised to be consistent with the topics and learning goals of the chapter.

**Chapter 5** Four new or revised learning goals have been introduced in the ninth edition to help students focus on key concepts. A comprehensive art program is critical to teaching and learning properties of gases, liquids, and solids. We have introduced five new or revised figures and nine new or revised figure captions, as well as three new photos to illustrate the effects of temperature and pressure on the behavior of the states of matter and the conversion between solids, liquids, and gases. Section 5.1, discussing the properties of gases and the ideal gas laws, has been revised to enhance clarity. Two revised examples and thirteen new or revised questions and problems were used to enhance problem-solving skills. The medical perspective, *Blood Gases and Respiration* has been moved to Chapter 6, where it accompanies the discussion of Henry's law. The Summary and Chapter Map were revised to assist students in organizing concepts as well as seeing the relationships that exist between the concepts discussed in the chapter.

**Chapter 6** Several learning goals have been added or revised. Eight of the chapter examples have been modified with reworked solutions in order to enhance clarity. The discussion pertaining to osmosis, osmotic pressure, and osmolarity has been amended. Twenty new or revised questions and problems have been added to correlate to the new and revised material within the chapter. The Summary and Chapter Map have been improved for better alignment with the discussions pertaining to concentration and concentration-dependent properties.

**Chapter 7** As in other chapters, we have paid special attention to the learning goals and introduction, revising where appropriate, to lead the students to understand three topics: thermodynamics, kinetics, and equilibrium. These topics are a critical part of any discussion of chemical and physical change. Opportunities for visual learning have been enhanced with three new or revised figures, six new or revised figure captions, and six new photographs. Section 7.4, dealing with equilibrium, was revised to enhance clarity. Eight new or revised questions and problems have been added to provide greater

opportunity for students to learn by doing. The Summary and Chapter Map have been revised to reflect changes in the chapter material.

**Chapter 8** The emphasis of this chapter has been changed to focus primarily on acids and bases. Oxidation and reduction content has been moved to Chapter 4. Ten new learning goals have been added to correlate to the new and revised content. The Introduction and Section 8.1, Acids and Bases, have been rewritten to incorporate acids and bases commonly used in organic chemistry. Topics revised include acid and base theories, the amphiprotic nature of water, conjugate acid-base pairs, acid and base strength, self-ionization of water, and $K_w$. The revision includes new figures and images. Five new or revised examples, two new practice problems, and thirty-six new or revised questions and problems provide students with an opportunity to practice solving problems correlating to the learning goals emphasized. The Summary and Chapter Map have been revised in alignment with the changes to the chapter content.

**Chapter 9** Two new learning goals have been added to help students identify essential concepts. The topic of nuclear chemistry can be difficult for students to conceptualize. To help overcome this problem, we have introduced three new or revised figures, twelve new or revised figure captions, and eleven new photos. Section 9.7 has been updated, including additional radiation measurement units. Thirteen new or revised questions and problems have been added, as well as four revised examples, reflecting an increased emphasis on improving the student's problem-solving skills. Both the Summary and Chapter Map have been revised to help students understand the basic concepts and their interrelationships.

**Chapter 10** A new perspective, *Kitchen Chemistry: Alkanes in our Food,* including two For Further Understanding questions, has been added to the revised Chapter 10. Six new margin notes, many with associated art, have been added to help students understand line formulas, alkyl groups, the classification of carbon atoms, identification and numbering of parent carbon chains in nomenclature, and placement of substituents above and below a cycloalkane ring. A new figure has been added to facilitate student comprehension of the variety of bonding patterns in organic molecules. Several topics have been rewritten to provide students with a deeper understanding of the content. These include the discussion of families of organic compounds, functional groups, physical properties of hydrocarbons, classification of carbon atoms and alkyl groups, nomenclature, free rotation around a bond, and halogenation. Six new problems have been added to accompany the revised content.

**Chapter 11** A new perspective, *Kitchen Chemistry: Pumpkin Pie Spice: An Autumn Tradition,* including two For Further Understanding questions, has been added to the revised Chapter 11. A new Example, *Writing Equations for the Hydrogenation of a Cycloalkane,* has been added, along with a set of practice problems and a set of recommended practice problems to help students master the concept. Two new problems have been added to accompany the revisions in the text. The revisions, along with new margin notes and text art, are intended to enhance student learning and understanding. Topics revised include physical characteristics, nomenclature, geometric isomers, and parts of the section on the reactions of alkenes and alkynes. A new table, and accompanying text, on saturated and unsaturated fatty acids has been added to help students recognize the practical applications of the chemistry being studied.

**Chapter 12** A new Example, *Using the Common System of Nomenclature to Name Alcohols,* has been added, along with a set of practice problems and a set of recommended practice problems to help students master the concept. The *Medical Perspective: Fetal Alcohol Syndrome,* has been updated to reflect the more recently described Fetal Alcohol Spectrum Disorder. New text art has been designed to help students understand the physical properties of alcohols and the nature of intramolecular hydrogen bonding. Revision of the discussion of intramolecular hydrogen bonding, along with the new text art, provides students with a clear idea of the importance of hydrogen bonding in biological systems. The information on general anesthetics has been updated, and sections on physical properties, dehydration reactions, and oxidation of alcohols have been revised for greater clarity.

**Chapter 13** A new *Human Perspective: Powerful Weak Attractions,* including two For Further Understanding questions, has been added to the revised Chapter 13. New text art has been added to the discussion of the common names of ketones and to clarify oxidation products of aldehydes under acidic or basic conditions. Other new text art clarifies the structure of hemiacetals and acetals. Three examples have been modified to include a structure of practical interest or to clarify the principle being applied. Revisions to the text included a reorganization of the discussion of structure and physical properties and additional details to clarify the IUPAC nomenclature of ketones.

**Chapter 14** A new *Medical Perspective: Esters for Appetite Control,* including two For Further Understanding questions, has been added. Five new text art diagrams have been added to support the revisions of the text with regard to the structure and physical properties of carboxylic acids and esters, as well as the action of soaps and the significance of phosphoester compounds in nature. Other revisions in the text include the preparation of carboxylic acids, the properties and nomenclature of carboxylic acid salts, and the structure, physical properties, and nomenclature of esters. Unnecessary content regarding acid anhydrides has been deleted.

**Chapter 15** New text art, with the associated text revisions, has been designed to assist student understanding of the physical properties and nomenclature of amines, the nomenclature of alkylammonium salts, neutralization reactions, and preparation of amides from acid chlorides. Along with revision of the nature of neutralization reactions, hydrolysis of amides, and nomenclature of amides, the synthesis and structure of primary, secondary, and tertiary amides is introduced in this edition. To complement these changes, the chapter map has been revised and three new key terms have been introduced. Four new problems have been added to allow students to test their understanding of the new materials.

**Chapter 16** A new *Medical Perspective: Human Milk Oligosaccharides,* including two For Further Understanding questions, has been added. A new Example, *Identifying a Chiral Compound,* has been added, along with a set of practice problems and a set of recommended practice problems to allow students to test their mastery of the concept. A new figure (16.13) shows the action of the enzymes α-amylase, β-amylase, and maltase. The section on meso compounds has been revised completely and two new problems have been included.

**Chapter 17** Section 17.2 has been reorganized so that ω-fatty acids are discussed prior to the section on prostaglandins. The reactions of fatty acids and glycerides has also been reorganized and revised for greater clarity. All text art in the section on sphingolipids has been redesigned as line formulas to enhance student understanding of the structures.

**Chapter 18** Two new perspectives have been added to Chapter 18: *A Medical Perspective: Medications from Venoms* and *A Human Perspective: The New Protein.* Sections 18.4, 18.5, and 18.7 have been revised to streamline the text and clarify concepts.

**Chapter 19** *A Medical Perspective: HIV Protease Inhibitors and Pharmaceutical Drug Design* has been updated to reflect the variety of new drugs available to treat the infection in adults and children. The discussion of transferases has been rewritten and new text art designed to provide students with an example that they will study later in the chapters on metabolism. Text revisions include Section 19.3 and passages in Sections 19.4, 19.6, 19.7, and 19.8. In all cases, the revisions streamline and simplify concepts to promote more effective student learning.

**Chapter 20** A new *Medical Perspective: Epigenomics,* including two For Further Understanding questions, has been added. The more recently described non-invasive prenatal testing procedure has been included in *A Medical Perspective: Molecular Genetics and Detection of Human Genetic Disorders.* The sections on the chemical composition of DNA and RNA and on chromatin structure have been revised for clarity. Section 20.8, Recombinant DNA, has been rewritten to reduce some of the historical methodologies so that students will focus on the potential of more recent advances.

**Chapter 21** *A Medical Perspective: High Fructose Corn Syrup* has been  updated with information on the recent studies demonstrating the impact of glucose and fructose on the hypothalamus of humans. In each of Sections 21.1–21.6, the text has been revised to simplify concepts. Section 21.7 has been reorganized for greater clarity.

**Chapter 22** A new *Medical Perspective, Babies with Three Parents,* including two For Further Understanding questions, has been added. Throughout the chapter, the text has been revised to streamline the writing and clarify the concepts.

**Chapter 23** Section 23.5 has been revised extensively to avoid redundancy with information presented in earlier chapters. Six new problems have been added to this chapter.

## Applications

Each chapter contains applications that present short stories about real-world situations involving one or more topics students will encounter within the chapter. There are over 100 applications throughout the text, so students are sure to find many topics that spark their interest. Global climate change,

DNA fingerprinting, the benefits of garlic, and gemstones are just a few examples of application topics.

- **Medical Perspectives** relate chemistry to a health concern or a diagnostic application.
- **Green Chemistry** explores environmental topics, including the impact of chemistry on the ecosystem and how these environmental changes affect human health.
- **Human Perspectives** delve into chemistry and society and include such topics as gender issues in science and historical viewpoints.
- **Chemistry at the Crime Scene** focuses on forensic chemistry, applying the principles of chemistry to help solve crimes.
- **Kitchen Chemistry** discusses the chemistry associated with everyday foods and cooking methods.

## Learning Tools

In designing the original learning system we asked ourselves: "If we were students, what would help us organize and understand the material covered in this chapter?" Based on the feedback of reviewers and users of our text, we include a variety of learning tools:

- **Chapter Overview** pages begin each chapter, listing learning goals and the chapter outline. Both students and professor can see, all in one place, the plan for the chapter.
- **Learning Goal Icons** mark the sections and examples in the chapter that focus on each learning goal.
- **Chapter Cross-References** help students locate pertinent background material. These references to previous chapters, sections, and perspectives are noted in the margins of the text. Marginal cross references also alert students to upcoming topics related to the information currently being studied.
- **End-of-Chapter Questions and Problems** are arranged according to the headings in the chapter outline, with further subdivision into Foundations (basic concepts) and Applications.
- **Chapter Maps** are included just before the End-of-Chapter Summaries to provide students with an overview of the chapter—showing connections among topics, how concepts are related, and outlining the chapter hierarchy.
- **Chapter Summaries** are now a bulleted list format of chapter concepts by major sections, with the integrated bold-faced **Key Terms** appearing in context. This more succinct format helps students to quickly identify and review important chapter concepts and to make connections with the incorporated Key Terms. Each Key Term is defined and listed alphabetically in the **Glossary** at the end of the book.
- **Answers to Practice Problems** are supplied at the end of each chapter so that students can quickly check their understanding of important problem-solving skills and chapter concepts.
- **Summary of Reactions** in the organic chemistry chapters highlight each major reaction type on a tan background. Major chemical reactions are summarized by equations at the end of the chapter, facilitating review.

## Problem Solving and Critical Thinking

Perhaps the best preparation for a successful and productive career is the development of problem-solving and critical thinking skills. To this end, we created a variety of problems that require recall, fundamental calculations, and complex reasoning. In this edition, we have used suggestions from our reviewers, as well as from our own experience, to enhance our 2300 problems. This edition includes new problems and hundreds of example problems with step-by-step solutions.

- **In-Chapter Examples, Solutions, and Practice Problems:** Each chapter includes examples that show the student, step-by-step, how to properly reach the correct solution to model problems. Each example contains a practice problem, as well as a referral to further practice questions. These questions allow students to test their mastery of information and to build self-confidence. The answers to the practice problems can be found at the end of each chapter so students can check their understanding.
- **Color-Coding System for In-Chapter Examples:** In this edition, we also introduced a color-coding and label system to help alleviate the confusion that students frequently have when trying to keep track of unit conversions. Introduced in Chapter 1, this color coding system has been used throughout the problem-solving chapters.

$$3.01 \; \cancel{\text{mol S}} \times \frac{32.06 \text{ g S}}{1 \; \cancel{\text{mol S}}} = 96.5 \text{ g S}$$

Data Given $\times$ Conversion Factor = Desired Result

- **In-Chapter and End-of-Chapter Questions and Problems:** We have created a wide variety of paired concept problems. The answers to the odd-numbered questions are found in the back of the book as reinforcement for students as they develop problem-solving skills. However, students must then be able to apply the same principles to the related even-numbered problems.
- **Challenge Problems:** Each chapter includes a set of challenge problems. These problems are intended to engage students to integrate concepts to solve more complex problems. They make a perfect complement to the classroom lecture because they provide an opportunity for in-class discussion of complex problems dealing with daily life and the health care sciences.

Over the course of the last nine editions, hundreds of reviewers have shared their knowledge and wisdom with us, as well as the reactions of their students to elements of this book. Their contributions, as well as our own continuing experience in the area of teaching and learning science, have resulted in a text that we are confident will provide a strong foundation in chemistry, while enhancing the learning experience of students.

## The Art Program

Today's students are much more visually oriented than previous generations. We have built upon this observation through the use of color, figures, and three-dimensional computer-generated models. This art program enhances the readability of the text and provides alternative pathways to learning.

- **Dynamic Illustrations:** Each chapter is amply illustrated using figures, tables, and chemical formulas. All of these illustrations are carefully annotated for clarity. To help students better understand difficult concepts, there are approximately 350 illustrations and 250 photos in the ninth edition.

- **Color-Coding Scheme:** We have color-coded equations so that chemical groups being added or removed in a reaction can be quickly recognized.

  1. **Red print** is used in chemical equations or formulas to draw the reader's eye to key elements or properties in a reaction or structure.

  2. **Blue print** is used when additional features must be highlighted.

  3. **Green background** screens denote generalized chemical and mathematical equations. In the organic chemistry chapters, the Summary of Reactions at the end of the chapter is also highlighted for ease of recognition.

  4. Yellow backgrounds illustrate energy, stored either in electrons or groups of atoms, in the general and biochemistry sections of the text. In the organic chemistry section of the text, yellow background screens also reveal the parent chain of an organic compound.

  5. There are situations in which it is necessary to adopt a unique color convention tailored to the material in a particular chapter. For example, in Chapter 18, the structures of amino acids require three colors to draw attention to key features of these molecules. For consistency, blue is used to denote the acid portion of an amino acid and red is used to denote the basic portion of an amino acid. Green print is used to denote the R groups, and a yellow background screen directs the eye to the α-carbon.

- **Computer-Generated Models:** The ability of students to understand the geometry and three-dimensional structure of molecules is essential to the understanding of organic and biochemical reactions. Computer-generated models are used throughout the text because they are both accurate and easily visualized.

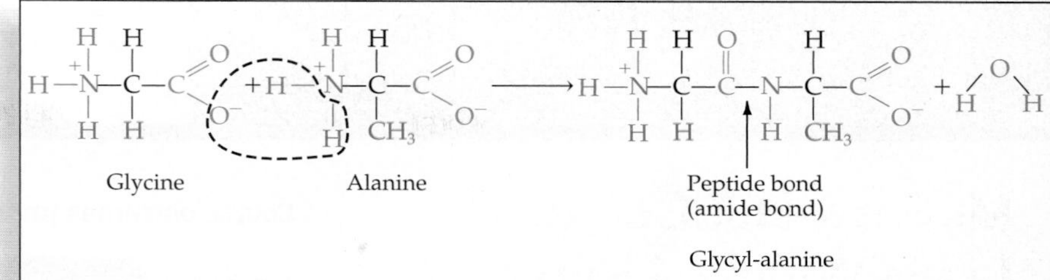

Glycine          Alanine          Peptide bond (amide bond)

Glycyl-alanine

The molecule formed by condensing two amino acids is called a *dipeptide*. The amino acid with a free α-N$^+$H$_3$ group is known as the amino terminal, or sim-

Because amines are bases, they react with acids to form alkylammonium salts.

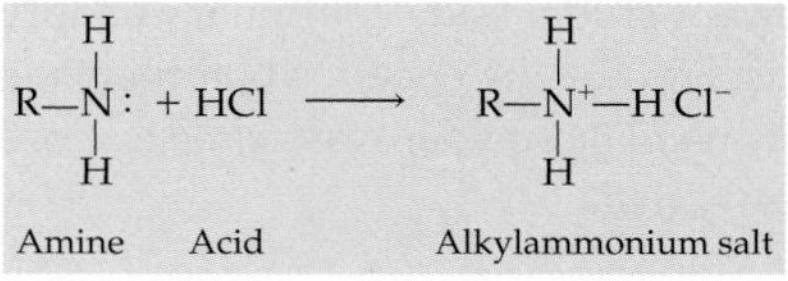

Amine    Acid          Alkylammonium salt

The reaction of methylamine with hydrochloric acid shown is typical of these reactions.

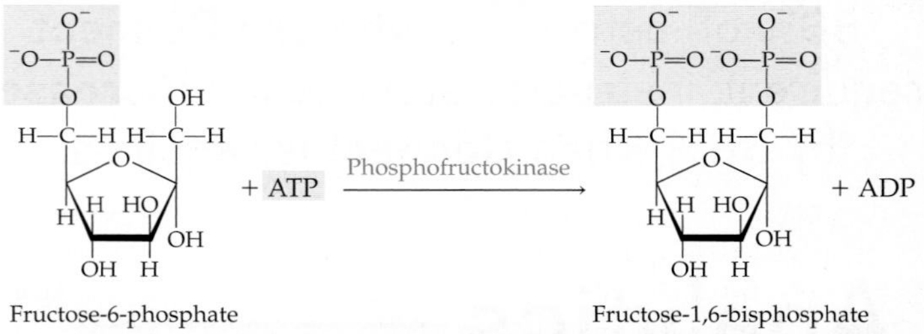

Fructose-6-phosphate          Phosphofructokinase          Fructose-1,6-bisphosphate

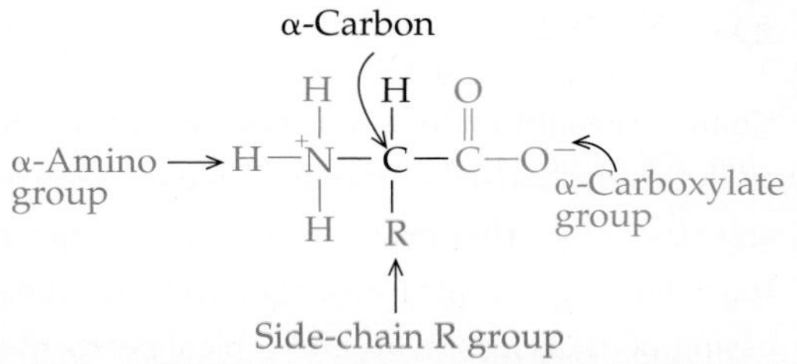

+ ATP          + ADP

α-Carbon

α-Amino group          α-Carboxylate group

Side-chain R group

# McGraw-Hill Connect®
# Learn Without Limits

Connect is a teaching and learning platform that is proven to deliver better results for students and instructors.

Connect empowers students by continually adapting to deliver precisely what they need, when they need it, and how they need it, so your class time is more engaging and effective.

**Course outcomes improve with Connect.**

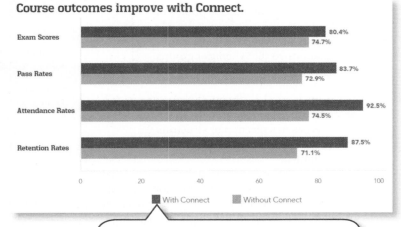

| | With Connect | Without Connect |
|---|---|---|
| Exam Scores | 80.4% | 74.7% |
| Pass Rates | 83.7% | 72.9% |
| Attendance Rates | 92.5% | 74.5% |
| Retention Rates | 87.5% | 71.1% |

Using **Connect** improves passing rates by **10.8%** and retention by **16.4%**.

88% of instructors who use **Connect** require it; instructor satisfaction **increases** by 38% when **Connect** is required.

# Analytics

## Connect Insight®

Connect Insight is Connect's new one-of-a-kind visual analytics dashboard—now available for both instructors and students—that provides at-a-glance information regarding student performance, which is immediately actionable. By presenting assignment, assessment, and topical performance results together with a time metric that is easily visible for aggregate or individual results, Connect Insight gives the user the ability to take a just-in-time approach to teaching and learning, which was never before available. Connect Insight presents data that empowers students and helps instructors improve class performance in a way that is efficient and effective.

**Connect helps students achieve better grades**

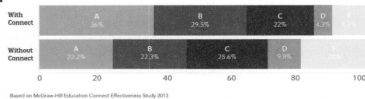

| | A | B | C | D | F |
|---|---|---|---|---|---|
| With Connect | 36% | 29.5% | 22% | 4.3% | |
| Without Connect | 22.2% | 22.3% | 25.6% | 9.8% | |

Based on McGraw-Hill Education Connect Effectiveness Study 2013

Students can view their results for any **Connect** course.

# Mobile

Connect's new, intuitive mobile interface gives students and instructors flexible and convenient, anytime–anywhere access to all components of the Connect platform.

# Adaptive

THE FIRST AND ONLY **ADAPTIVE READING EXPERIENCE** DESIGNED TO TRANSFORM THE WAY STUDENTS READ

More students earn **A's** and **B's** when they use McGraw-Hill Education **Adaptive** products.

## SmartBook®

Proven to help students improve grades and study more efficiently, SmartBook contains the same content within the print book, but actively tailors that content to the needs of the individual. SmartBook's adaptive technology provides precise, personalized instruction on what the student should do next, guiding the student to master and remember key concepts, targeting gaps in knowledge and offering customized feedback, driving the student toward comprehension and retention of the subject matter. Available on smartphones and tablets, SmartBook puts learning at the student's fingertips—anywhere, anytime.

Over **4 billion questions** have been answered making McGraw-Hill Education products more intelligent, reliable precise.

STUDENTS WANT

Mc Graw Hill Education **SMARTBOOK®**

**95%** of students reported **SmartBook** to be a more effective way of reading material

**100%** of students want to use the Practice Quiz feature available within **SmartBook** to help them study

**100%** of students reported having reliable access to off-campus wifi

**90%** of students say they would purchase **SmartBook** over print alone

**95%** reported that **SmartBook** would impact their study skills in a positive way

McGraw Hill Education

*Findings based on a 2015 focus group survey at Pellissippi State Community College administered by McGraw-Hill Education

## For the Instructor

- **Instructor's Manual:** Written and developed for the ninth edition by the authors, this ancillary contains many useful suggestions for organizing flipped classrooms, lectures, instructional objectives, perspectives on readings from the text, answers to the even-numbered problems from the text, a list of each chapter's key problems and concepts, and more. The Instructor's Manual is available through the Instructor Resources in the Connect Library tab.
- **Laboratory Manual for General, Organic, and Biological Chemistry:** Authored by Applegate, Neely, and Sakuta to be the most current lab manual available for the GOB course, incorporating the most modern instrumentation and techniques. Illustrations and chemical structures were developed by the authors to conform to the most recent IUPAC conventions. A problem-solving methodology is also utilized throughout the laboratory exercises. There are two online virtual labs for Nuclear Chemistry and Gas Laws. This Laboratory Manual is also designed with flexibility in mind to meet the differing lengths of GOB courses and the variety of instrumentation available in GOB labs. Helpful instructor materials are also available on this companion website, including answers, solution recipes, best practices with common student issues and TA advice, sample syllabi, and a calculation sheet for the Density lab.
- **Presentation Tools:** Build instructional material wherever, whenever, and however you want with assets such as photos, artwork, and other media that can be used to create customized lectures, visually enhanced tests and quizzes, compelling course websites, or attractive printed support materials. The Presentation Tools can be accessed from the Instructor Resources in the Connect Library tab. Instructors can still access the animations from the OLC for use in their presentations.
- **More than 300 animations available through Connect:** They supplement the textbook material in much the same way as instructor demonstrations. However, they are only a few mouse-clicks away, any time, day or night. Because many students are visual learners and quite computer-literate, the animations add another dimension of learning; they bring a greater degree of reality to the written word.

## For the Student

- **Student Study Guide/Solutions Manual:** A separate Student Study Guide/Solutions Manual, prepared by Danaè Quirk Dorr, is available. It contains the answers and complete solutions for the odd-numbered problems. It also offers students a variety of exercises and keys for testing their comprehension of basic, as well as difficult, concepts.
- **Schaum's Outline of General, Organic, and Biological Chemistry:** Written by George Odian and Ira Blei, this supplement provides students with more than 1 400 solved problems with complete solutions. It also teaches effective problem-solving techniques.

## Acknowledgments

We are thankful to our families, whose patience and support made it possible for us to undertake this project. We are also grateful to our many colleagues at McGraw-Hill for their support, guidance, and assistance. In particular, we would like to thank Sherry Kane, Content Project Manager, Mary Hurley, Developmental Editor, Andrea Pellerito, Brand Manager, and Tamara Hodge, Marketing Manager.

The following individuals helped write and review learning goal-oriented content for **LearnSmart for General, Organic, & Biochemistry:**

David G. Jones,   *Vistamar School*

Adam I. Keller,   *Columbus State Community College*

A revision cannot move forward without the feedback of professors teaching the course. The following reviewers have our gratitude and assurance that their comments received serious consideration. The following professors provided reviews, participated in focus groups, or otherwise provided valuable advice as our textbook has evolved to its current form:

Augustine Agyeman,   *Clayton State University*

Phyllis Arthasery,   *Ohio University*

EJ Behrman,   *The Ohio State University*

C. Bruce Bradley,   *Spartanburg Community College*

Thomas Gilbert,   *Northern Illinois University*

Mary Hadley,   *Minnesota State University, Mankato*

Emily Halvorson,   *Pima Community College*

James Hardy,   *The University of Akron*

Amy Hanks,   *Brigham Young University-Idaho*

Theresa Hill,   *Rochester Community and Technical College*

Shirley Hino,   *Santa Rosa Junior College*

Narayan Hosmane,   *Northern Illinois University*

Colleen Kelley,   *Pima Community College*

Myung-Hoon Kim,   *Georgia Perimeter College*

Charlene Kozerow,   *University of Maine*

Andrea Leonard,   *University of Louisiana at Lafayette*

Lauren E. H. McMills,   *Ohio University*

Jonathan McMurry,   *Kennesaw State University*

Cynthia Molitor,   *Lourdes College*

Matthew Morgan,   *Georgia Perimeter College, Covington*

Melekeh Nasiri,   *Woodland Community College*

Glenn Nomura,   *Georgia Perimeter College*

Kenneth O'Connor,   *Marshall University*

Dwight Patterson,   *Middle Tennessee State University*

Allan Pinhas,   *University of Cincinnati, Cincinnati*

Jerry Poteat,   *Georgia Perimeter College*

Michael E. Rennekamp,   *Columbus State Community College*

Raymond Sadeghi,   *University of Texas at San Antonio*

Paul Sampson,   *Kent State University*

Shirish Shah,   *Towson University*

Buchang Shi,   *Eastern Kentucky University*

Heather Sklenicka,   *Rochester Community and Technical College*

Sara Tate,   *Northeast Lakeview College*

Kimberley Taylor,   *University of Arkansas at Little Rock*

Susan Tansey Thomas,   *University of Texas at San Antonio*

Nathan Tice,   *Eastern Kentucky University*

Steven Trail,   *Elgin Community College*

David A. Tramontozzi,   *Macomb Community College*

Pearl Tsang,   *University of Cincinnati*

Michael Van Dyke,   *Western Carolina University*

Wendy Weeks,   *Pima Community College*

Gregg Wilmes,   *Eastern Michigan University*

Yakov Woldman,   *Valdosta State University*

# METHODS AND MEASUREMENT
# Chemistry

1

## LEARNING GOALS

1 Explain the relationship between chemistry, matter, and energy.

2 Discuss the approach to science, the scientific method, and distinguish among the terms *hypothesis, theory,* and *scientific law.*

3 Distinguish between data and results.

4 Describe the properties of the solid, liquid, and gaseous states.

5 Classify matter according to its composition.

6 Provide specific examples of physical and chemical properties and physical and chemical changes.

7 Distinguish between intensive and extensive properties.

8 Identify the major units of measure in the English and metric systems.

9 Report data and calculate results using scientific notation and the proper number of significant figures.

10 Distinguish between *accuracy* and *precision* and their representations: *error* and *deviation.*

11 Convert between units of the English and metric systems.

12 Know the three common temperature scales, and convert values from one scale to another.

13 Use density, mass, and volume in problem solving, and calculate the specific gravity of a substance from its density.

Chemistry is the study of anything that has mass and occupies space.

## OUTLINE

# INTRODUCTION

Louis Pasteur, a chemist and microbiologist, said, "Chance favors the prepared mind." In the history of science and medicine, there are many examples in which individuals made important discoveries because they recognized the value of an unexpected observation.

One such example is the use of ultraviolet (UV) light to treat infant jaundice. Infant jaundice is a condition in which the skin and the whites of the eyes appear yellow because of high levels of the bile pigment bilirubin in the blood. Bilirubin is a breakdown product of the oxygen-carrying blood protein hemoglobin. If bilirubin accumulates in the body, it can cause brain damage and death. The immature liver of the baby cannot remove the bilirubin.

In 1956, an observant nurse in England noticed that when jaundiced babies were exposed to sunlight, the jaundice faded. Research based on her observation showed that the UV light changes the bilirubin into another substance, which can be excreted. To this day, jaundiced newborns undergoing phototherapy are treated with UV light. Historically, newborns were diagnosed with jaundice based only on their physical appearance. However, it has been determined that this method is not always accurate. Now, it is common to use either an instrument or a blood sample to measure the amount of bilirubin present in the serum.

In this first chapter of your study of chemistry, you will learn about the scientific method: the process of developing hypotheses to explain observations and the design of experiments to test those hypotheses.

You will also see that measurement of properties of matter, and careful observation and recording of data, are essential to scientific inquiry. So too is assessment of the precision and accuracy of measurements. Measurements (data) must be reported to allow others to determine their significance. Therefore, an understanding of significant figures, and the ability to represent data in the most meaningful units, enables other scientists to interpret data and results.

The goal of this chapter is to help you develop the skills needed to represent and communicate data and results from scientific inquiry.

## 1.1    The Discovery Process

## LEARNING GOAL

**1** Explain the relationship between chemistry, matter, and energy.

Models In Chemistry, p. 4

### Chemistry

**Chemistry** is the study of matter, its chemical and physical properties, the chemical and physical changes it undergoes, and the energy changes that accompany those processes.

**Matter** is anything that has mass and occupies space. The air we breathe, our bodies, our planet earth, our universe; all are made up of an immense variety and quantity of particles, collectively termed matter. Matter undergoes change. Sometimes this change occurs naturally or we change matter when we make new substances (creating drugs in a pharmaceutical laboratory). All of these changes involve **energy,** the ability to do work to accomplish some change. Hence, we may describe chemistry as a study of matter and energy and their interrelationship.

Chemistry is an experimental science. A traditional image of a chemist is someone wearing a white coat and safety goggles while working in solitude in a laboratory. Although much chemistry is still accomplished in a traditional laboratory setting, over the last 40 years the boundaries of the laboratory have expanded to include the power of modern technology. For example, searching the scientific literature for information no longer involves a trip to the library as it is now done very quickly via the Internet. Computers are also invaluable in the laboratory because they control sophisticated instrumentation that measures, collects, processes, and interprets information. The behavior of matter can also be modeled using sophisticated computer programs.

Additionally, chemistry is a collaborative process. The solitary scientist, working in isolation, is a relic of the past. Complex problems dealing with topics such as the environment, disease, forensics, and DNA require input from other scientists and mathematicians who can bring a wide variety of expertise to problems that are chemical in nature.

The boundaries between the traditional sciences of chemistry, physics, and biology, as well as mathematics and computer science, have gradually faded. Medical practitioners, physicians, nurses, and medical technologists use therapies that contain elements of all these disciplines. The rapid expansion of the pharmaceutical industry is based on recognition of the relationship between the function of an organism and its basic chemical makeup. Function is a consequence of changes that chemical substances undergo.

For these reasons, an understanding of basic chemical principles is essential for anyone considering a medically related career; indeed, a worker in any science-related field will benefit from an understanding of the principles and applications of chemistry.

Investigating the causes of the rapid melting of glaciers is a global application of chemistry. How does this illustrate the interaction of matter and energy?

## The Scientific Method

The **scientific method** is a systematic approach to the discovery of new information. How do we learn about the properties of matter, the way it behaves in nature, and how it can be modified to make useful products? Chemists do this by using the scientific method to study the way in which matter changes under carefully controlled conditions.

The scientific method is not a "cookbook recipe" that, if followed faithfully, will yield new discoveries; rather, it is an organized approach to solving scientific problems. Every scientist brings his or her own curiosity, creativity, and imagination to scientific study. Yet, scientific inquiry does involve some of the "cookbook recipe" approach.

Characteristics of the scientific process include the following:

LEARNING GOAL

2 Discuss the approach to science, the scientific method, and distinguish among the terms *hypothesis*, *theory*, and *scientific law*.

- *Observation.* The description of, for example, the color, taste, or odor of a substance is a result of observation. The measurement of the temperature of a liquid or the size or mass of a solid results from observation.
- *Formulation of a question.* Humankind's fundamental curiosity motivates questions of why and how things work.
- *Pattern recognition.* When a cause-and-effect relationship is found, it may be the basis of a generalized explanation of substances and their behavior.
- *Theory development.* When scientists observe a phenomenon, they want to explain it. The process of explaining observed behavior begins with a hypothesis. A **hypothesis** is simply an attempt to explain an observation, or series of observations. If many experiments support a hypothesis, it may attain the status of a theory. A **theory** is a hypothesis supported by extensive testing (experimentation) that explains scientific observations and data and can accurately predict new observations and data.
- *Experimentation.* Demonstrating the correctness of hypotheses and theories is at the heart of the scientific method. This is done by carrying out carefully designed experiments that will either support or disprove the hypothesis or theory. A scientific experiment produces **data.** Each piece of data is the individual result of a single measurement or observation.

    A **result** is the outcome of an experiment. Data and results may be identical, but more often, several related pieces of data are combined, and logic is used to produce a result.
- *Information summarization.* A **scientific law** is nothing more than the summary of a large quantity of information. For example, the law of conservation of matter states that matter cannot be created or destroyed, only converted from one form to another. This statement represents a massive body of chemical information gathered from experiments.

LEARNING GOAL

3 Distinguish between data and results.

## EXAMPLE 1.1    Distinguishing Between Data and Results

In many cases, a drug is less stable in the presence of moisture, and excess moisture can hasten the breakdown of the active ingredient, leading to loss of potency. Bupropion (Wellbutrin) is an antidepressant that is moisture sensitive. Describe an experiment that will allow for the determination of the quantity of water gained by a certain quantity of bupropion when it is exposed to air.

### Solution

To do this experiment, we must first weigh the buproprion sample, and then expose it to the air for a period of time and reweigh it. The change in weight,

$$[\text{weight}_{\text{final}} - \text{weight}_{\text{initial}}] = \text{weight difference}$$

indicates the weight of water taken up by the drug formulation. The initial and final weights are individual bits of *data*; by themselves they do not answer the question, but they do provide the information necessary to calculate the answer: the results. The difference in weight and the conclusions based on the observed change in weight are the *results* of the experiment.

*Note:* This is actually not a very good experiment because many conditions were not measured. Measurement of the temperature, humidity of the atmosphere, and the length of time that the drug was exposed to the air would make the results less ambiguous.

### Practice Problem 1.1

Describe an experiment that demonstrates that the boiling point of water changes when salt (sodium chloride) is added to the water.

▶ For Further Practice: **Questions 1.35 and 1.36.**

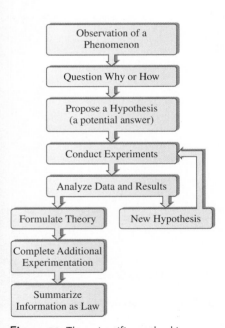

**Figure 1.1** The scientific method is an organized way of doing science that incorporates a degree of trial and error. If the data analysis and results do not support the initial hypothesis, the cycle must begin again.

The scientific method involves the interactive use of hypotheses, development of theories, and thorough testing of theories using well-designed experiments. It is summarized in Figure 1.1.

## Models in Chemistry

Hypotheses, theories, and laws are frequently expressed using mathematical equations. These equations may confuse all but the best of mathematicians. For this reason, a *model* of a chemical unit or system is often used to help illustrate an idea. A good model based on everyday experience, although imperfect, gives a great deal of information in a simple fashion.

Consider the fundamental unit of methane, the major component of natural gas, which is composed of one carbon (symbolized by C) atom and four hydrogen (symbolized by H) atoms.

A geometrically correct model of methane can be constructed from balls and sticks. The balls represent the individual atoms of hydrogen and carbon, and the sticks correspond to the attractive forces that hold the hydrogen and carbon together. The model consists of four balls representing hydrogen symmetrically arranged around a center ball representing carbon.

# A Human Perspective

## The Scientific Method

The discovery of penicillin by Alexander Fleming is an example of the scientific method at work. Fleming was studying the growth of bacteria. One day, his experiment was ruined because colonies of mold were growing on his plates. From this failed experiment, Fleming made an observation that would change the practice of medicine: Bacterial colonies could not grow in the area around the mold colonies. Fleming hypothesized that the mold was making a chemical compound that inhibited the growth of the bacteria. He performed a series of experiments designed to test this hypothesis.

The success of the scientific method is critically dependent upon carefully designed experiments that will either support or disprove the hypothesis. This is exactly what Fleming did.

In one experiment, he used two sets of tubes containing sterile nutrient broth. To one set he added mold cells. The second set (the control tubes) remained sterile. The mold was allowed to grow for several days. Then the broth from each of the tubes (experimental and control) was passed through a filter to remove any mold cells. Next, bacteria were placed in each tube. If Fleming's hypothesis was correct, the tubes in which the mold had grown would contain the chemical that inhibits growth, and the bacteria would not grow. On the other hand, the control tubes (which were never used to grow mold) would allow bacterial growth. This is exactly what Fleming observed.

Within a few years this *antibiotic*, penicillin, was being used to treat bacterial infections in patients.

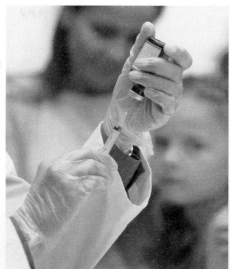

A nurse administers an injection of penicillin to a young patient.

### For Further Understanding

▶ What is the purpose of the control tubes used in this experiment?

▶ Match the features of this article with the flowchart items in Figure 1.1.

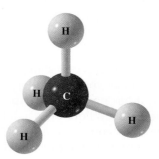

Color-coding the balls distinguishes one type of atom from another; the geometrical form of the model, all of the angles and dimensions of a tetrahedron, are the same for each methane unit found in nature. Methane is certainly not a collection of balls and sticks, but such models are valuable because they help us understand the chemical behavior of methane and other more complex substances.

The structure-properties concept has advanced so far that compounds are designed and synthesized in the laboratory with the hope that they will perform very specific functions, such as curing diseases that have been resistant to other forms of treatment. Figure 1.2 shows some of the variety of modern technology that has its roots in scientific inquiry.

Chemists and physicists have used the observed properties of matter to develop models of the individual units of matter. These models collectively make up what we now know as the atomic theory of matter, which is discussed in detail in Chapter 2.

**Figure 1.2** Examples of technology originating from scientific inquiry: (a) synthesis of a new drug, (b) blood pressure app for a smartphone, (c) preparation of solid-state electronics, and (d) use of a gypsy moth sex attractant for insect control.

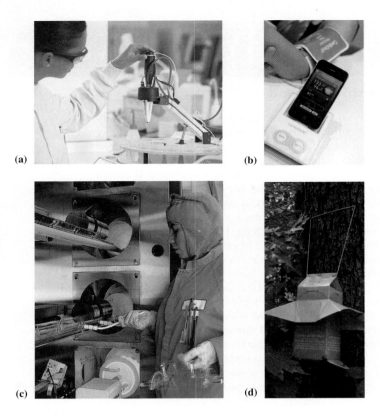

(a)

(b)

(c)

(d)

## 1.2    The Classification of Matter

Matter is a large and seemingly unmanageable concept because it includes everything that has mass and occupies space. Chemistry becomes manageable as we classify matter according to its **properties**—that is, the characteristics of the matter. Matter will be classified in two ways in this section, by *state* and by *composition*.

### States of Matter

*We will examine each of the three states of matter in detail in Chapter 5.*

There are three *states of matter:* the **gaseous state,** the **liquid state,** and the **solid state.** A gas is made up of particles that are widely separated. In fact, a gas will expand to fill any container; it has no definite shape or volume. In contrast, particles of a liquid are closer together; a liquid has a definite volume but no definite shape; it takes on the shape of its container. A solid consists of particles that are close together and often have a regular and predictable pattern of particle arrangement (crystalline). The particles in a solid are much more organized than the particles in a liquid or a gas. As a result, a solid has both fixed volume and fixed shape. Attractive forces, which exist between all particles, are very pronounced in solids and much less so in gases.

### Composition of Matter

We have seen that matter can be classified by its state as a solid, liquid, or gas. Another way to classify matter is by its composition. This very useful system, described in the following paragraphs and summarized in Figure 1.3, will be utilized throughout the textbook.

All matter is either a *pure substance* or a *mixture*. A **pure substance** has only one component. Pure water is a pure substance. It is made up only of particles containing two hydrogen (symbolized by H) atoms and one oxygen (symbolized by O) atom—that is, water molecules ($H_2O$).

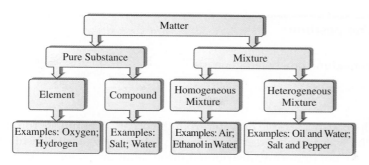

There are different types of pure substances. Elements and compounds are both pure substances. An **element** is a pure substance that generally cannot be changed into a simpler form of matter. Hydrogen and oxygen, for example, are elements. Alternatively, a **compound** is a substance resulting from the combination of two or more elements in a definite, reproducible way. The elements hydrogen and oxygen, as noted earlier, may combine to form the compound water, $H_2O$.

A **mixture** is a combination of two or more pure substances in which each substance retains its own identity. Ethanol, the alcohol found in beer, and water can be combined in a mixture. They coexist as pure substances because they do not undergo a chemical reaction. A mixture has variable composition; there are an infinite number of combinations of quantities of ethanol and water that can be mixed. For example, the mixture may contain a small amount of ethanol and a large amount of water or vice versa. Each is, however, an ethanol-water mixture.

A mixture may be either *homogeneous* or *heterogeneous* (Figure 1.4). A **homogeneous mixture** has uniform composition. Its particles are well mixed, or thoroughly intermingled. A homogeneous mixture, such as alcohol and water, is described as a *solution*. Air, a mixture of gases, is an example of a gaseous solution. A **heterogeneous mixture** has a nonuniform composition. A mixture of salt and pepper is a good example of a heterogeneous mixture. Concrete is also composed of a heterogeneous mixture of materials (various types and sizes of stone and sand with cement in a nonuniform mixture).

At present, more than 100 elements have been characterized. A complete listing of the elements and their symbols is found on the inside front cover of this textbook.

*A detailed discussion of solutions (homogeneous mixtures) and their properties is presented in Chapter 6.*

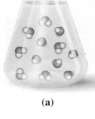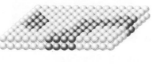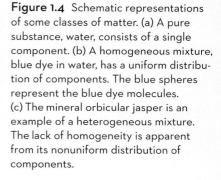

**(a)** **(b)** **(c)**

**Figure 1.4** Schematic representations of some classes of matter. (a) A pure substance, water, consists of a single component. (b) A homogeneous mixture, blue dye in water, has a uniform distribution of components. The blue spheres represent the blue dye molecules. (c) The mineral orbicular jasper is an example of a heterogeneous mixture. The lack of homogeneity is apparent from its nonuniform distribution of components.

## EXAMPLE 1.2    Classifying Matter by Composition

Is seawater a pure substance, a homogeneous mixture, or a heterogeneous mixture?

**5**  Classify matter according to its composition.

### Solution

Imagine yourself at the beach, filling a container with a sample of water from the ocean. Examine it. You would see a variety of solid particles suspended in the water: sand, green vegetation, perhaps even a small fish! Clearly, it is a mixture, and one in which the particles are not uniformly distributed throughout the water; hence, it is a heterogeneous mixture.

### Practice Problem 1.2

Is each of the following materials a pure substance, a homogeneous mixture, or a heterogeneous mixture?

a. ethanol
b. blood
c. an Alka-Seltzer tablet fizzing in water
d. oxygen being delivered from a hospital oxygen tank

▶ For Further Practice: **Questions 1.57 and 1.58.**

**Question 1.1**  Intravenous therapy may be used to introduce a saline solution into a patient's vein. Is this solution a pure substance, a homogeneous mixture, or a heterogeneous mixture?

**Question 1.2**  Cloudy urine can be a symptom of a bladder infection. Classify this urine as a pure substance, a homogeneous mixture, or a heterogeneous mixture.

## Physical Properties and Physical Change

**6**  Provide specific examples of physical and chemical properties and physical and chemical changes.

Water is the most common example of a substance that can exist in all three states over a reasonable temperature range (Figure 1.5). Conversion of water from one state to another constitutes a *physical change*. A **physical change** produces a recognizable difference in the appearance of a substance without causing any change in its composition or identity. For example, we can warm an ice cube and it will melt, forming liquid water. Clearly its appearance has changed; it has been transformed from

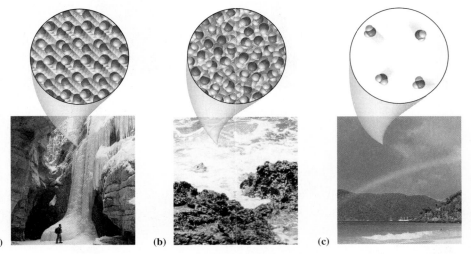

(a)                    (b)                    (c)

**Figure 1.5**  The three states of matter exhibited by water: (a) solid, as ice; (b) liquid, as ocean water; (c) gas, as humidity in the air.

the solid to the liquid state. It is, however, still water; its composition and identity remain unchanged. A physical change has occurred. We could in fact demonstrate the constancy of composition and identity by refreezing the liquid water, re-forming the ice cube. This melting and freezing cycle could be repeated over and over. This very process is a hallmark of our global weather changes. The continual interconversion of the three states of water in the environment (snow, rain, and humidity) clearly demonstrates the retention of the identity of water particles or *molecules.*

A **physical property** can be observed or measured without changing the composition or identity of a substance. As we have seen, melting ice is a physical change. We can measure the temperature when melting occurs; this is the *melting point* of water. We can also measure the *boiling point* of water, when liquid water becomes a gas. Both the melting and boiling points of water, and of any other substance, are physical properties.

A practical application of separation of materials based upon their differences in physical properties is shown in Figure 1.6.

**Figure 1.6** An example of separation based on differences in physical properties. Magnetic iron is separated from nonmagnetic substances. A large-scale version of this process is important in the recycling industry.

## Chemical Properties and Chemical Change

We have noted that physical properties can be exhibited, measured, or observed without any change in identity or composition. In contrast, **chemical properties** do result in a change in composition and can be observed only through chemical reactions. In a **chemical reaction,** a chemical substance is converted to one or more different substances by rearranging, removing, replacing, or adding atoms. For example, the process of photosynthesis can be shown as

$$\text{carbon dioxide} + \text{water} \xrightarrow[\text{Chlorophyll}]{\text{Light}} \text{sugar} + \text{oxygen}$$

This chemical reaction involves the conversion of carbon dioxide and water (the *reactants*) to a sugar and oxygen (the *products*). The physical properties of the reactants and products are clearly different. We know that carbon dioxide and oxygen are gases at room temperature, and water is a liquid at this temperature; the sugar is a solid white powder. A chemical property of carbon dioxide is its ability to form sugar under certain conditions. The process of formation of this sugar is the *chemical change.* The term *chemical reaction* is synonymous with **chemical change.**

Light is the energy needed to make the reaction happen. Chlorophyll is the energy absorber, converting light energy to chemical energy.

---

**EXAMPLE 1.3**  **Classifying Change**

Can the process that takes place when an egg is fried be described as a physical or chemical change?

**Solution**

Examine the characteristics of the egg before and after frying. Clearly, some significant change has occurred. Furthermore, the change appears irreversible. More than a simple physical change has taken place. A chemical reaction (actually, several) must be responsible; hence, there is a chemical change.

**LEARNING GOAL**

**6** Provide specific examples of physical and chemical properties and physical and chemical changes.

**Practice Problem 1.3**

Classify each of the following as either a chemical change or a physical change:
- a. water boiling to become steam
- b. butter becoming rancid
- c. burning wood
- d. melting of ice in spring
- e. decaying of leaves in winter

▶ For Further Practice: **Questions 1.51 and 1.52.**

**Question 1.3** Classify each of the following as either a chemical property or a physical property:
  a. color          b. flammability          c. hardness

**Question 1.4** Classify each of the following as either a chemical property or a physical property:
  a. odor          b. taste          c. temperature

## Intensive and Extensive Properties

The mass of a pediatric patient (in kg) is an extensive property that is commonly used to determine the proper dosage of medication [in milligrams (mg)] prescribed. Although the mass of the medication is also an extensive property, the dosage (in mg/kg) is an intensive property. This calculated dosage should be the same for every pediatric patient.

It is important to recognize that properties can also be classified according to whether they depend on the size of the sample. Consequently, there is a fundamental difference between properties such as color and melting point and properties such as mass and volume.

An **intensive property** is a property of matter that is *independent* of the *quantity* of the substance. Boiling and melting points are intensive properties. For example, the boiling point of one single drop of water is exactly the same as the boiling point of a liter (L) of water.

An **extensive property** *depends* on the *quantity* of a substance. Mass and volume are extensive properties. There is an obvious difference between 1 gram (g) of silver and 1 kilogram (kg) of silver; the quantities and, incidentally, the monetary values, differ substantially.

---

**EXAMPLE 1.4** **Differentiating Between Intensive and Extensive Properties**

Is temperature an intensive or extensive property?

**Solution**

Imagine two glasses, each containing 100 g of water, and each at 25°C. Now pour the contents of the two glasses into a larger glass. You would predict that the mass of the water in the larger glass would be 200 g (100 g + 100 g) because mass is an *extensive property,* dependent on quantity. However, we would expect the temperature of the water to remain the same (not 25°C + 25°C); hence, temperature is an *intensive property* . . . independent of quantity.

**Practice Problem 1.4**

Pure water freezes at 0°C. Is this an intensive or extensive property? Why?

▶ For Further Practice: **Questions 1.41 and 1.42.**

---

**Question 1.5** Label each property as intensive or extensive:
  a. the length of my pencil          b. the color of my pencil

**Question 1.6** Label each property as intensive or extensive:
  a. the shape of leaves on a tree          b. the number of leaves on a tree

## 1.3 The Units of Measurement

The study of chemistry requires the collection of data through measurement. The quantities that are most often measured include mass, length, and volume. Measurements require the determination of an amount followed by a **unit,** which defines the basic quantity being measured. A weight of 3 *ounces* (oz) is clearly quite different than 3 *pounds* (lb). A number that is not followed by the correct unit usually conveys no useful information.

The *English system of measurement* is a collection of unrelated units used in the United States in business and industry. However, it is not used in scientific work, primarily because it is difficult to convert one unit to another. In fact, the English "system" is not really a system at all; it is simply a collection of units accumulated throughout English history. Table 1.1 shows relationships among common English units of weight, length, and volume.

The United States has begun efforts to convert to the metric system. The *metric system* is truly systematic. It is composed of a set of units that are related to each other decimally; in other words, as powers of ten. Because the metric system is a decimally based system, it is inherently simpler to use and less ambiguous. Table 1.2 shows the meaning of the prefixes used in the metric system.

The metric system was originally developed in France just before the French Revolution in 1789. The more extensive version of this system is the *Systéme International*, or *S.I. system*. Although the S.I. system has been in existence for over 50 years, it has yet to gain widespread acceptance. Because the S.I. system is truly systematic, it utilizes certain units, especially for pressure, that many find unwieldy.

In this text, we will use the metric system, not the S.I. system, and we will use the English system only to the extent of converting from it to the more systematic metric system.

Now let's look at the major metric units for mass, length, volume, and time in more detail. In each case, we will compare the unit to a familiar English unit.

The photo shows 3 oz of grapes versus a 3-lb cantaloupe. Clearly units are important.

## Mass

**Mass** describes the quantity of matter in an object. The terms *weight* and *mass*, in common usage, are often considered synonymous. They are not, in fact. **Weight** is the force of gravity on an object:

$$\text{Weight} = \text{mass} \times \text{acceleration due to gravity}$$

LEARNING GOAL

**8**  Identify the major units of measure in the English and metric systems.

*The mathematical process of converting between units will be covered in detail in Section 1.5.*

The table of common prefixes used in the metric system relates values to the base units. For example, it defines 1 mg as being equivalent to $10^{-3}$ g and 1 kg as being equivalent to $10^3$ g.

### TABLE 1.1 Some Common Relationships Used in the English System

| | |
|---|---|
| Weight | 1 pound (lb) = 16 ounces (oz) |
| | 1 ton (t) = 2000 pounds (lb) |
| Length | 1 foot (ft) = 12 inches (in) |
| | 1 yard (yd) = 3 feet (ft) |
| | 1 mile (mi) = 5280 feet (ft) |
| Volume | 1 quart (qt) = 32 fluid ounces (fl oz) |
| | 1 quart (qt) = 2 pints (pt) |
| | 1 gallon (gal) = 4 quarts (qt) |

### TABLE 1.2 Some Common Prefixes Used in the Metric System

| Prefix | Abbreviation | Meaning | Decimal Equivalent | Equality with major metric units (g, m, or L are represented by $x$ in each) |
|---|---|---|---|---|
| mega | M | $10^6$ | 1,000,000. | $1\ \text{M}x = 10^6 x$ |
| kilo | k | $10^3$ | 1000. | $1\ \text{k}x = 10^3 x$ |
| deka | da | $10^1$ | 10. | $1\ \text{da}x = 10^1 x$ |
| deci | d | $10^{-1}$ | 0.1 | $1\ \text{d}x = 10^{-1} x$ |
| centi | c | $10^{-2}$ | 0.01 | $1\ \text{c}x = 10^{-2} x$ |
| milli | m | $10^{-3}$ | 0.001 | $1\ \text{m}x = 10^{-3} x$ |
| micro | μ | $10^{-6}$ | 0.000001 | $1\ \mu x = 10^{-6} x$ |
| nano | n | $10^{-9}$ | 0.000000001 | $1\ \text{n}x = 10^{-9} x$ |

**Figure 1.7** Three common balances that are useful for the measurement of mass. (a) A two-pan comparison balance for approximate mass measurement suitable for routine work requiring accuracy to 0.1 g (or perhaps 0.01 g). (b) A top-loading single-pan electronic balance that is similar in accuracy to (a) but has the advantages of speed and ease of operation. The revolution in electronics over the past 20 years has resulted in electronic balances largely supplanting the two-pan comparison balance in routine laboratory usage. (c) An analytical balance of this type is used when the highest level of precision and accuracy is required.

(a)

(c)

(b)

When gravity is constant, mass and weight are directly proportional. But gravity is not constant; it varies as a function of the distance from the center of the earth. Therefore, weight cannot be used for scientific measurement because the weight of an object may vary from one place on the earth to the next.

Mass, on the other hand, is independent of gravity; it is a result of a comparison of an unknown mass with a known mass called a *standard mass*. Balances are instruments used to measure the mass of materials.

The metric unit for mass is the gram (g). A common English unit for mass is the pound (lb).

$$1 \text{ lb} = 454 \text{ g}$$

Examples of balances commonly used for the determination of mass are shown in Figure 1.7.

## Length

The standard metric unit of *length,* the distance between two points, is the meter (m). A meter is close to the English yard (yd).

$$1 \text{ yd} = 0.914 \text{ m}$$

### LEARNING GOAL

**8**  Identify the major units of measure in the English and metric systems.

## Volume

The standard metric unit of *volume,* the space occupied by an object, is the liter (L). A liter is the volume occupied by 1000 g of water at 4 degrees Celsius (°C).

The English quart (qt) is similar to the liter.

$$1 \text{ qt} = 0.946 \text{ L} \quad \text{or} \quad 1.06 \text{ qt} = 1 \text{ L}$$

Volume can be derived using the formula

$$V = \text{length} \times \text{width} \times \text{height}$$

Therefore, volume is commonly reported with a length cubed unit. A cube with the length of each side equal to 1 m will have a volume of 1 m × 1 m × 1 m, or 1 m$^3$.

$$1 \text{ m}^3 = 1000 \text{ L}$$

The relationships among the units L, mL, and cm$^3$ are shown in Figure 1.8.

Typical laboratory devices used for volume measurement are shown in Figure 1.9. These devices are calibrated in units of milliliters (mL) or microliters (μL); 1 mL is, by definition, equal to 1 cm$^3$. The volumetric flask is designed to *contain* a specified volume, and the graduated cylinder, pipet, and buret *dispense* a desired volume of liquid.

## Time

The standard metric unit of time is the second (s). The need for accurate measurement of time by chemists may not be as apparent as that associated with mass, length, and volume. It is necessary, however, in many applications. In fact, matter may be characterized by measuring the time required for a certain process to occur. The rate of a chemical reaction is a measure of change as a function of time.

## 1.4   The Numbers of Measurement

A measurement has two parts: a number and a unit. The English and metric units of mass, length, volume, and time were discussed in Section 1.3. In this section, we will learn to handle the numbers associated with the measurements.

Information-bearing figures in a number are termed *significant figures*. Data and results arising from a scientific experiment convey information about the way in which the experiment was conducted. The degree of uncertainty or doubt associated with a measurement or series of measurements is indicated by the number of figures used to represent the information.

### Significant Figures

Consider the following situation: A student was asked to obtain the length of a section of wire. In the chemistry laboratory, several different types of measuring devices are usually available. Not knowing which was most appropriate, the

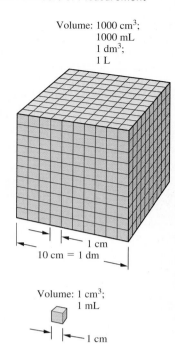

Volume: 1000 cm$^3$;
1000 mL
1 dm$^3$;
1 L

1 cm
10 cm = 1 dm

Volume: 1 cm$^3$;
1 mL
1 cm

**Figure 1.8** The relationships among various volume units.

### LEARNING GOAL

**9**  Report data and calculate results using scientific notation and the proper number of significant figures.

**Figure 1.9** Common laboratory equipment used for the measurement of volume. Graduated (a) cylinders, (b) pipets, and (c) burets are used for the delivery of liquids. A graduated cylinder is usually used for measurement of approximate volume; it is less accurate and precise than either pipets or burets. (d) Volumetric flasks are used to contain a specific volume.

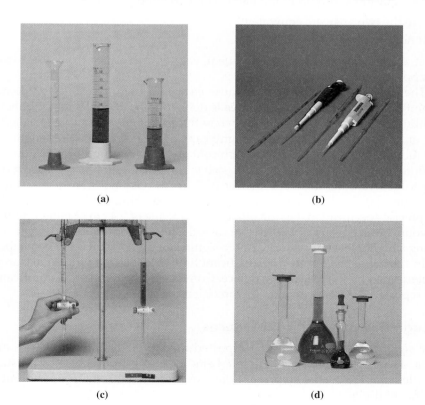

(a)

(b)

(c)

(d)

student decided to measure the object using each device that was available in the laboratory. To make each measurement, the student determined the mark nearest to the end of the wire. This is depicted in the figure below; the red bar represents the wire being measured. In each case, the student estimated one additional digit by mentally subdividing the marks into ten equal divisions. The following data were obtained:

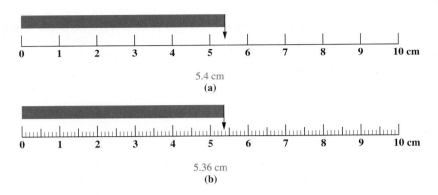

5.4 cm
(a)

5.36 cm
(b)

In case (a), we are certain that the object is at least 5 cm long and equally certain that it is *not* 6 cm long because the end of the object falls between the calibration lines 5 and 6. We can only estimate between 5 and 6, because there are no calibration indicators between 5 and 6. The end of the wire appears to be approximately four-tenths of the way between 5 and 6, hence 5.4 cm. The 5 is known with certainty, and 4 is estimated.

In case (b), the ruler is calibrated in tenths of a centimeter. The end of the wire is at least 5.3 cm and not 5.4 cm. Estimation of the second decimal place between the two closest calibration marks leads to 5.36 cm. In this case, 5.3 is certain, and the 6 is estimated (or uncertain).

Two questions should immediately come to mind:

1. Are the two answers equivalent?

2. If not, which answer is correct?

In fact, the two answers are *not* equivalent, yet *both* are correct. How do we explain this apparent discrepancy?

The data are not equivalent because each is known to a different degree of certainty. The term **significant figures** is defined to be all digits in a number representing data or results that are known with certainty *plus one uncertain digit*. The answer 5.36 cm, containing three significant figures, specifies the length of the wire more precisely than 5.4 cm, which contains only two significant figures.

Both answers are correct because each is consistent with the measuring device used to generate the data. An answer of 5.36 cm obtained from a measurement using ruler (a) would be *incorrect* because the measuring device is not capable of that precise specification. On the other hand, a value of 5.4 cm obtained from ruler (b) would be erroneous as well; in that case, the measuring device is capable of generating a higher level of certainty (more significant digits) than is actually reported.

In summary, the number of significant figures associated with a measurement is determined by the measuring device. Conversely, the number of significant figures reported is an indication of the precision of the measurement itself.

| The uncertain digit results from an estimation. |

| The uncertain digit represents the degree of doubt in a single measurement. |

## Recognition of Significant Figures

Only *significant* digits should be reported as data or results. However, are all digits, as written, significant digits? Let's look at a few examples illustrating the rules that are used to represent data and results with the proper number of significant digits.

- All nonzero digits are significant.

   7.314 has *four* significant digits.
- The number of significant digits is independent of the position of the decimal point.

   73.14 has *four* significant digits, as does 7.314.
- Zeros located between nonzero digits are significant.

   60.052 has *five* significant figures.
- Zeros at the end of a number (often referred to as trailing zeros) are significant or not significant depending upon the existence of a decimal point in the number.
   - If there *is* a decimal point, any trailing zeros are significant.

      4.70 has *three* significant figures.

      1000. has *four* significant figures because the decimal point is included.
   - If the number *does not* contain a decimal point, trailing zeros are not significant.

      1000 has *one* significant figure.
- Zeros to the left of the first nonzero integer are not significant; they serve only to locate the position of the decimal point.

   0.0032 has *two* significant figures.

**Question 1.7** How many significant figures are contained in each of the following numbers?

   a. 7.26  c. 700.2  e. 0.0720
   b. 726  d. 7.0  f. 720

**Question 1.8** How many significant figures are contained in each of the following numbers?

   a. 0.042  c. 24.0  e. 204
   b. 4.20  d. 240  f. 2.04

## Scientific Notation

It is often difficult to express very large numbers to the proper number of significant figures using conventional notation. The solution to this problem lies in the use of **scientific notation,** which involves the representation of a number that is greater than 1 and less than 10 which is multiplied by 10 raised to the power of a whole number.

The conversion is illustrated as:

$$6200 = 6.2 \times 1000 = 6.2 \times 10^3$$

If we wish to express 6200 with three significant figures, we can write it as:

$$6.20 \times 10^3$$

The trailing zero becomes significant with the existence of the decimal point in the number. Note also that the exponent of 3 has no bearing on the number of significant figures. The value of $6.20 \times 10^{14}$ also contains three significant figures.

■RULE: To convert a number greater than one to scientific notation, the original decimal point is moved $x$ places to the left, and the resulting number is multiplied by $10^x$. The exponent ($x$) is a *positive* number equal to the number of places the original decimal point was moved.

Scientific notation is also useful in representing numbers less than one. The conversion is illustrated as:

$$0.0062 = 6.2 \times \frac{1}{1000} = 6.2 \times \frac{1}{10^3} = 6.2 \times 10^{-3}$$

LEARNING GOAL

**9** Report data and calculate results using scientific notation and the proper number of significant figures.

Scientific notation is also referred to as exponential notation. When a number is not written in scientific notation, it is said to be in standard form.

By convention, in the exponential form, we represent the number with one digit to the left of the decimal point.

Scientific notation is written in the format: $y \times 10^x$, in which $y$ represents a number between 1 and 10, and $x$ represents a positive or negative whole number.

■RULE:   To convert a number less than one to scientific notation, the original decimal point is moved $x$ places to the right, and the resulting number is multiplied by $10^{-x}$. The exponent $(-x)$ is a *negative* number equal to the number of places the original decimal point was moved.

When a number is exceedingly large or small, scientific notation must be used to enter the number into a calculator. For example, the mass of a single helium atom is a rather cumbersome number as written:

$$0.000000000000000000000006692 \text{ g}$$

Most calculators only allow for the input of nine digits. Scientific notation would express this number as $6.692 \times 10^{-24}$ g.

**Question 1.9**   Represent each of the following numbers in scientific notation, showing only significant digits:

|   |   |   |
|---|---|---|
| a. 0.0024 | c. 224 | e. 72.420 |
| b. 0.0180 | d. 673,000 | f. 0.83 |

**Question 1.10**   Represent each of the following numbers in scientific notation, showing only significant digits:

|   |   |   |
|---|---|---|
| a. 48.20 | c. 0.126 | e. 0.0520 |
| b. 480.0 | d. 9,200 | f. 822 |

## Accuracy and Precision

The terms *accuracy* and *precision* are often used interchangeably in everyday conversation. However, they have very different meanings when discussing scientific measurement.

**Accuracy** is the degree of agreement between the true value and the measured value. The measured value may be a single number (such as the mass of an object) or the average value of a series of replicate measurements of the same quantity (reweighing the same object several times). We represent accuracy in terms of **error,** the numerical difference between the measured and true value.

Error is an unavoidable consequence of most laboratory measurements (except counted numbers, discussed on p. 17), but not for the reasons you might expect. Spills and contamination are certainly problems in a laboratory, but proper training and a great deal of practice eliminates most of these human errors. Still, errors, *systematic* and *random,* remain.

Systematic errors cause results to be generally higher than the true value or generally lower than the true value. An example would be something as simple as dust on a balance pan, causing each measurement to be higher than the true value. The causes of systematic error can often be discovered and removed. Even after correcting for systematic error we are still left with random error. Random error is an unavoidable, intrinsic consequence of measurement. Replicate measurements of the same quantity will produce some results greater than the true value and some less than the true value.

When possible, we prefer to make as many replicate measurements of the same quantity to "cancel out" the high (+) and low (−) fluctuations.

**Precision** is a measure of the agreement within a set of replicate measurements. Just as accuracy is measured in terms of error, precision is represented by **deviation,** the amount of variation present in a set of replicate measurements.

It is important to recognize that accuracy and precision are not the same thing. It is possible to have one without the other. However, when scientific measurements are carefully made, the two most often go hand in hand; high-quality data are characterized by high levels of precision and accuracy.

In Figure 1.10, bull's-eye (a) shows the goal of all experimentation: accuracy *and* precision. Bull's-eye (b) shows the results to be repeatable (good precision); however,

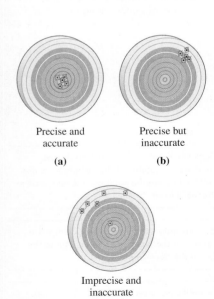

Precise and accurate

**(a)**

Precise but inaccurate

**(b)**

Imprecise and inaccurate

**(c)**

**Figure 1.10**   An illustration of precision and accuracy in replicate experiments.

some error in the experimental procedure has caused the results to center on an incorrect value. This error is systematic, occurring in each replicate measurement. Occasionally, an experiment may show "accidental" accuracy. The precision is poor, but the average of replicate measurements leads to a correct value. We don't want to rely on accidental success; the experiment should be repeated until the precision inspires faith in the accuracy of the method. Modern measuring devices in chemistry, equipped with powerful computers with immense storage capacity, are capable of making literally thousands of individual replicate measurements to enhance the quality of the result. In bull's-eye (c), we see a representation of poor precision and poor accuracy. Often, poor precision is accompanied by poor accuracy.

In summary, the presence of error and deviation in most measurements is the real basis for significant figures: all the *certain* digits plus one *uncertain* digit.

## Exact (Counted) and Inexact Numbers

*Inexact numbers,* by definition, have uncertainty (the degree of doubt in the final significant digit). *Exact numbers,* on the other hand, have no uncertainty. Exact numbers may arise from a definition; there are *exactly* 60 min in 1 h or there are exactly 1000 mL in 1 L.

Exact numbers are a consequence of counting. Counting the number of dimes in your pocket or the number of letters in the alphabet are examples. The fact that exact numbers have no uncertainty means that they do not limit the number of significant figures in the result of a calculation.

For example, we may wish to determine the mass of three bolts purchased from the hardware store. Each bolt has a mass of 12.97 g. The total mass is determined by:

$$3 \times 12.97 \text{ g} = 38.91 \text{ g}$$

The number of significant figures in the result is governed by the data (mass of the bolt) and not by the counted (*exact*) number of bolts.

In Section 1.5, we will learn how to convert between units. A good rule of thumb to follow when performing these types of calculations is to use the measured quantity, *not* the conversion factor in order to determine the number of significant figures in the answer.

## Rounding Numbers

The use of a calculator generally produces more digits for a result than are justified by the rules of significant figures on the basis of the data input. For example, your calculator may show:

$$3.84 \times 6.72 = 25.8048$$

The most correct answer would be 25.8, dropping 048. A convenient way to show this is:

$$3.84 \times 6.72 = 25.8048 \approx 25.8$$

The rule for multiplication and significant figures dictates three significant figures in the answer.

A number of acceptable conventions for rounding exist. Throughout this book, we will use the following:

■RULE:   When the number to be dropped is less than five, the preceding number is not changed. When the number to be dropped is five or larger, the preceding number is increased by one unit.

**Question 1.11**   Round each of the following numbers to three significant figures.
   a. 61.40      b. 6.171      c. 0.066494      d. 63.669      e. 8.7715

**Question 1.12**   Round each of the following numbers to two significant figures.
   a. 6.2262      b. 3895      c. 6.885      d. 2.2247      e. 0.0004109

LEARNING GOAL

**9** Report data and calculate results using scientific notation and the proper number of significant figures.

Remember the distinction between the words *zero* and *nothing*. *Zero* is one of the 10 digits and conveys as much information as 1, 2, and so forth. *Nothing* implies no information; the digits in the positions indicated by *x* could be 0, 1, 2, or any other.

*See the rules for rounding discussed earlier in this section.*

## Significant Figures in Calculation of Results

### Addition and Subtraction

If we combine the following numbers:

$$37.68$$
$$108.428$$
$$6.71864$$

our calculator will show a final result of

$$152.82664$$

Clearly the answer, with eight digits, defines the total much more accurately than *any* of the individual quantities being combined. This cannot be correct; *the answer cannot have greater significance than any of the quantities that produced the answer.* We rewrite the problem:

$$
\begin{array}{r}
37.68xxx \\
108.428xx \\
+\quad 6.71864 \\
\hline
152.82664
\end{array}
$$
(should be 152.83)

where $x$ = no information; $x$ may be any integer from 0 to 9. Adding 4 to two unknown numbers (in the rightmost column) produces no information. Similar logic prevails for the previous two columns. Thus, five digits remain, all of which are significant. Conventional rules for rounding would dictate a final answer of 152.83.

**Question 1.13** Report the result of each of the following to the proper number of significant figures:
  a. $4.26 + 3.831 =$    b. $8.321 - 2.4 =$    c. $16.262 + 4.33 - 0.40 =$

**Question 1.14** Report the result of each of the following to the proper number of significant figures:
  a. $7.939 + 6.26 =$    b. $2.4 - 8.321 =$    c. $2.333 + 1.56 - 0.29 =$

Adding numbers that are in scientific notation requires a bit more consideration. The numbers must either be converted to standard form or converted to numbers that have the same exponents. Example 1.5 demonstrates this point.

---

**EXAMPLE 1.5**    **Determining Significant Figures When Adding Numbers in Scientific Notation**

LEARNING GOAL

**9** Report data and calculate results using scientific notation and the proper number of significant figures.

Report the result of the following addition to the proper number of significant figures and in scientific notation.

$$9.47 \times 10^{-6} + 9.3 \times 10^{-5}$$

### Solution

There are two strategies that may be used in order to arrive at the correct answer.

**First solution strategy.**
When both numbers are converted to standard form, they can be added together. The initial answer is not the correct answer because it does not have the proper number of significant figures.

$$0.00000947$$
$$+ \ 0.000093xx$$
$$0.0001024\,7$$

After rounding, the answer 0.000102 can then be converted to the final answer, which in scientific notation is $1.02 \times 10^{-4}$.

**Second solution strategy.**

When both numbers have the same power of 10 exponent, they can be added together. In this example, $9.47 \times 10^{-6}$ is converted to $0.947 \times 10^{-5}$.

$$9.47 \times 10^{-6} = 0.947 \times 10^{-5}$$

$$0.947 \times 10^{-5}$$
$$+ \ 9.3xx \times 10^{-5}$$
$$10.247 \times 10^{-5}$$

As in the first solution strategy, the initial answer is rounded to the proper number of significant figures, $10.2 \times 10^{-5}$ which is written in scientific notation as $1.02 \times 10^{-4}$.

**Practice Problem 1.5**

Report the result of the addition of $6.72 \times 10^5 + 7.4 \times 10^4$ to the proper number of significant figures and in scientific notation.

▶ For Further Practice: **Questions 1.79 b, d; 1.80 d, e.**

**Question 1.15**   Report the result of the following addition to the proper number of significant figures and in scientific notation.

$$8.23 \times 10^{-4} + 6.1 \times 10^{-5}$$

**Question 1.16**   Report the result of the following addition to the proper number of significant figures and in scientific notation.

$$4.80 \times 10^8 + 9.149 \times 10^2$$

## Multiplication and Division

In the preceding discussion of addition and subtraction, the position of the decimal point in the quantities being combined had a bearing on the number of significant figures in the answer. In multiplication and division, this is not the case. The decimal point position is irrelevant when determining the number of significant figures in the answer. It is the number of significant figures in the data that is important. Consider

$$\frac{4.237 \times 1.21 \times 10^{-3} \times 0.00273}{11.125} = 1.26 \times 10^{-6}$$

The answer is limited to three significant figures; the answer can have *only* three significant figures because two numbers in the calculation, $1.21 \times 10^{-3}$ and $0.00273$, have three significant figures and "limit" the answer. *The answer can be no more precise than the least precise number from which the answer is derived. The least precise number is the number with the fewest significant figures.*

**LEARNING GOAL**

**9**  Report data and calculate results using scientific notation and the proper number of significant figures.

**EXAMPLE 1.6** | **Determining Significant Figures When Multiplying Numbers in Scientific Notation**

LEARNING GOAL

Report the result of the following operation to the proper number of significant figures and in scientific notation.

**9** Report data and calculate results using scientific notation and the proper number of significant figures.

$$\frac{2.44 \times 10^4}{91}$$

**Solution**

Often problems that combine multiplication and addition can be broken into parts. This allows each part to be solved in a stepwise fashion.

**Step 1.** The numerator operation can be completed.

$$2.44 \times 10^4 = 24{,}400$$

**Step 2.** This value can now be divided by the value in the denominator.

$$\frac{24{,}400}{91} = 268$$

**Step 3.** The answer is limited to two significant figures. This is because of the two numbers in the calculation, 2.244 and 91, the number 91 has fewer significant figures and limits the number of significant figures in the answer. The answer in scientific notation is $2.7 \times 10^2$.

---

**Practice Problem 1.6**

Report the result of the following operation to the proper number of significant figures and in scientific notation.

$$\frac{837}{1.8 \times 10^{-2}}$$

▶ For Further Practice: **1.79 a, c, e and 1.80 a, b, c.**

---

**Question 1.17**   Report the result of each of the following operations using the proper number of significant figures:

a. $63.8 \times 0.80 =$

b. $\dfrac{63.8}{0.80} =$

c. $\dfrac{16.4 \times 78.11}{22.1} =$

d. $\dfrac{42.2}{21.38 \times 2.3} =$

e. $\dfrac{4.38 \times 10^8}{0.9462} =$

f. $\dfrac{6.1 \times 10^{-4}}{0.3025} =$

**Question 1.18**   Report the result of each of the following operations using the proper number of significant figures:

a. $\dfrac{27.2 \times 15.63}{1.84} =$

b. $\dfrac{13.6}{18.02 \times 1.6} =$

c. $\dfrac{4.79 \times 10^5}{0.7911} =$

d. $3.58 \times 4.0 =$

e. $\dfrac{3.58}{4.0} =$

f. $\dfrac{11.4 \times 10^{-4}}{0.45} =$

## 1.5   Unit Conversion

To convert from one unit to another, we must have a *conversion factor* or series of conversion factors that relate two units. The proper use of these conversion factors is called the *factor-label method* or *dimensional analysis*. This method is used for two kinds of conversions: to convert from one unit to another within the *same system* or to convert units from *one system to another*.

## Conversion of Units within the Same System

Based on the information presented in Table 1.1, Section 1.3, we know that in the English system,

$$1 \text{ gal} = 4 \text{ qt}$$

Dividing both sides of the equation by the same term does not change its identity. These ratios are equivalent to unity (1); therefore

$$\frac{1 \text{ gal}}{1 \text{ gal}} = \frac{4 \text{ qt}}{1 \text{ gal}} = 1$$

Multiplying any other expression by either of these ratios will not change the value of the term because multiplication of any number by 1 produces the original value. However, the units will change.

## Factor-Label Method

When the expressions are written as ratios, they can be used as conversion factors in the factor-label method. For example, if you were to convert 12 gal to quarts, you must decide which conversion factor to use,

$$\frac{1 \text{ gal}}{4 \text{ qt}} \quad \text{or} \quad \frac{4 \text{ qt}}{1 \text{ gal}}$$

Since you are converting 12 gal (Data Given) to qt (Desired Result), it is important to choose a conversion factor with gal in the denominator and qt in the numerator. That way, when the initial quantity (12 gal) is multiplied by the conversion factor, the original unit (gal) will cancel, leaving you with the unit qt in the answer.

$$12 \text{ gal} \times \frac{4 \text{ qt}}{1 \text{ gal}} = 48 \text{ qt}$$

Data Given × Conversion Factor = Desired Result

If the incorrect ratio was selected as a conversion factor, the answer would be incorrect.

$$12 \text{ gal} \times \frac{1 \text{ gal}}{4 \text{ qt}} = \frac{3 \text{ gal}^2}{\text{qt}} \quad \text{(incorrect units)}$$

Therefore, the factor-label method is a self-indicating system. The product will only have the correct units if the conversion factor is set up properly.

The factor-label method is also useful when more than one conversion factor is needed to convert the data given to the desired result. The use of a series of conversion factors is illustrated in Example 1.7.

LEARNING GOAL

**11**   Convert between units of the English and metric systems.

The speed of an automobile is indicated in both English (mi/h) and metric (km/h) units.

Conversion factors are used to relate units through the process of the factor-label method (dimensional analysis).

---

| EXAMPLE 1.7 | **Using English System Conversion Factors** |
| --- | --- |

Convert $3.28 \times 10^4$ ounces to tons.

### Solution

Using the equalities provided in Table 1.1, the data given in ounces (oz) can be directly converted to a bridging data result in pounds (lb), so lb can be converted to the desired result in tons (t). The possible conversion factors are

$$\frac{1 \text{ lb}}{16 \text{ oz}} = \frac{16 \text{ oz}}{1 \text{ lb}} \quad \text{and} \quad \frac{2000 \text{ lb}}{1 \text{ t}} = \frac{1 \text{ t}}{2000 \text{ lb}}$$

LEARNING GOAL

**11**   Convert between units of the English and metric systems.

*Continued…*

**Step 1.** Since the initial value is in oz, the conversion factor with oz in the denominator should be used first.

$$3.28 \times 10^4 \; \cancel{oz} \times \frac{1 \text{ lb}}{16 \; \cancel{oz}} = 2.05 \times 10^3 \text{ lb}$$

Data Given × Conversion Factor = Initial Data Result

If the other conversion factor relating oz and lb was used, the resulting units would have been $oz^2/lb$, and the answer would have been incorrect.

**Step 2.** Now that $3.28 \times 10^4$ oz has been converted to $2.05 \times 10^3$ lb, the conversion factor relating lb to t is used. The conversion factor with lb in the denominator and t in the numerator is the only one that leads to the correct answer.

$$2.05 \times 10^3 \; \cancel{lb} \times \frac{1 \text{ t}}{2000 \; \cancel{lb}} = 1.03 \text{ t}$$

Initial Data Result × Conversion Factor = Desired Result

This calculation may also be done in a single step by arranging the factors in a chain:

$$3.28 \times 10^4 \; \cancel{oz} \times \frac{1 \; \cancel{lb}}{16 \; \cancel{oz}} \times \frac{1 \text{ t}}{2000 \; \cancel{lb}} = 1.03 \text{ t}$$

Data Given × Conversion Factor × Conversion Factor = Desired Result

*Helpful Hint:* After the conversion factors have been selected and set up in the solution to the problem, it is important to also cancel the units that can be canceled. This process will allow for you to verify that you have set up the problem correctly. In addition, the unit ton represents a significantly larger quantity than the unit ounce. Therefore, one would expect a small number of tons to equal a large number of ounces.

## Practice Problem 1.7

Convert 360 ft to mi.

▶ For Further Practice: **Questions 1.91 a, b and 1.92 a, b.**

Table 1.2 is located in Section 1.3.

Conversion of units within the metric system may be accomplished by using the factor-label method as well. Unit prefixes that dictate the conversion factor facilitate unit conversion (refer to Table 1.2). Example 1.8 demonstrates this process.

## EXAMPLE 1.8    Using Metric System Conversion Factors

**LEARNING GOAL**

Convert 0.0047 kg to mg.

**11** Convert between units of the English and metric systems.

### Solution

Using the equalities provided in Table 1.2, the data given in kg can be directly converted to a bridging data result in g, so g can be converted to the desired result in mg. The possible conversion factors are

$$\frac{10^3 \text{ g}}{1 \text{ kg}} = \frac{1 \text{ kg}}{10^3 \text{ g}} \quad \text{and} \quad \frac{10^{-3} \text{ g}}{1 \text{ mg}} = \frac{1 \text{ mg}}{10^{-3} \text{ g}}$$

**Step 1.** Since the initial value is in kg, the conversion factor with kg in the denominator should be used first.

$$0.0047 \; \cancel{kg} \times \frac{10^3 \text{ g}}{1 \; \cancel{kg}} = 4.7 \text{ g}$$

Data Given × Conversion Factor = Initial Data Result

If the other conversion factor relating kg and g was used, the resulting units would have been $kg^2/g$, and the answer would have been incorrect.

**Step 2.** Now that 0.0047 kg has been converted to 4.7 g, the conversion factor relating g to mg is used. The conversion factor with g in the denominator and mg in the numerator is the only one that leads to the correct answer.

$$4.7 \, \cancel{g} \times \frac{1 \, mg}{10^{-3} \, \cancel{g}} = 4.7 \times 10^3 \, mg$$

Initial Data Result $\times$ Conversion Factor = Desired Result

This calculation may also be done in a single step by arranging the factors in a chain:

$$0.0047 \, \cancel{kg} \times \frac{10^3 \, \cancel{g}}{1 \, \cancel{kg}} \times \frac{1 \, mg}{10^{-3} \, \cancel{g}} = 4.7 \times 10^3 \, mg$$

Data Given $\times$ Conversion Factor $\times$ Conversion Factor = Desired Result

*Helpful Hint:* After the conversion factors have been selected and set up in the solution to the problem, it is important to also cancel the units that can be canceled. This process will allow for you to verify that you have set up the problem correctly. In addition, the unit mg represents a significantly smaller quantity than the unit kg. Therefore, one would expect a large number of mg to equal a small number of kg.

### Practice Problem 1.8

a. 750 cm to mm
b. $1.5 \times 10^8$ microliters to centiliters
c. 0.00055 Mg to kg

▶ For Further Practice: **Questions 1.95 and 1.96.**

## Conversion of Units Between Systems

The conversion of a quantity expressed in a unit of one system to an equivalent quantity in the other system (English to metric or metric to English) requires the use of a relating unit, a conversion unit that relates the two systems. Examples are shown in Table 1.3.

The conversion may be represented as a three-step process:

**Step 1.** Conversion from the unit given in the problem to a relating unit.

Data Given $\times$ Conversion Unit = Relating Unit

**Step 2.** Conversion to the other system using the relating unit.

Relating Unit $\times$ Conversion Unit = Initial Data Result

**Step 3.** Conversion within the desired system to unit required by the problem.

Initial Data Result $\times$ Conversion Unit = Desired Result

Example 1.9 demonstrates a conversion from the English system to the metric system.

**TABLE 1.3  Relationships Between Common English and Metric Units**

| Quantity | English | | Metric |
|---|---|---|---|
| Mass | 1 pound | = | 454 grams |
| Length | 1 yard | = | 0.914 meter |
| Volume | 1 quart | = | 0.946 liter |

**EXAMPLE 1.9**    **Using Both English and Metric System Conversion Factors**

LEARNING GOAL

11   Convert between units of the English and metric systems.

Convert 4.00 oz to kg.

### Solution

Based on the English system relationships provided in Tables 1.1 and 1.3, the data given in oz should be converted to a relating data result in lb, so lb can be converted to the g. Then, using the prefix equalities in Table 1.2, the initial data result in g can be converted to the desired result in kg. The possible conversion factors are:

$$\frac{16 \text{ oz}}{1 \text{ lb}} = \frac{1 \text{ lb}}{16 \text{ oz}} \quad \text{and} \quad \frac{454 \text{ g}}{1 \text{ lb}} = \frac{1 \text{ lb}}{454 \text{ g}} \quad \text{and} \quad \frac{10^3 \text{ g}}{1 \text{ kg}} = \frac{1 \text{ kg}}{10^3 \text{ g}}$$

**Step 1.** Since the initial value is in oz, the conversion factor with oz in the denominator should be used first because it relates the data given to a relating unit.

$$4.00 \text{ oz} \times \frac{1 \text{ lb}}{16 \text{ oz}} = 0.250 \text{ lb}$$

Data Given × Conversion Factor = Relating Unit

If the other conversion factor relating oz and lb was used, the resulting units would have been $\text{oz}^2/\text{lb}$, and the answer would have been incorrect.

**Step 2.** Now that 4.00 oz has been converted to 0.250 lb, the conversion factor relating lb to g is used. The conversion factor with lb in the denominator and g in the numerator is the only one that leads to the correct answer.

$$0.250 \text{ lb} \times \frac{454 \text{ g}}{1 \text{ lb}} = 114 \text{ g}$$

Relating Unit × Conversion Factor = Initial Data Result

**Step 3.** In the final step of this conversion, the conversion is within the desired system of units required by the problem. The conversion factor relating g and kg with g in the denominator and kg in the numerator is the only one that leads to the correct answer.

$$114 \text{ g} \times \frac{1 \text{ kg}}{10^3 \text{ g}} = 0.114 \text{ kg}$$

Initial Data Result × Conversion Factor = Desired Result

This calculation may also be done in a single step by arranging the factors in a chain:

$$4.00 \text{ oz} \times \frac{1 \text{ lb}}{16 \text{ oz}} \times \frac{454 \text{ g}}{1 \text{ lb}} \times \frac{1 \text{ kg}}{10^3 \text{ g}} = 0.114 \text{ kg}$$

Data Given × Conversion Factor × Conversion Factor × Conversion Factor = Desired Result

*Helpful Hint:* After the conversion factors have been selected and set up in the solution to the problem, it is important to also cancel the units that can be canceled. This process will allow for you to verify that you have set up the problem correctly. In addition, the unit oz represents a smaller quantity than the unit kg. Therefore, one would expect a large number of oz to equal a small number of kg.

### Practice Problem 1.9

Convert:

a. 0.50 in to m

b. 0.75 qt to L

c. 56.8 g to oz

d. 0.50 in to cm

e. 0.75 qt to mL

f. 56.8 mg to oz

▶ For Further Practice: **Questions 1.93 a, b and 1.94 a, b.**

# A Medical Perspective

## Curiosity and the Science That Leads to Discovery

Curiosity is one of the most important human traits. Small children constantly ask, "Why?" As we get older, our questions become more complex, but the curiosity remains. Curiosity is also the basis of the scientific method. A scientist observes an event, wonders why it happened, and sets out to answer the question. Dr. Eric Wieschaus's story provides an example of curiosity that led to the discovery of gene pathways that are currently the target of new medicines.

As a child, Dr. Wieschaus dreamed of being an artist, but during the summer following his junior year of high school, he took part in a science program and found his place in the laboratory. When he was a sophomore in college, he accepted a job preparing fly food in a *Drosophila* (fruit fly) lab. Then, while learning about mitosis (cell division) in his embryology course, he became excited about the process of embryonic development. He was fascinated watching how a fertilized frog egg underwent cell division with little cellular growth or differentiation until it formed an embryo. Then, when the embryo grew, the cells in the various locations within the embryo developed differently. As a direct result of his observations, he became determined to understand why certain embryonic cells developed the way they did.

Throughout graduate school, his interest in solving this mystery continued. In his search for the answer, he devised different types of experiments in order to collect data that could explain what caused certain embryonic cells to differentiate into their various shapes, sizes, and positions within the growing embryo. It is these cellular differentiations that determine which cells may become tissues, organs, muscles, or nerves. Although many of his experiments failed, some of the experiments that he completed using normal embryonic cells provided data that led to his next series of experiments in which he used mutated embryos.

After graduate school, Dr. Wieschaus and his colleague, Dr. Christiane Nüsslein-Volhard, used a trial-and-error approach to determine which of the fly's 20,000 genes were essential to embryonic development. They used a chemical to create random mutations in the flies. The mutated flies were bred, and the fly families were analyzed under a microscope. Although the fly embryos are only 0.18 mm in length, the average adult female fly is 2.5 mm long. This allowed for the physical characteristics that resulted from mutated genes to be observed. An artist at heart, Dr. Wieschaus enjoyed this visual work.

Each day was exciting because he knew that at any moment, he could find the answer that he had been seeking for so long. After many years, the team was able to find the genes that controlled the cellular development process within *Drosophila*. The hedgehog gene was one of several genes they

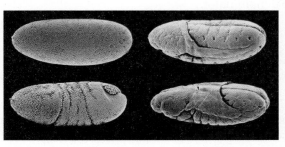

Discoveries about the Drosophila embryo have led to advances in medicine.

identified. It controls a pathway that provides cells with the information they need to develop.

Although it was initially discovered while *Drosophila* embryos were being studied, the hedgehog gene has roles in other adult animals. It has been found that if the hedgehog pathway becomes impaired in humans, basal cell carcinoma (BCC), the most common form of skin cancer, develops. The curiosity that led to the hedgehog gene also led to the discovery of an entirely new type of cancer drug, the first Food and Drug Administration (FDA) approved drug for patients with advanced BCC. This and other types of gene-controlled pathways are allowing for the creation of drugs that target specific diseases. Since these drugs can be designed to be selective, they should also have fewer side effects.

The curiosity that enabled Dr. Wieschaus to advance the field of medicine also catalyzed the development of chemistry. We will see the product of this fundamental human characteristic as we study the work of many extraordinary chemists throughout this textbook.

### For Further Understanding

▶ What is the length of the fruit fly embryo in cm?
▶ What is the length of the fruit fly embryo in inches?

---

When a unit is raised to a power, the corresponding conversion factor must also be raised to that power. This ensures that the units cancel properly. Example 1.10 demonstrates how to convert units that are squared or cubed.

**EXAMPLE 1.10**    **Using Conversion Factors Involving Exponents**

LEARNING GOAL

Convert 1.5 m$^2$ to cm$^2$.

**11**   Convert between units of the English and metric systems.

**Solution**

This problem is similar to the conversion problems performed in the previous examples. However, in solving this problem using the factor-label method, the unit exponents must be included.

Using the metric system equalities provided in Table 1.2, the data given in m$^2$ can be directly converted to the desired result in cm$^2$. The possible conversion factors are

$$\frac{10^{-2} \text{ m}}{1 \text{ cm}} = \frac{1 \text{ cm}}{10^{-2} \text{ m}}$$

Since the initial value is in m$^2$, the conversion factor with cm in the denominator should be used. If the incorrect conversion factor was used, the units would not cancel and the result would be m$^4$ in the numerator and cm$^2$ in the denominator.

$$1.5 \text{ m}^2 \times \frac{1 \text{ cm}}{10^{-2} \text{ m}} \times \frac{1 \text{ cm}}{10^{-2} \text{ m}} = 1.5 \times 10^4 \text{ cm}^2$$

Data Given × (Conversion Factor)$^2$ = Desired Result

*Helpful Hint:* When converting a value with a squared unit, the impact of the conversion factor is much greater than if the unit had no exponent. Without the squared unit, the two numbers would be different by a factor of 100; whereas in this example, the two numbers are different by a factor of 10,000.

**Practice Problem 1.10**

Convert:

  a. 1.5 cm$^2$ to m$^2$              b. 3.6 m$^2$ to cm$^2$

▶ For Further Practice: **Question 1.97.**

Sometimes the unit to be converted is in the denominator. Be sure to set up your conversion factor accordingly. Example 1.11 demonstrates this process.

**EXAMPLE 1.11**    **Converting Units in the Denominator**

LEARNING GOAL

The density of air is 1.29 g/L. What is the value in g/mL? (Note: Density will be discussed in more detail in Section 1.6.)

**11**   Convert between units of the English and metric systems.

**Solution**

This problem requires the use of one conversion factor. According to the metric system equalities relating mL and L provided in Table 1.2, the possible conversion factors are

$$\frac{10^{-3} \text{ L}}{1 \text{ mL}} = \frac{1 \text{ mL}}{10^{-3} \text{ L}}$$

Since the data given has L in the denominator, the conversion factor with L in the numerator should be used. If the incorrect conversion factor was used, the units would not cancel and the result would be g and mL in the numerator and L$^2$ in the denominator.

$$\frac{1.29 \text{ g}}{\cancel{L}} \times \frac{10^{-3} \cancel{L}}{1 \text{ mL}} = 1.29 \times 10^{-3} \frac{\text{g}}{\text{mL}}$$

Data Given × Conversion Factor = Desired Result

*Helpful Hint:* If the incorrect conversion factor was used, the units would not cancel and the result would be g and mL in the numerator and $L^2$ in the denominator.

---

**Practice Problem 1.11**

Convert 0.791 g/mL to kg/L.

▶ For Further Practice: **Question 1.98.**

---

It is difficult to overstate the importance of paying careful attention to units and unit conversions. Just one example of the tremendous cost that can result from a "small error," is the loss of a 125 million-dollar Mars-orbiting satellite because of failure to convert from English to metric units during one phase of its construction. As a consequence of this error, the satellite established an orbit too close to Mars and burned up in the Martian atmosphere along with 125 million dollars of the National Aeronautics and Space Administration (NASA) budget.

## 1.6 Additional Experimental Quantities

In Section 1.3, we introduced the experimental quantities of mass, length, volume, and time. We will now introduce other commonly measured and derived quantities.

### Temperature

**Temperature** is the degree of "hotness" of an object. This may not sound like a very "scientific" definition, and, in a sense, it is not. Intuitively, we know the difference between a "hot" and a "cold" object, but developing a precise definition to explain this is not easy. We may think of the temperature of an object as a measure of the amount of heat in the object. However, this is not strictly true. An object increases in temperature because its heat content has increased and vice versa; however, the relationship between heat content and temperature depends on the quantity and composition of the material.

Many substances, such as mercury, expand as their temperature increases, and this expansion provides us with a way to measure temperature and temperature changes. If the mercury is contained within a sealed tube, as it is in a thermometer, the height of the mercury is proportional to the temperature. A mercury thermometer may be calibrated, or scaled, in different units, just as a ruler can be. Three common temperature scales are *Fahrenheit* (°F), *Celsius* (°C), and *Kelvin* (K). Two convenient reference temperatures that are used to calibrate a thermometer are the freezing and boiling temperatures of water. Figure 1.11 shows the relationship between the scales and these reference temperatures.

Although Fahrenheit temperature is most familiar to us, Celsius and Kelvin temperatures are used exclusively in scientific measurements. It is often necessary to convert a temperature reading from one scale to another. To convert from Fahrenheit to Celsius, we use the following formula:

$$T_{°C} = \frac{T_{°F} - 32}{1.8}$$

**LEARNING GOAL**

**12** Know the three common temperature scales, and convert values from one scale to another.

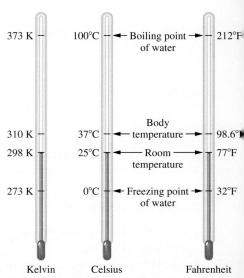

**Figure 1.11** The freezing point and boiling point of water, body temperature, and room temperature expressed in the three common units of temperature.

To convert from Celsius to Fahrenheit, we solve this formula for °F, resulting in

$$T_{\mathrm{°F}} = \left(1.8 \times T_{\mathrm{°C}}\right) + 32$$

To convert from Celsius to Kelvin, we use the formula

$$T_{\mathrm{K}} = T_{\mathrm{°C}} + 273.15$$

The Kelvin symbol does not have a degree sign. The degree sign implies a value that is *relative* to some standard. Kelvin is an *absolute* scale.

---

**EXAMPLE 1.12**   **Converting from Fahrenheit to Celsius and Kelvin**

LEARNING GOAL

Normal body temperature is 98.6°F. Calculate the corresponding temperature in both degrees Celsius and Kelvin units and report the answer to the appropriate number of significant figures.

**12**   Know the three common temperature scales, and convert values from one scale to another.

**Solution**

Using the expression relating °C and °F,

$$T_{\mathrm{°C}} = \frac{T_{\mathrm{°F}} - 32}{1.8}$$

Substituting the information provided,

$$= \frac{98.6 - 32}{1.8} = \frac{66.6}{1.8}$$

results in:

$$= 37.0\,\mathrm{°C}$$

To calculate the corresponding temperature in Kelvin units, use the expression relating K and °C.

$$T_{\mathrm{K}} = T_{\mathrm{°C}} + 273.15$$

Substituting the value obtained in the first part,

$$= 37.0 + 273.15$$

results in:

$$= 310.2\,\mathrm{K}$$

According to Figure 1.11, these three temperatures are at the same place on each thermometer. Therefore, 98.6°F, 37.0°C, and 310.2 K are equivalent.

**Practice Problem 1.12**

a. The freezing temperature of water is 32°F. Calculate the freezing temperature of water in Celsius units and Kelvin units.

b. When a patient is ill, his or her temperature may increase to 104°F. Calculate the temperature of this patient in Celsius units and Kelvin units.

▶ For Further Practice: **Questions 1.115 and 1.116.**

## Energy

Energy, the ability to do work, may be categorized as either **kinetic energy,** the energy of motion, or **potential energy,** the energy of position. Kinetic energy may be considered as energy in action; potential energy is stored energy. All energy is either kinetic or potential.

Another useful way of classifying energy is by form. The principal forms of energy include light, heat, electrical, mechanical, nuclear, and chemical energy. All of these forms of energy share the following set of characteristics:

- Energy cannot be created or destroyed.
- Energy may be converted from one form to another.
- Conversion of energy from one form to another always occurs with less than 100% efficiency. Energy is not lost (remember, energy cannot be destroyed) but, rather, is not useful. We use gasoline to move our cars from place to place; however, much of the energy stored in the gasoline is released as heat.
- All chemical reactions involve either a "gain" or a "loss" of energy.

Energy absorbed or liberated in chemical reactions is usually in the form of heat energy. Heat energy may be represented in units of *calories* (cal) or *joules* (J), their relationship being

$$1 \text{ cal} = 4.18 \text{ J}$$

One calorie is defined as the amount of heat energy required to increase the temperature of 1 g of water 1°C.

Heat energy measurement is a quantitative measure of heat content. It is an extensive property, dependent upon the quantity of material. Temperature, as we have mentioned, is an intensive property, independent of quantity.

Not all substances have the same capacity for holding heat; 1 g of iron and 1 g of water, even if they are at the same temperature, do *not* contain the same amount of heat energy. One gram of iron will absorb and store 0.108 cal of heat energy when the temperature is raised 1°C. In contrast, 1 g of water will absorb almost ten times as much energy, 1.00 cal, when the temperature is increased an equivalent amount.

Units for other forms of energy will be introduced in later chapters.

**Question 1.19**   Convert 595 cal to units of J.

**Question 1.20**   Convert $2.00 \times 10^2$ J to units of cal.

## Concentration

**Concentration** is a measure of the number or mass of particles of a substance that are contained in a specified volume. Examples include:

- The concentration of oxygen in the air
- Pollen counts, given during the hay fever seasons, which are simply the number of grains of pollen contained in a measured volume of air
- The amount of an illegal drug in a certain volume of blood, indicating the extent of drug abuse
- The proper dose of an antibiotic, based on a patient's weight

We will describe many situations in which concentration is used to predict useful information about chemical reactions (Chapters 6–8, for example). In Chapter 6, we calculate a numerical value for concentration from experimental data.

Water in the environment (lakes, oceans, and streams) has a powerful effect on the climate because of its ability to store large quantities of energy. In summer, water stores heat energy and moderates temperatures of the surrounding area. In winter, some of this stored energy is released to the air as the water temperature falls; this prevents the surroundings from experiencing extreme changes in temperature.

The *kilocalorie* (kcal) is the familiar nutritional calorie. It is also known as the large Calorie (C); note that in this term the C is uppercase to distinguish it from the normal calorie. The large Calorie is 1000 normal calories. Refer to A Human Perspective: Food Calories (p. 30) for more information.

## Food Calories

The body gets its energy through the processes known collectively as metabolism, which will be discussed in detail in Chapters 21–23. The primary energy sources for the body are carbohydrates, fats, and proteins, which we obtain from the foods we eat. The amount of energy available from a given foodstuff is related to the Calories (C) available in the food. Calories are a measure of energy that can be derived from food. One (food) Calorie (symbolized by C) equals 1000 (metric) calories (symbolized by cal):

$$1 \text{ C} = 1000 \text{ cal} = 1 \text{ kcal}$$

The energy available in food can be measured by completely burning the food; in other words, using the food as fuel. The energy given off in the form of heat is directly related to the amount of chemical energy, the energy stored in chemical bonds, that is available in the food. Food provides energy to the body through various metabolic pathways.

The classes of food molecules are not equally energy-rich. When oxidized via metabolic pathways, carbohydrates and proteins provide the cell with 4 C/g, whereas fats generate approximately 9 C/g.

In addition, as with all processes, not all the available energy can be efficiently extracted from the food; a certain percentage is always released to the surroundings as heat. The average person requires between 2000 and 3000 C/day to maintain normal body functions such as the regulation of body temperature and muscle movement. If a person takes in more C than the body uses, the person will gain weight. Conversely, if a person uses more C than are ingested, the individual will lose weight.

Excess C are stored in the form of fat, the form that provides the greatest amount of energy per g. Too many C leads to too much fat. Similarly, a lack of C (in the form of food) forces the body to raid its storehouse, the fat. Weight is lost in this process as the fat is consumed. Unfortunately, it always seems easier to add fat to the storehouse than to remove it.

The "rule of thumb" is that 3500 C are equivalent to approximately 1 lb of body fat. You have to take in 3500 C more than you use to gain 1 lb, and you have to expend 3500 C more than you normally use to lose 1 lb. If you eat as few as 100 C/day beyond your body's needs, you could gain about 10–11 lb per year (yr):

$$\frac{100 \text{ C}}{\text{day}} \times \frac{365 \text{ day}}{1 \text{ yr}} \times \frac{1 \text{ lb}}{3500 \text{ C}} = \frac{10.4 \text{ lb}}{\text{yr}}$$

A frequently recommended procedure for increasing the rate of weight loss involves a combination of dieting (taking in fewer C) and exercise. Running, swimming, jogging, and cycling are particularly efficient forms of exercise. Running burns 0.11 C/min for every lb of body weight, and swimming burns approximately 0.05 C/min for every lb of body weight.

### For Further Understanding

▶ Sarah runs 1 h each day, and Nancy swims 2 h each day. Assuming that Sarah and Nancy are the same weight, which girl burns more calories in 1 week?

▶ Would you expect a runner to burn more calories in summer or winter? Why?

---

## Density and Specific Gravity

Both mass and volume are functions of the *amount* of material present (extensive properties). **Density,** the ratio of mass to volume,

$$\text{Density } (d) = \frac{\text{mass}}{\text{volume}} = \frac{m}{V}$$

**TABLE 1.4** Densities of Some Common Materials

| Substance | Density (g/mL) | Substance | Density (g/mL) |
|---|---|---|---|
| Air | 0.00129 (at 0°C) | Mercury | 13.6 |
| Ammonia | 0.000771 (at 0°C) | Methanol | 0.792 |
| Benzene | 0.879 | Milk | 1.028–1.035 |
| Blood | 1.060 | Oxygen | 0.00143 (at 0°C) |
| Bone | 1.7–2.0 | Rubber | 0.9–1.1 |
| Carbon dioxide | 0.001963 (at 0°C) | Turpentine | 0.87 |
| Ethanol | 0.789 | Urine | 1.010–1.030 |
| Gasoline | 0.66–0.69 | Water | 1.000 (at 4°C) |
| Gold | 19.3 | Water | 0.998 (at 20°C) |
| Hydrogen | 0.000090 (at 0°C) | Wood (balsa, least dense; ebony and teak, most dense) | 0.3–0.98 |
| Kerosene | 0.82 | | |
| Lead | 11.3 | | |

**Figure 1.12** Density (mass/volume) is a unique property of a material. A mixture of wood, water, brass, and mercury is shown, with the cork—the least dense—floating on water. Brass, with a density greater than water but less than liquid mercury, floats on the interface between these two liquids.

is *independent* of the amount of material (intensive property). Density is a useful way to characterize or identify a substance because each substance has a unique density (Figure 1.12).

In density calculations, mass is usually represented in g, and volume is given in either mL, cm³, or cc:

$$1 \text{ mL} = 1 \text{ cm}^3 = 1 \text{ cc}$$

The unit of density would therefore be g/mL, g/cm³, or g/cc. It is important to recognize that because the units of density are a ratio of mass to volume, density can be used as a conversion factor when the factor-label method is used to solve for either mass or volume from density data.

A 1-mL sample of air and 1-mL sample of iron have different masses. There is much more mass in 1 mL of iron; its density is greater. Density measurements were used to distinguish between real gold and "fool's gold" during the gold rush era. Today, the measurement of the density of a substance is still a valuable analytical technique. The densities of a number of common substances are shown in Table 1.4.

---

**EXAMPLE 1.13** | **Calculating the Density of a Solid**

LEARNING GOAL

A 2.00 cm³ sample of aluminum (symbolized Al) is found to weigh 5.40 g. Calculate the density of Al in units of g/cm³ and g/mL.

**13** Use density, mass, and volume in problem solving, and calculate the specific gravity of a substance from its density.

**Solution**

The density expression is:

$$d = \frac{m}{V}, \text{ in which mass is usually in g, and volume is in either mL or cm}^3.$$

Substituting the information given in the problem,

$$d = \frac{5.40 \text{ g}}{2.00 \text{ cm}^3} = 2.70 \text{ g/cm}^3$$

*Continued…*

According to Table 1.2, 1 mL = 1 cm³. Therefore, we can use this identity as a conversion factor to obtain the answer in g/mL. The cm³ unit is placed in the numerator so that it cancels, and the mL unit is placed in the denominator because it will provide the correct unit for the product.

$$\frac{2.70 \text{ g}}{1 \text{ cm}^3} \times \frac{1 \text{ cm}^3}{1 \text{ mL}} = 2.70 \text{ g/mL}$$

Initial Data Result × Conversion Factor = Desired Result

The density of water, 1.0 g/mL, can be found on Table 1.4. Since aluminum is more dense than water, it should have a density greater than 1.0 g/mL.

### Practice Problem 1.13

A 0.500 mL sample of a metal has a mass of 6.80 g. Calculate the density of the metal in units of g/mL and g/cm³.

▶ For Further Practice: **Questions 1.121 and 1.122.**

---

### EXAMPLE 1.14 | Using the Density to Calculate the Mass of a Liquid

LEARNING GOAL

Calculate the mass, in g, of 10.0 mL of mercury (symbolized Hg) if the density of mercury is 13.6 g/mL.

**13** Use density, mass, and volume in problem solving, and calculate the specific gravity of a substance from its density.

#### Solution

First, it must be determined which density conversion factor is correct for this problem.

$$\frac{13.6 \text{ g Hg}}{1 \text{ mL Hg}} \quad \text{or} \quad \frac{1 \text{ mL Hg}}{13.6 \text{ g Hg}}$$

Since the data given is in mL, only the first conversion factor will result in a product with the unit g. Using the factor-label method, the answer can be calculated.

$$10.0 \text{ mL Hg} \times \frac{13.6 \text{ g Hg}}{1 \text{ mL Hg}} = 136 \text{ g Hg}$$

Data Given × Conversion Factor = Desired Result

### Practice Problem 1.14

The density of ethanol (200 proof or pure alcohol) is 0.789 g/mL at 20°C. Calculate the mass of a 30.0-mL sample.

▶ For Further Practice: **Questions 1.125 and 1.126.**

---

### EXAMPLE 1.15 | Calculating the Mass of a Gas from Its Density

LEARNING GOAL

Air has a density of 0.0013 g/mL. What is the mass of a 6.0 L sample of air?

**13** Use density, mass, and volume in problem solving, and calculate the specific gravity of a substance from its density.

#### Solution

This problem can be solved using the factor-label method. Since the data given is in L, the first conversion factor used should relate L to mL, one of the units in the density expression.

$$6.0 \, \cancel{\text{L air}} \times \frac{10^3 \text{ mL air}}{1 \, \cancel{\text{L air}}} = 6.0 \times 10^3 \text{ mL air}$$

Data Given × Conversion Factor = Initial Data Result

Since the units of density are in fraction form, the value of density is a ratio that can be used as a conversion factor.

$$\frac{0.0013 \text{ g air}}{1 \text{ mL}} \quad \text{or} \quad \frac{1 \text{ mL}}{0.0013 \text{ g air}}$$

The density conversion factor with mL in the denominator is the only one that will result in the product unit of g.

$$6.0 \times 10^3 \, \cancel{\text{mL air}} \times \frac{0.0013 \text{ g air}}{1 \, \cancel{\text{mL air}}} = 7.8 \text{ g air}$$

Initial Data Result × Conversion Factor = Desired Result

## Practice Problem 1.15

What mass of air, in g, would be found in a 2.0-L party balloon?

▶ For Further Practice: **Questions 1.123 and 1.124.**

---

**EXAMPLE 1.16**    **Using the Density to Calculate the Volume of a Liquid**

Calculate the volume, in mL, of a liquid that has a density of 1.20 g/mL and a mass of 5.00 g.

LEARNING GOAL

**13**  Use density, mass, and volume in problem solving, and calculate the specific gravity of a substance from its density.

### Solution

It must first be determined which density conversion factor is correct for this problem.

$$\frac{1.20 \text{ g liquid}}{1 \text{ mL liquid}} \quad \text{or} \quad \frac{1 \text{ mL liquid}}{1.20 \text{ g liquid}}$$

Since the data given for the liquid is in g, the conversion factor with g in the denominator is chosen. Using the factor-label method, the answer can be calculated.

$$5.00 \, \cancel{\text{g liquid}} \times \frac{1 \text{ mL liquid}}{1.20 \, \cancel{\text{g liquid}}} = 4.17 \text{ mL liquid}$$

Data Given × Conversion Factor = Desired Result

*Helpful Hint:* Notice in the solution that density is inverted with the volume in the numerator and the mass in the denominator. This enables the units to cancel.

## Practice Problem 1.16

Calculate the volume, in mL, of 10.0 g of a saline solution that has a density of 1.05 g/mL.

▶ For Further Practice: **Questions 1.131 and 1.136.**

# A Medical Perspective

## Assessing Obesity: The Body-Mass Index

Density, the ratio of two extensive properties, mass and volume, is an intensive property that can provide useful information about the identity and properties of a substance. The Body-Mass Index (BMI) is also a ratio of two extensive properties, the weight and height (actually the square of the height) of an individual. As a result, the BMI is also an intensive property. It is widely used by physical trainers, medical professionals, and life insurance companies to quantify obesity, which is a predictor of a variety of potential medical problems.

In metric units, the Body-Mass Index is expressed:

$$BMI = \frac{weight\ (kg)}{height\ (m^2)}$$

This can be converted to the English system by using conversion factors. The number 703 is the commonly used conversion factor to convert from English units (in and lb) to metric units (m and kg) that are the units in the definition of BMI.

The conversion is accomplished in the following way:

Weight and height (metric)    Weight and height (English)
↓    ↓

$$BMI = \frac{kg}{m^2} = \frac{lb}{in^2} \times \frac{1\ kg}{2.205\ lb} \times \left( \frac{39.37\ in}{1\ m} \right)^2$$

$$= \frac{lb}{in^2} \times 703 \frac{kg \cdot in^2}{lb \cdot m^2}$$

The units of the conversion factor are generally not shown, and the BMI in English units is reduced to:

$$BMI = \frac{weight\ in\ lb}{(height\ in\ in)^2} \times 703$$

Online BMI calculators generally use this form of the equation.

An individual with a BMI of 25 or greater is considered overweight; if the BMI is 30 or greater, the individual is described as obese. However, for some individuals, the BMI may underestimate or overestimate body fat. For example, it is common for an athlete with a muscular build to have a high BMI that does not accurately reflect his or her body fat.

BMI values for a variety of weights and heights are shown as a function of individuals' height and weight. Once known, the BMI can be used as a guideline in the design of suitable diet and exercise programs.

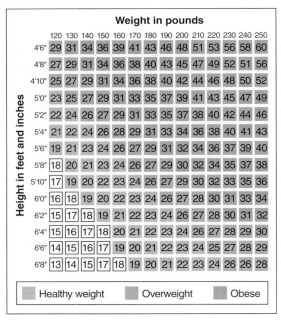

| Weight in pounds | | | | | | | | | | | | | | |
|---|---|---|---|---|---|---|---|---|---|---|---|---|---|---|
| | 120 | 130 | 140 | 150 | 160 | 170 | 180 | 190 | 200 | 210 | 220 | 230 | 240 | 250 |
| 4'6" | 29 | 31 | 34 | 36 | 39 | 41 | 43 | 46 | 48 | 51 | 53 | 56 | 58 | 60 |
| 4'8" | 27 | 29 | 31 | 34 | 36 | 38 | 40 | 43 | 45 | 47 | 49 | 52 | 51 | 56 |
| 4'10" | 25 | 27 | 29 | 31 | 34 | 36 | 38 | 40 | 42 | 44 | 46 | 48 | 50 | 52 |
| 5'0" | 23 | 25 | 27 | 29 | 31 | 33 | 35 | 37 | 39 | 41 | 43 | 45 | 47 | 49 |
| 5'2" | 22 | 24 | 26 | 27 | 29 | 31 | 33 | 35 | 37 | 38 | 40 | 42 | 44 | 46 |
| 5'4" | 21 | 22 | 24 | 26 | 28 | 29 | 31 | 33 | 34 | 36 | 38 | 40 | 41 | 43 |
| 5'6" | 19 | 21 | 23 | 24 | 26 | 27 | 29 | 31 | 32 | 34 | 36 | 37 | 39 | 40 |
| 5'8" | 18 | 20 | 21 | 23 | 24 | 26 | 27 | 29 | 30 | 32 | 34 | 35 | 37 | 38 |
| 5'10" | 17 | 19 | 20 | 22 | 23 | 24 | 26 | 27 | 29 | 30 | 32 | 33 | 35 | 36 |
| 6'0" | 16 | 18 | 19 | 20 | 22 | 23 | 24 | 26 | 27 | 28 | 30 | 31 | 33 | 34 |
| 6'2" | 15 | 17 | 18 | 19 | 21 | 22 | 23 | 24 | 26 | 27 | 28 | 30 | 31 | 32 |
| 6'4" | 15 | 16 | 17 | 18 | 20 | 21 | 22 | 23 | 24 | 26 | 27 | 28 | 29 | 30 |
| 6'6" | 14 | 15 | 16 | 17 | 19 | 20 | 21 | 22 | 23 | 24 | 25 | 27 | 28 | 29 |
| 6'8" | 13 | 14 | 15 | 17 | 18 | 19 | 20 | 21 | 22 | 23 | 24 | 26 | 26 | 28 |

Height in feet and inches

☐ Healthy weight   ☐ Overweight   ☐ Obese

Developed by the National Center for Health Statistics in collaboration with the National Center for Chronic Disease Prevention and Health Promotion

### For Further Understanding

▶ Refer to A Human Perspective: Food Calories (p. 30) and describe connections between these two perspectives.
▶ Calculate your BMI in both metric and English units. Do they agree? Explain why or why not.

---

Specific gravity is frequently referenced to water at 4°C, its temperature of maximum density (1.000 g/mL). Other reference temperatures may be used. However, the temperature must be specified.

For convenience, values of density are often related to a standard, well-known reference, the density of pure water at 4°C. This "referenced" density is called the **specific gravity,** the ratio of the density of the object in question to the density of pure water at 4°C.

$$Specific\ gravity = \frac{density\ of\ object\ (g/mL)}{density\ of\ water\ (g/mL)}$$

# A Human Perspective

## Quick and Useful Analysis

Measurement of the specific gravity of a liquid is fast, easy, and nondestructive of the sample. Changes in specific gravity over time can provide a wealth of information. Two examples follow:

Living cells carry out a wide variety of chemical reactions, which produce molecules and energy essential for the proper function of living organisms. Urine, a waste product, contains a wide variety of by-products from these chemical processes. It can be analyzed to indicate abnormalities in cell function or even unacceptable personal behavior (recall the steroid tests in Olympic competition).

Many of these tests must be performed by using sophisticated and sensitive instrumentation. However, a very simple test, the measurement of the specific gravity of urine, can be an indicator of diabetes mellitus or dehydration. The normal range for human urine specific gravity is 1.010–1.030.

A hydrometer, a weighted glass bulb inserted in a liquid, may be used to determine specific gravity. The higher it floats in the liquid, the more dense the liquid. A hydrometer that is calibrated to indicate the specific gravity of urine is called a urinometer.

Winemaking is a fermentation process (Chapter 12). The flavor, aroma, and composition of wine depend upon the extent of fermentation. As fermentation proceeds, the specific gravity of the wine gradually changes. Periodic measurement of the specific gravity during fermentation enables the wine-maker to determine when the wine has reached its optimal composition.

### For Further Understanding

▶ Give reasons that may account for such a broad range of "normal" values for urine specific gravity.
▶ Could the results for a diabetes test depend on food or medicine consumed prior to the test?

Monitoring the winemaking process.

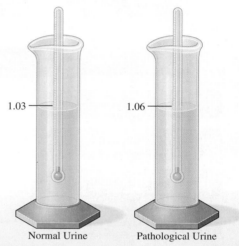
A hydrometer is used in the measurement of the specific gravity of urine.

Specific gravity is a *unitless* term. Because the density of water at 4.0°C is 1.00 g/mL, the numerical values for the density and specific gravity of a substance are equal. That is, an object with a density of 2.00 g/mL has a specific gravity of 2.00 at 4°C.

Routine hospital tests involving the measurement of the specific gravity of urine and blood samples are frequently used as diagnostic tools. For example, diseases such as kidney disorders and diabetes change the composition of urine. This compositional change results in a corresponding change in the specific gravity. This change is easily measured and provides the basis for a quick preliminary diagnosis. This topic is discussed in greater detail in A Human Perspective: Quick and Useful Analysis (above).

## LEARNING GOAL

**13** Use density, mass, and volume in problem solving, and calculate the specific gravity of a substance from its density.

# CHAPTER MAP

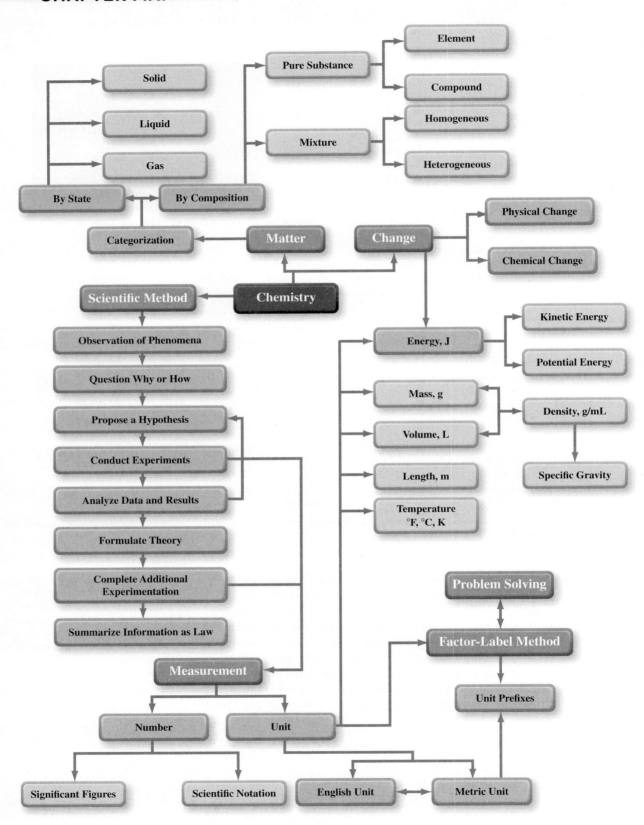

# SUMMARY

## 1.1 The Discovery Process

▶ **Chemistry** is the study of matter, its chemical and physical properties, the chemical and physical changes it undergoes, and the energy changes that accompany those processes.

▶ **Matter** is anything that has mass and occupies space.

▶ Matter gains and loses **energy** at it undergoes change.

▶ The **scientific method** is a systematic approach to the discovery of new information. Characteristics of the scientific method include:
  • Observation of a phenomenon.
  • Formulation of a question concerning the observation.
  • Presentation of a **hypothesis,** or answer to the question.
  • Experimentation, with the collection and analysis of **data** and **results** in an attempt to support or disprove the hypothesis.
  • The ultimate goal of the process is to form a **theory,** a hypothesis supported by extensive testing.
  • A scientific **law** is the summary of a large quantity of information.

## 1.2 The Classification of Matter

▶ It is useful to classify matter according to its **properties.**

▶ Matter can be classified by state as a **solid, liquid,** or **gas.**

▶ Matter can also be classified by composition, which groups matter as either a **pure substance** or **mixture.**

▶ Pure substances can be further subdivided into **elements** or **compounds.**

▶ Mixtures can be subdivided into **homogeneous** mixtures or **heterogeneous** mixtures.

▶ Properties of matter can be classified as:
  • a **physical property**—observed without changing the composition of the matter or
  • a **chemical property**—observed as the matter is converted to a new substance

▶ Properties can also be classified as:
  • **intensive**—a property that does not depend on the quantity of matter or
  • **extensive**—a property that does depend on the quantity of matter

▶ The changes that matter can undergo can be classified as **physical change** or **chemical change.** Chemical change is synonymous with **chemical reaction.**

## 1.3 The Units of Measurement

▶ The **unit** of a measurement is as vital as the number.

▶ The metric system has an advantage over the English system because metric units are systematically related to each other by powers of ten.

▶ **Mass** is a measure of the quantity of matter. **Weight** is the force of gravity on an object. The metric unit for mass is the gram. A common English mass unit is the pound.

▶ **Length** is the distance between two points. The metric unit is the meter, which is similar, but not equal to the English yard.

▶ **Volume** is the space occupied by an object. The metric unit of the liter is similar to the English quart.

▶ The metric unit of time is the second.

## 1.4 The Numbers of Measurement

▶ **Significant figures** are all digits in a measurement known with certainty plus one uncertain digit. It is important to be able to:
  • Read a measuring device to the correct number of significant figures.
  • Recognize the number of significant figures in a given written measurement.
  • Report answers to calculations to the correct number of significant figures. The rules for addition and subtraction are different from the rules for multiplication and division.
  • Follow the rules for rounding numbers as digits are dropped from the calculation to give the correct number of significant figures.

▶ **Scientific notation** is a way to express a number as a power of ten.

▶ Measurements always have a certain degree of **deviation** and **error** associated with them. Care must be taken to obtain a measurement with minimal error and high **accuracy** and **precision.**

## 1.5 Unit Conversion

▶ Conversions between units can be accomplished using the factor-label method.

▶ Conversion factors are fractions in which the numerator and denominator are equivalent in magnitude, and thus, the conversion factor is equivalent to one.

▶ In the factor-label method, the undesired unit is eliminated because it cancels out with a unit in the conversion factor.

▶ When a unit is squared or cubed, the conversion factor must also be squared or cubed.

## 1.6 Additional Experimental Quantities

▶ **Temperature** is the degree of "hotness" of an object. Common units include Celsius, Kelvin, and Fahrenheit. Equations are used to convert between the units.

▶ **Energy,** the ability to do work, is categorized as **kinetic energy** or **potential energy.** Common units of energy are the calorie and the joule.

▶ **Concentration** is a measure of the amount of a substance contained in a specified amount of a mixture.

▶ **Density** is the ratio of mass to volume and is an intensive property.
  • Density is typically reported as g/mL or $g/cm^3$.
  • Density can be used as a conversion factor to convert between the mass and volume of an object.

▶ **Specific gravity** is the ratio of the density of an object to the density of pure water at 4°C. It is numerically equal to density but has no units.

# ANSWERS TO PRACTICE PROBLEMS

**1.1** Fill two beakers with identical volumes of water. Add salt (several grams) to one of the beakers of water. Insert a thermometer into each beaker, and slowly heat the beakers. Record the temperature of each liquid when boiling is observed.

**1.2**   **a.** Pure substance      **c.** Heterogeneous mixture
      **b.** Heterogeneous mixture    **d.** Pure substance

**1.3**   **a.** Physical change      **d.** Physical change
      **b.** Chemical change      **e.** Chemical change
      **c.** Chemical change

**1.4** Intensive property; the freezing point of a glass of pure water and a gallon of pure water is the same. The freezing point is independent of the quantity of the substance.

**1.5** $7.46 \times 10^5$

**1.6** $4.7 \times 10^4$

**1.7** $6.82 \times 10^{-2}$ mi

**1.8**   **a.** $7.5 \times 10^3$ mm
      **b.** $1.5 \times 10^4$ cL
      **c.** 0.55 kg

**1.9**   **a.** $1.3 \times 10^{-2}$ m        **d.** 1.3 cm
      **b.** 0.71 L              **e.** $7.1 \times 10^2$ mL
      **c.** 2.00 oz           **f.** $2.00 \times 10^{-3}$ oz

**1.10**  **a.** $1.5 \times 10^{-4}$ m$^2$       **b.** $3.6 \times 10^4$ cm$^2$

**1.11** 0.791 kg/L

**1.12**  **a.** 0°C                **b.** 40°C
       273 K                   313 K

**1.13** 13.6 g/mL
      13.6 g/cm$^3$

**1.14** 23.7 g ethanol

**1.15** 2.6 g air

**1.16** 9.52 mL saline

# QUESTIONS AND PROBLEMS

The answers to the odd-numbered questions and problems in this section are provided at the back of the book. In addition, the Student Study Guide/Solutions Manual provides complete solutions to the odd-numbered questions and problems as well as additional problems.

## The Discovery Process

### Foundations

**1.21** Define chemistry and explain how burning wood is related to chemistry.
**1.22** Define energy and explain the importance of energy in chemistry.
**1.23** Why is experimentation an important part of the scientific method?
**1.24** Why is observation a critical starting point for any scientific study?
**1.25** What data would be required to estimate the total cost of gasoline needed to drive from New York City to Washington, D.C.?
**1.26** What data would be required to estimate the mass of planet earth?
**1.27** What are the characteristics of methane emphasized by the following model?

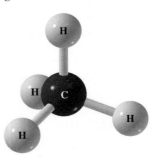

**1.28** The model of methane in Question 1.27 has limitations, as do all models. What are these limitations?

### Applications

**1.29** Discuss the difference between *hypothesis* and *theory*.
**1.30** Discuss the difference between *theory* and *scientific law*.
**1.31** We use aspects of the scientific method in our everyday lives. Provide one example of formulating a hypothesis as an aid in solving a practical problem.
**1.32** Describe an application of reasoning involving the scientific method that has occurred in your day-to-day life.
**1.33** Experimentation has shown that stem cell research has the potential to provide replacement "parts" for the human body. Is this statement a theory of scientific law? Explain your reasoning.
**1.34** Observed increases in global temperatures are caused by elevated levels of carbon dioxide. Is this statement a theory or a scientific law? Explain your reasoning.
**1.35** Describe an experiment demonstrating that the freezing point of water changes when salt (sodium chloride) is added to water.
**1.36** Describe an experiment that would enable you to determine the mass (g) of solids suspended in a 1-L sample of seawater.

## The Classification of Matter

### Foundations

**1.37** List the three states of matter.
**1.38** Explain the differences among the three states of matter in terms of volume and shape.

**1.39** Distinguish between a pure substance and a mixture.

**1.40** Give examples of pure substances and mixtures.

**1.41** Describe what is meant by an intensive property and give an example.

**1.42** Describe what is meant by an extensive property and give an example.

**1.43** Distinguish between a homogeneous mixture and a heterogeneous mixture.

**1.44** Distinguish between an intensive property and an extensive property.

**1.45** Explain the difference between chemical properties and physical properties.

**1.46** List the differences between chemical changes and physical changes.

**1.47** Label each of the following as pertaining to either a solid, liquid, or gas.
  **a.** It expands to fill the container.
  **b.** It has a fixed shape.
  **c.** The particles are in a predictable pattern of arrangement.

**1.48** Label each of the following as pertaining to either a solid, liquid, or gas.
  **a.** It has a fixed volume, but not a fixed shape.
  **b.** The attractive forces between particles are very pronounced.
  **c.** The particles are far apart.

### Applications

**1.49** Draw a diagram representing a heterogeneous mixture of two different substances. Use two different colored spheres to represent the two different substances.

**1.50** Draw a diagram representing a homogeneous mixture of two different substances. Use two different colored spheres to represent the two different substances.

**1.51** Label each of the following as either a physical change or a chemical reaction:
  **a.** An iron nail rusts.
  **b.** An ice cube melts.
  **c.** A limb falls from a tree.

**1.52** Label each of the following as either a physical change or a chemical reaction:
  **a.** A puddle of water evaporates.
  **b.** Food is digested.
  **c.** Wood is burned.

**1.53** Label each of the following properties of sodium as either a physical property or a chemical property:
  **a.** Sodium is a soft metal (can be cut with a knife).
  **b.** Sodium reacts violently with water to produce hydrogen gas and sodium hydroxide.

**1.54** Label each of the following properties of sodium as either a physical property or a chemical property:
  **a.** When exposed to air, sodium forms a white oxide.
  **b.** The density of sodium metal at 25°C is 0.97 g/cm$^3$.

**1.55** Label each of the following as either a pure substance or a mixture:
  **a.** saliva
  **b.** table salt (sodium chloride)
  **c.** wine
  **d.** helium inside of a balloon

**1.56** Label each of the following as either a pure substance or a mixture:
  **a.** sucrose (table sugar)    **c.** urine
  **b.** orange juice    **d.** tears

**1.57** Label each of the following as either a homogeneous mixture or a heterogeneous mixture:
  **a.** a carbonated soft drink    **c.** gelatin
  **b.** a saline solution    **d.** margarine

**1.58** Label each of the following as either a homogeneous mixture or a heterogeneous mixture:
  **a.** gasoline    **c.** concrete
  **b.** vegetable soup    **d.** hot coffee

**1.59** Classify the matter represented in the following diagram by state and by composition.

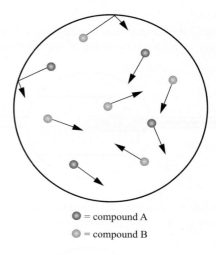

= compound A
= compound B

**1.60** Classify the matter represented in the following diagram by state and by composition.

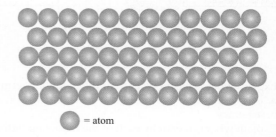

= atom

**1.61** Plant varieties may be distinguished, one from another, by observing properties of their leaves.
  **a.** Suggest two extensive properties of leaves that would be useful in the process.
  **b.** Suggest two intensive properties of leaves that would be useful in the process.

**1.62** Would you expect that intensive properties or extensive properties would be more useful in distinguishing among plant varieties by inspecting their leaves?

### The Units of Measurement

#### Foundations

**1.63** Mass is the measure of what property of matter?

**1.64** Explain the difference between mass and weight.

**1.65** Define length.

**1.66** What metric unit for length is similar to the English yd?

**1.67** How is the metric unit of L defined?

**1.68** What English unit of volume is similar to a L?

## Applications

**1.69**  Rank the following from shortest to longest length.

mm, km, m

**1.70**  Rank the following from least to greatest mass.

cg, μg, Mg

## The Numbers of Measurement

### Foundations

**1.71**  Determine the temperature reading of the following thermometer to the correct number of significant figures.

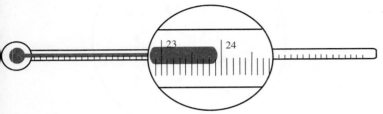

**1.72**  Determine the temperature reading of the following thermometer to the correct number of significant figures.

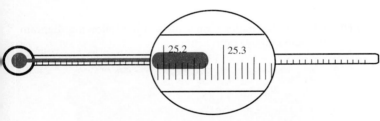

**1.73**  Explain what is meant by each of the following terms:
a. precision
b. accuracy

**1.74**  Explain what is meant by each of the following terms:
a. error
b. uncertainty

**1.75**  How many significant figures are represented in each of the following numbers?
a. 10.0            d. 2.062
b. 0.214           e. 10.50
c. 0.120           f. 1050

**1.76**  How many significant figures are represented in each of the following numbers?
a. $3.8 \times 10^{-3}$      d. 24
b. $5.20 \times 10^{2}$      e. 240
c. 0.00261         f. 2.40

**1.77**  Round the following numbers to three significant figures:
a. $3.873 \times 10^{-3}$     d. 24.3387
b. $5.202 \times 10^{-2}$     e. 240.1
c. 0.002616        f. 2.407

**1.78**  Round the following numbers to three significant figures:
a. 123700          d. 53.2995
b. 0.00285792      e. 16.96
c. $1.421 \times 10^{-3}$     f. 507.5

## Applications

**1.79**  Perform each of the following operations, reporting the answer with the proper number of significant figures:
a. (23)(657)                    d. $1157.23 - 17.812$
b. $0.00521 + 0.236$            e. $\dfrac{(1.987)(298)}{0.0821}$
c. $\dfrac{18.3}{3.0576}$

**1.80**  Perform each of the following operations, reporting the answer with the proper number of significant figures:
a. $\dfrac{(16.0)(0.1879)}{45.3}$     d. $18 + 52.1$
b. $\dfrac{(76.32)(1.53)}{0.052}$     e. $58.17 - 57.79$
c. (0.0063)(57.8)

**1.81**  Express the following numbers in scientific notation (use the proper number of significant figures):
a. 12.3            e. 92,000,000
b. 0.0569          f. 0.005280
c. −1527           g. 1.279
d. 0.000000789     h. −531.77

**1.82**  Express each of the following numbers in standard notation:
a. $3.24 \times 10^{3}$      e. $-8.21 \times 10^{-2}$
b. $1.50 \times 10^{4}$      f. $2.9979 \times 10^{8}$
c. $4.579 \times 10^{-1}$    g. $1.50 \times 10^{0}$
d. $-6.83 \times 10^{5}$     h. $6.02 \times 10^{23}$

**1.83**  The following four measurements were made for an object whose true mass is 4.56 g.

4.55 g, 4.56 g, 4.56 g, 4.57 g

Describe the measurements in terms of their accuracy and their precision.

**1.84**  The following four measurements were made for an object whose true volume is 17.55 mL.

18.69 mL, 18.69 mL, 18.70 mL, 18.71 mL

Describe the measurements in terms of their accuracy and their precision.

## Unit Conversion

### Foundations

**1.85**  Give a reason why the metric system is a more convenient system than the English system of measurement.

**1.86**  Why is it important to *always* include units when recording measurements?

**1.87**  Give the abbreviation and meaning of the following metric prefixes:
a. kilo            c. micro
b. centi

**1.88**  Fill in the blank with the missing abbreviation and name the prefix.
a. $10^{6}$ m $= 1$ _____m      c. $10^{-9}$ g $= 1$ _____g
b. $10^{-3}$ L $= 1$ _____L

**1.89**  Write the two conversion factors that can be written for the relationship between ft and in.

**1.90**  Write the two conversion factors that can be written for the relationship between cm and in.

**1.91** Convert 2.0 lb to:
   **a.** oz
   **b.** t
   **c.** g
   **d.** mg
   **e.** dag

**1.92** Convert 5.0 qt to:
   **a.** gal
   **b.** pt
   **c.** L
   **d.** mL
   **e.** μL

**1.93** Convert 3.0 g to:
   **a.** lb
   **b.** oz
   **c.** kg
   **d.** cg
   **e.** mg

**1.94** Convert 3.0 m to:
   **a.** yd
   **b.** in
   **c.** ft
   **d.** cm
   **e.** mm

**1.95** Convert $1.50 \times 10^4$ μg to mg.

**1.96** Convert $7.5 \times 10^{-3}$ cm to mm.

**1.97** A typical office has 144 ft² of floor space. Calculate the floor space in m² (use the proper number of significant figures).

**1.98** Tire pressure is measured in units of lb/in². Convert 32 lb/in² to g/cm² (use the proper number of significant figures).

## Applications

**1.99** A 150 lb adult has approximately 9 pt of blood. How many L of blood does the individual have?

**1.100** If a drop of blood has a volume of 0.05 mL, how many drops of blood are in the adult described in Question 1.99?

**1.101** A patient's temperature is found to be 38.5°C. To what Fahrenheit temperature does this correspond?

**1.102** A newborn is 21 in in length and weighs 6 lb 9 oz. Describe the baby in metric units.

**1.103** Which distance is shorter: 5.0 cm or 5.0 in?

**1.104** Which volume is smaller: 50.0 mL or 0.500 L?

**1.105** Which mass is smaller: 5.0 mg or 5.0 μg?

**1.106** Which volume is smaller: 1.0 L or 1.0 qt?

**1.107** A new homeowner wished to know the perimeter of his property. He found that the front boundary and back boundary were measured in meters: 85 m and 95 m, respectively. The side boundaries were measured in feet: 435 ft and 515 ft.
   **a.** Describe the problem-solving strategy used to determine the perimeter in km.
   **b.** Calculate the perimeter in km.

**1.108** Sally and Gertrude were comparing their weight-loss regimens. Sally started her diet weighing 193 lb. In 1 year she weighed 145 lb. Gertrude started her diet weighing 80 kg. At the end of the year, she weighed 65 kg. Who lost the most weight?
   **a.** Describe the problem-solving strategy used to determine who was more successful.
   **b.** Calculate the weight lost in lb and kg by Sally and Gertrude.

## Additional Experimental Quantities

### Foundations

**1.109** List three major temperature scales.

**1.110** Rank the following temperatures from coldest to hottest: zero degrees Celsius, zero degrees Fahrenheit, zero Kelvin

**1.111** List and define the two subgroups of energy.

**1.112** Label each of the following statements as true or false. If false, correct the statement.
   **a.** Energy can be created or destroyed.
   **b.** Energy can be converted from electrical energy to light energy.
   **c.** Conversion of energy from one form to another can occur with 100% efficiency.
   **d.** All chemical reactions involve either a gain or loss of energy.

**1.113** List each of the following as an intensive or extensive property.
   **a.** mass      **b.** volume      **c.** density

**1.114** What is the relationship between density and specific gravity?

## Applications

**1.115** Convert 50.0°F to:
   **a.** °C                    **b.** K

**1.116** The weather station posted that the low for the day would be −10°F. Convert −10.0°F to:
   **a.** °C                    **b.** K

**1.117** The thermostat shows that the room temperature is 20.0°C. Convert 20.0°C to:
   **a.** K                     **b.** °F

**1.118** Convert 300.0 K to:
   **a.** °C                    **b.** °F

**1.119** The combustion of a peanut releases 6 kcal of heat. Convert this energy to J.

**1.120** The energy available from the world's total petroleum reserve is estimated at $2.0 \times 10^{22}$ J. Convert this energy to kcal.

**1.121** Calculate the density of a $3.00 \times 10^2$ g object that has a volume of 50.0 mL.

**1.122** Calculate the density of 50.0 g of an isopropyl alcohol–water mixture (commercial rubbing alcohol) that has a volume of 63.6 mL.

**1.123** What volume, in L, will $8.00 \times 10^2$ g of air occupy if the density of air is 1.29 g/L?

**1.124** In Question 1.123, you calculated the volume of $8.00 \times 10^2$ g of air with a density of 1.29 g/L. The temperature of the air sample was lowered and the density increased to 1.50 g/L. Calculate the new volume of the air sample.

**1.125** What is the mass, in g, of a piece of iron that has a volume of $1.50 \times 10^2$ mL and a density of 7.20 g/mL?

**1.126** What is the mass of a femur (leg bone) having a volume of 118 cm³? The density of bone is 1.8 g/cm³.

**1.127** For the treatment of cystic fibrosis, it has been found that inhaling a mist of saline solution can clear mucous from the lungs. This solution is made by dissolving 7 g of salt in 1 L of sterile water. If this is to be done twice per day for 1 year, how many g of salt will be needed?

**1.128** You are given a piece of wood that is either maple, teak, or oak. The piece of wood has a volume of $1.00 \times 10^2$ cm³ and a mass of 98 g. The densities of maple, teak, and oak are as follows:

| Wood | Density (g/cm³) |
| --- | --- |
| Maple | 0.70 |
| Teak | 0.98 |
| Oak | 0.85 |

What is the identity of the piece of wood?

**1.129** You are given three bars of metal. Each is labeled with its identity (lead, uranium, platinum). The lead bar has a mass of $5.0 \times 10^1$ g and a volume of 6.36 cm³. The uranium bar has a mass of 75 g and a volume of 3.97 cm³. The platinum bar has a mass of 2140 g and a volume of $1.00 \times 10^2$ cm³. Which of these metals has the lowest density? Which has the greatest density?

**1.130** Refer to Question 1.129. Suppose that each of the bars had the same mass. How could you determine which bar had the lowest density and which had the highest density?

**1.131** The density of methanol at 20°C is 0.791 g/mL. What is the volume of a 10.0 g sample of methanol?

**1.132** The density of methanol at 20°C is 0.791 g/mL. What is the mass of a 50.0 mL sample of methanol?

**1.133** It is common for a dehydrated patient to provide a urine sample that has a specific gravity of 1.04. Using the density of water at 37°C (0.993 g/mL), calculate the density of the urine sample.

**1.134** The specific gravity of a patient's urine sample was measured to be 1.008. Given that the density of water is 1.000 g/mL at 4°C, what is the density of the urine sample?

**1.135** The density of grain alcohol is 0.789 g/mL. Given that the density of water at 4°C is 1.00 g/mL, what is the specific gravity of grain alcohol?

**1.136** The density of mercury is 13.6 g/mL. If a sample of mercury weighs 272 g, what is the volume of the sample in mL?

**1.137** The density of whole human blood in a healthy individual is 1.04 g/mL. Given that the density of water at 37°C is 0.993 g/mL, what is the specific gravity of whole human blood?

**1.138** Assume the Body-Mass Index (BMI) is calculated using the expression BMI = weight (kg)/height² (m²). If a patient has a height of 1.6 m and a BMI of 38 kg/m², what is the patient's weight in both kg and lb?

## CHALLENGE PROBLEMS

1. An instrument used to detect metals in drinking water can detect as little as 1 μg of mercury in 1 L of water. Mercury is a toxic metal; it accumulates in the body and is responsible for the deterioration of brain cells. Calculate the number of mercury atoms you would consume if you drank 1 L of water that contained 1 μg of mercury. (The mass of one mercury atom is $3.3 \times 10^{-22}$ g.)

2. Yesterday's temperature was 40°F. Today it is 80°F. Bill tells Sue that it is twice as hot today. Sue disagrees. Do you think Sue is correct or incorrect? Why or why not?

3. Aspirin has been recommended to minimize the chance of heart attacks in persons who have already had one or more occurrences. If a patient takes one aspirin tablet per day for 10 years, how many pounds of aspirin will the patient consume? (Assume that each tablet is approximately 325 mg.)

4. The diameter of an aluminum atom is 250 picometers (pm) (1 pm = $10^{-12}$ m). How many aluminum atoms must be placed end-to-end to make a "chain" of aluminum atoms 1 ft long?

# The Structure of the Atom and the Periodic Table

**2**

## LEARNING GOALS

1 Describe the properties of protons, neutrons, and electrons.

2 Interpret atomic symbols, and calculate the number of protons, neutrons, and electrons for atoms.

3 Distinguish between the terms *atom* and *isotope,* and use isotope notations and natural abundance values to calculate atomic masses.

4 Summarize the history of the development of atomic theory, beginning with Dalton.

5 Describe the role of spectroscopy and the importance of electromagnetic radiation in the development of atomic theory.

6 State the basic postulates of Bohr's theory, its utility, and its limitations.

7 Recognize the important subdivisions of the periodic table: periods, groups (families), metals, and nonmetals.

8 Identify and use the specific information about an element that can be obtained from the periodic table.

9 Describe the relationship between the electronic structure of an element and its position in the periodic table.

10 Write electron configurations, shorthand electron configurations, and orbital diagrams for atoms and ions.

11 Discuss the octet rule, and use it to predict the charges and the numbers of protons and electrons in cations and anions formed from neutral atoms.

12 Utilize the periodic table trends to estimate the relative sizes of atoms and ions, as well as relative magnitudes of ionization energy and electron affinity.

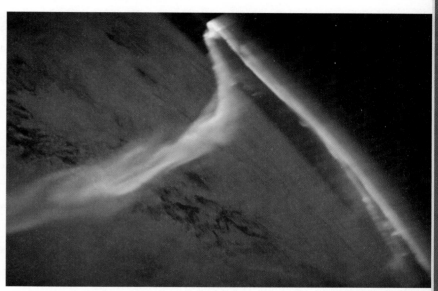

The southern lights, as seen from the space station. The connections between the energy of light and the energy of matter help us understand the structure of atoms.

## OUTLINE

## INTRODUCTION

Why does ice float on water? Why don't oil and water mix? Why does blood transport oxygen to our cells, and why does carbon monoxide inhibit this process? Questions such as these are best answered after we understand the behavior of matter at the atomic level.

In this chapter, we shall learn about the properties of the most important particles that make up the atom, and we will study the experiments that led to theories that attempt to explain the structure of the atom. These theories enable us to explain the behavior of atoms as well as compounds, such as water and carbon monoxide, resulting from the combination of atoms.

The atomic structure of each element is unique. However, the atomic structures of all the elements share many common characteristics. The unifying principle that links the elements is the periodic law. This law gives rise to an organized "map" of the elements that relates the structure of individual atoms of the various elements to their chemical and physical properties. This "map" is the periodic table.

As we study the periodic law and periodic table, we shall see that chemical and physical properties of elements follow directly from the electronic structure of their atoms. A thorough familiarity with the arrangement of the periodic table is vital to the study of chemistry. It enables us to predict the structure and properties of each element, and it serves as the basis for developing an understanding of chemical bonding, the process of forming compounds by combining atoms of various elements. The properties of these compounds are fundamentally related to the properties of the elements that comprise them.

## LEARNING GOAL

**1** Describe the properties of protons, neutrons, and electrons.

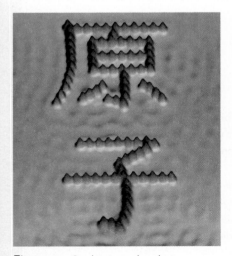

**Figure 2.1** Sophisticated techniques, such as scanning tunneling electron microscopy, provide visual evidence for the structure of atoms and molecules. Each dot represents the image of a single iron atom. Even more amazing, the iron atoms have been arranged on a copper surface in the form of the Chinese characters representing the word *atom*.

## 2.1   Composition of the Atom

The basic structural unit of an element is the **atom,** which is the smallest unit of an element that retains the chemical properties of that element. A tiny sample of the element copper, too small to be seen by the naked eye, is composed of billions of copper atoms arranged in some orderly fashion. Each atom is incredibly small. With the development of the scanning tunneling electron microscope in 1981, we are now able to "see" surface images of individual atoms (Figure 2.1).

### Electrons, Protons, and Neutrons

We know that the atom is composed of three primary particles: the *proton,* the *neutron,* and the *electron.* Although other subatomic fragments with unusual names (neutrinos, gluons, quarks, and so forth) have also been discovered, we shall concern ourselves only with the primary particles: the protons, neutrons, and electrons.

We can consider the atom to be composed of two distinct regions:

1. The **nucleus** is a small, dense, positively charged region in the center of the atom. The nucleus is composed of positively charged **protons** and uncharged **neutrons.**
2. Surrounding the nucleus is a diffuse region of negative charge populated by **electrons,** the source of the negative charge. Electrons are very low in mass compared to protons and neutrons.

The properties of these particles are summarized in Table 2.1.

Atoms of various types differ in their number of protons, neutrons, and electrons. The number of protons determines the identity of the atom. As such, the number of protons is *characteristic* of the element. When the number of protons is equal to the number of electrons, the atom is neutral because the charges are balanced and effectively cancel one another. Thus, all atoms have the same number of electrons as protons.

**TABLE 2.1 Selected Properties of the Three Basic Subatomic Particles**

| Name | Charge | Mass (amu) | Mass (g) |
|---|---|---|---|
| Electron (e$^-$) | $-1$ | $5.486 \times 10^{-4}$ | $9.1094 \times 10^{-28}$ |
| Proton (p$^+$) | $+1$ | $1.007$ | $1.6726 \times 10^{-24}$ |
| Neutron (n) | $0$ | $1.009$ | $1.6750 \times 10^{-24}$ |

We may represent an element symbolically as follows:

Mass number → $A$

$_Z X$ ← Element symbol

Atomic number → $Z$

The **atomic number** ($Z$) is equal to the number of protons in the atom, and the **mass number** ($A$) is equal to the *sum* of the number of protons and neutrons (the mass of the electrons is so small that it is insignificant in comparison to the mass of the nucleus).

The atomic number is the whole number associated with the atom on the periodic table. The mass number is not found on the periodic table.

Since,

mass number = number of protons + number of neutrons

to determine the number of neutrons, we can rearrange the equation to give:

number of neutrons = mass number − number of protons

Since number of protons = atomic number

number of neutrons = mass number − atomic number

number of neutrons = $A - Z$

**LEARNING GOAL**

**2** Interpret atomic symbols, and calculate the number of protons, neutrons, and electrons for atoms.

---

**EXAMPLE 2.1** **Determining the Composition of an Atom**

**LEARNING GOAL**

**2** Interpret atomic symbols, and calculate the number of protons, neutrons, and electrons for atoms.

Calculate the number of protons, neutrons, and electrons in an atom of fluorine. The atomic symbol for the fluorine atom is $_9^{19}$ F.

**Solution**

The atomic symbol provided gives us both the atomic number and the mass number.

**Step 1.** The atomic number, $Z$, is 9. Therefore, there are 9 protons.

**Step 2.** The number of protons is equal to the number of electrons in an atom. There are 9 electrons.

**Step 3.** The mass number, $A$ is equal to 19. The number of neutrons = $A - Z$.
Since the number of neutrons is equal to $19 - 9 = 10$, there are 10 neutrons.

*Helpful Hint:* Since the mass number is the sum of the number of protons and neutrons, it is the number with the greater value provided in the atomic symbol. The atomic number, which directly provides us with the number of protons, can also be found on the periodic table.

**Practice Problem 2.1**

Calculate the number of protons, neutrons, and electrons in each of the following atoms:

a. $_{16}^{32}$ S

b. $_{11}^{23}$ Na

c. $_1^1$ H

d. $_{94}^{244}$ Pu

▶ For Further Practice: **Questions 2.27 and 2.28.**

## Isotopes

**Isotopes** are atoms of the same element having different masses *because they contain different numbers of neutrons.* In other words, isotopes have different mass numbers. For example, all of the following are isotopes of hydrogen:

$$^1_1\text{H} \qquad\qquad ^2_1\text{H} \qquad\qquad ^3_1\text{H}$$
Hydrogen       Deuterium       Tritium

Isotopes are often written with the name of the element followed by the mass number. For example, the isotopes $^{12}_6\text{C}$ and $^{14}_6\text{C}$ may be written as carbon-12 (or C-12) and carbon-14 (or C-14), respectively.

> **Question 2.1**   How many protons, neutrons, and electrons are present in a single atom of:
> a. bromine-79          b. bromine-81          c. iron-56

> **Question 2.2**   How many protons, neutrons, and electrons are present in a single atom of:
> a. phosphorus-30          b. sulfur-32          c. chlorine-35

*A detailed discussion of the use of radioactive isotopes in the diagnosis and treatment of diseases is found in Chapter 9.*

Isotopes are useful in many clinical situations. For example, certain isotopes (radioactive isotopes) of elements emit particles and energy that can be used to trace the behavior of biochemical systems. The chemical behavior of these isotopes is identical to the other isotopes of the same element. However, their nuclear behavior is unique. As a result, a radioactive isotope can be substituted for the "nonradioactive" isotope, and its biochemical activity can be followed by monitoring the particles or energy emitted by the isotope as it passes through the body.

As stated earlier, the atomic number is the whole number associated with every element on the periodic table. The other number associated with each element on the periodic table is its **atomic mass,** the *weighted* average of the masses of each isotope that makes up the element. Atomic mass is measured in *atomic mass units (amu).*

$$1 \text{ amu} = 1.6605 \times 10^{-24} \text{ grams (g)}$$

Notice in Table 2.1 that the masses of protons and neutrons are both approximately 1.0 amu. Since the atomic mass is equal to the mass of protons and neutrons, the atomic mass of a hydrogen-2 atom containing one proton and one neutron would be 2.0 amu.

*The vast majority of hydrogen on our planet is hydrogen-1. Hydrogen-2 is often termed deuterium and hydrogen-3, tritium.*

If we examine the periodic table, we see that the atomic mass of hydrogen is 1.008 amu. Three natural isotopes of hydrogen exist, H-1, H-2, and H-3. The atomic mass of hydrogen, given as 1.008 amu, is not an average of 1, 2, and 3 (which would be 2), it is a weighted average. There is more H-1 in nature than there is H-2 and H-3. The percentage of each isotope, as found in nature, is called its *natural abundance.* A weighted average takes into account the natural abundance of each isotope.

Example 2.2 demonstrates the calculation of the atomic mass of chlorine.

---

| **EXAMPLE 2.2** | **Determining Atomic Mass from Two Isotopes** |

Calculate the atomic mass of naturally occurring chlorine if 75.77% of the chlorine atoms are $^{35}_{17}\text{Cl}$ and 24.23% of chlorine atoms are $^{37}_{17}\text{Cl}$.

### Solution

The mass of each isotope is derived from the isotope notation. The atomic mass derived from the weighted average of isotope masses will be between 35 amu and 37 amu. Since there is more chlorine-35 than chlorine-37, we expect the weighted average to be closer to 35 amu.

**Step 1.** Convert each percentage to a decimal fraction.

$$75.77\% \text{ chlorine-35} \times \frac{1}{100\%} = 0.7577 \text{ chlorine-35}$$

$$24.23\% \text{ chlorine-37} \times \frac{1}{100\%} = 0.2423 \text{ chlorine-37}$$

**Step 2.** Determine the contribution of each isotope to the total atomic mass by multiplying the decimal fraction by the mass of the isotope.

For chlorine-35:   $0.7577 \times 35.0 \text{ amu} = 26.5 \text{ amu}$

For chlorine-37:   $0.2423 \times 37.0 \text{ amu} = 8.97 \text{ amu}$

**Step 3.** Add the mass contributed by each isotope.

Atomic mass $= 26.5 \text{ amu} + 8.97 \text{ amu} = 35.5 \text{ amu}$

*Helpful Hint:* The value obtained, 35.5 amu, is between 35.0 amu and 37.0 amu. As expected from the natural abundance values, it is closer to 35.0 amu. The periodic table provides the value of 35.45 amu for the atomic mass of chlorine.

### Practice Problem 2.2

The element nitrogen has two naturally occurring isotopes. One of these has a mass of 14.0 amu and a natural abundance of 99.63%; the other isotope has a mass of 15.0 amu and a natural abundance of 0.37%. Calculate the atomic mass of nitrogen.

▶ For Further Practice: **Question 2.37.**

---

**EXAMPLE 2.3** | **Determining Atomic Mass from Three Isotopes**

LEARNING GOAL

The element neon has three naturally occurring isotopes. Neon-20 has a natural abundance of 90.48%, neon-21 has a natural abundance of 0.27%, and neon-22 has a natural abundance of 9.25%. Calculate the atomic mass of neon.

**3** Distinguish between the terms *atom* and *isotope*, and use isotope notations and natural abundance values to calculate atomic masses.

#### Solution

Remember the mass of each isotope is derived from the isotope notation. Since the isotope of the greatest abundance is neon-20, the atomic mass value should be close to 20.0 amu. The atomic mass will be greater than 20.0 amu because the less abundant isotopes have masses greater than 20.0 amu.

**Step 1.** Convert each percentage to a decimal fraction.

$$90.48\% \text{ neon-20} \times \frac{1}{100\%} = 0.9048 \text{ neon-20}$$

$$0.27\% \text{ neon-21} \times \frac{1}{100\%} = 0.0027 \text{ neon-21}$$

$$9.25\% \text{ neon-22} \times \frac{1}{100\%} = 0.0925 \text{ neon-22}$$

**Step 2.** Determine the contribution of each isotope to the total atomic mass by multiplying the decimal fraction by the mass of the isotope.

For neon-20:   $0.9048 \times 20.0 \text{ amu} = 18.1 \text{ amu}$

For neon-21:   $0.0027 \times 21.0 \text{ amu} = 0.057 \text{ amu}$

For neon-22:   $0.0925 \times 22.0 \text{ amu} = 2.04 \text{ amu}$

*Continued…*

**Step 3.** Add the masses contributed by each isotope.

$$\text{Atomic mass} = 18.1 \text{ amu} + 0.057 \text{ amu} + 2.04 \text{ amu} = 20.2 \text{ amu}$$

*Helpful Hint:* The calculated value of 20.2 amu is slightly greater than the mass of the most abundant isotope. This value is also close to the atomic mass of neon provided on the periodic table, 20.18 amu.

---

### Practice Problem 2.3

Calculate the atomic mass of naturally occurring boron if 19.9% of the boron atoms are $^{10}_{5}$B and 80.1% are $^{11}_{5}$B.

---

▶ For Further Practice: **Question 2.38.**

---

LEARNING GOAL

**4** Summarize the history of the development of atomic theory, beginning with Dalton.

Compound formed from elements X and Y

**(b)**

**Figure 2.2** An illustration of John Dalton's atomic theory. (a) Atoms of the same element are identical but different from atoms of any other element. (b) Atoms combine in whole-number ratios to form compounds.

## 2.2  Development of Atomic Theory

With this overview of our current understanding of the structure of the atom, we now look at a few of the most important scientific discoveries that led to modern atomic theory.

### Dalton's Theory

The first experimentally based theory of atomic structure was proposed in the early 1800s by John Dalton, an English schoolteacher. Dalton proposed the following description of atoms:

1. All matter consists of tiny particles called atoms.
2. An atom cannot be created, divided, destroyed, or converted to any other type of atom.
3. Atoms of a particular element have identical properties.
4. Atoms of different elements have different properties.
5. Atoms of different elements combine in simple whole-number ratios to produce compounds (stable combinations of atoms).
6. Chemical change involves joining, separating, or rearranging atoms.

Although Dalton's theory was founded on meager and primitive experimental information, we regard much of it as correct today. The discovery of the process of nuclear fission (fission is the process of "splitting" atoms that led to the development of the atomic bomb during World War II) disproved the postulate that atoms cannot be created or destroyed. The postulate that all the atoms of a particular element are identical was disproved by the discovery of isotopes.

Fusion, fission, radioactivity, and isotopes are discussed in some detail in Chapter 9. Figure 2.2 uses a simple model to illustrate Dalton's theory.

### Evidence for Subatomic Particles: Electrons, Protons, and Neutrons

The next major discoveries occurred almost a century later (1879–1897). Although Dalton pictured atoms as indivisible, various experiments, particularly those of William Crookes and Eugene Goldstein, indicated that the atom is composed of charged (+ and −) particles.

Crookes connected two metal electrodes (metal disks connected to a source of electricity) at opposite ends of a sealed glass vacuum tube. When the electricity was turned on, rays of light were observed to travel between the two electrodes. They were called *cathode rays* because they traveled from the *cathode* (the negative electrode) to the *anode* (the positive electrode).

Atoms of element X     Atoms of element Y

**(a)**

# Chemistry at the Crime Scene

## Microbial Forensics

We have learned that not all atoms of the same element are identical; usually elements are a mixture of two or more isotopes, differing in mass because they contain different numbers of neutrons. Furthermore, the atomic mass is the weighted average of the masses of these various isotopes.

It seems to follow from this that the relative amounts of these isotopes would be the same, no matter where in the world we obtain a sample of the element. In reality, this is not true. There exist small, but measurable, differences between elemental isotopic ratios; these differences correlate with their locations.

Water, of course, contains oxygen atoms, and a small fraction of these atoms are oxygen-18. We know that lakes and rivers across the United States contain oxygen-18 in different concentrations. Ocean water is richer in oxygen-18. Consequently, freshwater supplies closest to oceans are similarly enriched, perhaps because water containing oxygen-18 is a bit heavier and falls to earth more rapidly, before the clouds are carried inland, far from the coast. Scientists have been able to map the oxygen-18 distribution throughout the United States, creating contour maps, similar to weather maps, showing regions of varying concentrations of the isotope.

How can we use these facts to our advantage? The Federal Bureau of Investigation (FBI) has an interest in ascertaining the origin of microbes that may be used by terrorists. If we could carefully measure the ratio of oxygen-18 to oxygen-16 in weaponized biological materials, it might be possible to match this ratio to that found in water supplies in a specific location. We would then have an indication of the region where the material was cultured, perhaps leading to the arrest and prosecution of the perpetrators of the terrorist activity.

This is certainly not an easy task. However, the FBI has assembled an advisory board of science and forensic experts to study this and other approaches to tracking the origin of biological weapons of mass destruction. Just like the "smoking gun," these strategies, termed *microbial forensics*, could lead to more effective prosecution and a safer society for all of us.

### For Further Understanding

▶ Use the Internet to determine other useful information that can be obtained by measuring the ratio of oxygen-18 to oxygen-16.

▶ How might the approach, described above, be applied to determining the origin of an oil spill at sea?

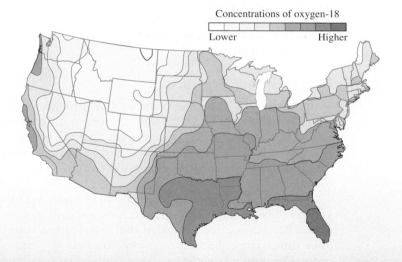

Concentrations of oxygen-18
Lower          Higher

Later experiments by J. J. Thomson, an English scientist, demonstrated the electrical and magnetic properties of cathode rays (Figure 2.3). The rays were deflected toward the positive pole of an external electric field. Because opposite charges attract, this indicates the negative character of the rays. Similar experiments with an external magnetic field showed a deflection as well; hence these cathode rays also have magnetic properties.

A change in the material used to fabricate the electrode disks brought about no change in the experimental results. This suggested that the ability to produce cathode rays is a characteristic of all materials.

**Figure 2.3** Illustration of an experiment demonstrating the charge properties of cathode rays. In the absence of an electric field, cathode rays will strike the fluorescent screen at A. In the presence of an electric field, the beam will be deflected to point B. Similar deflections are observed when a magnetic field is applied.

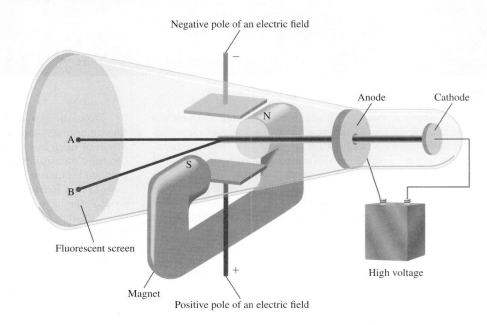

In 1897, Thomson announced that cathode rays are streams of negative particles of energy. These particles are *electrons*. Similar experiments, conducted by Goldstein, led to the discovery of particles that are equal in charge to the electron but opposite in sign. These particles, much heavier than electrons (actually 1837 times as heavy), are called *protons.*

As we have seen, the third fundamental atomic particle is the *neutron.* It has a mass virtually identical (it is less than 1% heavier) to that of the proton and has zero charge. The existence of the neutron was first proposed in the early 1920s, but it was not until 1932 that James Chadwick, an English physicist, experimentally demonstrated its existence.

## Evidence for the Nucleus

In the early 1900s, it was believed that protons and electrons were uniformly distributed throughout the atom. However, an experiment by Hans Geiger led Ernest Rutherford (in 1911) to propose that the majority of the mass and positive charge of the atom was actually located in a small, dense region, the *nucleus,* with small, negatively charged electrons occupying a much larger volume outside of the nucleus.

To understand how Rutherford's theory resulted from the experimental observations of Geiger, let us examine this experiment in greater detail. Rutherford and others had earlier demonstrated that some atoms spontaneously "decay" to produce three types of radiation: alpha (α), beta (β), and gamma (γ) radiation. This process is known as *natural radioactivity.* Geiger used materials that were naturally radioactive, such as *radium,* as projectile sources, "firing" the alpha particles produced at a thin metal foil (gold leaf) target. He then observed the interaction of the metal and alpha particles with a detection screen (Figure 2.4) and found that:

- Most alpha particles passed through the foil without being deflected.
- A small fraction of the particles were deflected, some even *directly back to the source.*

Rutherford interpreted this to mean that most of the atom is empty space, because most alpha particles were not deflected. Further, most of the mass and positive charge must be located in a small, dense region; collision of the heavy and positively charged alpha particle with this small dense and positive region (the nucleus) caused the great deflections. Rutherford summarized his astonishment

LEARNING GOAL

**4**  Summarize the history of the development of atomic theory, beginning with Dalton.

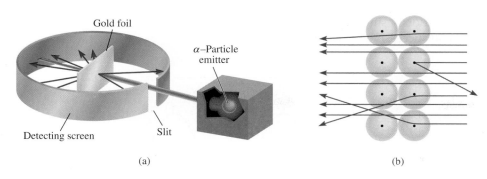

Gold foil

α–Particle
emitter

Detecting screen

Slit

(a)

(b)

**Figure 2.4** (a) The alpha-particle scattering experiment. Most alpha particles passed through the foil without being deflected; a few were deflected from their path by nuclei in the gold atoms. (b) An enlarged view of the particles passing through the atoms. The nuclei, shown as black dots, deflect some of the alpha particles.

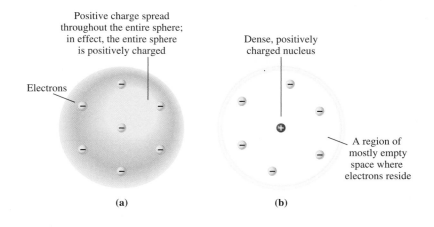

Positive charge spread
throughout the entire sphere;
in effect, the entire sphere
is positively charged

Electrons

Dense, positively
charged nucleus

A region of
mostly empty
space where
electrons reside

**(a)**

**(b)**

**Figure 2.5** (a) A model of the atom (credited to Thomson) prior to the work of Geiger and Rutherford. (b) A model of the atom supported by the alpha-particle scattering experiments of Geiger and Rutherford.

at observing the deflected particles: "It was almost as incredible as if you fired a 15-inch shell at a piece of tissue and it came back and hit you."

The significance of Rutherford's contribution cannot be overstated. It caused a revolutionary change in the way that scientists pictured the atom (Figure 2.5). His discovery of the nucleus is fundamental to our understanding of chemistry. Chapter 9 will provide much more information about the nucleus and its unique properties.

## 2.3   Light, Atomic Structure, and the Bohr Atom

The Rutherford model of the atom leaves us with a picture of a tiny, dense, positively charged nucleus containing protons and surrounded by electrons. The electron arrangement, or configuration, is not clearly detailed. More information is needed to ascertain the relationship of the electrons to each other and to the nucleus.

When dealing with dimensions on the order of $10^{-9}$ m (the atomic level), conventional methods for measurement of location and distance of separation become impossible. An alternative approach to determine structure involves the measurement of *energy* rather than the *position* of the atomic particles. For example, information obtained from the absorption or emission of *light* by atoms can yield valuable insight into structure. Such studies are referred to as **spectroscopy.**

### Electromagnetic Radiation

Light is **electromagnetic radiation.** Electromagnetic radiation travels in *waves* from a source. The most recognizable source of this radiation is the sun. We are aware of a rainbow, in which visible white light from the sun is broken up into several characteristic bands of different colors. Similarly, visible white light, when passed through a glass prism, is separated into its various component colors (Figure 2.6). These various colors are simply light of differing *wavelengths*. Light is propagated

LEARNING GOAL

**5** Describe the role of spectroscopy and the importance of electromagnetic radiation in the development of atomic theory.

**Figure 2.6** The visible spectrum of light. Light passes through a prism, producing a continuous spectrum. Color results from the way in which our eyes interpret the various wavelengths.

as a collection of sine waves, and the wavelength is the distance between identical points on successive waves:

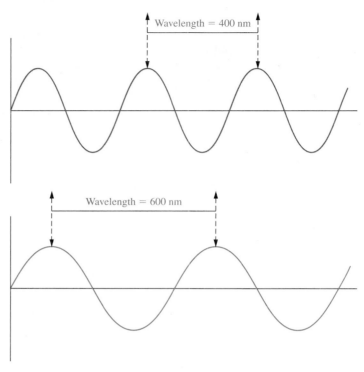

All electromagnetic radiation travels at a speed of $3.0 \times 10^8$ m/s, the **speed of light.** However, each wavelength of light, although traveling with identical velocity, has its own characteristic energy. A collection of all electromagnetic radiation, including each of these wavelengths, is referred to as the *electromagnetic spectrum.* For convenience in discussing this type of radiation, we subdivide electromagnetic radiation into various spectral regions, which are characterized by physical properties of the radiation, such as its *wavelength* or its *energy* (Figure 2.7). Some of these regions are quite familiar to us from our everyday experiences; the visible and microwave regions are two common examples. A variety of applications of electromagnetic radiation are discussed in Green Chemistry: Practical Applications of Electromagnetic Radiation, on p. 54.

## Photons

Experimental studies by Max Planck in the early part of the twentieth century, and interpretation of his results by Albert Einstein, led us to believe that light is made up of particles we call *photons*. A **photon** is a particle of light. You may ask, "How can light that we have described as energy that moves from location to location as a wave also be described as a particle?" The best non-mathematical answer we can give is that light exhibits both wave and particle properties, depending on the type of measurement being made. We say that light has a dual nature, both wave and particle. Owing to the fact that the relationship between the wavelength and energy of a photon is known, scientists can calculate the energy of any photon when its wavelength has been measured. Photons with large wavelengths are lower in energy than photons with small wavelengths.

## The Bohr Atom

If hydrogen gas is placed in an evacuated tube and an electric current is passed through the gas, light is emitted. Not all wavelengths (or energies) of light are emitted—only certain wavelengths that are characteristic of the gas in the tube. This is referred to as an *emission spectrum* (Figure 2.8). If a different gas, such as

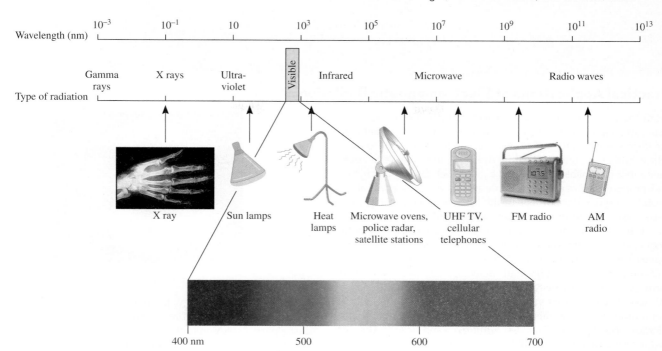

**Figure 2.7** The electromagnetic spectrum. Note that the visible spectrum is only a small part of the total electromagnetic spectrum.

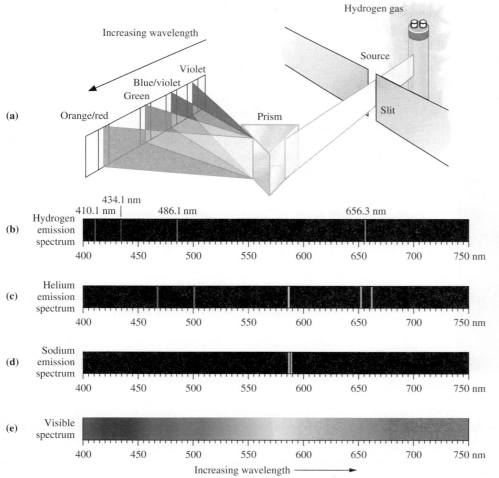

**Figure 2.8** (a) The emission spectrum of hydrogen. Certain wavelengths of light, characteristic of the atom, are emitted upon electrical excitation. The line spectrum of hydrogen (b) is compared with the line spectra of helium (c), sodium (d), and the spectrum of visible light (e).

## Practical Applications of Electromagnetic Radiation

From the preceding discussion of the interaction of electromagnetic radiation with matter—spectroscopy—you might be left with the impression that the utility of such radiation is limited to theoretical studies of atomic structure. Although this is a useful application that has enabled us to learn a great deal about the structure and properties of matter, it is by no means the only application. Useful, everyday applications of the theories of light energy and transmission are all around us. Let's look at just a few examples.

Transmission of sound and pictures is conducted at radio frequencies (RF) or radio wavelengths. We are immersed in radio waves from the day we are born. Radios, televisions, cell phones, and computers (via Wi-Fi) are all "detectors" of radio waves. This form of electromagnetic radiation is believed to cause no physical harm because of its very low energy. However, the Federal Communications Commission (FCC) has adopted guidelines for RF radiation exposure. The FCC authorizes and licenses devices and facilities that generate RF to ensure public safety.

X-rays are electromagnetic radiation, and they travel at the speed of light just like radio waves. However, because of their higher energy, they can pass through the human body and leave an image of the body's interior on a photographic film. X-ray photographs are invaluable for medical diagnosis. However, caution is advised in exposing oneself to X-rays, because the high energy can remove electrons from biological molecules, causing subtle and potentially harmful changes in their chemistry.

The sunlight that passes through our atmosphere provides the basis for a potentially useful technology for supplying heat and electricity: *solar energy*. Light is captured by absorbers, referred to as *solar collectors*, which convert the light energy into heat energy. This heat can be transferred to water circulating beneath the collectors to provide heat and hot water for homes or industry. Wafers of a silicon-based material can convert light

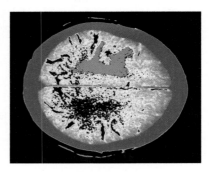

An image of a tumor detected by a CT scanner.

energy to electrical energy; many believe that if the efficiency of these processes can be improved, such approaches may provide at least a partial solution to the problems of rising energy costs and pollution associated with our fossil fuel–based energy economy.

*Microwave radiation* for cooking, *infrared* (IR) lamps for heating and IR photography, *ultraviolet* (UV) lamps used to kill microorganisms on environmental surfaces, *gamma radiation* from nuclear waste, the *visible* light from the lamp you are using while reading this chapter—all are forms of the same type of energy that, for better or worse, plays such a large part in our twenty-first century technological society.

Electromagnetic radiation and spectroscopy also play a vital role in the field of diagnostic medicine. They are routinely used as diagnostic and therapeutic tools in the detection and treatment of disease.

The radiation therapy used in the treatment of several types of cancer has been responsible for saving many lives and extending the span of many others. When radiation is used as a treatment, it destroys cancer cells. This topic will be discussed in detail in Chapter 9.

As a diagnostic tool, spectroscopy has the benefit of providing data quickly and reliably; it can also provide information that might not be available through any other means. Additionally, spectroscopic procedures are often nonsurgical, outpatient procedures. Such procedures involve less risk, can be more routinely performed, and are more acceptable to the general public than surgical procedures. The potential cost savings because of the elimination of many unnecessary surgical procedures is an added benefit.

The most commonly practiced technique uses the CT scanner, an acronym for *computerized tomography*. In this technique, X-rays are directed at the tissue of interest. As the X-rays pass through the tissue, detectors surrounding the tissue gather the signal, compare it to the original X-ray beam, and, using the computer, produce a three-dimensional image of the tissue.

The intensity of IR radiation from a solid or liquid is an indicator of relative temperature. This has been used to advantage in the design of IR cameras, which can obtain images without the benefit of the visible light that is necessary for conventional cameras. This IR photograph shows the coastline surrounding the city of San Francisco.

### For Further Understanding

▶ Diane says that a medical X-ray is risky, but a CT scan is risk free. Is Diane correct? Explain your answer.

▶ Why would the sensors (detectors) for a cell phone and an IR camera have to be designed differently?

helium, is used, a different spectrum with different wavelengths of light is observed. The reason for this behavior was explained by Niels Bohr as he gave us our first look into the electronic structure of the atom.

Niels Bohr studied the emission spectrum of hydrogen (Figure 2.8b) and developed a model to explain the line spectrum observed in this one electron atom. (Refer to Figure 2.9 throughout this discussion.) Bohr hypothesized that surrounding each atomic nucleus were certain fixed **energy levels** that could be occupied by the electron. This is referred to as the *quantization* of energy, meaning energy can have certain values but cannot have amounts between those values. The levels were analogous to orbits of planets around the sun and were numbered according to their relative distance from the nucleus ($n = 1, 2, 3, \ldots$).

An atom is in the **ground state** when the electrons of the atom are in the lowest possible energy levels. Hydrogen is in the ground state when its electron is in the $n = 1$ level. The electron can absorb energy and be promoted to a higher energy level, farther from the nucleus; that is, elevated to an **excited state** (any $n > 1$). Once in the excited state, the electron spontaneously emits energy in the form of a photon of light of the exact energy and wavelength necessary to return to the ground state. This process is called *relaxation*. The photon of light emitted appears as a specific line (*spectral line*) on the emission spectrum. Bohr was able to use the values of the wavelengths of light emitted to calculate the energy of an electron in each of the energy levels.

The major features of the Bohr theory are summarized as follows:

- Electrons are found only in *allowed energy levels.*
- The allowed energy levels are quantized energy levels, or orbits.
- Atoms absorb energy by excitation of electrons to higher energy levels, farther from the nucleus.
- Atoms release energy by relaxation of electrons to lower energy levels, closer to the nucleus.
- Energy that is emitted upon relaxation is observed as a single wavelength of light, a collection of photons, each having the same wavelength.
- Energy differences may be calculated from the wavelengths of light emitted.
- These *spectral lines* are a result of electron transitions between allowed energy levels in the atom.

## Modern Atomic Theory

The Bohr model was an immensely important contribution to the understanding of atomic structure. The idea that electrons exist in specific energy states and that the emission of energy in the form of a photon is required for an electron to move

The line spectrum of each known element is unique. Consequently, spectroscopy is a very useful tool for identifying elements.

### LEARNING GOAL

**6** State the basic postulates of Bohr's theory, its utility, and its limitations.

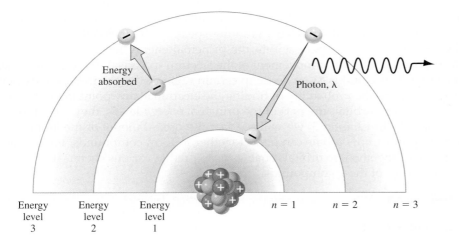

**Figure 2.9** The electron, shown in yellow, absorbs energy as it is promoted from the $n = 2$ energy level to the $n = 3$ excited state. The electron then undergoes *relaxation* as it returns to the $n = 1$ orbit (the ground state). The relaxation of the electron results in the release of one photon of light with a specific wavelength associated with the $n = 3 \longrightarrow n = 1$ transition.

Energy absorbed

Photon, $\lambda$

Energy level 3    Energy level 2    Energy level 1    $n = 1$    $n = 2$    $n = 3$

# A Human Perspective

## Atomic Spectra and the Fourth of July

At one time or another, we have all marveled at the bright, multicolored display of light and sounds characteristic of a fireworks show. These sights and sounds are produced by chemical reactions that generate the energy necessary to excite a variety of elements to their higher-energy electronic states. Light emission results from relaxation of the excited atoms to the ground state. Each atom releases light of specific wavelengths. The visible wavelengths are seen as colored light.

Fireworks use chemical reactions to produce energy. We know from experience that when oxygen reacts with a type of fuel, energy is released. The fuel in most fireworks preparations is sulfur or aluminum. Since each of these fuels reacts slowly with the oxygen in the air, a more potent solid-state source of oxygen, potassium perchlorate ($KClO_4$), is used in packaging the fireworks. The potassium perchlorate reacts with the fuel (an oxidation-reduction reaction, Chapter 4), producing a bright white flash of light. The heat produced excites the various other elements packaged with the fuel and oxidant.

Sodium salts, such as sodium chloride, furnish sodium ions, which, when excited, produce yellow light. Red colors arise from salts of strontium, which emit several shades of red corresponding to wavelengths in the 600- to 700-nm region of the visible spectrum. Copper salts produce blue radiation, because copper emits in the 400- to 500-nm spectral region.

The beauty of fireworks is a direct result of the skill of the manufacturer. Selection of the proper oxidant, fuel, and color-producing elements is critical to the production of a spectacular display. Packaging these chemicals in proper quantities so they can be stored and used safely is an equally important consideration.

### For Further Understanding

▶ Explain why excited sodium emits a yellow color. (Refer to Figure 2.8.)
▶ How does this story illustrate the interconversion of potential and kinetic energy?

A fireworks display is a dramatic illustration of light emission by excited atoms.

from a higher to a lower energy state provided the linkage between atomic structure and atomic spectra. However, some limitations of this model quickly became apparent. Although it explained the hydrogen spectrum, it provided only a crude approximation of the spectra for atoms with more than one electron. Subsequent development of more sophisticated experimental techniques demonstrated that there are problems with the Bohr theory even in the case of hydrogen.

Although Bohr's concept of principal energy levels is still valid, restriction of electrons to fixed orbits is too rigid. All current evidence shows that electrons do *not*, in fact, orbit the nucleus. We now speak of the *probability* of finding an electron in a *region* of space within the principal energy level, referred to as an **atomic orbital.** The rapid movement of the electron spreads the charge into a *cloud* of charge. This cloud is more dense in certain regions, the **electron density** being proportional to the probability of finding the electron at any point in time. Insofar as these atomic orbitals are part of the principal energy levels, they are referred to as sublevels. In Chapter 3, we will see that the orbital model of the atom can be used to predict how atoms can bond together to form compounds. Furthermore, electron arrangement in orbitals enables us to predict various chemical and physical properties of these compounds.

**Question 2.3** What is meant by the term *electron density*?

**Question 2.4** How do *orbits* and *orbitals* differ?

The theory of atomic structure has progressed rapidly, from a very primitive level to its present point of sophistication. Before we proceed, let us insert a note of caution. We must not think of the present picture of the atom as final. Scientific inquiry continues, and we should view the present theory as a step in an evolutionary process. *Theories are subject to constant refinement,* as was noted in our discussion of the scientific method.

## 2.4    The Periodic Law and the Periodic Table

In 1869, Dmitri Mendeleev, a Russian, and Lothar Meyer, a German, working independently, found ways of arranging elements in order of increasing atomic mass such that elements with similar properties were grouped together in a *table of elements*. The **periodic law** is embodied by Mendeleev's statement, "the elements, if arranged according to their atomic weights (masses), show a distinct *periodicity* (regular variation) of their properties." The *periodic table* (Figure 2.10) is a visual representation of the periodic law.

Chemical and physical properties of elements correlate with the electronic structure of the atoms that make up the elements. In turn, the electronic structure

**LEARNING GOAL**

**7** Recognize the important subdivisions of the periodic table: periods, groups (families), metals, and nonmetals.

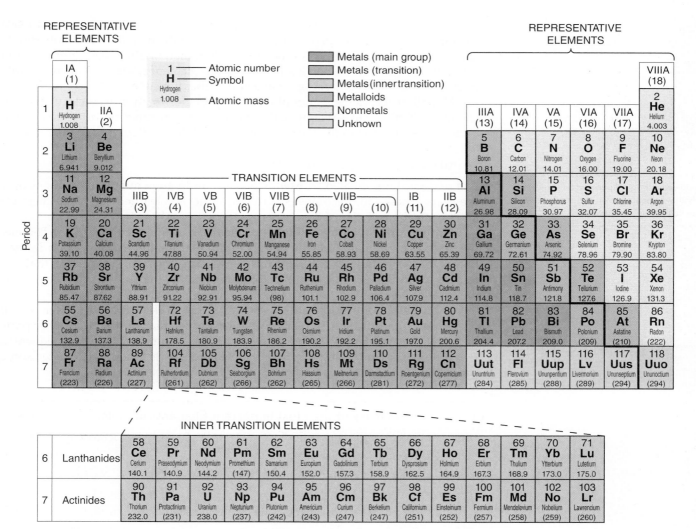

**Figure 2.10** Classification of the elements: the periodic table.

correlates with the position on the periodic table. We will examine these connections in Section 2.5; however, the scientists who first arranged the elements did not know about their electronic structure.

A thorough familiarity with the arrangement of the periodic table allows us to predict electronic structure and physical and chemical properties of the various elements. It also serves as the basis for understanding chemical bonding.

The concept of "periodicity" may be illustrated by examining a portion of the modern periodic table. The elements in the second row (beginning with lithium, Li, and proceeding to the right) show a marked difference in properties. However, sodium (Na) has properties similar to those of lithium, and sodium is therefore placed below lithium; once sodium is fixed in this position, the elements Mg through Ar have properties remarkably similar (though not identical) to those of the elements just above them. The same is true throughout the complete periodic table.

Mendeleev arranged the elements in his original periodic table in order of increasing atomic mass. However, as our knowledge of atomic structure increased, atomic numbers became the basis for the organization of the table. Remarkably, his table was able to predict the existence of elements not known at the time.

The modern periodic law states that *the physical and chemical properties of the elements are periodic functions of their atomic numbers.* If we arrange the elements in order of increasing number of protons, the properties of the elements repeat at regular intervals.

We will use the periodic table as our "map," just as a traveler would use a road map. A short time spent learning how to read the map (and remembering to carry it along on your trip!) is much easier than memorizing every highway and intersection. The information learned about one element relates to an entire family of elements grouped as a recognizable unit within the table.

Not all of the elements are of equal importance to an introductory study of chemistry. Table 2.2 lists twenty of the elements that are most important to biological systems, along with their symbols and a brief description of their functions.

## Numbering Groups in the Periodic Table

The periodic table created by Mendeleev has undergone numerous changes over the years. These modifications occurred as more was learned about the chemical and physical properties of the elements.

**Groups** or *families* are columns of elements in the periodic table. The elements of a particular group or family share many similarities, as in a human family. The similarities extend to physical and chemical properties that are related to similarities in electronic structure (that is, the way in which electrons are arranged in an atom).

The labeling of groups with Roman numerals followed by the letter *A* or *B* was standard, until 1983, in North America and Russia. However, in other parts of the world, the letters *A* and *B* were used in a different way. Consequently, two different periodic tables were in widespread use. This certainly created some confusion.

Mendeleev's original periodic table included only the elements known at the time, fewer than half of the current total.

**TABLE 2.2** Summary of the Most Important Elements in Biological Systems

| Roles in Biological Systems | Element Symbols |
| --- | --- |
| Components of major biological molecules | H, C, O, N, P, S |
| Responsible for fluid balance and nerve transmission | K, Na, Cl |
| Necessary for bones and nerve function | Ca, Mg |
| In very small quantities, essential for human metabolism | Zn, Sr, Fe, Cu, Co, Mn |
| "Heavy metals," toxic to living systems | Cd, Hg, Pb |

In 1983, the International Union of Pure and Applied Chemistry (IUPAC) recommended that a third system, using numbers 1–18 to label the groups, replace both of the older systems. Unfortunately, multiple systems now exist, and this can cause confusion for both students and experienced chemists.

The periodic tables in this textbook are "double labeled." Both the old (Roman numeral) and new (1–18) systems are used to label the groups. The label that you use is simply a guide to reading the table; the real source of information is the structure of the table itself. The following sections will show you how to extract useful information from this structure.

Group A elements are called **representative elements,** and Group B elements are **transition elements.** Certain families also have common names. For example, Group IA (or 1) elements are also known as the **alkali metals**; Group IIA (or 2), the **alkaline earth metals**; Group VIIA (or 17), the **halogens**; and Group VIIIA (or 18), the **noble gases.**

*Representative elements* are also known as *main-group elements.* These terms are synonymous.

## Periods

A **period** is a horizontal row of elements in the periodic table. The periodic table consists of seven periods containing two, eight, eight, eighteen, eighteen, thirty-two, and thirty-two elements. Note that the *lanthanide series,* a collection of fourteen elements that are chemically and physically similar to the element lanthanum, is a part of period six. It is written separately for convenience of presentation and is inserted between lanthanum (La), atomic number 57, and hafnium (Hf), atomic number 72. Similarly, the *actinide series,* consisting of fourteen elements similar to the element actinium, is inserted between actinium, atomic number 89, and rutherfordium, atomic number 104.

**LEARNING GOAL**

**7** Recognize the important subdivisions of the periodic table: periods, groups (families), metals, and nonmetals.

## Metals and Nonmetals

A **metal** is a substance whose atoms tend to lose electrons during chemical change. A **nonmetal,** on the other hand, is a substance whose atoms may gain electrons.

A close inspection of the periodic table reveals a bold zigzag line running from top to bottom, beginning to the left of boron (B) and ending between ununseptium (Uus) and ununoctium (Uuo). This line acts as the boundary between *metals,* to the left, and *nonmetals,* to the right. Elements straddling the boundary have properties intermediate between those of metals and nonmetals. These elements are referred to as **metalloids.** Commonly encountered metalloids include boron (B), silicon (Si), germanium (Ge), arsenic (As), antimony (Sb), and tellurium (Te).

Metals and nonmetals may be distinguished by differences in their physical properties in addition to their chemical tendency to lose or gain electrons. Metals have a characteristic luster and generally conduct heat and electricity well. Most (except mercury) are solids at room temperature. Nonmetals, on the other hand, are poor conductors, and several are gases at room temperature.

Note that aluminum (in spite of the fact that it borders the zigzag line) is classified as a metal, not a metalloid.

**Question 2.5**  Using the periodic table, write the symbol for each of the following and label as a metal, metalloid, or nonmetal.
- a. sodium
- b. radium
- c. manganese
- d. magnesium

**Question 2.6**  Using the periodic table, write the symbol for each of the following and label as a metal, metalloid, or nonmetal.
- a. sulfur
- b. oxygen
- c. phosphorus
- d. nitrogen

Copper is a metal that has many uses. Can you provide other uses of copper?

# A Medical Perspective

## Copper Deficiency and Wilson's Disease

An old adage tells us that we should consume all things in moderation. This is true for many of the trace minerals, such as copper. Too much copper in the diet causes toxicity and too little copper results in a serious deficiency disease.

Copper is extremely important for the proper functioning of the body. It aids in the absorption of iron from the intestine and facilitates iron metabolism. It is critical for the formation of hemoglobin and red blood cells in the bone marrow. Copper is also necessary for the synthesis of collagen, a protein that is a major component of the connective tissue. It is essential to the central nervous system in two important ways. First, copper is needed for the synthesis of norepinephrine and dopamine, two chemicals that are necessary for the transmission of nerve signals. Second, it is required for the formation of the myelin sheath (a layer of insulation) around nerve cells. Release of cholesterol from the liver depends on copper, as does bone development and proper function of the immune and blood clotting systems.

The estimated safe and adequate daily dietary intake (ESADDI) for adults is 1.5–3.0 milligrams (mg). Meats, cocoa, nuts, legumes, and whole grains provide significant amounts of copper.

Although getting enough copper in the diet would appear to be relatively simple, it is estimated that Americans often ingest only marginal levels of copper, and we absorb only 25–40% of that dietary copper. Despite these facts, it appears that copper deficiency is not a serious problem in the United States.

Individuals who are at risk for copper deficiency include people who are recovering from abdominal surgery, which causes decreased absorption of copper from the intestine. Others at risk are premature babies and people who are sustained solely by intravenous feedings that are deficient in copper. In addition, people who ingest high doses of antacids or take excessive supplements of zinc, iron, or vitamin C can develop copper deficiency because of reduced copper absorption. Because copper is involved in so many processes in the body, it is not surprising that the symptoms of copper deficiency are many and diverse. They include anemia; decreased red and white blood cell counts; heart disease; increased levels of serum cholesterol; loss of bone; defects in the nervous system, immune system, and connective tissue; and abnormal hair.

Just as too little copper causes serious problems, so does an excess of copper. At doses greater than about 15 mg, copper causes toxicity that results in vomiting. The effects of extended exposure to excess copper are apparent when we look at Wilson's disease. This is a genetic disorder in which excess copper cannot be removed from the body and accumulates in the cornea of the eye, liver, kidneys, and brain. The symptoms include a greenish ring around the cornea, cirrhosis of the liver, copper in the urine, dementia and paranoia, drooling, and progressive tremors. As a result of the condition, the victim generally dies in early adolescence. Wilson's disease can be treated with medication and diet modification with moderate success, if it is recognized early, before permanent damage has occurred to any tissues.

### For Further Understanding

▸ Why is there an upper limit on the recommended daily amount of copper?

▸ Iron is another essential trace metal in our diet. Use the Internet to find out if upper limits exist for daily iron consumption.

---

See Section 2.1 for an explanation of atomic number and atomic mass.

## LEARNING GOAL

**8** Identify and use the specific information about an element that can be obtained from the periodic table.

## Information Contained in the Periodic Table

Both the atomic number and the average atomic mass of each element are readily available from the periodic table. For example,

| 20 | ←—— atomic number |
|---|---|
| **Ca** | ←—— symbol |
| Calcium | ←—— name |
| 40.08 | ←—— atomic mass |

More detailed periodic tables may also include such information as the electron arrangement, relative sizes of atoms and ions, and most probable ion charges.

**Question 2.7**  Refer to the periodic table and find the following information:
  a. the symbol of the element with an atomic number of 40
  b. the atomic mass of the element sodium (Na)
  c. the element whose atoms contain 24 protons
  d. the known element that should most resemble the recently discovered element ununseptium, with an atomic number of 117

**Question 2.8**    Refer to the periodic table, and find the following information:
a. the symbol of the noble gas in period 3
b. the element in Group IVA (or 14) with the smallest mass
c. the only metalloid in Group IIIA (or 13)
d. the element whose atoms contain 18 protons

**Question 2.9**    For each of the following element symbols, give the name of the element, its atomic number, and its atomic mass.
a. He                  b. F                  c. Mn

**Question 2.10**    For each of the following element symbols, give the name of the element, its atomic number, and its atomic mass.
a. Mg                  b. Ne                  c. Se

## 2.5    Electron Arrangement and the Periodic Table

A primary objective of studying chemistry is to understand the way in which atoms join together to form chemical compounds. This *bonding process* is a direct consequence of the arrangement of the electrons in the atoms that combine. The **electron configuration** describes the arrangement of electrons in atoms. The organization of the periodic table, originally developed from careful measurement of properties of the elements, also correlates well with similarities in electron configuration. This reveals a very important fact: the properties of collections of atoms (bulk properties) are a direct consequence of their electron arrangement.

**LEARNING GOAL**

**9**  Describe the relationship between the electronic structure of an element and its position in the periodic table.

### The Quantum Mechanical Atom

As we noted in Section 2.3, the success of Bohr's theory was short-lived. Emission spectra of multi-electron atoms (recall that the hydrogen atom has only one electron) could not be explained by Bohr's theory. Evidence that electrons have wave properties was problematic. Bohr stated that electrons in atoms had very specific locations, now termed *principal energy levels*. The very nature of waves, spread out in space, defies such an exact model of electrons in atoms. Furthermore, the exact model is contradictory to theory and subsequent experiments.

The basic concept of the Bohr theory, that the energy of an electron in an atom is quantized, was refined and expanded by an Austrian physicist, Erwin Schröedinger. He described electrons in atoms in probability terms, developing equations that emphasize the wavelike character of electrons. Although Schröedinger's approach was founded on complex mathematics, we can readily use models of electron probability regions to enable us to gain insight into atomic structure without needing to understand the underlying mathematics.

Schröedinger's theory, often described as quantum mechanics, incorporates Bohr's principal energy levels ($n = 1$, 2, and so forth); however, it proposes that each of these levels is made up of one or more sublevels. Each sublevel, in turn, contains one or more atomic orbitals. In the following section, we shall look at each of these regions in more detail and learn how to predict the way that electrons are arranged in stable atoms.

### Principal Energy Levels, Sublevels, and Orbitals

**Principal Energy Levels**

Bohr concluded that electrons in atoms do not roam freely in space; rather they are confined to certain specific regions of space outside of the nucleus of an atom.

**Principal energy levels** (analogous to Bohr's orbits) are regions where electrons may be found, and have integral values designated $n = 1$, $n = 2$, $n = 3$, and so forth. The principal energy level is related to the average distance from the nucleus. An $n = 1$ level is closest to the nucleus; the larger the value of $n$, the greater the average distance of an electron in that level from the nucleus.

The maximum number of electrons that a principal energy level can hold is equal to $2(n)^2$. For example:

| Principal Energy | $2(n)^2$ | Maximum Number of Electrons |
|---|---|---|
| $n = 1$ | $2(1)^2$ | $2e^-$ |
| $n = 2$ | $2(2)^2$ | $8e^-$ |
| $n = 3$ | $2(3)^2$ | $18e^-$ |

## Sublevels

A **sublevel** is a set of equal-energy orbitals within a principal energy level. The sublevels, or subshells, are symbolized as $s$, $p$, $d$, and so forth; they increase in energy in the following order:

$$s < p < d$$

We specify both the principal energy level and type of sublevel when describing the location of an electron—for example, $1s$, $2s$, $2p$. Energy level designations for the first three principal energy levels are as follows:

- The first principal energy level ($n = 1$) has one possible sublevel: $1s$.
- The second principal energy level ($n = 2$) has two possible sublevels: $2s$ and $2p$.
- The third principal energy level ($n = 3$) has three possible sublevels: $3s$, $3p$, and $3d$.

## Orbitals

An **atomic orbital** is a specific region of a sublevel containing a maximum of two electrons.

Figure 2.11 depicts models of three $s$ orbitals. Each $s$ orbital is spherically symmetrical, much like a Ping-Pong ball. Its volume represents a region where there is a high probability of finding electrons of similar energy. This probability decreases as we approach the outer region of the atom. The nucleus is at the center of the $s$ orbital. At that point, the probability of finding the electron is zero; electrons cannot reside in the nucleus. Only one $s$ orbital can be found in any $n$ level. Atoms with many electrons, occupying a number of $n$ levels, have an $s$ orbital in each $n$ level. Consequently $1s$, $2s$, $3s$, and so forth are possible orbitals.

Figure 2.12 illustrates the shapes of the three possible $p$ orbitals within a given level. Each has the same shape, and that shape appears much like a dumbbell; these three orbitals differ only in the direction they extend into space. Imaginary coordinates $x$, $y$, and $z$ are superimposed on these models to emphasize this fact. These three orbitals, termed $p_x$, $p_y$, and $p_z$, may coexist in a single atom.

Figure 2.13 depicts the shapes of the five possible $d$ orbitals within a given $n$ level. These $d$ orbitals are important in determining the properties of the transition metals.

Higher-energy orbitals ($f$, $g$, and so forth) also exist, but they are important only in the description of the electron arrangements of the heaviest elements.

It is important to remember that the *shape* of the orbital represents regions in the atom (but outside of the nucleus) where electrons *may* be found. Not all orbitals are occupied by electrons; the shaded regions really represent the probability of finding the electrons in specific regions of the atom.

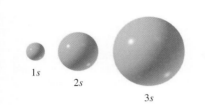

**Figure 2.11** Representation of $s$ orbitals.

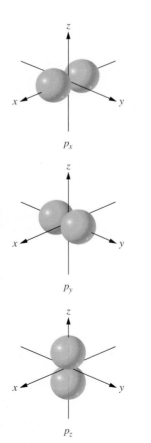

**Figure 2.12** Representation of the three $p$ orbitals, $p_x$, $p_y$, and $p_z$.

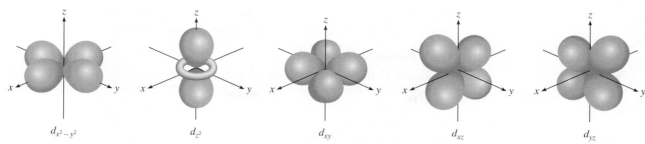

**Figure 2.13** Representation of the five *d* orbitals.

### Electrons in Sublevels

We can deduce the maximum electron capacity of each sublevel based on the information just given.

For the *s* sublevel:

$$1 \text{ orbital} \times \frac{2e^- \text{ capacity}}{\text{orbital}} = 2e^- \text{ capacity}$$

For the *p* sublevel:

$$3 \text{ orbitals} \times \frac{2e^- \text{ capacity}}{\text{orbital}} = 6e^- \text{ capacity}$$

For the *d* sublevel:

$$5 \text{ orbitals} \times \frac{2e^- \text{ capacity}}{\text{orbital}} = 10e^- \text{ capacity}$$

### Electron Spin

As we have noted, each atomic orbital has a maximum capacity of two electrons. The electrons are perceived to *spin* on an imaginary axis, and the two electrons in the same orbital must have opposite spins: clockwise and counterclockwise. Their behavior is analogous to two ends of a magnet. Remember, electrons have magnetic properties. The electrons exhibit sufficient magnetic attraction to hold themselves together despite the natural repulsion that they "feel" for each other, owing to their similar charge (remember, like charges repel). Electrons must have opposite spins to coexist in an orbital. Two electrons in one orbital that possess opposite spins are referred to as *paired* electrons. The number and arrangement of unpaired electrons in an atom are responsible for the magnetic properties of elements (Figure 2.14).

## Electron Configurations

We can write the electron arrangement (electron configuration) for an atom of any element if we know a few simple facts. We need to know the number of electrons in the atom, which is readily available from the periodic table. (Remember, the number of electrons in a neutral atom is equal to the atomic number.) We know that each principal energy level has a maximum capacity of $2(n)^2$ electrons. No more than two electrons can be placed in any orbital, and each principal energy level, *n*, can contain only *n* subshells. Additionally, the aufbau principle, the Pauli exclusion principle, and Hund's rule will complete our strategy.

### Aufbau Principle

The *aufbau,* or building up, *principle* helps us to represent the electron configuration of atoms of various elements. According to this principle, electrons fill the lowest energy orbital that is available. Figure 2.15 is a useful way of depicting the

**Figure 2.14** A compass is a familiar direction-finder that aligns the magnetic field of the compass needle with the earth's natural magnetic field. Unpaired electrons in iron atoms (in the needle and in the earth) are responsible for the magnetic fields.

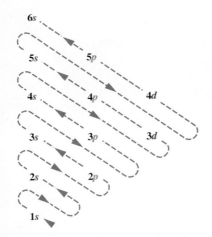

**Figure 2.15** A useful way to remember the filling order for electrons in atoms. Begin adding electrons at the bottom (lowest energy) and follow the arrows. Thus, orbitals fill in the order 1s, then 2s, then 2p, then 3s, and so forth.

We can also use the periodic table to determine the order in which orbitals are filled. See Figure 2.16.

theoretical order in which orbitals fill with electrons. It is easily memorized and will prove to be a useful guide to constructing electron configurations for the elements.

### Pauli Exclusion Principle

Wolfgang Pauli was a renowned quantum physicist who is credited with providing the most complete explanation of the relationship between electrons in orbitals. Although the theory behind the *Pauli exclusion principle* is rooted in the mathematics of quantum theory, the practical application is straightforward: Each orbital can hold up to two electrons with the electrons spinning in opposite directions (paired).

### Hund's Rule

All electrons in atoms are typically in their lowest energy state, termed the *ground state,* at room temperature. *Hund's rule* is a consequence of this: When there is a set of orbitals of equal energy (for example, three *p* orbitals in the *n* = 2 level), each orbital becomes half-filled (one electron per orbital) before any become completely filled (two electrons).

## Guidelines for Writing Electron Configurations of Atoms

- Obtain the total number of electrons in the atom from the atomic number found on the periodic table. The number of electrons equals the number of protons for an atom.
- Electrons in atoms occupy the lowest energy orbitals that are available, beginning with 1s.
- Fill subshells according to the order depicted in Figure 2.15:
  - 1s, 2s, 2p, 3s, 3p, 4s, 3d, 4p, 5s, 4d, 5p, 6s, . . .
- Remember:
  - The *s* sublevel has one orbital and can hold two electrons.
  - The *p* sublevel has three orbitals. The electrons will half-fill before completely filling the orbitals for a maximum of six electrons.
  - The *d* sublevel has five orbitals. Again, the electrons will half-fill before completely filling the orbitals for a maximum of ten electrons.

Now let us look at several examples:

### Hydrogen

Hydrogen is the simplest atom; it has only one electron. That electron must be in the lowest principal energy level (*n* = 1) and the lowest orbital (*s*). We indicate the number of electrons in a region with a *superscript,* so we write $1s^1$. The electron configuration for hydrogen is $1s^1$.

An alternate way of depicting electron arrangement in atoms is the *orbital diagram.* Each orbital is represented as a box, and each electron as an arrow, indicating the relative direction of its spin. The orbital diagram for hydrogen is:

1s

### Helium

Helium has two electrons, which will fill the lowest energy level. The ground state (lowest energy) electron configuration for helium is $1s^2$, and the corresponding orbital diagram is:

1s

The arrows show paired (opposite) spins, in accordance with the Pauli exclusion principle.

## Lithium

Lithium has three electrons. The first two are configured the same as helium. The third must go into the orbital of the lowest energy in the second principal energy level; therefore, the configuration is $1s^2 2s^1$.
The orbital diagram is:

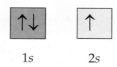

## Beryllium

Beryllium has four electrons. The first three are configured the same as lithium. The fourth electron fills the $2s$ orbital; therefore, the configuration is $1s^2 2s^2$, and the orbital diagram is:

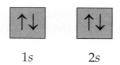

## Boron

Boron has five electrons. The first four are configured the same as beryllium. The fifth electron must go into the $2p$ level; therefore, the configuration is $1s^2 2s^2 2p^1$.
The orbital diagram is:

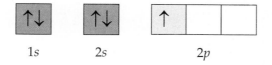

## Carbon

Carbon has six electrons. The first five are configured the same as boron. The sixth electron, according to Hund's rule, enters a second $2p$ orbital, with the same spin as the fifth electron. The electron configuration for carbon is $1s^2 2s^2 2p^2$, and the orbital diagram is:

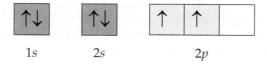

Note that Hund's rule requires the two $p$ electrons to occupy different $2p$ orbitals.

## Nitrogen

Nitrogen, following the same logic, is $1s^2, 2s^2, 2p^3$, and the orbital diagram is:

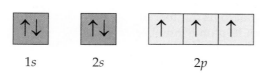

## Oxygen, Fluorine, and Neon

Each of these elements adds one more electron, pairing one of the three unpaired electrons, resulting in:

for oxygen, $1s^2\,2s^2\,2p^4$ and

| $\uparrow\downarrow$ | $\uparrow\downarrow$ | $\uparrow\downarrow$ | $\uparrow$ | $\uparrow$ |
|---|---|---|---|---|
| $1s$ | $2s$ | | $2p$ | |

for fluorine, $1s^2\,2s^2\,2p^5$ and

| $\uparrow\downarrow$ | $\uparrow\downarrow$ | $\uparrow\downarrow$ | $\uparrow\downarrow$ | $\uparrow$ |
|---|---|---|---|---|
| $1s$ | $2s$ | | $2p$ | |

for neon, $1s^2\,2s^2\,2p^6$ and

| $\uparrow\downarrow$ | $\uparrow\downarrow$ | $\uparrow\downarrow$ | $\uparrow\downarrow$ | $\uparrow\downarrow$ |
|---|---|---|---|---|
| $1s$ | $2s$ | | $2p$ | |

## Sodium Through Argon

Electrons in these elements retain the basic $1s^2\,2s^2\,2p^6$ arrangement of the preceding element, neon; new electrons enter the third principal energy level:

| Na | $1s^2\,2s^2\,2p^6\,3s^1$ |
|----|--------------------------|
| Mg | $1s^2\,2s^2\,2p^6\,3s^2$ |
| Al | $1s^2\,2s^2\,2p^6\,3s^2\,3p^1$ |
| Si | $1s^2\,2s^2\,2p^6\,3s^2\,3p^2$ |
| P  | $1s^2\,2s^2\,2p^6\,3s^2\,3p^3$ |
| S  | $1s^2\,2s^2\,2p^6\,3s^2\,3p^4$ |
| Cl | $1s^2\,2s^2\,2p^6\,3s^2\,3p^5$ |
| Ar | $1s^2\,2s^2\,2p^6\,3s^2\,3p^6$ |

The $3p$ orbital can hold a maximum of six $e^-$.

We have seen that elements in the periodic table are classified as either representative or transition. Representative elements consist of all Group IA–VIIIA (or 1, 2, and 13–18) elements. All others are transition elements. The guidelines we have developed for writing electron configurations work well for representative elements. Electron configurations for transition elements include several exceptions to the rules, due to more complex interactions among electrons that occur in atoms with large numbers of electrons.

Let us now look at the electron configuration for tin, a representative element with a large number of electrons; hence, a more complex electronic structure.

---

### EXAMPLE 2.4    Writing the Electron Configuration

Write the electron configuration for tin.

**Solution**

Since tin is a neutral atom, its number of electrons is equal to its number of protons. The number of protons can be determined from its atomic number which is found on the periodic table.

### LEARNING GOAL

**10** Write electron configurations, shorthand electron configurations, and orbital diagrams for atoms and ions.

**Step 1.** Tin (Sn) has an atomic number of 50; thus, we must place fifty electrons in atomic orbitals.

**Step 2.** Recall the total electron capacities of orbital types: $s$, two electrons; $p$, six electrons; and $d$, ten electrons. The order of filling the orbitals (Figure 2.15) is $1s$, $2s$, $2p$, $3s$, $3p$, $4s$, $3d$, $4p$, $5s$, $4d$, $5p$, $6s$.

**Step 3.** The electron configuration is as follows:

$$1s^2 2s^2 2p^6 3s^2 3p^6 4s^2 3d^{10} 4p^6 5s^2 4d^{10} 5p^2$$

*Helpful Hint:*

As a check, count electrons in the electron configuration (add all of the superscript numbers) to ensure we have accounted for all fifty electrons of the Sn atom.

## Practice Problem 2.4

Write the electron configuration for an atom of:

   a. sulfur      b. calcium      c. potassium      d. phosphorus

▶ For Further Practice: **Questions 2.85 and 2.86.**

---

**EXAMPLE 2.5**    **Writing the Electron Configuration and Orbital Diagram**

LEARNING GOAL

Write the electron configuration and orbital diagram for silicon.

**10**  Write electron configurations, shorthand electron configurations, and orbital diagrams for atoms and ions.

**Solution**

Since silicon is a neutral atom, its number of electrons is equal to its number of protons. The number of protons can be determined from its atomic number, which is found on the periodic table.

**Step 1.** Silicon (Si) has an atomic number of 14; thus, we must place fourteen electrons in atomic orbitals.

**Step 2.** Recall the total electron capacities of orbital types ($s$, two electrons; $p$, six electrons; $d$, ten electrons). The order of filling the orbitals (Figure 2.15) is $1s$, $2s$, $2p$, $3s$, $3p$, $4s$, $3d$, $4p$, $5s$, $4d$, $5p$, $6s$.

**Step 3.** The electron configuration is as follows:

$$1s^2 2s^2 2p^6 3s^2 3p^2$$

**Step 4.** Writing the orbital diagram follows from the electron configuration. Remember that Hund's rule tells us to enter $p$ electrons unpaired until each orbital contains one electron.

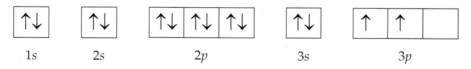

*Helpful Hint:*

Be sure to count the electrons (superscript numbers) in the electron configuration to ensure that all fourteen electrons are accounted for.

## Practice Problem 2.5

Write the orbital diagram for an atom of:

   a. sulfur      b. calcium      c. potassium      d. phosphorus

▶ For Further Practice: **Questions 2.87 and 2.88.**

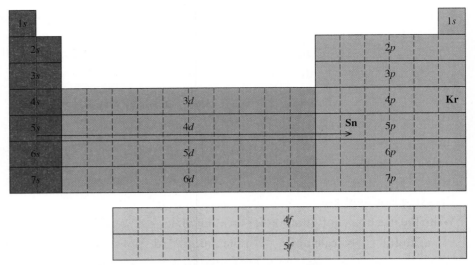

**Figure 2.16** The shape of the periodic table shows four distinct regions corresponding to the type of subshell that is filling with electrons. Starting with 1s at the top left of the periodic table and proceeding from left to right and down, the same order of sublevels as shown in Figure 2.15 can be obtained. Take time to examine both figures to see the connection. The application of this figure in writing the shorthand notation for tin is detailed in Example 2.6.

## Electron Configurations and the Periodic Table

Mendeleev's periodic table was based on extensive observation of physical and chemical properties. Its unusual shape is nicely explained by electron configurations resulting from atomic orbital theory. Elements in the same group (column) have the same outer shell electron configuration. Group IA(1) is $ns^1$, Group IIA(2) is $ns^2$, and so forth. The prefix $n$ corresponds to the period (row) containing the element whose principal energy level (also $n$) is filling. The link between electron configuration and physical properties is, in fact, the periodic table and its unusual shape!

This relationship is shown in Figure 2.16.

## Shorthand Electron Configurations

Using the periodic table and the layout of sublevels depicted in Figure 2.16, a shorthand version of the electron configuration can be obtained. To use the shorthand method, write the symbol of the nearest noble gas (with an atomic number less than the element for which you are determining the shorthand electron configuration) in square brackets. Then finish the electron configuration by writing all additional sublevels that contain electrons.

For example, the full electron configuration of a sodium atom is:

$$1s^2 2s^2 2p^6 3s^1$$

The noble gas that comes before sodium is neon. Putting [Ne] in the configuration accounts for the first ten electrons. The shorthand electron configuration is given as:

$$[Ne]3s^1$$

The advantage to this method is that the electron configurations of atoms with a large number of electrons can be written quickly by examining the periodic table. Example 2.6 demonstrates this method.

| EXAMPLE 2.6 | Writing Shorthand Electron Configurations |
|---|---|

Use the periodic table to write the shorthand electron configuration of tin.

LEARNING GOAL

10  Write electron configurations, shorthand electron configurations, and orbital diagrams for atoms and ions.

**Solution**

**Step 1.** Locate tin (Sn) on the periodic table. Tin has the atomic number 50.

**Step 2.** Krypton is the nearest noble gas that comes before Sn. The symbol for krypton (element 36) is first written in square brackets:

$$[Kr]$$

**Step 3.** Move to the left side of the periodic table (element 37) and put electrons in the next available sublevels, counting element blocks to determine the number of electrons in the sublevel. Finish at element Sn (Figure 2.16). This gives:

$$[Kr] 5s^2 4d^{10} 5p^2$$

*Helpful Hint:* The atomic number for the noble gas used in the shorthand electronic configuration must be less than the atomic number for tin. The difference between the two atomic numbers (for Kr and Sn) indicates the number of electrons necessary to complete the shorthand electron configuration for tin.

**Practice Problem 2.6**

Write the shorthand electron configuration for:

   a. sulfur     b. silicon     c. selenium     d. iron

▶ For Further Practice: **Questions 2.93 and 2.94.**

## 2.6 Valence Electrons and the Octet Rule

### Valence Electrons

If we picture two spherical objects that we wish to join together, perhaps with glue, the glue can be applied to the surfaces and the two objects can then be brought into contact. We can extend this analogy to two atoms that are modeled as spherical objects. Although this is not a perfect analogy, it is apparent that the surface interaction is of primary importance. Although the positively charged nucleus and "interior" electrons certainly play a role in bonding, we can most easily understand the process by considering only the outermost electrons. We refer to these as *valence electrons*. **Valence electrons** are the outermost electrons in an atom, which are involved, or have the potential to become involved, in the bonding process.

Metals tend to have fewer valence electrons than nonmetals.

For representative elements, the number of valence electrons in an atom corresponds to the number of the *group* in which the atom is found. For example, elements such as hydrogen and sodium (in fact, all alkali metals, Group IA or 1) have one valence electron. From left to right in period 2, beryllium, Be (Group IIA or 2), has two valence electrons; boron, B (Group IIIA or 13), has three; carbon, C (Group IVA or 14), has four; and so forth.

### The Octet Rule

Elements in the last family (Group VIIIA or 18), the noble gases, have eight valence electrons, except for helium, which has two. These elements are extremely stable and were often termed *inert gases* because they do not readily bond to other elements, although some of the larger ones (lower on the periodic table) can be made to do so under extreme experimental conditions. A full $n = 1$ energy level (as in helium) or an outer *octet* of electrons (eight valence electrons, two in the s and six in the *p* sublevel) is responsible for this unique stability.

LEARNING GOAL

11  Discuss the octet rule, and use it to predict the charges and the numbers of protons and electrons in cations and anions formed from neutral atoms.

| EXAMPLE 2.7 | Determining Electron Arrangement | LEARNING GOAL |
|---|---|---|

Provide the total number of electrons, total number of valence electrons, and energy level in which the valence electrons are found for the silicon (Si) atom.

**10** Write electron configurations, shorthand electron configurations, and orbital diagrams for atoms and ions.

### Solution

**Step 1.** Determine the position of silicon in the periodic table. Silicon has an atomic number of 14. Silicon is found in Group IVA (or 14) and period 3 of the table.

**Step 2.** The atomic number provides the number of protons in an atom. Since this is a neutral atom, the number of protons is equal to the number of electrons. Silicon therefore has fourteen electrons.

**Step 3.** Because silicon is in Group IVA (or 14), only four of the fourteen electrons are valence electrons.

**Step 4.** The third period corresponds to the $n = 3$ energy level. Silicon's four valence electrons are in the third principal energy level.

### Practice Problem 2.7

For each of the following elements, provide the total number of electrons and valence electrons in its atoms as well as the number of the energy level in which the valence electrons are found:

   a. Na        b. Mg        c. S        d. Cl        e. Ar

▶ For Further Practice: **Questions 2.101 and 2.102.**

Atoms of elements in other groups are more reactive than the noble gases because in the process of chemical reaction they try to achieve a more stable "noble gas" configuration by gaining or losing electrons. This is the basis of the **octet rule,** which states that elements usually react in such a way as to attain the electron configuration of the noble gas closest to them in the periodic table (a stable octet of electrons). In chemical reactions, they will gain, lose, or share the minimum number of electrons necessary to attain this more stable energy state. The octet rule, although simple in concept, is a remarkably reliable predictor of chemical change, especially for representative elements.

The shorthand electron configuration highlights the valence electrons by placing them after the noble gas core.

### Ions

Ions are often formed in chemical reactions, when one or more electrons are transferred from one substance to another.

**Ions** are electrically charged particles that result from a gain of one or more electrons by the parent atom (forming negative ions, or **anions**) or a loss of one or more electrons from the parent atom (forming positive ions, or **cations**).

Formation of an anion may occur as follows:

$$\underset{\text{Neutral atom}}{\text{F}} + 1e^- \longrightarrow \underset{\substack{\text{Gain of an Electron} \\ \text{Anion formed}}}{\text{F}^-}$$

Alternatively, formation of a cation of sodium may proceed as follows:

$$\underset{\text{Neutral atom}}{\text{Na}} \longrightarrow 1e^- + \underset{\substack{\text{Loss of an Electron} \\ \text{Cation formed}}}{\text{Na}^+}$$

Note that the electrons gained are written as reactants to the left of the reaction arrow, whereas the electrons lost are written as products to the right of the reaction arrow.

**EXAMPLE 2.8** | **Determining Ion Proton and Electron Composition**

Determine the number of protons and electrons in $Sr^{2+}$.

**LEARNING GOAL**

**11** Discuss the octet rule, and use it to predict the charges and the numbers of protons and electrons in cations and anions formed from neutral atoms.

**Solution**

**Step 1.** Locate Sr, strontium, on the periodic table and determine its atomic number. Sr has the atomic number 38. Therefore, a neutral atom of Sr has 38 protons and 38 electrons. Since the number of protons in an ion is the same as in a neutral atom, there are 38 protons in $Sr^{2+}$.

**Step 2.** Determine whether electrons were gained or lost in order to form the ion. Sr is a metallic element, and metals lose electrons to form cations.

**Step 3.** Using the charge of the ion, determine how many electrons were lost. An ion with a $2^+$ charge is produced by the loss of two electrons from the neutral atom.

$$Sr \longrightarrow 2e^- + Sr^{2+}$$

Since the neutral atom, Sr, has a 38 electrons, a loss of two electrons in ion formation leaves 36 electrons in the ion $Sr^{2+}$.

*Helpful Hint:* Sr is found in Group IIA (or 2). Therefore, a neutral atom of Sr has two valence electrons. Metals lose valence electrons to form cations.

**Practice Problem 2.8**

Determine the number of protons and electrons in $As^{3-}$.

▶ For Further Practice: **Questions 2.103 and 2.104.**

**Question 2.11** Determine the number of protons and electrons in each of the following ions:

a. $O^{2-}$          b. $Mg^{2+}$          c. $Fe^{3+}$

**Question 2.12** Determine the number of protons and electrons in each of the following ions:

a. $Ni^{2+}$          b. $Br^-$          c. $N^{3-}$

## Ion Formation and the Octet Rule

Metals and nonmetals differ in the way in which they form ions. Metallic elements (located at the left of the periodic table) tend to form positively charged *cations*, by the loss of electrons to obtain a noble gas configuration.

**LEARNING GOAL**

**11** Discuss the octet rule, and use it to predict the charges and the numbers of protons and electrons in cations and anions formed from neutral atoms.

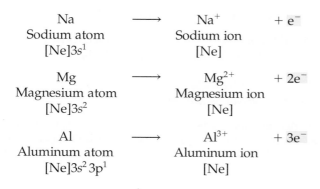

The prefix *iso* (Greek *isos*) means equal.

These cations are particularly stable because they are **isoelectronic** (that is, they have the same electron configuration) with their nearest noble gas neighbor, Ne, and have an octet of electrons in their outermost energy level.

Sodium is typical of each element in its group. Knowing that sodium, a Group IA (or 1) atom, forms a $1^+$ ion leads to the prediction that H, Li, K, Rb, Cs, and Fr also will form $1^+$ ions. Furthermore, magnesium, which forms a $2^+$ ion, is typical of each element in its group (IIA or 2): $Be^{2+}$, $Ca^{2+}$, $Sr^{2+}$, and so forth are the resulting ions.

Nonmetallic elements, located at the right of the periodic table, tend to gain electrons to become isoelectronic with the nearest noble gas element, forming negative charged *anions*.

Consider:

$$\begin{array}{ccc} \text{F} & + 1e^- \longrightarrow & \text{F}^- \\ \text{Fluorine atom} & & \text{Fluoride ion} \\ [\text{He}]2s^2\,2p^5 & & [\text{He}]2s^2\,2p^6 \text{ or [Ne]} \end{array}$$

$$\begin{array}{ccc} \text{O} & + 2e^- \longrightarrow & \text{O}^{2-} \\ \text{Oxygen atom} & & \text{Oxide ion} \\ [\text{He}]2s^2\,2p^4 & & [\text{He}]2s^2\,2p^6 \text{ or [Ne]} \end{array}$$

$$\begin{array}{ccc} \text{N} & + 3e^- \longrightarrow & \text{N}^{3-} \\ \text{Nitrogen atom} & & \text{Nitride ion} \\ [\text{He}]2s^2\,2p^3 & & [\text{He}]2s^2\,2p^6 \text{ or [Ne]} \end{array}$$

As in the case of cation formation, each of these anions has an octet of electrons in its outermost energy level.

The element fluorine, forming $F^-$, indicates that the other halogens, Cl, Br, and I, behave as a true group and form $Cl^-$, $Br^-$, and $I^-$ ions. Also, oxygen and the other nonmetals in its group (VIA or 16) form $2^-$ ions; nitrogen and phosphorus (both of Group V or 15) form $3^-$ ions. It is important to recognize that ions are formed by gain or loss of *electrons*. No change occurs in the nucleus; the number of protons remains the same.

---

| **EXAMPLE 2.9** | **Writing Shorthand Electron Configurations for Ions** | LEARNING GOAL |

Write the electron configuration and shorthand electron configuration for $Sb^{3-}$.

**10**  Write electron configurations, shorthand electron configurations, and orbital diagrams for atoms and ions.

**Solution**

**Step 1.** Locate antimony (Sb) on the periodic table. Antimony is in Group V (or 15) and has the atomic number 51.

**Step 2.** Determine the number of electrons for the ion. Since $Sb^{3-}$ indicates that the ion has three more electrons than a neutral atom of Sb, the total number of electrons in $Sb^{3-}$ can be calculated:

$$\begin{array}{ccccc} 51e^- & + & 3e^- & = & 54e^- \\ \text{Electrons in Sb} & & \text{Electrons gained} & & \text{Electrons in Sb}^{3-} \end{array}$$

**Step 3.** Recall the total electron capacities of the orbital types: *s*, two electrons; *p*, six electrons; *d*, ten electrons. The order of filling the orbitals (Figure 2.15) is 1*s*, 2*s*, 2*p*, 3*s*, 3*p*, 4*s*, 3*d*, 4*p*, 5*s*, 4*d*, 5*p*, 6*s*.

**Step 4:** The electron configuration is as follows:

$$1s^2 2s^2 2p^6 3s^2 3p^6 4s^2 3d^{10} 4p^6 5s^2 4d^{10} 5p^6$$

**Step 5:** Determine if the ion is isoelectronic with its nearest noble gas neighbor. Since $Sb^{3-}$ is isoelectronic with Xe, xenon, all fifty-four electrons of $Sb^{3-}$ are indicated by the symbol Xe in square brackets. The shorthand electron configuration for $Sb^{3-}$ is [Xe].

*Helpful Hint:* By adding together the superscripts in the electron configuration, you can confirm that fifty-four electrons were used. Since the noble gas xenon also has fifty-four electrons, it has the same electronic configuration as $Sb^{3-}$.

## Practice Problem 2.9

Write the electron configuration and shorthand electron configuration for $Cs^{1+}$.

▶ For Further Practice: **Questions 2.111 and 2.112.**

**Question 2.13**  Write the electron configuration and shorthand electron configuration for each of the following ions:
   a. $K^+$                          c. $Se^{2-}$
   b. $Ca^{2+}$                      d. $Br^-$

**Question 2.14**  Write the electron configuration and shorthand electron configuration for each of the following ions:
   a. $Rb^+$                         c. $S^{2-}$
   b. $Sr^{2+}$                      d. $I^-$

---

**EXAMPLE 2.10** | **Determining Isoelectronic Ions and Atoms**

**LEARNING GOAL**

Provide the charge of the most probable ion resulting from Se. With what element is the ion isoelectronic?

**11**  Discuss the octet rule, and use it to predict the charges and the numbers of protons and electrons in cations and anions formed from neutral atoms.

### Solution

**Step 1.**  Locate selenium (Se) on the periodic table. Since it is in Group VIA (or 16), it is a nonmetal. Nonmetallic elements gain electrons to form anions.

**Step 2.**  Find the noble gas that is selenium's nearest neighbor. Krypton, Kr, has an octet of electrons in its outermost level and will be isoelectronic with the anion formed by Se.

**Step 3.**  Determine the number of electrons that Se will need to gain to become isoelectronic with Kr. A neutral atom of Se has thirty-four electrons because it has an atomic number of 34, indicating it has thirty-four protons. Kr has thirty-six electrons because it has an atomic number of 36. The difference between 36 and 34 is 2. Therefore, Se will gain two electrons to form $Se^{2-}$.

*Helpful Hint:* An element's location on the periodic table can also allow general predictions to be made regarding anion formation. Elements in Group VII (or 17) tend to form anions with a $1^-$ charge. Elements in Group VI (or 16) tend to form anions with a $2^-$ charge. Elements in Group V (or 15) tend to form anions with a $3^-$ charge. Since Se is in Group VI (or 16), it should form an anion with a $2^-$ charge.

## Practice Problem 2.10

Provide the charge of the most probable ion resulting from radium. With what element is the ion isoelectronic?

▶ For Further Practice: **Questions 2.107 and 2.108.**

**Question 2.15**  Give the charge of the most probable ion resulting from each of the following elements. With what element is the ion isoelectronic?
   a. K                    c. S                    e. P
   b. Sr                   d. Mg                   f. Be

# A Medical Perspective

## Dietary Calcium

"Drink your milk!" "Eat all of your vegetables!" These imperatives are almost universal memories from our childhood. Our parents knew that calcium, present in abundance in these foods, is an essential element for the development of strong bones and healthy teeth.

Many studies, spanning the fields of biology, chemistry, and nutrition science, indicate that the benefits of calcium go far beyond bones and teeth. This element has been found to play a role in the prevention of disease throughout our bodies.

Calcium is the most abundant mineral (metal) in the body. It is ingested as the calcium ion ($Ca^{2+}$) either in its "free" state or "combined," as a part of a larger compound; calcium dietary supplements often contain ions in the form of calcium carbonate. The acid naturally present in the stomach produces the calcium ion:

$$CaCO_3 + 2H^+ \longrightarrow Ca^{2+} + H_2O + CO_2$$

| calcium | stomach | calcium | water | carbon |
|---------|---------|---------|-------|--------|
| carbonate | acid | ion | | dioxide |

Calcium is responsible for a variety of body functions including:

- transmission of nerve impulses
- release of "messenger compounds" that enable communication among nerves
- blood clotting
- hormone secretion
- growth of living cells throughout the body

The body's storehouse of calcium is bone tissue. When the supply of calcium from external sources, such as through the diet, is insufficient, the body uses a mechanism to compensate for this shortage. With vitamin D in a critical role, this mechanism removes calcium from bone to enable other functions to continue to take place. It is evident then that prolonged dietary calcium deficiency can weaken the bone structure. Unfortunately, current studies show that as much as 75% of the American population may not be consuming sufficient amounts of calcium. Developing an understanding of the role of calcium in premenstrual syndrome, cancer, and blood pressure regulation is the goal of three current research areas.

*Calcium and premenstrual syndrome (PMS).* Dr. Susan Thys-Jacobs, a gynecologist at St. Luke's-Roosevelt Hospital Center in New York City, and colleagues at eleven other medical centers are conducting a study of calcium's ability to relieve the discomfort of PMS. They believe that women with chronic PMS have calcium blood levels that are normal only because calcium is continually being removed from the bone to maintain an adequate supply in the blood. To complicate the situation, vitamin D levels in many young women are very low (as much as 80% of a person's vitamin D is made in the skin, upon exposure to sunlight; many of us now minimize our exposure to the sun because of concerns about ultraviolet radiation and skin cancer). Because vitamin D plays an essential role in calcium metabolism, even if sufficient calcium is consumed, it may not be used efficiently in the body.

*Colon cancer.* The colon is lined with a type of cell (epithelial cell) that is similar to those that form the outer layers of skin. Various studies have indicated that by-products of a high-fat diet are irritants to these epithelial cells and produce abnormal cell growth in the colon. Dr. Martin Lipkin, formerly of Rockefeller University in New York, and his colleagues have shown that calcium ions may bind with these irritants, reducing their undesirable effects. It is believed that a calcium-rich diet, low in fat, and perhaps the use of a calcium supplement can prevent or reverse this abnormal colon cell growth, delaying or preventing the onset of colon cancer.

*Blood pressure regulation.* Dr. David McCarron, a blood pressure specialist at the Oregon Health Sciences University, believes that dietary calcium levels may have a significant influence on hypertension (high blood pressure). Preliminary studies show that a diet rich in low-fat dairy products, fruits, and vegetables, all high in calcium, may produce a significant lowering of blood pressure in adults with mild hypertension.

The take-home lesson appears clear: a high-calcium, low-fat diet promotes good health in many ways. Once again, our parents were right!

### For Further Understanding

▶ Distinguish between "free" and "combined" calcium in the diet.
▶ Why might calcium supplements be ineffective in treating all cases of calcium deficiency?

---

**Question 2.16** Which of the following pairs of atoms and ions are isoelectronic?

a. $Cl^-$, $Ar$       c. $Mg^{2+}$, $Na^+$      e. $O^{2-}$, $F^-$
b. $Na^+$, $Ne$      d. $Li^+$, $Ne$      f. $N^{3-}$, $Cl^-$

The transition metals tend to form cations by losing electrons, just like the representative metals. Metals, whether representative or transition, share this characteristic. However, the transition elements are characterized as "variable valence" elements; depending on the type of substance with which they react, they may form more than one stable ion. For example, iron has two stable ionic forms:

$$Fe^{2+} \text{ and } Fe^{3+}$$

Copper can exist as

$$Cu^+ \text{ and } Cu^{2+}$$

and elements such as vanadium (V) and manganese (Mn) each can form four different stable ions.

Predicting the charge of an ion or the various possible ions for a given transition metal is not an easy task. Energy differences between valence electrons of transition metals are small and not easily predicted from the position of the element in the periodic table. In fact, in contrast to representative metals, the transition metals show great similarities within a *period* as well as within a *group*.

## 2.7 Trends in the Periodic Table

### Atomic Size

Many atomic properties correlate with electronic structure; hence, with their position in the periodic table. Although correlations are not always perfect, the periodic table remains an excellent guide to the prediction of properties.

If our model of the atom is a tiny sphere whose radius is determined by the distance between the center of the nucleus and the boundary of the region where the valence electrons have a probability of being located, the size of the atom will be determined principally by two factors.

1. The energy level (n level) in which the outermost electrons are found increases as we go *down* a group. (Recall that the outermost n level correlates with period number.) Thus, the size of atoms should increase from top to bottom of the periodic table as we fill successive energy levels of the atoms with electrons (Figure 2.17).
2. Across a period, as the magnitude of the positive charge of the nucleus increases, its "pull" on the atom's valence electrons increases. This results in a contraction of the atomic radius from left to right across a period. Hence, atomic size decreases from left to right on the periodic table. Examine Figure 2.17 and notice that there are exceptions.

### Ion Size

Positive ions (cations) are smaller than their parent atoms. The cation has more protons than electrons. The decrease in the number of electrons pulls the remaining electrons closer to the nucleus. Also, cation formation often results in the loss of all outer-shell electrons, resulting in a significant decrease in radius.

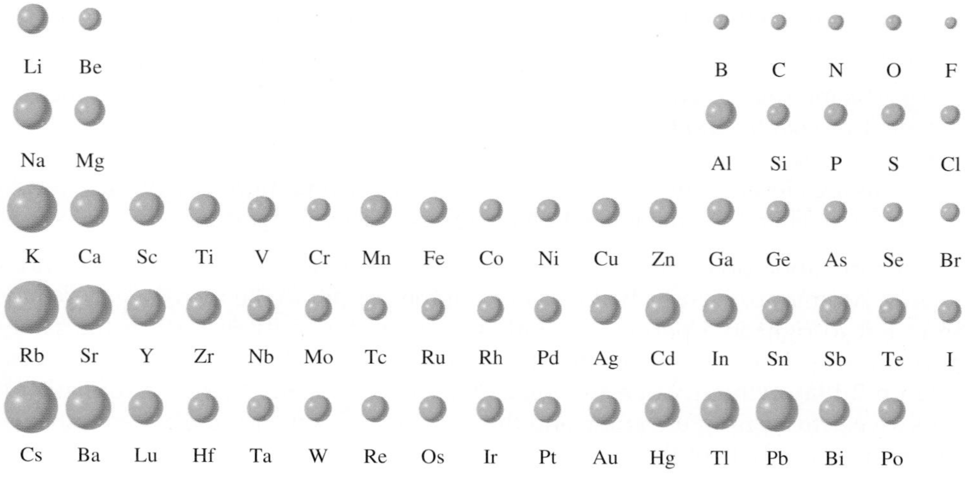

**LEARNING GOAL**

**12** Utilize the periodic table trends to estimate the relative sizes of atoms and ions, as well as relative magnitudes of ionization energy and electron affinity.

*The radius of an atom is traditionally defined as one-half of the distance between the nuclei of adjacent bonded atoms.*

**Figure 2.17** Variation in the size of atoms as a function of their position in the periodic table. Note the decrease in size from left to right and the increase in size as we proceed down the table, although some exceptions do exist. (Lanthanide and actinide elements are not included here.)

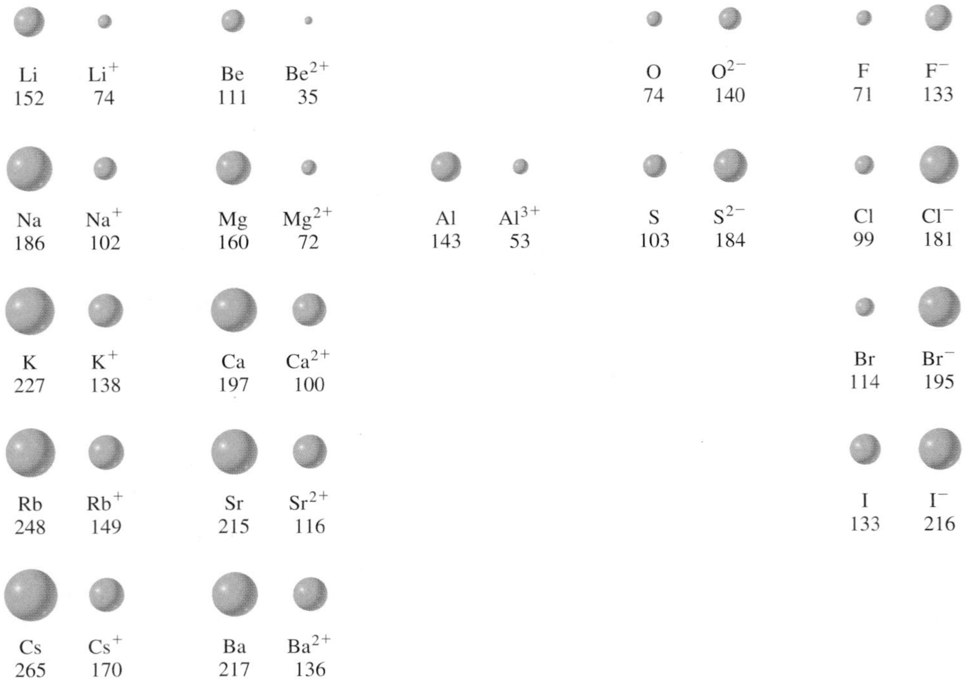

**Figure 2.18** The relative size of ions and their parent atoms. Atomic radii are provided in units of picometers (pm).

| Li | Li$^+$ | Be | Be$^{2+}$ | | | O | O$^{2-}$ | F | F$^-$ |
| 152 | 74 | 111 | 35 | | | 74 | 140 | 71 | 133 |

| Na | Na$^+$ | Mg | Mg$^{2+}$ | Al | Al$^{3+}$ | S | S$^{2-}$ | Cl | Cl$^-$ |
| 186 | 102 | 160 | 72 | 143 | 53 | 103 | 184 | 99 | 181 |

| K | K$^+$ | Ca | Ca$^{2+}$ | | | | | Br | Br$^-$ |
| 227 | 138 | 197 | 100 | | | | | 114 | 195 |

| Rb | Rb$^+$ | Sr | Sr$^{2+}$ | | | | | I | I$^-$ |
| 248 | 149 | 215 | 116 | | | | | 133 | 216 |

| Cs | Cs$^+$ | Ba | Ba$^{2+}$ |
| 265 | 170 | 217 | 136 |

Negative ions (anions) are larger than their parent atoms. The anion has more electrons than protons. Owing to the excess negative charge, the nuclear "pull" on each individual electron is reduced. The electrons are held less tightly, resulting in a larger anion radius in contrast to the neutral atom.

Ions with multiple positive charge are even *smaller* than their corresponding monopositive ion. Thus, $Cu^{2+}$ is smaller than $Cu^+$.

Figure 2.18 depicts the relative sizes of several atoms and their corresponding ions.

## Ionization Energy

The energy required to remove an electron from an isolated atom is the **ionization energy.** The process for sodium is represented as follows:

$$\text{ionization energy} + Na \longrightarrow Na^+ + e^-$$

The magnitude of the ionization energy should correlate with the strength of the attractive force between the nucleus and the outermost electron.

- Reading *down* a group, the ionization energy decreases because the atom's size is increasing. The outermost electron is progressively farther from the nuclear charge, and hence, easier to remove.
- Reading *across* a period, atomic size decreases because the outermost electrons are closer to the nucleus, more tightly held, and more difficult to remove. Therefore, the ionization energy generally increases.

A correlation does indeed exist between trends in atomic size and ionization energy. Atomic size generally *decreases* from the bottom to the top of a group and from left to right in a period. Ionization energies generally *increase* in the same periodic way. Note also that ionization energies are highest for the noble gases (Figure 2.19a). A high value for ionization energy means that it is difficult to remove electrons from the atom, and this, in part, accounts for the extreme stability and nonreactivity of the noble gases.

**LEARNING GOAL**

**12** Utilize the periodic table trends to estimate the relative sizes of atoms and ions, as well as relative magnitudes of ionization energy and electron affinity.

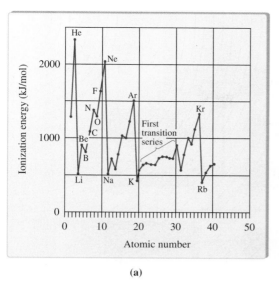

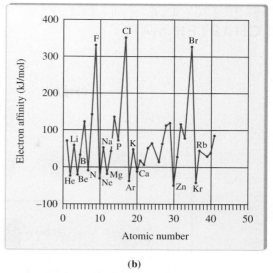

(a)                                                                    (b)

**Figure 2.19** (a) The ionization energies of the first forty elements versus their atomic numbers. Note the very high values for elements located on the right in the periodic table, and low values for those on the left. Some exceptions to the trends are evident. (b) The periodic variation of electron affinity. Note the very low values for the noble gases and the elements on the far left of the periodic table. These elements do not form negative ions. In contrast, F, Cl, and Br readily form negative ions.

## Electron Affinity

The energy change when a single electron is added to an isolated atom is the **electron affinity.** If we consider ionization energy in relation to positive ion formation (remember that the magnitude of the ionization energy tells us the ease of *removal* of an electron, hence the ease of forming positive ions), then electron affinity provides a measure of the ease of forming negative ions. A large electron affinity, meaning a large release of energy, indicates that the atom becomes more stable as it becomes a negative ion (through gaining an electron). Consider the gain of an electron by a bromine atom:

$$Br + e^- \longrightarrow Br^- + energy$$

Electron affinity

Periodic trends for electron affinity are as follows:

- Electron affinities generally decrease down a group.
- Electron affinities generally increase across a period.

Remember these trends are not absolute. Exceptions exist, as seen in the many irregularities in Figure 2.19b.

**Question 2.17** Using periodic trends, rank Be, N, and F in order of increasing
a. atomic size                b. ionization energy         c. electron affinity

**Question 2.18** Using periodic trends, rank Br, I, and F in order of increasing
a. atomic size                b. ionization energy         c. electron affinity

**LEARNING GOAL**

**12** Utilize the periodic table trends to estimate the relative sizes of atoms and ions, as well as relative magnitudes of ionization energy and electron affinity.

Remember: ionization energy and electron affinity are predictable from *trends* in the periodic table. As with most trends, exceptions occur.

# CHAPTER MAP

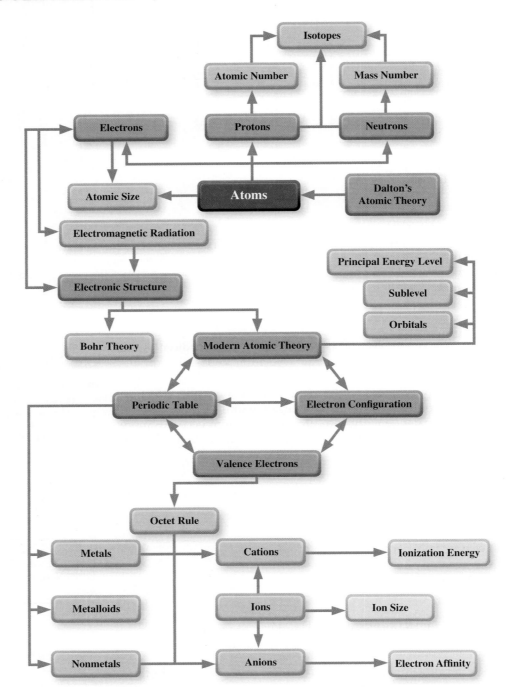

# SUMMARY

## 2.1 Composition of the Atom

▶ The basic structural unit of an element is the **atom.**

▶ The **nucleus** is the very small and very dense core at the center of the atom containing:

- Protons—positively charged particles. The number of protons is indicated by the **atomic number,** Z.
- Neutrons—neutral particles. The number of neutrons is calculated from the **mass number** minus the atomic number, A–Z.

▶ **Electrons** are negatively charged particles that are located in a diffuse region. For a neutral atom, the number of electrons equals the number of protons.

▶ **Isotopes** are atoms of the same element that have a different number of neutrons. Isotopes of the same element have the same chemical properties.

▶ The **atomic mass** is the weighted average of the masses of the isotopes of an element in atomic mass units; $1 \text{ amu} = 1.66 \times 10^{-24}$ grams (g).

## 2.2 Development of Atomic Theory

▶ Dalton's atomic theory gave the first experimentally based concept of the atom.

▶ Dalton proposed that atoms were indivisible. Subsequent experiments by Thomson, Rutherford, and others led to the discovery that the atom contains subatomic particles (electrons, protons, and neutrons) and is divisible.

## 2.3 Light, Atomic Structure, and the Bohr Atom

▶ **Spectroscopy** is the study of the interaction of light and matter and led to the understanding of the electronic structure of the atom.

▶ Features of light (**electromagnetic radiation**) include:

- The **speed of light** equals $3.0 \times 10^8$ m/s.
- Light has a wave nature and the wavelength of light determines the energy of the light. The shorter the wavelength, the greater the energy.
- Light has a particle nature. The particles are called photons.

▶ **Niels Bohr** used the emission spectrum of hydrogen to give the first model of the electronic structure of the atom. Some important features of his model include the following:

- Electrons can exist only in certain allowed **energy levels** ($n = 1, 2, 3 \ldots$); that is, energy is *quantized.* Bohr called these levels orbits.
- Electrons can gain energy and be promoted from the **ground state** to a higher energy level (**excited state**).
- Electrons can lose energy in the form of a photon and return to a lower energy level.
- The energy difference between the levels can be determined from the wavelength of the emitted light.
- Bohr's model could not explain the emission spectra of systems with more than one electron.

▶ The modern view of the electronic structure of the atom describes **atomic orbitals,** which are regions in space with a high probability of containing electrons; that is, a high **electron density.**

## 2.4 The Periodic Law and the Periodic Table

▶ The **periodic law** relates the structure of elements to their chemical and physical properties. The modern periodic table groups the elements according to these properties.

▶ **Periods** are horizontal rows, numbered 1 through 7 from top to bottom. The lanthanide series is part of period 6; the actinide series is part of period 7.

▶ Vertical columns are referred to as **groups** or families. Two common numbering systems are used in this textbook:

- Roman numeral system: IA–VIIIA for **representative elements,** IB–VIIIB for **transition elements.**
- IUPAC system: 1–18.

▶ Four common names of groups are:

- Alkali metals (IA, 1)
- Alkaline earth metals (IIA, 2)
- Halogens (VIIA, 17)
- Noble gases (VIIIA, 18)

▶ A bold zigzag line from boron leading to the right and down separates the **metals** from the **nonmetals.**

▶ The elements bordering the line (except aluminum) are **metalloids.**

▶ The blocks on the periodic table commonly give the atomic symbol, name, atomic number, and atomic mass.

## 2.5 Electron Arrangement and the Periodic Table

▶ Electrons are identified by their location in the atom.

▶ **Principal energy levels,** $n$, give the general distance from the nucleus. Electrons that are higher in energy and further from the nucleus have larger $n$ values.

▶ Each principal energy level, $n$, can have a maximum of $2(n)^2$ electrons located in it.

▶ Each principal energy level contains **sublevels,** named $s$, $p$, and $d$. The number of the principal energy level gives the number of sublevels.

- For $n = 1$, there is one sublevel: $1s$.
- For $n = 2$, there are two sublevels: $2s$, $2p$.
- For $n = 3$, there are three sublevels: $3s$, $3p$, $3d$.

▶ Each sublevel contains atomic orbitals, named the same as the sublevel. Each atomic orbital contains a maximum of 2 electrons.

- $s$ sublevels contain one orbital, and a maximum of 2 electrons.
- $p$ sublevels contain three orbitals, and a maximum of 6 electrons.
- $d$ sublevels contain five orbitals, and a maximum of 10 electrons.

▶ The **electron configuration,** shorthand electron configuration, and orbital diagram are three ways to designate where all electrons are located in an atom in its ground state.

## 2.6 Valence Electrons and the Octet Rule

▶ **Valence electrons** are the outermost electrons in the atom. These are the electrons that are involved in bonding as elements form compounds.

▶ The **octet rule** states that atoms usually react in such a way as to obtain a noble gas configuration.

▶ The octet rule can be used to predict the charge of atoms when they become **ions.**

  • Metals tend to lose electrons to become positively charged **cations.**
  • Nonmetals tend to gain electrons to become negatively charged **anions.**
  • Atoms gain and lose electrons to obtain a noble gas configuration; that is, to be **isoelectronic** with the nearest noble gas.

## 2.7 Trends in the Periodic Table

▶ **Atomic size *decreases* from left to right and from bottom to top in the periodic table.**

  • Cations are smaller than their parent atoms.
  • Anions are larger than their parent atoms.

▶ **Ionization energy** is the energy required to remove an electron from an isolated atom.

  • Ionization energy *increases* from left to right and from bottom to top in the periodic table. The noble gases have the highest ionization energy.

▶ **Electron affinity** is the energy change when a single electron is added to an isolated atom.

  • Elements with a high electron affinity will *release* a large amount of energy.
  • Electron affinity *increases* from left to right and up a group. The halogens have the greatest electron affinity.

# ANSWERS TO PRACTICE PROBLEMS

**2.1**  a.  16 protons, 16 electrons, 16 neutrons
  b.  11 protons, 11 electrons, 12 neutrons
  c.  1 proton, 1 electron, 0 neutrons
  d.  94 protons, 94 electrons, 150 neutrons

**2.2**  14.0 amu

**2.3**  10.8 amu

**2.4**  a.  sulfur: $1s^2\, 2s^2\, 2p^6\, 3s^2\, 3p^4$
  b.  calcium: $1s^2\, 2s^2\, 2p^6\, 3s^2\, 3p^6\, 4s^2$
  c.  potassium: $1s^2\, 2s^2\, 2p^6\, 3s^2\, 3p^6\, 4s^1$
  d.  phosphorus: $1s^2\, 2s^2\, 2p^6\, 3s^2\, 3p^3$

**2.5**  a.
  b.

**c.**
**d.**

**2.6**  a.  $[\text{Ne}]3s^2\, 3p^4$          c.  $[\text{Ar}]4s^2 3d^{10} 4p^4$
  b.  $[\text{Ne}]3s^2\, 3p^2$          d.  $[\text{Ar}]4s^2 3d^6$

**2.7**  a.  Total electrons = 11, valence electrons = 1, energy level = 3
  b.  Total electrons = 12, valence electrons = 2, energy level = 3
  c.  Total electrons = 16, valence electrons = 6, energy level = 3
  d.  Total electrons = 17, valence electrons = 7, energy level = 3
  e.  Total electrons = 18, valence electrons = 8, energy level = 3

**2.8**  33 protons, 36 electrons

**2.9**  [Xe]

**2.10**  $Ra^{2+}$ is isoelectronic with Rn.

# QUESTIONS AND PROBLEMS

## Composition of the Atom

### Foundations

**2.19**  Explain the difference between the mass number and the atomic mass of an element.

**2.20**  Why is the number of electrons not part of the mass number of an atom?

**2.21**  Fill in the blanks:
  a.  Isotopes of an element differ in mass because the atoms have a different number of _____.
  b.  The atomic number gives the number of _____ in the nucleus.
  c.  The mass number of an atom is due to the number of _____ and _____ in the nucleus.
  d.  Electrons surround the _____ and have a _____ charge.

**2.22**  Identify which of the following isotopic symbols is incorrect.

$$^{12}_{6}\text{C} \qquad ^{13}_{7}\text{C} \qquad ^{12}\text{C}$$

**2.23**  Identify the major difference and the major similarity among isotopes of an element.

**2.24**  Label each of the following statements as true or false:
  a.  An atom with an atomic number of 7 and a mass of 14 is identical to an atom with an atomic number of 6 and a mass of 14.
  b.  Neutral atoms have the same number of electrons as protons.
  c.  The mass number of an atom is due to the sum of the number of protons, neutrons, and electrons.

**2.25**  Label each of the following statements as true or false.
  a.  Isotopes are atoms of the same element with different numbers of neutrons.

**b.** Isotopes are atoms with the same number of protons but different numbers of neutrons.

**c.** Isotopes are atoms with the same atomic number but different mass numbers.

**2.26** The nuclei of three different atoms are depicted in the diagrams below. Which ones are isotopes, if any?

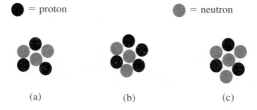

● = proton          ● = neutron

(a)          (b)          (c)

## Applications

**2.27** Calculate the number of protons, neutrons, and electrons in:
   **a.** $^{136}_{56}$Ba        **b.** $^{209}_{84}$Po        **c.** $^{113}_{48}$Cd

**2.28** Calculate the number of protons, neutrons, and electrons in:
   **a.** $^{37}_{17}$Cl        **b.** $^{23}_{11}$Na        **c.** $^{84}_{36}$Kr

**2.29** An atom has nine protons, ten neutrons, and nine electrons. Write the symbol of the atom.

**2.30** An atom has nineteen protons, twenty neutrons, and nineteen electrons. Write the symbol of the atom.

**2.31** **a.** How many protons are in the nucleus of the isotope Rn-220?
   **b.** How many neutrons are in the nucleus of the isotope Rn-220?

**2.32** **a.** How many protons are in the nucleus of the isotope In-115?
   **b.** How many neutrons are in the nucleus of the isotope In-115?

**2.33** Selenium-80 is a naturally occurring isotope used in over-the-counter supplements.
   **a.** How many protons are found in one atom of selenium-80?
   **b.** How many neutrons are found in one atom of selenium-80?

**2.34** Iodine-131 is an isotope used in thyroid therapy.
   **a.** How many protons are found in one atom of iodine-131?
   **b.** How many neutrons are found in one atom of iodine-131?

**2.35** Write symbols for each isotope:
   **a.** Each atom contains one proton and zero neutrons.
   **b.** Each atom contains six protons and eight neutrons.

**2.36** Write symbols for each isotope:
   **a.** Each atom contains one proton and two neutrons.
   **b.** Each atom contains 92 protons and 146 neutrons.

**2.37** The element copper has two naturally occurring isotopes. One of these has a mass of 62.93 amu and a natural abundance of 69.09%. A second isotope has a mass of 64.9278 amu and a natural abundance of 30.91%. Calculate the atomic mass of copper.

**2.38** The element lithium has two naturally occurring isotopes. One of these has a mass of 6.0151 amu and a natural abundance of 7.49%. A second isotope has a mass of 7.0160 amu and a natural abundance of 92.51%. Calculate the atomic mass of lithium.

## Development of Atomic Theory

### Foundations

**2.39** What are the major postulates of Dalton's atomic theory?

**2.40** What points of Dalton's theory are no longer current?

**2.41** Describe the experiment that provided the basis for our understanding of the nucleus.

**2.42** Describe the series of experiments that characterized the electron.

**2.43** Note the major accomplishment of each of the following:
   **a.** Dalton          **c.** Chadwick
   **b.** Crookes        **d.** Goldstein

**2.44** Note the major accomplishment of each of the following:
   **a.** Thomson        **c.** Geiger
   **b.** Rutherford     **d.** Bohr

## Applications

**2.45** What is a cathode ray? Which subatomic particle is detected?

**2.46** Use the concept of charges to explain why cathode rays are specifically deflected toward the positive pole by external electric fields and magnetic fields.

**2.47** List at least three properties of the electron.

**2.48** Use the concept of charges to explain why an alpha particle fired toward the nucleus is deflected away from the nucleus.

**2.49** Prior to Rutherford's gold foil experiments and the understanding of the existence of a nucleus, how did scientists view the atom?

**2.50** Explain how Rutherford concluded that the atom is principally empty space.

## Light, Atomic Structure, and the Bohr Atom

### Foundations

**2.51** What is meant by the term *spectroscopy?*

**2.52** What is meant by the term *electromagnetic spectrum?*

**2.53** Describe electromagnetic radiation according to its wave nature.

**2.54** Describe electromagnetic radiation according to its particle nature.

**2.55** Is the following statement true or false?
   Light of higher energy travels at a faster speed than light of lower energy.

**2.56** What is the relationship between the energy of light and its wavelength?

**2.57** Which form of radiation has greater energy, microwave or infrared? Explain your reasoning.

**2.58** Which form of radiation has the longer wavelength, ultraviolet or infrared? Explain your reasoning.

**2.59** Describe the process that occurs when electrical energy is applied to a sample of hydrogen gas.

**2.60** When electrical energy is applied to an element in its gaseous state, light is produced. How does the light differ among elements?

## Applications

**2.61** Critique this statement: Electrons can exist in any position outside of the nucleus.

**2.62** Critique this statement: Promotion of electrons is accompanied by a release of energy.

**2.63** List three of the most important points of the Bohr theory.

**2.64** Give two reasons why the Bohr theory did not stand the test of time.

**2.65** What was the major contribution of Bohr's atomic model?

**2.66** What was the major deficiency of Bohr's atomic model?

## The Periodic Law and the Periodic Table

### Foundations

**2.67** Provide the atomic number, atomic mass, and name of the element represented by each of the following symbols:
   **a.** Na          **c.** Mg
   **b.** K          **d.** B

**2.68** Provide the atomic number, atomic mass, and name of the element represented by each of the following symbols:
   **a.** Ca          **c.** Co
   **b.** Cu          **d.** Si

**2.69** Which group of the periodic table is known as the alkali metals? List their symbols.

**2.70** Which group of the periodic table is known as the alkaline earth metals? List their symbols.

**2.71** Which group of the periodic table is known as the halogens? List their names.

**2.72** Which group of the periodic table is known as the noble gases? List their names.

### Applications

**2.73** For each of the elements Na, Ni, Al, P, Cl, and Ar, provide the following information:
   **a.** Which are metals?
   **b.** Which are representative metals?
   **c.** Which are inert or noble gases?

**2.74** For each of the elements Ca, K, Cu, Zn, Br, and Kr, provide the following information:
   **a.** Which are metals?
   **b.** Which are representative metals?
   **c.** Which are inert or noble gases?

**2.75** Using the information below, for Group IA (1) elements:

| Element | Atomic Number | Melting Point (°C) |
|---------|---------------|--------------------|
| Li | 3 | 180.5 |
| Na | 11 | 97.8 |
| K | 19 | 63.3 |
| Rb | 37 | 38.9 |
| Cs | 55 | 28.4 |

Prepare a graph relating melting point and atomic number. How does this demonstrate the periodic law?

**2.76** Use the graph prepared in Question 2.75 to predict the melting point of francium (Fr).

## Electron Arrangement and the Periodic Table

### Foundations

**2.77** Distinguish between a principal energy level and a sublevel.

**2.78** Distinguish between a sublevel and an orbital.

**2.79** Sketch a diagram and describe our current model of an $s$ orbital.

**2.80** How is a $2s$ orbital different from a $1s$ orbital?

**2.81** What is the maximum number of electrons in each of the following energy levels?
   **a.** $n = 1$          **b.** $n = 2$          **c.** $n = 3$

**2.82** For any given principal energy level, what is the maximum number of electrons that can exist in the following subshells?
   **a.** $s$          **b.** $p$          **c.** $d$

**2.83** State the Pauli exclusion principle. Explain how it is used to determine the number of electrons that can exist in a $d$ subshell.

**2.84** State Hund's rule. Determine whether the following orbital diagrams violate Hund's rule.

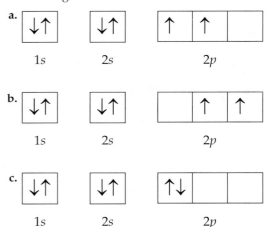

### Applications

**2.85** Using the periodic table, write the electron configuration of each of the following atoms:
   **a.** Al          **b.** Na          **c.** Sc

**2.86** Using the periodic table, write the electron configuration of each of the following atoms:
   **a.** Ca          **b.** Fe          **c.** Cl

**2.87** Using the periodic table, write the electron configuration and orbital diagram of each of the following atoms:
   **a.** B          **b.** S          **c.** Ar

**2.88** Using the periodic table, write the electron configuration and orbital diagram of each of the following atoms:
   **a.** V          **b.** Cd          **c.** Te

**2.89** Which of the following electron configurations are not possible? Why?
   **a.** $1s^2 1p^2$          **c.** $2s^2 2s^2 2p^6 2d^1$
   **b.** $1s^2 2s^2 2p^2$          **d.** $1s^2 2s^3$

**2.90** For each incorrect electron configuration in Question 2.89, assume that the number of electrons is correct, identify the element, and write the correct electron configuration.

**2.91** Determine whether the following orbital diagrams are correct. If there is an error, fix the diagram.

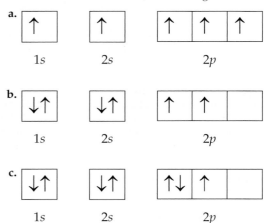

**2.92** Identify the element for each of the orbital diagrams (once corrected) in Question 2.91.

**2.93** Use the periodic table and determine the shorthand electron configuration of each of the following atoms.
**a.** Zr  **b.** Br  **c.** K

**2.94** Use the periodic table and determine the shorthand electron configuration of each of the following atoms.
**a.** I  **b.** Al  **c.** V

## Valence Electrons and the Octet Rule

### Foundations

**2.95** How does the total number of electrons differ from the number of valence electrons in an atom?

**2.96** How can the periodic table be used to determine the number of valence electrons in a representative element atom?

**2.97** State the octet rule.

**2.98** How can the octet rule be used to determine the number of electrons gained or lost by an atom as it becomes an ion?

**2.99** Do metals tend to gain or lose electrons? Do they become cations or anions?

**2.100** Do nonmetals tend to gain or lose electrons? Do they become cations or anions?

### Applications

**2.101** How many total electrons and valence electrons are found in an atom of each of the following elements? What is the number of the principal energy level in which the valence electrons are found?
**a.** H  **d.** F
**b.** Na  **e.** Ne
**c.** B  **f.** He

**2.102** How many total electrons and valence electrons are found in an atom of each of the following elements? What is the number of the principal energy level in which the valence electrons are found?
**a.** Mg  **d.** Br
**b.** K  **e.** Ar
**c.** C  **f.** Xe

**2.103** Determine the number of protons and electrons in each of the following ions.
**a.** $Cl^-$  **c.** $Fe^{2+}$
**b.** $Ca^{2+}$

**2.104** Determine the number of protons and electrons in each of the following ions.
**a.** $S^{2-}$  **c.** $Cd^{2+}$
**b.** $K^+$

**2.105** Predict the number of valence electrons in an atom of:
**a.** calcium  **c.** cesium
**b.** potassium  **d.** barium

**2.106** Predict the number of valence electrons in an atom of:
**a.** carbon  **c.** sulfur
**b.** phosphorus  **d.** chlorine

**2.107** Give the most probable ion formed from each of the following elements:
**a.** Li  **c.** S
**b.** Ca

**2.108** Give the most probable ion formed from each of the following elements.
**a.** O  **c.** Al
**b.** Br

**2.109** Which of the following pairs of atoms and/or ions are isoelectronic with one another?
**a.** $O^{2-}$, Ne  **b.** $S^{2-}$, $Cl^-$

**2.110** Which of the following pairs of atoms and/or ions are isoelectronic with one another?
**a.** $F^-$, $Cl^-$  **b.** $K^+$, Ar

**2.111** Write the electron configuration and shorthand electron configuration of each of the following ions:
**a.** $I^-$  **c.** $Se^{2-}$
**b.** $Ba^{2+}$  **d.** $Al^{3+}$

**2.112** Write the electron configuration and shorthand electron configuration of each of the following biologically important ions:
**a.** $Ca^{2+}$  **c.** $K^+$
**b.** $Mg^{2+}$  **d.** $Cl^-$

## Trends in the Periodic Table

### Foundations

**2.113** What is the trend for atom size from left to right across a period?

**2.114** What is the trend for atom size from top to bottom down a group?

**2.115** Define ionization energy.

**2.116** Define electron affinity.

**2.117** Write an equation for the removal of an electron from a gaseous atom of sodium.

**2.118** Write an equation for the addition of an electron to a gaseous atom of chlorine.

**2.119** Arrange each of the following lists of elements in order of increasing atomic size:
**a.** N, O, F  **c.** Cl, Br, I
**b.** Li, K, Cs  **d.** Ra, Be, Mg

**2.120** Arrange each of the following lists of elements in order of increasing atomic size:
**a.** Al, Si, P  **c.** Sr, Ca, Ba
**b.** In, Ga, Al  **d.** P, N, Sb

**2.121** Arrange each of the following lists of elements in order of increasing ionization energy:
**a.** N, O, F  **b.** Li, K, Cs

**2.122** Arrange each of the following lists of elements in order of increasing ionization energy:
**a.** Cl, Br, I  **b.** Ra, Be, Mg

**2.123** Arrange each of the following lists of elements in order of decreasing electron affinity:
**a.** Na, Li, K  **b.** Sr, Sn, Te

**2.124** Arrange each of the following lists of elements in order of decreasing electron affinity:
**a.** Mg, P, Cl  **b.** Br, I, Cl

### Applications

**2.125** **a.** Explain why a positive ion is always smaller than its parent atom.
**b.** Explain why a fluoride ion is commonly found in nature but a fluorine atom is not.

**2.126** **a.** Explain why a negative ion is always larger than its parent atom.
**b.** Explain why a sodium ion is commonly found in nature but a sodium atom is not.

**2.127** $Cl^-$ and Ar are isoelectronic. Which is larger? Why?

**2.128** $K^+$ and Ar are isoelectronic. Which is larger? Why?

## CHALLENGE PROBLEMS

1. A natural sample of chromium, taken from the ground, will contain four isotopes: Cr-50, Cr-52, Cr-53, and Cr-54. Predict which isotope is in greatest abundance. Explain your reasoning.
2. Crookes's cathode ray tube experiment inadvertently supplied the basic science for a number of modern high-tech devices. List a few of these devices and describe how they involve one or more aspects of this historic experiment.
3. Name five elements that you came in contact with today. Were they in a combined form or did they exist in the form of atoms? Were they present in a pure form or in mixtures? If mixtures, were they heterogeneous or homogeneous? Locate each in the periodic table by providing the group and period designation—for example: Group IIA (or 2), period 3.
4. The periodic table is incomplete. It is possible that new elements will be discovered from experiments using high-energy particle accelerators. Predict as many properties as you can that might characterize the element that has the atomic number 118. Use the Internet to find the properties of element 118, and evaluate your predictions.
5. The element titanium is now being used as a structural material for bone and joint replacement (shoulders, knees). Predict properties that you would expect for such applications; utilize the Internet to look up the properties of titanium and evaluate your answer.

6. Imagine that you have undertaken a voyage to an alternate universe. Using your chemical skills, you find a collection of elements quite different than those found here on earth. After measuring their properties and assigning symbols for each, you wish to organize them as Mendeleev did for our elements. Design a periodic table using the information you have gathered:

| Symbol | Mass (amu) | Reactivity | Electrical Conductivity |
|--------|------------|------------|-------------------------|
| A | 2.0 | High | High |
| B | 4.0 | High | High |
| C | 6.0 | Moderate | Trace |
| D | 8.0 | Low | 0 |
| E | 10.0 | Low | 0 |
| F | 12.0 | High | High |
| G | 14.0 | High | High |
| H | 16.0 | Moderate | Trace |
| I | 18.0 | Low | 0 |
| J | 20.0 | None | 0 |
| K | 22.0 | High | High |
| L | 24.0 | High | High |

Predict the reactivity and conductivity of an element with a mass of 30.0 amu. What element in our universe does this element most closely resemble?

# Structure and Properties of Ionic and Covalent Compounds

## LEARNING GOALS

1 Draw Lewis symbols for representative elements and their respective ions.

2 Classify compounds as having ionic, polar covalent, or nonpolar covalent bonds.

3 Write the formula of a compound when provided with the name or elemental composition of the compound.

4 Name inorganic compounds using standard naming conventions, and recall the common names of frequently used substances.

5 Predict differences in physical state, melting and boiling points, solid-state structure, and solution chemistry that result from differences in bonding.

6 Draw Lewis structures for covalent compounds and polyatomic ions.

7 Explain how the presence or absence of multiple bonding relates to bond length, bond energy, and stability.

8 Use Lewis structures to predict the geometry of molecules.

9 Describe the role that molecular geometry plays in determining the polarity of compounds.

10 Use polarity to determine solubility and predict the melting and boiling points of compounds.

Large gypsum ($CaSO_4 \cdot 2H_2O$) crystals located in a mine in Mexico. The 55-ton crystals reflect the structure seen on the atomic level.

## OUTLINE

# INTRODUCTION

A chemical compound is formed when two or more atoms of different elements are joined by attractive forces called chemical bonds. These bonds result from either a transfer of electrons from one atom to another (the ionic bond) or a sharing of electrons between two atoms (the covalent bond). The elements, once converted to a compound, cannot be recovered by any physical process. A chemical reaction must take place to regenerate the individual elements. The chemical and physical properties of a compound are related to the structure of the compound, and this structure is, in turn, determined by the arrangement of electrons in the atoms that produced the compound. Properties such as solubility, boiling point, and melting point correlate well with the shape and charge distribution, hence, polarity, in the individual units of the compound.

You need to learn how to properly name and write formulas for ionic and covalent compounds. You should also become familiar with some of their properties and be able to relate these properties to the structure and bonding of the compounds.

## 3.1   Chemical Bonding

When two or more atoms form a chemical compound, the atoms are held together in a characteristic arrangement by attractive forces. The **chemical bond** is the force of attraction between any two atoms in a compound. This force of attraction overcomes the repulsion of the positively charged nuclei of the two atoms.

Interactions involving valence electrons are responsible for the chemical bond. We shall focus our attention on these electrons and the electron arrangement of atoms both before and after bond formation.

### Lewis Symbols

The **Lewis symbol,** developed by G. N. Lewis early in the twentieth century, uses the atomic symbol to represent the nucleus and core electrons and dots to represent valence electrons. Its principal advantage is that *only* valence electrons (those that may participate in bonding) are shown. Lewis symbolism is based on the octet rule that was introduced in Chapter 2.

To draw Lewis symbols, we first write the chemical symbol of the atom; this symbol represents the nucleus and all of the lower energy nonvalence electrons. The valence electrons are indicated by dots arranged around the atomic symbol.

Note that the number of dots corresponds to the number of electrons in the outermost shell of the atoms of the element (valence electrons). The four sides around the atomic symbol can each have two dots for a maximum of eight. This corresponds to the fact that a maximum of eight electrons are contained within the $s$ and $p$ subshells. When placing the dots around the symbol, start by placing one dot per side. When finished, each unpaired dot (representing an unpaired electron) is available to form a chemical bond with another atom.

### Principal Types of Chemical Bonds: Ionic and Covalent

Two principal classes of chemical bonds exist: ionic and covalent. Both involve valence electrons.

**Ionic bonding** involves a transfer of one or more electrons from one atom to another. **Covalent bonding** involves a sharing of electrons.

Before discussing each type, we should recognize that the distinction between ionic and covalent bonding is not always clear-cut. Some compounds are clearly ionic, and some are clearly covalent, but many others possess both ionic and covalent characteristics.

## LEARNING GOAL

**1** Draw Lewis symbols for representative elements and their respective ions.

*Recall that the number of valence electrons for a representative element can be determined from the Roman numeral above the group in the periodic table (see Figure 2.10).*

| **EXAMPLE 3.1** | **Drawing Lewis Symbols for Representative Elements** | LEARNING GOAL |

Draw the Lewis symbol for carbon, and indicate the number of bonds that carbon will form when chemically bonded to other atoms.

**1**  Draw Lewis symbols for representative elements and their respective ions.

**Solution**

Carbon is found in Group IVA (or 14) of the periodic table. Therefore, carbon has four valence electrons.

**Step 1.** The chemical symbol for carbon is written as

$$C$$

**Step 2.** The four dots representing the four valence electrons are placed around the C, with one dot on each side.

$$\cdot \overset{\displaystyle \cdot}{\underset{\displaystyle \cdot}{C}} \cdot$$

**Step 3.** Carbon is able to form four bonds because each unpaired electron (dot) is available to form a bond.

*Helpful Hint:* Since carbon has four valence electrons, it would need four more electrons in order to satisfy the octet rule.

**Practice Problem 3.1**

Draw the Lewis symbol for oxygen, and indicate the number of bonds that oxygen will form when bonded to other atoms.

▶ For Further Practice: **Questions 3.13 and 3.14.**

### Ionic Bonding

Representative elements form ions that obey the octet rule. Ions of opposite charge attract each other, and this attraction is the essence of the ionic bond. As a result, when metals and nonmetals combine, it is usually through the formation of an ionic bond. Consider the reaction of a sodium atom and a chlorine atom to produce sodium chloride:

$$Na + Cl \longrightarrow NaCl$$

Recall that the sodium atom, a metal, has

- a low ionization energy (it readily loses an electron) and
- a low electron affinity (it does not want more electrons).

If sodium loses its valence electron, it will become isoelectronic (same electron configuration) with neon, a very stable noble gas atom. This tells us that the sodium atom would be a good electron donor, forming the sodium cation:

$$Na\cdot \longrightarrow Na^+ + e^-$$

Recall that the chlorine atom, a nonmetal, has

- a high ionization energy (it will not easily give up an electron) and
- a high electron affinity (it readily accepts another electron).

Chlorine will gain one more electron. By doing so, it will complete an octet (eight outermost electrons) and be isoelectronic with argon, a stable noble gas. Therefore, chlorine behaves as a willing electron acceptor, forming a chloride anion:

$$:\overset{\displaystyle \cdot\cdot}{\underset{\displaystyle \cdot\cdot}{Cl}}\cdot \; + \; e^- \longrightarrow \left[ :\overset{\displaystyle \cdot\cdot}{\underset{\displaystyle \cdot\cdot}{Cl}}: \right]^-$$

LEARNING GOALS

**1**  Draw Lewis symbols for representative elements and their respective ions.

**2**  Classify compounds as having ionic, polar covalent, or nonpolar covalent bonds.

*Refer to Section 2.7 for a discussion of ionization energy and electron affinity.*

Square brackets are placed around Lewis symbols of anions.

When a sodium atom reacts with a chlorine atom, the electron released by sodium (*electron donor*) is the electron received by chlorine (*electron acceptor*):

$$Na\cdot \longrightarrow Na^+ + e^-$$

$$e^- + \cdot \ddot{\underset{\cdot\cdot}{Cl}}: \longrightarrow \left[ :\ddot{\underset{\cdot\cdot}{Cl}}: \right]^-$$

An **ionic bond** is the *electrostatic force*, the attraction of opposite charges, between the resulting cation and anion (in this case, the $Na^+$ and the $Cl^-$). The electrostatic force is quite strong and holds the ions together as an *ion pair*: $Na^+Cl^-$. The essential features of ionic bonding are the following:

- Metals tend to form cations because they have low ionization energies and low electron affinities.
- Nonmetals tend to form anions because they have high ionization energies and high electron affinities.
- Ions are formed by the transfer of electrons.
- The oppositely charged ions formed are held together by an electrostatic force.
- Reactions between metals and nonmetals tend to form ionic compounds.

---

**EXAMPLE 3.2**    **Drawing Lewis Symbols for Ions**

LEARNING GOAL

**1**   Draw Lewis symbols for representative elements and their respective ions.

When there is a reaction between potassium and bromine, ions form. Using Lewis symbols, write the reactions showing how electrons are lost or gained when potassium and bromine become ions.

**Solution**

The periodic table is used to determine the number of valence electrons associated with each atom.

**Step 1.** Potassium is in Group IA (or 1); it has one valence electron that should be represented by one dot on the atom.

$$\cdot K$$

**Step 2.** Potassium has low ionization energy and low electron affinity, which makes it a good electron donor. In the reaction shown below, the cation formed does not have any valence electrons.

$$\cdot K \longrightarrow K^+ + e^-$$

**Step 3.** Bromine is in Group VIIA (or 17); it has seven valence electrons that should be represented by seven dots on the atom.

$$\cdot \ddot{\underset{\cdot\cdot}{Br}}:$$

**Step 4.** Bromine has high ionization energy and high electron affinity, which make it a good electron acceptor. The anion formed will have eight valence electrons because bromine gains one electron to form a stable octet. Square brackets are often placed around Lewis symbols of anions to more easily distinguish the ion charge from the electrons.

$$\cdot \ddot{\underset{\cdot\cdot}{Br}}: + e^- \longrightarrow \left[ :\ddot{\underset{\cdot\cdot}{Br}}: \right]^-$$

*Helpful Hint:* Lewis symbols for cations should not have any dots because the atoms lose their valence electrons in the process of ion formation. Whereas, with the exception of hydrogen, Lewis symbols for anions should contain eight dots because the atoms gained electrons in the process of attaining a stable octet.

---

**Practice Problem 3.2**

When there is a reaction between calcium and oxygen, ions form. Using Lewis symbols, write the reactions showing how electrons are lost or gained when calcium and oxygen become ions.

▶ For Further Practice: **Questions 3.23 and 3.24.**

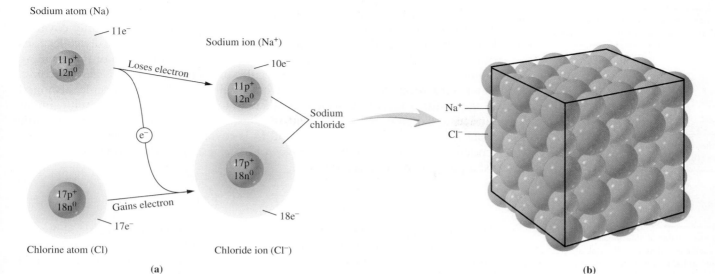

**Figure 3.1** The arrangement of ions in a crystal of NaCl (sodium chloride, table salt). (a) A sodium atom loses one electron to become a smaller sodium ion, and a chlorine atom gains that electron, becoming a larger chloride ion. (b) Attraction of $Na^+$ and $Cl^-$ forms NaCl ion pairs that aggregate in a three-dimensional crystal lattice structure. (c) An enlarged view of NaCl crystals, magnified 400x, shows their cubic geometry. Each tiny crystal contains billions and billions of sodium and chloride ions.

Although ionic compounds are sometimes referred to as ion pairs, in the solid state these ion pairs do not actually exist as individual units. The positive ions exert attractive forces on several negative ions, and the negative ions are attracted to several positive centers. Positive and negative ions arrange themselves in a regular three-dimensional repeating array to produce a stable arrangement known as a **crystal lattice.** The lattice structure for the ionic compound sodium chloride is shown in Figure 3.1.

## Covalent Bonding

The octet rule is not just for ionic compounds. In covalent bonding, atoms share electrons to complete the octet of electrons for each of the atoms participating in the bond. Consider the bond formed between two hydrogen atoms, producing the diatomic form of hydrogen: $H_2$.

An individual hydrogen atom is not stable; however, if it were to gain a second electron, it would be isoelectronic with the stable electron configuration of helium. Since two identical hydrogen atoms have an equal tendency to gain or lose electrons, an electron transfer from one atom to the other is unlikely to occur under normal conditions. Each atom may attain a noble gas structure only by *sharing* its electron with the other, as shown with Lewis symbols and a Lewis structure:

$$H\cdot + \cdot H \longrightarrow H : H$$

LEARNING GOAL

**2** Classify compounds as having ionic, polar covalent, or nonpolar covalent bonds.

Lewis symbols represent atoms and ions. Lewis structures represent covalent compounds.

A diatomic molecule is one that is composed of two atoms joined by a covalent bond.

Fourteen valence electrons are arranged in such a way that each fluorine atom is surrounded by eight electrons. The octet rule is satisfied for each fluorine atom.

When electrons are shared rather than transferred, the *shared electron pair* is referred to as a *covalent bond* (Figure 3.2). Compounds containing only covalent bonds are called *covalent compounds*. Covalent compounds are typically collections of *molecules*. **Molecules** are neutral (uncharged) species made up of two or more atoms joined by covalent bonds. Molecules are represented by *Lewis structures*. **Lewis structures** depict valence electrons of all atoms in the molecule, arranged to satisfy the octet rule. Covalent bonds tend to form between atoms with similar tendencies to gain or lose electrons. For example, bonding within the diatomic molecules ($H_2$, $N_2$, $O_2$, $F_2$, $Cl_2$, $Br_2$, and $I_2$) is covalent because there can be no net tendency for electron transfer between identical atoms. The formation of $F_2$, for example, may be represented as

$$:\overset{..}{\underset{..}{F}}\cdot \;+\; \cdot\overset{..}{\underset{..}{F}}: \longrightarrow \;:\overset{..}{\underset{..}{F}}:\overset{..}{\underset{..}{F}}:$$

As in $H_2$, a single covalent bond is formed. The bonding electron pair, shown in blue, is said to be *localized*, or largely confined to the region between the two fluorine nuclei. Paired electrons around an atom that are not shared are termed **lone pairs.** The six lone pairs in $F_2$ are shown in red.

Two atoms do not have to be identical to form a covalent bond. Consider compounds such as the following:

$$H:\overset{..}{\underset{..}{F}}: \qquad H:\overset{..}{\underset{..}{O}}:H \qquad H:\overset{\displaystyle H}{\underset{\displaystyle H}{\overset{..}{C}}}:H \qquad H:\overset{\displaystyle H}{\underset{..}{N}}:H$$

As you examine each of these structures, notice the number of electrons associated with each atom. The octet rule is satisfied for each atom. The hydrogen atoms have two electrons (shared electrons with the atom to which they are attached), and the other (non-hydrogen) atoms have eight valence electrons, which are counted as follows:

- Fluorine (in HF) has two electrons shared with hydrogen and six lone-pair electrons (3 lone pairs).
- Oxygen (in $H_2O$) has four electrons shared with the two hydrogen atoms and four lone-pair electrons (2 lone pairs).
- Carbon (in $CH_4$) has eight electrons shared with the four hydrogen atoms.
- Nitrogen (in $NH_3$) has six electrons shared with the three hydrogen atoms and two lone-pair electrons (1 lone pair).

In each of these cases, bond formation satisfies the octet rule. A total of eight electrons surrounds each atom other than hydrogen. Hydrogen is an exception because it has only two electrons (corresponding to the electronic structure of helium).

## Polar Covalent Bonding and Electronegativity

### The Polar Covalent Bond

Covalent bonding is the sharing of an electron pair by two atoms. However, just as we may observe in our day-to-day activities, sharing is not always equal. In a molecule like $H_2$ (or any other diatomic molecule), the electrons, on average, spend the same amount of time in the vicinity of each atom; the electrons have no preference because both atoms are identical.

Now consider a diatomic molecule composed of two different elements; HF is a common example. It has been experimentally shown that the electrons in the H—F bond between hydrogen and fluorine atoms are not equally shared; the electrons spend more time in the vicinity of the fluorine atom. This unequal sharing results in a **polar covalent bond.** One end of the bond (in this case, the F atom) is more electron rich (higher electron density), hence, more negative. The other end

Two hydrogen atoms approach at high velocity.

Hydrogen nuclei begin to attract each other's electrons.

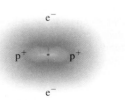

Hydrogen atoms form the hydrogen molecule; atoms are held together by sharing the bonding electron pair.

**Figure 3.2** Covalent bonding in hydrogen.

of the bond (in this case, the H atom) is less electron rich (lower electron density), hence, more positive. These two ends can be described as follows (Figure 3.3):

- Somewhat positive end (partial positive), denoted with a $\delta^+$ symbol.
- Somewhat negative end (partial negative), denoted with a $\delta^-$ symbol.

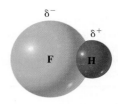

Elements whose atoms strongly attract electrons are described as electronegative elements. Linus Pauling, a chemist noted for his theories on chemical bonding, developed a scale of relative electronegativities that correlates reasonably well with the positions of the elements in the periodic table, and allows for us to use the predictive power of the periodic table to determine whether a particular bond is polar or nonpolar covalent. Electronegative elements that tend to form anions (by gaining electrons) are found to the right of the table, whereas the elements that tend to form cations (by losing electrons) are located on the left side of the table.

**Figure 3.3** Polar covalent bonding in HF. Fluorine is electron rich ($\delta^-$) and hydrogen is electron deficient ($\delta^+$) due to unequal electron sharing.

## Electronegativity

**Electronegativity** (EN) is a measure of the ability of an atom to attract electrons in a chemical bond. Elements with high EN have a greater ability to attract electrons than do elements with low EN. Pauling developed a method to assign values of EN to many of the elements in the periodic table. These values range from a low of 0.7 to a high of 4.0, with 4.0 being the most electronegative element.

Figure 3.4 shows that the most electronegative elements (excluding the nonreactive noble gas elements) are located in the upper right corner of the periodic table, whereas the least electronegative elements are found in the lower left corner of the table. In general, EN values increase as we proceed left to right and bottom to top of the table. Like other periodic trends, numerous exceptions occur.

If we picture the covalent bond as a competition for electrons between two positive centers, it is the difference in EN, $\Delta EN$, that determines the extent of polarity. Consider the calculation of the EN difference in $H_2$ or H—H:

Linus Pauling is the only person to receive two Nobel Prizes in very unrelated fields; the chemistry award in 1954 and 8 years later, the Nobel Peace Prize. His career is a model of interdisciplinary science, with important contributions ranging from chemical physics to molecular biology.

$$\Delta EN = \begin{bmatrix} EN\ of \\ hydrogen \end{bmatrix} - \begin{bmatrix} EN\ of \\ hydrogen \end{bmatrix}$$

$$\Delta EN = 2.1 - 2.1 = 0 \quad \text{A nonpolar covalent bond}$$

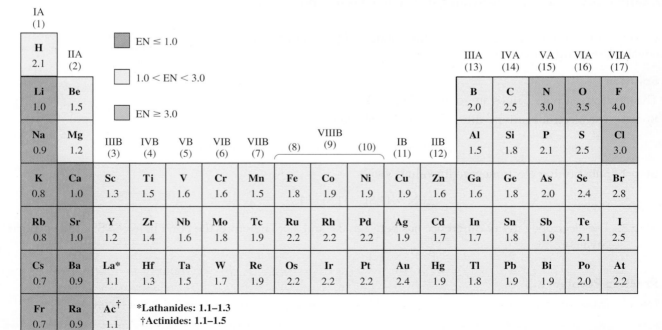

**Figure 3.4** Electronegativities of the elements.

By convention, the EN difference is calculated by subtracting the less electronegative element's value from the value for the more electronegative element. In this way, negative numbers are avoided.

The bond in $H_2$ is nonpolar covalent. The difference in electronegativity between two identical atoms is zero. This can also be calculated for $Cl_2$ or Cl—Cl:

$$\Delta EN = \left[\begin{array}{c} EN\ of \\ chlorine \end{array}\right] - \left[\begin{array}{c} EN\ of \\ chlorine \end{array}\right]$$

$$\Delta EN = 3.0 - 3.0 = 0 \quad \text{A nonpolar covalent bond}$$

Bonds between *identical* atoms are *always* nonpolar covalent. Although, strictly speaking, any EN difference, no matter how small, produces a polar bond, the degree of polarity for bonds with EN differences less than 0.5 is minimal. Consequently, we shall classify these bonds as nonpolar. Now consider HCl or H—Cl:

$$\Delta EN = \left[\begin{array}{c} EN\ of \\ chlorine \end{array}\right] - \left[\begin{array}{c} EN\ of \\ hydrogen \end{array}\right]$$

$$\Delta EN = 3.0 - 2.1 = 0.9 \quad \text{A polar covalent bond}$$

The EN difference is greater than 0.5 and less than 2.0. By definition, this means that the bond in HCl is polar covalent. An EN difference of 2.0 is generally accepted as the boundary between polar covalent and ionic bonds.

When the EN difference is calculated for NaCl:

$$\Delta EN = \left[\begin{array}{c} EN\ of \\ chlorine \end{array}\right] - \left[\begin{array}{c} EN\ of \\ sodium \end{array}\right]$$

$$\Delta EN = 3.0 - 0.9 = 2.1 \quad \text{An ionic bond}$$

The EN difference of 2.1 is greater than 2.0, and the bond in NaCl is ionic. Recall that metals and nonmetals usually react to produce ionic compounds resulting from the transfer of one or more electrons from the metal to the nonmetal.

---

**EXAMPLE 3.3**    **Using Electronegativity to Classify Bond Polarity**

LEARNING GOAL

Use electronegativity values to classify the bonds in $SiO_2$ as ionic, polar covalent, or nonpolar covalent.

**2** Classify compounds as having ionic, polar covalent, or nonpolar covalent bonds.

**Solution**

The electronegativity values are found in Figure 3.4.

**Step 1.** The electronegativity difference can be calculated using the equation

$$\Delta EN = [EN\ of\ oxygen] - [EN\ of\ silicon]$$

**Step 2.** Substituting electronegativity values yields,

$$\Delta EN = [3.5] - [1.8] = 1.7$$

**Step 3.** The electronegativity difference lies between 0.5 and 2.0. Therefore, the bond between Si and O is polar covalent.

**Practice Problem 3.3**

Use electronegativity values to classify the bond in $O_2$ as ionic, polar covalent, or nonpolar covalent.

▶ For Further Practice: **Questions 3.21 and 3.22.**

## 3.2   Naming Compounds and Writing Formulas of Compounds

**Nomenclature** is the assignment of a correct and unambiguous name to each and every chemical compound. Assigning a name to a structure or deducing the structure from a name is a necessary first step in any discussion of these compounds. The system for naming ionic compounds is different from the system for naming covalent compounds.

LEARNING GOAL

**3** Write the formula of a compound when provided with the name or elemental composition of the compound.

### Ionic Compounds

The **formula** is the representation of the fundamental compound using chemical symbols and numerical subscripts. It is the "shorthand" symbol for a compound such as

$$NaCl \quad \text{and} \quad MgF_2$$

The *formula* of an ionic compound is the smallest whole-number ratio of ions in the substance.

The formula identifies the number and type of the various atoms that make up the compound unit. The number of like atoms in the unit is shown by the use of a subscript. The presence of only one atom is understood when no subscript is present.

The formula $NaCl$ indicates that each ion pair consists of one sodium cation ($Na^+$) and one chloride anion ($Cl^-$). Similarly, the formula $MgF_2$ indicates that one magnesium cation, $Mg^{2+}$, and two fluoride anions, $2\ F^-$, combine to form the compound.

### Writing Formulas of Ionic Compounds from the Identities of the Component Ions

It is important to be able to write the formula of an ionic compound when provided with the identities of the ions that make up the compound. The charge of each ion can usually be determined from the group (family) on the periodic table in which the parent element is found. The cations and anions must combine in such a way that the resulting formula unit has a net charge of zero.

---

**EXAMPLE 3.4**   **Determining the Formula of an Ionic Compound**

LEARNING GOAL

**3** Write the formula of a compound when provided with the name or elemental composition of the compound.

Predict the formula of the compound formed from the combination of ions of aluminum and sulfur.

**Solution**

Determine the charges of the ions from the periodic table. Use subscripts to create a neutral compound.

**Step 1.**   Aluminum is in Group IIIA (or 13); it has three valence electrons. Loss of these electrons produces $Al^{3+}$.

$$\cdot \overset{\cdot}{Al} \longrightarrow Al^{3+} + 3e^-$$

**Step 2.**   Sulfur is in Group VIA (or 16); it has six valence electrons. A gain of two electrons (to create a stable octet) produces $S^{2-}$.

$$\cdot \overset{\cdot\cdot}{\underset{\cdot\cdot}{S}} \cdot + 2e^- \longrightarrow \left[ :\overset{\cdot\cdot}{\underset{\cdot\cdot}{S}} : \right]^{2-}$$

**Step 3.**   In order to combine $Al^{3+}$ and $S^{2-}$ to yield a unit charge of zero, the least common multiple of 3 and 2, which is 6, is used. Each charge is multiplied by a different factor to achieve a charge of $6^+$ and $6^-$.

$$\text{For Al: } 2Al^{3+} = 6^+ \text{ charge}$$
$$\text{For S: } 3S^{2-} = 6^- \text{ charge}$$

*Continued…*

**Step 4.** The subscript 2 is used to indicate that the formula unit contains two aluminum ions. The subscript 3 is used to indicate that the formula unit contains three sulfide ions. Thus, the formula of the compound is $Al_2S_3$.

*Helpful Hint:* Electrons are transferred when this neutral ionic compound is formed. When 2 Al atoms form 2 $Al^{3+}$ cations, there are a total of $(2 \times 3e^-)$ six electrons produced. Since each S requires two electrons to form each $S^{2-}$, 3S atoms require a total of $(3 \times 2e^-)$ six electrons.

---

### Practice Problem 3.4

Predict the formulas of the compounds formed from the combination of ions of the following elements:

   a. calcium and nitrogen
   b. magnesium and bromine
   c. magnesium and nitrogen

▶ For Further Practice: **Questions 3.27 and 3.28.**

---

### LEARNING GOAL

**4** Name inorganic compounds using standard naming conventions, and recall the common names of frequently used substances.

### Writing Names of Ionic Compounds from the Formulas of the Compounds

In naming ionic compounds, the name of the cation appears first, followed by the name of the anion. If the ionic compound consists of a metal cation and a non-metal anion, the cation has the name of the metal; the anion is named using the *stem* of the nonmetal name joined to the suffix *-ide*. Some examples follow.

| Formula | Cation | and | Anion Stem | + ide | = | Compound Name |
|---------|--------|-----|------------|-------|---|---------------|
| NaCl    | sodium |     | chlor      | + ide |   | sodium chloride |
| $Na_2O$ | sodium |     | ox         | + ide |   | sodium oxide |
| $Li_2S$ | lithium |    | sulf       | + ide |   | lithium sulfide |
| $AlBr_3$ | aluminum |  | brom       | + ide |   | aluminum bromide |
| CaO     | calcium |    | ox         | + ide |   | calcium oxide |

The metals that exist with only one possible cation charge are the Group IA (or 1) and IIA (or 2) metals, which have $1^+$ and $2^+$ charges, respectively, as well as $Ag^+$, $Cd^{2+}$, $Zn^{2+}$, and $Al^{3+}$.

If the cation and anion exist in only one common charged form, there is no ambiguity between formula and name. Sodium chloride *must be* NaCl, and lithium sulfide *must be* $Li_2S$, so that the sum of positive and negative charges is zero. With many elements, such as the transition metals, several ions of different charge may exist. $Fe^{2+}$, $Fe^{3+}$ and $Cu^+$, $Cu^{2+}$ are two common examples. Clearly, an ambiguity exists if we use the name iron for both $Fe^{2+}$ and $Fe^{3+}$ or copper for both $Cu^+$ and $Cu^{2+}$. Two systems have been developed to avoid this problem: the *Stock system* and the *common nomenclature system*.

In the Stock system (systematic name), a Roman numeral placed immediately after the name of the ion indicates the magnitude of the cation's charge. In the older common nomenclature system, the suffix *-ous* indicates the lower ionic charge, and the suffix *-ic* indicates the higher ionic charge. Consider the examples in Table 3.1.

Systematic names are easier and less ambiguous than common names. Whenever possible, we will use this system of nomenclature. The older, common names (-ous, -ic) are less specific; furthermore, they often use the Latin names of the elements (for example, iron compounds use *ferr-*, from *ferrum*, the Latin word for iron).

| EXAMPLE 3.5 | Naming an Ionic Compound Using the Stock System |
|---|---|

LEARNING GOAL

**4** Name inorganic compounds using standard naming conventions, and recall the common names of frequently used substances.

Name $MnO_2$.

**Solution**

**Step 1.** Based on the formula, it can be concluded that this compound is ionic.

**Step 2.** Name the cation as the metal name followed by the anion stem with the *-ide* suffix.

Hence, manganese oxide.

**Step 3.** Determine if a Roman numeral is needed.

Since Mn is not a Group IA (or 1) or IIA (or 2) metal, nor is it Ag, Cd, Zn, or Al, a Roman numeral *is* needed.

**Step 4.** Determine the charge of the metal. This is determined by using two pieces of information: (1) the charge of the anion, and (2) the overall charge of the compound is zero.

(1)  The charge of oxide is $2^-$, and there are two $O^{2-}$ ions.

$$2 \times (2^-) = 4^-$$

(2)  There must be a $4^+$ charge on the metal to balance the $4^-$ of oxide.

**Step 5.** Insert a Roman numeral stating this charge (IV) after the metal name. This gives manganese(IV) oxide.

**Practice Problem 3.5**

Name $CrBr_2$.

▶ For Further Practice: **Questions 3.39 and 3.40.**

**Monatomic ions** are ions consisting of a single atom. Common monatomic ions are listed in Table 3.2. The ions that are particularly important in biological systems are highlighted in red.

**Polyatomic ions,** such as the hydroxide ion, $OH^-$, are composed of two or more atoms bonded together. These ions, although bonded to other ions with ionic bonds, are themselves held together by covalent bonds.

**TABLE 3.1 Systematic (Stock) and Common Names for Iron and Copper Ions**

| **For systematic name:** | | | |
|---|---|---|---|
| Formula | Cation Charge | Cation Name | Systematic Name |
| $FeCl_2$ | 2 + | Iron(II) | Iron(II) chloride |
| $FeCl_3$ | 3 + | Iron(III) | Iron(III) chloride |
| $Cu_2O$ | 1 + | Copper(I) | Copper(I) oxide |
| $CuO$ | 2 + | Copper(II) | Copper(II) oxide |
| **For common nomenclature:** | | | |
| Formula | Cation Charge | Cation Name | Common -ous/ic Name |
| $FeCl_2$ | 2 + | Ferr*ous* | Ferrous chloride |
| $FeCl_3$ | 3 + | Ferr*ic* | Ferric chloride |
| $Cu_2O$ | 1 + | Cupr*ous* | Cuprous oxide |
| $CuO$ | 2 + | Cupr*ic* | Cupric oxide |

**TABLE 3.2 Common Monatomic Cations and Anions**

| Cation | Name | Anion | Name |
|--------|------|-------|------|
| $H^+$ | Hydrogen ion | $H^-$ | Hydride ion |
| $Li^+$ | Lithium ion | $F^-$ | Fluoride ion |
| $Na^+$ | Sodium ion | $Cl^-$ | Chloride ion |
| $K^+$ | Potassium ion | $Br^-$ | Bromide ion |
| $Cs^+$ | Cesium ion | $I^-$ | Iodide ion |
| $Be^{2+}$ | Beryllium ion | $O^{2-}$ | Oxide ion |
| $Mg^{2+}$ | Magnesium ion | $S^{2-}$ | Sulfide ion |
| $Ca^{2+}$ | Calcium ion | $N^{3-}$ | Nitride ion |
| $Ba^{2+}$ | Barium ion | $P^{3-}$ | Phosphide ion |
| $Al^{3+}$ | Aluminum ion | | |
| $Ag^+$ | Silver ion | | |

*Note:* The ions of principal biological importance are highlighted in red.

The polyatomic ion has an *overall* positive or negative charge. Some common polyatomic ions are listed in Table 3.3. You should memorize the formulas, charges, and names of these polyatomic ions, especially those highlighted in red.

**TABLE 3.3 Common Polyatomic Cations and Anions**

| Ion | Name |
|-----|------|
| $H_3O^+$ | Hydronium |
| $NH_4^+$ | Ammonium |
| $NO_2^-$ | Nitrite |
| $NO_3^-$ | Nitrate |
| $SO_3^{2-}$ | Sulfite |
| $SO_4^{2-}$ | Sulfate |
| $HSO_4^-$ | Hydrogen sulfate |
| $OH^-$ | Hydroxide |
| $CN^-$ | Cyanide |
| $PO_4^{3-}$ | Phosphate |
| $HPO_4^{2-}$ | Hydrogen phosphate |
| $H_2PO_4^-$ | Dihydrogen phosphate |
| $CO_3^{2-}$ | Carbonate |
| $HCO_3^-$ | Bicarbonate |
| $ClO^-$ | Hypochlorite |
| $ClO_2^-$ | Chlorite |
| $ClO_3^-$ | Chlorate |
| $ClO_4^-$ | Perchlorate |
| $CH_3COO^-$ (or $C_2H_3O_2^-$) | Acetate |
| $MnO_4^-$ | Permanganate |
| $Cr_2O_7^{2-}$ | Dichromate |
| $CrO_4^{2-}$ | Chromate |
| $O_2^{2-}$ | Peroxide |

*Note:* The most commonly encountered ions are highlighted in red.

When naming compounds containing polyatomic ions, the same rules apply. That is, name the cation and then the anion. Use Roman numerals where appropriate.

| Formula | Cation | Anion | Compound Name |
|---------|--------|-------|---------------|
| $NH_4Cl$ | $NH_4^+$ | $Cl^-$ | ammonium chloride |
| $Ca(OH)_2$ | $Ca^{2+}$ | $OH^-$ | calcium hydroxide |
| $Na_2SO_4$ | $Na^+$ | $SO_4^{2-}$ | sodium sulfate |
| $NaHCO_3$ | $Na^+$ | $HCO_3^-$ | sodium bicarbonate |
| $Cu(NO_3)_2$ | $Cu^{2+}$ | $NO_3^-$ | copper(II) nitrate |

Sodium bicarbonate may also be named sodium hydrogen carbonate, a preferred and less ambiguous name. Likewise, $Na_2HPO_4$ is named sodium hydrogen phosphate, and other ionic compounds are named similarly.

**Question 3.1**  Name each of the following compounds:
  a. KCN                b. MgS               c. $Mg(CH_3COO)_2$

**Question 3.2**  Name each of the following compounds:
  a. $Li_2CO_3$           b. $FeBr_2$             c. $CuSO_4$

## Writing Formulas of Ionic Compounds from the Names of the Compounds

It is also important to be able to write the correct formula when given the compound name. To do this, we must be able to predict the charge of monatomic ions and remember the charge and formula of polyatomic ions. Equally important, the relative number of positive and negative ions in the unit must result in a net charge of zero for compounds that are electrically neutral. When more than one polyatomic ion needs to be represented in the formula of the neutral compound, the polyatomic ion portion of the formula is placed within parentheses before the subscript. Two examples follow.

**LEARNING GOAL**

**3** Write the formula of a compound when provided with the name or elemental composition of the compound.

---

**EXAMPLE 3.6**  **Writing a Formula From the Name of an Ionic Compound**

Write the formula of sodium sulfate.

**LEARNING GOAL**

**3** Write the formula of a compound when provided with the name or elemental composition of the compound.

**Solution**

The charges of monatomic ions can be determined from the periodic table. The polyatomic ions should be memorized.

**Step 1.** Determine the charges of the ions:

sodium sulfate

Group IA (or 1) metal $\longrightarrow$ $Na^+$    $SO_4^{2-}$ $\longleftarrow$ Polyatomic ion

**Step 2.** Balance the charges. Two positive charges are needed to balance the two negative charges of sulfate. The subscript 2 is used following Na to indicate this.
Hence, the formula is $Na_2SO_4$.

*Helpful Hint:* Overall, this compound is neutral. Therefore, when the 2 $Na^+$ charge component is added to the 1 $SO_4^{2-}$ charge component, the sum should be zero.

$$(2 \times 1^+) + (1 \times 2^-) = 0$$

*Continued…*

### Practice Problem 3.6

Write the formula for each of the following compounds:

    a. calcium carbonate            b. copper(I) sulfate

▶ For Further Practice: **Questions 3.41 and 3.42.**

---

**EXAMPLE 3.7**    **Writing a Formula From the Name of an Ionic Compound**

Write the formula of magnesium phosphate.

LEARNING GOAL

**3**   Write the formula of a compound when provided with the name or elemental composition of the compound.

**Solution**

The charges of monatomic ions can be determined from the periodic table. The polyatomic ions should be memorized.

**Step 1.** Determine the charges of the ions:

magnesium phosphate

Group IIA (or 2) metal  ⟶  $Mg^{2+}$   $PO_4^{3-}$  ⟵  Polyatomic ion

**Step 2.** Balance the charges. The least common multiple for 2 and 3 is 6. Obtain $6^+$ and $6^-$ charges using subscripts. Three $Mg^{2+}$ and two $PO_4^{3-}$ are needed. The subscript 3 is written after magnesium, and the polyatomic ion, phosphate, is placed within parentheses and followed with the subscript 2. Hence, the formula is $Mg_3(PO_4)_2$.

*Helpful Hint:* Overall, this compound is neutral. Therefore, when the 3 $Mg^{2+}$ charge component is added to the 2 $PO_4^{3-}$ charge component, the sum should be zero. $(3 \times 2^+) + (2 \times 3^-) = 0$

---

### Practice Problem 3.7

Write the formula for each of the following compounds:

    a. iron(III) sulfide        b. calcium sulfate        c. aluminum oxide

▶ For Further Practice: **Questions 3.43 and 3.44.**

---

LEARNING GOAL

**4**   Name inorganic compounds using standard naming conventions, and recall the common names of frequently used substances.

By convention, the prefix *mono-* is often omitted from the second element as well (dinitrogen oxide, not dinitrogen monoxide). In other cases, common usage retains the prefix (carbon monoxide, not carbon oxide).

## Covalent Compounds

### Naming Covalent Compounds

Most covalent compounds are formed by the reaction of nonmetals. We saw earlier that ionic compounds are not composed of single units but are a part of a massive three-dimensional crystal structure in the solid state. Covalent compounds typically exist as discrete molecules in the solid, liquid, and gas states. This is a distinctive feature of covalently bonded substances.

    The conventions for naming covalent compounds follow:

1. The names of the elements are written in the order in which they appear in the formula.
2. A prefix (Table 3.4) indicating the number of each kind of atom found in the unit is placed before the name of the element.
3. If only one atom of a particular kind is the first element present in the molecule, the prefix *mono-* is usually omitted from that first element.
4. The stem of the name of the last element is used with the suffix *-ide.*
5. The final vowel in a prefix is often dropped before *oxide.*

# A Medical Perspective

## Unwanted Crystal Formation

Conventional wisdom says that the painful symptoms associated with the presence of stones in the bladder and kidneys are just one more problem associated with aging. Unfortunately, recent observations by many clinicians and physicians across the country seem to indicate that these problems are not limited to the elderly. Children as young as 5 years old are developing kidney stones while doctors search for reasons to explain this phenomenon.

Kidney stones most often result from the combination of calcium cations ($Ca^{2+}$) with anions such as oxalate ($C_2O_4^{2-}$) and phosphate ($PO_4^{3-}$). Calcium oxalate and calcium phosphate are ionic compounds that are only sparingly soluble in water. They grow in a three-dimensional crystal lattice. When the crystals become large enough to inhibit the flow of urine

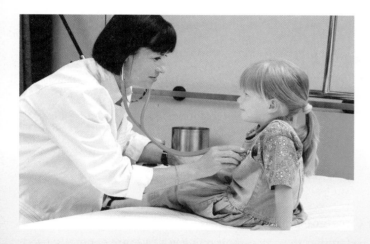

in the kidney or bladder, painful symptoms necessitate some strategy to remove the stones.

Conditions that favor stone formation are the same as those that favor the formation of the same material in a beaker: high concentrations of the ions and insufficient water to dissolve the stones.

Many physicians believe that children who tend to form stones share several behavioral characteristics. They do not drink enough water, and they consume too much salt. Salt in the diet appears to favor the transport of calcium ions to the kidney. Potato chips, French fries, and other snack foods, as well as processed foods such as frozen dinners, sandwich meats, canned soups, and sport drinks are very high in salt content. Obesity appears associated with stone formation, but this may be linked to the unhealthy diet of many children.

Although limiting calcium ion intake would appear to inhibit stone formation (remember, the stones are calcium compounds), reduction of calcium in the diet is not the answer! Dietary calcium is actually beneficial because it binds with oxalate ions before they reach the kidneys. Dietary calcium is important in preventing osteoporosis and dental caries as well. The take-home lesson? A balanced diet, in moderation, with minimal salt intake, especially in the formative years, is recommended.

### For Further Understanding

Consult reliable references to support your answers to the following:

▶ Write the formulas for calcium oxalate and calcium phosphate.

▶ Describe one useful function of phosphate ions in the diet.

**TABLE 3.4** Prefixes Used to Denote Numbers of Atoms in a Compound

| Prefix | Number of Atoms |
| --- | --- |
| Mono- | 1 |
| Di- | 2 |
| Tri- | 3 |
| Tetra- | 4 |
| Penta- | 5 |
| Hexa- | 6 |
| Hepta- | 7 |
| Octa- | 8 |
| Nona- | 9 |
| Deca- | 10 |

---

| EXAMPLE 3.8 | Naming a Covalent Compound |
|---|---|

Name the covalent compound $N_2O_4$.

**Solution**

**Step 1.** According to the formula provided, there are two nitrogen atoms and four oxygen atoms.

**Step 2.** Prefixes are used to denote the numbers of atoms in the compound. *Di-* means two, and *tetra-* means four.

**Step 3.** The last element listed in the formula is oxygen. The stem of the name, *ox*, is used with the suffix *-ide*.

**Step 4.** *Tetra-* reduces to *tetr-* by dropping the final vowel because it precedes oxide.

The name is dinitrogen tetroxide.

**LEARNING GOAL**

**4** Name inorganic compounds using standard naming conventions, and recall the common names of frequently used substances.

---

**Practice Problem 3.8**

Name each of the following compounds:

   a. $B_2O_3$    b. NO    c. ICl    d. $PCl_3$    e. $PCl_5$    f. $P_2O_5$

---

▶ For Further Practice: **Questions 3.51 and 3.52.**

---

The following are examples of other covalent compounds.

| Formula | Name |
|---|---|
| $N_2O$ | dinitrogen monoxide |
| $NCl_3$ | nitrogen trichloride |
| $SiO_2$ | silicon dioxide |
| $CF_4$ | carbon tetrafluoride |
| CO | carbon monoxide |
| $CO_2$ | carbon dioxide |

### Writing Formulas of Covalent Compounds

Many compounds are so familiar to us that their *common names* are generally used. For example, $H_2O$ is water, $NH_3$ is ammonia, $CH_4$ is methane, $C_2H_5OH$ (ethanol) is ethyl alcohol, and $C_6H_{12}O_6$ is glucose. It is useful to be able to correlate both systematic and common names with the corresponding molecular formula and vice versa.

When common names are used, formulas of covalent compounds can be written *only* from memory. You *must* remember that water is $H_2O$, ammonia is $NH_3$, and so forth. This is the major disadvantage of common names. Because of their widespread use, they cannot be avoided and must be memorized.

Compounds named by using numeric prefixes are easily converted to formulas. Consider the following examples.

---

| EXAMPLE 3.9 | Writing the Formula of a Covalent Compound |
|---|---|

Write the formula of dinitrogen tetroxide.

**Solution**

Use prefix meanings to determine subscripts.

**LEARNING GOAL**

**3** Write the formula of a compound when provided with the name or elemental composition of the compound.

**Step 1.** Nitrogen has the prefix *di-* which indicates two nitrogen atoms.

**Step 2.** Oxygen has the prefix *tetr-* which indicates four oxygen atoms.

**Step 3.** Hence, the formula is $N_2O_4$.

---

**Practice Problem 3.9**

Write the formula of each of the following compounds:

  a. diphosphorus pentoxide
  b. silicon dioxide
  c. carbon tetrabromide
  d. oxygen difluoride

▶ For Further Practice: **Questions 3.53 and 3.54.**

---

## 3.3 Properties of Ionic and Covalent Compounds

**LEARNING GOAL**

**5** Predict differences in physical state, melting and boiling points, solid-state structure, and solution chemistry that result from differences in bonding.

The differences in ionic and covalent bonding result in markedly different properties for ionic and covalent compounds. Because covalent compounds are typically made up of molecules—distinct units—they have less of a tendency to form an extended structure in the solid state. Ionic compounds, with ions joined by electrostatic attraction, form a crystal lattice composed of enormous numbers of positive and negative ions in an extended three-dimensional network. The effects of this basic structural difference are summarized in this section.

### Physical State

All ionic compounds (for example, NaCl, KCl, and $NaNO_3$) are solids at room temperature; covalent compounds may be solids (glucose), liquids (water, ethanol), or gases (carbon dioxide, methane). The three-dimensional crystal structure that is characteristic of ionic compounds holds them in a rigid, solid arrangement, whereas molecules of covalent compounds may be fixed, as in a solid, or more mobile, a characteristic of liquids and gases.

### Melting and Boiling Points

The **melting point** is the temperature at which a solid is converted to a liquid, and the **boiling point** is the temperature at which a liquid is converted to a gas at a specified pressure. Considerable energy is required to break apart the uncountable numbers of ionic interactions within an ionic crystal lattice and convert the ionic substance to a liquid or a gas. As a result, the melting and boiling temperatures for ionic compounds are generally higher than those of covalent compounds, whose molecules interact less strongly in the solid state. A typical ionic compound, sodium chloride, has a melting point of 801°C; methane, a covalent compound, melts at −182°C.

*Although melting and boiling temperatures for ionic compounds are generally higher than those for covalent compounds, exceptions do exist; quartz, a covalent compound of silicon dioxide with an extremely high melting point, is a familiar example.*

### Structure of Compounds in the Solid State

Ionic solids are *crystalline*, characterized by a regular structure, whereas covalent solids may either be crystalline or have no regular structure. In the latter case, they are said to be *amorphous.*

# A Medical Perspective

## Rebuilding Our Teeth

Tooth decay (dental caries) is an unpleasant fact of life. Aging, diet, and improper dental hygiene lead to the breakdown of a critical building block of teeth: hydroxyapatite, $Ca_5(PO_4)_3OH$. The hydroxyapatite forms a three-dimensional crystalline structure, and this structural unit is the principal component in the exterior, the enamel part of the tooth. Hydroxyapatite is also a major component in the dentin, which is directly underneath the enamel.

Hydroxyapatite breakdown causes the super-strong enamel to become porous and weak. The pores created are ideal hiding places for bacteria that form acids from foods (especially sugars), which hasten the decay of the tooth. The traditional remedy is the familiar whine of the drill, removing the decayed material, and unfortunately, some of the unaffected tooth. This step is followed by filling with a carbon-based polymer material or metal amalgam. In extreme cases, removal of the entire tooth is the only suitable remedy.

Researchers at a variety of institutions, such as the University of California, San Francisco, are studying other alternatives, collectively termed *remineralization.* What if teeth, in the early stages of enamel decay, were exposed to solutions containing calcium, phosphate, and fluoride ions? Could the hydroxyapatite be rebuilt through the uptake of its critical components, calcium and phosphate ions? Can the hydroxide ion in the hydroxyapatite be replaced by fluoride ion, producing a more decay-resistant $Ca_5(PO_4)_3F$?

Although conventional drill and fill procedures will be with us for the foreseeable future, early remineralization research is encouraging. Already toothpastes and mouthwashes containing calcium, phosphate, and/or fluoride ions are commercially available. Regular use of these products may at least extend the life of our valuable and irreplaceable natural teeth.

### For Further Understanding

▶ Examine the labels of a variety of toothpastes and mouthwashes. Do these products contain any of the ions discussed above? Describe their potential benefit.

▶ Many mouthwashes claim to kill bacteria. How can this reduce the incidence of tooth decay?

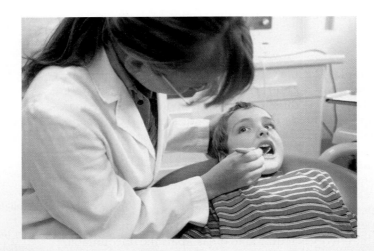

## Solutions of Ionic and Covalent Compounds

In Chapter 1, we saw that mixtures are either heterogeneous or homogeneous. A homogeneous mixture is a solution. Many ionic solids dissolve in solvents, such as water. An ionic solid, if soluble, will form cations and anions in solution by **dissociation.**

*The role of the solvent in the dissolution of solids is discussed in Section 6.1.*

Because ions in water are capable of carrying (conducting) a current of electricity, we refer to ionic compounds dissolved in water as **electrolytes,** and the solution is termed an *electrolytic solution.* Dissolved covalent solids usually retain their neutral (molecular) character and are **nonelectrolytes.** The solution is not an electrical conductor.

# 3.4 Drawing Lewis Structures of Molecules and Polyatomic Ions

## Lewis Structures of Molecules

In Section 3.1, we used Lewis symbols of individual atoms to help us understand the bonding process. Lewis symbols for atoms are building blocks that enable construction of *Lewis structures* for compounds and polyatomic ions that depict the role of valence electrons in bonding and structure. To begin to explain the relationship between molecular structure and molecular properties, we will first need a set of guidelines to help us write Lewis structures for molecules and polyatomic ions:

**Step 1.** *Use chemical symbols for the various elements to write the skeletal structure of the compound.* To accomplish this, place the bonded atoms next to one another. This is relatively easy for simple compounds; however, as the number of atoms in the compound increases, the possible number of arrangements increases dramatically. We may be told the pattern of arrangement of the atoms in advance; if not, we can make an intelligent guess and see if a reasonable Lewis structure can be constructed. Three considerations are very important here:

1. *The least electronegative atom will usually be the central atom and often the element written first in the formula.*

2. *Hydrogen and fluorine must occupy terminal (non-central) positions.*

3. *Carbon often forms chains of carbon-carbon covalent bonds.*

**Step 2.** *Determine the number of valence electrons associated with each atom; combine them to determine the total number of valence electrons in the compound.* If we are representing polyatomic cations or anions, we must account for the charge on the ion. Specifically:

1. *For polyatomic cations, subtract one electron for each unit of positive charge. This accounts for the fact that the positive charge arises from electron loss.*

2. *For polyatomic anions, add one electron for each unit of negative charge. This accounts for excess negative charge resulting from electron gain.*

**Step 3.** *Connect the central atom to each of the surrounding atoms with single bonds.* Connection of the atoms uses two electrons per bond. Keep a count of how many valence electrons you placed in the Lewis structure so as not to exceed the previously determined number.

**Step 4.** *Place electrons as lone pairs around the terminal atoms to complete the octet for each.* Remember that hydrogen only needs two electrons. Hydrogen's electron requirement is satisfied simply by a single bond between it and the central atom. Remember to keep a count of electrons used and do not exceed the number of available electrons. Once the terminal atoms have their octet rule satisfied, do the same for the central atom (if you have enough electrons to do so).

**Step 5.** *If the octet rule is not satisfied for all the atoms, move one or more lone pairs on a terminal atom in to make a bond with the central atom.* Double and triple bonds may be formed to ensure that all atoms have an octet.

**Step 6.** *After you are satisfied with the Lewis structure that you have constructed, perform a final electron count.* Count each electron used in the structure; the total must match the number of electrons available.

Now, let us see how these guidelines are applied in the examples that follow.

**LEARNING GOAL**

**6** Draw Lewis structures for covalent compounds and polyatomic ions.

The central atom is often the element farthest to the left and/or lowest in the periodic table.

The central atom is often the element in the compound for which there is only one atom.

Hydrogen is *never* the central atom.

*Sometimes the octet rule is satisfied for all atoms but electrons are left over from the valence electron count. This problem is addressed later in this section under Lewis Structures and Exceptions to the Octet Rule.*

| EXAMPLE 3.10 | Drawing Lewis Structures of Covalent Compounds | LEARNING GOAL |

Draw the Lewis structure of carbon dioxide, $CO_2$.

**6** Draw Lewis structures for covalent compounds and polyatomic ions.

**Solution**

**Step 1.** Draw a skeletal structure of the molecule, arranging the atoms in their most probable order.

For $CO_2$, two possibilities exist:

C   O   O    and    O   C   O

Our strategy dictates that the least electronegative atom (the one written first in the formula), in this case carbon, is the central atom. Hence, the skeletal structure O   C   O may be presumed correct.

**Step 2.** Next, determine the number of valence electrons on each atom and add them to arrive at the total for the compound.
For $CO_2$,

$$1 \text{ C atom} \times 4 \text{ valence electrons} = 4 \text{ e}^-$$
$$2 \text{ O atoms} \times 6 \text{ valence electrons} = 12 \text{ e}^-$$
$$\overline{\phantom{2 \text{ O atoms} \times 6 \text{ valence electrons} = 12 \text{ e}^-}}$$
$$16 \text{ e}^- \text{ total}$$

**Step 3.** Now use electron pairs to connect the central atom, C, to each oxygen with a single bond.

O:C:O

**Step 4.** Distribute the electrons around the terminal atoms in pairs, in an attempt to satisfy the octet rule.

:Ö:C:Ö:

**Step 5.** At this point, all sixteen electrons have been used. This structure satisfies the octet rule for each oxygen atom, but not the carbon atom (only four electrons surround the carbon). Therefore, this structure is modified by moving two electrons from each oxygen atom to a position between C and O, so that each oxygen and carbon atom is surrounded by eight electrons, and the octet rule is satisfied.

Ö::C::Ö

In this structure, four electrons (two electron pairs) are located between C and each O, and these electrons are shared in covalent bonds. Because a **single bond** is composed of two electrons (one electron pair) and four electrons "bond" the carbon atom to each oxygen atom in this structure, there must be two bonds between each oxygen atom and the carbon atom, a **double bond:**

The notation for a single bond : is equivalent to — (one pair of electrons).
The notation for a double bond : : is equivalent to = (two pairs of electrons).

The Lewis structure can be written with dashes to indicate bonds,

Ö=C=Ö

**Step 6.** A final electron count indicates that there are eight electron pairs (4 bonding pairs and 4 lone pairs), and they correspond to sixteen valence electrons (8 pair $\times$ 2 e$^-$/pair). Furthermore, there are eight electrons around each atom, and the octet rule is satisfied. Therefore,

Ö=C=Ö

is a satisfactory way to depict the structure of $CO_2$.

*Helpful Hint:* Each bond represents a bonding electron pair (2 electrons).

# A Medical Perspective

## Blood Pressure and the Sodium Ion/Potassium Ion Ratio

When you have a physical exam, the physician measures your blood pressure. This indicates the pressure of blood against the walls of the blood vessels each time the heart pumps. A blood pressure reading is always characterized by two numbers. With every heartbeat there is an increase in pressure; this is the systolic blood pressure. When the heart relaxes between contractions, the pressure drops; this is the diastolic pressure. Thus, the blood pressure is expressed as two values—for instance, 117/72—measured in millimeters (mm) of mercury. Hypertension is simply defined as high blood pressure. To the body it means that the heart must work too hard to pump blood, and this can lead to heart failure or heart disease.

Heart disease accounts for 50% of all deaths in the United States. Epidemiological studies correlate the following major risk factors with heart disease: heredity, gender, race, age, diabetes, cigarette smoking, high blood cholesterol, and hypertension. Obviously, we can do little about our age, gender, and genetic heritage, but we can stop smoking, limit dietary cholesterol, and maintain a normal blood pressure.

The number of Americans with hypertension is alarmingly high: sixty-seven million adults and children. Sixteen million of these individuals take medication to control blood pressure, at a cost of nearly 2.5 billion dollars each year. In many cases, blood pressure can be controlled without medication by increasing physical activity, losing weight, decreasing consumption of alcohol, and limiting intake of sodium.

It has been estimated that the average American ingests 7.5–10 grams (g) of salt ($NaCl$) each day. Because $NaCl$ is about 40% (by mass) sodium ions, this amounts to 3–4 g of sodium daily. Until 1989, the Food and Nutrition Board of the National Academy of Sciences National Research Council's defined *e*stimated *s*afe and *a*dequate *d*aily *d*ietary *i*ntake (ESADDI) of sodium ions was 1.1–3.3 g. Clearly, Americans exceed this recommendation.

Recently, studies have shown that excess sodium is not the sole consideration in the control of blood pressure. More important is the sodium ion/potassium ion ($Na^+/K^+$) ratio. That ratio should be about 0.6; in other words, our diet should contain about 67% more potassium than sodium. Does the typical American diet fall within this limit? Definitely not! Young American males (25–30 years old) consume a diet with a $Na^+/K^+ = 1.07$, and the diet of females of the same age range has a $Na^+/K^+ = 1.04$. It is little wonder that so many Americans suffer from hypertension.

How can we restrict sodium in the diet, while increasing potassium? A variety of foods are low in sodium and high in potassium. These include fresh fruits and vegetables and fruit juices, a variety of cereals, unsalted nuts, and cooked dried beans (legumes). Unfortunately, some high-sodium, low-potassium foods are very popular. Most of these are processed or prepared foods. This points out how difficult it can be to control sodium in the diet. The majority of the sodium we ingest comes from commercially prepared foods. The consumer must read the nutritional information printed on cans and packages to determine whether the sodium levels are within acceptable limits.

### For Further Understanding

▶ Find several processed food products, and use the labels to calculate the sodium ion/potassium ion ratio.

▶ Describe each product you have chosen in terms of its suitability for inclusion in the diet of a person with moderately elevated blood pressure.

---

### Practice Problem 3.10

Draw a Lewis structure for each of the following compounds:

    a. water         b. methane

▶ For Further Practice: **Questions 3.79 and 3.80.**

---

Many compounds have more than one central atom. Example 3.11 illustrates how to draw structures for these compounds.

## Lewis Structures of Polyatomic Ions

The strategies for writing the Lewis structures of polyatomic ions are similar to those for neutral compounds. There is, however, one major difference: the charge on the ion must be accounted for when computing the total number of valence electrons.

### LEARNING GOAL

**6** Draw Lewis structures for covalent compounds and polyatomic ions.

**EXAMPLE 3.11**    **Drawing Lewis Structures for Compounds with Multiple Central Atoms**

LEARNING GOAL

Draw the Lewis structure for ethane, $C_2H_4$.

**6**  Draw Lewis structures for covalent compounds and polyatomic ions.

### Solution

**Step 1.** Carbon often forms carbon-carbon chains, and hydrogen atoms must occupy terminal positions. This gives the skeletal structure:

$$\begin{array}{ccc} H & & H \\ & C \quad C & \\ H & & H \end{array}$$

**Step 2.** Determine the number of valence electrons for each atom, and add them to obtain the total for the compound.

$$2\,C \text{ atoms} \times 4 \text{ valence electrons} = 8\,e^-$$
$$4\,H \text{ atoms} \times 1 \text{ valence electrons} = 4\,e^-$$
$$\overline{\hspace{4cm}}$$
$$12\,e^- \text{ total}$$

**Step 3.** Connect the atoms with single bonds:

$$\begin{array}{ccc} H & & H \\ \diagdown & & \diagup \\ & C - C & \\ \diagup & & \diagdown \\ H & & H \end{array}$$

Because each bond represents a bonding electron pair, it can be determined that ten electrons (5 bonds × 2 e⁻/bond = 10 e⁻) are represented in this step.

**Step 4.** Since hydrogen's octet is satisfied by a single bond, additional electrons cannot be added to the terminal hydrogens. The two electrons remaining can be added to one of the carbons to satisfy its octet as follows:

$$\begin{array}{ccc} H & & H \\ \diagdown & & \diagup \\ & \overset{..}{C} - C & \\ \diagup & & \diagdown \\ H & & H \end{array}$$

**Step 5.** The carbon on the right has only six valence electrons. The lone pair of electrons on the left carbon can be modified by moving them to a position where the carbon atoms form a double bond.

$$\begin{array}{ccc} H & & H \\ \diagdown & & \diagup \\ & C = C & \\ \diagup & & \diagdown \\ H & & H \end{array}$$

**Step 6.** A final electron count will verify that the number of electrons used in the structure matches the number of electrons determined in step 2. The six bonding pairs correspond to twelve valence electrons (6 bonds × 2 e⁻/bond = 12 electrons). Therefore, the structure above is the correct Lewis structure.

*Helpful Hint:* Compounds that consist of only carbon and hydrogen (hydrocarbons) are often written to convey information concerning connectivity. The compound in this example can be written as $CH_2CH_2$ (a condensed formula). Writing it this way indicates that the carbons are connected to each other and that each carbon has two hydrogen atoms connected to it.

### Practice Problem 3.11

Draw a Lewis structure for each of the following compounds:

a. $N_2H_4$     b. $CH_3CH_2CH_3$     c. HCN

▶ For Further Practice: **Questions 3.83 and 3.84.**

**EXAMPLE 3.12**    **Drawing Lewis Structures of Polyatomic Anions**

Draw the Lewis structure of the carbonate ion, $CO_3^{2-}$.

**6** Draw Lewis structures for covalent compounds and polyatomic ions.

**Solution**

**Step 1.** Carbon is less electronegative than oxygen. Therefore, carbon is the central atom. The carbonate ion has the following skeletal structure and charge:

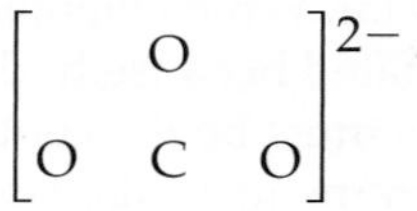

$$\begin{bmatrix} & O & \\ O & C & O \end{bmatrix}^{2-}$$

The use of square brackets with the charge outside of the brackets is standard when drawing Lewis structures for polyatomic anions.

**Step 2.** The total number of valence electrons is determined by adding one electron for each unit of negative charge:

$$\begin{aligned} 1\ C\ atom\ \times 4\ valence\ electrons &= 4\ e^- \\ 3\ O\ atoms \times 6\ valence\ electrons &= 18\ e^- \\ electrons\ for\ 2^-\ charge &= 2\ e^- \\ \hline 24\ e^-\ total \end{aligned}$$

**Step 3.** Connect the O atoms to the central atom using single bonds. This step uses six of the valence electrons.

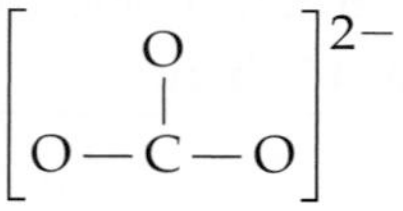

$$\begin{bmatrix} & O & \\ & | & \\ O & \!\!-C-\!\! & O \end{bmatrix}^{2-}$$

**Step 4.** Start placing lone-pair electrons around the terminal atoms, giving each an octet. Do not exceed the twenty-four available electrons.

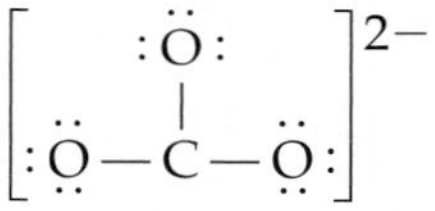

$$\begin{bmatrix} & :\ddot{O}: & \\ & | & \\ :\ddot{O}\!\!-&C&\!\!-\ddot{O}: \end{bmatrix}^{2-}$$

**Step 5.** The central atom only has six valence electrons surrounding it. Move a lone pair from one of the O atoms to form another bond with C. In this example, a lone pair from the top O was moved to make a second bond between it and the C.

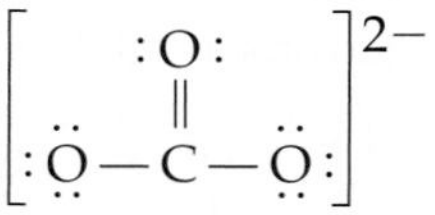

$$\begin{bmatrix} & :O: & \\ & \| & \\ :\ddot{O}\!\!-&C&\!\!-\ddot{O}: \end{bmatrix}^{2-}$$

**Step 6.** A final electron count indicates that each atom has eight valence electrons surrounding it. Overall, there are four bonding electron pairs (4 bonds × $2e^-$/bond = $8e^-$) and eight lone electron pairs (8 lone pairs × $2e^-$/lone pair = $16e^-$), which when combined total twenty-four electrons.

**Practice Problem 3.12**

Draw the Lewis structure of $O_2^{2-}$.

▶ For Further Practice: **Questions 3.85 and 3.86.**

**EXAMPLE 3.13**   **Drawing Lewis Structures of Polyatomic Anions**

Draw the Lewis structure of the acetate ion, $CH_3COO^-$.

**6**  Draw Lewis structures for covalent compounds and polyatomic ions.

### Solution

This species has multiple central atoms and a negative charge.

**Step 1.** The acetate ion, a commonly encountered anion, has a skeletal structure that is more complex than any of the examples we have studied thus far. Which element should we choose as the central atom? We have three choices: H, O, and C. H is eliminated because hydrogen can never be the central atom. Oxygen is more electronegative than carbon, so carbon must be the central atom. There are two carbon atoms; often they are joined. Further clues are obtained from the formula itself; $CH_3COO^-$ implies three hydrogen atoms attached to the first carbon atom and two oxygen atoms joined to the second carbon. A plausible skeletal structure is:

$$
\begin{bmatrix}
& H & & O \\
H & C & C & \\
& H & & O
\end{bmatrix}^{-}
$$

**Step 2.** The pool of valence electrons for anions is determined by adding one electron for each unit of negative charge:

$$
\begin{aligned}
2\,\text{C atoms} \times 4 \text{ valence electrons} &= \phantom{0}8\,e^- \\
3\,\text{H atoms} \times 1 \text{ valence electron} &= \phantom{0}3\,e^- \\
2\,\text{O atoms} \times 6 \text{ valence electrons} &= 12\,e^- \\
\underline{1 \text{ electron for } 1^- \text{ charge}} &= \underline{\phantom{0}1\,e^-} \\
& \quad\ 24\,e^- \text{ total}
\end{aligned}
$$

**Step 3.** Use bonds to connect the terminal atoms to the two central carbon atoms.

$$
\begin{bmatrix}
& H & & O \\
& | & & \diagup \\
H & - C - C & \\
& | & & \diagdown \\
& H & & O
\end{bmatrix}^{-}
$$

This step used twelve valence electrons (6 bonds × $2e^-$/bond).

**Step 4.** Starting with terminal O atoms, place lone-pair electrons around the atoms to give each an octet. (Remember to keep in mind the twenty-four electrons available, and do not put lone-pair electrons around H.)

$$
\begin{bmatrix}
& H & & :\ddot{O}: \\
& | & & \diagup \\
H & - C - C & \\
& | & & \diagdown \\
& H & & :\underset{\cdot\cdot}{O}:
\end{bmatrix}^{-}
$$

This structure uses all twenty-four electrons, but one of the C atoms only has six valence electrons.

**Step 5.** Move one of the lone pairs from an O to create an additional bond between C and O.

$$
\begin{bmatrix}
& H & & :O: \\
& | & & /\!/ \\
H & - C - C & \\
& | & & \diagdown \\
& H & & :\underset{\cdot\cdot}{O}:
\end{bmatrix}^{-}
$$

**Step 6.** A final electron count indicates that there are seven bonding electron pairs (7 bonds $\times$ 2e$^-$/bond = 14e$^-$) and five lone electron pairs (5 lone pairs $\times$ 2e$^-$/lone pair = 10e$^-$), which confirms that all twenty-four electrons are used. The octet rule is satisfied for all atoms in the Lewis structure.

---

**Practice Problem 3.13**

Draw a Lewis structure illustrating the bonding in each of the following polyatomic ions:

    a. the bicarbonate ion, $HCO_3{}^-$

    b. the phosphate ion, $PO_4{}^{3-}$

▶ For Further Practice: **Questions 3.87 and 3.88.**

---

## Lewis Structure, Stability, Multiple Bonds, and Bond Energies

**LEARNING GOAL**

**7** Explain how the presence or absence of multiple bonding relates to bond length, bond energy, and stability.

Hydrogen, oxygen, and nitrogen are present in the atmosphere as diatomic gases, $H_2$, $O_2$, and $N_2$. Although they are all covalent molecules, their stability and reactivity are quite different. Hydrogen is an explosive material, sometimes used as a fuel. Oxygen, although more stable than hydrogen, reacts with fuels in combustion. The explosion of the space shuttle *Challenger* resulted from the reaction of massive amounts of hydrogen and oxygen. Nitrogen, on the other hand, is extremely nonreactive. Because nitrogen makes up about 80% of the atmosphere, it dilutes the oxygen, which accounts for only about 20% of the atmosphere.

The great difference in reactivity among these three gases can be explained, in part, in terms of their bonding characteristics. The Lewis structure for $H_2$ (two valence electrons, one from each atom) is

$$H - H$$

For oxygen (twelve valence electrons, six from each atom), the only Lewis structure that satisfies the octet rule is

$$\ddot{O} = \ddot{O}$$

The Lewis structure of $N_2$ (ten valence electrons, five from each atom) must be

$$: N \equiv N :$$

Therefore:

    $H_2$ has a *single bond* (two bonding electrons).

    $O_2$ has a *double bond* (four bonding electrons).

    $N_2$ has a *triple bond* (six bonding electrons).

A **triple bond,** in which three pairs of electrons are shared by two atoms, is very stable. More energy is required to break a triple bond than a double bond, and a double bond is stronger than a single bond. Stability is related to the bond energy. The **bond energy** is the amount of energy, in units of kilocalories (kcal) or kilojoules (kJ), required to break a bond holding two atoms together. Bond energy is therefore a *measure* of stability. The values of bond energies decrease in the order *triple bond > double bond > single bond*. The H—H bond energy is 436 kJ/mol. This amount of energy is necessary to break a H—H bond. In contrast, the O=O bond energy is 499 kJ/mol, and the N≡N bond energy is 941 kJ/mol.

The bond length is related to the presence or absence of multiple bonding. The distance of separation of two nuclei is greatest for a single bond, less for a double bond, and still less for a triple bond. The *bond length* decreases in the order *single bond > double bond > triple bond*.

The term *bond order* is sometimes used to distinguish among single, double, and triple bonds. A bond order of one corresponds to a single bond, two corresponds to a double bond, and three corresponds to a triple bond.

The mole (mol) is simply a unit denoting quantity. Just as a *dozen* eggs represents twelve eggs, a mole of bonds is $6.022 \times 10^{23}$ bonds (see Chapter 4).

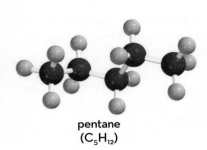

pentane
($C_5H_{12}$)

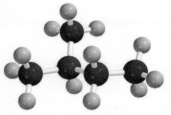

2-methylbutane
($C_5H_{12}$)

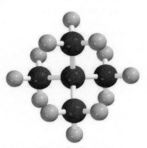

2,2-dimethylpropane
($C_5H_{12}$)

---

The compound pentane, above, is the "straight chain" isomer. Notice that the carbons are attached in a chain; however, they are not actually in a *straight* line.

---

**Question 3.3**   Contrast a single and a double bond with regard to:
   a.  distance of separation of the bonded nuclei
   b.  strength of the bond

How are the distance of separation and bond strength related?

**Question 3.4**   Two nitrogen atoms in a nitrogen molecule are held together more strongly than the two chlorine atoms in a chlorine molecule. Explain this fact by comparing their respective Lewis structures.

## Isomers

**Isomers** are compounds that share the same molecular formula but have different structures. Hydrocarbons (compounds that contain only hydrogen and carbon atoms) frequently exhibit this property. For example, $C_4H_{10}$ has two isomeric forms. One isomer, termed butane, has a structure characterized by the four carbon atoms being linked in a chain; the other, termed methylpropane, has a three-carbon chain, with the fourth carbon attached to the middle carbon.

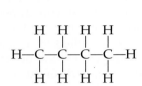

Butane ($C_4H_{10}$)

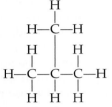

Methylpropane ($C_4H_{10}$)

Notice that both structures, although clearly different, contain four carbon atoms and ten hydrogen atoms. Owing to their structural differences, each has a different melting point and boiling point. In fact, all of their physical properties differ. These differences in properties clearly show that, in fact, isomers are different compounds.

As the size of the hydrocarbon increases, the number of possible isomers increases dramatically. A five-carbon hydrocarbon has three isomers, but a thirty-carbon hydrocarbon has over 400 million possible isomers. Petroleum is largely a complex mixture of hydrocarbons, and the principal reason for this complexity lies in the tremendous variety of possible isomers present.

The three isomers of $C_5H_{12}$ (a five-carbon hydrocarbon) are depicted in the figure in the margin.

## Lewis Structures and Resonance

In some cases, we find that it is possible to write more than one Lewis structure that satisfies the octet rule for a particular compound. Consider sulfur dioxide, $SO_2$. Its skeletal structure is

O   S   O

Total valence electrons may be calculated as follows:

$$
\begin{aligned}
1 \text{ sulfur atom} \times 6 \text{ valence } e^- &= 6\ e^- \\
+2 \text{ oxygen atoms} \times 6 \text{ valence } e^- &= 12\ e^- \\
\hline
&18\ e^- \text{ total}
\end{aligned}
$$

The resulting Lewis structures are

$$\ddot{O}=\ddot{S}-\ddot{O}: \quad \text{and} \quad :\ddot{O}-\ddot{S}=\ddot{O}$$

Both satisfy the octet rule. However, experimental evidence shows no double bond in $SO_2$. The two sulfur-oxygen bonds are equivalent. Apparently, neither structure accurately represents the structure of $SO_2$, and neither actually exists. The actual structure is said to be an average or *hybrid* of these two Lewis structures. When a compound has two or more Lewis structures that contribute to the real structure, we say that the compound displays the property of **resonance.** The contributing Lewis structures are *resonance forms.* The true structure, a hybrid of the resonance forms, is known as a *resonance hybrid* and may be represented as:

$$\ddot{O}\!=\!\ddot{S}\!-\!\ddot{O}\!: \quad \longleftrightarrow \quad :\!\ddot{O}\!-\!\ddot{S}\!=\!\ddot{O}$$

A common analogy might help to clarify this concept. A horse and a donkey may be crossbred to produce a hybrid, the mule. The mule doesn't look or behave exactly like either parent, yet it has attributes of both. The resonance hybrid of a molecule has properties of each resonance form but is not identical to any one form. Unlike the mule, resonance hybrids *do not actually exist.* Rather, they comprise a model that results from the failure of any one Lewis structure to agree with experimentally obtained structural information.

The presence of resonance enhances molecular stability. The more resonance forms that exist, the greater the stability of the molecule they represent. This concept is important in understanding the chemical reactions of many complex organic molecules and is used extensively in organic chemistry.

It is a misconception to picture the real molecule as oscillating back and forth among the various resonance structures. Resonance is a modeling strategy designed to help us visualize electron arrangements too complex to be adequately explained by the simple Lewis structure.

---

**EXAMPLE 3.14**  **Drawing Resonance Hybrids of Covalently Bonded Compounds**

Draw the possible resonance structures of the nitrate ion, $NO_3^-$, and represent them as a resonance hybrid.

LEARNING GOAL

**6** Draw Lewis structures for covalent compounds and polyatomic ions.

**Solution**

**Step 1.** Nitrogen is less electronegative than oxygen; therefore, nitrogen is the central atom and the skeletal structure is:

$$\left[\begin{array}{ccc} & O & \\ O & N & O \end{array}\right]^-$$

**Step 2.** The pool of valence electrons for anions is determined by adding one electron for each unit of negative charge:

$$1\,\text{N atom} \times 5 \text{ valence electrons} = 5\,e^-$$
$$3\,\text{O atoms} \times 6 \text{ valence electrons} = 18\,e^-$$
$$\underline{1 \text{ electron for } 1^- \text{ charge} \qquad\quad = 1\,e^-}$$
$$24\,e^- \text{ total}$$

**Step 3.** First, connect O atoms to the N atom using single bonds.

$$\left[\begin{array}{c} O \\ | \\ O\!-\!N\!-\!O \end{array}\right]^-$$

This step used twelve valence electrons (3 bonds $\times$ 2 e$^-$/bond).

**Step 4.** Place lone-pair electrons around the terminal O atoms until each atom has an octet. Do not exceed twenty-four electrons.

$$\left[\begin{array}{c} :\ddot{O}: \\ | \\ :\ddot{O}\!-\!N\!-\!\ddot{O}: \end{array}\right]^-$$

This structure uses twenty-four electrons; however, the central atom only has six valence electrons.

*Continued…*

**Step 5.** Shift a lone pair on one of the O atoms to become a bond between the O and N. To draw all possible resonance structures, this shift is drawn for each of the oxygen atoms.

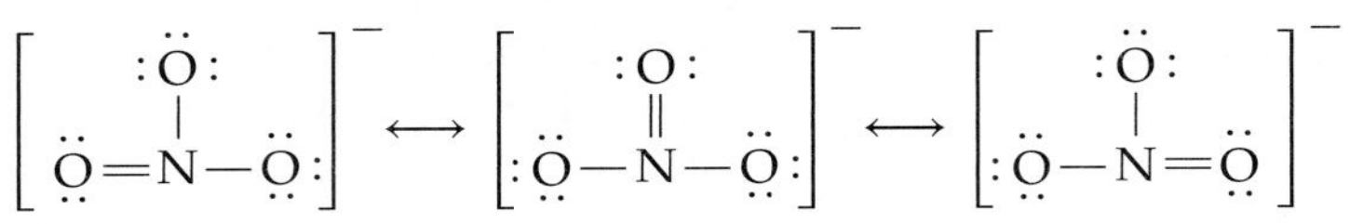

$$
\left[
\begin{array}{c}
:\ddot{O}: \\
| \\
\ddot{O}=N-\ddot{O}:
\end{array}
\right]^{-}
\longleftrightarrow
\left[
\begin{array}{c}
:O: \\
\| \\
:\ddot{O}-N-\ddot{O}:
\end{array}
\right]^{-}
\longleftrightarrow
\left[
\begin{array}{c}
:\ddot{O}: \\
| \\
:\ddot{O}-N=\ddot{O}
\end{array}
\right]^{-}
$$

**Step 6.** A final count of electrons indicates that there are four pairs of bonding electrons (4 bonds × 2 e⁻/bond = 8 e⁻) and eight lone electron pairs (8 lone pairs × 2 e⁻/lone pair = 16 e⁻) in each of these resonance structures. All 24 electrons are used, and the octet rule is obeyed for each atom.

### Practice Problem 3.14

a. $SeO_2$, like $SO_2$, has two resonance forms. Draw their Lewis structures.

b. Explain any similarities between the structures for $SeO_2$ and $SO_2$ in light of periodic relationships.

▶ For Further Practice: **Questions 3.89 and 3.90.**

## Lewis Structures and Exceptions to the Octet Rule

The octet rule is remarkable in its ability to realistically model bonding and structure in covalent compounds. But, like any model, it does not adequately describe all systems. Beryllium, boron, and aluminum, in particular, tend to form compounds in which they are surrounded by fewer than eight electrons. This situation is termed an *incomplete octet*.

Other molecules, such as nitric oxide:

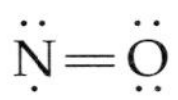

$$\ddot{N}=\ddot{O}$$

are termed *odd-electron* molecules. Note that it is impossible to pair all electrons to achieve an octet simply because the compound contains an odd number of valence electrons.

Elements in the third period and beyond may involve *d* orbitals and form an *expanded octet*, with ten or even twelve electrons surrounding the central atom. Example 3.15 illustrates the expanded octet.

---

**EXAMPLE 3.15** | **Drawing Lewis Structures of Covalently Bonded Compounds that Are Exceptions to the Octet Rule**

Draw the Lewis structure of $SF_4$.

LEARNING GOAL

**6** Draw Lewis structures for covalent compounds and polyatomic ions.

### Solution

**Step 1.** Sulfur is the central atom with four fluorine atoms surrounding the sulfur.

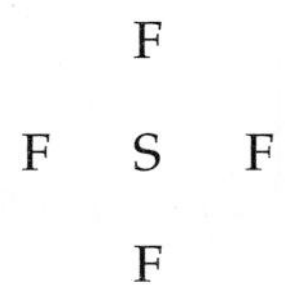

$$
\begin{array}{ccc}
 & F & \\
F & S & F \\
 & F &
\end{array}
$$

**Step 2.** The total number of valence electrons is:

$$1 \text{ sulfur atom} \quad \times 6 \text{ valence e}^- = \quad 6 \text{ e}^-$$
$$\underline{4 \text{ fluorine atoms} \times 7 \text{ valence e}^- = 28 \text{ e}^-}$$
$$= 34 \text{ e}^- \text{ total}$$

**Step 3.** Connect the four fluorine atoms with single bonds to the sulfur. This uses eight electrons (4 bonds $\times$ 2 e$^-$/bond).

$$
\begin{array}{ccc}
 & \text{F} & \\
 & | & \\
\text{F} - & \text{S} & - \text{F} \\
 & | & \\
 & \text{F} &
\end{array}
$$

**Step 4.** Give each terminal atom eight valence electrons.

$$
\begin{array}{ccc}
 & :\ddot{\text{F}}: & \\
 & | & \\
:\ddot{\text{F}} - & \text{S} & - \ddot{\text{F}}: \\
 & | & \\
 & :\ddot{\text{F}}: &
\end{array}
$$

**Step 5.** The octet rule *is* satisfied for all atoms. However, we have only used thirty-two electrons and we must use all thirty-four electrons. The two extra electrons will be placed on the central atom.

$$
\begin{array}{ccc}
 & :\ddot{\text{F}}: & \\
 & |.. & \\
:\ddot{\text{F}} - & \text{S} & - \ddot{\text{F}}: \\
 & | & \\
 & :\ddot{\text{F}}: &
\end{array}
$$

**Step 6.** A final count of electrons confirms that all thirty-four have been used. There are four pairs of bonding electrons (4 bonds $\times$ 2e$^-$/bond = 8 e$^-$) and thirteen lone electron pairs (13 lone pairs $\times$ 2 e$^-$/lone pair = 26 e$^-$) in this Lewis structure. $SF_4$ is an example of a compound with an expanded octet. The central sulfur atom is surrounded by ten electrons.

---

### Practice Problem 3.15

    a. Draw the Lewis structure of $SeCl_4$.
    b. Draw the Lewis structure of $SF_6$.
    c. Draw the Lewis structure of $BCl_3$.

▶ For Further Practice: **Questions 3.93–3.96.**

---

## Lewis Structures and Molecular Geometry; VSEPR Theory

The shape of a molecule plays a large part in determining its properties and reactivity. We may predict the shapes of various molecules by inspecting their Lewis structures for the orientation of their electron pairs. The covalent bond, for instance, in which bonding electrons are localized between the nuclear centers of the atoms, is *directional*; the bond has a specific orientation in space between the bonded atoms. The specific orientation of electron pairs in covalent molecules imparts a characteristic shape to the molecules. Consider the following series of molecules whose Lewis structures are shown.

LEARNING GOAL

**8**   Use Lewis structures to predict the geometry of molecules.

---

Electrostatic forces in ionic bonds are *nondirectional*; they have no specific orientation in space.

$BeH_2$          H—Be—H          $BeH_2$ and $BF_3$ are exceptions to the octet rule. The central atoms are not surrounded by eight electrons, and the octets are incomplete.

$BF_3$          :F̈—B̈—F̈:

$CH_4$          H—C—H with H above and H below

$NH_3$          H—N̈—H with H below

$H_2O$          H—Ö—H

The electron pairs around the central atom of the molecule arrange themselves to minimize electronic repulsion. This means that the electron pairs arrange themselves so that they can be as far from each other as possible. We may use this fact to predict molecular shape. This approach is termed the **valence-shell electron-pair repulsion (VSEPR) theory.**

Let's see how the VSEPR theory can be used to describe the bonding and structure of each of the preceding molecules.

### $BeH_2$

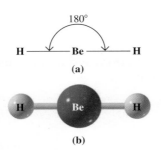

**Figure 3.5** Bonding and geometry in beryllium hydride, $BeH_2$. (a) Linear geometry in $BeH_2$. (b) Computer-generated model of linear $BeH_2$.

As illustrated in the Lewis structure above, beryllium hydride has two bonded atoms around the beryllium atom. These bonding electron pairs have minimum repulsion if they are located as far apart as possible while still bonding the hydrogen atoms to the central atom. This results in a **linear** geometric structure or shape. The *bond angle,* the angle between the H—Be and Be—H bonds, formed by the two bonding pairs is 180° (Figure 3.5).

$BeF_2$, $CS_2$, and HCN are other examples of molecules that exhibit linear geometry. Multiple bonds are treated identically to single bonds in VSEPR theory. For example, the Lewis structure of HCN is H—C≡N:. The bonded atoms on either side of carbon are positioned 180° from each other. Instead of counting bonding electrons to predict molecular shape, it is more appropriate to count bonded atoms. The central atom has two bonded atoms.

### $BF_3$

Boron trifluoride has three bonded atoms around the central atom. The Lewis structure, as illustrated above, shows boron as electron deficient. Placing the bonding electron pairs in a plane, forming a triangle, minimizes the electron-pair repulsion in this molecule, as depicted in Figure 3.6.

Such a structure is **trigonal planar,** and each F—B—F bond angle is 120°. We also find that compounds with central atoms in the same group of the periodic table have similar geometry. Aluminum, in the same group as boron, produces compounds such as $AlH_3$, which is also trigonal planar.

### $CH_4$

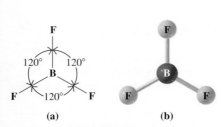

**Figure 3.6** Bonding and geometry in boron trifluoride, $BF_3$. (a) Trigonal planar geometry in $BF_3$. (b) Computer-generated model of trigonal planar $BF_3$.

Methane has four bonded atoms around carbon. Here, minimum electron repulsion is achieved by arranging the electrons at the corners of a tetrahedron (Figure 3.7). Each H—C—H bond angle is 109.5°. Methane has a three-dimensional **tetrahedral** structure or shape. Silicon, in the same group as carbon, forms compounds such as $SiCl_4$ and $SiH_4$ that also have tetrahedral shapes.

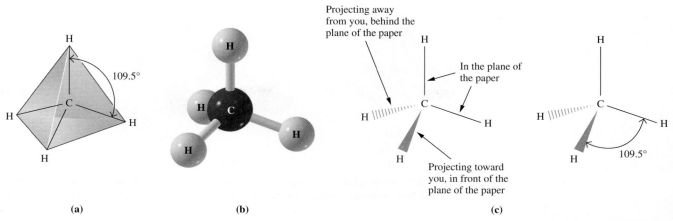

**Figure 3.7** Representations of the three-dimensional structure of methane, $CH_4$. (a) Tetrahedral methane structure. (b) Computer-generated model of tetrahedral methane. (c) Three-dimensional representation showing the H—C—H bond angle.

## $NH_3$

Ammonia has three bonded atoms and one lone pair about the central atom. In contrast to methane, in which all four electron pairs are bonding, ammonia has three pairs of bonding electrons and one nonbonding lone pair of electrons. We might expect $CH_4$ and $NH_3$ to have electron-pair arrangements that are similar but not identical. The lone pair in ammonia is more negative than the bonding pairs because some of the negative charge on the bonding pairs is offset by the presence of the hydrogen atoms with their positive nuclei. Thus, the arrangement of electron pairs in ammonia is distorted.

The hydrogen atoms in ammonia are pushed closer together than in methane (Figure 3.8). The bond angle is 107° because lone pair–bond pair repulsions are greater than bond pair–bond pair repulsions. The structure or shape is termed *trigonal pyramidal,* and the molecule is termed a **trigonal pyramidal** molecule.

## $H_2O$

Water has two bonded atoms and two lone pairs about the central atom. These four electron pairs are approximately tetrahedral to each other; however, because of the difference between bonding and nonbonding electrons, noted earlier, the tetrahedral relationship is only approximate.

The **bent** structure has a bond angle of 104.5°, which is 5° smaller than the tetrahedral angle, because of the repulsive effects of the lone pairs of electrons (Figure 3.9).

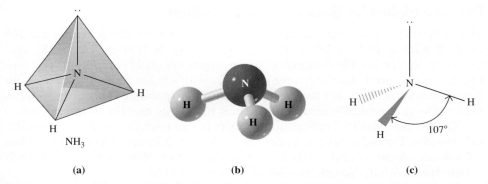

**Figure 3.8** The structure of the ammonia molecule. (a) Trigonal pyramidal ammonia structure. (b) Computer-generated model of trigonal pyramidal ammonia. (c) A three-dimensional sketch showing the H—N—H bond angle.

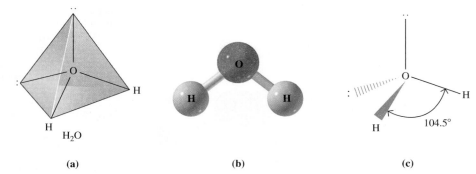

**Figure 3.9**  The structure of the water molecule. (a) Bent water structure. (b) Computer-generated model of bent water. (c) A three-dimensional sketch showing the H—O—H bond angle in water.

**TABLE 3.5**  **Molecular Geometry: The Shape of a Molecule Is Affected by the Number of Bonded Atoms and the Number of Nonbonded Lone Electron Pairs Around the Central Atom**

| Bonded Atoms | Nonbonding Lone Electron Pairs | Bond Angle | Molecular Geometry | Example | Structure or Shape |
|---|---|---|---|---|---|
| 2 | 0 | 180° | Linear | $CO_2$ | |
| 3 | 0 | 120° | Trigonal planar | $SO_3$ | |
| 2 | 1 | <120° | Bent | $SO_2$ | |
| 4 | 0 | 109.5° | Tetrahedral | $CH_4$ | |
| 3 | 1 | ~107° | Trigonal pyramidal | $NH_3$ | |
| 2 | 2 | ~104.5° | Bent | $H_2O$ | |

**LEARNING GOAL**

**8**   Use Lewis structures to predict the geometry of molecules.

The characteristics of linear, trigonal planar, trigonal pyramidal, bent, and tetrahedral shapes are summarized in Table 3.5.

## Periodic Molecular Geometry Relationships

The molecules considered previously contain the central atoms Be (Group IIA or 2), B (Group IIIA or 13), C (Group IVA or 14), N (Group VA or 15), and O (Group VIA or 16). We may expect that a number of other compounds containing the same central atom will have structures with similar geometries. This is an approximation, not always true, but still useful in expanding our ability to write reasonable, geometrically accurate structures for a large number of compounds.

The periodic similarity of group members is also useful in predictions involving bonding. Consider oxygen, sulfur, and selenium (Group VIA or 16). Each has six valence electrons and needs two more electrons to complete its octet. Each should react with hydrogen, forming $H_2O$, $H_2S$, and $H_2Se$.

If we recall that $H_2O$ is a bent molecule with the following Lewis structure and shape,

$$\text{H}-\overset{\cdot\cdot}{\underset{\cdot\cdot}{\text{O}}}-\text{H}$$

it follows that $H_2S$ and $H_2Se$ would also be bent molecules with similar Lewis structures and shapes.

$$H - \overset{..}{\underset{..}{S}} - H \qquad \overset{S}{\underset{H}{\diagup}} \diagdown_{H}$$

$$H - \overset{..}{\underset{..}{Se}} - H \qquad \overset{Se}{\underset{H}{\diagup}} \diagdown_{H}$$

This logic applies equally well to the other representative elements.

**Question 3.5**   Draw the Lewis structures and shapes of each of the following molecules. Identify the molecular geometry of each shape using VSEPR.
  a. $PH_3$      b. $SiH_4$

**Question 3.6**   Draw the Lewis structures and shapes of each of the following molecules. Identify the molecular geometry of each shape using VSEPR.
  a. $C_2H_4$      b. $C_2H_2$

## More Complex Molecules

For compounds containing more than one central atom, geometry is determined at each central atom. Dimethyl ether, $CH_3$—O—$CH_3$, has three distinct central atoms as shown in the Lewis structure

$$\begin{array}{ccc} H & & H \\ | & & | \\ H-C- & \overset{..}{\underset{..}{O}} & -C-H \\ | & & | \\ H & & H \end{array}$$

Each carbon atom has four bonded atoms, giving a tetrahedral geometry with bond angles of 109.5°.

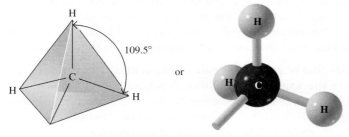

The oxygen has two bonded atoms and two lone pairs, giving a bent geometry with a 104° bond angle, as shown in Figure 3.10.

Trimethylamine, $(CH_3)_3N$, is a member of the amine family. Its Lewis structure is depicted as

$$\begin{array}{ccc} H & & H \\ | & & | \\ H-C- & \overset{..}{N} & -C-H \\ | & | & | \\ H & | & H \\ & H-C-H & \\ & | & \\ & H & \end{array}$$

As in the case of dimethyl ether, two different central atoms are present. Carbon and nitrogen determine the geometry of amines. In this case, each carbon atom is bonded to four atoms and has a tetrahedral geometry like that shown for methane. The nitrogen atom should have the bonded carbon atoms in a pyramidal arrangement, similar to the hydrogen atoms in ammonia, as seen in Figure 3.11. This creates a pyramidal geometry around nitrogen. H—N—H bond angles in ammonia are 107°; experimental information shows a very similar C—N—C bond angle in trimethylamine.

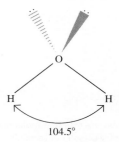

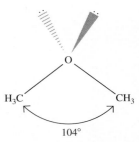

**Figure 3.10**   A comparison of the bonding in water and dimethyl ether.

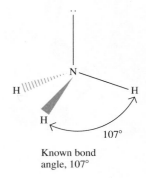

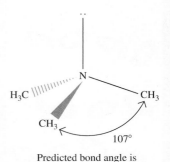

**Figure 3.11**   A comparison of the bonding in ammonia and trimethylamine.

It is essential to represent a molecule in its correct geometric form, using the Lewis and VSEPR theories, in order to understand its physical and chemical behavior. In the rest of this section, we use these models to predict molecular behavior.

## Lewis Structures and Polarity

As discussed in Section 3.1, covalent bonds can be polar or nonpolar. In this section, we will examine all the bonds that make up a molecule to determine if the *molecule* is polar or nonpolar. Polar molecules, when placed in an electric field, align themselves with the field (Figure 3.12). These molecules are said to have a *dipole* (having two "poles" or ends, one pole is more negative and the other pole is more positive). Nonpolar molecules do not align with an electric field. It is important to determine if a molecule is polar or nonpolar because this information helps predict properties of solubility as well as the melting point and boiling point. These properties will be discussed in Section 3.5.

The hydrogen molecule is the simplest nonpolar molecule. The electrons that make up the bond are shared equally between the two atoms (see Figure 3.2). Any molecule made up of only nonpolar bonds is a nonpolar molecule.

A diatomic molecule that is made up of two elements with different electronegativities will contain a polar bond. Since this bond is polar, the molecule is polar. We used the partial positive and partial negative symbols ($\delta^+$ and $\delta^-$) in Section 3.1 to represent the polar bond. We can also represent this polar bond using a vector (arrow) pointing in the direction of the most electronegative element in the bond.

$$\overset{\delta^+}{H}-\overset{\delta^-}{F} \qquad \overset{\longrightarrow}{H-F}$$

If a molecule contains more than one polar bond, the molecule *may* or *may not* be polar. Think of the polarity of a bond as a rope tied around the central atom pulling in the direction of the more electronegative atom. (Or in the case of lone pairs, the pull will always be in the direction of the lone pair.) Each terminal-atom to central-atom connection is a separate tug-of-war. If all the pulls are equal, the molecule is nonpolar; otherwise, the molecule is polar. To determine if a molecule with polar bonds is polar or nonpolar, draw the Lewis structure and follow these guidelines:

**Molecules that have no lone pair on the central atom and where all terminal atoms are the same are *nonpolar.*** For example, the molecule $CO_2$ has two bonded O atoms and no lone pairs on the central atom. It is linear and nonpolar. The molecule $CCl_4$ has no lone pairs on the central atom and four bonded Cl atoms. Its shape is tetrahedral, and it is nonpolar.

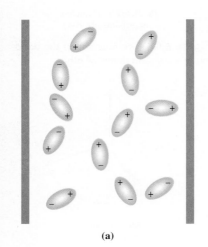

**Molecules with one lone pair on the central atom are *polar.*** Ammonia is an example. Its nitrogen atom has three bonded H atoms and one lone pair. The shape of ammonia is trigonal pyramidal. Because the nitrogen atom is more electronegative than the H atoms, the vectors (arrows) point toward nitrogen. The pull of lone-pair electrons is always away from the H atoms, and ammonia is a polar molecule.

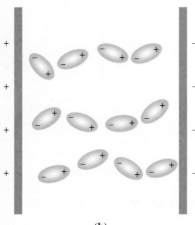

**Molecules that have more than one lone pair on the central atom are *usually polar,* but there are exceptions.** The Lewis structure of water has two lone

**Figure 3.12** The green ovals represent polar molecules (a) in the absence of an electric field and (b) under the influence of an electric field.

pairs and two bonded H atoms on the central atom of oxygen. Water is a bent molecule, and it is polar.

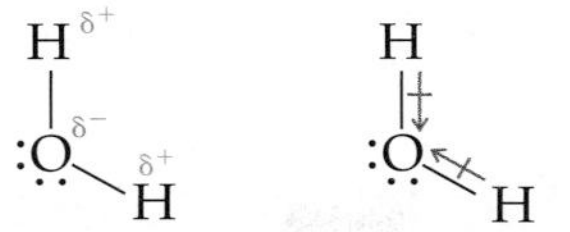

$$H^{\delta+}$$
$$| _{\delta-}$$
$$:O \underset{H}{\overset{\delta+}{\diagdown}}$$

$$H$$
$$|\updownarrow$$
$$:O \overset{\displaystyle \leftarrow}{\diagdown}$$
$$H$$

The electron density is shifted away from the hydrogens toward oxygen in the water molecule.

**Molecules that are made up of only carbon and hydrogen (hydrocarbons) are nonpolar.** The C—H bond has an electronegativity difference of 0.4; hence, the C—H bond is essentially nonpolar. Furthermore, the combined effects of the numerous C—H bonds effectively cancel, rendering the molecule nonpolar.

---

**EXAMPLE 3.16**  **Determining if a Molecule Is Polar Covalent or Nonpolar Covalent**

Is $PCl_3$ a polar or nonpolar covalent compound?

**9** Describe the role that molecular geometry plays in determining the polarity of compounds.

**Solution**

To determine polarity, the geometry must be determined. To determine geometry, draw the Lewis structure.

**Step 1.** Follow all steps to correctly draw the Lewis structure.

| Skeletal Structure | Count Valence Electrons | Distribute Valence Electrons |
|---|---|---|
| Cl<br><br>Cl   P   Cl | $1\,P \times 5\,e^- = 5\,e^-$<br>$3\,Cl \times 7\,e^- = 21\,e^-$<br>$\overline{\phantom{xxxx}26\,e^- \text{ total}}$ | 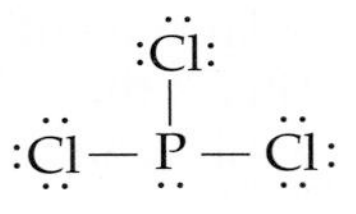 $:\!\ddot{C}l\!:$<br>$\,\,\,\,\,\vert$<br>$:\!\ddot{C}l\!-\!\ddot{P}\!-\!\ddot{C}l\!:$ |

**Step 2.** Examine the central atom to determine if the molecule is polar. The molecule has three chlorine atoms and one lone pair. The one lone pair makes the trigonal pyramidal molecule polar covalent.

*Helpful Hint:* Vectors can also be used in determining the polarity of this compound. The vectors should point in the direction of each electronegative Cl atom.

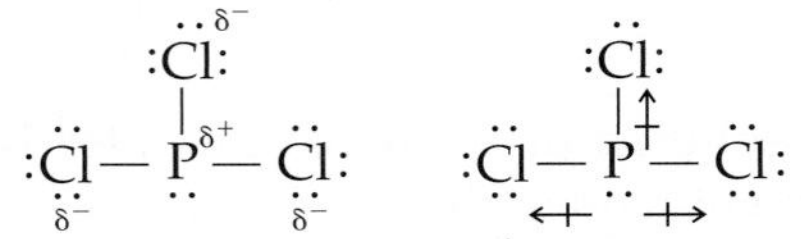

$$:\ddot{C}l:^{\delta-}$$
$$|^{\delta+}$$
$$:\ddot{C}l - P - \ddot{C}l:$$
$$_{\delta-} \qquad _{\delta-}$$

$$:\ddot{C}l:$$
$$|\updownarrow$$
$$:\ddot{C}l - P - \ddot{C}l:$$
$$\leftarrow \quad \rightarrow$$

---

**Practice Problem 3.16**

Determine whether the $AsCl_3$ molecule is polar.

---

▶ For Further Practice: **Questions 3.99 and 3.100.**

---

**Question 3.7**  Predict which of the following bonds are polar, and, if polar, use a vector to indicate in which direction the electrons are pulled:
   a. O—S    b. C≡N    c. Cl—Cl    d. I—Cl

**Question 3.8**  Predict which of the following bonds are polar, and, if polar, use a vector to indicate in which direction the electrons are pulled:
   a. Si—Cl    b. S—Cl    c. H—C    d. C—C

**Question 3.9**  Using Lewis structures and VSEPR, predict whether each of the following molecules is polar:
   a. $CS_2$    b. $NF_3$    c. HCl    d. $SiCl_4$

**Question 3.10**   Using Lewis structures and VSEPR, predict whether each of the following molecules is polar:

   a. $CO_2$        b. $SCl_2$        c. BrCl        d. $BCl_3$

# 3.5   Properties Based on Molecular Geometry and Intermolecular Forces

**Intramolecular forces** are attractive forces *within* molecules. They are the chemical bonds that determine the shape and polarity of individual molecules. **Intermolecular forces,** on the other hand, are forces *between* molecules.

It is important to distinguish between these two kinds of forces. It is the *intermolecular* forces that determine such properties as the solubility of one substance in another and the freezing and boiling points of liquids. But, at the same time, we must realize that these forces are a direct consequence of the *intramolecular* forces within the individual units, the molecules.

In this section, we will see some of the consequences of bonding that are directly attributable to differences in intermolecular forces (solubility, boiling and melting points). In Section 5.2, we will investigate, in some detail, the nature of the intermolecular forces themselves.

## Solubility

*The solute is the substance that is present in a lesser quantity, and the solvent is the substance that is present in a greater amount.*

**Solubility** is defined as the maximum amount of solute that dissolves in a given amount of solvent at a specified temperature. Polar molecules are most soluble in polar solvents, whereas nonpolar molecules are most soluble in nonpolar solvents. This is the rule of *"like dissolves like."* Substances of similar polarity are mutually soluble, and large differences in polarity lead to insolubility.

### Case I: Ammonia and Water

*The interaction of water and ammonia is an example of a particularly strong intermolecular force, the hydrogen bond; this phenomenon is discussed in Chapter 5.*

Ammonia is soluble in water because both ammonia and water are polar molecules:

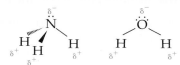

Dissolution of ammonia in water is a consequence of the intermolecular forces present among the ammonia and water molecules. The $\delta^-$ end (a nitrogen) of the ammonia molecule is attracted to the $\delta^+$ end (a hydrogen) of the water molecule; at the same time the $\delta^+$ end (a hydrogen) of the ammonia molecule is attracted to the $\delta^-$ end (an oxygen) of the water molecule. These attractive forces thus "pull" ammonia into water (and water into ammonia), and the ammonia molecules are randomly distributed throughout the solvent, forming a homogeneous solution (Figure 3.13).

### Case II: Oil and Water

Oil and water do not mix; oil is a nonpolar substance composed primarily of molecules containing carbon and hydrogen. Water molecules, on the other hand, are quite polar. The potential solvent, water molecules, have partially charged ends, whereas the molecules of oil do not. As a result, water molecules exert their attractive forces on other water molecules, not on the molecules of oil; the oil remains insoluble, and because it is less dense than water, the oil simply floats on the surface of the water. This is illustrated in Figure 3.14.

## Boiling Points of Liquids and Melting Points of Solids

Boiling a liquid requires energy. The energy is used to overcome the intermolecular attractive forces in the liquid, driving the molecules into the less-associated gas phase.

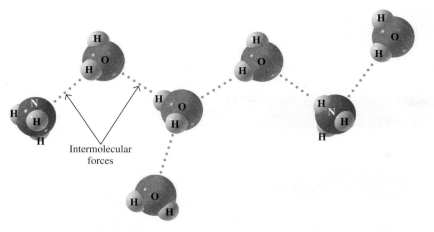

**Figure 3.13** The interaction of polar covalent water molecules (the solvent) with polar covalent solute molecules, ammonia, results in the formation of a solution.

**TABLE 3.6 Melting and Boiling Points of Selected Compounds in Relation to Their Bonding Type**

| Formula (Name) | Bonding Type | M.P. (°C) | B.P. (°C) |
|---|---|---|---|
| $N_2$ (nitrogen) | Nonpolar covalent | −210 | −196 |
| $O_2$ (oxygen) | Nonpolar covalent | −219 | −183 |
| $NH_3$ (ammonia) | Polar covalent | −78 | −33 |
| $H_2O$ (water) | Polar covalent | 0 | 100 |
| NaCl (sodium chloride) | Ionic | 801 | 1413 |
| KBr (potassium bromide) | Ionic | 730 | 1435 |

The amount of energy required to accomplish this is related to the boiling temperature. This, in turn, depends on the strength of the intermolecular attractive forces in the liquid, which parallels the polarity. This is not the only determinant of the boiling point. Molecular mass is also an important consideration. The larger the mass of the molecule, the more difficult it becomes to convert the collection of molecules to the gas phase.

A similar argument can be made for the melting points of solids. The ease of conversion of a solid to a liquid also depends on the magnitude of the attractive forces in the solid. The situation actually becomes very complex for ionic solids because of the complexity of the crystal lattice.

As a general rule, polar compounds have strong attractive (intermolecular) forces, and their boiling and melting points tend to be higher than those of nonpolar substances of similar molecular mass.

Melting and boiling points of a variety of substances are included in Table 3.6.

**Question 3.11** Predict which compound in each of the following pairs should have the higher melting and boiling points (Hint: Write the Lewis structure and determine whether the compound is ionic, polar covalent, or nonpolar covalent.):

    a. $H_2O$ and $C_2H_4$      b. CO and $CH_4$      c. $NH_3$ and $N_2$      d. $Cl_2$ and ICl

**Question 3.12** Predict which compound in each of the following pairs should have the higher melting and boiling points (Hint: Write the Lewis structure and determine whether the compound is ionic, polar covalent, or nonpolar covalent.):

    a. $C_2H_6$ and $CH_4$      c. $F_2$ and $Br_2$
    b. CO and NO      d. $CHCl_3$ and $Cl_2$

**Figure 3.14** The interaction of polar water molecules and nonpolar oil molecules. The familiar salad dressing—oil and vinegar—forms two layers. The oil does not dissolve in vinegar, an aqueous solution of acetic acid.

# CHAPTER MAP

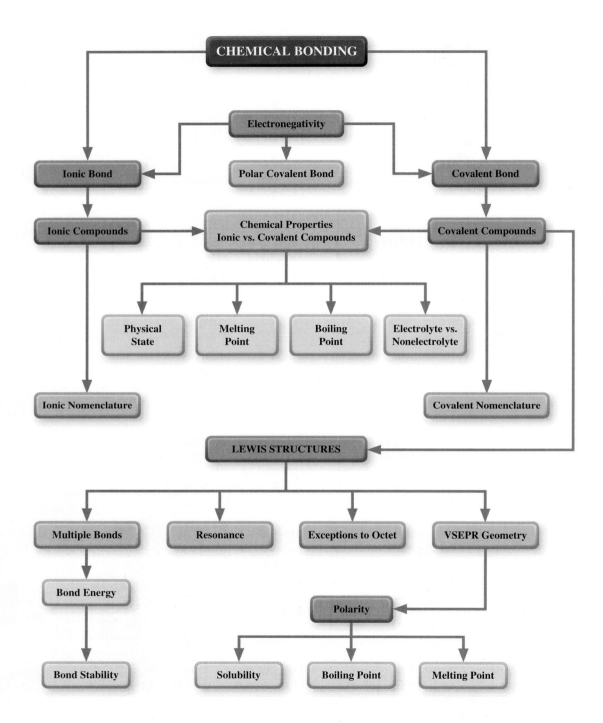

# SUMMARY

## 3.1 Chemical Bonding

▶ **Lewis symbols** show valence electrons on atoms and ions.

▶ **Chemical bonding**—the attractive force between atoms in a compound can be classified as

- **Covalent**, atoms sharing electrons
  - **Polar covalent** and **nonpolar covalent**
- **Ionic**, consisting of cations and anions

▶ **Electronegativity** is a measure of the ability of an atom to attract electrons in a chemical bond, and the difference in electronegativity is used in classifying chemical bonds.

- Difference of 0.5 and less—nonpolar covalent
- Difference between 0.5 and 2.0—polar covalent
- Difference of 2.0 or larger—ionic

## 3.2 Naming Compounds and Writing Formulas of Compounds

▶ The system for naming compounds (**nomenclature**) is different for ionic and covalent compounds.

- Ionic compounds: name cation followed by the anion. Use Roman numeral to denote the charge on the cation, when required.
- The charge of a **monatomic ion** can be determined for main-group elements from the periodic table.
- Know the names and charges of the **polyatomic ions**.
- Covalent compounds: name first element first and then second element (with -ide ending). Use prefixes of di-, tri-, etc., to denote the number of atoms of each element in the compound.

▶ When writing **formulas** for neutral ionic compounds, be sure the number of positive charges equals the number of negative charges.

▶ When writing **formulas** for covalent compounds, use the prefix before the element name as the subscript for the element.

## 3.3 Properties of Ionic and Covalent Compounds

▶ Covalent compounds are typically made up of discrete units called **molecules**.

▶ Ionic compounds form a **crystal lattice** composed of cations and anions extended out in a three-dimensional network.

▶ Ionic compounds have higher **melting points** and **boiling points** than covalent compounds.

▶ When ionic compounds dissolve in water, the ions **dissociate** and the solution conducts electricity. These compounds are **electrolytes**.

▶ When covalent compounds dissolve in water, the compound does not dissociate. They are **nonelectrolytes**.

## 3.4 Drawing Lewis Structures of Molecules and Polyatomic Ions

▶ To draw a **Lewis structure**, all valence electrons are placed around the atoms of the compound as bonding electron pairs or **lone pairs** in order to satisfy the octet rule for each atom.

- The least electronegative atom is central.
- Hydrogen and fluorine occupy terminal positions.
- Carbon has a tendency to form chains.

▶ If the octet rule cannot be satisfied with **single bonds** connecting the atoms, then **double bonds** and **triple bonds** are used.

▶ **Bond energy** determines the stability of a bond. The bond energy trend is as follows:

- Single < double < triple

▶ The bond length trend is the reverse.

- Triple < double < single

▶ **Isomers** are compounds that have the same molecular formula but have different structures. Hydrocarbons have many possible isomers.

▶ When two or more Lewis structures contribute to the molecular structure, the compound displays **resonance**. The true structure is a hybrid of the drawn resonance forms. Stability of a compound increases with the number of resonance structures that can be drawn.

▶ Some molecules have exceptions to the octet rule, these include:

- Odd-electron compounds
- Incomplete octets
- Expanded octets

▶ The shapes of molecules can be predicted using **valence-shell electron-pair repulsion (VSEPR) theory.** Possible shapes include:

- Linear
- Trigonal planar
- Tetrahedral
- Bent
- Trigonal pyramidal

▶ The geometry of a molecule and the knowledge of the polarity of a bond can be used to determine if a molecule is polar (has a dipole) or is nonpolar.

## 3.5 Properties Based on Molecular Geometry and Intermolecular Forces

▶ **Intermolecular forces** are attractive forces between molecules. **Intramolecular forces** are chemical bonds.

▶ Polar molecules are generally attracted to each other more strongly than are nonpolar molecules.

▶ **Solubility** is the maximum amount of solute that dissolves in a given amount of solvent at a specific temperature.

- Polar molecules are soluble in polar solvents.
- Nonpolar molecules are soluble in nonpolar solvents.

▶ Polar molecules (of similar mass) have higher melting points and boiling points than nonpolar molecules.

# ANSWERS TO PRACTICE PROBLEMS

**3.1** $: \overset{\displaystyle .}{\underset{\displaystyle .}{O}} :$

Oxygen has two unpaired electrons. Therefore, it is capable of forming two bonds.

**3.2** $: Ca \longrightarrow Ca^{2+} + 2e^-$

$: \overset{\displaystyle .}{O} : + 2e^- \longrightarrow [: \overset{\displaystyle ..}{\underset{\displaystyle ..}{O}} :]^{2-}$

**3.3** Nonpolar covalent

**3.4**  **a.** $Ca_3N_2$ (three $Ca^{2+}$ and two $N^{3-}$)
  **b.** $MgBr_2$ (one $Mg^{2+}$ and two $Br^-$)
  **c.** $Mg_3N_2$ (three $Mg^{2+}$ and two $N^{3-}$)

**3.5** Chromium(II) bromide

**3.6**  **a.** $CaCO_3$    **b.** $Cu_2SO_4$

**3.7**  **a.** $Fe_2S_3$    **b.** $CaSO_4$    **c.** $Al_2O_3$

**3.8**  **a.** Diboron trioxide
  **b.** Nitrogen monoxide
  **c.** Iodine monochloride
  **d.** Phosphorus trichloride
  **e.** Phosphorus pentachloride
  **f.** Diphosphorus pentoxide

**3.9**  **a.** $P_2O_5$    **b.** $SiO_2$    **c.** $CBr_4$    **d.** $OF_2$

**3.10**  **a.** :Ö—H
          |
          H

  **b.**      H
           |
       H—C—H
           |
           H

**3.11**  **a.**     H   H
             |   |
          H—N—N—H
             ..  ..

  **b.**     H   H   H
             |   |   |
          H—C—C—C—H
             |   |   |
             H   H   H

  **c.** H—C≡N:

**3.12** $\left[ : \overset{\displaystyle ..}{\underset{\displaystyle ..}{O}} - \overset{\displaystyle ..}{\underset{\displaystyle ..}{O}} : \right]^{2-}$

**3.13**  **a.**
$$\left[ : \overset{\displaystyle ..}{\underset{\displaystyle ..}{O}} - \overset{\overset{\textstyle :O:}{\|}}{\underset{\displaystyle ..}{C}} - \overset{\displaystyle ..}{\underset{\displaystyle ..}{O}} - H \right]^{-}$$

**b.** $$\left[ \begin{array}{c} :O: \\ | \\ : \overset{..}{O} - P - \overset{..}{O} : \\ | \\ :O: \end{array} \right]^{3-}$$

**3.14**  **a.** $\overset{..}{O} = \overset{..}{Se} - \overset{..}{O} : \longleftrightarrow : \overset{..}{O} - \overset{..}{Se} = \overset{..}{O}$

**b.** Since both S and Se are in the same family (Group VIA or 16), they have the same number of valence electrons, and therefore, should form the same kinds of bonds.

**3.15**  **a.**      :Cl:
              |
       :Cl—Se—Cl:
              |
             :Cl:

**b.**      :F:   :F:
          :F—S—F:
           :F:   :F:

**c.**        :Cl:
              |
       :Cl—B—Cl:

**3.16** $AsCl_3$ is polar.

# QUESTIONS AND PROBLEMS

## Chemical Bonding

### Foundations

**3.13** Draw the appropriate Lewis symbol for each of the following atoms:
  **a.** H    **b.** He    **c.** Si    **d.** N

**3.14** Draw the appropriate Lewis symbol for each of the following atoms:
  **a.** Be    **b.** B    **c.** F    **d.** S

**3.15** Draw the appropriate Lewis symbol for each of the following ions:
  **a.** $Li^+$    **b.** $Mg^{2+}$    **c.** $Cl^-$    **d.** $P^{3-}$

**3.16** Draw the appropriate Lewis symbol for each of the following ions:
  **a.** $Be^{2+}$    **b.** $Al^{3+}$    **c.** $O^{2-}$    **d.** $S^{2-}$

**3.17** Describe the differences between covalent bonding and ionic bonding.

**3.18** Describe the difference between nonpolar covalent and polar covalent bonding.

**3.19** What is the periodic trend of electronegativity?

**3.20** What role does electronegativity play in determining the bonding between atoms in a compound?

**3.21** Use electronegativity values to classify the bonds in each of the following compounds as ionic, polar covalent, or nonpolar covalent.
**a.** $MgCl_2$    **b.** $CO_2$    **c.** $H_2S$    **d.** $NO_2$

**3.22** Use electronegativity values to classify the bonds in each of the following compounds as ionic, polar covalent, or nonpolar covalent.
**a.** $CaCl_2$    **b.** $CO$    **c.** $ICl$    **d.** $H_2$

## Applications

**3.23** When there is a reaction between each of these pairs of atoms, ions form. Using Lewis symbols, write the reactions showing how electrons are lost or gained when these atoms become ions.
**a.** Li + Br    **b.** Mg + Cl    **c.** P + H

**3.24** When there is a reaction between each of these pairs of atoms, ions form. Using Lewis symbols, write the reactions showing how electrons are lost or gained when these atoms become ions.
**a.** Na + O    **b.** Na + S    **c.** Si + H

**3.25** Explain, using Lewis symbols and the octet rule, why helium is so nonreactive.

**3.26** Explain, using Lewis symbols and the octet rule, why neon is so nonreactive.

## Naming Compounds and Writing Formulas of Compounds

### Foundations

**3.27** Predict the formula of the compound formed from the combination of ions of magnesium and sulfur.

**3.28** Predict the formula of the compound formed from the combination of ions of calcium and fluorine.

**3.29** Name each of the following ions:
**a.** $Na^+$    **b.** $Cu^+$    **c.** $Mg^{2+}$

**3.30** Name each of the following ions:
**a.** $Cu^{2+}$    **b.** $Fe^{2+}$    **c.** $Fe^{3+}$

**3.31** Name each of the following ions:
**a.** $HCO_3^-$    **b.** $H_3O^+$    **c.** $CO_3^{2-}$

**3.32** Name each of the following ions:
**a.** $ClO^-$    **b.** $NH_4^+$    **c.** $CH_3COO^-$

**3.33** Write the formula for each of the following monatomic ions:
**a.** the potassium ion    **b.** the nickel(II) ion

**3.34** Write the formula for each of the following monatomic ions:
**a.** the calcium ion    **b.** the chromium(VI) ion

**3.35** Write the formula for each of the following polyatomic ions:
**a.** the sulfate ion    **b.** the nitrate ion

**3.36** Write the formula for each of the following polyatomic ions:
**a.** the phosphate ion    **b.** the cyanide ion

## Applications

**3.37** Predict the formula of a compound formed from:
**a.** aluminum and oxygen
**b.** lithium and sulfur

**3.38** Predict the formula of a compound formed from:
**a.** boron and hydrogen
**b.** magnesium and phosphorus

**3.39** Name each of the following compounds:
**a.** $MgCl_2$    **b.** $AlCl_3$    **c.** $Cu(NO_3)_2$

**3.40** Name each of the following compounds:
**a.** $Na_2O$    **b.** $Fe(OH)_3$    **c.** $CaBr_2$

**3.41** Write the correct formula for each of the following:
**a.** sodium chloride
**b.** magnesium bromide

**3.42** Write the correct formula for each of the following:
**a.** potassium oxide    **b.** potassium nitride

**3.43** Write the correct formula for each of the following:
**a.** silver cyanide
**b.** ammonium chloride

**3.44** Write the correct formula for each of the following:
**a.** magnesium carbonate
**b.** magnesium bicarbonate

**3.45** Write the correct formula for each of the following:
**a.** copper(II) oxide    **b.** iron(III) oxide

**3.46** Write the correct formula for each of the following:
**a.** manganese(II) oxide
**b.** manganese(III) oxide

**3.47** Write a suitable formula for:
**a.** sodium nitrate    **b.** magnesium nitrate

**3.48** Write a suitable formula for:
**a.** aluminum nitrate    **b.** potassium nitrate

**3.49** Write a suitable formula for:
**a.** ammonium iodide    **b.** ammonium sulfate

**3.50** Write a suitable formula for:
**a.** ammonium acetate    **b.** ammonium cyanide

**3.51** Name each of the following compounds:
**a.** $NO_2$    **b.** $SeO_3$    **c.** $SO_3$

**3.52** Name each of the following compounds:
**a.** $N_2O_4$    **b.** $CCl_4$    **c.** $N_2O_5$

**3.53** Write a suitable formula for:
**a.** silicon dioxide    **b.** sulfur dioxide

**3.54** Write a suitable formula for:
**a.** diphosphorus pentoxide
**b.** dioxygen difluoride

## Properties of Ionic and Covalent Compounds

### Foundations

**3.55** Contrast ionic and covalent compounds with respect to their solid-state structures.

**3.56** Contrast ionic and covalent compounds with respect to their behaviors in solution.

**3.57** Contrast ionic and covalent compounds with respect to their relative boiling points.

**3.58** Contrast ionic and covalent compounds with respect to their relative melting points.

## Applications

**3.59** Would KCl be expected to be a solid at room temperature? Why?

**3.60** Would $CCl_4$ be expected to be a solid at room temperature? Why?

**3.61** Would $H_2O$ or $CCl_4$ be expected to have a higher boiling point? Why?

**3.62** Would $H_2O$ or $CCl_4$ be expected to have a higher melting point? Why?

**3.63** Would $MgCl_2$ in $H_2O$ form an electrolytic solution? Why?

**3.64** Would $C_6H_{12}O_6$ in $H_2O$ form an electrolytic solution? Why?

## Drawing Lewis Structures of Molecules and Polyatomic Ions

### Foundations

**3.65** When drawing a Lewis structure, how can the central atom be determined?

**3.66** When drawing a Lewis structure, which elements can never be a central atom?

**3.67** How is the positive charge of a polyatomic *cation* incorporated when determining the number of valence electrons to be used in a Lewis structure?

**3.68** How is the negative charge of a polyatomic *anion* incorporated when determining the number of valence electrons to be used in a Lewis structure?

**3.69** Rank the following in order of increasing bond energy:

single bond, double bond, triple bond

**3.70** Rank the following in order of increasing bond length:

single bond, double bond, triple bond

**3.71** Which will have more isomers: $C_4H_{10}$ or $C_5H_{12}$? Why?

**3.72** Will the number of isomers increase or decrease with the number of carbon atoms in a hydrocarbon? Explain your reasoning.

**3.73** Discuss the concept of resonance, being certain to define the terms *resonance, resonance form,* and *resonance hybrid.*

**3.74** Why is resonance an important concept in bonding?

**3.75** What is the bond angle of a trigonal planar molecule?

**3.76** What is the bond angle of a tetrahedral molecule?

**3.77** True or false? Molecules that have only nonpolar bonds will always be nonpolar. Explain your reasoning.

**3.78** True or false? Molecules that have only polar bonds will always be polar. Explain your reasoning.

### Applications

**3.79** Give the Lewis structure for each of the following compounds:
    **a.** $NCl_3$    **b.** $CH_3OH$    **c.** $CS_2$    **d.** $CH_2Cl_2$

**3.80** Give the Lewis structure for each of the following compounds:
    **a.** $HNO_3$    **b.** $CCl_4$    **c.** $PBr_3$    **d.** $CH_3CH_2OH$

**3.81** Acetaldehyde has the molecular formula $C_2H_4O$. Draw the Lewis structure of acetaldehyde.

**3.82** Formaldehyde, $H_2CO$, in water solution has been used as a preservative for biological specimens. Draw the Lewis structure of formaldehyde.

**3.83** Acetone, $C_3H_6O$, is a common solvent. It is found in such diverse materials as nail polish remover and industrial solvents. Draw its Lewis structure if its skeletal structure is

O

C    C    C

**3.84** Ethylamine is an example of an important class of organic compounds. The molecular formula of ethylamine is $CH_3CH_2NH_2$. Draw its Lewis structure.

**3.85** Draw the Lewis structure of $NO^+$.

**3.86** Draw the Lewis structure of $NO_2^-$.

**3.87** Draw the Lewis structure of $OH^-$.

**3.88** Draw the Lewis structure of $HS^-$.

**3.89** The acetate ion exhibits resonance. Draw two resonance forms of the acetate ion.

**3.90** Ozone, $O_3$, has two resonance forms. Draw each form.

**3.91** All of the following Lewis structures are incorrect. Find the errors and write the correct structures.

    **a.** $:\!C\!=\!\ddot{O}:$

    **b.** $:\!\ddot{H}\!-\!\ddot{O}\!-\!\ddot{H}:$

    **c.** $:\!\ddot{O}\!-\!\ddot{C}\!-\!\ddot{O}:$

**3.92** All of the following Lewis structures are incorrect. Find the errors and write the correct structures.

    **a.**

    **c.**

    **b.**

**3.93** $BeCl_2$ has an incomplete octet around the beryllium atom. Draw the Lewis structure of $BeCl_2$.

**3.94** $B(OH)_3$ has an incomplete octet around the boron atom. Draw the Lewis structure of $B(OH)_3$.

**3.95** $SeF_6$ has an expanded octet around the selenium atom. Draw the Lewis structure of $SeF_6$.

**3.96** Noble gases in the third period and beyond can undergo covalent bonding. All have an expanded octet. Draw the Lewis structure of $XeF_2$.

**3.97** Draw the Lewis structure of each of the following compounds and predict its geometry using the VSEPR theory.
    **a.** $SO_2$        **b.** $SO_3$

**3.98** Draw the Lewis structure of each of the following compounds and predict its geometry using the VSEPR theory.
    **a.** $SeO_2$      **b.** $SeO_3$

**3.99** Predict the polarity of each compound in Question 3.97.

**3.100** Predict the polarity of each compound in Question 3.98.

## Properties Based on Molecular Geometry and Intermolecular Forces

### Foundations

**3.101** Which of the following compounds have polar bonds but are nonpolar covalent compounds?
    **a.** $CO_2$      **b.** $NF_3$      **c.** $CF_4$

**3.102** Which of the following compounds have polar bonds but are nonpolar covalent compounds?
    **a.** $SO_2$      **b.** $CF_4$      **c.** $NH_3$

**3.103** What is the relationship between the polarity of a bond and the polarity of the molecule?

**3.104** What effect does polarity have on the solubility of a compound in water?

**3.105** Using the VSEPR theory, predict the geometry, polarity, and water solubility of each compound in Question 3.79.

**3.106** Using the VSEPR theory, predict the geometry, polarity, and water solubility of each compound in Question 3.80.

**3.107** What effect does polarity have on the melting point of a pure compound?

**3.108** What effect does polarity have on the boiling point of a pure compound?

### Applications

**3.109** Would you expect KCl to dissolve in water?

**3.110** Would you expect ethylamine (Question 3.84) to dissolve in water?

**3.111** In each of the following pairs of compounds, choose the compound with the higher boiling point.
   **a.** $N_2$ and $NH_3$     **b.** $CS_2$ and $CF_4$     **c.** NaCl and $Cl_2$

**3.112** In each of the following pairs of compounds, choose the compound with the higher melting point.
   **a.** KF and $F_2$     **b.** CO and $O_2$     **c.** $NBr_3$ and $CCl_4$

## CHALLENGE PROBLEMS

1. Predict differences in our global environment that may have arisen if the freezing point and boiling point of water were 20°C higher than they are.

2. Would you expect the compound $C_2S_2H_4$ to exist? Why or why not?

3. Draw the resonance forms of the carbonate ion. What conclusions, based on this exercise, can you draw about the stability of the carbonate ion?

4. Which of the following compounds would be predicted to have the higher boiling point? Explain your reasoning.

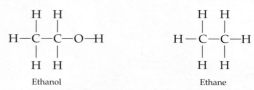

Ethanol                              Ethane

5. Why does the octet rule not work well for compounds of lanthanide and actinide elements? Suggest a number other than eight that may be more suitable.

# 4

# Calculations, Chemical Changes, and the Chemical Equation

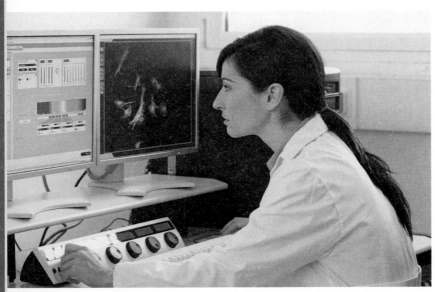

Sophisticated computer-based instrumentation is used to follow the progress of a chemical reaction.

## OUTLINE

## LEARNING GOALS

1   Calculate the mass of an atom using the atomic mass unit.

2   Use the relationship between Avogadro's number and the mole to perform calculations.

3   Determine molar mass, and demonstrate how it is used in mole and mass conversion calculations.

4   Use chemical formulas to calculate the formula mass and molar mass of a compound.

5   Describe the functions served by the chemical equation, the basis for chemical calculations.

6   Classify chemical reactions by type: combination, decomposition, or replacement.

7   Balance chemical equations given the identity of products and reactants.

8   Write net ionic equations, and use solubility rules to predict the formation of a precipitate.

9   Distinguish between an acid and a base.

10   Write oxidation and reduction half-reactions, and identify oxidizing agents and reducing agents.

11   Compare and contrast voltaic and electrolytic cells.

12   Describe examples of redox processes.

13   Use a chemical equation and a given number of moles or mass of a reactant or product to calculate the number of moles or mass of a reactant or product.

14   Calculate theoretical and percent yields.

# INTRODUCTION

In this chapter, we define the mole (mol), the fundamental unit of measure of chemical arithmetic. We will learn to write and balance chemical equations and use these tools to perform calculations of chemical quantities. We will also see that chemical reactions are classified according to their unique patterns and characteristics.

If a pharmaceutical company wishes to manufacture 1000 kilograms (kg) of a product next year, many calculations of chemical quantities based on chemical equations would be required. The company would first have to determine the amount of each starting material that would need to be ordered. This answer would be used in determining how much the process will cost as well as the product's price per gram.

We often need to predict the quantity of a product produced from the reaction of a given amount of material. This calculation is possible. It is equally possible to calculate the amount of a material that would be necessary to produce a desired amount of product.

What is required is a recipe: a procedure to follow. The basis for our recipe is the chemical equation. A properly written chemical equation provides all of the necessary information for the chemical calculation. That critical information is the combining ratio of elements or compounds that must interact in order to produce a certain amount of product or products.

It is also necessary to understand how elements and compounds interact during a chemical reaction. When dissolved in water, some compounds react and form a product that is a solid. Other compounds react and produce salt and water, while some compounds react to produce large amounts of energy along with carbon dioxide and water. We will use chemical equations to classify reactions as precipitation, acid-base, and oxidation-reduction. We will also study some of the practical applications that are based on these reactions.

Many chemical calculations are made during the production of a pharmaceutical product.

---

## 4.1   The Mole Concept and Atoms

Atoms are exceedingly small, yet their masses have been experimentally determined for each of the elements. The unit of measurement for these determinations is the **atomic mass unit** (amu):

$$1 \text{ amu} = 1.661 \times 10^{-24} \text{ g}$$

### The Mole and Avogadro's Number

The exact value of the amu is defined in relation to a standard, just as the units of the metric system represent defined quantities. The carbon-12 isotope has been chosen and is assigned a mass of exactly 12 amu. Hence, this standard reference point defines an amu as exactly one-twelfth the mass of a carbon-12 atom.

The periodic table provides atomic masses in amu. These atomic masses are average values, based on the contribution of all naturally occurring isotopes of the particular element. For example, the average mass of a carbon atom is 12.01 amu and, using the conversion factor based on the relationship between amu and grams, shown above, we can calculate the mass of a carbon atom in units of grams:

$$\frac{12.01 \text{ amu C}}{\text{C atom}} \times \frac{1.661 \times 10^{-24} \text{ g C}}{1 \text{ amu C}} = 1.995 \times 10^{-23} \frac{\text{g C}}{\text{C atom}}$$

In everyday work, chemists use much larger quantities of matter (typically g or kg). Therefore, the mole is a more practical unit than the amu for defining a "collection" of atoms. The **mole** (mol) is the amount of a substance that contains as many atoms, molecules, or ions as are found in exactly 12 g of the carbon-12

### LEARNING GOAL

**1**   Calculate the mass of an atom using the atomic mass unit.

isotope. That number, experimentally determined, is **Avogadro's number,** named in honor of the nineteenth-century Italian scientist, Amadeo Avogadro.

Avogadro's number is expressed as:

$$1 \text{ mol of atoms} = 6.022 \times 10^{23} \text{ atoms of an element}$$

The practice of defining a unit for a quantity of small objects is common; a *dozen* eggs, a *ream* of paper, and a *gross* of pencils are well-known examples. Similarly, a mol is $6.022 \times 10^{23}$ individual units of anything. We could, if we desired, speak of a mol of eggs or a mol of pencils. However, in chemistry we use the mol to represent a specific quantity of atoms, ions, or molecules.

The mol and the amu are related. The atomic mass of an element corresponds to the average mass of a single atom in amu, and the *molar mass* is the mass of a mole of atoms in grams.

The mass of 1 mol of atoms, in g, is defined as the **molar mass.** Consider this relationship for sodium in Example 4.1.

---

| **EXAMPLE 4.1** | **Relating Atomic Mass Units to Molar Mass** | **LEARNING GOALS** |

Calculate the mass, in g, of Avogadro's number of sodium atoms.

**Solution**

Avogadro's number represents the relationship between $6.022 \times 10^{23}$ atoms and 1 mol.

**Step 1.**  Since the data given is Avogadro's number of atoms, it should be written as a conversion factor with the number of atoms in the numerator.

$$\frac{6.022 \times 10^{23} \text{ atoms Na}}{1 \text{ mol Na}}$$

**Step 2.**  The periodic table indicates that the average mass of one sodium atom = 22.99 amu. This can be used as a conversion factor with atoms Na in the denominator.

$$\frac{6.022 \times 10^{23} \text{ atoms Na}}{1 \text{ mol Na}} \times \frac{22.99 \text{ amu Na}}{1 \text{ atom Na}} = \frac{138.4 \times 10^{23} \text{ amu Na}}{1 \text{ mol Na}}$$

Data Given × Conversion Factor = Initial Data Result

**Step 3.**  As previously noted, 1 amu = $1.661 \times 10^{-24}$ g. The conversion factor written with g in the numerator and amu in the denominator is the only one that leads to the answer in g/mol, or the molar mass of sodium.

$$\frac{138.4 \times 10^{23} \text{ amu Na}}{1 \text{ mol Na}} \times \frac{1.661 \times 10^{-24} \text{ g Na}}{1 \text{ amu Na}} = \frac{22.99 \text{ g Na}}{1 \text{ mol Na}}$$

Initial Data Result × Conversion Factor = Desired Result

This calculation may also be done in a single step by arranging the factors in a chain.

$$\frac{6.022 \times 10^{23} \text{ atoms Na}}{1 \text{ mol Na}} \times \frac{22.99 \text{ amu Na}}{1 \text{ atom Na}} \times \frac{1.661 \times 10^{-24} \text{ g Na}}{1 \text{ amu Na}} = \frac{22.99 \text{ g Na}}{1 \text{ mol Na}}$$

Data Given × Conversion Factor × Conversion Factor = Desired Result

The average mass of one atom of sodium, in units of amu, is numerically identical to the mass of Avogadro's number of atoms, expressed in units of g. Hence, the molar mass of sodium is 22.99 g Na/mol.

*Helpful Hint:* The use of conversion factors is discussed in Section 1.5.

---

**LEARNING GOALS**

**1**  Calculate the mass of an atom using the atomic mass unit.

**2**  Use the relationship between Avogadro's number and the mole to perform calculations.

**Practice Problem 4.1**

Calculate the mass, in g, of Avogadro's number of:

a. aluminum atoms    b. mercury atoms

▶ For Further Practice: **Questions 4.21 and 4.22.**

The sodium example is not unique. The relationship holds for every element in the periodic table.

Because Avogadro's number of particles (atoms) is 1 mol, it follows that the average mass of one atom of hydrogen is 1.008 amu and the mass of 1 mol of hydrogen atoms is 1.008 g, or the average mass of one atom of carbon is 12.01 amu and the mass of 1 mol of carbon atoms is 12.01 g.

In fact, 1 mol of atoms of *any element* contains the same number, Avogadro's number, of atoms, $6.022 \times 10^{23}$ atoms.

The difference in mass of a mol of two different elements can be quite striking (Figure 4.1). For example, a mol of hydrogen atoms is 1.008 g, and a mol of lead atoms is 207.19 g.

**Figure 4.1** The comparison of approximately 1 mol each of silver (as Morgan and Peace dollars), gold (as Canadian Maple Leaf coins), and copper (as pennies) shows the considerable difference in mass (as well as economic value) of equivalent mol of different substances.

## Calculating Atoms, Moles, and Mass

Performing calculations based on a chemical equation requires a facility for relating the number of atoms of an element to a corresponding number of mol of that element and ultimately to their mass in g. Such calculations involve the use of conversion factors. The use of conversion factors was first described in Chapter 1.

Examples 4.2–4.6 demonstrate the use of conversion factors to proceed from the information *provided* in the problem (data given) to the information *requested* by the problem (desired result).

| **EXAMPLE 4.2** | **Converting Moles to Atoms** |
| --- | --- |

How many iron atoms are present in 3.0 mol of iron metal?

**LEARNING GOAL**

**2** Use the relationship between Avogadro's number and the mole to perform calculations.

**Solution**

**Step 1.** The calculation is based on the choice of the appropriate conversion factor. The relationship, 1 mol Fe = $6.022 \times 10^{23}$ atoms Fe, can be represented with atoms Fe in the numerator and mol Fe in the denominator.

$$\frac{6.022 \times 10^{23} \text{ atoms Fe}}{1 \text{ mol Fe}}$$

**Step 2.** Using this conversion factor, we have

$$3.0 \ \cancel{\text{mol Fe}} \times \frac{6.022 \times 10^{23} \text{ atoms Fe}}{1 \ \cancel{\text{mol Fe}}} = 18 \times 10^{23} \text{ atoms of Fe, or}$$

Data Given × Conversion Factor = Desired Result

$$= 1.8 \times 10^{24} \text{ atoms of Fe (2 significant figures)}$$

**Practice Problem 4.2**

How many oxygen atoms are present in 2.50 mol of:

a. oxygen atoms    b. diatomic oxygen

▶ For Further Practice: **Questions 4.23 and 4.24.**

| EXAMPLE 4.3 | Converting Atoms to Moles |
|---|---|

Calculate the number of mol of sulfur represented by $1.81 \times 10^{24}$ atoms of sulfur.

**2**  Use the relationship between Avogadro's number and the mole to perform calculations.

**Solution**

**Step 1.**  Just as in the previous example, the calculation is based on the choice of the appropriate conversion factor. The relationship, 1 mol S = $6.022 \times 10^{23}$ atoms S, can be represented with mol S in the numerator and atoms S in the denominator.

$$\frac{1 \text{ mol S}}{6.022 \times 10^{23} \text{ atoms S}}$$

**Step 2.**  $1.81 \times 10^{24} \text{ atoms S} \times \dfrac{1 \text{ mol S}}{6.022 \times 10^{23} \text{ atoms S}} = 3.01 \text{ mol S}$

Data Given × Conversion Factor = Desired Result

Note that this conversion factor is the inverse of that used in Example 4.2. Remember, the conversion factor must cancel units that should not appear in the final answer.

**Practice Problem 4.3**

How many mol of sodium are represented by $9.03 \times 10^{23}$ atoms of sodium?

▶ For Further Practice: **Questions 4.25 and 4.26.**

| EXAMPLE 4.4 | Converting Moles to Mass |
|---|---|

What is the mass, in g, of 3.01 mol of sulfur?

**3**  Determine molar mass, and demonstrate how it is used in mole and mass conversion calculations.

**Solution**

The molar mass is the mass of a mole of atoms in grams.

**Step 1.**  The molar mass can be calculated using information provided on the periodic table. One mol of sulfur has a mass of 32.06 g. This relationship, 1 mol S = 32.06 g S, can be represented as a conversion factor with g S in the numerator and mol S in the denominator.

$$\frac{32.06 \text{ g S}}{1 \text{ mol S}}$$

**Step 2.**  Using this conversion factor (ensuring that the units *mol S* cancel):

$$3.01 \text{ mol S} \times \frac{32.06 \text{ g S}}{1 \text{ mol S}} = 96.5 \text{ g S}$$

Data Given × Conversion Factor = Desired Result

**Practice Problem 4.4**

What is the mass, in g, of 3.50 mol of the element helium?

▶ For Further Practice: **Questions 4.27 and 4.28.**

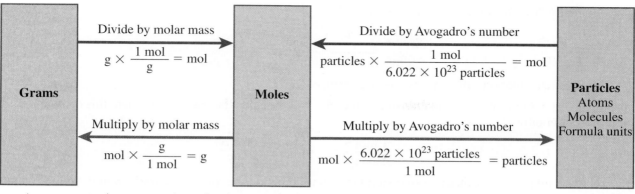

**Figure 4.2** Interconversion between numbers of mol, particles, and g. The mol concept is central to chemical calculations involving measured quantities of matter.

---

## EXAMPLE 4.5 | Converting Mass to Moles

Calculate the number of mol of sulfur in 1.00 kg of sulfur.

### Solution

The data given has units of kg. This will need to first be converted to g. From g, the number of mol can be calculated.

**Step 1.** Convert kg S to g S. Using the relationship, 1 kg S = $10^3$ g S, as a conversion factor with g S in the numerator and kg S in the denominator will result in an answer in g S.

**Step 2.** Convert g S to the desired result in mol S using the molar mass relationship as a conversion factor. Molar mass can be determined from the periodic table, 1 mol S = 32.06 g.

**Step 3.** The calculation may be done in a single step by arranging the factors in a chain:

$$1.00 \; \cancel{kg \, S} \times \frac{10^3 \; \cancel{g \, S}}{1 \; \cancel{kg \, S}} \times \frac{1 \; mol \; S}{32.06 \; \cancel{g \, S}} = 31.2 \; mol \; S$$

Data Given × Conversion Factor × Conversion Factor = Desired Result

### LEARNING GOAL

**3** Determine molar mass, and demonstrate how it is used in mole and mass conversion calculations.

---

### Practice Problem 4.5

Calculate the number of mol of silver in a silver ring that has a mass of 3.42 g.

▶ For Further Practice: **Questions 4.31 and 4.32.**

---

The conversion between the three principal measures of quantity of matter—the number of g (mass), the number of mol, and the number of individual particles (atoms, ions, or molecules)—is essential to the art of problem solving in chemistry. Their interrelationship is depicted in Figure 4.2.

---

## EXAMPLE 4.6 | Converting Grams to Number of Atoms

Calculate the number of atoms of sulfur in 1.00 g of sulfur.

### Solution

It is generally useful to map out a pattern for the required conversion. We are given the number of grams and need the number of atoms that correspond to that mass. Figure 4.2 illustrates that the mole concept is central to solving this problem.

### LEARNING GOALS

**2** Use the relationship between Avogadro's number and the mole to perform calculations.

**3** Determine molar mass, and demonstrate how it is used in mole and mass conversion calculations.

*Continued…*

Begin by "tracing a path" to the answer:

$$\boxed{\begin{array}{c}\text{grams}\\\text{sulfur}\end{array}}\xrightarrow[\text{1}]{\text{Step}}\boxed{\begin{array}{c}\text{moles}\\\text{sulfur}\end{array}}\xrightarrow[\text{2}]{\text{Step}}\boxed{\begin{array}{c}\text{atoms}\\\text{sulfur}\end{array}}$$

Two transformations, or conversions, are required:

**Step 1.** Convert g S to mol S. The relationship, 1 mol S = 32.06 g S, can be used to complete this conversion. Consider either

$$\frac{1 \text{ mol S}}{32.06 \text{ g S}} \quad \text{or} \quad \frac{32.06 \text{ g S}}{1 \text{ mol S}}$$

If we want g S to cancel, the conversion factor with mol S in the numerator and g S in the denominator is the correct choice, resulting in

$$1.00 \ \cancel{\text{g S}} \times \frac{1 \text{ mol S}}{32.06 \ \cancel{\text{g S}}} = 0.0312 \text{ mol S}$$

Data Given × Conversion Factor = Relating Unit

**Step 2.** Convert mol S to atoms S.

The relationship, 1 mol S = $6.022 \times 10^{23}$ atoms S, can be used to convert mol S to atoms S. The mol S must cancel; therefore

$$0.0312 \ \cancel{\text{mol S}} \times \frac{6.022 \times 10^{23} \text{ atom S}}{1 \ \cancel{\text{mol S}}} = 1.88 \times 10^{22} \text{ atoms S}$$

Relating Unit × Conversion Factor = Desired Result

The calculation may also be done in a single step:

$$1.00 \ \cancel{\text{g S}} \times \frac{1 \ \cancel{\text{mol S}}}{32.06 \ \cancel{\text{g S}}} \times \frac{6.022 \times 10^{23} \text{ atoms S}}{1 \ \cancel{\text{mol S}}} = 1.88 \times 10^{22} \text{ atoms S}$$

Data Given × Conversion Factor × Conversion Factor = Desired Result

### Practice Problem 4.6

How many oxygen atoms are present in 40.0 g of oxygen molecules?

▶ For Further Practice: **Questions 4.35 and 4.36.**

**Question 4.1**   What is the mass, in g, of $1.00 \times 10^{12}$ mercury (Hg) atoms?

**Question 4.2**   How many mol of lead (Pb) atoms are equivalent to six billion lead atoms?

## 4.2   The Chemical Formula, Formula Mass, and Molar Mass

### The Chemical Formula

Compounds are pure substances. They are composed of two or more elements that are chemically combined. A **chemical formula** is a combination of symbols of the various elements that make up the compound. It serves as a convenient way to represent a compound. The chemical formula is based on the formula unit. The **formula unit** is the smallest collection of atoms or ions that provides two important pieces of information:

• the identity of the atoms or ions present in the compound and
• the relative numbers of each type of atom or ion.

Let's look at the following formulas:

- *Hydrogen gas,* $H_2$. This indicates that two atoms of hydrogen are chemically bonded forming diatomic hydrogen, hence the subscript two.
- *Water,* $H_2O$. Water is composed of molecules that contain two atoms of hydrogen (subscript two) and one atom of oxygen (lack of a subscript means *one* atom).
- *Sodium chloride,* NaCl. One ion of sodium and one ion of chlorine combine to make sodium chloride.
- *Calcium hydroxide,* $Ca(OH)_2$. Calcium hydroxide contains one ion of calcium and two atoms each of oxygen and hydrogen. One atom of oxygen and one atom of hydrogen are contained in one hydroxide ion (a polyatomic ion). These two hydroxide ions furnish two atoms of both oxygen and hydrogen. Recall that the subscript outside the parentheses applies to *all* atoms inside the parentheses.
- *Ammonium sulfate,* $(NH_4)_2SO_4$. Ammonium sulfate contains two ammonium ions ($NH_4^+$) and one sulfate ion ($SO_4^{2-}$). Each ammonium ion contains one nitrogen and four hydrogen atoms. The formula shows that ammonium sulfate contains two nitrogen atoms, eight hydrogen atoms, one sulfur atom, and four oxygen atoms.
- *Copper(II) sulfate pentahydrate,* $CuSO_4 \cdot 5H_2O$. This is an example of a compound that has water incorporated in its structure. Compounds containing one or more water molecules as an integral part of their structure are termed **hydrates.** Copper sulfate pentahydrate has five units of water (or ten H atoms and five O atoms) in addition to one copper atom, one sulfur atom, and four oxygen atoms for a total atomic composition of:

> 1 copper atom
> 1 sulfur atom
> 9 oxygen atoms
> 10 hydrogen atoms

Note that the symbol for water is preceded by a dot, indicating that, although the water is a formula unit capable of standing alone, in this case it is a part of a larger structure. Copper sulfate also exists as a structure free of water, $CuSO_4$. This form is described as anhydrous (no water) copper sulfate. The physical and chemical properties of a hydrate often differ markedly from the anhydrous form (Figure 4.3).

## Formula Mass and Molar Mass

Just as the atomic mass of an element is the average atomic mass for one atom of the naturally occurring element, expressed in amu, the **formula mass** of a compound is the sum of the atomic masses of all atoms in the compound, as represented by its formula. To calculate the formula mass of a compound we *must* know the correct chemical formula. The formula mass is expressed in amu.

When working in the laboratory, we do not deal with individual molecules; instead, we use units of mol or g. Eighteen grams of water (less than 1 ounce) contain approximately Avogadro's number of water molecules ($6.022 \times 10^{23}$ molecules). Defining our working units as mol and g makes good chemical sense.

We earlier concluded that the atomic mass of an element in amu from the periodic table corresponds to the mass of a mol of atoms of that element in units of grams per mole (g/mol). It follows that *molar mass,* the mass of a mol of compound, is numerically equal to the formula mass in amu.

In Example 4.7, $H_2O$ is a covalent compound. In Example 4.8, $Ca_3(PO_4)_2$ is an ionic compound. As we have seen, it is not technically correct to describe ionic compounds as molecules; similarly, the term *molecular mass* is not appropriate for $Ca_3(PO_4)_2$. The term *formula mass* may be used to describe the formula unit of a substance, whether it is made up of ions, ion pairs, or molecules. We shall use the term *formula mass* in a general way to represent each of these species.

Figure 4.4 illustrates the difference between molecules and ion pairs.

It is possible to determine the correct chemical formula of a compound from experimental data.

**(a)** **(b)**

**Figure 4.3** The marked difference in color of (a) hydrated and (b) anhydrous copper sulfate is clear evidence that they are, in fact, different compounds.

### LEARNING GOAL

**4** Use chemical formulas to calculate the formula mass and molar mass of a compound.

**Figure 4.4** Formula units of (a) sodium chloride, an ionic compound, and (b) methane, a covalent compound.

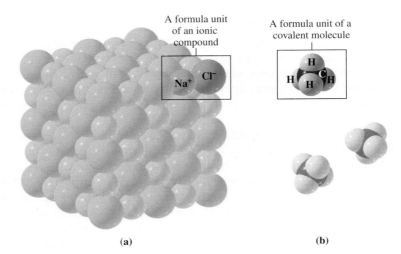

A formula unit of an ionic compound

A formula unit of a covalent molecule

(a)

(b)

---

| EXAMPLE 4.7 | **Calculating Formula Mass and Molar Mass** | LEARNING GOAL |

Calculate the formula mass and molar mass of water, $H_2O$.

**4** Use chemical formulas to calculate the formula mass and molar mass of a compound.

**Solution**

The formula mass is expressed in amu, and the molar mass is expressed in g/mol.

**Step 1.** Each water molecule contains two hydrogen atoms and one oxygen atom. The periodic table provides atomic weights in amu.

**Step 2.** Addition of the masses of all of the hydrogen and oxygen atoms in the water molecule results in the formula mass of water.

$$2 \text{ H atoms} \times 1.008 \text{ amu/H atom} = \phantom{0}2.016 \text{ amu}$$
$$\underline{1 \text{ O atom} \phantom{s} \times 16.00 \text{ amu/O atom} = 16.00 \phantom{0} \text{ amu}}$$
$$18.02 \phantom{0} \text{ amu}$$

**Step 3.** The formula mass of a single molecule of $H_2O$ is 18.02 amu. The formula mass and molar mass are related; the formula mass, in amu, is numerically equal to the molar mass, in units of g/mol. Therefore, the mass of a mol of $H_2O$ is 18.02 g, and the molar mass is 18.02 g/mol.

*Helpful Hint:* Adding 2.016 and 16.00 shows a result of 18.016 on your calculator. Proper use of significant figures (Chapter 1) dictates rounding that result to 18.02.

---

**Practice Problem 4.7**

Calculate the formula mass and molar mass of $NH_3$ (ammonia).

---

▶ For Further Practice: **Questions 4.40 and 4.41.**

---

| EXAMPLE 4.8 | **Calculating Formula Mass and Molar Mass** | LEARNING GOAL |

Calculate the formula mass and molar mass of calcium phosphate.

**4** Use chemical formulas to calculate the formula mass and molar mass of a compound.

**Solution**

**Step 1.** The calcium ion is $Ca^{2+}$, and the phosphate ion is $PO_4^{3-}$. To form a neutral unit, three $Ca^{2+}$ must combine with two $PO_4^{3-}$; $[3 \times (2^+)]$ calcium ion charges are balanced by $[2 \times (3^-)]$ phosphate ion charges.

**Step 2.** Thus, for calcium phosphate, $Ca_3(PO_4)_2$, the subscript two for phosphate dictates that there are two phosphorus atoms and eight oxygen atoms ($2 \times 4$) in the formula unit.

**Step 3.** Addition of the masses of all of the calcium, phosphorus, and oxygen atoms in the compound results in the formula mass of calcium phosphate.

$$
\begin{array}{l}
3 \text{ Ca atoms} \times 40.08 \text{ amu/Ca atom} = 120.24 \text{ amu} \\
2 \text{ P atoms} \times 30.97 \text{ amu/P atom} = \phantom{0}61.94 \text{ amu} \\
8 \text{ O atoms} \times 16.00 \text{ amu/O atom} = 128.00 \text{ amu} \\
\hline
\phantom{8 \text{ O atoms} \times 16.00 \text{ amu/O atom} = } 310.18 \text{ amu}
\end{array}
$$

**Step 4.** The formula mass of calcium phosphate is 310.18 amu, and the molar mass is 310.18 g/mol.

*Helpful Hint:* Writing ionic formulas from compound names is explained in Section 3.2.

---

**Practice Problem 4.8**

Calculate the formula mass and molar mass of $CoCl_2 \cdot 6H_2O$ (cobalt chloride hexahydrate).

▶ For Further Practice: **Questions 4.43 and 4.44.**

---

**Question 4.3**   Caffeine occurs naturally in coffee and tea and is present in many soft drinks. The formula of caffeine is $C_8H_{10}N_4O_2$. Calculate the formula mass and molar mass of caffeine.

**Question 4.4**   The formula of ascorbic acid, commonly known as vitamin C, is $C_6H_8O_6$. Calculate the formula mass and molar mass of vitamin C.

## 4.3   The Chemical Equation and the Information It Conveys

### A Recipe for Chemical Change

The **chemical equation** is the shorthand notation for a chemical reaction. It describes all the substances that react and all the products that form. **Reactants,** or starting materials, are all substances that undergo change in a chemical reaction; **products** are substances produced by a chemical reaction.

The chemical equation also describes the physical state of the reactants and products. It tells us whether the reaction occurs and identifies the solvent and experimental conditions employed, such as heat, light, or electrical energy added to the system.

Most important, the relative number of mol of reactants and products appears in the equation. According to the **law of conservation of mass,** matter cannot be either gained or lost in the process of a chemical reaction. The total mass of the products must be equal to the total mass of the reactants. In other words, the law of conservation of mass tells us that we must have a balanced chemical equation.

### Features of a Chemical Equation

Consider the decomposition of calcium carbonate:

$$
\underset{\text{calcium carbonate}}{CaCO_3(s)} \xrightarrow{\Delta} \underset{\text{calcium oxide}}{CaO(s)} + \underset{\text{carbon dioxide}}{CO_2(g)}
$$

**LEARNING GOAL**

**5**  Describe the functions served by the chemical equation, the basis for chemical calculations.

This equation reads: One mole of solid calcium carbonate decomposes upon heating to produce one mole of solid calcium oxide and one mole of gaseous carbon dioxide.

The factors involved in writing equations of this type are described as follows:

1. **The identity of products and reactants must be specified using chemical symbols.** In some cases, it is possible to predict the products of a reaction. More often, the reactants and products must be verified by chemical analysis. (Generally, you will be given information regarding the identity of the reactants and products.)
2. **Reactants are written to the left of the reaction arrow ($\rightarrow$), and products are written to the right.** The direction in which the arrow points indicates the direction in which the reaction proceeds. In the decomposition of calcium carbonate, the reactant on the left ($CaCO_3$) is converted to products on the right ($CaO + CO_2$) during the course of the reaction.
3. **The physical states of reactants and products may be shown in parentheses.** For example:

   - $CaO(s)$ means that calcium oxide is a solid.
   - $CO_2(g)$ indicates that carbon dioxide is in the gaseous state.
   - Alternatively, ($l$) indicates a substance is present as a liquid, and ($aq$) tells us a substance is present as an aqueous solution which means it is dissolved in water.

4. **The symbol $\Delta$ over the reaction arrow means that heat energy is necessary for the reaction to occur.** Often this and other special conditions are noted above or below the reaction arrow. For example, "light" means that a light source provides energy necessary for the reaction.
5. **The equation must be balanced.** All of the atoms of every reactant must also appear in the products, although in different compounds. We will treat this topic in detail later in this chapter.

*Reactions that utilize light energy are termed* photochemical reactions.

## The Experimental Basis of a Chemical Equation

The chemical equation must represent a chemical change: One or more substances are changed into new substances, with different chemical and physical properties. Evidence for the reaction may be based on observations such as

- the release of carbon dioxide gas when a carbonate is heated,
- the formation of a solid (or precipitate) when solutions of iron ions and hydroxide ions are mixed,
- the production of heat when using hot packs for treatment of injury, and
- the change in color of a solution upon addition of a second substance.

*See A Medical Perspective: Hot and Cold Packs in Chapter 7.*

Many reactions are not so obvious. Sophisticated instruments are available to chemists that allow the detection of subtle changes in chemical systems that would otherwise go unnoticed. Such instruments may measure

- heat or light absorbed or emitted as the result of a reaction,
- changes in the way the sample behaves in an electric or magnetic field before and after a reaction, and
- changes in electrical properties before and after a reaction.

Whether we use our senses or a million-dollar computerized instrument, the "bottom line" is the same: We are measuring a change in one or more chemical or physical properties in an effort to understand the changes taking place in a chemical system, the conversion of reactants to new products.

Disease can be described as a chemical system (actually a biochemical system) gone awry. Here, too, the underlying changes may not be obvious. Just as technology has helped chemists see subtle chemical changes in the laboratory, medical diagnosis has been revolutionized in our lifetimes using very similar technology. Some of these techniques are described in A Medical Perspective: Magnetic Resonance Imaging, in Chapter 9.

## Strategies for Writing Chemical Equations

Chemical reactions generally follow one of a few simple patterns: combination, decomposition, and single- or double-replacement. Recognizing the underlying pattern will improve your ability to write chemical equations and understand chemical reactions.

**LEARNING GOAL**

**6** Classify chemical reactions by type: combination, decomposition, or replacement.

### Combination Reactions

**Combination reactions** involve the joining of two or more elements or compounds, producing a product of different composition. The general form of a combination reaction is

$$A + B \longrightarrow AB$$

in which $A$ and $B$ represent reactant elements or compounds and $AB$ is the product.

Examples include

- combination of a metal and a nonmetal to form a salt,

$$Ca(s) + Cl_2(g) \longrightarrow CaCl_2(s)$$

- combination of hydrogen and chlorine molecules to produce hydrogen chloride,

$$H_2(g) + Cl_2(g) \longrightarrow 2HCl(g)$$

- formation of water from hydrogen and oxygen molecules,

$$2H_2(g) + O_2(g) \longrightarrow 2H_2O(g)$$

- reaction of magnesium oxide and carbon dioxide to produce magnesium carbonate,

$$MgO(s) + CO_2(g) \longrightarrow MgCO_3(s)$$

### Decomposition Reactions

**Decomposition reactions** produce two or more products from a single reactant. The general form of these reactions is the reverse of a combination reaction:

$$AB \longrightarrow A + B$$

Some examples are

- the heating of calcium carbonate to produce calcium oxide and carbon dioxide,

$$CaCO_3(s) \xrightarrow{\Delta} CaO(s) + CO_2(g)$$

- the removal of water from a hydrated material,

$$CuSO_4 \cdot 5H_2O(s) \longrightarrow CuSO_4(s) + 5H_2O(g)$$

*Hydrated compounds are described in the previous section.*

## Replacement Reactions

Replacement reactions include both *single-replacement* and *double-replacement*. In a **single-replacement reaction,** one atom replaces another in the compound, producing a new compound:

$$A + BC \longrightarrow AC + B$$

Examples include

In a single-replacement reaction, an element *replaces* an ion. In the first example, zinc metal is converted to $Zn^{2+}$ and replaces $Cu^{2+}$ in the $CuSO_4$. $Cu^{2+}$, in turn, is converted to copper metal.

- the replacement of copper by zinc in copper sulfate,

$$Zn(s) + CuSO_4(aq) \longrightarrow ZnSO_4(aq) + Cu(s)$$

- the replacement of aluminum by sodium in aluminum nitrate,

$$3Na(s) + Al(NO_3)_3(aq) \longrightarrow 3NaNO_3(aq) + Al(s)$$

A **double-replacement reaction,** on the other hand, involves *two compounds* undergoing a "change of partners." Two compounds react by exchanging atoms to produce two new compounds:

$$AB + CD \longrightarrow AD + CB$$

Examples include

Two ions *swap positions* in double-replacement reactions.

- the reaction of an acid (hydrochloric acid) and a base (sodium hydroxide) to produce water and salt, sodium chloride,

$$HCl(aq) + NaOH(aq) \longrightarrow H_2O(l) + NaCl(aq)$$

- the formation of solid barium sulfate from barium chloride and potassium sulfate,

$$BaCl_2(aq) + K_2SO_4(aq) \longrightarrow BaSO_4(s) + 2KCl(aq)$$

**Question 4.5**   Classify each of the following reactions as decomposition (D), combination (C), single-replacement (SR), or double-replacement (DR):

a. $HNO_3(aq) + KOH(aq) \longrightarrow KNO_3(aq) + H_2O(aq)$

b. $Al(s) + 3NiNO_3(aq) \longrightarrow Al(NO_3)_3(aq) + 3Ni(s)$

c. $KCN(aq) + HCl(aq) \longrightarrow HCN(aq) + KCl(aq)$

d. $MgCO_3(s) \longrightarrow MgO(s) + CO_2(g)$

**Question 4.6**   Classify each of the following reactions as decomposition (D), combination (C), single-replacement (SR), or double-replacement (DR):

a. $2Al(OH)_3(s) \xrightarrow{\Delta} Al_2O_3(s) + 3H_2O(g)$

b. $Fe_2S_3(s) \xrightarrow{\Delta} 2Fe(s) + 3S(s)$

c. $Na_2CO_3(aq) + BaCl_2(aq) \longrightarrow BaCO_3(s) + 2NaCl(aq)$

d. $C(s) + O_2(g) \xrightarrow{\Delta} CO_2(g)$

## 4.4  Balancing Chemical Equations

**LEARNING GOAL**

**7**  Balance chemical equations given the identity of products and reactants.

The chemical equation shows the *molar quantity* of reactants needed to produce a certain *molar quantity* of products. The relative number of mol of each product and reactant is indicated by placing a whole-number *coefficient* before the formula of each substance in the chemical equation. A coefficient of two (for example, 2Na) indicates that 2 mol of sodium are involved in the reaction. The coefficient one is understood, not written. Therefore, $Cl_2$ indicates 1 mol of chlorine is involved in the reaction that results in the formation of 2 mol of sodium chloride. This information is summarized in the equation:

$$2Na(s) + Cl_2(g) \longrightarrow 2NaCl(s)$$

The equation is balanced because there are two Na and two Cl on each side of the reaction arrow. Now consider the equation:

$$CaCO_3(s) \overset{\Delta}{\longrightarrow} CaO(s) + CO_2(g)$$

It is balanced as written. On the reactant side we have one mol of $CaCO_3$, which is:

> 1 mol Ca
>
> 1 mol C
>
> 3 mol O

The coefficients indicate *relative* numbers of mol: 10 mol of $CaCO_3$ produce 10 mol of CaO; 0.5 mol of $CaCO_3$ produce 0.5 mol of CaO; and so forth.

On the product side there are one mol of CaO and one mol of $CO_2$, which is:

> 1 mol Ca
>
> 1 mol C
>
> 3 mol O

*Therefore, the law of conservation of mass is obeyed*, and the equation is balanced as written.

Now consider the reaction of aqueous hydrogen chloride with solid calcium metal:

$$HCl(aq) + Ca(s) \longrightarrow CaCl_2(aq) + H_2(g)$$

The equation, as written, is not balanced.

| Reactants | Products |
|---|---|
| 1 mol H atoms | 2 mol H atoms |
| 1 mol Cl atoms | 2 mol Cl atoms |
| 1 mol Ca atoms | 1 mol Ca atoms |

We need 2 mol of both H and Cl on the left, or reactant, side. We must remember that *we cannot alter any chemical substance in the process of balancing the equation*. We can *only* introduce coefficients into the equation. Changing subscripts changes the identity of the substances involved, and that is not permitted. The equation must represent the reaction accurately. The correct equation is

Coefficients placed in front of the formula indicate the relative numbers of mol of compound (represented by the formula) that are involved in the reaction. Subscripts placed to the lower right of the atomic symbol indicate the relative number of atoms in the compound.

$$2HCl(aq) + Ca(s) \longrightarrow CaCl_2(aq) + H_2(g)$$
Balanced equation

Water ($H_2O$) and hydrogen peroxide ($H_2O_2$) illustrate the effect a subscript can have. The two compounds show marked differences in physical and chemical properties.

Many equations are balanced by trial and error. After the identity of the products and reactants, the physical states, and the reaction conditions are known, the following steps provide a method for correctly balancing a chemical equation:

Do not dismantle a polyatomic ion. It will retain its identity on both reactant and product sides.

**Step 1.** Count the number of mol of atoms of each element on both the reactant side and the product side.

**Step 2.** Determine which elements are not balanced.

Generally, when using trial and error, save H and O for the very end of the process.

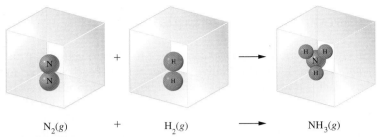

$$N_2(g) \quad + \quad H_2(g) \quad \longrightarrow \quad NH_3(g)$$

**(a)** Unbalanced equation.  The law of conservation of mass is not obeyed.

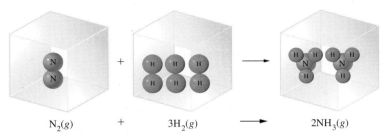

$$N_2(g) \quad + \quad 3H_2(g) \quad \longrightarrow \quad 2NH_3(g)$$

**(b)** Balanced equation.  The species are correct, and the law of conservation of mass is obeyed.

**Figure 4.5**  Balancing the equation $N_2(g) + H_2(g) \longrightarrow NH_3(g)$

**Step 3.** Balance one element at a time using coefficients. It is often most efficient to begin by balancing the atoms in the most complicated formulas.

**Step 4.** When you believe that you have successfully balanced the equation, check, as in step 1, to be certain that mass conservation has been achieved.

Let us apply these steps to the reaction of nitrogen and hydrogen (Figure 4.5).

$$N_2(g) + H_2(g) \longrightarrow NH_3(g)$$

**Step 1.**

| Reactants | Products |
|---|---|
| 2 mol N atoms | 1 mol N atoms |
| 2 mol H atoms | 3 mol H atoms |

**Step 2.** The numbers of mol of N and H are not balanced.

**Step 3.** Insertion of a 3 before $H_2(g)$ on the reactant side and a 2 before $NH_3(g)$ on the product side.

$$N_2(g) + 3H_2(g) \longrightarrow 2NH_3(g)$$

**Step 4.** Check to confirm that mass conservation has been achieved:

| Reactants | Products |
|---|---|
| 2 mol N atoms | 2 mol N atoms |
| 6 mol H atoms | 6 mol H atoms |

Hence, the equation is balanced. The balanced reaction equation used in industrial production of ammonia is illustrated in Figure 4.5.

Examples 4.9–4.10 illustrate equation-balancing strategies for a variety of commonly encountered situations.

**EXAMPLE 4.9**   **Balancing Equations**

Balance the following equation: Propane gas, $C_3H_8$, a fuel, reacts with oxygen gas to produce carbon dioxide and water vapor. The reaction is

$$C_3H_8(g) + O_2(g) \longrightarrow CO_2(g) + H_2O(g)$$

**Solution**

**Step 1.** Count the number of mol of atoms of each element on both the reactant side and the product side.

| Reactants | Products |
|---|---|
| 3 mol C atoms | 1 mol C atoms |
| 8 mol H atoms | 2 mol H atoms |
| 2 mol O atoms | 3 mol O atoms |

**Step 2.** Note that C, H, and O atoms are not balanced.

**Step 3.** First, balance the carbon atoms; save hydrogen and oxygen for later. There are 3 mol of carbon atoms on the left and only 1 mol of carbon atoms on the right. We need $3CO_2$ on the right side of the equation:

$$C_3H_8(g) + O_2(g) \longrightarrow 3CO_2(g) + H_2O(g)$$

Next, balance the hydrogen atoms; there are 8 mol of hydrogen atoms on the left and 2 mol of hydrogen atoms on the right. We need to place a 4 in front of $H_2O$ on the right side of the equation:

$$C_3H_8(g) + O_2(g) \longrightarrow 3CO_2(g) + 4H_2O(g)$$

There are now 2 mol of oxygen atoms (2 mol of O from 1 mol $O_2$) on the left and 10 mol of oxygen atoms on the right (4 mol O from 4 mol $H_2O$ and 6 mol O from 3 mol $CO_2$). To balance, we must have $5O_2$ (10 mol oxygen atoms) on the left side of the equation:

$$C_3H_8(g) + 5O_2(g) \longrightarrow 3CO_2(g) + 4H_2O(g)$$

**Step 4.** *Remember:* In every case, be sure to check the final equation to confirm that the law of conservation of mass is obeyed. There are 3 mol of C atoms, 8 mol of H atoms, and 10 mol of O atoms on each side of the reaction arrow.

**Practice Problem 4.9**

Balance the chemical equation:

$$C_2H_5OH(l) + O_2(g) \longrightarrow CO_2(g) + H_2O(g)$$

▶ For Further Practice: **Questions 4.69 and 4.70.**

**EXAMPLE 4.10**   **Balancing Equations**

Balance the following equation: Aqueous ammonium sulfate reacts with aqueous lead nitrate to produce aqueous ammonium nitrate and solid lead sulfate. The reaction is

$$(NH_4)_2SO_4(aq) + Pb(NO_3)_2(aq) \longrightarrow NH_4NO_3(aq) + PbSO_4(s)$$

**Solution**

In this double-replacement reaction, the polyatomic ions remain as intact units. Therefore, we can balance them as we would balance molecules rather than as atoms.

*Continued…*

**Step 1.** Count the number of mol of ions of each compound on both reactant and product side:

| Reactants | Products |
|-----------|----------|
| 2 mol $NH_4^+$ | 1 mol $NH_4^+$ |
| 1 mol $SO_4^{2-}$ | 1 mol $SO_4^{2-}$ |
| 1 mol $Pb^{2+}$ | 1 mol $Pb^{2+}$ |
| 2 mol $NO_3^-$ | 1 mol $NO_3^-$ |

**Step 2.** Note that $NH_4^+$ and $NO_3^-$ are not balanced.

**Step 3.** There are two ammonium ions on the left and only one ammonium ion on the right. To balance, the coefficient 2 is placed before $NH_4NO_3$ on the product side of the equation. Hence

$$(NH_4)_2SO_4(aq) + Pb(NO_3)_2(aq) \longrightarrow 2NH_4NO_3(aq) + PbSO_4(s)$$

**Step 4.** No further steps are necessary. The equation is now balanced. There are two ammonium ions, two nitrate ions, one lead ion, and one sulfate ion on each side of the reaction arrow.

---

### Practice Problem 4.10

Balance the chemical equation:

$$S_2Cl_2(s) + NH_3(g) \longrightarrow N_4S_4(s) + NH_4Cl(s) + S_8(s)$$

▶ For Further Practice: **Questions 4.71 and 4.72.**

---

## 4.5 Precipitation Reactions

Precipitation reactions include any chemical change in solution that results in one or more insoluble product(s). The insoluble product is termed a **precipitate.** For aqueous solution reactions, the product is insoluble in water.

An understanding of precipitation reactions is useful in many ways. They may explain natural phenomena, such as the formation of stalagmites and stalactites in caves; these are simply precipitates in rocklike form. Kidney stones may result from the precipitation of calcium oxalate ($CaC_2O_4$).

How do you know whether a precipitate will form? Readily available solubility tables, such as Table 4.1, make prediction rather easy.

Example 4.11 illustrates the process.

### LEARNING GOAL

**8** Write net ionic equations, and use solubility rules to predict the formation of a precipitate.

---

Precipitation reactions may be written as net ionic equations. See Section 4.6.

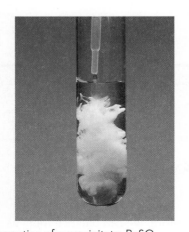

Formation of a precipitate, $BaSO_4$.

### TABLE 4.1 Solubilities of Some Common Ionic Compounds

| Soluble Compounds Contain | Exceptions |
|---------------------------|------------|
| Alkali metal ions ($Li^+$, $Na^+$, $K^+$, $Rb^+$, $Cs^+$) or the ammonium ion ($NH_4^+$) | |
| Nitrate ($NO_3^-$), bicarbonate ($HCO_3^-$), or chlorate ($ClO_3^-$) | |
| Halides ($Cl^-$, $Br^-$, $I^-$) | Compounds containing halides of $Ag^+$, $Hg_2^{2+}$, or $Pb^{2+}$ |
| Sulfate ($SO_4^{2-}$) | Compounds containing sulfate of $Ag^+$, $Ca^{2+}$, $Sr^{2+}$, $Ba^{2+}$, $Hg_2^{2+}$, or $Pb^{2+}$ |
| **Insoluble Compounds Contain** | **Exceptions** |
| Carbonate ($CO_3^{2-}$), phosphate ($PO_4^{3-}$), chromate ($CrO_4^{2-}$), or sulfide ($S^{2-}$) | Compounds containing alkali metal ions or the ammonium ion |
| Hydroxide ($OH^-$) | Compounds containing alkali metal ions or the $Ba^{2+}$ ion |

| EXAMPLE 4.11 | Predicting Whether Precipitation Will Occur |
|---|---|

Will a precipitate form if two solutions of the soluble salts NaCl and $AgNO_3$ are mixed?

**8** Write net ionic equations, and use solubility rules to predict the formation of a precipitate.

### Solution

**Step 1.** These soluble salts form ions in aqueous solutions. If a cation from one compound reacts with an anion from another compound, it will be a double-replacement reaction, which involves a "change of partners."

$$NaCl(aq) + AgNO_3(aq) \longrightarrow AgCl(?) + NaNO_3(?)$$

**Step 2.** Refer to Table 4.1 to determine the solubility of AgCl and $NaNO_3$. We predict that $NaNO_3$ is soluble and AgCl is not:

$$NaCl(aq) + AgNO_3(aq) \longrightarrow AgCl(s) + NaNO_3(aq)$$

**Step 3.** The fact that solid AgCl is predicted to form classifies this reaction as a precipitation reaction.

*Helpful Hints:* (*aq*) indicates a soluble species; (*s*) indicates a solid, an insoluble species.

### Practice Problem 4.11

Predict whether the following reactants, when mixed in aqueous solution, undergo a precipitation reaction. Write a balanced equation for each precipitation reaction.

a. potassium chloride and silver nitrate

b. potassium carbonate and calcium hydroxide

c. sodium hydroxide and ammonium chloride

d. sodium hydroxide and iron(II) chloride

▶ For Further Practice: **Questions 4.77 and 4.78.**

## 4.6   Net Ionic Equations

### Writing Net Ionic Equations

The equation that we developed in Example 4.11 is written as a *molecular equation.* Although technically correct and properly balanced, it conveys no information about the way the products and reactants exist in solution, other than the precipitate. In reality, all four species are ionic compounds; both reactants and one product are actually *dissociated* in solution, existing as ions. Only the product, AgCl, is associated. Our solubility rules predicted that AgCl is a solid, crystalline precipitate. A more useful representation would show all of the reactants and products in the form in which they are actually present in solution, solid AgCl surrounded by an aqueous collection of ions. This is an *ionic equation.* Even greater clarity can be achieved by removing the ions that do not change during the course of the reaction, *spectator ions,* to produce a *net ionic equation.* The net ionic equation only shows the chemical species that actually undergo change. This is the approach that is most faithful to our original concept of a chemical equation: an accurate depiction of chemical *change.* The process we use to write a net ionic equation for a precipitation reaction is as follows:

1. Write a balanced molecular equation for the process being considered. Use the solubility rules to identify any precipitates.
2. Write the ionic equation showing all reactants and products as free ions unless they are precipitates.
3. Ions that appear on both sides of the equation are *spectator ions* (they do not undergo change) and are cancelled out. What remains is the net ionic equation.
4. Ensure that charges and numbers of atoms are balanced, just as they must be in a conventional equation.

Example 4.12 shows how this procedure is applied.

| **EXAMPLE 4.12** | **Writing Net Ionic Equations** | | LEARNING GOAL |
|---|---|---|---|

In Example 4.11, we considered the reaction of NaCl and $AgNO_3$. We wrote the chemical equation for this process in the form of a molecular equation. Now, write this process as a net ionic equation.

**8** Write net ionic equations, and use solubility rules to predict the formation of a precipitate.

**Solution**

**Step 1.** Write the balanced molecular equation. In Example 4.11, we found:

$$NaCl(aq) + AgNO_3(aq) \longrightarrow AgCl(s) + NaNO_3(aq)$$

**Step 2.** AgCl is a precipitate and should be written in its associated form; all others are not, and should be written in ionic form:

$$Na^+(aq) + Cl^-(aq) + Ag^+(aq) + NO_3^-(aq) \longrightarrow AgCl(s) + Na^+(aq) + NO_3^-(aq)$$

This is the form of the ionic equation.

**Step 3.** $Na^+(aq)$ and $NO_3^-(aq)$ appear on both sides of the equation and are spectator ions that cancel out because they are unchanged during the course of the reaction:

$$\cancel{Na^+(aq)} + Cl^-(aq) + Ag^+(aq) + \cancel{NO_3^-(aq)} \longrightarrow AgCl(s) + \cancel{Na^+(aq)} + \cancel{NO_3^-(aq)}$$

**Step 4.** We must now ensure that both net charge and number of atoms of each kind are the same on both sides of the reaction arrow.

**Counting charges:**
**Reactants:** One positive charge, $Ag^+(aq)$, and one negative charge, $Cl^-(aq)$, result in a net charge of zero.
**Products:** AgCl has a zero charge.

**Counting atoms:**
**Reactants:** One Ag and one Cl atom
**Products:** One Ag and one Cl atom

Charges and numbers of atoms are balanced. The net ionic equation representing the precipitation of silver chloride is:

$$Ag^+(aq) + Cl^-(aq) \longrightarrow AgCl(s)$$

---

**Practice Problem 4.12**

Write net ionic equations for the following reactions:

a. $BaCl_2(aq) + ZnSO_4(aq) \longrightarrow$

b. $AgNO_3(aq) + Na_2SO_4(aq) \longrightarrow$

▶ For Further Practice: **Questions 4.81 and 4.82.**

---

Net ionic equations are useful, not only for precipitation reactions, but for any process involving ionic compounds in aqueous solution. We will see net ionic equations representing acid-base reactions in Chapter 8.

**Question 4.7**   A solution of $Na_2S$ is mixed with a solution of $CuCl_2$. A black precipitate is formed. Write the net ionic equation for the reaction, and identify the black precipitate.

**Question 4.8**   A solution of $Na_2CO_3$ is mixed with a solution of $CaCl_2$. A white precipitate is formed. Write the net ionic equation for the reaction, and identify the white precipitate.

# 4.7    Acid-Base Reactions

Another approach to the classification of chemical reactions is based on the gain or loss of hydrogen ions. **Acid-base reactions** involve the transfer of a *hydrogen ion,* $H^+$, from one reactant (the acid) to another (the base).

A common example of an acid-base reaction involves hydrochloric acid and sodium hydroxide:

$$\underset{\text{Acid}}{HCl(aq)} + \underset{\text{Base}}{NaOH(aq)} \longrightarrow \underset{\text{Water}}{H_2O(l)} + \underset{\text{Salt}}{NaCl(aq)}$$

A hydrogen cation, $H^+$, is transferred from the acid to the base, producing water and a salt in solution. When equal molar quantities of acid and base are mixed, the resulting reaction is termed a **neutralization reaction.** The net ionic equation for this process is

$$H^+(aq) + OH^-(aq) \longrightarrow H_2O(l)$$

Acid and base properties and reactions are important in virtually all aspects of chemistry and biochemistry; for this reason, they are considered in much greater detail in Chapter 8.

# 4.8    Oxidation-Reduction Reactions

Oxidation-reduction reactions are responsible for many types of chemical change. Corrosion of metals, combustion of fossil fuels, the operation of a battery, and biochemical energy-harvesting reactions are a few examples. In this section, we explore the basic concepts underlying this class of chemical reactions.

## Oxidation and Reduction

LEARNING GOAL

**10** Write oxidation and reduction half-reactions, and identify oxidizing agents and reducing agents.

**Oxidation** is defined as a loss of electrons, loss of hydrogen atoms, or gain of oxygen atoms.

*Magnesium metal,* is, for example, oxidized to a *magnesium ion,* losing two electrons when it reacts with a nonmetal such as chlorine:

$$Mg \longrightarrow Mg^{2+} + 2e^-$$

**Reduction** is defined as a gain of electrons, gain of hydrogen atoms, or loss of oxygen atoms.

*Diatomic chlorine* is reduced to *chloride ions* by gaining electrons when it reacts with a metal such as magnesium:

$$Cl_2 + 2e^- \longrightarrow 2Cl^-$$

Oxidation and reduction are complementary processes and are often termed *redox reactions.* The *oxidation half-reaction* produces electrons that are the reactants for the *reduction half-reaction.* The combination of two half-reactions, one oxidation and one reduction, produces the complete reaction:

Oxidation half-reaction:   $Mg \longrightarrow Mg^{2+} + 2e^-$
Reduction half-reaction:   $Cl_2 + 2e^- \longrightarrow 2Cl^-$
Complete redox reaction:   $Mg + Cl_2 \longrightarrow Mg^{2+} + 2Cl^-$

Half-reactions, one oxidation and one reduction, are exactly that: one-half of a complete reaction. The two half-reactions combine to produce the complete reaction. Note that the electrons cancel: in the electron transfer process, no free electrons remain.

Passing an electrical current through water causes an oxidation-reduction reaction. The products are $H_2$ and $O_2$ in a 2:1 ratio. Is this ratio of products predicted by the equation for the decomposition of water, $2H_2O(l) \longrightarrow 2H_2(g) + O_2(g)$? Explain.

Oxidation cannot occur without reduction, and vice versa. The reducing agent becomes oxidized and the oxidizing agent becomes reduced.

In the preceding reaction, magnesium metal is the **reducing agent.** It releases electrons for the reduction of chlorine. Chlorine is the **oxidizing agent.** It accepts electrons from the magnesium, which is oxidized.

The characteristics of oxidizing and reducing agents may be summarized as follows:

| Oxidizing Agent | Reducing Agent |
| --- | --- |
| • Is reduced | • Is oxidized |
| • Gains electrons | • Loses electrons |
| • Causes oxidation | • Causes reduction |

Oxidation-reduction processes are more difficult to identify using half-reactions when covalent compounds are involved. For example, consider the reaction of methane with oxygen:

$$\overset{\displaystyle \text{Loses H}}{CH_4(g) + 2O_2(g) \longrightarrow CO_2(g) + 2H_2O(g)}$$
$$\underset{\displaystyle \text{Gains H}}{}$$

Our definitions of oxidation and reduction make it clear that this is an oxidation-reduction reaction. Carbon has lost hydrogen and gained oxygen, becoming $CO_2$ (our definition of oxidation). Oxygen has gained hydrogen, becoming water (the gain of hydrogen indicates reduction).

Consider the reaction of aluminum with atmospheric oxygen:

$$\overset{\displaystyle \text{Gains O}}{4Al(s) + 3O_2(g) \longrightarrow 2Al_2O_3(s)}$$

Aluminum is strong, and its low density makes it ideal for the wings and cabin exterior of airplanes. Aluminum oxide forms on the metal surface, and this oxide coating protects the metal from further reaction.

It is evident that aluminum has been oxidized because it gains oxygen atoms.

**Question 4.9**    Write the oxidation half-reaction, the reduction half-reaction, and the complete reaction for the formation of calcium sulfide from the elements Ca and S. Remember, the electron gain *must* equal the electron loss.

**Question 4.10**    Write the oxidation half-reaction, the reduction half-reaction, and the complete reaction for the formation of calcium iodide from calcium metal and $I_2$. Remember, the electron gain *must* equal the electron loss.

**Question 4.11**    Identify the oxidizing agent, reducing agent, substance oxidized, and substance reduced in the reaction described in Question 4.9.

**Question 4.12**    Identify the oxidizing agent, reducing agent, substance oxidized, and substance reduced in the reaction described in Question 4.10.

## Voltaic Cells

LEARNING GOAL

**11**    Compare and contrast voltaic and electrolytic cells.

When zinc metal is dipped into a copper(II) sulfate solution, zinc atoms are oxidized to zinc ions and copper(II) ions are reduced to copper metal, which deposits on the surface of the zinc metal (Figure 4.6). This reaction is summarized as follows:

$$\overset{\displaystyle \text{Oxidation/e}^- \text{ loss}}{Zn(s) + Cu^{2+}(aq) \longrightarrow Zn^{2+}(aq) + Cu(s)}$$
$$\underset{\displaystyle \text{Reduction/e}^- \text{ gain}}{}$$

In the reduction of aqueous copper(II) ions by zinc metal, electrons flow from the zinc rod directly to copper(II) ions in the solution. If electron transfer from the zinc rod to the copper ions in solution could be directed through an external

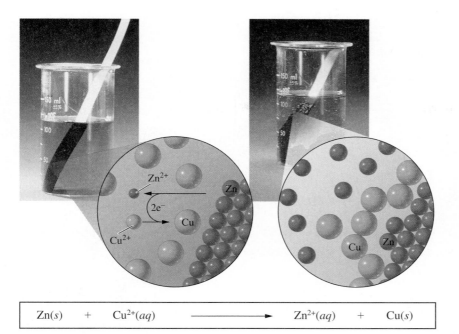

**Figure 4.6**  The spontaneous reaction of zinc metal and $Cu^{2+}$ ions is the basis of the voltaic cell depicted in Figure 4.7.

$$Zn(s) \quad + \quad Cu^{2+}(aq) \quad \longrightarrow \quad Zn^{2+}(aq) \quad + \quad Cu(s)$$

electrical circuit, this spontaneous oxidation-reduction reaction could be used to produce an electrical current that could perform some useful function.

However, when zinc metal in one container is connected by a copper wire with a copper(II) sulfate solution in a separate container, no current flows through the wire. A complete, or continuous, circuit is necessary for current to flow. To complete the circuit, we connect the two containers with a tube filled with a solution of an electrolyte such as potassium chloride. This tube is described as a *salt bridge.*

Current now flows through the external circuit (Figure 4.7). The device shown in Figure 4.7 is an example of a *voltaic cell.* A **voltaic cell** is an *electrochemical* cell that converts stored *chemical* energy into *electrical* energy.

This cell consists of two *half-cells.* The oxidation half-reaction occurs in one half-cell, and the reduction half-reaction occurs in the other half-cell. The sum of the two half-cell reactions is the overall oxidation-reduction reaction that describes the cell. The electrode at which oxidation occurs is called the **anode,** and the electrode at which reduction occurs is the **cathode.** In the device shown in Figure 4.7, the zinc metal is the anode. At this electrode, the zinc atoms are oxidized to zinc ions:

*Solutions of ionic salts are good conductors of electricity (Chapter 6).*

$$\text{Anode half-reaction: } Zn(s) \longrightarrow Zn^{2+}(aq) + 2e^{-}$$

Electrons released at the anode travel through the external circuit to the cathode (the copper rod) where they are transferred to copper(II) ions in the solution. Copper(II) ions are reduced to copper atoms that deposit on the copper metal surface, the cathode:

$$\text{Cathode half-reaction: } Cu^{2+}(aq) + 2e^{-} \longrightarrow Cu(s)$$

The sum of these half-cell reactions is the voltaic cell reaction:

$$Zn(s) + Cu^{2+}(aq) \longrightarrow Zn^{2+}(aq) + Cu(s)$$

Voltaic cells are found in many aspects of our lives, as a convenient and reliable source of electrical energy, the battery. Batteries convert stored chemical energy to an electrical current to power a wide array of different commercial appliances: radios, cellphones, computers, flashlights, and a host of other useful devices.

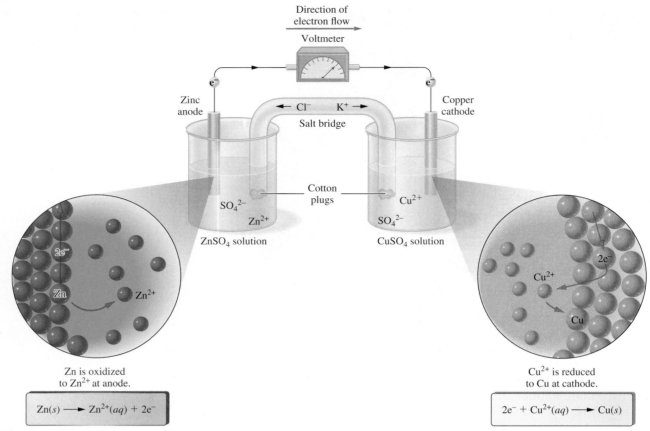

**Figure 4.7** A voltaic cell generating electrical current by the reaction:

$$Zn(s) + Cu^{2+}(aq) \longrightarrow Zn^{2+}(aq) + Cu(s)$$

Each electrode consists of the pure metal, zinc or copper. Zinc is oxidized, releasing electrons that flow to the copper, reducing $Cu^{2+}$ to Cu. The salt bridge completes the circuit, and the voltmeter displays the voltage (or chemical potential) associated with the reaction.

Technology has made modern batteries smaller, safer, and more dependable than our crudely constructed copper-zinc voltaic cell. A new generation of bio-compatible batteries are now available and can be implanted in the human body as part of a pacemaker circuit used to improve heart rhythm.

## Electrolysis

**Electrolysis** reactions use electrical energy to cause nonspontaneous oxidation-reduction reactions to occur. One common application of electrolysis is the rechargeable battery. When it is being used to power a device, such as a laptop computer, it behaves as a voltaic cell. After some time, the chemical reaction approaches completion and the voltaic cell "runs down." The cell reaction is reversible, and the battery is plugged into a battery charger. The charger is really an external source of electrical energy that reverses the chemical reaction in the battery, bringing it back to its original state. The cell has been operated as an electrolytic cell. Removal of the charging device turns the cell back into a voltaic device, ready to spontaneously react to produce electrical current once again.

Another common example of electrolysis is electroplating. This process is used to cover less expensive and unappealing metal objects with a thin, chemi-cally stable, and (usually) lustrous surface. Chromium (chrome plating) and silver (silver-plated dinnerware) are most common.

The object to be plated (for example, a spoon or fork) is the cathode (negative charge) in an electrolytic cell. The solution surrounding the cathode contains silver ions ($Ag^+$) that migrate to the cathode, undergoing reduction:

$$\text{Cathode half-reaction: } Ag^+(aq) + e^- \longrightarrow Ag(s)$$

The silver metal remains on the surface of the object being plated. The spoon or fork has the appearance of expensive silver at a fraction of the cost.

**Question 4.13** Chrome plating involves the reduction of $Cr^{3+}(aq)$ at the surface of the electrode to be electroplated.
  a. Must the electrode that is being electroplated have a positive or negative charge? Why?
  b. Is this electrode termed the cathode or the anode?
  c. Write the reduction reaction for $Cr^{3+}(aq)$.

**Question 4.14** $Cu^{2+}(aq)$ can be reduced in an electrolytic cell to prepare high-purity copper metal.
  a. Does this reduction take place at the positive or negative electrode of the electrolytic cell? Why?
  b. In this electrode termed the cathode or the anode?
  c. Write the reduction reaction for $Cu^{2+}(aq)$.

## Applications of Oxidation and Reduction

Oxidation-reduction reactions are important in many areas as diverse as industrial manufacturing and biochemical processes.

### Corrosion

The deterioration of metals caused by an oxidation-reduction reaction is termed **corrosion.** Metal atoms are converted to metal ions; the structure, hence the properties, changes dramatically and usually for the worse.

Millions of dollars are spent annually in an attempt to remedy damage resulting from corrosion. A current area of chemical research is concerned with the development of corrosion-inhibiting processes. In one type of corrosion, elemental iron is oxidized to iron(III) oxide (rust):

$$4Fe(s) + 3O_2(g) \longrightarrow 2Fe_2O_3(s)$$

### Combustion

Burning fossil fuel (coal, oil, gasoline, and natural gas) releases energy. This energy is used to heat our homes, offices, and classrooms. The combustion of gasoline is used for transportation. The simplest fossil fuel and major component of natural gas is methane, $CH_4$, and its oxidation reaction is written:

$$CH_4(g) + 2O_2(g) \longrightarrow CO_2(g) + 2H_2O(g)$$

Methane is a hydrocarbon because its chemical formula contains only hydrogens and carbon. The complete oxidation of any hydrocarbon (including those in gasoline, heating oil, and liquid propane) produces carbon dioxide and water. The unseen product, energy, released by these reactions is of paramount importance. The water and carbon dioxide are viewed as waste products, and the carbon dioxide contributes to the *greenhouse effect* (Chapter 5) and global warming.

### Bleaching

Bleaching agents are most often oxidizing agents. Since sodium hypochlorite (NaOCl) is an effective oxidizing agent, it is active ingredient in a variety of laundry products advertised for their stain-removing capabilities. Stains are a result of colored compounds adhering to surfaces. Oxidation of these compounds produces

**LEARNING GOAL**

**12** Describe examples of redox processes.

At the same time that iron is oxidized, $O_2$ is being reduced to $O^{2-}$ and is incorporated into the structure of iron(III) oxide. Electrons lost by iron reduce oxygen. This again shows that oxidation and reduction reactions go hand in hand.

*See Chapters 21–23 for the details of these energy-harvesting cellular oxidation-reduction reactions.*

Some reactions of metals with oxygen are very rapid. A dramatic example is the reaction of magnesium with oxygen.

$$2Mg(s) + O_2(g) \longrightarrow 2MgO(s)$$

products that are not colored or compounds that are subsequently easily removed from the surface, thus removing the stain.

### Metabolism

When ethanol is metabolized in the liver, it is oxidized to acetaldehyde (the molecule partially responsible for hangovers). Continued oxidation of acetaldehyde produces acetic acid, which is eventually oxidized to $CO_2$ and $H_2O$. These reactions, summarized as follows, are catalyzed by liver enzymes.

$$CH_3CH_2OH \xrightarrow[\text{enzymes}]{\text{liver}} CH_3\overset{\overset{O}{\|}}{C}H \xrightarrow[\text{enzymes}]{\text{liver}} CH_3\overset{\overset{O}{\|}}{C}OH \xrightarrow[\text{enzymes}]{\text{liver}} CO_2 + H_2O$$

ethanol                acetaldehyde            acetic acid

It is more difficult to recognize these reactions as oxidations because neither the product nor the reactant carries a charge. In previous examples, we looked for an increase in positive charge, signifying a loss of electrons, as an indication that an oxidation had occurred. An increase in positive charge (or decrease in negative charge) would signify oxidation.

Once again our descriptions of oxidation and reduction are useful in identifying these reactions. Recall:

> Oxidation is the *gain* of oxygen or *loss* of hydrogen.
> Reduction is the *loss* of oxygen or *gain* of hydrogen.

This strategy is most useful for recognizing oxidation and reduction of *organic compounds* and organic compounds of biological interest, *biochemical compounds*.

In our example of the conversion of ethanol to acetaldehyde, ethanol has six hydrogen atoms per molecule; the product acetaldehyde has four hydrogen atoms per molecule. This represents a loss of two hydrogen atoms per molecule. Therefore, ethanol has been oxidized to acetaldehyde. In a subsequent step, the acetaldehyde is oxidized to acetic acid (the active ingredient in vinegar).

Acetaldehyde has one oxygen atom per molecule; acetic acid has two. An increase in the number of oxygen atoms per molecule indicates oxidation has occurred. In the process of fermentation of grapes to make wine, the ethanol formed may convert to acetic acid over time, and vinegar, rather than wine, is the result.

Organic compounds and their structures and reactivity are the focus of Chapters 10 through 15, and biochemical compounds are described in Chapters 16 through 23.

### Chemical Control of Microbes

Many common antiseptics and disinfectants are oxidizing agents. An antiseptic is used to destroy pathogens associated with living tissue. A disinfectant is a substance that is used to kill or inhibit the growth of pathogens, disease-causing microorganisms, on environmental surfaces.

Hydrogen peroxide is an effective antiseptic that is commonly used to cleanse cuts and abrasions. We are all familiar with the furious bubbling (due to the rapid release of oxygen gas) that occurs as catalase, an enzyme from our cells, catalyzes the breakdown of $H_2O_2$:

$$2H_2O_2(aq) \longrightarrow 2H_2O(l) + O_2(g)$$

At higher concentrations (3–6%), $H_2O_2$ is used as a disinfectant. It is particularly useful for disinfection of soft contact lenses, utensils, and surgical implants because there is no residual toxicity. Concentrations of 6–25% are even used for complete sterilization of environmental surfaces. Disinfectants such as $H_2O_2$ solutions are critically important in the fight against outbreaks of highly infectious diseases such as Ebola and influenza.

## 4.9  Calculations Using the Chemical Equation

### General Principles

The calculation of quantities of products and reactants based on a balanced chemical equation is termed *stoichiometry* and is important in many fields. The synthesis of drugs and other complex molecules on a large scale is conducted on the basis of a balanced equation. This minimizes the waste of expensive chemical compounds used in these reactions. Similarly, the ratio of fuel and air in a home furnace or automobile must be adjusted carefully, according to their combining ratio, to maximize energy conversion, minimize fuel consumption, and minimize pollution.

In carrying out chemical calculations, we apply the following guidelines:

1. The chemical formulas of all reactants and products must be known.
2. The basis for the calculations is a balanced equation because the conservation of mass must be obeyed. If the equation is not properly balanced, the calculation is meaningless.
3. The calculations are performed in terms of mol. The coefficients in the balanced equation represent the relative number of mol of products and reactants.

We have seen that the number of mol of products and reactants often differs in a balanced equation. For example,

$$C(s) + O_2(g) \longrightarrow CO_2(g)$$

is a balanced equation. Two mol of reactants combine to produce 1 mol of product:

$$1 \text{ mol C} + 1 \text{ mol O}_2 \longrightarrow 1 \text{ mol CO}_2$$

However, 1 mol of C *atoms* and 2 mol of O *atoms* produce 1 mol of C *atoms* and 2 mol of O *atoms*. In other words, the number of mol of reactants and products may differ, but the number of mol of atoms cannot. The formation of $CO_2$ from C and $O_2$ may be described as follows:

$$C(s) + O_2(g) \longrightarrow CO_2(g)$$
$$1 \text{ mol C} + 1 \text{ mol O}_2 \longrightarrow 1 \text{ mol CO}_2$$
$$12.0 \text{ g C} + 32.0 \text{ g O}_2 \longrightarrow 44.0 \text{ g CO}_2$$

### Using Conversion Factors

**Conversion Between Moles and Grams**

The mol is the basis of our calculations. However, mol are generally measured in g. A facility for interconversion of mol and g is fundamental to chemical arithmetic (see Figure 4.2). Conversion from mol to g, and vice versa, requires only the formula mass of the compound of interest. These calculations, discussed earlier in this chapter, are reviewed in Example 4.13.

**EXAMPLE 4.13**   **Converting Between Moles and Mass**

LEARNING GOAL

**3**  Determine molar mass, and demonstrate how it is used to solve mole and mass conversion calculations.

a. Convert 1.00 mol of oxygen gas, $O_2$, to g.

**Solution**

**Step 1.** Use the following path:

$$\text{mol O}_2 \longrightarrow \text{g O}_2$$

*Continued…*

**Step 2.** The molar mass of oxygen ($O_2$) is 32.00 g $O_2$, and the conversion factor becomes:

$$\frac{32.00 \text{ g } O_2}{1 \text{ mol } O_2}$$

**Step 3.** Using the conversion factor (ensure that mol $O_2$ cancel):

$$1.00 \text{ } \cancel{\text{mol } O_2} \times \frac{32.00 \text{ g } O_2}{1 \text{ } \cancel{\text{mol } O_2}} = 32.0 \text{ g } O_2$$

Data Given × Conversion Factor = Desired Result

b. How many g of carbon dioxide are contained in 10.0 mol of carbon dioxide?

**Solution**

**Step 1.** Use the following path:

$$\boxed{\text{mol } CO_2} \longrightarrow \boxed{\text{g } CO_2}$$

**Step 2.** The molar mass of $CO_2$ is 44.01 g $CO_2$, and the conversion factor becomes:

$$\frac{44.01 \text{ g } CO_2}{1 \text{ mol } CO_2}$$

**Step 3.** Using the conversion factor (ensure that mol $CO_2$ cancel):

$$10.0 \text{ } \cancel{\text{mol } CO_2} \times \frac{44.01 \text{ g } CO_2}{1 \text{ } \cancel{\text{mol } CO_2}} = 4.40 \times 10^2 \text{ g } CO_2$$

Data Given × Conversion Factor = Desired Result

*Helpful Hint:* Note that each conversion factor can be inverted, producing a second possible conversion factor. Only one will allow the appropriate unit cancellation.

---

**Practice Problem 4.13**

Perform each of the following conversions:

   a. 5.00 mol of water to g of water      c. $1.00 \times 10^{-5}$ mol of $C_6H_{12}O_6$ to micrograms (μg) of $C_6H_{12}O_6$
   b. 25.0 g of LiCl to mol of LiCl         d. 35.0 g of $MgCl_2$ to mol of $MgCl_2$

▶ For Further Practice: **Questions 4.33 and 4.34.**

---

**LEARNING GOAL**

**13**  Use a chemical equation and a given number of moles or mass of a reactant or product to calculate the number of moles or mass of a reactant or product.

**Conversion of Moles of Reactants to Moles of Products**

In Example 4.9, we balanced the equation for the reaction of propane and oxygen as follows:

$$C_3H_8(g) + 5O_2(g) \longrightarrow 3CO_2(g) + 4H_2O(g)$$

In this reaction, 1 mol of $C_3H_8$ corresponds to, or results in,

   5 mol of $O_2$ being consumed and
   3 mol of $CO_2$ being formed and
   4 mol of $H_2O$ being formed.

This information may be written in the form of a conversion factor, the molar ratio:

$$\frac{1 \text{ mol C}_3\text{H}_8}{5 \text{ mol O}_2}$$     *Translated:* 1 mol of $C_3H_8$ reacts with 5 mol of $O_2$.

$$\frac{1 \text{ mol C}_3\text{H}_8}{3 \text{ mol CO}_2}$$     *Translated:* 1 mol of $C_3H_8$ produces 3 mol of $CO_2$.

$$\frac{1 \text{ mol C}_3\text{H}_8}{4 \text{ mol H}_2\text{O}}$$     *Translated:* 1 mol of $C_3H_8$ produces 4 mol of $H_2O$.

Conversion factors based on the chemical equation permit us to perform a variety of calculations.

Let us look at Examples 4.14–4.16; each is based on the combustion of propane and the equation that we balanced in Example 4.9.

---

**EXAMPLE 4.14**    **Calculating Mass of Reactant from Moles of Reactant**

Calculate the number of g of $O_2$ that will react with 1.00 mol of $C_3H_8$. The balanced equation is: $C_3H_8(g) + 5O_2(g) \longrightarrow 3CO_2(g) + 4H_2O(g)$.

**LEARNING GOAL**

**13** Use a chemical equation and a given number of moles or mass of a reactant or product to calculate the number of moles or mass of a reactant or product.

**Solution**

**Step 1.** Our path is:

$$\boxed{\text{mol } C_3H_8} \longrightarrow \boxed{\text{mol } O_2} \longrightarrow \boxed{\text{g } O_2}$$

**Step 2.** Two conversion factors are necessary to solve this problem:

- conversion from mol of $C_3H_8$ to mol of $O_2$ and
- conversion of mol of $O_2$ to g of $O_2$.

The balanced equation indicates that the conversion factor relating the two reactants is based on 1 mol $C_3H_8 = 5$ mol $O_2$. The conversion factor that relates mol to g is constructed from the molar mass, 32.00 g $O_2 = 1$ mol $O_2$.

**Step 3.** Set up conversion factors to cancel mol $C_3H_8$ and mol $O_2$:

$$1.00 \text{ mol C}_3\text{H}_8 \times \frac{5 \text{ mol O}_2}{1 \text{ mol C}_3\text{H}_8} \times \frac{32.00 \text{ g O}_2}{1 \text{ mol O}_2} = 1.60 \times 10^2 \text{ g O}_2$$

Data Given × Conversion Factor × Conversion Factor = Desired Result

---

**Practice Problem 4.14**

When potassium cyanide (KCN) reacts with hydrochloric acid, hydrogen cyanide (HCN), a poisonous gas, is produced. The equation is

$$KCN(aq) + HCl(aq) \longrightarrow KCl(aq) + HCN(g)$$

Calculate the number of g of KCN that will react with 1.00 mol of HCl.

▶ For Further Practice: **Questions 4.101 and 4.102.**

**EXAMPLE 4.15** **Calculating Mass of Product from Moles of Reactant**

LEARNING GOAL

Calculate the number of g of $CO_2$ produced from the combustion of 1.00 mol of $C_3H_8$ using the balanced equation from Example 4.14.

**13**  Use a chemical equation and a given number of moles or mass of a reactant or product to calculate the number of moles or mass of a reactant or product.

**Solution**

**Step 1.** Use the following path:

$$\begin{array}{ccc} \text{mol} & \text{mol} & \text{g} \\ C_3H_8 & \longrightarrow & CO_2 & \longrightarrow & CO_2 \end{array}$$

**Step 2.** The balanced equation indicates that the conversion factor relating the reactant $C_3H_8$ to the product $CO_2$ is based on 1 mol $C_3H_8$ = 3 mol $CO_2$. The conversion factor that relates mol to g is constructed from the molar mass, 44.01 g $CO_2$ = 1 mol $CO_2$.

**Step 3.** Set up conversion factors to cancel mol $C_3H_8$ and mol $CO_2$:

$$1.00 \ \text{mol } C_3H_8 \times \frac{3 \ \text{mol } CO_2}{1 \ \text{mol } C_3H_8} \times \frac{44.01 \ \text{g } CO_2}{1 \ \text{mol } CO_2} = 132 \ \text{g } CO_2$$

Data Given × Conversion Factor × Conversion Factor = Desired Result

**Practice Problem 4.15**

Fermentation is a critical step in the process of winemaking. The reaction is

$$C_6H_{12}O_6(aq) \longrightarrow 2CH_3CH_2OH(aq) + 2CO_2(g)$$
$$\text{glucose} \qquad\qquad \text{ethanol}$$

Calculate the number of g of ethanol produced from the fermentation of 5.00 mol of glucose.

▶ For Further Practice: **Questions 4.103 and 4.104.**

**EXAMPLE 4.16** **Calculating Mass of Reactant from Mass of Product**

LEARNING GOAL

Calculate the number of g of $C_3H_8$ required to produce 36.0 g of $H_2O$ using the balanced equation from Example 4.14.

**13**  Use a chemical equation and a given number of moles or mass of a reactant or product to calculate the number of moles or mass of a reactant or product.

**Solution**

**Step 1.** Use the following path:

$$\begin{array}{cccc} \text{g} & \text{mol} & \text{mol} & \text{g} \\ H_2O & \longrightarrow & H_2O & \longrightarrow & C_3H_8 & \longrightarrow & C_3H_8 \end{array}$$

**Step 2.** It is necessary to convert g of $H_2O$ to mol of $H_2O$, mol of $H_2O$ to mol of $C_3H_8$, and mol of $C_3H_8$ to g of $C_3H_8$. The molar mass of $H_2O$ (18.0 g $H_2O$ = 1 mol $H_2O$) is the conversion factor that will convert from g $H_2O$ to mol $H_2O$. The balanced equation indicates that the conversion factor relating the reactant $C_3H_8$ to the product $H_2O$ is based on 1 mol $C_3H_8$ = 4 mol $H_2O$. The conversion factor that relates mol to g is constructed from the molar mass, 44.09 g $C_3H_8$ = 1 mol $C_3H_8$.

# A Human Perspective

## The Chemistry of Automobile Air Bags

Each year, thousands of individuals are killed or seriously injured in automobile accidents. Perhaps most serious is the front-end collision. The car decelerates or stops virtually on impact; the momentum of the passengers, however, does not stop, and the driver and passengers are thrown forward toward the dashboard and the windshield. Suddenly, passive parts of the automobile, such as control knobs, the rearview mirror, the steering wheel, the dashboard, and the windshield, become lethal weapons.

Automobile engineers have been aware of these problems for a long time. They have made a series of design improvements to lessen the potential problems associated with front-end impact. Smooth switches rather than knobs, recessed hardware, and padded dashboards are examples. These changes, coupled with the use of lap and shoulder belts, which help to immobilize occupants of the car, have decreased the frequency and severity of occupant impact and lowered the death rate for this type of accident.

An almost ideal protection would be a soft, fluffy pillow, providing a cushion against impact. Such a device, an air bag inflated only on impact, is now standard equipment for the protection of the driver and front-seat passenger.

How does it work? Ideally, it inflates only when severe front-end impact occurs; it inflates very rapidly [in approximately 40 milliseconds (ms)], then deflates to provide a steady deceleration, cushioning the occupants from impact. A variety of simple chemical reactions make this a reality.

Our strategy uses sodium azide, $NaN_3$. When solid sodium azide is detonated by mechanical energy produced by an electrical current, it decomposes to form solid sodium and nitrogen gas:

$$2NaN_3(s) \longrightarrow 2Na(s) + 3N_2(g)$$

State trooper inspects accident with airbag deployment

The nitrogen gas inflates the air bag, cushioning the driver and front-seat passenger.

The solid sodium azide has a high density (characteristic of solids) and thus occupies a small volume. It can easily be stored in the center of a steering wheel or in the dashboard. The rate of detonation is very rapid. The reaction produces 3 mol of $N_2$ gas for every 2 mol of $NaN_3$. The $N_2$ gas occupies a large volume relative to the solid $NaN_3$ because, like all gases, its density is low.

Figuring out how much sodium azide is needed to produce enough nitrogen to properly inflate the bag is an example of a practical application of the chemical arithmetic we are learning in this chapter.

### For Further Understanding

▸ Why is nitrogen gas preferred for this application?
▸ If this reaction occurs in 5 ms, how many seconds (s) does this represent?

---

**Step 3.** Set up conversion factors to cancel g $H_2O$, mol $H_2O$, and mol $C_3H_8$:

$$36.0 \text{ g } H_2O \times \frac{1 \text{ mol } H_2O}{18.0 \text{ g } H_2O} \times \frac{1 \text{ mol } C_3H_8}{4 \text{ mol } H_2O} \times \frac{44.09 \text{ g } C_3H_8}{1 \text{ mol } C_3H_8} = 22.0 \text{ g } C_3H_8$$

Data Given × Conversion Factor × Conversion Factor × Conversion Factor = Desired Result

### Practice Problem 4.16

The balanced equation for the combustion of ethanol (ethyl alcohol) is

$$C_2H_5OH(l) + 3O_2(g) \longrightarrow 2CO_2(g) + 3H_2O(g)$$

a. How many mol of $O_2$ will react with 1 mol of ethanol?
b. How many g of $O_2$ will react with 1 mol of ethanol?
c. How many g of $CO_2$ will be produced by the combustion of 1 mol of ethanol?

▸ For Further Practice: **Questions 4.105 and 4.106.**

Let's consider an example that requires us to write and balance the chemical equation, use conversion factors, and calculate the amount of a reactant consumed in the chemical reaction.

---

**EXAMPLE 4.17**   | **Calculating Reactant Quantities**

LEARNING GOAL

**13**   Use a chemical equation and a given number of moles or mass of a reactant or product to calculate the number of moles or mass of a reactant or product.

Calcium hydroxide may be used to neutralize (completely react with) aqueous hydrochloric acid. Calculate the number of g of hydrochloric acid that would be neutralized by 0.500 mol of solid calcium hydroxide.

**Solution**

**Step 1.** The chemical formulas for $Ca(OH)_2$ and HCl are used to write the unbalanced equation that includes the products of this acid-base reaction, calcium chloride and water:

$$Ca(OH)_2(s) + HCl(aq) \longrightarrow CaCl_2(aq) + H_2O(l)$$

**Step 2.** Balance the equation:

$$Ca(OH)_2(s) + 2HCl(aq) \longrightarrow CaCl_2(aq) + 2H_2O(l)$$

**Step 3.** Use the following path:

$$\boxed{\begin{array}{c} \text{mol} \\ Ca(OH)_2 \end{array}} \longrightarrow \boxed{\begin{array}{c} \text{mol} \\ HCl \end{array}} \longrightarrow \boxed{\begin{array}{c} \text{g} \\ HCl \end{array}}$$

**Step 4.** Determine the necessary conversions:

- mol of $Ca(OH)_2$ to mol of HCl and
- mol of HCl to g of HCl

The balanced equation indicates that the conversion factor relating the two reactants is based on 1 mol $Ca(OH)_2$ = 2 mol HCl. The conversion factor that relates mol HCl to g HCl is constructed from the molar mass, 36.46 g HCl = 1 mol HCl.

**Step 5.**

$$0.500 \ \text{mol} \ Ca(OH)_2 \times \frac{2 \ \text{mol HCl}}{1 \ \text{mol} \ Ca(OH)_2} \times \frac{36.46 \ \text{g HCl}}{1 \ \text{mol HCl}} = 36.5 \ \text{g HCl}$$

Data Given × Conversion Factor × Conversion Factor = Desired Result

This reaction is illustrated in Figure 4.8.

*Helpful Hints:*

1. Writing ionic formulas from compound names is explained in Section 3.2.
2. Recall that the reaction between an acid and a base produces a salt and water (Section 4.7 and further discussed in Chapter 8).
3. Remember to balance the chemical equation; the proper coefficients are essential parts of the subsequent calculations.

---

**Practice Problem 4.17**

Metallic iron reacts with $O_2$ gas to produce iron(III) oxide.

a. Write and balance the equation.   b. Calculate the number of g of iron needed to produce 5.00 g of product.

▶ For Further Practice: **Questions 4.109 and 4.110.**

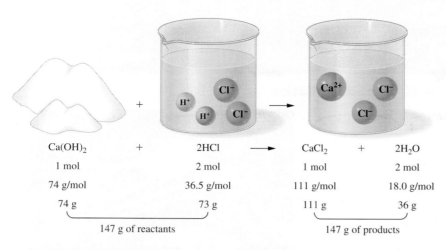

$$Ca(OH)_2 \quad + \quad 2HCl \quad \longrightarrow \quad CaCl_2 \quad + \quad 2H_2O$$

| 1 mol | 2 mol | 1 mol | 2 mol |
| 74 g/mol | 36.5 g/mol | 111 g/mol | 18.0 g/mol |
| 74 g | 73 g | 111 g | 36 g |

147 g of reactants                    147 g of products

**Figure 4.8** An illustration of the law of conservation of mass. In this example, 1 mol of calcium hydroxide and 2 mol of hydrogen chloride react to produce 3 mol of product (2 mol of water and 1 mol of calcium chloride). The total mass, in g, of reactant(s) consumed is equal to the total mass, in g, of product(s) formed. *Note:* In reality, HCl does not exist as discrete molecules in water. The HCl separates to form $H^+$ and $Cl^-$. Ionization in water will be discussed with the chemistry of acids and bases in Chapter 8.

---

**EXAMPLE 4.18**    **Calculating Reactant Quantities**

LEARNING GOAL

**13** Use a chemical equation and a given number of moles or mass of a reactant or product to calculate the number of moles or mass of a reactant or product.

What mass of sodium hydroxide, NaOH, would be required to produce 8.00 g of the antacid milk of magnesia, $Mg(OH)_2$, by the reaction of $MgCl_2$ with NaOH?

**Solution**

**Step 1.**  Write and balance the equation:

$$MgCl_2(aq) + 2NaOH(aq) \longrightarrow Mg(OH)_2(s) + 2NaCl(aq)$$

**Step 2.**  Determine the strategy:

The equation tells us that 2 mol of NaOH form 1 mol of $Mg(OH)_2$. If we calculate the number of mol of $Mg(OH)_2$ in 8.00 g of $Mg(OH)_2$, we can determine the number of mol of NaOH necessary and then the mass of NaOH required:

$$\boxed{\text{g } Mg(OH)_2} \longrightarrow \boxed{\text{mol } Mg(OH)_2} \longrightarrow \boxed{\text{mol } NaOH} \longrightarrow \boxed{\text{g } NaOH}$$

**Step 3.**  The conversion factor to convert g $Mg(OH)_2$ to mol $Mg(OH)_2$ is:

$$58.3 \text{ g } Mg(OH)_2 = 1 \text{ mol } Mg(OH)_2$$

Therefore, using the molar mass of $Mg(OH)_2$,

$$8.00 \text{ g } Mg(OH)_2 \times \frac{1 \text{ mol } Mg(OH)_2}{58.3 \text{ g } Mg(OH)_2} = 0.137 \text{ mol } Mg(OH)_2$$

**Step 4.**  Two moles of NaOH react to give 1 mol of $Mg(OH)_2$. Therefore, using the molar ratio,

$$0.137 \text{ mol } Mg(OH)_2 \times \frac{2 \text{ mol } NaOH}{1 \text{ mol } Mg(OH)_2} = 0.274 \text{ mol } NaOH$$

**Step 5.**  The conversion factor to convert mol to mass NaOH is: 40.0 g of NaOH = 1 mol of NaOH. Therefore, using the molar mass of NaOH,

$$0.274 \text{ mol } NaOH \times \frac{40.0 \text{ g } NaOH}{1 \text{ mol } NaOH} = 11.0 \text{ g } NaOH$$

This calculation may also be done in a single step:

$$8.00 \text{ g } Mg(OH)_2 \times \frac{1 \text{ mol } Mg(OH)_2}{58.3 \text{ g } Mg(OH)_2} \times \frac{2 \text{ mol } NaOH}{1 \text{ mol } Mg(OH)_2} \times \frac{40.0 \text{ g } NaOH}{1 \text{ mol } NaOH} = 11.0 \text{ g } NaOH$$

Data Given × Conversion Factor × Conversion Factor × Conversion Factor = Desired Result

*Continued…*

# A Medical Perspective

## Carbon Monoxide Poisoning: A Case of Combining Ratios

A fuel, such as methane, $CH_4$, burned in an excess of oxygen produces carbon dioxide and water:

$$CH_4(g) + 2O_2(g) \longrightarrow CO_2(g) + 2H_2O(g)$$

The same combustion in the presence of insufficient oxygen produces carbon monoxide and water:

$$2CH_4(g) + 3O_2(g) \longrightarrow 2CO(g) + 4H_2O(g)$$

The combustion of methane, repeated over and over in millions of gas furnaces that use natural gas as a fuel, is responsible for heating many of our homes in the winter. The furnace is designed to operate under conditions that favor the first reaction and minimize the second; excess oxygen is available from the surrounding atmosphere. Furthermore, the vast majority of exhaust gases (containing principally CO, $CO_2$, $H_2O$, and unburned fuel) are removed from the home through the chimney. However, if the chimney becomes obstructed, or the burner malfunctions, carbon monoxide levels within the home can rapidly reach hazardous levels.

Why is exposure to carbon monoxide hazardous? Hemoglobin, an iron-containing compound in our blood, binds with $O_2$ and transports it throughout the body. Carbon monoxide also combines with hemoglobin, thereby blocking oxygen transport. The binding affinity of hemoglobin for carbon monoxide is about 200 times greater than for $O_2$. Therefore, to maintain $O_2$ binding and transport capability, our exposure to carbon monoxide must be minimal. Proper ventilation and a suitable oxygen-to-fuel ratio are essential for any combustion process in the home, automobile, or workplace. In recent years, carbon monoxide sensors have been developed. These sensors sound an alarm when potentially toxic levels of CO are reached. Warning devices like this have helped to create a safer indoor environment.

The example we have chosen is an illustration of what is termed the *law of multiple proportions*. This law states that identical reactants may produce different products, depending on their combining ratio. The experimental conditions (in this

A carbon monoxide meter detects the concentration of the odorless and colorless gas and sounds an alarm when the concentration reaches preset levels.

case, the quantity of available oxygen) determine the preferred path of the chemical reaction.

**For Further Understanding**

▸ Why may new, stricter insulation standards for homes and businesses inadvertently increase the risk of carbon monoxide poisoning?

▸ Explain the link between smoking and carbon monoxide that has motivated many states and municipalities to ban smoking in restaurants, offices, and other indoor spaces.

*Helpful Hint:* Mass is a laboratory unit, whereas mol is a calculation unit. The laboratory balance is calibrated in units of mass (g). Although mol are essential for this type of calculation, the starting point and objective are often in mass units. As a result, our path is often g $\longrightarrow$ mol $\longrightarrow$ g.

### Practice Problem 4.18

Barium carbonate decomposes upon heating to barium oxide and carbon dioxide.

    a. Write and balance the equation.

    b. Calculate the number of g of carbon dioxide produced by heating 50.0 g of barium carbonate.

▸ For Further Practice: **Questions 4.111 and 4.112.**

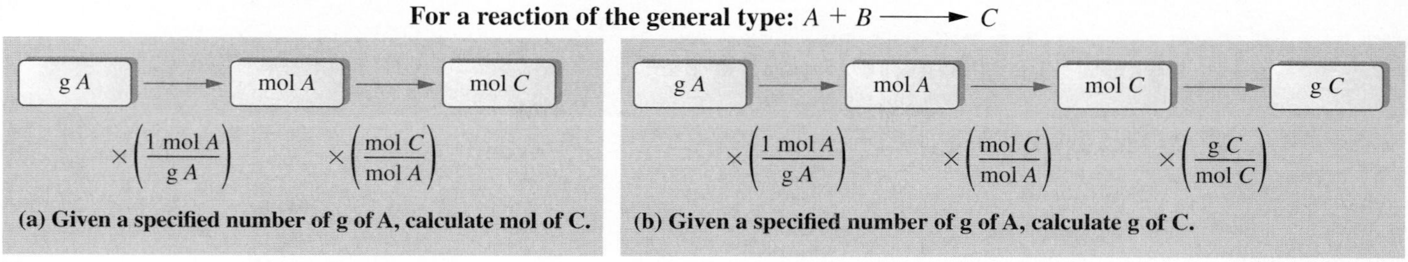
For a reaction of the general type: A + B → C
g A → mol A → mol C
× (1 mol A / g A) × (mol C / mol A)
(a) Given a specified number of g of A, calculate mol of C.
g A → mol A → mol C → g C
× (1 mol A / g A) × (mol C / mol A) × (g C / mol C)
(b) Given a specified number of g of A, calculate g of C.

**Figure 4.9** A general problem-solving strategy, using molar quantities.

A general problem-solving strategy is summarized in Figure 4.9. By systematically applying this strategy, you will be able to solve virtually any problem requiring calculations based on the chemical equation.

## Theoretical and Percent Yield

LEARNING GOAL

**14** Calculate theoretical and percent yields.

The **theoretical yield** is the *maximum* amount of product that can be produced (in an ideal world). In the "real" world, it is difficult to produce the amount calculated as the theoretical yield. This is true for a variety of reasons. Some experimental error is unavoidable. Moreover, many reactions simply do not go to completion; some amount of reactant remains at the end of the reaction, and the *actual* amount of product is less than the *theoretical* (predicted) amount. We will study these processes, termed *equilibrium reactions* in Chapter 7.

The **percent yield,** the ratio of the actual and theoretical yields multiplied by 100%, is often used to show the relationship between predicted and experimental quantities. Thus,

$$\% \text{ yield} = \frac{\text{actual yield}}{\text{theoretical yield}} \times 100\%$$

In Example 4.15, the theoretical yield of $CO_2$ is 132 g. For this reaction, let's assume that a chemist actually obtained 125 g $CO_2$. This is the actual yield and would normally be provided as a part of the data in the problem.

Calculate the percent yield as follows:

$$\% \text{ yield} = \frac{\text{actual yield}}{\text{theoretical yield}} \times 100\%$$

$$= \frac{125 \text{ g } CO_2}{132 \text{ g } CO_2} \times 100\% = 94.7\%$$

## EXAMPLE 4.19 Calculation of Percent Yield

LEARNING GOAL

**14** Calculate theoretical and percent yields.

Assume that the theoretical yield of iron in the process

$$2Al(s) + Fe_2O_3(s) \longrightarrow Al_2O_3(l) + 2Fe(l)$$

was 30.0 g. If the actual yield of iron was 25.0 g, calculate the percent yield.

**Solution**

$$\% \text{ yield} = \frac{\text{actual yield}}{\text{theoretical yield}} \times 100\%$$

$$= \frac{25.0 \text{ g}}{30.0 \text{ g}} \times 100\%$$

$$= 83.3\%$$

*Continued...*

# A Medical Perspective

## Pharmaceutical Chemistry: The Practical Significance of Percent Yield

In recent years, the major pharmaceutical industries have introduced a wide variety of new drugs targeted to cure or alleviate the symptoms of a host of diseases that afflict humanity.

The vast majority of these drugs are synthetic; they are made in a laboratory or by an industrial process. These substances are complex molecules that are patiently designed and constructed from relatively simple molecules in a series of chemical reactions. A series of ten to twenty "steps," or sequential reactions, is not unusual to put together a final product that has the proper structure, geometry, and reactivity for efficacy against a particular disease.

Although a great deal of research occurs to ensure that each of the steps in the overall process is efficient (having a large percent yield), the overall process is still very inefficient (low percent yield). This inefficiency, and the research needed to minimize it, at least in part determines the cost and availability of both prescription and over-the-counter preparations.

Consider a hypothetical five-step sequential synthesis. If each step has a percent yield of 80%, our initial impression might be that this synthesis is quite efficient. However, on closer inspection we find quite the contrary to be true.

The overall yield of the five-step reaction is the product of the decimal fraction of the percent yield of each of the sequential reactions. So, if the decimal fraction corresponding to 80% is 0.80:

$$0.80 \times 0.80 \times 0.80 \times 0.80 \times 0.80 = 0.33$$

Converting the decimal fraction to percentage:

$$0.33 \times 100\% = 33\% \text{ yield}$$

Many reactions are considerably less than 80% efficient, especially those that are used to prepare large molecules with complex arrangements of atoms. Imagine a more realistic scenario in which one step is only 20% efficient (a 20% yield) and the other four steps are 50%, 60%, 70%, and 80% efficient. Repeating the calculation with these numbers (after conversion to decimal fractions):

$$0.20 \times 0.50 \times 0.60 \times 0.70 \times 0.80 = 0.0336$$

Converting the decimal fraction to a percentage:

$$0.0336 \times 100\% = 3.36\% \text{ yield}$$

A 3.36% yield refects a very inefficient process.

If we apply this logic to a fifteen- or twenty-step synthesis, we gain some appreciation of the difficulty of producing modern pharmaceutical products. Add to this the challenge of predicting the most appropriate molecular structure that will have the desired biological effect and be relatively free of side effects. All these considerations give new meaning to the term *wonder drug* that has been attached to some of the more successful synthetic products.

We will study some of the elementary steps essential to the synthesis of a wide range of pharmaceutical compounds in later chapters, beginning with Chapter 10.

### For Further Understanding

▶ Explain the possible connection of this perspective to escalating costs of pharmaceutical products.
▶ Can you describe other situations, not necessarily in the field of chemistry, where multiple-step processes contribute to inefficiency?

---

### Practice Problem 4.19

Given the reaction represented by the balanced equation

$$CH_4(g) + 3Cl_2(g) \longrightarrow 3HCl(g) + CHCl_3(g)$$

a. Calculate the number of g of $CHCl_3$ that could be produced by mixing 105 g $Cl_2$ with excess $CH_4$.
b. If 10.0 g $CHCl_3$ were actually produced, calculate the % yield.

▶ For Further Practice: **Questions 4.117 and 4.118.**

**Question 4.15**   It is believed that the reaction responsible for the depletion of ozone in the atmosphere is:

$$O_3(g) + NO(g) \longrightarrow O_2(g) + NO_2(g)$$

a. If 50.0 g of $O_3$ react with excess NO, how many g of $NO_2$ will be produced?
b. If the actual yield of $NO_2$ is 25.0 g, what is the % yield?

**Question 4.16**   The reaction:

$$2NO(g) + O_2(g) \longrightarrow 2NO_2(g)$$

is one step in the process of forming atmospheric smog.

a. How many g of $NO_2$ can be produced by the reaction of excess $O_2$ with 50.0 g of NO?
b. If the actual yield of $NO_2$ is 50.0 g, what is the % yield?

## A Special Case—The Limiting Reactant

We have learned that reactants combine in molar proportions dictated by the coefficients in the balanced equation. However, we often encounter situations where the reactants are not mixed to match the theoretical proportions. In cases such as this, one reactant will be completely consumed, leaving some of the other reactant unchanged. In effect, the extent of the reaction is *limited* by the amount of the reactant that is completely consumed. This completely consumed reactant is termed the *limiting reactant*. In order to correctly calculate the amount of product formed, the *theoretical yield*, we must base the amount of product formed on the number of mol of the compound "in short supply," the limiting reactant.

Imagine that you are making cheeseburgers. You have ten buns, four slices of cheese, and five meat patties. What is the limiting ingredient? How many cheeseburgers can you make? What are the leftover ingredients? If you can answer these questions, you can do limiting reactant problems.

We know that ten buns could make ten cheeseburgers if we had ten meat patties and ten slices of cheese. But we do not, so it is obvious that we cannot make ten cheeseburgers, even though we certainly have enough buns. It can be reasoned that only four cheeseburgers are possible. We are limited by the availability of only four slices of cheese. In our example, cheese is the limiting reactant. Furthermore, five minus four, or one meat patty and ten minus four, or six buns, would be left over as shown in Figure 4.10.

The strategy outlined above is the same as that used in solving problems involving limiting reactants.

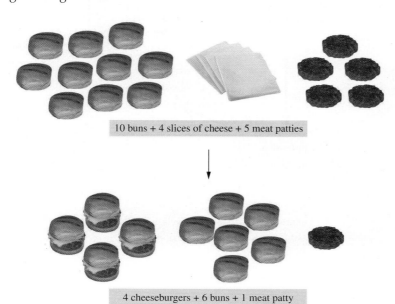

10 buns + 4 slices of cheese + 5 meat patties

4 cheeseburgers + 6 buns + 1 meat patty

**Figure 4.10**  In this illustration, the number of cheese slices limits the number of cheeseburgers that can be made. The cheese slices are the limiting reactant.

# CHAPTER MAP

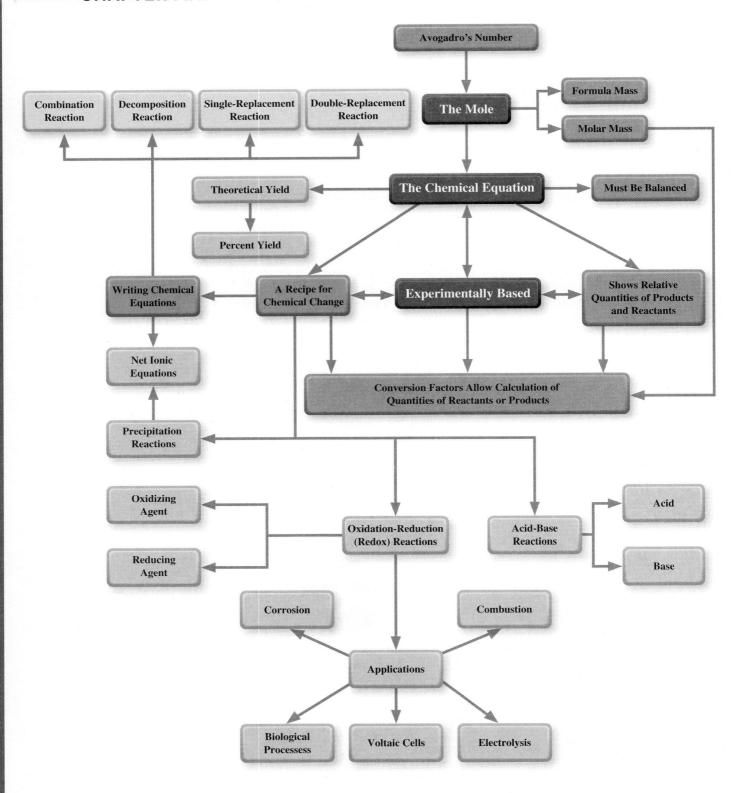

# SUMMARY

## 4.1 The Mole Concept and Atoms

▶ Atoms are exceedingly small, yet their masses have been experimentally determined for each of the elements. The unit of measurement for these determinations is the **atomic mass unit,** (amu):

$$1 \text{ amu} = 1.661 \times 10^{-24} \text{ g}$$

▶ The periodic table provides atomic masses in amu. A more practical unit for defining a "collection" of atoms is the **mole** (mol):

1 mol of atoms = $6.022 \times 10^{23}$ atoms of an element

This number is referred to as **Avogadro's number.**

▶ The **atomic mass** of a given element is the average mass of a single atom in amu. The mass of 1 mol of atoms, in grams, is termed the **molar mass** of the element. One mole of atoms of any element contains the same number, Avogadro's number, of atoms.

## 4.2 The Chemical Formula, Formula Mass, and Molar Mass

▶ Compounds are pure substances composed of two or more elements that are chemically combined. They are represented by their **chemical formula,** a combination of symbols of the various elements that make up the compounds. The chemical formula is based on the **formula unit.** This is the smallest collection of atoms that provides the identity of the atoms present in the compound and the relative numbers of each type of atom.

▶ Just as the mass of a mol of atoms is based on the atomic mass, the mass of a mol of a compound is based on the **formula mass.** The formula mass is calculated by adding the masses of all the atoms or ions of which the unit is composed. To calculate the formula mass, the formula unit must be known. The formula mass of 1 mol of a compound is its **molar mass** in units of g/mol.

## 4.3 The Chemical Equation and the Information It Conveys

▶ The **chemical equation** is the shorthand notation for a chemical reaction. It describes all of the substances that react to produce the product(s). **Reactants,** or starting materials, are all substances that undergo change in a chemical reaction; **products** are substances produced by a chemical reaction.

▶ According to the **law of conservation of mass,** matter can neither be gained nor lost in the process of a chemical reaction. The law of conservation of mass states that we must have a balanced chemical equation.

▶ Features of a chemical equation include the following:
- The identity of products and reactants must be specified.
- Reactants are written to the left of the reaction arrow ($\rightarrow$) and products to the right.
- The physical states of reactants and products are shown in parentheses.

- If heat energy is necessary for the reaction to occur, the symbol $\Delta$ is written over the reaction arrow.
- The equation must be balanced.

▶ Chemical reactions involve the **combination** of reactants to produce products, the **decomposition** of reactant(s) into products, or the **replacement** of one or more elements in a compound to yield products. Replacement reactions are subclassified as either **single-** or **double-**replacement.

## 4.4 Balancing Chemical Equations

▶ The chemical equation enables us to determine the quantity of reactants needed to produce a certain molar quantity of products. The chemical equation expresses these quantities in terms of mol.

▶ The relative number of mol of each reactant and product is indicated by placing a whole-number coefficient before the formula of each substance in the chemical equation.

▶ Many equations are balanced by trial and error. If the identity of the reactants and products, the physical states, and the reaction conditions are known, the following steps provide a method for correctly balancing a chemical equation:
- Count the number of atoms of each element on both reactant and product sides.
- Determine which atoms are not balanced.
- Balance one element at a time using coefficients.
- After you believe that you have successfully balanced the equation, check to be certain that mass conservation has been achieved.

## 4.5 Precipitation Reactions

▶ Reactions that produce products with similar characteristics are often classified together. The formation of an insoluble solid, a **precipitate,** is very common. Such reactions are precipitation reactions and are represented using net ionic equations.

## 4.6 Net Ionic Equations

▶ **Net ionic equations** show the chemical species that actually undergo change. Other ions that retain their identity throughout the chemical reaction are termed *spectator ions.*

## 4.7 Acid-Base Reactions

▶ **Acid-base reactions** involve the transfer of a hydrogen cation, $H^+$, from one reactant (the acid) to another (the base).

▶ The reaction of an acid with a base to produce a salt and water is referred to as **neutralization.**

## 4.8 Oxidation-Reduction Reactions

▶ **Oxidation** is defined as a loss of electrons, loss of hydrogen atoms, or gain of oxygen atoms.

▶ **Reduction** is defined as a gain of electrons, gain of hydrogen atoms, or loss of oxygen atoms.

▶ Oxidation and reduction are complementary processes. The oxidation half-reaction produces one or more electrons that are the reactants for the reduction half-reaction. The combination of two half-reactions, one oxidation and one reduction, produces the complete *redox* reaction.

▶ The **reducing agent** releases electrons for the reduction of a second substance to occur. The **oxidizing agent** accepts electrons, causing the oxidation of a second substance to take place.

▶ The deterioration of metals caused by an oxidation-reduction process is termed **corrosion.**

▶ The complete oxidation of hydrocarbons produces energy, carbon dioxide, and water in a process termed **combustion.**

▶ A **voltaic cell** is an electrochemical cell that converts chemical energy into electrical energy. The best-known example of a voltaic cell is the storage battery. **Electrolysis** is the opposite of a battery. It converts electrical energy into chemical potential energy. The electrode at which oxidation occurs is called the **anode,** and the electrode at which reduction occurs is the **cathode.**

## 4.9 Calculations Using the Chemical Equation

▶ Calculations involving chemical quantities are based on the following requirements:
- The basis for the calculations is a balanced equation.
- The calculations are performed using mole-based conversion factors.
- The conservation of mass must be obeyed.

▶ The mol is the basis for calculations. However, masses are generally measured in g. Therefore, you must be able to interconvert mol and g to perform chemical arithmetic.

▶ The calculated amount assumes complete conversion of reactant to product. This amount is the **theoretical yield.** Most reactions are not complete; some reactant(s) remains and the actual amount is less than the theoretical amount. The **percent yield** is the ratio of the actual to theoretical yields multiplied by 100%.

- The *limiting reactant* should be completely consumed in the reaction and will limit the amount of product formed. Identifying the limiting reactant is often important in theoretical yield calculations.

## ANSWERS TO PRACTICE PROBLEMS

**4.1**  **a.** $26.98 \dfrac{\text{g Al}}{\text{mol Al}}$

**b.** $200.59 \dfrac{\text{g Hg}}{\text{mol Hg}}$

**4.2**  **a.** $1.51 \times 10^{24}$ oxygen atoms
**b.** $3.01 \times 10^{24}$ oxygen atoms

**4.3**  1.50 mol Na

**4.4**  14.0 g He

**4.5**  $3.17 \times 10^{-2}$ mol Ag

**4.6**  $1.51 \times 10^{24}$ O atoms

**4.7**  17.04 amu and 17.04 g/mol

**4.8**  237.95 amu and 237.95 g/mol

**4.9**  $C_2H_5OH(l) + 3O_2(g) \longrightarrow 2CO_2(g) + 3H_2O(g)$

**4.10**  $6S_2Cl_2(s) + 16NH_3(g) \longrightarrow N_4S_4(s) + 12NH_4Cl(s) + S_8(s)$

**4.11**  **a.** $KCl(aq) + AgNO_3(aq) \longrightarrow KNO_3(aq) + AgCl(s)$
**b.** $K_2CO_3(aq) + Ca(OH)_2(aq) \longrightarrow 2KOH(aq) + CaCO_3(s)$
**c.** $NaOH(aq) + NH_4Cl(aq) \longrightarrow$ no reaction
**d.** $2NaOH(aq) + FeCl_2(aq) \longrightarrow 2NaCl(aq) + Fe(OH)_2(s)$

**4.12**  **a.** $Ba^{2+}(aq) + SO_4^{2-}(aq) \longrightarrow BaSO_4(s)$
**b.** $2Ag^+(aq) + SO_4^{2-}(aq) \longrightarrow Ag_2SO_4(s)$

**4.13**  **a.** $90.1$ g $H_2O$        **c.** $1.80 \times 10^3$ µg $C_6H_{12}O_6$
**b.** $0.590$ mol LiCl        **d.** $0.368$ mol $MgCl_2$

**4.14**  65.1 g KCN

**4.15**  $4.61 \times 10^2$ g ethanol

**4.16**  **a.** 3 mol $O_2$
**b.** 96.00 g $O_2$
**c.** 88.0 g $CO_2$

**4.17**  **a.** $4Fe(s) + 3O_2(g) \longrightarrow 2Fe_2O_3(s)$
**b.** 3.50 g Fe

**4.18**  **a.** $BaCO_3(s) \xrightarrow{\Delta} BaO(s) + CO_2(g)$
**b.** 11.2 g $CO_2$

**4.19**  **a.** 58.9 g $CHCl_3$
**b.** 17.0% yield

## QUESTIONS AND PROBLEMS

### The Mole Concept and Atoms

**Foundations**

**4.17**  What is the average mass (in amu) of:
  **a.** Hg          **b.** Kr          **c.** Mg
**4.18**  What is the average mass (in amu) of:
  **a.** Zr          **b.** Cs          **c.** Ca
**4.19**  What is the average molar mass of:
  **a.** Si          **b.** Ag          **c.** As
**4.20**  What is the average molar mass of:
  **a.** S          **b.** Na          **c.** Hg

**4.21** What is the mass, in g, of Avogadro's number of argon atoms?

**4.22** What is the mass, in g, of Avogadro's number of iron atoms?

## Applications

**4.23** How many carbon atoms are present in $1.0 \times 10^{-4}$ mol of carbon?

**4.24** How many mercury atoms are present in $1.0 \times 10^{-10}$ mol of mercury?

**4.25** How many mol of arsenic correspond to $1.0 \times 10^2$ atoms of arsenic?

**4.26** How many mol of sodium correspond to $1.0 \times 10^{15}$ atoms of sodium?

**4.27** How many g of neon are contained in 2.00 mol of neon atoms?

**4.28** How many g of carbon are contained in 3.00 mol of carbon atoms?

**4.29** What is the mass, in g, of 1.00 mol of helium atoms?

**4.30** What is the mass, in g, of 1.00 mol of nitrogen atoms?

**4.31** Calculate the number of mol corresponding to:
  **a.** 20.0 g He    **b.** 0.040 kg Na    **c.** 3.0 g $Cl_2$

**4.32** Calculate the number of mol corresponding to:
  **a.** 0.10 g Ca    **b.** 4.00 g Fe    **c.** 2.00 kg $N_2$

**4.33** What is the mass, in g, of 15.0 mol of silver?

**4.34** What is the mass, in g, of 15.0 mol of carbon?

**4.35** Calculate the number of silver atoms in 15.0 g of silver.

**4.36** Calculate the number of carbon atoms in 15.0 g of carbon.

## The Chemical Formula, Formula Mass, and Molar Mass

### Foundations

**4.37** Distinguish between the terms *molecule* and *ion pair*.

**4.38** Distinguish between the terms *formula mass* and *molar mass*.

**4.39** Calculate formula mass and the molar mass of each of the following formula units:
  **a.** NaCl    **b.** $Na_2SO_4$    **c.** $Fe_3(PO_4)_2$

**4.40** Calculate formula mass and the molar mass of each of the following formula units:
  **a.** $S_8$    **b.** $(NH_4)_2SO_4$    **c.** $CO_2$

**4.41** Calculate formula mass and the molar mass of oxygen gas, $O_2$.

**4.42** Calculate formula mass and the molar mass of ozone, $O_3$.

**4.43** Calculate formula mass and the molar mass of $CuSO_4 \cdot 5H_2O$.

**4.44** Calculate formula mass and the molar mass of $CaCl_2 \cdot 2H_2O$.

### Applications

**4.45** Calculate the number of mol corresponding to:
  **a.** 15.0 g NaCl    **b.** 15.0 g $Na_2SO_4$

**4.46** Calculate the number of mol corresponding to:
  **a.** 15.0 g $NH_3$    **b.** 16.0 g $O_2$

**4.47** Calculate the mass in g corresponding to:
  **a.** 1.000 mol $H_2O$    **c.** 10.0 mol He
  **b.** 2.000 mol NaCl    **d.** $1.00 \times 10^2$ mol $H_2$

**4.48** Calculate the mass in g corresponding to:
  **a.** 0.400 mol $NH_3$    **c.** 2.00 mol $CH_4$
  **b.** 0.800 mol $BaCO_3$    **d.** 0.400 mol $Ca(NO_3)_2$

**4.49** How many g are required to have 0.100 mol of each of the following?
  **a.** $CH_4$ (methane)    **c.** NaOH
  **b.** $CaCO_3$    **d.** $H_2SO_4$

**4.50** How many g are required to have 0.100 mol of each of the following?
  **a.** $C_6H_{12}O_6$ (glucose)
  **b.** NaCl
  **c.** $C_2H_5OH$ (ethanol)
  **d.** $Ca_3(PO_4)_2$

**4.51** How many mol are in 50.0 g of each of the following substances?
  **a.** KBr    **c.** $CS_2$
  **b.** $MgSO_4$    **d.** $Al_2(CO_3)_3$

**4.52** How many mol are in 50.0 g of each of the following substances?
  **a.** $Br_2$    **c.** $Sr(OH)_2$
  **b.** $NH_4Cl$    **d.** $LiNO_3$

## The Chemical Equation and the Information It Conveys

### Foundations

**4.53** What law is the ultimate basis for a balanced chemical equation?

**4.54** List the general types of information that a chemical equation provides.

**4.55** What is a reactant? On which side of the reaction arrow are reactants found?

**4.56** What is a product? On which side of the reaction arrow are products found?

**4.57** What is the meaning of $\Delta$ over the reaction arrow?

**4.58** What is the meaning of $(s)$, $(l)$, $(g)$, and $(aq)$ immediately following the symbol for a chemical substance?

### Applications

**4.59** Classify each of the following reactions as decomposition (D), combination (C), single-replacement (SR), or double-replacement (DR):
  **a.** $2KClO_3(s) \xrightarrow{\Delta} 2KCl(s) + 3O_2(g)$
  **b.** $K_2CO_3(aq) + Ca(OH)_2(aq) \longrightarrow CaCO_3(s) + 2KOH(aq)$
  **c.** $CaO(aq) + H_2O(l) \longrightarrow Ca(OH)_2(aq)$
  **d.** $Ca(s) + Sn(NO_3)_2(aq) \longrightarrow Sn(aq) + Ca(NO_3)_2(aq)$

**4.60** Classify each of the following reactions as decomposition (D), combination (C), single-replacement (SR), or double-replacement (DR):
  **a.** $KOH(s) + CO_2(g) \longrightarrow KHCO_3(s)$
  **b.** $K_2CO_3(aq) \xrightarrow{\Delta} K_2O(g) + CO_2(g)$
  **c.** $H_2SO_4(aq) + 2 NaOH(aq) \longrightarrow Na_2SO_4(aq) + 2 H_2O(l)$
  **d.** $2AgNO_3(aq) + Zn(s) \longrightarrow 2Ag(s) + Zn(NO_3)_2(aq)$

**4.61** What is the meaning of the subscript in a chemical formula?

**4.62** What is the meaning of the coefficient in a chemical equation?

## Balancing Chemical Equations

### Foundations

**4.63** When you are balancing an equation, why must the subscripts in the chemical formulas remain unchanged?

**4.64** Describe the process of checking to ensure that an equation is properly balanced.

## Applications

**4.65** Balance each of the following equations:

a. $C_2H_6(g) + O_2(g) \longrightarrow CO_2(g) + H_2O(g)$

b. $K_2O(s) + P_4O_{10}(s) \longrightarrow K_3PO_4(s)$

c. $MgBr_2(aq) + H_2SO_4(aq) \longrightarrow HBr(g) + MgSO_4(aq)$

d. $C_2H_5OH(l) + O_2(g) \longrightarrow CO_2(g) + H_2O(g)$

**4.66** Balance each of the following equations:

a. $C_6H_{12}O_6(s) + O_2(g) \longrightarrow CO_2(g) + H_2O(g)$

b. $H_2O(l) + P_4O_{10}(s) \longrightarrow H_3PO_4(aq)$

c. $PCl_5(g) + H_2O(l) \longrightarrow HCl(aq) + H_3PO_4(aq)$

d. $C_6H_{12}O_6(s) \longrightarrow C_2H_6O(l) + CO_2(g)$

**4.67** Complete, then balance, each of the following equations:

a. $Ca(s) + F_2(g) \longrightarrow$

b. $Mg(s) + O_2(g) \longrightarrow$

c. $H_2(g) + N_2(g) \longrightarrow$

**4.68** Complete, then balance, each of the following equations:

a. $Li(s) + O_2(g) \longrightarrow$

b. $Ca(s) + N_2(g) \longrightarrow$

c. $Al(s) + S(s) \longrightarrow$

**4.69** Balance each of the following equations:

a. $C_4H_{10}(g) + O_2(g) \longrightarrow H_2O(g) + CO_2(g)$

b. $Au_2S_3(s) + H_2(g) \longrightarrow Au(s) + H_2S(g)$

c. $Al(OH)_3(s) + HCl(aq) \longrightarrow AlCl_3(aq) + H_2O(l)$

d. $(NH_4)_2Cr_2O_7(s) \longrightarrow Cr_2O_3(s) + N_2(g) + H_2O(g)$

**4.70** Balance each of the following equations:

a. $Fe_2O_3(s) + CO(g) \longrightarrow Fe_3O_4(s) + CO_2(g)$

b. $C_6H_6(l) + O_2(g) \longrightarrow CO_2(g) + H_2O(g)$

c. $I_4O_9(s) + I_2O_6(s) \longrightarrow I_2(s) + O_2(g)$

d. $KClO_3(s) \longrightarrow KCl(s) + O_2(g)$

**4.71** Write a balanced equation for each of the following reactions:

a. Ammonia is formed by the reaction of nitrogen and hydrogen.

b. Hydrochloric acid reacts with sodium hydroxide to produce water and sodium chloride.

c. Glucose, a sugar, $C_6H_{12}O_6$, is oxidized in the body to produce water and carbon dioxide.

d. Sodium carbonate, upon heating, produces sodium oxide and carbon dioxide.

**4.72** Write a balanced equation for each of the following reactions:

a. Nitric acid reacts with calcium hydroxide to produce water and calcium nitrate.

b. Butane ($C_4H_{10}$) reacts with oxygen to produce water and carbon dioxide.

c. Sulfur, present as an impurity in coal, is burned in oxygen to produce sulfur dioxide.

d. Hydrofluric acid (HF) reacts with glass ($SiO_2$) in the process of etching to produce silicon tetrafluoride and water.

## Precipitation Reactions

### Foundations

**4.73** Which of the following ionic compounds will form a precipitate in water?

a. $Na_2SO_4$            c. $BaCO_3$

b. $BaSO_4$             d. $K_2CO_3$

**4.74** Which of the following ionic compounds will form a precipitate in water?

a. $PbCO_3$            c. $Pb(NO_3)_2$

b. $Na_2CO_3$           d. $Na_2NO_3$

### Applications

**4.75** Will a precipitate form if solutions of the soluble salts $Pb(NO_3)_2$ and KI are mixed?

**4.76** Will a precipitate form if solutions of the soluble salts $AgNO_3$ abd NaOH are mixed?

**4.77** Solutions containing $(NH_4)_2CO_3(aq)$ and $CaCl_2(aq)$ are mixed. Will a precipitate form? If so, write its formula.

**4.78** Solutions containing $Mg(NO_3)_2(aq)$ and $NaOH(aq)$ are mixed. Will a precipitate form? If so, write its formula.

## Net Ionic Equations

### Foundations

**4.79** Describe the difference between the terms *ionic equation* and *net ionic equation.*

**4.80** Describe the steps used in writing the net ionic equation for a reaction.

### Applications

**4.81** Write the net ionic equation for the reaction of $NaBr(aq)$ with $AgNO_3(aq)$.

**4.82** Write the net ionic equation for the reaction of $Pb(NO_3)_2(aq)$ with $K_2S(aq)$.

## Acid-Base Reactions

### Foundations

**4.83** Does an acid gain or lose a hydrogen cation, $H^+$, during an acid-base reaction?

**4.84** During an acid-base reaction, what term is used to describe the reactant that gains a hydrogen cation, $H^+$?

### Applications

**4.85** Identify the acid and base in the following reaction:

$$HCN\ (aq) + KOH\ (aq) \longrightarrow KCN\ (aq) + H_2O\ (l)$$

**4.86** Identify the acid and base in the following reaction:

$$HBr\ (aq) + NaOH\ (aq) \longrightarrow NaBr\ (aq) + H_2O\ (l)$$

## Oxidation-Reduction Reactions

### Foundations

**4.87** During an oxidation process in an oxidation-reduction reaction, does the species oxidized gain or lose electrons?

**4.88** During an oxidation-reduction reaction, is the oxidizing agent oxidized or reduced?

**4.89** During an oxidation-reduction reaction, is the reducing agent oxidized or reduced?

**4.90** Do metals tend to be good oxidizing agents or good reducing agents?

### Applications

**4.91** In the following reaction, identify the oxidized species, reduced species, oxidizing agent, and reducing agent:

$$Cl_2(aq) + 2KI(aq) \longrightarrow 2KCl(aq) + I_2(aq)$$

**4.92**   In the following reaction, identify the oxidized species, reduced species, oxidizing agent, and reducing agent:

$$Zn(s) + Cu^{2+}(aq) \longrightarrow Zn^{2+}(aq) + Cu(s)$$

**4.93**   Write the oxidation and reduction half-reactions for the equation in Question 4.91.

**4.94**   Write the oxidation and reduction half-reactions for the equation in Question 4.92.

**4.95**   Explain the relationship between oxidation-reduction and voltaic cells.

**4.96**   Compare and contrast a battery and electrolysis.

**4.97**   Describe one application of voltaic cells.

**4.98**   Describe one application of electrolytic cells.

## Calculations Using the Chemical Equation

### Foundations

**4.99**   Why is it essential to use balanced equations to solve mol problems?

**4.100**  Describe the steps used in the calculation of g of product resulting from the reaction of a specified number of g of reactant.

### Applications

**4.101**  How many g of $B_2H_6$ will react with 3.00 mol of $O_2$?

$$B_2H_6(l) + 3O_2(g) \longrightarrow B_2O_3(s) + 3H_2O(l)$$

**4.102**  How many g of Al will react with 3.00 mol of $O_2$?

$$4Al(s) + 3O_2(g) \longrightarrow 2Al_2O_3(s)$$

**4.103**  Calculate the number of moles of $CrCl_3$ that could be produced from 50.0 g $Cr_2O_3$ according to the equation

$$Cr_2O_3(s) + 3CCl_4(l) \longrightarrow 2CrCl_3(s) + 3COCl_2(aq)$$

**4.104**  A 3.5-g sample of water reacts with $PCl_3$ according to the following equation:

$$3H_2O(l) + PCl_3(g) \longrightarrow H_3PO_3(aq) + 3HCl(aq)$$

How many mol of $H_3PO_3$ are produced?

**4.105**  For the reaction

$$N_2(g) + H_2(g) \longrightarrow NH_3(g)$$

a. Balance the equation.
b. How many mol of $H_2$ would react with 1 mol of $N_2$?
c. How many mol of product would form from 1 mol of $N_2$?
d. If 14.0 g of $N_2$ were initially present, calculate the number of mol of $H_2$ required to react with all of the $N_2$.
e. For conditions outlined in part (d), how many g of product would form?

**4.106**  Aspirin (acetylsalicylic acid) may be formed from salicylic acid and acetic acid as follows:

$$C_7H_6O_3(aq) + CH_3COOH(aq) \longrightarrow C_9H_8O_4(s) + H_2O(l)$$

Salicylic     Acetic     Aspirin
acid        acid

a. Is this equation balanced? If not, complete the balancing.
b. How many mol of aspirin may be produced from $1.00 \times 10^2$ mol salicylic acid?

c. How many g of aspirin may be produced from $1.00 \times 10^2$ mol salicylic acid?
d. How many g of acetic acid would be required to react completely with the $1.00 \times 10^2$ mol salicylic acid?
e. For the conditions outlined in part (d), how many g of aspirin would form?

**4.107**  The proteins in our bodies are composed of molecules called amino acids. One amino acid is methionine; its molecular formula is $C_5H_{11}NO_2S$. Calculate:
a. the formula mass of methionine
b. the number of oxygen atoms in a mol of this compound
c. the mass of oxygen in a mol of the compound
d. the mass of oxygen in 50.0 g of the compound

**4.108**  Triglycerides (Chapters 17 and 23) are used in biochemical systems to store energy; they can be formed from glycerol and fatty acids. The molecular formula of glycerol is $C_3H_8O_3$. Calculate:
a. the formula mass of glycerol
b. the number of oxygen atoms in a mol of this compound
c. the mass of oxygen in a mol of the compound
d. the mass of oxygen in 50.0 g of the compound

**4.109**  Joseph Priestley discovered oxygen in the eighteenth century by using heat to decompose mercury(II) oxide:

$$2HgO(s) \xrightarrow{\Delta} 2Hg(l) + O_2(g)$$

How many g of oxygen is produced from $1.00 \times 10^2$ g HgO?

**4.110**  Dinitrogen monoxide (also known as nitrous oxide and used as an anesthetic) can be made by heating ammonium nitrate:

$$NH_4NO_3(s) \xrightarrow{\Delta} N_2O(g) + 2H_2O(g)$$

How many g of dinitrogen monoxide can be made from $1.00 \times 10^2$ g of ammonium nitrate?

**4.111**  The burning of acetylene ($C_2H_2$) in oxygen is the reaction in the oxyacetylene torch. How many g of $CO_2$ is produced by burning 20.0 kg of acetylene in an excess of $O_2$? The unbalanced equation is

$$C_2H_2(g) + O_2(g) \xrightarrow{\Delta} CO_2(g) + H_2O(g)$$

**4.112**  The reaction of calcium hydride with water can be used to prepare hydrogen gas:

$$CaH_2(s) + 2H_2O(l) \longrightarrow Ca(OH)_2(aq) + 2H_2(g)$$

How many g of hydrogen gas are produced in the reaction of $1.00 \times 10^2$ g calcium hydride with water?

**4.113**  Various members of a class of compounds called alkenes (Chapter 11) react with hydrogen to produce a corresponding alkane (Chapter 10). Termed hydrogenation, this type of reaction is used to produce products such as margarine. A typical hydrogenation reaction is

$$C_{10}H_{20}(l) + H_2(g) \longrightarrow C_{10}H_{22}(s)$$

Decene          Decane

How many g of decane can be produced in a reaction of excess decene with 1.00 g hydrogen?

**4.114** Chemical Control of Microbes (Section 4.8) describes the breakdown of the antiseptic $H_2O_2$ with the balanced equation

$$2H_2O_2(aq) \longrightarrow 2H_2O(l) + O_2(g)$$

Assuming there is an unlimited amount of the enzyme, how many g of $O_2$ would be produced from $1.00 \times 10^{-1}$ g of $H_2O_2$?

**4.115** A rocket can be powered by the reaction between dinitrogen tetroxide and hydrazine:

$$N_2O_4(l) + 2N_2H_4(l) \longrightarrow 3N_2(g) + 4H_2O(g)$$

An engineer designed the rocket to hold 1.00 kg $N_2O_4$ and excess $N_2H_4$. How many g of $N_2$ would be produced according to the engineer's design?

**4.116** A 4.00-g sample of $Fe_3O_4$ reacts with $O_2$ to produce $Fe_2O_3$:

$$4Fe_3O_4(s) + O_2(g) \longrightarrow 6Fe_2O_3(s)$$

Determine the number of g of $Fe_2O_3$ produced.

**4.117** If the actual yield of decane in Question 4.113 is 65.4 g, what is the % yield?

**4.118** If the actual yield of oxygen gas in Question 4.114 is $1.10 \times 10^{-2}$ g, what is the % yield?

**4.119** If the % yield of nitrogen gas in Question 4.115 is 75.0%, what is the actual yield of nitrogen?

**4.120** If the % yield of $Fe_2O_3$ in Question 4.116 is 90.0%, what is the actual yield of $Fe_2O_3$?

## CHALLENGE PROBLEMS

1. Which of the following has fewer mol of carbon: 100 g of $CaCO_3$ or 0.5 mol of $CCl_4$?

2. Which of the following has fewer mol of carbon: $6.02 \times 10^{22}$ molecules of $C_2H_6$ or 88 g of $CO_2$?

3. How many molecules are found in each of the following?
   **a.** 1.0 lb of sucrose, $C_{12}H_{22}O_{11}$ (table sugar)
   **b.** 1.57 kg of $N_2O$ (anesthetic)

4. How many molecules are found in each of the following?
   **a.** $4 \times 10^5$ tons (t) of $SO_2$ (produced by the 1980 eruption of the Mount St. Helens volcano)
   **b.** 25.0 lb of $SiO_2$ (major constituent of sand)

5. Based on the information in Questions 4.15 and 4.16, it appears that we could solve some of our atmospheric problems by reducing the amount of NO that we put into the air. Use the Internet to determine the sources of atmospheric NO. Can we control atmospheric NO? If so, how?

# 5

# GASES, LIQUIDS, AND SOLIDS
# States of Matter

## LEARNING GOALS

1 Perform conversions between units of pressure.

2 Describe the major points of the kinetic molecular theory of gases.

3 Explain the relationship between the kinetic molecular theory and the physical properties of measurable quantities of gases.

4 Describe the behavior of gases expressed by the gas laws: Boyle's law, Charles's law, combined gas law, Avogadro's law, the ideal gas law, and Dalton's law.

5 Use gas law equations to calculate conditions and changes in conditions of gases.

6 Use molar volume and standard temperature and pressure (STP) to perform calculations.

7 Discuss the limitations to the ideal gas model as it applies to real gases.

8 Describe properties of the liquid state in terms of the properties of the individual molecules that comprise the liquid.

9 Describe the processes of melting, boiling, evaporation, condensation, and sublimation.

10 Describe the dipolar attractions known collectively as van der Waals forces.

11 Describe hydrogen bonding and its relationship to boiling and melting temperatures.

12 Relate the properties of the various classes of solids (ionic, covalent, molecular, and metallic) to the structure of these solids.

Volcanic activity is a dramatic example of interconversion among the states of matter.

## OUTLINE

# INTRODUCTION

Major differences among solids, liquids, and gases are due to the relationships among particles. These relationships include:

- the average distance of separation of particles in each state,
- the kinds of interactions among the particles, and
- the degree of organization of particles.

We have already discovered that the solid state is the most organized, with particles close together, allowing significant interactions among the particles. This results in high melting and boiling points for solid substances. Large amounts of energy are needed to overcome the attractive forces and disrupt the orderly structure.

Substances that are gases, on the other hand, are disordered, with particles widely separated and weak interactions among particles. Their melting and boiling points are relatively low. Gases at room temperature must be cooled a great deal for them to liquefy or solidify. For example, the melting and boiling points of $N_2$ are $-210°C$ and $-196°C$, respectively.

Liquids are intermediate in character. The molecules of a liquid are close together, like those of solids. However, the molecules of a liquid are disordered, like those of a gas.

Can a substance such as $N_2$ gas or $CO_2$ gas also exist as a liquid, or even as a solid? We will see that a reduction in temperature or an increase in pressure can force atoms or molecules closer together, allowing them to behave as liquids or solids. Dry ice, for example, is solid carbon dioxide.

Changes in state are described as physical changes. When a substance undergoes a change in state, many of its physical properties change. For example, when ice forms from liquid water, changes occur in density and hardness, but it is still water. Table 5.1 summarizes the important differences in physical properties among gases, liquids, and solids.

Liquid nitrogen is commonly used in cryopreservation when biological samples need to be stored at temperatures below $-196°C$.

*Section 1.2 introduces the properties of the three states of matter.*

## 5.1   The Gaseous State

### Ideal Gas Concept

An **ideal gas** is simply a model of the way that gas particles (molecules or atoms) behave at the atomic/molecular level. The behavior of the individual particles can be inferred from the measurable behavior of samples of real gases. We can easily measure temperature, volume, pressure, and quantity (number of moles) of real

**TABLE 5.1 A Comparison of Physical Properties of Gases, Liquids, and Solids**

|  | Gas | Liquid | Solid |
|---|---|---|---|
| **Volume and Shape** | Expands to fill the volume of its container; consequently, it takes the shape of the container | Has a fixed volume at a given mass and temperature; volume principally dependent on its mass and secondarily on temperature; it assumes the shape of its container | Has a fixed volume; volume principally dependent on its mass and secondarily on temperature; it has a definite shape |
| **Density** | Low (typically ~$10^{-3}$ g/mL) | High (typically ~1 g/mL) | High (typically 1–10 g/mL) |
| **Compressibility** | High | Very low | Virtually incompressible |
| **Particle Motion** | Virtually unrestricted | Molecules or atoms "slide" past each other | Vibrate about a fixed position |
| **Intermolecular Distance** | Very large | Molecules or atoms are close to each other | Molecules, ions, or atoms are close to each other |

gases. Similarly, when we systematically change one of these properties, we can determine the effect on each of the others. For example, putting more molecules in a balloon (the act of blowing up a balloon) causes its volume to increase in a predictable way. In fact, careful measurements show a direct proportionality between the number of molecules and the volume of the balloon, an observation made by Amadeo Avogadro more than 200 years ago.

## Measurement of Properties of Gases

There are four basic gas laws:

Boyle's law
Charles's law
Avogadro's law
Dalton's law

Two laws are derived from these basic laws: the combined gas law and the ideal gas law. These laws involve the relationships among pressure ($P$), volume ($V$), temperature ($T$), and number of moles ($n$) of gas. We are already familiar with the measurements of temperature, volume, and mass (allowing the calculation of number of mol). The measurement of **pressure** is a measurement of force per unit area.

Gas pressure is a result of the force exerted by the collision of particles with the walls of the container. The pressure of a gas may be measured with a **barometer,** invented by Evangelista Torricelli in the mid-1600s.

The most common type of barometer is the mercury barometer. An early version is depicted in Figure 5.1. A tube, sealed at one end, is filled with mercury and inverted in a dish of mercury. The pressure of the atmosphere pushing down on the mercury surface in the dish supports the column of mercury. The height of the column is proportional to the atmospheric pressure. The tube can be calibrated to give a numerical reading in millimeters (mm), centimeters (cm), or inches (in) of mercury. A commonly used unit of measurement is the atmosphere (atm). One standard atmosphere (1 atm) of pressure is equivalent to a height of mercury that is equal to

760 mm Hg (millimeters of mercury)
76.0 cm Hg (centimeters of mercury)
1 mm of Hg is also = 1 torr, in honor of Torricelli.

The English system equivalent of the standard atmosphere is 14.7 lb/in$^2$ (pounds per square inch, abbreviated psi) or 29.9 in Hg (inches of mercury). A recommended, yet less frequently used, systematic unit is the pascal (or kilopascal), named in honor of Blaise Pascal, a seventeenth-century French mathematician and scientist:

$$1 \text{ atm} = 1.01 \times 10^5 \text{ Pa (pascal)} = 101 \text{ kPa (kilopascal)}$$

Atmospheric pressure is due to the cumulative force of the molecules of air ($N_2$ and $O_2$, for the most part) that are attracted to the earth's surface by gravity.

**Question 5.1** Express each of the following in units of atm:
a. 725 mm Hg    b. 29.0 cm Hg    c. 555 torr    d. 95 psi

**Question 5.2** Express each of the following in units of atm:
a. 10.0 torr    b. 61.0 cm Hg    c. 275 mm Hg    d. 124 psi

## Kinetic Molecular Theory of Gases

The kinetic molecular theory of gases provides a reasonable explanation of the behavior of gases. The bulk properties of a gas result from the action of the individual molecules comprising the gas.

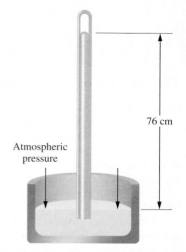

**Figure 5.1** A mercury barometer of the type invented by Torricelli. The mercury in the tube is supported by atmospheric pressure, and the height of the column of mercury is a function of the magnitude of the surrounding atmospheric pressure.

### LEARNING GOAL

**1** Perform conversions between units of pressure.

Pressure equivalencies are used to construct factors that allow conversions from one pressure unit to another. The use of conversion factors was introduced in Chapter 1.

# A Human Perspective

## The Demise of the Hindenburg

One of the largest and most luxurious airships of the 1930s, the Hindenburg, completed thirty-six transatlantic flights within a year after its construction. It was the flagship of a new era of air travel. But, on May 6, 1937, while making a landing approach near Lakehurst, New Jersey, the hydrogen-filled airship exploded and burst into flames. In this tragedy, thirty-seven of the ninety-six passengers were killed and many others were injured.

We may never know the exact cause. Many believe that the massive ship [it was more than 800 feet (ft) long] struck an overhead power line. Others speculate that lightning ignited the hydrogen, and some believe that sabotage may have been involved.

In retrospect, such an accident was inevitable. Hydrogen gas is very reactive, it combines with oxygen readily and rapidly, and this reaction liberates a large amount of energy. Explosions are the result of rapid, energy-releasing reactions.

Why was hydrogen chosen? Hydrogen is the lightest element. One mole of hydrogen has a mass of 2 grams (g). Hydrogen can be easily prepared in pure form, an essential requirement; more than seven million cubic feet (ft$^3$) of hydrogen were needed for each airship. Hydrogen has a low density; hence, it provides great lift. The lifting power of a gas is based on the difference in density of the gas and the surrounding air (air is composed of gases with much greater molar masses; N$_2$ is 28 g/mol and O$_2$ is 32 g/mol). Engineers believed that the hydrogen would be safe when enclosed by the hull of the airship.

Today, airships are filled with helium (molar mass is 4 g/mol), which is far less reactive than hydrogen, and are used

The Hindenburg

principally for advertising and television. A blimp, with its corporate logo prominently displayed, can be seen hovering over almost every significant outdoor sporting event.

### For Further Understanding

▶ Would a gas such as methane (CH$_4$) provide lifting power for an airship? Why or why not?

▶ What property would immediately rule out methane as a replacement gas for hydrogen in an airship?

Kinetic energy (K.E.) is equal to $\frac{1}{2}mv^2$, in which $m$ = mass and $v$ = velocity. Thus, increased velocity at higher temperature correlates with an increase in kinetic energy.

The **kinetic molecular theory** can be summarized as follows:

1. Gases are made up of tiny atoms or molecules that are in constant, random motion. The particles are moving along a linear path, changing direction only as a result of collisions.
2. The distance of separation among these atoms or molecules is very large in comparison to the size of the individual atoms or molecules. In other words, a gas is mostly empty space.
3. All of the atoms and molecules behave independently. No attractive or repulsive forces exist between atoms or molecules in a gas.
4. Atoms and molecules collide with each other and with the walls of the container without *losing* energy. The energy is *transferred* from one atom or molecule to another. These collisions cause random changes in direction.
5. The average kinetic energy of the atoms or molecules increases or decreases in proportion to absolute temperature. As the temperature increases, the speed and kinetic energy of the atoms or molecules increase.

## Properties of Gases and the Kinetic Molecular Theory

We know that gases are easily *compressible*. The reason is that a gas is mostly empty space, providing space for the particles to be pushed closer together.

Gases will *expand* to fill any available volume because they move freely with sufficient energy to overcome their attractive forces.

Gases readily *diffuse* through each other simply because they are in continuous motion and paths are readily available owing to the large space between adjacent atoms or molecules. Light molecules diffuse rapidly; heavier molecules diffuse more slowly (Figure 5.2).

Gases have a *low density*. Density is defined as mass per volume. Because gases are mostly empty space, they have a low mass per volume.

Gases exert *pressure* on their containers. Pressure is a force per unit area resulting from collisions of gas particles with the walls of their container.

Gases behave most *ideally at low pressures and high temperatures*. At low pressures, the average distance of separation among atoms or molecules is greatest, minimizing interactive forces. At high temperatures, the atoms and molecules are in rapid motion and are able to overcome interactive forces more easily.

**LEARNING GOAL**

**3** Explain the relationship between the kinetic molecular theory and the physical properties of measurable quantities of gases.

## Boyle's Law

The Irish scientist Robert Boyle found that the volume of a gas varies *inversely* with the pressure exerted by the gas if the number of mol and temperature of gas are held constant. This relationship is known as **Boyle's law.**

Mathematically, the *product* of pressure ($P$) and volume ($V$) is a constant, $k_b$:

$$PV = k_b$$

This relationship is illustrated in Figure 5.3.

Boyle's law is often used to calculate the volume resulting from a pressure change or vice versa. We consider

$$P_i V_i = k_b$$

with the subscript $i$ representing the *initial* condition and

$$P_f V_f = k_b$$

with the subscript $f$ representing the *final* condition. Because $PV$, initial or final, is constant and is equal to $k_b$,

$$P_i V_i = P_f V_f$$

Consider a gas occupying a volume of 10.0 liters (L) at 1.00 atm of pressure. The product, $P_i V_i = (1.00 \text{ atm})(10.0 \text{ L})$, is a constant, $k_b$, that is equal to 10.0 L · atm. Doubling the pressure, to 2.00 atm, decreases the volume by a factor of two:

$$(2.00 \text{ atm})(V_f) = 10.0 \text{ L} \cdot \text{atm}$$
$$V_f = 5.00 \text{ L}$$

Tripling the pressure decreases the volume by a factor of three:

$$(3.00 \text{ atm})(V_f) = 10.0 \text{ L} \cdot \text{atm}$$
$$V_f = 3.33 \text{ L}$$

**LEARNING GOAL**

**4** Describe the behavior of gases expressed by the gas laws: Boyle's law, Charles's law, combined gas law, Avogadro's law, the ideal gas law, and Dalton's law.

**(a)**

**(b)**

**Figure 5.2** Gaseous diffusion. (a) Ammonia (17.0 g/mol) and hydrogen chloride (36.5 g/mol) are introduced into the ends of a glass tube containing indicating paper. Red indicates the presence of hydrogen chloride and green indicates ammonia. (b) Note that ammonia has diffused much farther than hydrogen chloride in the same amount of time. This is a verification of the kinetic molecular theory. Light molecules move faster than heavier molecules at a specified temperature.

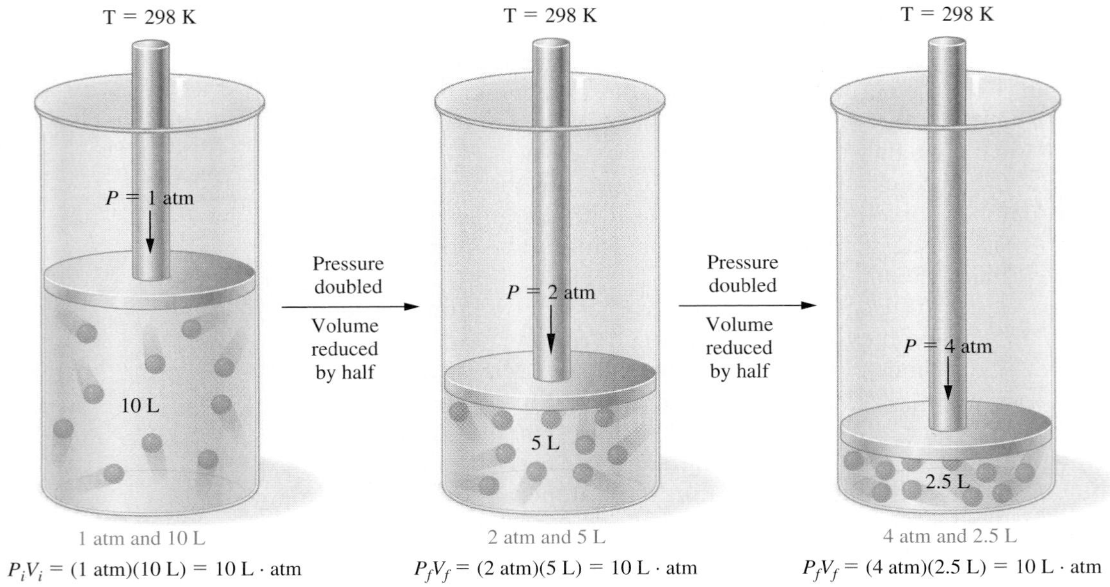

**Figure 5.3** An illustration of Boyle's law. Note the inverse relationship of pressure and volume. Since *PV* is a constant, increases in pressure decrease the volume.

---

**EXAMPLE 5.1**    **Calculating a Final Pressure**

A sample of oxygen, at 25°C, occupies a volume of $5.00 \times 10^2$ milliliters (mL) at 1.50 atm pressure. What pressure must be applied to compress the gas to a volume of $1.50 \times 10^2$ mL, with no temperature change?

LEARNING GOAL

**5** Use gas law equations to calculate conditions and changes in conditions of gases.

**Solution**

**Step 1.** Boyle's law applies directly, because there is no change in temperature or number of mol (no gas enters or leaves the container).

**Step 2.** Begin by identifying each term in the Boyle's law expression:

$$P_i = 1.50 \text{ atm}$$
$$P_f = ?$$
$$V_i = 5.00 \times 10^2 \text{ mL}$$
$$V_f = 1.50 \times 10^2 \text{ mL}$$

**Step 3.** The Boyle's law expression is:

$$P_i V_i = P_f V_f$$

**Step 4.** Solving for $P_f$:

$$P_f = \frac{P_i V_i}{V_f}$$

**Step 5.** Substituting:

$$P_f = \frac{(1.50 \text{ atm})(5.00 \times 10^2 \text{ mL})}{1.50 \times 10^2 \text{ mL}}$$
$$= 5.00 \text{ atm}$$

*Helpful Hint:* The calculation can be done with any volume units. It is important only that the initial and final volume units be the *same*.

## Practice Problem 5.1

Complete the following table:

| Sample Number | Initial Pressure (atm) | Final Pressure (atm) | Initial Volume (L) | Final Volume (L) |
|---|---|---|---|---|
| 1 | X | 5.0 | 1.0 | 7.5 |
| 2 | 5.0 | X | 1.0 | 0.20 |
| 3 | 1.0 | 0.50 | X | 0.30 |
| 4 | 1.0 | 2.0 | 0.75 | X |

▶ For Further Practice: **Questions 5.39 and 5.40.**

## Charles's Law

Jacques Charles, a French scientist, studied the relationship between gas volume and temperature. This relationship, **Charles's law,** states that the volume of a gas varies *directly* with the absolute temperature (K) if pressure and number of mol of gas are constant.

Mathematically, the *ratio* of volume (V) and temperature (T) is a constant, $k_c$:

$$\frac{V}{T} = k_c$$

This relationship is illustrated in Figure 5.4. In a way analogous to Boyle's law, we may establish a set of initial conditions represented with the subscript i,

$$\frac{V_i}{T_i} = k_c$$

and final conditions represented with the subscript f,

$$\frac{V_f}{T_f} = k_c$$

LEARNING GOAL

**4**  Describe the behavior of gases expressed by the gas laws: Boyle's law, Charles's law, combined gas law, Avogadro's law, the ideal gas law, and Dalton's law.

Temperature is a measure of the energy of molecular motion. The Kelvin scale is *absolute;* that is, directly proportional to molecular motion. Celsius and Fahrenheit are simply numerical scales based on the melting and boiling points of water. It is for this reason that Kelvin is used for energy-dependent relationships such as the gas laws.

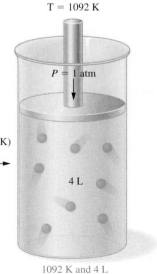

T = 273 K         T = 546 K         T = 1092 K

P = 1 atm

P = 1 atm

P = 1 atm

Temperature (K) doubled

Volume doubled

Temperature (K) doubled

Volume doubled

1 L         2 L         4 L

273 K and 1 L         546 K and 2 L         1092 K and 4 L

$$\frac{V_i}{T_i} = \frac{1\,L}{273\,K} = 3.66 \times 10^{-3}\,L \cdot K^{-1} \qquad \frac{V_f}{T_f} = \frac{2\,L}{546\,K} = 3.66 \times 10^{-3}\,L \cdot K^{-1} \qquad \frac{V_f}{T_f} = \frac{4\,L}{1092\,K} = 3.66 \times 10^{-3}\,L \cdot K^{-1}$$

**Figure 5.4** An illustration of Charles's law. Note the direct relationship between temperature and volume. Since V/T is a constant, increases in temperature will increase the volume.

Remember that this equation is only valid at constant number of mol ($n$) and pressure ($P$).

Because $k_c$ is a constant, we may equate them, resulting in

$$\frac{V_i}{T_i} = \frac{V_f}{T_f}$$

and we may use this expression to solve some practical problems.

Consider a gas occupying a volume of 10.0 L at 273 K. The ratio $V/T$ is a constant, $k_c$. Doubling the temperature, to 546 K, increases the volume to 20.0 L, as shown here:

$$\frac{10.0\text{ L}}{273\text{ K}} = \frac{V_f}{546\text{ K}}$$
$$V_f = 20.0\text{ L}$$

Tripling the temperature, to 819 K, increases the volume by a factor of three:

$$\frac{10.0\text{ L}}{273\text{ K}} = \frac{V_f}{819\text{ K}}$$
$$V_f = 30.0\text{ L}$$

## EXAMPLE 5.2 Calculating a Final Volume

LEARNING GOAL

**5** Use gas law equations to calculate conditions and changes in conditions of gases.

A balloon filled with helium has a volume of $4.0 \times 10^3$ L at 25°C. What volume will the balloon occupy at 50°C if the pressure surrounding the balloon remains constant?

### Solution

**Step 1.** Summarize the data, remembering that the temperature must be converted to Kelvin before Charles's law is applied:

$$T_i = 25°\text{C} + 273 = 298\text{ K}$$
$$T_f = 50°\text{C} + 273 = 323\text{ K}$$
$$V_i = 4.0 \times 10^3\text{ L}$$
$$V_f = ?$$

**Step 2.** Using the Charles's law expression relating initial and final conditions:

$$\frac{V_i}{T_i} = \frac{V_f}{T_f}$$

**Step 3.** Rearrange and solve for $V_f$:

$$V_f = \frac{V_i T_f}{T_i}$$

**Step 4.** Substituting our data, we get

$$V_f = \frac{V_i T_f}{T_i} = \frac{(4.0 \times 10^3\text{ L})(323\text{ }\cancel{\text{K}})}{298\text{ }\cancel{\text{K}}} = 4.3 \times 10^3\text{ L}$$

### Practice Problem 5.2

A sample of nitrogen gas has a volume of 3.00 L at 25°C. What volume will it occupy at each of the following temperatures if the pressure and number of mol are constant?

a. 100°C b. 150°F c. 273 K d. 546 K e. 0°C f. 373 K

▸ For Further Practice: **Questions 5.47 and 5.48.**

The behavior of a fixed-volume hot-air balloon is a commonplace consequence of Charles's law. The balloon rises because air expands when heated (Figure 5.5). The volume of the balloon is fixed because the balloon is made of an inelastic material; as a result, when the air expands as described by Charles' law, some of it must be forced out. Hence, the density of the remaining air is less (less mass contained in the same volume), and the balloon rises. Turning down the heat reverses the process, and the balloon descends.

## Combined Gas Law

Boyle's law describes the inverse proportional relationship between volume and pressure; Charles's law shows the direct proportional relationship between volume and temperature. Often, a sample of gas (a fixed number of mol of gas) undergoes change involving volume, pressure, and temperature simultaneously.

The **combined gas law** is one equation that describes such processes. It can be derived from Boyle's law and Charles's law and takes the form:

$$\frac{P_i V_i}{T_i} = \frac{P_f V_f}{T_f}$$

Let's look at two examples that use this expression.

**Figure 5.5** Charles's law predicts that the volume of air in the balloon will increase when heated.

---

| EXAMPLE 5.3 | **Using the Combined Gas Law** |
| --- | --- |

If 0.100 L of $N_2$ at 27.0°C and 1.00 atm is compressed to a pressure of 10.0 atm at 77.0°C, calculate the new volume of $N_2$.

**LEARNING GOAL**

**5** Use gas law equations to calculate conditions and changes in conditions of gases.

**Solution**

**Step 1.** Summarize the data, remembering that the temperature must be converted to Kelvin before the combined gas law is applied:

$$P_i = 1.00 \text{ atm} \qquad\qquad P_f = 10.0 \text{ atm}$$
$$V_i = 0.100 \text{ L} \qquad\qquad V_f = ? \text{ L}$$
$$T_i = 27.0°C + 273.15 = 300.2 \text{ K} \qquad T_f = 77.0°C + 273.15 = 350.2 \text{ K}$$

**Step 2.** The combined gas law expression is:

$$\frac{P_i V_i}{T_i} = \frac{P_f V_f}{T_f}$$

**Step 3.** Rearrange:

$$P_f V_f T_i = P_i V_i T_f$$

and solve for $V_f$:

$$V_f = \frac{P_i V_i T_f}{P_f T_i}$$

**Step 4.** Substituting gives

$$V_f = \frac{(1.00 \text{ atm})(0.100 \text{ L})(350.2 \text{ K})}{(10.0 \text{ atm})(300.2 \text{ K})}$$
$$= 0.0117 \text{ L}$$

*Continued…*

## Practice Problem 5.3

Hydrogen sulfide, $H_2S$, has the characteristic odor of rotten eggs. If a sample of $H_2S$ gas at 760.0 torr and 25.0°C in a 2.00-L container is allowed to expand into a 10.0-L container at 25.0°C, what is the pressure, in atmospheres, in the 10.0-L container?

▶ For Further Practice: **Questions 5.57 and 5.58.**

## EXAMPLE 5.4   Using the Combined Gas Law

LEARNING GOAL

**5** Use gas law equations to calculate conditions and changes in conditions of gases.

A sample of helium gas has a volume of 1.27 L at 149 K and 5.00 atm. When the gas is compressed to 0.320 L at 50.0 atm, the temperature increases markedly. What is the final temperature?

### Solution

**Step 1.** Summarize the data:

$$P_i = 5.00 \text{ atm} \quad P_f = 50.0 \text{ atm}$$
$$V_i = 1.27 \text{ L} \quad V_f = 0.320 \text{ L}$$
$$T_i = 149 \text{ K} \quad T_f = ? \text{ K}$$

**Step 2.** The combined gas law expression is

$$\frac{P_i V_i}{T_i} = \frac{P_f V_f}{T_f}$$

**Step 3.** Rearrange:

$$P_f V_f T_i = P_i V_i T_f$$

and solve for $T_f$:

$$T_f = \frac{P_f V_f T_i}{P_i V_i}$$

**Step 4.** Substituting gives

$$T_f = \frac{(50.0 \text{ atm})(0.320 \text{ L})(149 \text{ K})}{(5.00 \text{ atm})(1.27 \text{ L})}$$
$$= 375 \text{ K}$$

## Practice Problem 5.4

Cyclopropane, $C_3H_6$, is used as a general anesthetic. If a sample of cyclopropane stored in a 2.00-L container at 10.0 atm and 25.0°C is transferred to a 5.00-L container at 5.00 atm, what is the resulting temperature?

▶ For Further Practice: **Questions 5.59 and 5.60.**

LEARNING GOAL

**4** Describe the behavior of gases expressed by the gas laws: Boyle's law, Charles's law, combined gas law, Avogadro's law, the ideal gas law, and Dalton's law.

## Avogadro's Law

The relationship between the volume and number of mol of a gas at constant temperature and pressure is known as **Avogadro's law.** It states that equal volumes of any ideal gas contain the same number of mol if measured under the same conditions of temperature and pressure.

Mathematically, the *ratio* of volume ($V$) to number of mol ($n$) is a constant, $k_a$:

$$\frac{V}{n} = k_a$$

Consider 1 mol of gas occupying a volume of 10.0 L; using logic similar to the application of Boyle's and Charles's laws, 2 mol of the gas would occupy 20.0 L,

3 mol would occupy 30.0 L, and so forth. As we have done with the previous laws, we can formulate a useful expression relating initial and final conditions:

$$\frac{V_i}{n_i} = \frac{V_f}{n_f}$$

**EXAMPLE 5.5**  **Using Avogadro's Law**

LEARNING GOAL

If 5.50 mol of CO occupy 20.6 L, how many L will 16.5 mol of CO occupy at the same temperature and pressure?

**5** Use gas law equations to calculate conditions and changes in conditions of gases.

**Solution**

**Step 1.** The quantities volume and number of moles are related through Avogadro's law. Summarizing the data:

$$V_i = 20.6 \text{ L} \qquad V_f = ? \text{ L}$$
$$n_i = 5.50 \text{ mol} \qquad n_f = 16.5 \text{ mol}$$

**Step 2.** Using the mathematical expression for Avogadro's law:

$$\frac{V_i}{n_i} = \frac{V_f}{n_f}$$

**Step 3.** Rearranging to solve for $V_f$:

$$V_f = \frac{V_i n_f}{n_i}$$

**Step 4.** Substitution yields:

$$V_f = \frac{(20.6 \text{ L})(16.5 \cancel{\text{ mol}})}{(5.50 \cancel{\text{ mol}})}$$
$$= 61.8 \text{ L of CO}$$

**Practice Problem 5.5**

a. A 1.00-mol sample of hydrogen gas occupies 22.4 L. How many mol of hydrogen are needed to fill a 100.0-L container at the same pressure and temperature?

b. How many mol of hydrogen are needed to triple the volume occupied by 0.25 mol of hydrogen, assuming no changes in pressure or temperature?

▶ For Further Practice: **Questions 5.63 and 5.64.**

## Molar Volume of a Gas

The volume occupied by *1 mol* of any gas is referred to as its **molar volume.** At **standard temperature and pressure (STP)**, the molar volume of any gas is 22.4 L. STP conditions are defined as follows:

LEARNING GOAL

**6** Use molar volume and standard temperature and pressure (STP) to perform calculations.

$$T = 273 \text{ K (or 0°C)}$$
$$P = 1 \text{ atm}$$

Thus, 1 mol of $N_2$, $O_2$, $CO_2$, $H_2$, or He all occupy the *same volume, 22.4 L,* at STP.

## Gas Densities

It is also possible to compute the density of various gases at STP. If we recall that density is the mass/unit volume,

Gas densities are most often expressed in units of g/L. Recall that units of g/mL are generally preferred for solids and liquids.

$$d = \frac{m}{V}$$

and that 1 mol of helium weighs 4.00 g,

$$d_{He} = \frac{4.00 \text{ g}}{22.4 \text{ L}} = 0.178 \text{ g/L at STP}$$

or, because 1 mol of nitrogen weighs 28.0 g, then

$$d_{N_2} = \frac{28.0 \text{ g}}{22.4 \text{ L}} = 1.25 \text{ g/L at STP}$$

The large difference in gas densities of helium and nitrogen (which makes up about 80% of the air) accounts for the lifting power of helium. A balloon filled with helium will rise through a predominantly nitrogen atmosphere because its gas density is less than 15% of the density of the surrounding atmosphere:

$$\frac{d_{He}}{d_{N_2}} \times 100\% = \% \text{ density}$$

$$\frac{0.178 \text{ g/L}}{1.25 \text{ g/L}} \times 100\% = 14.2\%$$

Heating a gas, such as air, will decrease its density and have a lifting effect as well.

## The Ideal Gas Law

Boyle's law (relating volume and pressure), Charles's law (relating volume and temperature), and Avogadro's law (relating volume to the number of mol) may be combined into a single expression relating all four terms. This expression is the **ideal gas law:**

$$PV = nRT$$

in which $R$ is a constant based on $k_b$, $k_c$, and $k_a$ (Boyle's, Charles's, and Avogadro's law constants) and is referred to as the *ideal gas constant:*

$$R = 0.0821 \text{ L} \cdot \text{atm} \cdot \text{K}^{-1} \cdot \text{mol}^{-1}$$

which is identical to

$$R = 0.0821 \frac{\text{L} \cdot \text{atm}}{\text{K} \cdot \text{mol}}$$

if the units

atmospheres for $P$,
liters for $V$,
moles for $n$,
and
Kelvin for $T$

are used.

Consider some examples of the application of the ideal gas equation.

### LEARNING GOAL

**4** Describe the behavior of gases expressed by the gas laws: Boyle's law, Charles's law, combined gas law, Avogadro's law, the ideal gas law, and Dalton's law.

---

**EXAMPLE 5.6** | **Calculating a Molar Volume**

Show by calculation that the molar volume of oxygen gas at STP is 22.4 L.

**Solution**

**Step 1.** At STP,

$$T = 273 \text{ K}$$
$$P = 1.00 \text{ atm}$$

and the other terms are

$$n = 1.00 \text{ mol}$$
$$R = 0.0821 \text{ L} \cdot \text{atm} \cdot \text{K}^{-1} \cdot \text{mol}^{-1}$$

### LEARNING GOALS

**5** Use gas law equations to calculate conditions and changes in conditions of gases.

**6** Use molar volume and standard temperature and pressure (STP) to perform calculations.

**Step 2.** The ideal gas expression is:

$$PV = nRT$$

**Step 3.** Rearrange and solve for $V$:

$$V = \frac{nRT}{P}$$

**Step 4.** Substitute and solve:

$$V = \frac{(1.00 \ \text{mol})(0.0821 \ \text{L} \cdot \text{atm} \cdot \text{K}^{-1} \cdot \text{mol}^{-1})(273 \ \text{K})}{(1.00 \ \text{atm})}$$

$$= 22.4 \ \text{L}$$

### Practice Problem 5.6

Explain why the molar volume of helium (or any other ideal gas) is 22.4 L.

▶ For Further Practice: **Questions 5.65 and 5.66.**

---

**EXAMPLE 5.7**    **Calculating the Number of Moles of a Gas**

LEARNING GOAL

Calculate the number of mol of helium in a 1.00-L balloon at 27°C and 1.00 atm of pressure.

**5** Use gas law equations to calculate conditions and changes in conditions of gases.

**Solution**

**Step 1.** The data are:

$$P = 1.00 \ \text{atm}$$
$$V = 1.00 \ \text{L}$$
$$T = 27°\text{C} + 273.15 = 3.00 \times 10^2 \ \text{K}$$
$$R = 0.0821 \ \text{L} \cdot \text{atm} \cdot \text{K}^{-1} \cdot \text{mol}^{-1}$$
$$n = ?$$

**Step 2.** The ideal gas expression is:

$$PV = nRT$$

**Step 3.** Rearrange and solve for $n$:

$$n = \frac{PV}{RT}$$

**Step 4.** Substitute and solve:

$$n = \frac{(1.00 \ \text{atm})(1.00 \ \text{L})}{(0.0821 \ \text{L} \cdot \text{atm} \cdot \text{K}^{-1} \cdot \text{mol}^{-1})(3.00 \times 10^2 \ \text{K})}$$

$$n = 0.0406 \ \text{or} \ 4.06 \times 10^{-2} \ \text{mol}$$

### Practice Problem 5.7

How many mol of $N_2$ gas will occupy a 5.00-L container at STP?

▶ For Further Practice: **Questions 5.69 and 5.70.**

## EXAMPLE 5.8 | Converting Mass to Volume

LEARNING GOAL

**5** Use gas law equations to calculate conditions and changes in conditions of gases.

Oxygen used in hospitals and laboratories is often obtained from cylinders containing liquefied oxygen. If a cylinder contains $1.00 \times 10^2$ kilograms (kg) of liquid oxygen, how many L of oxygen can be produced at 1.00 atm of pressure at room temperature (20.0°C)?

### Solution

**Step 1.** Summarize the data:

mass of oxygen ($O_2$) = $1.00 \times 10^2$ kg
$T = 20.0°C$
$P = 1.00$ atm
$V$ of $O_2$ = ?

**Step 2.** The number of moles of $O_2$ ($n$) is obtained by using two conversion factors based on 1000 g = 1 kg and the molar mass of $O_2$ (32.0 g/mol):

$$n = 1.00 \times 10^2 \ \cancel{kg \, O_2} \times \frac{10^3 \ \cancel{g \, O_2}}{1 \ \cancel{kg \, O_2}} \times \frac{1 \ mol \ O_2}{32.0 \ \cancel{g \, O_2}} = 3.13 \times 10^3 \ mol \ O_2$$

**Step 3.** Convert °C to K:

$$T = 20.0°C + 273.15 = 293.2 \ K$$

**Step 4.** The ideal gas expression is:

$$PV = nRT$$

**Step 5.** Rearrange and solve for $V$:

$$V = \frac{nRT}{P}$$

**Step 6.** Substitute and solve:

$$V = \frac{(3.13 \times 10^3 \ \cancel{mol})(0.0821 \ L \cdot atm \cdot \cancel{K^{-1}} \cdot \cancel{mol^{-1}})(293.2 \ \cancel{K})}{1.00 \ \cancel{atm}}$$

$$= 7.53 \times 10^4 \ L$$

### Practice Problem 5.8

What volume is occupied by 10.0 g $N_2$ at 30.0°C and a pressure of 750 torr?

▶ For Further Practice: **Questions 5.75 and 5.76.**

**Question 5.3**   A 20.0-L gas cylinder contains 4.80 g $H_2$ at 25°C. What is the pressure of this gas?

**Question 5.4**   At what temperature will 2.00 mol of He fill a 2.00-L container at standard pressure?

LEARNING GOAL

**4** Describe the behavior of gases expressed by the gas laws: Boyle's law, Charles's law, combined gas law, Avogadro's law, the ideal gas law, and Dalton's law.

## Dalton's Law of Partial Pressures

Our discussion of gases so far has presumed that we are working with a single pure gas. A *mixture* of gases exerts a pressure that is the *sum* of the pressures that each gas would exert if it were present alone under the same conditions. This is known as **Dalton's law** of partial pressures. Dalton's law is based on the assumption that the behavior of each gas in a mixture of gases is independent of all of the other gases.

# Green Chemistry

## The Greenhouse Effect and Global Climate Change

A greenhouse is a bright, warm, and humid environment for growing plants, vegetables, and flowers even during the cold winter months. It functions as a closed system in which the concentration of water vapor is elevated and visible light streams through the windows; this creates an ideal climate for plant growth.

Some of the visible light is absorbed by plants and soil in the greenhouse and released as infrared radiation. This radiated energy is blocked by the glass or absorbed by water vapor and carbon dioxide ($CO_2$). This trapped energy warms the greenhouse and is a form of solar heating: light energy is converted to heat energy. Hence, water vapor and carbon dioxide are termed *greenhouse gases.*

On a global scale, the same process takes place. Although more than half of the sunlight that strikes the earth's surface is reflected back into space, the fraction of light that is absorbed produces sufficient heat to sustain life. How does this happen? Greenhouse gases, such as $CO_2$, trap energy radiated from the earth's surface and store it in the atmosphere. This moderates our climate. The earth's surface would be much colder and more inhospitable if the atmosphere was not able to capture some reasonable amount of solar energy.

Can we have too much of a good thing? It appears so. Since 1900, the atmospheric concentration of $CO_2$ has increased from 296 parts per million (ppm) to over 350 ppm (approximately 17% increase). The energy demands of technological and population growth have caused massive increases in the combustion of organic matter and carbon-based fuels (coal, oil, and natural gas), adding over 50 billion tons of $CO_2$ to that already present in the atmosphere. Photosynthesis naturally removes $CO_2$ from the atmosphere. However, the removal of forestland to create living space and cropland has decreased the amount of vegetation available to consume atmospheric $CO_2$ through photosynthesis. The rapid destruction of the Amazon rain forest is just the latest of many examples.

Many gases, in addition to $H_2O$ and $CO_2$, behave as greenhouse gases. Any molecule in the gas phase that is capable of absorbing infrared radiation may behave as a greenhouse gas. Many, however, are unimportant in the global climate change discussion simply because they are not present in the atmosphere in significant quantity. Methane ($CH_4$), an infrared absorber, exists at higher levels and is a potent greenhouse gas. It has received little attention principally because we have relatively little control over its atmospheric levels.

If our greenhouse model is a correct representation of our atmosphere, an increase in $CO_2$ levels should contribute to global warming, perhaps changing our climate in unforeseen and undesirable ways.

### For Further Understanding

▶ What steps might be taken to decrease levels of $CO_2$ in the atmosphere over time?

▶ In what ways might our climate and our lives change as a consequence of significant global warming?

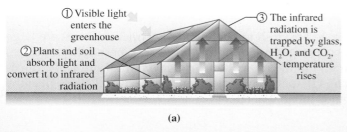

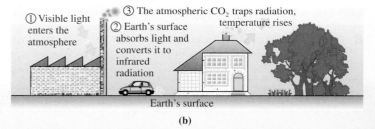

(a) A greenhouse traps solar radiation as heat. (b) Our atmosphere also acts as a solar collector. Carbon dioxide, like the windows of a greenhouse, allows the visible light to enter and traps the heat.

---

Stated another way, the total pressure of a mixture of gases is the sum of the **partial pressures.** That is,

$$P_t = p_1 + p_2 + p_3 + \cdots$$

in which $P_t$ = total pressure and $p_1, p_2, p_3, \ldots$, are the partial pressures of the component gases. For example, the total pressure of our atmosphere is equal to the sum of the pressures of $N_2$ and $O_2$ (the principal components of air):

$$P_{air} = p_{N_2} + p_{O_2}$$

The ideal gas law applies to mixtures of gases as well as pure gases.

Other gases, such as argon (Ar), carbon dioxide ($CO_2$), carbon monoxide (CO), and methane ($CH_4$) are present in the atmosphere at very low partial pressures. However, their presence may result in dramatic consequences; one such gas is carbon dioxide. Classified as a "greenhouse gas," it exerts a significant effect on our climate. Its role is described in Green Chemistry: The Greenhouse Effect and Global Climate Change.

## Ideal Gases Versus Real Gases

See Sections 3.5 and 5.2 for a discussion of interactions of polar molecules.

To this point we have assumed, in both theory and calculations, that all gases behave as ideal gases. However, in reality there is no such thing as an ideal gas. As we noted at the beginning of this section, the ideal gas is a model (a very useful one) that describes the behavior of individual atoms and molecules; this behavior translates to the collective properties of measurable quantities of these atoms and molecules. Limitations of the model arise from the fact that interactive forces, even between the widely spaced particles of gas, are not totally absent in any sample of gas.

Gases comprised of polar molecules have stronger attractive forces than gases made up of nonpolar molecules. Nonuniform charge distribution on polar molecules creates positive and negative regions, resulting in electrostatic attraction and deviation from ideality.

Calculations involving polar gases such as HF, NO, and $SO_2$ based on ideal gas equations (which presume no such interactions) are approximations. However, at low pressures, such approximations certainly provide useful information. Nonpolar molecules, on the other hand, are only weakly attracted to each other and behave much more ideally in the gas phase.

**LEARNING GOAL**

**7** Discuss the limitations to the ideal gas model as it applies to real gases.

Gases behave less ideally as their temperature decreases; they become more like the liquid phase as they approach their condensation temperature.

**Question 5.5**   Radon and nitrogen dioxide are gases at 25°C. Which exhibits more ideal behavior? Explain your answer.

**Question 5.6**   Hydrogen sulfide ($H_2S$) is a gas at 0°C. When its temperature is decreased, does it behave more or less ideally? Explain your answer.

## 5.2  The Liquid State

**LEARNING GOAL**

**8** Describe properties of the liquid state in terms of the properties of the individual molecules that comprise the liquid.

Molecules in the liquid state are close to one another. Attractive forces are large enough to keep the molecules together, in contrast to gases, whose cohesive forces are so low that gases expand to fill any volume. However, these attractive forces in liquids are not large enough to restrict movement, as in solids. Let's look at the various properties of liquids in more detail.

### Compressibility

Liquids are practically incompressible. In fact, the molecules are so close to one another that even the application of very high pressure does not significantly decrease the volume. This makes liquids ideal for the transmission of force, as in the brake lines of an automobile. The force applied by the driver's foot on the brake pedal does not compress the brake fluid in the lines; rather, it transmits the force directly to the brake pads, and the friction between the brake pads and rotors (that are attached to the wheels) stops the car.

### Viscosity

The **viscosity** of a liquid is a measure of its resistance to flow. Viscosity is a function of both the attractive forces between molecules and molecular geometry.

Molecules with complex structures, which do not "slide" smoothly past each other, and polar molecules tend to have higher viscosity than less structurally complex, less polar liquids. Glycerol, which is used in a variety of skin treatments, has the structural formula:

$$
\begin{array}{c}
\text{H} \\
| \\
\text{H—C—O—H} \\
| \\
\text{H—C—O—H} \\
| \\
\text{H—C—O—H} \\
| \\
\text{H}
\end{array}
$$

It is quite viscous, owing to its polar nature and its significant intermolecular attractive forces. This is certainly desirable in a skin treatment because its viscosity keeps it on the area being treated. Gasoline, on the other hand, is much less viscous and readily flows through the gas lines of your auto; it is composed of nonpolar molecules.

Viscosity generally decreases with increasing temperature. The increased kinetic energy at higher temperatures overcomes some of the intermolecular attractive forces. The temperature effect is an important consideration in the design of products that must remain fluid at low temperatures, such as motor oils and transmission fluids found in automobiles.

## Surface Tension

The **surface tension** of a liquid is a measure of the attractive forces exerted among molecules at the surface of the liquid. It is only the surface molecules that are not totally surrounded by other liquid molecules (the top of the molecule faces the atmosphere). These surface molecules are surrounded and attracted by fewer liquid molecules than the interior molecules. Hence, the net attractive forces on surface molecules are greater (greater force per molecule) because each surface molecule shares its attractive forces with fewer molecules. The resulting stronger attractive forces pull the surface molecules downward, into the body of the liquid. As a result, the surface molecules behave as a tight "skin" that covers the interior.

This increased surface force is responsible for the spherical shape of drops of liquid. Drops of water "beading" on a polished surface, such as a waxed automobile, illustrate this effect.

Because surface tension is related to the attractive forces exerted among molecules, surface tension generally decreases with an increase in temperature or a decrease in the polarity of molecules that make up the liquid.

A **surfactant** is a substance that can be added to a liquid to decrease surface tension. Surfactants have polar and nonpolar regions at opposite ends of their molecules. The polar ends of the molecules interact with polar liquids to decrease attractive forces at the surface (hence, lowering surface tension). Common surfactants include soaps and detergents that reduce water's surface tension; this promotes the interaction of water with grease and dirt, making them easier to remove. For more information on these interesting molecules, see Kitchen Chemistry: Solubility, Surfactants and the Dishwasher, Chapter 6.

**Question 5.7** What molecular properties favor high viscosity?

**Question 5.8** What molecular properties favor high surface tension?

## Vapor Pressure of a Liquid

Evaporation, condensation, and the meaning of the term *boiling point* are all related to the concept of liquid vapor pressure. Consider the following example. A liquid,

Skipping stones is possible due to the surface tension of water. Explain.

Compounds may be detected and identified because they have a measurable vapor pressure, as you will see in the discussion Chemistry at the Crime Scene: Explosives at the Airport.

### LEARNING GOAL

**9** Describe the processes of melting, boiling, evaporation, condensation, and sublimation.

such as water, is placed in a sealed container. After a time, the contents of the container are analyzed. Both liquid water and water vapor are found at room temperature, when we might expect water to be found only as a liquid. In this closed system, some of the liquid water was converted to a gas:

$$\text{energy} + H_2O(l) \longrightarrow H_2O(g)$$

How did this happen? The temperature is too low for conversion of a liquid to a gas by boiling. According to the kinetic molecular theory, liquid molecules are in continuous motion, with their *average* kinetic energy directly proportional to the Kelvin temperature. The word *average* is the key. Although the average kinetic energy is too low to allow "average" molecules to escape from the liquid phase to the gas phase, there exists a range of molecules with different energies, some low and some high, that make up the "average" (Figure 5.6). Thus, some of these high-energy molecules possess sufficient energy to escape from the bulk liquid.

At the same time, a fraction of these gaseous molecules lose energy (perhaps by collision with the walls of the container) and return to the liquid state:

$$H_2O(g) \longrightarrow H_2O(l) + \text{energy}$$

The process of conversion of liquid to gas, at a temperature too low to boil, is **evaporation.** The reverse process, conversion of the gas to the liquid state, is **condensation.** After some time, the rates of evaporation and condensation become *equal,* and this sets up a dynamic equilibrium between liquid and vapor states. The **vapor pressure of a liquid** is defined as the pressure exerted by the vapor *at equilibrium.*

$$H_2O(g) \rightleftharpoons H_2O(l)$$

The equilibrium process of evaporation and condensation of water is depicted in Figure 5.7.

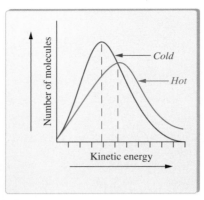

**Figure 5.6** The range of molecules with different kinetic energies is illustrated. The small number of high-energy molecules possess sufficient energy to evaporate. Note that the average values are indicated by dashed lines.

The process of evaporation of perspiration from the skin produces a cooling effect, because heat is absorbed and carried away by the evaporating molecules.

## Boiling Point and Vapor Pressure

The boiling point of a liquid is defined as the temperature at which the vapor pressure of the liquid becomes equal to the atmospheric pressure. The "normal" atmospheric pressure is 760 torr, or 1 atm, and the **normal boiling point** is the temperature at which the vapor pressure of the liquid is equal to 1 atm.

It follows from the definition that the boiling point of a liquid is not constant. It depends on the atmospheric pressure. At high altitudes, where the atmospheric pressure is low, the boiling point of a liquid, such as water, is lower than the normal boiling point (for water, 100°C). Alternatively, high atmospheric pressure increases the boiling point.

Apart from its dependence on the surrounding atmospheric pressure, the boiling point depends on the nature of the attractive forces between the liquid molecules. Polar liquids, such as water, with large intermolecular attractive forces have *higher* boiling points than nonpolar liquids, such as gasoline, which exhibit weak attractive forces.

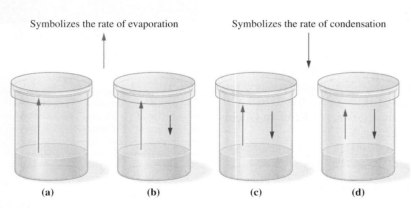

**Figure 5.7** Liquid water in equilibrium with water vapor. (a) Initiation: process of evaporation exclusively. (b, c) After a time, both evaporation and condensation occur, but evaporation predominates. (d) Dynamic equilibrium established. Rates of evaporation and condensation are equal.

**Question 5.9**    Distinguish between the terms *evaporation* and *condensation*.

**Question 5.10**    Distinguish between the terms *evaporation* and *boiling*.

## van der Waals Forces

LEARNING GOAL

**10** Describe the dipolar attractions known collectively as van der Waals forces.

Many physical properties of liquids, such as melting and boiling temperatures, can be explained in terms of their intermolecular forces. Attractive forces between polar molecules, **dipole-dipole interactions,** significantly decrease vapor pressure and increase the boiling point. However, nonpolar substances can exist as liquids as well; many are liquids and even solids at room temperature. What is the nature of the attractive forces in these nonpolar compounds?

In 1930, Fritz London demonstrated the presence of a weak attractive force between any two molecules, whether polar or nonpolar. He postulated that the electron distribution in molecules is not fixed; electrons are in continuous motion, relative to the nucleus. So, for a short time a nonpolar molecule could experience an *instantaneous dipole,* a short-lived polarity caused by a temporary dislocation of the electron cloud. These temporary dipoles could interact with other temporary dipoles, just as permanent dipoles interact in polar molecules (Figure 5.8). We now call these intermolecular forces **London dispersion forces.**

London dispersion forces and dipole-dipole interactions are collectively known as **van der Waals forces.** London dispersion forces exist among polar and nonpolar molecules because electrons are in constant motion in all molecules. Dipole-dipole attractions occur only among polar molecules. In addition to van der Waals forces, a special type of dipole-dipole force, the *hydrogen bond,* has a very significant effect on molecular properties, particularly in biological systems.

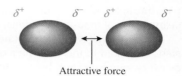

Attractive force

**Figure 5.8** London dispersion forces. A temporary dipole results when the electron distribution is unsymmetrical. The nucleus has a partial positive charge represented by $\delta^+$, and the electrons have a partial negative charge represented by $\delta^-$.

## Hydrogen Bonding

LEARNING GOAL

**11** Describe hydrogen bonding and its relationship to boiling and melting temperatures.

Typical forces in polar liquids, discussed earlier, are only about 1–2% as strong as ionic and covalent bonds. However, certain liquids have boiling points that are much higher than we would predict from these polar interactions alone. This indicates the presence of some strong intermolecular force. This attractive force is due to **hydrogen bonding.** Molecules in which a hydrogen atom is bonded to a small, highly electronegative atom such as nitrogen, oxygen, or fluorine exhibit this effect. The presence of a highly electronegative atom bonded to a hydrogen atom creates a large dipole:

*Recall that the most electronegative elements are in the upper right corner of the periodic table, and these elements exert strong electron attraction in molecules, as described in Chapter 3.*

$$
\begin{array}{ccc}
\overset{\delta^-}{N} & \overset{\delta^-}{O}\overset{\delta^-}{} & \delta^-:\overset{\delta^-}{F}:\delta^- \\
\underset{\delta^+\ \delta^+\ \delta^+}{H\ H\ H} & \underset{\delta^+\quad\ \delta^+}{H\quad H} & \underset{\delta^+}{H}
\end{array}
$$

Although the hydrogen bond is weaker than bonds formed *within* molecules (covalent and polar covalent *intra*molecular forces), it is the strongest attractive force *between* molecules (*inter*molecular force).

Consider the boiling points of four small molecules:

| $CH_4$ | $NH_3$ | $H_2O$ | HF |
|---|---|---|---|
| molar mass | molar mass | molar mass | molar mass |
| 16 g/mol | 17 g/mol | 18 g/mol | 20 g/mol |
| −161°C | −33°C | +100°C | +19.5°C |

# Chemistry at the Crime Scene

## Explosives at the Airport

The images flash across our television screens: a "bomb sniffing" dog being led through an airport or train station, pausing to sniff packages or passengers, looking for anything of a suspicious nature. Or, perhaps, we see a long line of people waiting to pass through a scanning device surrounded by what appears to be hundreds of thousands of dollars worth of electronic gadgetry.

At one level, we certainly know what is happening. These steps are taken to increase the likelihood that our trip, as well as everyone else's, will be as safe and worry-free as possible. From a scientific standpoint, we may wonder how these steps actually detect explosive materials. What do the dog and some electronic devices have in common? How can a dog sniff a solid or a liquid? Surely everyone knows that the nose can only sense gases, and explosive devices are solids or liquids, or a combination of the two.

One potential strategy is based on the concept of vapor pressure. We know that liquids, such as water, have a measurable vapor pressure at room temperature. In fact, most liquids and many solids have vapor pressures large enough to allow detection of the molecules in the gas phase. The challenge is finding devices that are sufficiently sensitive and selective, enabling them to detect low concentrations of molecules characteristic of explosives, without becoming confused by thousands of other compounds routinely present in the air.

Each explosive device has its own "signature," a unique mix of chemicals used in its manufacture and assembly. If only one, or perhaps a few, of these compounds has a measurable vapor pressure, it may be detected with a sensitive measuring device.

Dogs are renowned for their keen sense of smell, and some breeds are better than others. Dogs can be trained to signal the presence of certain scents by barking or exhibiting unusual agitation. A qualified handler can recognize these cues and alert appropriate authorities.

Scientific instruments are designed to mimic the scenario described here. A device, the mass spectrometer, can detect very low concentrations of molecules in the air. Additionally,

Specially trained dogs detect the specific scents of several common explosive materials.

it can distinguish certain "target" molecules, because each different compound has its own unique molar mass. Detection of molecules of interest generates an electrical signal, and an alarm is sounded.

Compounds with high vapor pressures are most easily detected. Active areas of forensic research involve designing a new generation of instruments that are even more sensitive and selective than those currently available. Decreased cost and increased portability and reliability will enable many sites not currently being monitored to have the same level of protection as major transit facilities.

### For Further Understanding

▶ Would you expect nonpolar or polar molecules of similar mass to be more easily detected? Why?

▶ Why must an explosives detection device be highly selective?

---

Clearly, ammonia, water, and hydrogen fluoride boil at significantly higher temperatures than methane. The N—H, O—H, and F—H bonds are far more polar than the C—H bond, owing to the high electronegativity of N, O, and F.

It is interesting to note that the boiling points increase as the electronegativity of the element bonded to hydrogen increases, with one exception: Fluorine, with the highest electronegativity, should cause HF to have the highest boiling point. This is not the case. The order of boiling points is

methane < ammonia < hydrogen fluoride < water

Why? To answer this question, we must look at the *number of potential bonding sites* in each molecule. Water has two partial positive sites (located at each hydrogen atom) and two partial negative sites (two lone pairs of electrons on the oxygen

Intramolecular hydrogen bonding between polar regions helps keep proteins folded in their proper three-dimensional structure. See Chapter 18.

atom); it can form hydrogen bonds at each site. This results in a complex network of attractive forces among water molecules in the liquid state, and the strength of the forces holding this network together accounts for water's unusually high boiling point. This network is depicted in Figure 5.9.

Ammonia and hydrogen fluoride can form only one hydrogen bond per molecule. Ammonia has three partial positive sites (three hydrogen atoms bonded to nitrogen) but only one partial negative site (the lone pair); the single partial negative site is the limiting factor. Hydrogen fluoride has only one partial positive site and three partial negative sites (three lone pairs); the single partial positive site is the limiting factor. Consequently, hydrogen fluoride, like ammonia, can form only one hydrogen bond per molecule. The network of attractive forces in ammonia and hydrogen fluoride is, therefore, much less extensive than that found in water, and their boiling points are considerably lower than that of water.

Hydrogen bonding has an extremely important influence on the behavior of many biological systems. Molecules such as proteins and DNA require extensive hydrogen bonding to maintain their structures and hence functions. DNA (deoxyribonucleic acid, Section 20.2) is a giant among molecules, with intertwined chains of atoms held together by thousands of hydrogen bonds.

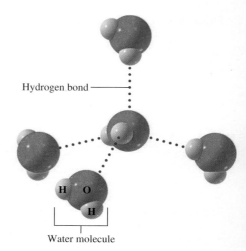

**Figure 5.9** Hydrogen bonding in water. Note that the central water molecule is hydrogen bonded to four other water molecules. The attractive force between the hydrogen ($\delta^+$) part of one water molecule and the oxygen ($\delta^-$) part of another water molecule constitutes the hydrogen bond.

**Question 5.11**   Arrange the following compounds in order of increasing boiling point:

$$CO_2 \qquad CH_3OH \qquad CH_3Cl$$

Explain your logic.

**Question 5.12**   Explain the large difference in boiling point (b.p.) for the isomers butanol and diethyl ether.

butanol
b.p. = 117°C

diethyl ether
b.p. = 34.5°C

## 5.3   The Solid State

The close packing of the particles of a solid results from attractive forces that are strong enough to restrict motion. This occurs because the kinetic energy of the particles is insufficient to overcome the attractive forces among particles. The particles are "locked" together in a defined and highly organized fashion. This results in a fixed shape and volume, and at the atomic level, only vibrational motion is observed.

### Properties of Solids

Solids are virtually incompressible, owing to the small distance between particles. Most will convert to liquids at a higher temperature, when the increased heat energy overcomes some of the attractive forces within the solid. The temperature at which a solid is converted to the liquid phase is its *melting point*. The melting point depends on the strength of the attractive forces in the solid, hence its structure. As we might expect, polar solids have higher melting points than nonpolar solids of the same molecular weight.

**LEARNING GOAL**

**12**   Relate the properties of the various classes of solids (ionic, covalent, molecular, and metallic) to the structure of these solids.

**Figure 5.10** Crystalline solids.

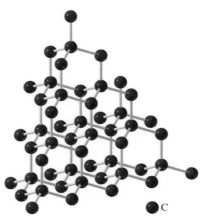

**(a)** The crystal structure of diamond.

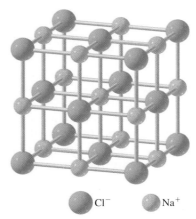

Cl⁻    Na⁺

**(b)** The crystal structure of sodium chloride.

**(c)** The crystal structure of methane, a frozen molecular solid. Only one methane molecule is shown in detail.

**(d)** The crystal structure of a metallic solid. The gray area represents mobile electrons around fixed metal cations.

*The chemical compositions and crystalline structures of various gemstones are discussed in A Human Perspective: Gemstones.*

A solid may be a **crystalline solid,** having a regular repeating structure, or an **amorphous solid,** having no organized structure. Diamond and sodium chloride (Figure 5.10) are examples of crystalline substances; glass, plastic, and concrete are examples of amorphous solids.

## Types of Crystalline Solids

Crystalline solids may exist in one of four general groups:

1. *Ionic solids.* The units that comprise an **ionic solid** are positive and negative ions. Electrostatic forces hold the crystal together. Ionic solids generally have high melting points and are hard and brittle. A common example of an ionic solid is sodium chloride.

2. *Covalent solids.* The units that comprise a **covalent solid** are atoms held together by covalent bonds. Covalent solids have very high melting points (1200°C to 2000°C or more is not unusual) and are extremely hard. They are insoluble in most solvents. Diamond is a covalent solid composed of covalently bonded carbon atoms. Diamonds are used for industrial cutting because they are so hard and as gemstones because of their crystalline beauty.

*Intermolecular forces are also discussed in Sections 3.5 and 5.2.*

3. *Molecular solids.* The units that make up a **molecular solid,** molecules, are held together by intermolecular attractive forces (London dispersion forces, dipole-dipole interactions, and hydrogen bonding). Molecular solids are usually soft and have low melting points. They are frequently volatile and are poor electrical conductors. A common example is ice (solid water; Figure 5.11).

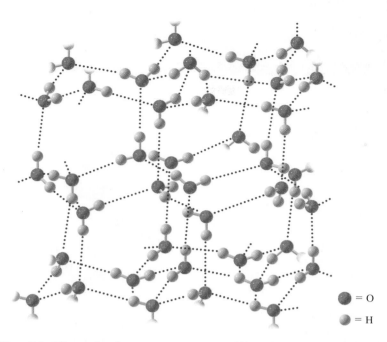

**Figure 5.11** The structure of ice, a molecular solid. Hydrogen bonding among water molecules produces a regular open structure that is less dense than liquid water.

= O

= H

4. *Metallic solids.* The units that comprise a **metallic solid** are metal atoms held together by metallic bonds. *Metallic bonds* are formed by the overlap of orbitals of metal atoms, resulting in regions of high electron density surrounding the positive metal nuclei. Electrons in these regions are extremely mobile. They are able to move freely from atom to atom through pathways that are, in reality, overlapping atomic orbitals. This results in the high *conductivity* (ability to carry electrical current) exhibited by many metallic solids. Silver and copper are common examples of metallic solids. Metals are easily shaped and are used for a variety of purposes. Most of these are practical applications such as hardware, cookware, and surgical and dental tools. Others are purely for enjoyment and decoration, such as silver and gold jewelry.

Solid-state chemistry is critically important to the semiconductor industry. "Chips," crystalline solids made of silicon and traces of other elements such as arsenic and germanium, are the "brains" behind our computers, cell phones, and a host of other electronic devices.

## Sublimation of Solids

**Sublimation** is the process in which some molecules in the solid state convert directly to the gaseous state.

As we saw in the discussion of the development of new devices for airport security (Chemistry at the Crime Scene: Explosives at the Airport, page 190), some molecular solids possess measurable vapor pressures. Recall that vapor pressure of a liquid is the key concept in explaining the conversion of a liquid to a gas by evaporation or by boiling. Certain molecular solids such as dry ice (frozen carbon dioxide) and moth balls (naphthalene) will, at room temperature, convert to a gas without passing through the liquid state because they have a sufficiently high vapor pressure. This process is termed *sublimation.*

If you live in a very cold climate, you may have observed that, over a period of several days, snow and ice "disappear," even though the temperature is continuously below the melting point of water. Snow and ice, molecular solids, have simply sublimed, converting from solid to water vapor.

**LEARNING GOAL**

**9** Describe the processes of melting, boiling, evaporation, condensation, and sublimation.

### Question 5.13
a. What properties are associated with ionic solids?
b. Provide two examples of ionic solids.

### Question 5.14
a. What properties are associated with molecular solids?
b. Provide two examples of molecular solids.

## Gemstones

When we think of the solid state, we may think of ice, the solid form of water; coal, a major energy source; or, perhaps, concrete and steel, bulwarks of the construction industry. All are commonplace materials with well-defined properties and applications. However, if we turn our thoughts toward beauty and value, diamonds often come to mind. Diamonds are valued for their sparkle, durability, and rarity. Diamonds are the most famous, but certainly not the only gemstones with desirable properties and high price tags.

The diamond market has a value of over twelve billion dollars per year and colored gemstones another six billion dollars. What are these gems made of, and why are they so valuable?

### Diamond

Most of the carbon deposits on earth are amorphous; they have no organized structure. Consequently, they do not share the properties of solids with regular, repeating structure. Much of this carbon is coal. A tiny fraction of the world's solid carbon exists as covalent solids. Recall that covalent solids have strong covalent bonds and a regular, repeating crystal structure. A diamond is a covalent solid comprised of carbon atoms arranged in a 3-dimensional crystalline structure (Figure 5.10a).

A one-carat diamond, which is only 0.20 g, has a retail value of thousands of dollars. Just how many thousands is a function of the regularity of the repeating pattern of carbon atoms and their freedom from the inclusion of impurities. The number of diamonds that meet the highest standards is very small.

### Rubies and Sapphires

These gemstones are variations of the mineral corundum, which is essentially $Al_2O_3$. Rubies and sapphires have similar crystalline structures; however, ruby is red and sapphire is blue. Why? Trace amounts of other elements make all the difference. Chromium replaces some aluminum ions in ruby ($Cr^{3+}$ replaces $Al^{3+}$). This alters the absorption spectrum of the material, favoring the transmission of red light (610 nm); hence, the ruby red color. Sapphire appears blue because of the presence of traces of $Fe^{2+}$ and $Ti^{4+}$. Light at the red end of the visible spectrum is absorbed by compounds formed from these trace ions. The blue light is transmitted and the sapphire appears blue.

### Emerald

The $Cr^{3+}$ ion is also responsible for the green color of emerald. It is a trace element incorporated into the base structure of the

A variety of gemstones. Variations in crystal structure, as well as the presence of trace metal ions, are responsible for differences in color and lustre.

mineral beryl (the origin of the name is beryllium, a key element in its structure). Beryl is $Be_3Al_2Si_6O_{18}$ and $Cr^{3+}$ (and vanadium ions as well) replaces $Al^{3+}$ in the crystal structure of the beryl. The resulting color is the familiar emerald green.

### Tanzanite

This blue gem is a product of a mineral with the formula $Ca_2Al_2(SiO_4)(Si_2O_7)O(OH)$. In contrast to other gems we have discussed, tanzanite was not discovered and characterized until the 1960s. It was first found in Tanzania, for which it is named. Once again, trace elements make all the difference between worthless rock and valuable gemstones. Vanadium ions, substituted for aluminum ions, are responsible for its deep blue color.

We owe the origin of gemstones to the pressure and temperature events associated with earth's formation. We have learned to make synthetic gemstones in the laboratory, but the gem connoisseurs of the world continue to show a preference for the natural product. Not surprisingly, they owe their value to their rarity and intrinsic beauty.

### For Further Understanding

► Predict the color of a gemstone that absorbs light mostly in the wavelength range 500–700 nm.

► Suggest a reason why a collection of sapphires may appear to be different shades of blue.

# CHAPTER MAP

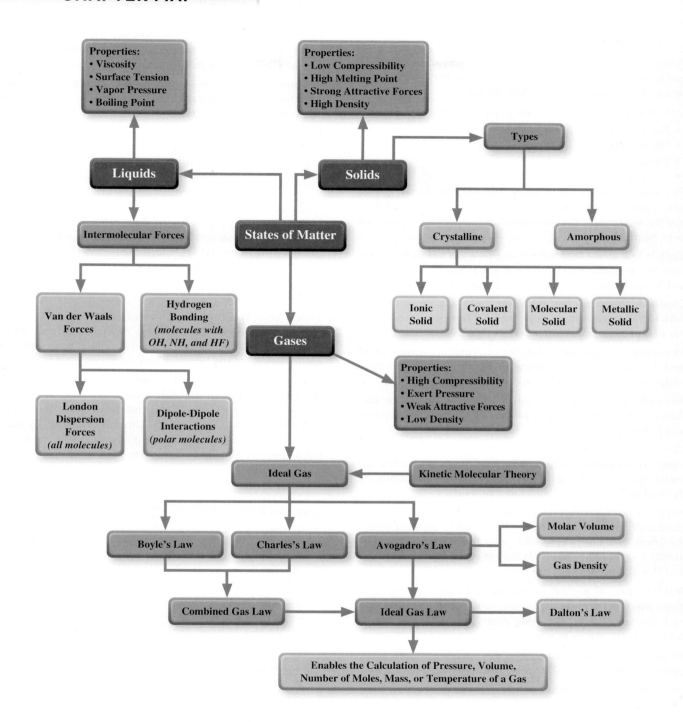

# SUMMARY

## 5.1 The Gaseous State

▶ Pressure, volume, temperature, and quantity (number of moles) characterize ideal gases. **Pressure** is the force per unit area and is measured using a **barometer.**

▶ One standard atmosphere (atm) of pressure is equivalent to

- 76.0 cm Hg
- 760 mm Hg
- 760 torr
- 14.7 psi

▶ The **kinetic molecular theory** describes an **ideal gas** in which gas particles exhibit no attractive or repulsive forces and the volumes of the individual gas particles are assumed to be negligible.

▶ **Boyle's law** states that the volume of a gas varies inversely with the pressure exerted by the gas if the number of mol and temperature of the gas are held constant ($PV = k_b$).

▶ **Charles's law** states that the volume of a gas varies directly with the absolute temperature (Kelvin) if pressure and number of mol of gas are constant ($V/T = k_c$).

▶ The **combined gas law** provides a convenient expression for performing gas law calculations involving the most common variables: pressure, volume, and temperature.

▶ **Avogadro's law** states that equal volumes of any gas contain the same number of mol if measured at constant temperature and pressure ($V/n = k_a$).

▶ The volume occupied by 1 mol of any gas is its **molar volume.** At **standard temperature and pressure** (STP), the molar volume of any ideal gas is 22.4 L. STP conditions are defined as 273 K (or 0°C) and 1 atm pressure.

▶ Boyle's law, Charles's law, and Avogadro's law may be combined into a single expression relating all four terms, the **ideal gas law:** $PV = nRT$. $R$ is the ideal gas constant ($0.0821 \text{ L} \cdot \text{atm} \cdot \text{K}^{-1} \cdot \text{mol}^{-1}$) if the units atm (for $P$), L (for $V$), mol (for $n$), and K (for $T$) are used.

▶ **Dalton's law of partial pressures** states that a mixture of gases exerts a pressure that is the sum of the pressures that each gas would exert if it were present alone under similar conditions ($P_t = p_1 + p_2 + p_3 + \cdots$).

▶ Because of their weak intermolecular forces, nonpolar gases behave more ideally. Polar gases behave more ideally with

- Increasing temperature
- Decreasing pressure

## 5.2 The Liquid State

▶ Liquids are practically incompressible because of the closeness of their molecules. The **viscosity** of a liquid is a measure of its resistance to flow. Viscosity generally decreases with increasing temperature. The **surface tension** of a liquid is a measure of the attractive forces at the surface of a liquid. **Surfactants** decrease surface tension.

▶ The conversion of liquid to vapor at a temperature below the boiling point of the liquid is **evaporation.** Conversion of the gas to the liquid state is **condensation.** The **vapor pressure** of the liquid is defined as the pressure exerted by the vapor at equilibrium at a specified temperature. The **normal boiling point** of a liquid is the temperature at which the vapor pressure of the liquid is equal to 1 atm.

▶ **Van der Waals forces** include **dipole-dipole interactions,** attractive forces between polar molecules, and **London dispersion forces,** attractive forces between molecules exhibiting temporary dipoles.

- Weak London dispersion forces are the only intermolecular force between nonpolar molecules.
- Generally, polar molecules have higher melting and boiling points than nonpolar molecules due to the presence of both dipole-dipole and London dispersion forces.

▶ Molecules in which a hydrogen atom is bonded to a nitrogen, oxygen, or fluorine atom exhibit **hydrogen bonding.** Hydrogen bonding in liquids is responsible for lower than expected vapor pressures and higher than expected boiling points.

## 5.3 The Solid State

▶ Solids have fixed shapes and volumes. They are incompressible, owing to the closeness of their particles. Solids may be **crystalline,** having a regular, repeating structure, or **amorphous,** having no organized structure.

▶ Crystalline solids may exist as **ionic solids, covalent solids, molecular solids,** or **metallic solids.** Electrons in metallic solids are extremely mobile, resulting in the high *conductivity* (ability to carry electrical current) exhibited by many metallic solids. **Sublimation** is a process whereby molecular solids convert directly from solid to gas.

# ANSWERS TO PRACTICE PROBLEMS

5.1   Sample 1: 38 atm
       Sample 2: 25 atm
       Sample 3: 0.15 L
       Sample 4: 0.38 L

5.2   **a.** 3.76 L          **c.** 2.75 L          **e.** 2.75 L
       **b.** 3.41 L          **d.** 5.50 L          **f.** 3.76 L

5.3   0.200 atm

5.4   99.5°C

5.5   **a.** 4.46 mol $H_2$        **b.** 0.75 mol $H_2$

5.6   The molar volume is based on 1 mol of *any* ideal gas. For any ideal gas, all quantities substituted in the ideal gas equation are independent of the identity of the ideal gas.

5.7   0.223 mol $N_2$

5.8   9.00 L

# QUESTIONS AND PROBLEMS

## Measurement of Properties of Gases

### Foundations

**5.15** Explain how the pressure of $O_2$ gas may be measured.

**5.16** Describe the molecular/atomic basis of gas pressure.

### Applications

**5.17** Express each of the following in units of atm:
a. 94.4 cm Hg
c. 150 mm Hg
b. 72.5 torr
d. 124 kPa

**5.18** Express each of the following in units of atm:
a. 128 cm Hg
c. 1405 mm Hg
b. 255 torr
d. 303 kPa

**5.19** Express each of the following in units of psi:
a. 54.0 cm Hg
c. 800 mm Hg
b. 155 torr
d. 1.50 atm

**5.20** Express each of the following in units of psi:
a. 12.5 cm Hg
c. 254 mm Hg
b. 46.0 torr
d. 0.48 atm

## Kinetic Molecular Theory of Gases

### Foundations

**5.21** Compare and contrast the gas, liquid, and solid states with regard to the average distance of particle separation.

**5.22** Compare and contrast the gas, liquid, and solid states with regard to the nature of the interactions among the particles.

### Applications

**5.23** Why are gases easily compressible?

**5.24** Why are gas densities much lower than those of liquids or solids?

**5.25** Why do gases expand to fill any available volume?

**5.26** Why do gases with lower molar masses diffuse more rapidly than gases with higher molar masses?

**5.27** Do gases exhibit more ideal behavior at low or high pressures? Why?

**5.28** Do gases exhibit more ideal behavior at low or high temperatures? Why?

**5.29** Use the kinetic molecular theory to explain why dissimilar gases mix more rapidly at high temperatures than at low temperatures.

**5.30** Use the kinetic molecular theory to explain why aerosol cans carry instructions warning against heating or disposing of the container in a fire.

## Boyle's Law

### Foundations

**5.31** State Boyle's law in words.

**5.32** State Boyle's law in equation form.

**5.33** The pressure on a fixed mass of a gas is tripled at constant temperature. Will the volume increase, decrease, or remain the same?

**5.34** By what factor will the volume of the gas in Question 5.33 change?

## Applications

A sample of helium gas was placed in a cylinder, and the volume of the gas was measured as the pressure was slowly increased. The results of this experiment are shown graphically.

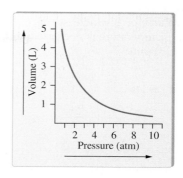

Questions 5.35–5.38 are based on this experiment.

**5.35** At what pressure does the gas occupy a volume of 5 L?

**5.36** What is the volume of the gas at a pressure of 5 atm?

**5.37** Calculate the Boyle's law constant at a volume of 2 L.

**5.38** Calculate the Boyle's law constant at a pressure of 2 atm.

**5.39** Calculate the pressure, in atm, required to compress a sample of helium gas from 20.9 L (at 1.00 atm) to 4.00 L.

**5.40** A balloon filled with helium gas at 1.00 atm occupies 15.6 L. What volume would the balloon occupy in the upper atmosphere at a pressure of 0.150 atm?

## Charles's Law

### Foundations

**5.41** State Charles's law in words.

**5.42** State Charles's law in equation form.

**5.43** Explain why the Kelvin scale is used for gas law calculations.

**5.44** The temperature on a summer day may be 90°F. Convert this value to Kelvin units.

### Applications

**5.45** The temperature of a gas is raised from 25°C to 50°C. Will the volume double if mass and pressure do not change? Why or why not?

**5.46** Verify your answer to Question 5.45 by calculating the temperature needed to double the volume of the gas.

**5.47** Determine the change in volume that takes place when a 2.00-L sample of $N_2(g)$ is heated from 250°C to 500°C.

**5.48** Determine the change in volume that takes place when a 2.00-L sample of $N_2(g)$ is heated from 250 K to 500 K.

**5.49** A balloon containing a sample of helium gas is warmed in an oven. If the balloon measures 1.25 L at room temperature (20°C), what is its volume at 80°C?

**5.50** The balloon described in Question 5.49 was then placed in a refrigerator at 39°F. Calculate its new volume.

**5.51** A balloon, filled with $N_2$, has a volume of 2.00 L at an indoor temperature of 68°F. When placed outdoors, the volume was observed to increase to 2.20 L. What is the outdoor temperature in °F?

**5.52** A balloon, filled with an ideal gas, has a volume of 5.00 L at 50°F. At what temperature (°F) would the balloon's volume double?

## Combined Gas Law

### Foundations

**5.53**  Will the volume of gas increase, decrease, or remain the same if the temperature is increased and the pressure is decreased? Explain.

**5.54**  Will the volume of gas increase, decrease, or remain the same if the temperature is decreased and the pressure is increased? Explain.

### Applications

Use the combined gas law,

$$\frac{P_i V_i}{T_i} = \frac{P_f V_f}{T_f}$$

to answer Questions 5.55 and 5.56.

**5.55**  Solve the combined gas law expression for the final volume.

**5.56**  Solve the combined gas law expression for the final temperature.

**5.57**  If 2.25 L of a gas at 16°C and 1.00 atm is compressed at a pressure of 125 atm at 20°C, calculate the new volume of the gas.

**5.58**  A sealed balloon filled with helium gas occupies 2.50 L at 25°C and 1.00 atm. When released, it rises to an altitude where the temperature is 20°C and the pressure is only 0.800 atm. Calculate the new volume of the balloon.

**5.59**  A 5.00-L balloon exerts a pressure of 2.00 atm at 30.0°C. What is the pressure that the sealed balloon exerts if the volume has increased to 7.0 L at 40°C?

**5.60**  If we double the pressure and temperature of the balloon in Question 5.59, what will its new volume be?

## Avogadro's Law

### Foundations

**5.61**  State Avogadro's law in words.

**5.62**  State Avogadro's law in equation form.

### Applications

**5.63**  If 5.00 g helium gas is added to a 1.00-L balloon containing 1.00 g of helium gas, what is the new volume of the balloon? Assume no change in temperature or pressure.

**5.64**  How many g of helium must be added to a balloon containing 8.00 g helium gas to double its volume? Assume no change in temperature or pressure.

## Molar Volume and the Ideal Gas Law

### Foundations

**5.65**  Will 1.00 mol of a gas always occupy 22.4 L?

**5.66**  Calculate the molar volume of $O_2$ gas at STP.

**5.67**  What are the units and numerical value of standard temperature?

**5.68**  What are the units and numerical value of standard pressure?

### Applications

**5.69**  A sample of nitrogen gas, stored in a 4.0-L container at 32°C, exerts a pressure of 5.0 atm. Calculate the number of mol of nitrogen gas in the container.

**5.70**  Calculate the pressure, in atmosphere, of 7.0 mol of carbon monoxide stored in a 30.0-L container at 65°C.

**5.71**  Calculate the volume of 44.0 g of carbon monoxide at STP.

**5.72**  Calculate the volume of 44.0 g of carbon dioxide at STP.

**5.73**  Calculate the density of carbon monoxide at STP.

**5.74**  Calculate the density of carbon dioxide at STP.

**5.75**  Calculate the number of mol of a gas that is present in a 7.55-L container at 45°C, if the gas exerts a pressure of 725 mm Hg.

**5.76**  Calculate the pressure (atm) exerted by 1.00 mol of gas contained in a 7.55-L cylinder at 45°C.

**5.77**  A sample of argon (Ar) gas occupies 65.0 mL at 22°C and 750 torr. What is the volume of this Ar gas sample at STP?

**5.78**  A sample of $O_2$ gas occupies 257 mL at 20°C and 1.20 atm. What is the volume of this $O_2$ gas sample at STP?

**5.79**  What is the temperature (°C) of 1.75 g of $O_2$ gas occupying 2.00 L at 1.00 atm?

**5.80**  How many g of $O_2$ gas occupy 10.0 L at STP?

**5.81**  Calculate the volume of 4.00 mol Ar gas at 8.25 torr and 27°C.

**5.82**  Calculate the volume of 6.00 mol $O_2$ gas at 30 cm Hg and 72°F.

## Dalton's Law of Partial Pressures

### Foundations

**5.83**  State Dalton's law in words.

**5.84**  State Dalton's law in equation form.

### Applications

**5.85**  A gas mixture has three components: $N_2$, $F_2$, and He. Their partial pressures are 0.40 atm, 0.16 atm, and 0.18 atm, respectively. What is the pressure of the gas mixture?

**5.86**  A gas mixture has three components, $N_2$, $F_2$, and He. The partial pressure of $N_2$ is 0.35 atm and $F_2$ is 0.45 atm. If the total pressure is 1.20 atm, what is the partial pressure of helium?

**5.87**  A gas mixture has a total pressure of 0.56 atm and consists of He and Ne. If the partial pressure of the He in the mixture is 0.27 atm, what is the partial pressure of the Ne in the mixture?

**5.88**  If we were to remove all of the helium from the mixture described in Question 5.86, what would the partial pressures of $N_2$ and $F_2$ be? Why? What is the new total pressure?

## Ideal Gases Versus Real Gases

### Foundations

**5.89**  Explain when limitations to the ideal gas model are observed.

**5.90**  $H_2O$ and $CH_4$ are gases at 150°C. Which exhibits more ideal behavior? Why?

### Applications

**5.91**  Would CO behave more like an ideal gas at 5 K or 50 K? Explain your reasoning.

**5.92**  Would CO behave more like an ideal gas at 2 atm or 20 atm? Explain your reasoning.

## The Liquid State

### Foundations

**5.93** Compare the strength of intermolecular forces in liquids with those in gases.

**5.94** Compare the strength of intermolecular forces in liquids with those in solids.

**5.95** What is the relationship between the temperature of a liquid and the vapor pressure of that liquid?

**5.96** What is the relationship between the strength of the attractive forces in a liquid and its vapor pressure?

**5.97** Describe the process occurring at the molecular level that accounts for the property of viscosity.

**5.98** Describe the process occurring at the molecular level that accounts for the property of surface tension.

### Applications

Questions 5.99–5.102 are based on the following:

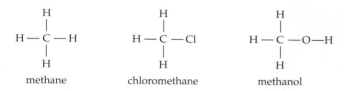

| methane | chloromethane | methanol |

**5.99** Which of these molecules exhibit London dispersion forces? Why?

**5.100** Which of these molecules exhibit dipole-dipole forces? Why?

**5.101** Which of these molecules exhibit hydrogen bonding? Why?

**5.102** Which of these molecules would you expect to have the highest boiling point? Why?

Questions 5.103 and 5.104 are based on the following:

| propane | isopropyl alcohol | propylene glycol |

**5.103** Predict the compound expected to have the greatest viscosity in the liquid state.

**5.104** Predict the compound expected to have the greatest surface tension in the liquid state.

## The Solid State

### Foundations

**5.105** Explain why solids are essentially incompressible.

**5.106** Distinguish between amorphous and crystalline solids.

**5.107** Describe one property that is characteristic of:
    **a.** ionic solids
    **b.** covalent solids

**5.108** Describe one property that is characteristic of:
    **a.** molecular solids
    **b.** metallic solids

### Applications

**5.109** Predict whether beryllium or carbon would be a better conductor of electricity in the solid state. Why?

**5.110** Why is diamond used as an industrial cutting tool?

**5.111** Mercury and chromium are toxic substances. Which element is more likely to be an air pollutant? Why?

**5.112** Why is the melting point of silicon much higher than that of argon, even though argon has a greater molar mass?

# CHALLENGE PROBLEMS

1. An elodea plant, commonly found in tropical fish aquaria, was found to produce $5.0 \times 10^{22}$ molecules of oxygen per hour (h). What volume of oxygen (at STP) would be produced in an 8-h period?

2. A chemist measures the volume of 1.00 mol of helium gas at STP and obtains a value of 22.4 L. After changing the temperature to 137 K, the experimental value was found to be 11.05 L. Verify the chemist's results using the ideal gas law and explain any apparent discrepancies.

3. A chemist measures the volumes of 1.00 mol of $H_2$ and 1.00 mol of CO and finds that they differ by 0.10 L. Which gas produced the larger volume? Do the results contradict the ideal gas law? Why or why not?

4. A 100.0-g sample of water was decomposed using an electric current (electrolysis), producing hydrogen gas and oxygen gas. Write the balanced equation for the process and calculate the volume of each gas produced (at STP). Explain any relationship you may observe between the volumes obtained and the balanced equation for the process.

5. An autoclave is used to sterilize surgical equipment. It is far more effective than steam produced from boiling water in the open atmosphere because it generates steam at a pressure of 2 atm. Explain why an autoclave is such an efficient sterilization device.

6. Imagine you have been asked to design a new solid material to be used in replacement bones and joints. What physical and chemical properties would you deem important?

# 6

# Solutions

Carbonated beverages are a commonplace example of a solution of a gas (solute) dissolved in a liquid (solvent). Based on your everyday experience, can you predict whether the solubility of carbon dioxide in water (or cola) would increase or decrease as the temperature of the solution increases?

## OUTLINE

## LEARNING GOALS

1   Distinguish among the terms *solution*, *solute*, and *solvent*.

2   Describe the properties and composition of various kinds of solutions.

3   Explain which factors influence the degree of solubility, and use trends to make predictions.

4   Describe the relationship between solubility and equilibrium.

5   Use Henry's law to calculate equilibrium solubility values for gases.

6   Calculate solution concentration in mass/volume percent, mass/mass percent, parts per thousand, and parts per million.

7   Determine the quantity of solute or solution from the concentration of solution.

8   Calculate the molarity of solution from mass or moles of solute.

9   Perform dilution calculations.

10   Describe and explain concentration-dependent solution properties.

11   Perform calculations involving colligative properties.

12   Describe why the chemical and physical properties of water make it a truly unique solvent.

13   Interconvert molar concentration of ions and milliequivalents/liter.

14   Explain the role of electrolytes in blood and their relationship to the process of dialysis.

# INTRODUCTION

A significant deterrent to achieving optimal athletic performance in strenuous competitive sports, especially in warm weather, is dehydration—the loss of body fluids through perspiration. Perspiration is an aqueous solution, and the loss of ions dissolved in water (the solvent) has a more negative impact on bodily function than the loss of the water itself.

This fact was not lost on researchers at the University of Florida in the 1960s. The University of Florida football team (the Florida Gators) plays much of its schedule in a very warm climate. This, coupled with the intense physical effort required and the heavy padding that must be worn to prevent injury, makes dehydration of the athletes a real concern.

The remedy, at that time, was to drink large volumes of water while consuming salt tablets, to replace the lost ions, or to consume high-sugar foods (often oranges) to provide energy. How much of each was pure guesswork. Often, the cure was worse than the problem, and cramping resulted.

The team doctor, along with medical researchers at the university, had an idea. Would it be possible to mix all three components in some proportion to produce a solution that achieved the desired effect without the unwanted side effect? The result of this research was a solution of ionic compounds and sugar dissolved in water, which was similar to the composition of the perspiration being lost, with flavoring added to make it palatable. The identity of the ions: sodium, potassium, and chloride, was certainly important, as were the concentrations of the ions in producing a solution that achieved the desired effect without inducing cramps.

The football team began using the "Gator-aid" solution and was victorious in the 1966 Orange Bowl, offering some proof that the solution had a positive effect on the team's performance. Now named Gatorade, it was the first "sports drink." Currently, several competing brands are available in the marketplace, differing slightly in composition, concentration, and flavor. They are widely used by college and professional teams, as well as the "weekend athlete." We should not forget that the most important ingredient in all sports drinks is the solvent: water. In fact, some argue that pure water is just as efficient a cell hydrator as sports drinks.

In this chapter, we will learn more about solutions, their composition and their concentration. We will see why some substances are soluble in water and others are not. We will see why the concentration of ions, such as sodium and potassium, is critical to the function and integrity of the cells in our bodies.

Many sports drink labels claim the product will replenish electrolytes. What does that mean?

---

## 6.1 Properties of Solutions

A **solution** is a homogeneous mixture of two or more substances. A solution is composed of one or more *solutes,* dissolved in a *solvent.* The **solute** is a component of a solution that is present in lesser quantity than the solvent. The **solvent** is the solution component present in the largest quantity. For example, when sugar (the solute) is added to water (the solvent), the sugar dissolves in the water to produce a solution. In those instances in which the solvent is water, we refer to the homogeneous mixture as an **aqueous solution,** from the Latin *aqua,* meaning "water."

The dissolution of a solid in a liquid is perhaps the most common example of solution formation. However, it is also possible to form solutions in gases and solids as well as in liquids. For example:

- Air is a gaseous mixture, but it is also a solution; oxygen and a number of trace gases are dissolved in the gaseous solvent, nitrogen.
- Metallic items, such as rings and bracelets, are homogeneous mixtures of two or more kinds of metal atoms in the solid state. These homogeneous mixtures are termed *alloys.*

**LEARNING GOAL**

**1** Distinguish among the terms *solution, solute,* and *solvent.*

Although solid and gaseous solutions are important in many applications, our emphasis will be on *liquid solutions* because so many important chemical reactions take place in liquid solutions.

## General Properties of Liquid Solutions

Liquid solutions are clear and transparent with no visible particles of solute. They may be colored or colorless, depending on the properties of the solute and solvent. Note that the terms *clear* and *colorless* do not mean the same thing; a clear solution has only one state of matter that can be detected; *colorless* simply means the absence of color.

Recall that solutions of **electrolytes** are formed from solutes that are soluble *ionic* compounds. These compounds dissociate in solution to produce ions that behave as charge carriers. Solutions of electrolytes are good conductors of electricity. For example, sodium chloride dissolving in water:

$$NaCl(s) \xrightarrow{\text{H}_2\text{O}} Na^+(aq) + Cl^-(aq)$$

Solid sodium             Dissolved sodium
chloride                      chloride

In contrast, solutions of **nonelectrolytes** are formed from nondissociating *molecular* solutes (nonelectrolytes), and these solutions are nonconducting. For example, dissolving sugar in water:

$$C_6H_{12}O_6(s) \xrightarrow{\text{H}_2\text{O}} C_6H_{12}O_6(aq)$$

Solid glucose        Dissolved glucose

A **true solution** is a homogeneous mixture with uniform properties throughout. In a true solution, the solute cannot be isolated from the solution by filtration. The particle size of the solute is about the same as that of the solvent, and solvent and solute pass directly through the filter paper. Furthermore, solute particles will not "settle out" after a time. All of the molecules of solute and solvent are intimately mixed. The continuous particle motion in solution maintains the homogeneous, random distribution of solute and solvent particles.

Volumes of solute and solvent are not additive; 1 liter (L) of alcohol mixed with 1 L of water does not result in exactly 2 L of solution. The volume of pure liquid is determined not only by the size of the individual molecules but also by the way in which the individual molecules "fit together." When two or more kinds of molecules are mixed, the interactions become more complex. Solvent interacts with solvent, solute interacts with solvent, and solute may interact with other solute. For example, mixing 1 L of water with 1 L of alcohol results in a solution volume measurably smaller than the anticipated 2 L.

## True Solutions, Colloidal Dispersions, and Suspensions

How can you recognize a solution? A clear liquid in a beaker may be a pure substance, a true solution, or a colloidal dispersion. Only chemical analysis, determining the identity of all substances in the liquid, can distinguish between a pure substance and a solution. A pure substance has *one* component, pure water being an example. A true solution will contain *more than one substance*, with the tiny particles homogeneously intermingled.

A **colloidal dispersion** also consists of solute particles distributed throughout a solvent. However, the distribution is not completely homogeneous, owing to the size of the colloidal particles. Particles with diameters of $1 \times 10^{-9}$ meter (m) to $2 \times 10^{-7}$ m are colloids. [Recall that $1 \times 10^{-9}$ m = 1 nanometer (nm), therefore $2 \times 10^{-7}$ m = 200 nm.] Particles smaller than 1 nm are solution particles; those larger than 200 nm are particles that are large enough to eventually settle to the bottom of the container. The settled particles are large enough to be observed by the naked eye; the collection of particles is termed a **precipitate,** a solid in contact with solvent.

*See Section 4.5 for more information on precipitates.*

To the naked eye, a colloidal dispersion and a true solution appear identical; neither solute nor colloid can be seen. However, a simple experiment, using only a bright light source, can readily make the distinction based upon differences in their interaction with light. Colloid particles are large enough to scatter light; solute particles are not. When a beam of light passes through a colloidal dispersion, the large particles scatter light, and the liquid appears hazy. We see this effect in sunlight passing through fog. Fog is a colloidal dispersion of tiny particles of liquid water dispersed throughout a gas, air. The haze is light scattered by droplets of water. You may have noticed that your automobile headlights are not very helpful in foggy weather. Visibility becomes worse rather than better because light scattering increases.

The light-scattering ability of colloidal dispersions is termed the *Tyndall effect.* True solutions, with very tiny particles, do not scatter light—no haze is observed—and true solutions are easily distinguished from colloidal dispersions by observing their light-scattering properties (Figure 6.1).

A **suspension** is a heterogeneous mixture that contains particles much larger than a colloidal dispersion; over time, these particles may settle, forming a second phase. A suspension is not a true solution, nor is it a precipitate.

**Question 6.1** Describe how you would distinguish experimentally between a pure substance and a true solution.

**Question 6.2** Describe how you would distinguish experimentally between a true solution and a colloidal dispersion.

## Degree of Solubility

In our discussion of the relationship of polarity and solubility, the rule *"like dissolves like"* was described as the fundamental condition for solubility. Polar solutes are soluble in polar solvents, and nonpolar solutes are soluble in nonpolar solvents. Thus, knowing a little bit about the structure of the molecule enables us to predict qualitatively the solubility of the compound.

The *degree* of **solubility,** *how much* solute can dissolve in a given volume of solvent, is a quantitative measure of solubility. It is difficult to predict the solubility of each and every compound. However, general solubility trends are based on the following considerations:

- *The magnitude of difference between polarity of solute and solvent.* The greater the difference, the less soluble is the solute.
- *Temperature.* An increase in temperature usually, but not always, increases solubility (Figure 6.2). Often, the effect is dramatic. For example, an increase in temperature from 0°C to 100°C increases the water solubility of $KNO_3$ from 10 grams per 100 grams $H_2O$ (10 g/100 g $H_2O$) to 240 g/100 g $H_2O$.
- *Pressure.* Pressure has little effect on the solubility of solids and liquids in liquids. However, the solubility of a gas in liquid is directly proportional to the applied pressure. Carbonated beverages, for example, are made by dissolving carbon dioxide in the beverage under high pressure (hence the term *carbonated*).

When a solution contains all the solute that can be dissolved at a particular temperature, it is a **saturated solution.** When solubility values are given—for example, 13.3 g of potassium nitrate in 100 g of water at 1°C—they refer to the concentration of a saturated solution.

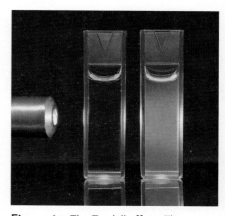

**Figure 6.1** The Tyndall effect. The sample on the right is a colloidal dispersion, which scatters the light. This scattered light is visible as a haze. The sample on the left is a true solution; no scattered light is observed.

**LEARNING GOAL**

**3** Explain which factors influence the degree of solubility, and use trends to make predictions.

*Section 3.5 describes solute-solvent interactions in detail.*

The term *qualitative* implies identity, and the term *quantitative* relates to quantity.

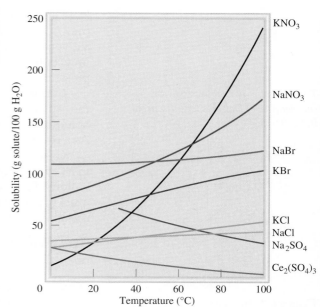

**Figure 6.2** The solubility of a variety of ionic compounds in water as a function of temperature. Note that $Na_2SO_4$ and $Ce_2(SO_4)_3$ become less soluble at higher temperatures.

As we have already noted, *increasing* the temperature generally increases the amount of solute a given solution may hold. Conversely, *cooling* a saturated solution often results in a decrease in the amount of solute in solution. The excess solute falls to the bottom of the container as a *precipitate* (a solid in contact with the solution). Occasionally, on cooling, the excess solute may remain in solution for a time. Such a solution is described as a **supersaturated solution.** This type of solution is inherently unstable. With time, excess solute will precipitate, and the solution will revert to a saturated solution, which is stable.

## Solubility and Equilibrium

**LEARNING GOAL**

**4** Describe the relationship between solubility and equilibrium.

*The concept of equilibrium was introduced in Section 5.2 and will be discussed in detail in Section 7.4.*

When an excess of solute (beyond the solubility limit) is added to a solvent, it begins to dissolve and continues until it establishes a *dynamic equilibrium* between dissolved and undissolved solute.

Initially, the rate of dissolution is large. After a time, the rate of the reverse process, precipitation, increases. The rates of dissolution and precipitation eventually become equal, and there is no further change in the composition of the solution. There is, however, a continual exchange of solute particles between solid and liquid phases because particles are in constant motion. The solution is saturated. The most precise definition of a saturated solution is a solution that is in equilibrium with undissolved solute.

## Solubility of Gases: Henry's Law

**LEARNING GOAL**

**5** Use Henry's law to calculate equilibrium solubility values for gases.

When a liquid and a gas are allowed to come to equilibrium, the amount of gas dissolved in the liquid reaches some maximum level. This quantity can be predicted from a very simple relationship. **Henry's law** states that the number of moles (mol) of a gas dissolved in a liquid at a given temperature is proportional to the pressure of the gas. In other words, the gas solubility is directly proportional to the pressure of that gas in the atmosphere that is in contact with the liquid.

Henry's law is expressed mathematically as

$$M = kP$$

Here, $M$ is the molar concentration of the gas in the liquid in units of moles/liter (mol/L). $P$ is the pressure (in atm) of the gas over the solution at equilibrium. For a given gas, $k$ is a constant that depends only on temperature. The constant, $k$, has units of mol/L · atm. In the event that more than one gas is present, $P$ is the partial pressure.

*The concept of partial pressure is a consequence of Dalton's law, discussed in Section 5.1.*

Carbonated beverages are bottled at high pressures of carbon dioxide. When the cap is removed, the fizzing results from the fact that the partial pressure of carbon dioxide in the atmosphere is much less than that used in the bottling process. As a result, the equilibrium quickly shifts to one of lower gas solubility.

Gases are most soluble at low temperatures, and the gas solubility decreases markedly at higher temperatures (Figure 6.3). This explains many common observations. For example, a chilled container of carbonated beverage that is opened quickly goes flat as it warms to room temperature. As the beverage warms up, the solubility of the carbon dioxide decreases.

**Question 6.3**   Explain why, over time, a bottle of soft drink goes "flat" after it is opened.

**Question 6.4**   Would the soft drink in Question 6.3 go "flat" faster if the bottle warmed to room temperature? Why?

The Henry's law constant, $k$, for $CO_2$ in aqueous solution is $3.1 \times 10^{-2}$ mol/(L · atm) at 25°C. Use this information to answer Questions 6.5 and 6.6.

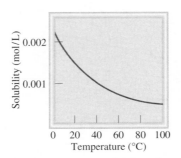

**Figure 6.3** The water solubility of $O_2$ gas decreases markedly as the temperature of the water increases; this may have significant environmental implications.

# A Human Perspective

## Scuba Diving: Nitrogen and the Bends

A deep-water diver's worst fear is the interruption of the oxygen supply through equipment malfunction, forcing his or her rapid rise to the surface in search of air. If a diver must ascend too rapidly, he or she may suffer a condition known as "the bends."

Key to understanding this problem is recognition of the tremendous increase in pressure that divers withstand as they descend, because of the weight of the water above them. At the surface, the pressure is approximately 1 atmosphere (atm). At a depth of 200 feet (ft), the pressure is approximately six times as great; hence, the blood concentration of $N_2$ increases dramatically. Oxygen solubility increases as well, although its effect is less serious ($O_2$ is 20% of air, $N_2$ is 80%). Recall that Henry's law tells us that the number of mol of gas dissolved in blood is directly proportional to the pressure of the gas.

As the diver quickly rises, the pressure decreases rapidly, and the nitrogen "boils" out of the blood, stopping blood flow and impairing nerve transmission. The joints of the body lock in a bent position, hence the name of the condition: the bends.

To minimize the problem, scuba tanks may be filled with mixtures of helium and oxygen rather than nitrogen and oxygen. Helium has a much lower solubility in blood and, like nitrogen, is inert. To avoid the bends, divers are advised to make several decompression stops while ascending to the water's surface. Such "time-outs" allow a more gradual equilibration of nitrogen concentration in the blood; the ideal is to

Scuba diving

achieve normal (or close to normal) levels upon reaching the surface. Tables and charts relating pressures and decompression times have been developed to aid divers.

### For Further Understanding

▶ Why are divers who slowly rise to the surface less likely to be adversely affected?

▶ What design features would be essential in deep-water manned exploration vessels?

---

**Question 6.5** An unopened bottle of soda contains $CO_2$ gas at 6.0 atm. Calculate the equilibrium solubility of $CO_2$ in the unopened soda at 25°C in units of mol/L.

**Question 6.6** After the soda in Question 6.5 is opened, the "fizz" shows a loss of $CO_2$. If the partial pressure of $CO_2$ in the atmosphere is $5.0 \times 10^{-4}$ atm, calculate the equilibrium $CO_2$ concentration in mol/L in the open bottle of soda.

## Henry's Law and Respiration

Henry's law helps to explain the process of respiration. Respiration depends on a rapid and efficient exchange of oxygen and carbon dioxide between the atmosphere and the blood. This transfer occurs through the lungs. The process, oxygen entering the blood and carbon dioxide released to the atmosphere, is accomplished in air sacs called *alveoli,* which are surrounded by an extensive capillary system. Equilibrium is quickly established between alveolar air and the capillary blood. The temperature of the blood is effectively constant. Therefore, the equilibrium concentrations of both oxygen and carbon dioxide are determined by the partial pressures of the gases (Henry's law). The oxygen is transported to cells, a variety of reactions take place, and the waste product of respiration, carbon dioxide, is brought back to the lungs to be expelled into the atmosphere.

*See A Medical Perspective: Blood Gases and Respiration.*

# A Medical Perspective

## Blood Gases and Respiration

Respiration must deliver oxygen to cells and carbon dioxide, the waste product, to the lungs to be exhaled. Henry's law helps to explain the way in which this process occurs.

Gases (such as $O_2$ and $CO_2$) move from a region of higher partial pressure to one of lower partial pressure in an effort to establish an equilibrium. At the interface of the lung, the membrane barrier between the blood and the surrounding atmosphere, the following situation exists: Atmospheric $O_2$ partial pressure is high, and atmospheric $CO_2$ partial pressure is low. The reverse is true on the other side of the membrane (blood). Thus, $CO_2$ is efficiently removed from the blood, and $O_2$ is efficiently moved into the bloodstream.

At the other end of the line, capillaries are distributed in close proximity to the cells that need to expel $CO_2$ and gain $O_2$. The partial pressure of $CO_2$ is high in these cells, and the partial pressure of $O_2$ is low, having been used up by the energy-harvesting reaction, the oxidation of glucose:

$$C_6H_{12}O_6 + 6O_2 \longrightarrow 6CO_2 + 6H_2O + energy$$

The $O_2$ diffuses into the cells (from a region of high to low partial pressure), and the $CO_2$ diffuses from the cells to the blood (again from a region of high to low partial pressure).

With each breath we take, oxygen is distributed to the cells and used to generate energy, and the waste product, $CO_2$, is expelled by the lungs.

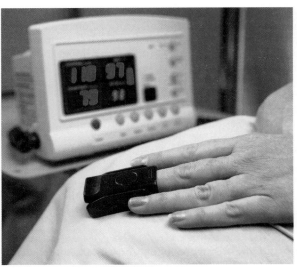

A pulse oximeter measures oxygen saturation which can be used to determine how well oxygen is being distributed to tissues.

### For Further Understanding

Use the Internet to investigate pulse oximetry and:

▸ Determine what the range of oxygen saturation should be for a healthy individual.
▸ Explain what happens as the partial pressure of carbon dioxide in the blood increases.

---

## 6.2  Concentration Based on Mass

Solution **concentration** is defined as the amount of solute dissolved in a given amount of solution. The concentration of a solution has a profound effect on the properties of a solution, both *physical* (melting and boiling points) and *chemical* (solution reactivity). Solution concentration may be expressed in many different units. Here, we consider concentration units based on mass.

### Mass/Volume Percent

The concentration of a solution is defined as the amount of solute dissolved in a specified amount of solution,

$$concentration = \frac{amount\ of\ solute}{amount\ of\ solution}$$

If we define the amount of solute as the *mass* of solute (in g) and the amount of solution in *volume* units (mL), concentration is expressed as the ratio

$$concentration = \frac{g\ of\ solute}{mL\ of\ solution}$$

### LEARNING GOAL

**6** Calculate solution concentration in mass/volume percent, mass/mass percent, parts per thousand, and parts per million.

This concentration can then be expressed as a percentage by multiplying the ratio by the factor 100%. This results in

$$\% \text{ concentration} = \frac{\text{g of solute}}{\text{mL of solution}} \times 100\%$$

The percent concentration expressed in this way is called **mass/volume percent**, or **% (m/V)**. Thus

$$\% \left( \frac{m}{V} \right) = \frac{\text{g of solute}}{\text{mL of solution}} \times 100\%$$

If the units of mass are other than g, or if the solution volume is in units other than mL, the proper conversion factor must be used to arrive at the units used in the equation.

Consider the following examples.

*Units and unit conversions were discussed in Chapter 1.*

---

### EXAMPLE 6.1 | Calculating Mass/Volume Percent

Calculate the mass/volume percent composition, or % (m/V), of 0.300 L of solution containing 15.0 g of glucose.

**LEARNING GOAL**

**6** Calculate solution concentration in mass/volume percent, mass/mass percent, parts per thousand, and parts per million.

**Solution**

**Step 1.** The expression for mass/volume percent is:

$$\% \left( \frac{m}{V} \right) = \frac{\text{g of solute}}{\text{mL of solution}} \times 100\%$$

**Step 2.** We must convert L to mL using the conversion factor based on 1000 mL = 1 L:

$$0.300 \, \cancel{L} \times \frac{10^3 \, \text{mL}}{1 \, \cancel{L}} = 3.00 \times 10^2 \, \text{mL}$$

**Step 3.** There are 15.0 g of glucose, the solute, and $3.00 \times 10^2$ mL of total solution. Therefore, substituting in our expression for mass/volume percent:

$$\% \left( \frac{m}{V} \right) = \frac{15.0 \, \text{g glucose}}{3.00 \times 10^2 \, \text{mL solution}} \times 100\%$$

$$= 5.00\% \left( \frac{m}{V} \right) \text{glucose}$$

---

### Practice Problem 6.1

a. Calculate the % (m/V) of 0.0600 L of solution containing 10.0 g NaCl.

b. Calculate the % (m/V) of 0.200 L of solution containing 15.0 g KCl.

c. 20.0 g of oxygen gas are diluted with 80.0 g of nitrogen gas in a 78.0-L container at standard temperature and pressure. Calculate the % (m/V) of oxygen gas.

d. 50.0 g of argon gas are diluted with 80.0 g of helium gas in a 476-L container at standard temperature and pressure. Calculate the % (m/V) of argon gas.

▶ For Further Practice: **Questions 6.31 and 6.32.**

**EXAMPLE 6.2** | **Calculating the Mass of Solute from a Mass/Volume Percent**

LEARNING GOAL

**7** Determine the quantity of solute or solution from the concentration of solution.

Calculate the number of g of NaCl in $5.00 \times 10^2$ mL of a 10.0% $\left(\dfrac{m}{V}\right)$ solution.

**Solution**

**Step 1.** The expression for mass/volume percent is:

$$\% \left(\frac{m}{V}\right) = \frac{\text{g of solute}}{\text{mL of solution}} \times 100\%$$

**Step 2.** Substitute the data from the problem:

$$10.0\% \left(\frac{m}{V}\right) = \frac{X \text{ g NaCl}}{5.00 \times 10^2 \text{ mL solution}} \times 100\%$$

**Step 3.** Multiply both sides by $5.00 \times 10^2$ mL solution to simplify:

$$X \text{ g NaCl} \times 100\% = \left[10.0\% \left(\frac{m}{V}\right)\right] (5.00 \times 10^2 \text{ mL solution})$$

Remember % (m/V) represents units % (g/mL). Therefore, after this calculation is complete, the only unit remaining is the mass unit, g.

**Step 4.** Divide both sides by 100% to isolate g NaCl on the left side of the equation:

$$X \text{ g NaCl} = 50.0 \text{ g NaCl}$$

*Helpful Hint:* The concentration % (m/V) may be used as a conversion factor to arrive at the same result. Two possibilities exist:

$$\frac{10.0\% \text{ g NaCl}}{1 \text{ mL solution}} \quad \text{and} \quad \frac{1 \text{ mL solution}}{10.0\% \text{ g NaCl}}$$

Only the former, 10.0% g NaCl/mL solution will result in the product unit, g NaCl.

$$(5.00 \times 10^2 \text{ mL solution}) \times \left(\frac{10.0\% \text{ g NaCl}}{1 \text{ mL solution}}\right) \times \left(\frac{1}{100\%}\right) = 50.0 \text{ g NaCl}$$

Data Given × Conversion Factor = Desired Result

**Practice Problem 6.2**

   a. Calculate the mass (in g) of sodium hydroxide required to make 2.00 L of a 1.00% (m/V) solution.
   b. Calculate the volume (in mL) of a 25.0% (m/V) solution containing 10.0 g NaCl.

▶ For Further Practice: **Questions 6.39 and 6.40.**

## Mass/Mass Percent

The **mass/mass percent,** or **% (m/m),** is most useful for mixtures of solids, whose masses are easily obtained. The expression used to calculate mass/mass percentage is analogous in form to % (m/V):

$$\% \left(\frac{m}{m}\right) = \frac{\text{g solute}}{\text{g solution}} \times 100\%$$

**EXAMPLE 6.3**   **Calculating Mass/Mass Percent**

LEARNING GOAL

Calculate the % (m/m) of platinum in a gold ring that contains 14.00 g gold and 4.500 g platinum.

**6**  Calculate solution concentration in mass/volume percent, mass/mass percent, parts per thousand, and parts per million.

**Solution**

**Step 1.**  Using our definition of mass/mass percent

$$\% \left(\frac{m}{m}\right) = \frac{\text{g solute}}{\text{g solution}} \times 100\%$$

**Step 2.**  Substituting,

$$\% \left(\frac{m}{m}\right) = \frac{4.500 \text{ g platinum}}{4.500 \text{ g platinum } + 14.00 \text{ g gold}} \times 100\%$$

$$= \frac{4.500 \text{ g platinum}}{18.50 \text{ g ring}} \times 100\%$$

$$= 24.32\% \text{ platinum}$$

**Practice Problem 6.3**

a. Calculate the % (m/m) of oxygen gas in a mixture containing 20.0 g of oxygen gas and 80.0 g of nitrogen gas.
b. Calculate the % (m/m) of argon gas in a mixture containing 50.0 g of argon gas and 80.0 g of helium gas.

▶ For Further Practice: **Questions 6.35 and 6.36.**

## Parts per Thousand (ppt) and Parts per Million (ppm)

LEARNING GOAL

The calculation of concentration in *parts per thousand* (ppt) or *parts per million* (ppm) is based on the same logic as mass/mass percent. Percentage is actually the number of parts of solute in 100 parts of solution. For example, a 5.00% (m/m) solution is made up of 5.00 g solute in 100 g solution.

**6**  Calculate solution concentration in mass/volume percent, mass/mass percent, parts per thousand, and parts per million.

$$5.00\% \left(\frac{m}{m}\right) = \frac{5.00 \text{ g solute}}{1.00 \times 10^2 \text{ g solution}} \times 100\%$$

It follows that a 5.00 ppt solution is made up of 5.00 g solute in 1000 g solution.

$$5.00 \text{ ppt} = \frac{5.00 \text{ g solute}}{1.00 \times 10^3 \text{ g solution}} \times 10^3 \text{ ppt}$$

Using similar logic, a 5.00 ppm solution is made up of 5.00 g solute in 1,000,000 g solution.

$$5.00 \text{ ppm} = \frac{5.00 \text{ g solute}}{1.00 \times 10^6 \text{ g solution}} \times 10^6 \text{ ppm}$$

The general expressions are:

$$\text{ppt} = \frac{\text{g solute}}{\text{g solution}} \times 10^3 \text{ ppt}$$

and

$$\text{ppm} = \frac{\text{g solute}}{\text{g solution}} \times 10^6 \text{ ppm}$$

Units of ppt and ppm are most often used for expressing the concentrations of very dilute solutions.

---

**EXAMPLE 6.4**   **Calculating ppt and ppm**

A 1.00-g sample of stream water was found to contain $1.0 \times 10^{-6}$ g lead. Calculate the concentration of lead in the stream water in units of % (m/m), ppt, and ppm. Which is the most suitable unit?

**Solution**

The expressions for mass/mass percent, parts per thousand, and parts per million are used.

**Step 1.**  mass/mass percent:

$$\% \left(\frac{m}{m}\right) = \frac{\text{g solute}}{\text{g solution}} \times 100\%$$

$$= \frac{1.0 \times 10^{-6} \text{ g Pb}}{1.00 \text{ g solution stream water}} \times 100\%$$

$$= 1.0 \times 10^{-4}\% \text{ (m/m)}$$

**Step 2.**  parts per thousand:

$$\text{ppt} = \frac{\text{g solute}}{\text{g solution}} \times 10^3 \text{ ppt}$$

$$= \frac{1.0 \times 10^{-6} \text{ g Pb}}{1.00 \text{ g solution stream water}} \times 10^3 \text{ ppt}$$

$$= 1.0 \times 10^{-3} \text{ ppt}$$

**Step 3.**  parts per million:

$$\text{ppm} = \frac{\text{g solute}}{\text{g solution}} \times 10^6 \text{ ppm}$$

$$= \frac{1.0 \times 10^{-6} \text{ g Pb}}{1.00 \text{ g solution stream water}} \times 10^6 \text{ ppm}$$

$$= 1.0 \text{ ppm}$$

Parts per million is the most reasonable unit because exponents are not required to express the numerical value.

**Practice Problem 6.4**

a. Calculate the ppt and ppm of oxygen gas in a mixture containing 20.0 g of oxygen gas and 80.0 g of nitrogen gas.
b. Calculate the ppt and ppm of argon gas in a mixture containing 50.0 g of argon gas and 80.0 g of helium gas.

▶ For Further Practice: **Questions 6.43 and 6.44.**

## 6.3   Concentration Based on Moles

LEARNING GOAL

**8** Calculate the molarity of solution from mass or moles of solute.

In our discussion of the chemical arithmetic of reactions in Chapter 4, we saw that the chemical equation represents the relative number of *moles* of reactants producing products. When chemical reactions occur in solution, it is most useful to represent their concentrations on a *molar* basis.

### Molarity

The most common mole-based concentration unit is molarity. **Molarity,** symbolized $M$, is defined as the number of mol of solute per L of solution, or

$$M = \frac{\text{mol solute}}{\text{L solution}}$$

## EXAMPLE 6.5   Calculating Molarity from Moles

Calculate the molarity of 2.0 L of solution containing 5.0 mol NaOH.

LEARNING GOAL

**8** Calculate the molarity of solution from mass or moles of solute.

### Solution

Using our expression for molarity

$$M = \frac{\text{mol solute}}{\text{L solution}}$$

Substituting,

$$M_{\text{NaOH}} = \frac{5.0 \text{ mol NaOH}}{2.0 \text{ L solution}}$$
$$= 2.5 \ M$$

### Practice Problem 6.5

Calculate the molarity of 2.5 L of solution containing 0.75 mol $MgCl_2$.

▶ For Further Practice: **Questions 6.47 and 6.48.**

Remember the need for conversion factors to convert from mass to number of mol. Consider the following example:

*Sections 1.3 and 1.5 discuss units and unit conversion.*

## EXAMPLE 6.6   Calculating Molarity from Mass

If 5.00 g glucose are dissolved in $1.00 \times 10^2$ mL of solution, calculate the molarity, $M$, of the glucose solution.

LEARNING GOAL

**8** Calculate the molarity of solution from mass or moles of solute.

### Solution

**Step 1.** To use our expression for molarity, it is necessary to convert from units of g of glucose to mol of glucose. The molar mass of glucose is $1.80 \times 10^2$ g/mol. Therefore

$$5.00 \ \cancel{g} \text{ glucose} \times \frac{1 \text{ mol glucose}}{1.80 \times 10^2 \ \cancel{g} \text{ glucose}} = 2.78 \times 10^{-2} \text{ mol glucose}$$

**Step 2.** We must convert mL to L:

$$1.00 \times 10^2 \ \cancel{\text{mL}} \text{ solution} \times \frac{1 \text{ L solution}}{10^3 \ \cancel{\text{mL}} \text{ solution}} = 1.00 \times 10^{-1} \text{ L solution}$$

**Step 3.** Substituting these quantities:

$$M_{\text{glucose}} = \frac{2.78 \times 10^{-2} \text{ mol glucose}}{1.00 \times 10^{-1} \text{ L solution}}$$
$$= 2.78 \times 10^{-1} \ M$$

### Practice Problem 6.6

Calculate the molarity, $M$, of KCl when 2.33 g KCl are dissolved in $2.50 \times 10^3$ mL of solution.

▶ For Further Practice: **Questions 6.53 and 6.54.**

## EXAMPLE 6.7    Calculating Volume from Molarity

LEARNING GOAL

Calculate the volume of a 0.750 $M$ sulfuric acid ($H_2SO_4$) solution containing 0.120 mol of solute.

**7**  Determine the quantity of solute or solution from the concentration of solution.

### Solution

**Step 1.**  Substituting in our basic expression for molarity, we obtain

$$0.750 \ M \ H_2SO_4 = \frac{0.120 \ \text{mol} \ H_2SO_4}{X \ \text{L solution}}$$

**Step 2.**  Rearranging to solve for volume (L):

$$X \ \text{L solution} = \frac{0.120 \ \text{mol} \ H_2SO_4}{0.750 \ \text{M} \ H_2SO_4}$$

Remember that $M$ represents mol/L.

$$X \ \text{L} = 0.160 \ \text{L}$$

*Helpful Hint:* Since the units of molarity are in fraction form, the value of molarity is a ratio that produces two possible conversion factors: $\dfrac{0.750 \ \text{mol} \ H_2SO_4}{1 \ \text{L solution}}$ and $\dfrac{1 \ \text{L solution}}{0.750 \ \text{mol} \ H_2SO_4}$

Only one will result in the product unit of L.

$$0.120 \ \text{mol} \ \cancel{H_2SO_4} \times \left( \frac{1 \ \text{L solution}}{0.750 \ \text{mol} \ \cancel{H_2SO_4}} \right) = 0.160 \ \text{L solution}$$

Data Given × Conversion Factor = Desired Result

### Practice Problem 6.7

Calculate the volume of a 0.200 $M$ KCl solution containing $5.00 \times 10^{-2}$ mol of solute.

▶ For Further Practice: **Questions 6.57 and 6.58.**

**Question 6.7**  Calculate the number of mol of solute in $5.00 \times 10^2$ mL of 0.250 $M$ HCl.

**Question 6.8**  Calculate the number of g of silver nitrate required to prepare 2.00 L of 0.500 $M$ $AgNO_3$.

### Dilution

LEARNING GOAL

**9**  Perform dilution calculations.

Laboratory reagents are often purchased as concentrated solutions (for example, 12 $M$ HCl or 6 $M$ NaOH) for reasons of safety, economy, and space limitations. We must often *dilute* such a solution to a larger volume to prepare a less concentrated solution for the experiment at hand. The approach to such a calculation is as follows.

We define

$$M_1 = \text{molarity of solution } before \text{ dilution}$$

$$M_2 = \text{molarity of solution } after \text{ dilution}$$

$$V_1 = \text{volume of solution } before \text{ dilution}$$

$$V_2 = \text{volume of solution } after \text{ dilution}$$

and

$$M = \frac{\text{mol solute}}{\text{L solution}}$$

This equation can be rearranged as:

$$\text{mol solute} = (M)(\text{L solution})$$

The number of mol of solute *before* and *after* dilution is unchanged, because dilution involves only the addition of extra solvent:

$$\text{mol}_1 \text{ solute} = \text{mol}_2 \text{ solute}$$

| Initial | Final |
| condition | condition |

or

$$(M_1)(\text{L}_1 \text{ solution}) = (M_2)(\text{L}_2 \text{ solution})$$

$$(M_1)(V_1) = (M_2)(V_2)$$

Knowing any three of these terms enables us to calculate the fourth.

---

**EXAMPLE 6.8**   **Calculating Molarity after Dilution**

LEARNING GOAL

Calculate the molarity of a solution made by diluting 0.050 L of 0.10 $M$ HCl solution to a volume of 1.0 L.

**9**  Perform dilution calculations.

**Solution**

**Step 1.**  Summarize the information provided in the problem:

$$M_1 = 0.10 \ M$$
$$M_2 = \text{Desired Result}$$
$$V_1 = 0.050 \text{ L}$$
$$V_2 = 1.0 \text{ L}$$

**Step 2.**  Use the dilution expression:

$$(M_1)(V_1) = (M_2)(V_2)$$

**Step 3.**  Solve for $M_2$, the final solution concentration:

$$M_2 = \frac{(M_1)(V_1)}{V_2}$$

**Step 4.**  Substituting,

$$M_2 = \frac{(0.10 \ M)(0.050 \ \cancel{L})}{(1.0 \ \cancel{L})}$$
$$= 0.0050 \ M \quad \text{or} \quad 5.0 \times 10^{-3} \ M \text{ HCl}$$

---

**Practice Problem 6.8**

What volume of 0.200 $M$ sugar solution can be prepared from 50.0 mL of 0.400 $M$ solution?

▶ For Further Practice: **Questions 6.60 and 6.61.**

| **EXAMPLE 6.9** | **Calculating a Dilution Volume** | **LEARNING GOAL** |

**9** Perform dilution calculations.

Calculate the volume, in L, of water that must be added to dilute 20.0 mL of 12.0 $M$ HCl to 0.100 $M$ HCl.

**Solution**

**Step 1.** Summarize the information provided in the problem:

$$M_1 = 12.0\ M$$
$$M_2 = 0.100\ M$$
$$V_1 = 20.0\ \text{mL} = 0.0200\ \text{L}$$
$$V_2 = \text{Desired Result}$$

**Step 2.** Then, using the dilution expression:

$$(M_1)(V_1) = (M_2)(V_2)$$

**Step 3.** Solve for $V_2$, the final volume:

$$V_2 = \frac{(M_1)(V_1)}{(M_2)}$$

**Step 4.** Substituting,

$$V_2 = \frac{(12.0\ \cancel{M})(0.0200\ \text{L})}{0.100\ \cancel{M}}$$
$$= 2.40\ \text{L solution}$$

Note that this is the *total final volume*. The amount of water added equals this volume *minus* the original solution volume, or

$$2.40\ \text{L} - 0.0200\ \text{L} = 2.38\ \text{L water}$$

**Practice Problem 6.9**

How would you prepare $1.0 \times 10^2$ mL of 2.0 $M$ HCl, starting with concentrated (12.0 $M$) HCl?

▶ For Further Practice: **Questions 6.59 and 6.62.**

The dilution equation is valid with any concentration units, such as % (m/V) *as well as* molarity, which are used in Examples 6.8 and 6.9. However, you must use the same units for both initial *and* final concentration values. Only in this way can you cancel units properly.

## 6.4   Concentration-Dependent Solution Properties

**LEARNING GOAL**

**10** Describe and explain concentration-dependent solution properties.

**Colligative properties** are solution properties that depend on the *concentration of the solute particles*, rather than the *identity of the solute*.

There are four colligative properties of solutions:

• vapor pressure lowering
• freezing point depression
• boiling point elevation
• osmotic pressure

Each of these properties has widespread practical applications. We look at each in some detail in this section.

## Vapor Pressure Lowering

**Raoult's law** states that, when a nonvolatile solute is added to a solvent, the vapor pressure of the solvent decreases in proportion to the concentration of the solute.

Perhaps the most important consequence of Raoult's law is the effect of the solute on the boiling point of a solution.

When a nonvolatile solute is added to a solvent, the boiling point of the solution is found to increase because it requires a higher temperature to form the gaseous state.

Raoult's law may be explained in molecular terms by using the following logic: Vapor pressure of a solution results from the escape of solvent molecules from the liquid to the gas phase, thus increasing the partial pressure of the gas-phase solvent molecules until the equilibrium vapor pressure is reached. Presence of solute molecules hinders the escape of solvent molecules, thus lowering the equilibrium vapor pressure (Figure 6.4).

**Figure 6.4** An illustration of Raoult's law: lowering of vapor pressure by addition of solute molecules. White units represent solvent molecules, and red units are solute molecules. Solute molecules present a barrier to escape of solvent molecules, thus decreasing the vapor pressure.

## Freezing Point Depression and Boiling Point Elevation

Freezing point depression may be explained by examining the equilibrium between liquid and solid states. At the freezing point, ice is in equilibrium with liquid water:

$$H_2O(l) \underset{(r)}{\overset{(f)}{\rightleftharpoons}} H_2O(s)$$

Solute molecules interfere with the rate at which liquid water molecules associate to form the solid state, decreasing the rate of the forward reaction. For a true equilibrium, the rate of the forward ($f$) and reverse ($r$) processes must be equal. Lowering the temperature eventually slows the rate of the reverse ($r$) process sufficiently to match the rate of the forward reaction. At the lower temperature, equilibrium is established, and the solution freezes.

*Recall that the concept of liquid vapor pressure was discussed in Section 5.2.*

Boiling point elevation can be explained by considering the definition of the boiling point; that is, the temperature at which the vapor pressure of the liquid equals the atmospheric pressure. Raoult's law states that the vapor pressure of a solution is decreased by the presence of a solute. Therefore, a higher temperature is necessary to raise the vapor pressure to the atmospheric pressure, hence the boiling point elevation.

*Section 7.4 discusses equilibrium.*

The extent of the freezing point depression ($\Delta T_f$) is proportional to the solute concentration over a limited range of concentration:

$$\Delta T_f = k_f \times \text{(solute particle concentration)}$$

The boiling point elevation ($\Delta T_b$) is also proportional to the solute concentration:

$$\Delta T_b = k_b \times \text{(solute particle concentration)}$$

If the value of the proportionality factor ($k_f$ or $k_b$) is known for the solvent of interest, the magnitude of the freezing point depression or boiling point elevation can be calculated for a solution of known concentration.

Solute concentration must be in *mole*-based units. The number of *particles* (molecules or ions) is critical here, not the *mass* of solute. One high mass molecule will have exactly the same effect on the freezing or boiling point as one low mass molecule. A mole-based unit, because it is related directly to Avogadro's number, will correctly represent the number of particles in solution.

We have already worked with one mole-based unit, *molarity*, and this concentration unit can be used to calculate either the freezing point depression or the boiling point elevation.

A second mole-based concentration unit, molality, is more commonly used in these types of situations. **Molality** (symbolized $m$) is defined as the number of mol of solute per kilogram (kg) of solvent in a solution:

$$m = \frac{\text{mol solute}}{\text{kg solvent}}$$

Molarity is temperature dependent simply because it is expressed as mol/L. Volume (L) is temperature dependent—most liquids expand measurably when heated and contract when cooled. Molality is mol/kg; both mol and mass (kg) are temperature independent.

Molality does not vary with temperature, whereas molarity is temperature dependent. For this reason, molality is the preferred concentration unit for studies such as freezing point depression and boiling point elevation, in which measurement of *change* in temperature is critical.

Practical applications that take advantage of freezing point depression of solutions by solutes include the following:

- Salt is spread on roads to melt ice in winter. The salt lowers the freezing point of the water, so it exists in the liquid phase below its normal freezing point, 0°C or 32°F.
- Solutes such as ethylene glycol, "antifreeze," are added to car radiators to prevent freezing by lowering the freezing point of the coolant.

We refer to the concentration of *particles* in our discussion of colligative properties. Why do we stress this term? The reason is that there is a very important difference between electrolytes and nonelectrolytes. That difference is the way that they behave when they dissolve. For example, if we dissolve 1 mol of glucose ($C_6H_{12}O_6$) in 1 kg of water,

$$1\ C_6H_{12}O_6(s) \xrightarrow{\ H_2O\ } 1\ C_6H_{12}O_6(aq)$$

1 mol (Avogadro's number, $6.022 \times 10^{23}$ particles) of glucose is present in solution. *Glucose is a covalently bonded nonelectrolyte.* Dissolving 1 mol of sodium chloride in 1 kg of water,

$$1\ NaCl(s) \xrightarrow{\ H_2O\ } 1\ Na^+(aq) + 1\ Cl^-(aq)$$

produces 2 mol of particles (1 mol of sodium ions and 1 mol of chloride ions). *Sodium chloride is an ionic electrolyte.*

$$1\text{ mol glucose} \longrightarrow 1\text{ mol of particles in solution}$$
$$1\text{ mol sodium chloride} \longrightarrow 2\text{ mol of particles in solution}$$

It follows that 1 mol of sodium chloride will decrease the vapor pressure, increase the boiling point, or depress the freezing point of 1 kg of water *twice as much* as 1 mol of glucose in the same quantity of water.

**Question 6.9**   Comparing pure water and a 0.10 $m$ glucose solution, which has the higher freezing point?

**Question 6.10**   Comparing pure water and a 0.10 $m$ glucose solution, which has the higher boiling point?

## Calculating Freezing Points and Boiling Points of Aqueous Solutions

LEARNING GOAL

**11**   Perform calculations involving colligative properties.

The freezing point depression constant for aqueous solutions is:

$$k_f = \frac{1.86°C}{m}$$

The expression for calculating the change (decrease) in freezing point of an aqueous solution is equal to the product of the freezing point depression constant and the molality of the particles in the solution:

$$\Delta T_f = (k_f)\,(m \text{ particles})$$

Correspondingly, for boiling point elevation:

$$k_b = \frac{0.52°C}{m}$$

and

$$\Delta T_b = (k_b)\,(m \text{ particles})$$

If we know the solution molality (mol solute/kg solvent), we can determine the particle molality,

$$m \text{ particles} = \frac{\text{mol solute}}{\text{kg solvent}} \times \frac{\text{mol particles}}{\text{mol solute}}$$

and calculate the decrease (freezing) or increase (boiling) in freezing or boiling temperature. Recalling that pure water freezes at 0°C and boils at 100°C, we can subtract $\Delta T_f$ from 0°C to obtain the solution freezing point and add $\Delta T_b$ to 100°C, resulting in the solution boiling point.

Let's review calculations of this type in Examples 6.10 and 6.11.

---

**EXAMPLE 6.10**  **Calculating Freezing and Boiling Points of Aqueous Solutions of Covalent, Nondissociating Solutes**

**LEARNING GOAL**

**11**  Perform calculations involving colligative properties.

Ethylene glycol, $H-O-\overset{\displaystyle H}{\underset{\displaystyle H}{C}}-\overset{\displaystyle H}{\underset{\displaystyle H}{C}}-O-H$, is a widely used automobile antifreeze.

a. Calculate the freezing point of an 8.38 $m$ aqueous solution of ethylene glycol.
b. Calculate the boiling point of an 8.38 $m$ aqueous solution of ethylene glycol.

**Solution**

We begin by recognizing that ethylene glycol is a nondissociating covalent compound. Consequently, 8.38 $m$ ethylene glycol solute is equivalent to 8.38 $m$ particles.

**For part a,**

**Step 1.** Using our expression for freezing point depression:

$$\Delta T_f = \left(\frac{1.86°C}{m}\right)(m \text{ particles})$$

and substituting molality of particles,

$$\Delta T_f = \left(\frac{1.86°C}{m}\right)(8.38\ m) = 15.6°C$$

**Step 2.** The solution freezing point is 15.6°C *below* 0.0°C, the freezing point of pure water. Therefore

$$\text{freezing point} = 0.0°C - 15.6°C = -15.6°C$$

**For part b,**

**Step 1.** Substituting our value for molality of particles into the boiling point elevation equation:

$$\Delta T_b = \left(\frac{0.52°C}{m}\right)(m \text{ particles})$$

$$= \left(\frac{0.52°C}{m}\right)(8.38\ m) = 4.4°C$$

**Step 2.** This means that the solution boiling point is 4.4°C *above* the boiling point of pure water. Therefore

$$\text{boiling point} = 100.0°C + 4.4°C = 104.4°C$$

*Continued…*

### Practice Problem 6.10

Calculate the boiling temperature and freezing temperature of a 1.5 $m$ solution of glucose ($C_6H_{12}O_6$). Remember that glucose is a covalent, nondissociating solute.

▸ For Further Practice: **Questions 6.73a and 6.74a.**

---

**EXAMPLE 6.11** | **Calculating Freezing and Boiling Points of Aqueous Solutions of Ionic, Dissociating Solutes**

Calcium chloride is used on roads and sidewalks to prevent ice formation in wintertime.

  a.  Calculate the freezing point of a 3.00 $m$ aqueous solution of $CaCl_2$.
  b.  Calculate the boiling point of a 3.00 $m$ aqueous solution of $CaCl_2$.

### Solution

Calcium chloride dissociates in water to form three particles for each $CaCl_2$:

$$\underbrace{CaCl_2(s)}_{\text{1 particle}} \xrightarrow{H_2O} \underbrace{Ca^{2+}(aq) + 2\,Cl^-(aq)}_{\text{3 particles}}$$

Consequently, a 3.00 $m$ $CaCl_2$ aqueous solution is

$$\frac{3\ m\ \text{particles}}{1\ m\ \cancel{CaCl_2}} \times 3.00\ \cancel{m\ CaCl_2} = 9.00\ m\ \text{particles}$$

**For part a,**

**Step 1.**  Using our expression for freezing point depression:

$$\Delta T_f = \left(\frac{1.86°C}{m}\right)(m\ \text{particles})$$

and substituting molality of particles

$$= \left(\frac{1.86°C}{\cancel{m}}\right)(9.00\ \cancel{m}) = 16.7°C$$

**Step 2.**  The solution freezing point is 16.7°C *below* 0.0°C, the freezing point of pure water. Therefore

$$\text{Freezing point} = 0.0°C - 16.7°C = -16.7°C$$

**For part b,**

**Step 1.**  Substituting our value for molality of particles into the boiling point elevation equation:

$$\Delta T_b = \left(\frac{0.52°C}{m}\right)(m\ \text{particles})$$

$$= \left(\frac{0.52°C}{\cancel{m}}\right)(9.00\ \cancel{m}) = 4.7°C$$

**Step 2.**  This means that the solution boiling point is 4.7°C *above* the boiling point of pure water. Therefore

$$\text{Boiling point} = 100.0°C + 4.7°C = 104.7°C$$

---

### Practice Problem 6.11

Calculate the boiling temperature and freezing temperature of a 1.5 $m$ solution of KCl. (Remember that 1 mol of KCl produces 2 mol of particles.)

▸ For Further Practice: **Questions 6.73b and 6.74b.**

# Osmosis, Osmotic Pressure, and Osmolarity

The biological cell membrane mediates the interaction of the cell with its environment and is responsible for the controlled passage of material into and out of the cell. One of the principal means of transport is termed *diffusion*. **Diffusion** is the net movement of solute or solvent molecules from an area of high concentration to an area of low concentration. This region where the concentration decreases over a distance is termed the **concentration gradient.** Because of the structure of the cell membrane, only small molecules are able to diffuse freely across this barrier. Large molecules and highly charged ions are restricted by the barrier. In other words, the cell membrane is behaving in a selective fashion. Such membranes are termed **selectively permeable membranes.**

Because a cell membrane is selectively permeable, it is not always possible for solutes to pass through it in response to a concentration gradient. In such cases, the solvent diffuses through the membrane. Such membranes, permeable to solvent but not to solute, are specifically called **semipermeable membranes.**

## Osmosis

**Osmosis** is the diffusion of a solvent (water in biological systems) through a semipermeable membrane in response to a (water) concentration gradient.

Suppose that we place a 0.5 M glucose solution in a dialysis bag that is composed of a membrane with pores that allow the passage of water molecules but not glucose molecules. Consider what will happen when we place this bag into a beaker of pure water. We have created a gradient in which there is a higher concentration of glucose inside the bag than outside, but the glucose cannot diffuse through the bag to achieve equal concentration on both sides of the membrane.

Now let's think about this situation in another way. We have a higher concentration of water molecules outside the bag (where there is only pure water) than inside the bag (where some of the water molecules are occupied in dipole-dipole interactions with solute particles and are consequently unable to move freely in the system). Because water can diffuse through the membrane, a net diffusion of water will occur through the membrane into the bag. This is the process of osmosis (Figure 6.5).

As you have probably already guessed, this system can never reach equilibrium (equal concentrations inside and outside the bag). Regardless of how much water diffuses into the bag, diluting the glucose solution, the concentration of glucose will always be higher inside the bag (and the accompanying free water concentration will always be lower).

## Osmotic Pressure and Osmolarity

What happens when the bag has taken in as much water as it can, when it has expanded as much as possible? Now the walls of the bag exert a force that will stop the *net* flow of water into the bag. **Osmotic pressure** is the pressure that must be exerted to stop the flow of water across a selectively permeable membrane by osmosis. Stated more precisely, the osmotic pressure of a solution is the net pressure with which water enters it by osmosis from a pure water compartment when the two compartments are separated by a semipermeable membrane.

The osmotic pressure can be calculated from the solution concentration at any temperature. How do we determine "solution concentration"? Recall that osmosis is a colligative property, dependent on the concentration of solute particles. Again, it becomes necessary to distinguish between solutions of electrolytes and nonelectrolytes. For example, a 1 M

## LEARNING GOAL

**10** Describe and explain concentration-dependent solution properties.

The terms *selectively permeable* or *differentially permeable* are used to describe biological membranes because such membranes restrict the passage of particles based both on size and charge. Even small ions, such as $H^+$, cannot pass freely across a cell membrane.

Cellophane is a familiar example of a semipermeable membrane.

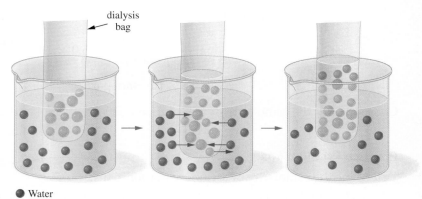

● Water
● Solute

**Figure 6.5** Osmosis across a membrane. The solvent, water, diffuses from outside the bag (the membrane) to the region of high solute concentration (inside the bag).

glucose solution consists of 1 mol of particles per L; glucose is a nonelectrolyte. A solution of 1 $M$ NaCl produces 2 mol of particles per L (1 mol of $Na^+$ and 1 mol of $Cl^-$). A 1 $M$ $CaCl_2$ solution is 3 $M$ in particles (1 mol of $Ca^{2+}$ and 2 mol of $Cl^-$ per L).

**Osmolarity,** the molarity of particles in solution, is used for osmotic pressure calculations. The equation relating the solution molarity to osmolarity is:

$$\text{osmolarity} = i \times M$$

where        $i$ = number of mol of particles/mol of solute

$M$ = molar concentration of the solute, in units of mol/L

We can use the value for the solution concentration of particles in conjunction with the ideal gas constant and the temperature of the solution to calculate the osmotic pressure of a solution, symbolized by $\pi$, using the following equation:

$$\pi = \text{osmolarity} \times R \times T$$

We know,                $\text{osmolarity} = i \times M$

Substituting,          $\pi = iMRT$

where,

$\pi$ = osmotic pressure of solution
$i$ = number of mol of particles/mol solute
$R$ = ideal gas constant (units of $L \cdot atm/K \cdot mol$)
$T$ = solution temperature (units of K)

---

**EXAMPLE 6.12**    **Calculating Solution Osmolarity**

Determine the osmolarity of $5.0 \times 10^{-3}$ $M$ $Na_3PO_4$.

**LEARNING GOAL**

**11** Perform calculations involving colligative properties.

**Solution**

**Step 1.** $Na_3PO_4$ is an ionic compound and produces an electrolytic solution:

$$Na_3PO_4 \xrightarrow{\ H_2O\ } 3Na^+ + PO_4^{3-}$$

1 mol of $Na_3PO_4$ yields 4 mol of product ions; consequently, $i$ = 4 mol particles/1 mol $Na_3PO_4$.

**Step 2.** Using our equation relating osmolarity and molarity (mol solute/L), and substituting,

$$\text{osmolarity} = i \times M$$

$$= \frac{4 \text{ mol particles}}{1 \text{ mol } Na_3PO_4} \times 5.0 \times 10^{-3} \frac{\text{mol } Na_3PO_4}{L}$$

$$= 2.0 \times 10^{-2} \text{ mol particles/L}$$

Consequently, the osmolarity of the solution is $2.0 \times 10^{-2}$ mol particles/L.

---

**Practice Problem 6.12**

Determine the osmolarity of the following solutions:

a. $5.0 \times 10^{-3}$ $M$ $NH_4NO_3$ (electrolyte)        b. $5.0 \times 10^{-3}$ $M$ $C_6H_{12}O_6$ (nonelectrolyte)

▶ For Further Practice: **Questions 6.83 and 6.84.**

**EXAMPLE 6.13** **Calculating Osmotic Pressure**

LEARNING GOAL

**11** Perform calculations involving colligative properties.

Calculate the osmotic pressure of a $5.0 \times 10^{-2}\ M$ solution of NaCl at 25°C (298 K).

**Solution**

**Step 1.** Using our definition of osmotic pressure, $\pi$:

$$\pi = i\,MRT$$

**Step 2.** One mol of NaCl produces two mol of particles ($Na^+$ and $Cl^-$). Therefore, $i = 2$ mol particles/1 mol NaCl.

**Step 3.** Substituting in our osmotic pressure expression:

$$= \frac{2\ \text{mol particles}}{1\ \text{mol NaCl}} \times 5.0 \times 10^{-2}\frac{\text{mol NaCl}}{L} \times 0.0821\frac{L \cdot atm}{K \cdot mol} \times 298\ K$$

$$= 2.4\ \text{atm}$$

**Practice Problem 6.13**

Calculate the osmotic pressure of each solution described in Practice Problem 6.12. Assume that the solutions are at 298 K.

▶ For Further Practice: **Questions 6.85 and 6.86.**

## Osmotic Pressure and Osmolarity in Red Blood Cells

Blood plasma has an osmolarity equivalent to a $0.30\ M$ glucose solution or a $0.15\ M$ NaCl solution. The latter is true because NaCl in solution dissociates into $Na^+$ and $Cl^-$ and thus contributes twice the number of solute particles as a glucose molecule that does not ionize. If red blood cells, which have an osmolarity equal to blood plasma, are placed in a $0.30\ M$ glucose solution, no net osmosis will occur because the osmolarity and water concentration inside the red blood cells are equal to those of the $0.30\ M$ glucose solution. The solutions inside and outside the red blood cells are said to be **isotonic** (*iso* means "same," and *tonic* means "strength") **solutions.** Because the osmolarity is the same inside and outside, the red blood cells will remain the same size (Figure 6.6b).

What happens if we now place the red blood cells into a **hypotonic solution,** in other words, a solution having a lower osmolarity than the cytoplasm of the cells? In this situation, there will be a net movement of water into the cells as water diffuses down its concentration gradient. The membranes of the red blood cells do not have the strength to exert a sufficient pressure to stop this flow of water, and the cells will swell and burst (Figure 6.6c). Alternatively, if we place the red blood cells into a **hypertonic solution** (one with a greater osmolarity than the cells), water will pass out of the cells, and they will shrink dramatically (Figure 6.6a).

These principles have important applications in the delivery of intravenous (IV) solutions into an individual (Figure 6.7). Normally, any fluids infused intravenously must have the correct osmolarity; they must be isotonic with the blood cells and the blood plasma. Such infusions are frequently either 5.5% dextrose (glucose) or "normal saline." The first solution is composed of 5.5 g of glucose per 100 mL of solution ($0.30\ M$), and the latter of 9.0 g of NaCl per 100 mL of solution ($0.15\ M$). In either case, they have the same osmotic pressure and osmolarity as the plasma and blood cells and can therefore be safely administered without upsetting the osmotic balance between the blood and the blood cells.

Practical examples of osmosis abound, including the following:

- A sailor, lost at sea in a lifeboat, dies of dehydration while surrounded by water. Seawater, because of its high salt concentration, dehydrates the cells of the body as a result of the large osmotic pressure difference between it and intracellular fluids.

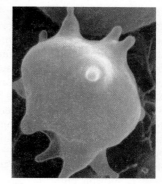

(a)

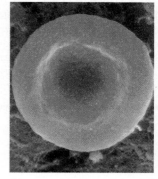

(b)

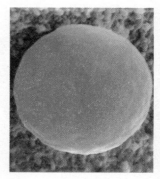

(c)

**Figure 6.6** Scanning electron micrographs of red blood cells exposed to (a) hypertonic, (b) isotonic, and (c) hypotonic solutions.

# A Medical Perspective

## Oral Rehydration Therapy

Diarrhea kills millions of children before they reach the age of 5 years. This is particularly true in third-world countries where sanitation, water supplies, and medical care are poor. In the case of diarrhea, death results from fluid loss, electrolyte imbalance, and hypovolemic shock (multiple organ failure due to insufficient perfusion). Cholera is one of the best-understood bacterial diarrheas. The organism *Vibrio cholera* survives passage through the stomach and reproduces in the intestine, where it produces a toxin called choleragen. The toxin causes the excessive excretion of $Na^+$, $Cl^-$, and $HCO_3^-$ from epithelial cells lining the intestine. The increased ion concentration (hypertonic solution) outside the cell results in the movement of massive quantities of water into the intestinal lumen. This causes the severe, abundant, clear vomit and diarrhea that can result in the loss of 10–15 L of fluid per day. Over the 4- to 6-day progress of the disease, a patient may lose from one to two times his or her body mass!

The need for fluid replacement is obvious. Oral rehydration is preferred over intravenous administration of fluids and electrolytes since it is noninvasive. In many third-world countries, it is the only therapy available in remote areas. The rehydration formula includes 50–80 g/L rice (or other starch), 3.5 g/L sodium chloride, 2.5 g/L sodium bicarbonate, and 1.5 g/L potassium chloride. Oral rehydration takes advantage of the cotransport of $Na^+$ and glucose across the cells lining the intestine. Thus, the glucose enters the cells, and $Na^+$ is carried along. Movement of these materials into the cells helps alleviate the osmotic imbalance, reduces the diarrhea, and corrects the fluid and electrolyte imbalance.

The disease runs its course in less than a week. In fact, antibiotics are not used to combat cholera. The only effective

A woman is shown filtering water through sari cloth.

therapy is oral rehydration, which reduces mortality to less than 1%. A much better option is prevention. In the photo above, a woman is shown filtering water through sari cloth. This simple practice has been shown to reduce the incidence of cholera significantly.

### For Further Understanding

▶ Explain dehydration in terms of osmosis.
▶ Explain why even severely dehydrated individuals continue to experience further fluid loss.

---

- A cucumber, soaked in brine, shrivels into a pickle. The water in the cucumber is drawn into the brine (salt) solution because of a difference in osmotic pressure (Figure 6.8).
- A Medical Perspective: Oral Rehydration Therapy describes one of the most lethal and pervasive examples of cellular fluid imbalance.

**Question 6.11** Refer to the intravenous solution in Figure 6.7 and calculate the osmolarity of its contents.

**Question 6.12** Is the solution osmolarity that you calculated in Question 6.11 isotonic with blood plasma? Why or why not?

## 6.5 Aqueous Solutions

### Water as a Solvent

Water is by far the most abundant substance on earth. It is an excellent solvent for most inorganic substances and is the principal biological solvent. Approximately 60% of the adult human body is water, and maintenance of this level is essential

**Figure 6.7** Composition and concentration are critically important in medical intervention. This solution is 0.15% (m/V) KCl and 5% (m/V) glucose.

for survival. These characteristics are a direct consequence of the molecular structure of water.

As we saw in Chapter 3, water is a bent molecule with a 104.5° bond angle. This angular structure, resulting from the effect of the two lone pairs of electrons around the oxygen atom, is responsible for the polar nature of water. The polarity, in turn, gives water its unique properties.

Because water molecules are polar, water is an excellent solvent for other polar substances ("like dissolves like"). Because much of the matter on earth is polar, hence at least somewhat water soluble, water has been described as the universal solvent. The term *universal solvent* is historical; for centuries, water was known to dissolve many commonly used substances. The solvent in blood is water, and it dissolves and transports compounds as diverse as potassium chloride, glucose, and protein throughout our bodies.

Water is readily accessible and easily purified. It is nontoxic and quite nonreactive. The high boiling point of water, 100°C, compared with molecules of similar size such as $N_2$ (b.p. = −196°C), is also explained by water's polar character. Strong dipole-dipole interactions between a $\delta^+$ hydrogen of one molecule and $\delta^-$ oxygen of a second, referred to as hydrogen bonding, create an interactive molecular network in the liquid phase (see Figure 5.9). The strength of these interactions requires more energy (higher temperature) for water to boil. The higher-than-expected boiling point enhances water's value as a solvent; often, reactions are carried out at higher temperatures to increase their rates. Other solvents, with lower boiling points, would simply boil away, and the reaction would stop.

This idea is easily extended to our own chemistry—because 60% of our bodies is water, we should appreciate the polarity of water on a hot day. As a biological solvent in the human body, water is involved in the transport of ions, nutrients, and waste into and out of cells. Water is also the solvent for biochemical reactions in cells and the digestive tract. Water is a reactant or product in some biochemical processes.

### LEARNING GOAL

**12**  Describe why the chemical and physical properties of water make it a truly unique solvent.

*See A Human Perspective: An Extraordinary Molecule, Chapter 7.*

*Refer to Sections 3.4 and 3.5 for a more complete description of the bonding, structure, and polarity of water.*

*Recall the discussion of intermolecular forces in Chapters 3 and 5.*

---

### EXAMPLE 6.14    Predicting Structure from Observable Properties

Sucrose is a common sugar, and we know that it is used as a sweetener when dissolved in many beverages. What does this allow us to predict about the structure of sucrose?

### LEARNING GOAL

**12**  Describe why the chemical and physical properties of water make it a truly unique solvent.

#### Solution

Sucrose is used as a sweetener in teas, coffee, and a host of soft drinks. The solvent in all of these beverages is water, a polar molecule. The rule "like dissolves like" implies that sucrose must also be a polar molecule. Without even knowing the formula or structure of sucrose, we can infer this important information from a simple experiment—dissolving sugar in our morning cup of coffee.

#### Practice Problem 6.14

Predict whether ammonia or methane would be more soluble in water. Explain your answer. (Hint: Refer to Section 5.2, the discussion of interactions in the liquid state.)

▶ For Further Practice: **Questions 6.101 and 6.102.**

(a)

(b)

**Figure 6.8** A cucumber (a) in an acidic salt solution undergoes considerable shrinkage on its way to becoming a pickle (b) because of osmosis.

# Kitchen Chemistry

## Solubility, Surfactants, and the Dishwasher

Each day we create a new supply of dirty dishes, glasses, pots and pans, and silverware. We may hand wash them, using one of the many commercially available detergents. Or, we may load them in an automatic dishwasher along with a solid or liquid detergent. Close the door, push a few buttons, and, in less than 1 hour, the dishes are clean and reasonably bacteria-free. How does this happen? It is a case of chemistry in action.

The fats, grease, and oils on the dishes are the potential solutes in the solvent water. The dissolution process is unlikely to happen if the solvent is pure water. Remember our rule "like dissolves like." The food residue is composed principally of nonpolar or very slightly polar molecules. Water, on the other hand, is extremely polar. We need some other substance to facilitate the interaction of the polar water and nonpolar food. That substance is a surfactant. Dishwashing detergents are a mixture of many components. Some have nothing to do with the cleaning process itself. Perfumes and dyes may be added to make the product more attractive to the consumer. Some components improve shelf life. The principal *active* ingredient is a surfactant. The role of the surfactant is to form a "bridge" between polar and nonpolar substances. Let us see how this happens.

Many surfactants exist, with a variety of chemical structures. However, all share one structural feature. They are molecules that have both a polar and nonpolar end. The polar end interacts with the solvent water, and the nonpolar end dissolves in the less polar (or nonpolar) food residue. Consequently, the surface tension of the water, which serves as a barrier between the water and food particles, is decreased (see Section 5.2). Agitation of the water removes the water/surfactant/residue aggregate from the surface that is being cleaned. This aggregate remains dissolved in the water until the rinse cycle sends it down the drain.

The structure of the typical surfactant, cocamido DEA,

**(nonpolar region)**　　　　　　**(polar region)**

is shown above. Note the combination of polar and nonpolar regions in the same molecule:

The $-OH$ groups interact with water; the carbon–hydrogen region (termed *hydrocarbon*) dissolves in the food residue.

The existence of polar and nonpolar sites within the same molecule is certainly the most important feature of a molecule used in a washing formulation. However, it is not the only desirable feature. The molecule should be nontoxic, inexpensive, readily soluble in water, and have a minimal adverse effect on the environment. It should be biodegradable, enabling bacteria, naturally occurring in water, to attack the bonds, destroying the molecules before they can damage aquatic ecosystems. Organic chemists (who study compounds containing mainly carbon and hydrogen atoms) are very adept at synthesizing molecules that optimize desirable properties while minimizing undesirable properties.

Thus, we see that carefully designed surfactants enable us to use clean, attractive, and sanitary utensils to prepare and serve our meals while minimizing the negative impact of our wastewater on the aquatic environment.

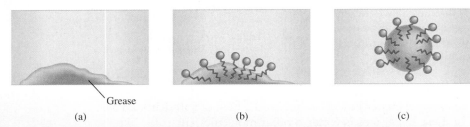

(a)　　　　　　　(b)　　　　　　　(c)

A surfactant at work. (a) Food residue (nonpolar) is not soluble in water. (b) Nonpolar ends of surfactant molecules dissolve in the food residue. (c) The food residue is removed from the surface and is solubilized in water.

## Concentration of Electrolytes in Solution

Recall (Sections 3.3 and 6.1) that an electrolyte is a material that dissolves in water to produce an *electrolytic solution* that conducts an electrical current. The behavior of many biological systems is critically dependent on the concentration of electrolytic solutions that are a part of these systems.

Molarity (mol/L) is the most commonly used concentration unit; however, another useful concentration unit is based on the *equivalent*. The **equivalent** (eq) is the number of moles of an ion corresponding to Avogadro's number of electrical charges. The resulting concentration unit is eq/L.

When discussing solutions of ionic compounds, molarity emphasizes the number of individual ions. A 1 molar solution of $Na^+$ contains Avogadro's number, $6.022 \times 10^{23}$, of $Na^+$ per L. In contrast, eq/L emphasize charge; 1 eq of $Na^+$ contains Avogadro's number of positive charges.

The concentration of any ion in aqueous solution, in units of eq/L, is equal to the product of the equivalents/mol of the ion and the molar concentration of the ion:

$$eq/L = \left(\frac{eq}{mol\ ion}\right)\left(\frac{mol\ ion}{L}\right)$$

Since

$$\frac{mol\ ion}{L} = M$$

$$eq/L = \left(\frac{eq}{mol\ ion}\right)(M)$$

The eq/mol of the ion is simply the number of charges on the ion, regardless of whether that charge is positive or negative. For example:

For $Na^+$, eq/mol is equal to 1
$Cl^-$, eq/mol is equal to 1
$Mg^{2+}$, eq/mol is equal to 2
$CO_3^{2-}$, eq/mol is equal to 2

and so forth.

The units milliequivalents/liter (meq/L) are often used when describing small amounts or a low concentration of ions. These units are routinely used when describing ions in blood, urine, and blood plasma.

We can convert between eq/L and meq/L using conversion factors based on the identity:

$$1\ eq = 10^3\ meq$$

---

**EXAMPLE 6.15**   **Calculating Ion Concentration**

For a solution that is $5.0 \times 10^{-3}\ M$ in phosphate ion ($PO_4^{3-}$)
  a. Calculate the concentration of phosphate ion in units of eq/L.
  b. Calculate the concentration of phosphate ion in units of meq/L.

**Solution**

**For part a,**

For $PO_4^{3-}$, the eq/mol is equal to 3. When the molarity concentration of the phosphate ion is expressed in mol/L, unit cancellation leads to the answer in eq/L. Substituting in the equation:

$$eq/L = \left(\frac{eq}{mol\ ion}\right)(M)$$

$$= \left(\frac{3\ eq}{mol\ PO_4^{3-}}\right)\left(\frac{5.0 \times 10^{-3}\ mol\ PO_4^{3-}}{L}\right)$$

$$= 1.5 \times 10^{-2}\ eq/L$$

*Continued…*

*Helpful Hint:* The eq of charge in this equation is always positive even if the ion is negative. It represents the number of eq of charge, not the sign of the charge.

**For part b,**

The conversion factor is based on the relationship $1 \text{ eq} = 10^3 \text{ meq}$:

$$\text{meq/L} = 1.5 \times 10^{-2} \frac{\text{eq}}{\text{L}} \times \frac{10^3 \text{ meq}}{\text{eq}} = 15 \text{ meq/L}$$

## Practice Problem 6.15

Calculate the number of eq/L of carbonate ion, $CO_3^{2-}$, in a solution that is $6.4 \times 10^{-4}$ $M$ carbonate ion.

▶ For Further Practice: **Questions 6.109 and 6.110.**

---

| EXAMPLE 6.16 | Calculating Electrolyte Concentrations |
|---|---|

LEARNING GOAL

A typical concentration of calcium ion in blood plasma is 4 meq/L. Represent this concentration in mol/L.

**13** Interconvert molar concentration of ions and milliequivalents/liter.

### Solution

**Step 1.** The data are given in meq/L, and the desired result is in mol/L ($M$). Therefore, meq/L must first be converted to eq/L using the conversion factor based on $1 \text{ eq} = 10^3 \text{ meq}$.

$$\frac{4 \text{ meq Ca}^{2+}}{1 \text{ L}} \times \frac{1 \text{ eq Ca}^{2+}}{10^3 \text{ meq Ca}^{2+}} = 4 \times 10^{-3} \frac{\text{eq Ca}^{2+}}{\text{L}}$$

**Step 2.** Our relationship between eq/L and mol/L ($M$) is:

$$\frac{\text{eq}}{\text{L}} = \left(\frac{\text{eq}}{\text{mol ion}}\right)(M)$$

**Step 3.** Rearranging and solving for $M$,

$$M = \left(\frac{\text{eq}}{\text{L}}\right)\left(\frac{\text{mol ion}}{\text{eq}}\right)$$

**Step 4.** The calcium ion has a $2^+$ charge (recall that calcium is in Group IIA of the periodic table; hence, there is a $2^+$ charge on the calcium ion). Substituting,

$$M = \left(\frac{4 \times 10^{-3} \text{ eq Ca}^{2+}}{\text{L}}\right)\left(\frac{1 \text{ mol Ca}^{2+}}{2 \text{ eq Ca}^{2+}}\right)$$

$$= \frac{2 \times 10^{-3} \text{ mol Ca}^{2+}}{\text{L}}$$

## Practice Problem 6.16

Sodium chloride [0.9% (m/V)] is a solution administered intravenously to replace fluid loss. It is frequently used to avoid dehydration. The sodium ion concentration is 15.4 meq/L. Calculate the sodium ion concentration in mol/L.

▶ For Further Practice: **Questions 6.113 and 6.114.**

**Question 6.13**   A typical concentration of chloride ion in blood plasma is 110 meq/L. Represent this concentration in mol/L.

**Question 6.14**   A typical concentration of magnesium ion in certain types of intravenous solutions is 3 meq/L. Represent this concentration in mol/L.

## Biological Effects of Electrolytes in Solution

The concentrations of cations, anions, and other substances in biological fluids are critical to health. Consequently, the osmolarity of body fluids is carefully regulated by the kidneys.

The two most important cations in body fluids are $Na^+$ and $K^+$. The sodium ion is the most abundant cation in the blood and intercellular fluids, whereas the potassium ion is the most abundant intracellular cation. In blood and intercellular fluid, the $Na^+$ concentration is 135 meq/L and the $K^+$ concentration is 3.5–5.0 meq/L. Inside the cell, the situation is reversed. The $K^+$ concentration is 125 meq/L and the $Na^+$ concentration is 10 meq/L.

If osmosis and simple diffusion were the only mechanisms for transporting water and ions across cell membranes, these concentration differences would not occur. One positive ion would be just as good as any other. However, the situation is more complex than this. Large protein molecules embedded in cell membranes actively pump sodium ions to the outside of the cell and potassium ions into the cell. This is termed *active transport* because cellular energy must be expended to transport those ions. Proper cell function in the regulation of muscles and the nervous system depends on the sodium ion/potassium ion ratio inside and outside of the cell.

If the $Na^+$ concentration in the blood becomes too low, urine output decreases, the mouth feels dry, the skin becomes flushed, and a fever may develop. The blood level of $Na^+$ may be elevated when large amounts of water are lost. Diabetes, certain high-protein diets, and diarrhea may cause elevated blood $Na^+$ level. In extreme cases, elevated $Na^+$ levels may cause confusion, stupor, or coma.

Concentrations of $K^+$ in the blood may rise to dangerously high levels following any injury that causes large numbers of cells to rupture, releasing their intracellular $K^+$. This may lead to death by heart failure. Similarly, very low levels of $K^+$ in the blood may also cause death from heart failure. This may occur following prolonged exercise that results in excessive sweating. When this happens, both body fluids and electrolytes must be replaced. Salt tablets containing both NaCl and KCl taken with water, and drinks such as Gatorade, effectively provide water and electrolytes and prevent serious symptoms.

The cationic charge in blood is neutralized by two major anions, $Cl^-$ and $HCO_3^-$. The chloride ion plays a role in acid-base balance, maintenance of osmotic pressure within an acceptable range, and oxygen transport by hemoglobin. The bicarbonate anion is the form in which most waste $CO_2$ is carried in the blood.

A variety of proteins are also found in the blood. Because of their larger size, they exist in colloidal dispersion. These proteins include blood-clotting factors, immunoglobulins (antibodies) that help us fight infection, and albumins that act as carriers of nonpolar, hydrophobic substances (fatty acids and steroid hormones) that cannot dissolve in water.

Additionally, blood is the medium for exchange of nutrients and waste products. Nutrients, such as the polar sugar glucose, enter the blood from the intestine or the liver. Because glucose molecules are polar, they dissolve in body fluids and are circulated to tissues throughout the body. As noted above, nonpolar nutrients are transported with the help of carrier proteins. Similarly, nitrogen-containing waste products, such as urea, are passed from cells to the blood. They are continuously and efficiently removed from the blood by the kidneys.

In cases of loss of kidney function, mechanical devices—dialysis machines—mimic the action of the kidney. The process of blood dialysis—hemodialysis—is discussed in A Medical Perspective: Hemodialysis.

**LEARNING GOAL**

**14**  Explain the role of electrolytes in blood and their relationship to the process of dialysis.

# A Medical Perspective

## Hemodialysis

As we have seen in Section 6.5, blood is the medium for exchange of both nutrients and waste products. The membranes of the kidneys remove waste materials such as urea and uric acid (Chapter 22), excess salts, and large quantities of water. This process of waste removal is termed **dialysis,** a process similar in function to osmosis (Section 6.4). Semipermeable membranes in the kidneys, dialyzing membranes, allow small molecules (principally water and urea) and ions in solution to pass through and ultimately collect in the bladder. From there they can be eliminated from the body.

Unfortunately, a variety of diseases can cause partial or complete kidney failure. Should the kidneys fail to perform their primary function, dialysis of waste products, urea and other waste products rapidly increase in concentration in the blood. This can become a life-threatening situation in a very short time.

The most effective treatment of kidney failure is the use of a machine, an artificial kidney, that mimics the function of the kidney. The artificial kidney removes waste from the blood using the process of hemodialysis (blood dialysis). The blood is pumped through a long semipermeable membrane, the dialysis membrane. The dialysis process is similar to osmosis. However, in addition to water molecules, larger molecules (including the waste products in the blood) and ions can pass across the membrane from the blood into a dialyzing fluid. The dialyzing fluid is isotonic with normal blood; it also is similar in its concentration of all other essential blood components. The waste materials move across the dialysis membrane (from a higher to a lower concentration, as in diffusion). A successful dialysis procedure selectively removes the waste from the body without upsetting the critical electrolyte balance in the blood.

Hemodialysis, although lifesaving, is not by any means a pleasant experience. The patient's water intake must be severely limited to minimize the number of times each week that treatment must be used. Many dialysis patients require two or three treatments per week, and each session may

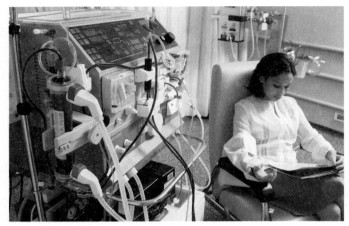

Dialysis patient

require one-half (or more) day of hospitalization, especially when the patient suffers from complicating conditions such as diabetes.

Improvements in technology, as well as the growth and sophistication of our health care delivery systems over the past several years, have made dialysis treatment much more patient friendly. Dialysis centers, specializing in the treatment of kidney patients, are now found in most major population centers. Smaller, more automated dialysis units are available for home use, under the supervision of a nurse. With the remarkable progress in kidney transplant success, dialysis is becoming, more and more, a temporary solution, sustaining life until a suitable kidney donor match can be found.

### For Further Understanding

▶ In what way is dialysis similar to osmosis?
▶ How does dialysis differ from osmosis?

# CHAPTER MAP

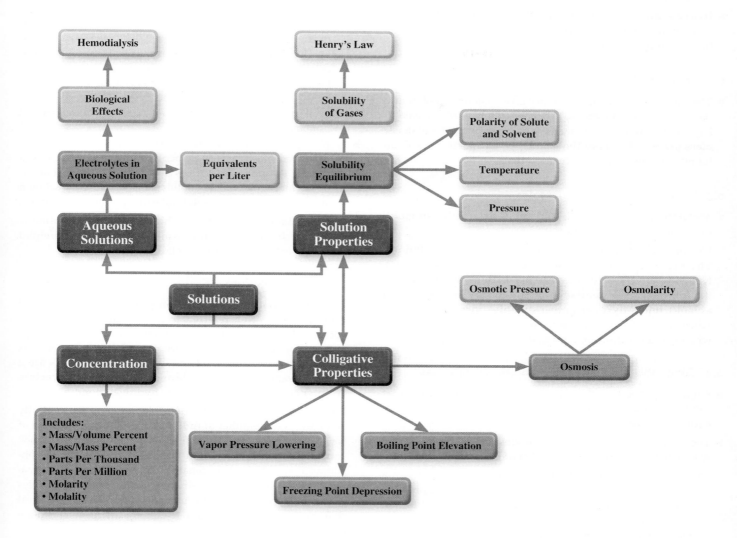

# SUMMARY

## 6.1 Properties of Solutions

▶ A **true solution** is a homogeneous mixture of two or more substances. A solution is composed of one or more **solutes,** dissolved in a **solvent.** When the solvent is water, the solution is called an **aqueous solution.**

▶ Liquid solutions are clear and transparent with no visible particles of solute. They may be colored or colorless, depending on the properties of the solute and solvent.

▶ In solutions of **electrolytes,** the solutes are ionic compounds that dissociate in solution to produce ions. They are good conductors of electricity. Solutions of nonelectrolytes are formed from nondissociating molecular solutes (nonelectrolytes), and their solutions do not conduct electricity.

▶ The rule "like dissolves like" is the fundamental condition for **solubility.** Polar solutes are soluble in polar solvents, and nonpolar solutes are soluble in nonpolar solvents.

▶ The degree of solubility depends on the difference between the polarity of solute and solvent, the temperature, and the pressure. Pressure considerations are significant only for solutions of gases.

▶ When a solution contains all the solute that can be dissolved at a particular temperature, it is **saturated.** Excess solute falls to the bottom of the container as a **precipitate.** Occasionally, on cooling, the excess solute may remain in solution for a time before precipitation. Such a solution is a **supersaturated solution.**

▶ When excess solute, the precipitate, contacts solvent, the dissolution process reaches a state of dynamic equilibrium.

▶ **Colloidal dispersions** have particle sizes between those of true solutions and precipitates. A **suspension** is a heterogeneous mixture that contains particles much larger than a colloidal dispersion. Over time, these particles may settle, forming a second phase.

▶ **Henry's law** describes the solubility of gases in liquids. At a given temperature, the solubility of a gas is proportional to the partial pressure of the gas.

## 6.2  Concentration Based on Mass

▶ The amount of solute dissolved in a given amount of solution is the solution **concentration.** The more widely used percentage-based concentration units are **mass/volume percent** and **mass/mass percent. Parts per thousand** (ppt) and **parts per million** (ppm) are used with very dilute solutions.

## 6.3  Concentration Based on Moles

▶ **Molarity,** symbolized *M*, is defined as the number of moles of solute per liter of solution.

▶ Dilution is often used to prepare less concentrated solutions. The expression for this calculation is $(M_1)(V_1) = (M_2)(V_2)$. Knowing any three of these terms enables us to calculate the fourth. The concentration of solute may be represented as mol/L (molarity) or any other suitable concentration units. However, both concentrations must be in the same units when using the dilution equation.

## 6.4  Concentration-Dependent Solution Properties

▶ Solution properties that depend on the concentration of solute particles, rather than the identity of the solute, are **colligative properties.**

▶ There are four colligative properties of solutions, all of which depend on the concentration of *particles* in solution:

• *Vapor pressure lowering. Raoult's law* states that when a nonvolatile solute is added to a solvent, the vapor pressure of the solvent decreases in proportion to the concentration of the solute.

• *Freezing point depression* and *boiling point elevation.* When a nonvolatile solid is added to a solvent, the freezing point of the resulting solution decreases, and the boiling point increases. The magnitudes of both the freezing point depression ($\Delta T_f$) and the boiling point elevation ($\Delta T_b$) are proportional to the solute particle concentration. Molality is commonly used in calculations involving colligative properties, because molality is temperature independent. **Molality** (*m*) of a solution is the number of mol of solute per kg of solvent.

• **Osmosis and osmotic pressure.** The cell membrane mediates the interaction of the cell with its environment and is responsible for the controlled passage of material into and out of the cell. One of the principal means of transport is termed *diffusion.* **Diffusion** is the net movement of solute or solvent molecules from an area of high concentration to an area of low concentration. This region where the concentration decreases over a distance is termed the **concentration gradient.** Because of the structure of the cell membrane, only small molecules are able to diffuse freely across this barrier. Large molecules and highly charged ions are restricted by the barrier. In other words, the cell membrane is behaving in a selective fashion. Such membranes are termed *selectively permeable membranes.* **Osmosis** is the movement of solvent (water) from a dilute solution to a more concentrated solution through a **semipermeable membrane.** The pressure that must be applied to the more concentrated solution to stop this flow is the **osmotic pressure.** The osmotic pressure, like the pressure exerted by a gas, may be treated quantitatively by using an equation similar in form to the ideal gas equation: $\pi = iMRT$. By convention, the molarity of particles used for osmotic pressure calculations is termed *osmolarity (mol particles/L).*

▶ In biological systems, if the concentration of the fluid surrounding red blood cells is higher than that inside the cell (a **hypertonic solution**), water flows from the cell, causing it to collapse. Too low a concentration of this fluid relative to the solution within the cell (a **hypotonic solution**) will cause the cell to rupture.

▶ Two solutions are **isotonic** if they have identical osmotic pressures. In that way, the osmotic pressure differential across the cell is zero, and no cell disruption occurs.

## 6.5  Aqueous Solutions

▶ The role of water in the solution process deserves special attention. It is often referred to as the "universal solvent" because of the large number of ionic and polar covalent compounds that are at least partially soluble in water. It is the principal biological solvent. These characteristics are a direct consequence of the molecular geometry and structure of water and its ability to undergo hydrogen bonding.

▶ When discussing solutions of ionic compounds, molarity emphasizes the number of individual ions. A 1 *M* solution of $Na^+$ contains Avogadro's number of sodium ions. In contrast, equivalents per liter (eq/L) emphasizes charge; a solution containing 1 eq of $Na^+$ per L contains Avogadro's number of positive charge. One equivalent of an ion is the number of moles of the ion corresponding to Avogadro's number of electrical charges. Changing from mol/L to eq/L (or the reverse) is done using conversion factors.

▶ Concentration of charge in these electrolytic solutions is even more important than the molar concentration of the ions that are responsible for the charge. Consequently, we often use concentration units (eq/L and meq/L) that emphasize charge rather than number of ions in solution.

▶ The concentrations of cations, anions, and other substances in biological fluids are critical to health. As a result, the osmolarity of body fluids is carefully regulated by the kidney using the process of dialysis.

## ANSWERS TO PRACTICE PROBLEMS

**6.1**  **a.** 16.7% (m/V) NaCl
**b.** 7.50% (m/V) KCl
**c.** $2.56 \times 10^{-2}$% (m/V) oxygen
**d.** $1.05 \times 10^{-2}$% (m/V) argon

**6.2**   **a.** 20.0 g NaOH
    **b.** 40.0 mL

**6.3**   **a.** 20.0% (m/m) oxygen
    **b.** 38.5% (m/m) argon

**6.4**   **a.** $2.00 \times 10^2$ ppt oxygen gas
    and
    $2.00 \times 10^5$ ppm oxygen gas
    **b.** $3.85 \times 10^2$ ppt argon gas
    and
    $3.85 \times 10^5$ ppm argon gas

**6.5**   0.30 $M$

**6.6**   $1.25 \times 10^{-2}\,M$

**6.7**   0.250 L

**6.8**   $1.00 \times 10^{-1}$ L (or $1.00 \times 10^2$ mL) of 0.200 $M$ sugar solution

**6.9**   To prepare the solution, dilute $1.7 \times 10^{-2}$ L of 12 $M$ HCl with sufficient water to produce $1.0 \times 10^2$ mL of total solution.

**6.10**   Boiling point = 100.8°C
    Freezing point = −2.8°C

**6.11**   Boiling point = 101.6°C
    Freezing point = −5.6°C

**6.12**   **a.** $1.0 \times 10^{-2}$ mol particles/L
    **b.** $5.0 \times 10^{-3}$ mol particles/L

**6.13**   **a.** 0.24 atm
    **b.** 0.12 atm

**6.14**   Ammonia is a polar substance, as is water. The rule "like dissolves like" predicts that ammonia would be water soluble. Methane, a nonpolar substance, would not be soluble in water.

**6.15**

$$\frac{1.3 \times 10^{-3} \text{ eq } CO_3^{2-}}{L}$$

**6.16**

$$1.54 \times 10^{-2}\,\frac{\text{mol } Na^+}{L}$$

# QUESTIONS AND PROBLEMS

## Properties of Solutions

### Foundations

**6.15**   Can a solution be both clear and red? Explain.

**6.16**   Two liters of liquid *A* are mixed with two liters of liquid *B*. The resulting volume is only 3.95 L. Explain what happened on the molecular level.

**6.17**   Which of the following solute(s) would form an electrolytic solution in water? Explain your reasoning.
    **a.** $NaNO_3$
    **b.** $C_6H_{12}O_6$
    **c.** $FeCl_3$

**6.18**   Which of the following solute(s) would form an electrolytic solution in water? Explain your reasoning.
    **a.** HCl
    **b.** $Na_2SO_4$
    **c.** Ethanol ($CH_3CH_2OH$)

**6.19**   Distinguish among the terms true solution, colloidal dispersion, and suspension.

**6.20**   Describe how you would distinguish experimentally between a colloidal dispersion and a suspension.

**6.21**   What is the difference between saturated and supersaturated solutions?

**6.22**   What happens when additional solute is added to a saturated solution that is being heated?

**6.23**   Intravenous (IV) therapy often involves colloidal dispersions. Albumin is an example. Describe some of the different properties expected for a colloidal dispersion of albumin versus a saline solution of NaCl.

**6.24**   An isotope of technetium, mixed with sulfur and colloidally dispersed in water, is frequently used in diagnosing various medical conditions because it is readily taken up by various tissues prior to excretion. Explain why this important mixture is not a true solution.

**6.25**   Is $CCl_4$ more likely to form a solution in water or benzene ($C_6H_6$)? Explain your reasoning.

**6.26**   Is $CH_3OH$ more likely to form a solution in water or benzene ($C_6H_6$)? Explain your reasoning.

### Applications

**6.27**   Fly fishermen in the Northeast have known for a long time that their chances of catching trout are much greater in early spring than in mid-August. Suggest an explanation based on solubility trends.

**6.28**   Fish kills (the sudden death of thousands of fish) often occur during periods of prolonged elevated temperatures. Pollution is often, but not always, the cause. Suggest another reason, based on solubility trends.

**6.29**   The Henry's law constant, *k,* for $O_2$ in aqueous solution is $1.3 \times 10^{-3}$ mol/(L · atm) at 25°C. When a diver is at a depth of 240 m, the pressure is approximately 25 atm. Calculate the equilibrium solubility of $O_2$ at this depth (25°C) in units of mol/L.

**6.30**   The Henry's law constant, *k,* for $N_2$ in aqueous solution is $6.1 \times 10^{-4}$ mol/(L · atm) at 25°C. When a diver is at a depth of 240 m, the pressure is approximately 25 atm. Calculate the equilibrium solubility of $N_2$ at this depth (25°C) in units of mol/L.

## Concentration Based on Mass

### Foundations

**6.31**   Calculate the composition of each of the following solutions in mass/volume %:
    **a.** 33.0 g sugar, $C_6H_{12}O_6$, in $5.00 \times 10^2$ mL solution
    **b.** 20.0 g NaCl in 1.00 L solution

**6.32** Calculate the composition of each of the following solutions in mass/volume %:
   **a.** 0.700 g KCl in 1.00 mL solution
   **b.** 95.2 g $MgCl_2$ in 0.250 L solution

**6.33** Calculate the composition of each of the following solutions in mass/volume %:
   **a.** 50.0 g ethanol dissolved in $5.00 \times 10^2$ mL solution
   **b.** 50.0 g ethanol dissolved in 1.00 L solution

**6.34** Calculate the composition of each of the following solutions in mass/volume %:
   **a.** 20.0 g benzene dissolved in $1.00 \times 10^2$ mL solution
   **b.** 20.0 g acetic acid dissolved in 2.50 L solution

**6.35** Calculate the composition of each of the following solutions in mass/mass %:
   **a.** 21.0 g NaCl in $1.00 \times 10^2$ g solution
   **b.** 21.0 g NaCl in $5.00 \times 10^2$ mL solution ($d = 1.12$ g/mL)

**6.36** Calculate the composition of each of the following solutions in mass/mass %:
   **a.** 1.00 g KCl in $1.00 \times 10^2$ g solution
   **b.** 50.0 g KCl in $5.00 \times 10^2$ mL solution ($d = 1.14$ g/mL)

### Applications

**6.37** A solution was prepared by dissolving 14.6 g of $KNO_3$ in sufficient water to produce 75.0 mL of solution. What is the mass/volume % of this solution?

**6.38** A solution was prepared by dissolving 12.4 g of $NaNO_3$ in sufficient water to produce 95.0 mL of solution. What is the mass/volume % of this solution?

**6.39** How many g of sugar would you use to prepare 100 mL of a 1.00 mass/volume % solution?

**6.40** How many mL of 4.0 mass/volume % $Mg(NO_3)_2$ solution would contain 1.2 g of magnesium nitrate?

**6.41** How many g of solute are needed to prepare each of the following solutions?
   **a.** $2.50 \times 10^2$ g of 0.900% (m/m) NaCl
   **b.** $2.50 \times 10^2$ g of 1.25% (m/m) $NaC_2H_3O_2$ (sodium acetate)

**6.42** How many g of solute are needed to prepare each of the following solutions?
   **a.** $2.50 \times 10^2$ g of 5.00% (m/m) $NH_4Cl$ (ammonium chloride)
   **b.** $2.50 \times 10^2$ g of 3.50% (m/m) $Na_2CO_3$

**6.43** A solution contains 1.0 mg of $Cu^{2+}$ per 0.50 kg solution. Calculate the concentration in ppt.

**6.44** A solution contains 1.0 mg of $Cu^{2+}$ per 0.50 kg solution. Calculate the concentration in ppm.

**6.45** Which solution is more concentrated: a 0.04% (m/m) solution or a 50 ppm solution?

**6.46** Which solution is more concentrated: a 20 ppt solution or a 200 ppm solution?

## Concentration Based on Moles

### Foundations

**6.47** Calculate the molarity of 5.0 L of solution containing 2.5 mol $HNO_3$.

**6.48** Calculate the molarity of 2.75 L of solution containing $1.35 \times 10^{-2}$ mol HCl.

**6.49** Calculate the molarity of a solution that contains 2.25 mol of $NaNO_3$ dissolved in 2.50 L.

**6.50** Calculate the molarity of a solution that contains 1.75 mol of $KNO_3$ dissolved in 3.00 L.

**6.51** Why is it often necessary to dilute solutions in the laboratory?

**6.52** Write the dilution expression and define each term.

### Applications

**6.53** Calculate the number of g of solute that would be needed to make each of the following solutions:
   **a.** $2.50 \times 10^2$ mL of 0.100 M NaCl
   **b.** $2.50 \times 10^2$ mL of 0.200 M $C_6H_{12}O_6$ (glucose)

**6.54** Calculate the number of g of solute that would be needed to make each of the following solutions:
   **a.** $2.50 \times 10^2$ mL of 0.100 M NaBr
   **b.** $2.50 \times 10^2$ mL of 0.200 M KOH

**6.55** How many g of glucose ($C_6H_{12}O_6$) are present in 1.75 L of a 0.500 M solution?

**6.56** How many g of sodium hydroxide are present in 675 mL of a 0.500 M solution?

**6.57** Calculate the volume of a 0.500 M sucrose solution (table sugar, $C_{12}H_{22}O_{11}$) containing 0.133 mol of solute.

**6.58** Calculate the volume of a $1.00 \times 10^{-2}$ M KOH solution containing $3.00 \times 10^{-1}$ mol of solute.

**6.59** It is desired to prepare 0.500 L of a 0.100 M solution of NaCl from a 1.00 M stock solution. How many mL of the stock solution must be taken for the dilution?

**6.60** A 50.0-mL sample of a 0.250 M sucrose solution was diluted to $5.00 \times 10^2$ mL. What is the molar concentration of the resulting solution?

**6.61** A 50.0-mL portion of a stock solution was diluted to 500.0 mL. If the resulting solution was 2.00 M, what was the molarity of the original stock solution?

**6.62** A 6.00-mL portion of an 8.00 M stock solution is to be diluted to 0.400 M. What will be the final volume after dilution?

**6.63** A 50.0-mL sample of 0.500 M NaOH was diluted to 500.0 mL. What is the new molarity?

**6.64** A 300.0-mL portion of $H_2O$ is added to 300.0 mL of 0.250 M $H_2SO_4$. What is the new molarity?

## Concentration-Dependent Solution Properties

### Foundations

**6.65** What is meant by the term *colligative property?*

**6.66** Name and describe four colligative solution properties.

**6.67** Explain, in terms of solution properties, why salt is used to melt ice in the winter.

**6.68** Explain, in terms of solution properties, why a wilted plant regains its "health" when watered.

**6.69** State Raoult's law.

**6.70** What is the major importance of Raoult's law?

**6.71** Why does 1 mol of $CaCl_2$ lower the freezing point of water more than 1 mol of NaCl?

**6.72** Using salt to try to melt ice on a day when the temperature is $-20°C$ will be unsuccessful. Why?

**6.73** **a.** Calculate the freezing temperature of 1.50 *m* urea, $N_2H_4CO$. Urea is a covalent compound.
   **b.** Calculate the freezing temperature of 1.50 *m* LiBr, an ionic compound.

**6.74** **a.** Calculate the boiling temperature of 1.50 *m* urea, $N_2H_4CO$. Urea is a covalent compound.
   **b.** Calculate the boiling temperature of 1.50 *m* LiBr, an ionic compound.

### Applications

Answer Questions 6.75–6.78 by comparing two solutions: 0.50 M sodium chloride (an ionic compound) and 0.50 M sucrose (a covalent compound).

**6.75** Calculate the freezing temperature of each solution. Assume that the molality of each solution is 0.50 $m$. (The molar and molal concentrations of dilute aqueous solutions are often identical, to two significant figures.)

**6.76** Calculate the boiling temperature of each solution. Assume that the molality of each solution is 0.50 $m$. (The molar and molal concentrations of dilute aqueous solutions are often identical, to two significant figures.)

**6.77** Which solution has the higher vapor pressure?

**6.78** Each solution is separated from water by a semipermeable membrane. Which solution has the higher osmotic pressure?

Answer Questions 6.79–6.82 based on the following scenario: Two solutions, A and B, are separated by a semipermeable membrane. For each case, predict whether there will be a net flow of water in one direction and, if so, which direction.

**6.79** A is pure water and B is 5% glucose.

**6.80** A is 0.10 $M$ glucose and B is 0.10 $M$ KCl.

**6.81** A is 0.10 $M$ NaCl and B is 0.10 $M$ KCl.

**6.82** A is 0.10 $M$ NaCl and B is 0.20 $M$ glucose.

**6.83** Determine the osmolarity of $5.0 \times 10^{-4}$ $M$ KNO$_3$ (electrolyte).

**6.84** Determine the osmolarity of $2.5 \times 10^{-4}$ $M$ C$_6$H$_{12}$O$_6$ (nonelectrolyte).

**6.85** Calculate the osmotic pressure of 0.50 $M$ KNO$_3$ (electrolyte).

**6.86** Calculate the osmotic pressure of 0.50 $M$ C$_6$H$_{12}$O$_6$ (nonelectrolyte).

In Questions 6.87–6.90, label each solution as isotonic, hypotonic, or hypertonic in comparison to 0.9% (m/V) NaCl (0.15 $M$ NaCl).

**6.87** 0.15 $M$ CaCl$_2$

**6.88** 0.35 $M$ glucose

**6.89** 0.15 $M$ glucose

**6.90** 3% (m/V) NaCl

## Aqueous Solutions

### Foundations

**6.91** What properties make water such a useful solvent?

**6.92** Sketch the "interactive network" of water molecules in the liquid state.

**6.93** Sketch the interaction of water with an ammonia molecule.

**6.94** Sketch the interaction of water with an ethanol, CH$_3$CH$_2$OH, molecule.

**6.95** Why is it important to distinguish between electrolytes and nonelectrolytes when discussing colligative properties?

**6.96** Name the two most important cations in biological fluids.

**6.97** Explain why a dialysis solution must have a low sodium ion concentration if it is designed to remove excess sodium ions from the blood.

**6.98** Explain why a dialysis solution must have an elevated potassium ion concentration when loss of potassium ions from the blood is a concern.

### Applications

**6.99** Solutions of ammonia in water are sold as window cleaner. Why do these solutions have a long "shelf life"?

**6.100** Why does water's abnormally high boiling point help to make it a desirable solvent?

**6.101** Sketch the interaction of a water molecule with a sodium ion.

**6.102** Sketch the interaction of a water molecule with a chloride ion.

**6.103** What type of solute dissolves readily in water?

**6.104** What type of solute dissolves readily in benzene (C$_6$H$_6$)?

**6.105** Describe the clinical effects of elevated concentrations of sodium ions in the blood.

**6.106** Describe the clinical effects of depressed concentrations of potassium ions in the blood.

**6.107** Describe conditions that can lead to elevated concentrations of sodium in the blood.

**6.108** Describe conditions that can lead to dangerously low concentrations of potassium in the blood.

**6.109** Calculate the number of eq/L of Ca$^{2+}$ in a solution that is $5.0 \times 10^{-2}$ $M$ in Ca$^{2+}$.

**6.110** Calculate the number of eq/L of SO$_4{}^{2-}$ in a solution that is $2.5 \times 10^{-3}$ $M$ in SO$_4{}^{2-}$.

**6.111** A physiological saline solution is labeled in part "154 meq/L of Na$^+$ and 154 meq/L of Cl$^-$."
  **a.** Calculate the number of mol of Na$^+$ in 1.00 L of solution.
  **b.** Calculate the number of mol of Cl$^-$ in 1.00 L of solution.

**6.112** A physiological solution designed to replace a patient's lost K$^+$ is 40 meq/L in K$^+$ and 40 meq/L in Cl$^-$.
  **a.** Calculate the number of mol of K$^+$ in 1.00L of solution.
  **b.** Calculate the number of mol of Cl$^-$ in 1.00L of solution.

**6.113** A potassium chloride solution that also contains 5% (m/V) dextrose is administered intravenously to treat some forms of malnutrition. The potassium ion concentration in this solution is 40 meq/L. Calculate the potassium ion concentration in mol/L.

**6.114** If the potassium ion concentration in the solution described in Question 6.113 was only 35 meq/L, calculate the potassium ion concentration in units of mol/L.

## CHALLENGE PROBLEMS

1. Which of the following compounds would cause the greater freezing point depression, per mol, in H$_2$O: C$_6$H$_{12}$O$_6$ (glucose) or NaCl?

2. Which of the following compounds would cause the greater boiling point elevation, per mol, in H$_2$O: MgCl$_2$ or HOCH$_2$CH$_2$OH (ethylene glycol, antifreeze)? (Hint: HOCH$_2$CH$_2$OH is covalent.)

3. Analytical chemists often take advantage of differences in solubility to separate ions. For example, adding Cl$^-$ to a solution of Cu$^{2+}$ and Ag$^+$ causes AgCl to precipitate; Cu$^{2+}$ remains in solution. Filtering the solution results in a separation. Design a scheme to separate the cations Ca$^{2+}$ and Pb$^{2+}$.

4. Using the strategy outlined in the above problem, design a scheme to separate the anions S$^{2-}$ and CO$_3{}^{2-}$.

5. Design an experiment that would enable you to measure the degree of solubility of a salt such as KI in water.

6. How could you experimentally distinguish between a saturated solution and a supersaturated solution?

7. Blood is essentially an aqueous solution, but it must transport a variety of nonpolar substances (hormones, for example). Colloidal proteins, termed *albumins*, facilitate this transport. Must these albumins be polar or nonpolar? Why?

# 7

# Energy, Rate, and Equilibrium

Describe the relationship between windmills and the topics discussed in this chapter.

## OUTLINE

## LEARNING GOALS

1  Correlate the terms *endothermic* and *exothermic* with heat flow between a *system* and its *surroundings*.

2  Explain what is meant by *enthalpy*, *entropy*, and *free energy* and demonstrate their implications.

3  Describe experiments that yield thermochemical information, and use experimental data to calculate the quantity of energy involved in reactions.

4  Describe the concept of reaction rate and the role of kinetics in chemical and physical change.

5  Describe the importance of *activation energy* and the *activated complex* in determining reaction rate.

6  Predict the way reactant structure, concentration, temperature, and catalysis affect the rate of a chemical reaction.

7  Write rate laws, and use these equations to calculate the effect of concentration on rate.

8  Recognize and describe equilibrium situations.

9  Write equilibrium constant expressions, and use these expressions to calculate equilibrium constants or equilibrium concentrations.

10  Use LeChatelier's principle to predict changes in equilibrium position.

# INTRODUCTION

In Chapter 4, we calculated quantities of matter involved in chemical change assuming that the reactions went to *completion*; that is, at least one reactant was *completely* used up and only product(s) remained at the end of the reaction. Often, this is not the case. There are many reactions, including processes occurring in living systems, that form product(s) but also have significant quantities of reactants still remaining. Additionally, we should be aware that all chemical reactions do not occur instantaneously. Reactions may occur rapidly (an explosion is one example) or over a period of minutes, hours, or even days. Some reactions are so slow that we may not observe their completion in our lifetime (corrosion is a common example).

Two concepts play important roles in determining the extent and speed of a chemical reaction: (1) thermodynamics, which deals with energy changes in chemical reactions, and (2) kinetics, which describes the rate or speed of a chemical reaction.

Although both thermodynamics and kinetics involve energy, they are two separate considerations. The laws of thermodynamics may predict that a reaction will occur, but the process may not be observed because the reaction is so slow; conversely, a reaction may be very fast because it is kinetically favorable yet produce very little product because it is thermodynamically unfavorable.

In this chapter, we investigate the fundamentals of thermodynamics and kinetics, with an emphasis on the critical role that energy changes play in chemical reactions. We consider physical change and chemical change, including the conversions that take place among the states of matter (solid, liquid, and gas). We use these concepts to explain the behavior of reactions that do not go to completion. These are termed *equilibrium reactions*. We develop the equilibrium constant expression and use LeChatelier's principle to demonstrate how equilibrium composition can be altered.

The Deepwater Horizon explosion was the result of a reaction between methane gas and oxygen gas.

## 7.1  Thermodynamics

**Thermodynamics** is the study of energy, work, and heat. It may be applied to chemical change, such as the calculation of the quantity of heat obtainable from the combustion of 1 gallon (gal) of fuel oil. Similarly, energy released or consumed in physical change, such as the boiling or freezing of water, may be determined.

There are three basic laws of thermodynamics:

1. Energy cannot be created or destroyed, only converted from one form to another.
2. The universe spontaneously tends toward increasing disorder or randomness.
3. The disorder of a pure, perfect crystal at absolute zero (0 Kelvin) is zero.

Only the first two laws of thermodynamics will be of concern here. They help us to understand why some chemical reactions may occur spontaneously and others do not. Whether we are synthesizing compounds in the laboratory, manufacturing industrial chemicals, or trying to determine causes of cancer, the ability to predict spontaneity is essential.

### The Chemical Reaction and Energy

John Dalton believed that chemical change involved joining, separating, or rearranging atoms. Two centuries later, this statement stands as an accurate description of chemical reactions. However, we now know much more about the energy changes that are an essential part of every reaction.

The kinetic molecular theory of gases was introduced in Section 5.1. The basic ideas of this theory will be useful to remember throughout the discussion

*Energy, its various forms, and commonly used energy units were introduced in Chapter 1.*

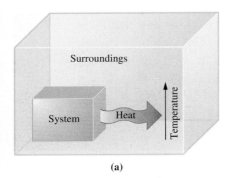

**(a)**

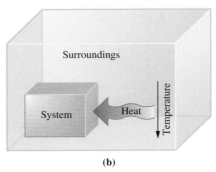

**(b)**

**Figure 7.1** Illustration of heat flow in (a) exothermic and (b) endothermic reactions.

of thermodynamics and kinetics. Keep in mind that molecules and atoms are in constant, random motion and frequently collide with each other. Remember that the average kinetic energy of the atoms or molecules increases with increasing temperature. In addition to these statements of the kinetic molecular theory, we will add the following concepts as they pertain to chemical reactions:

- some collisions, those with sufficient energy, will break bonds in molecules, and
- when reactant bonds are broken, new bonds may be formed and products result.

It is worth noting that we cannot measure an absolute value for energy stored in a chemical system. We can only measure the *change* in energy (energy absorbed or released) as a chemical reaction occurs. Also, it is often both convenient and necessary to establish a boundary between the *system* and its *surroundings*.

The **system** contains the process under study. The **surroundings** encompass the rest of the universe. Our universe is composed of the system and its surroundings. Energy is lost from the system to the surroundings or energy is gained by the system at the expense of the surroundings. This energy change, most often in the form of heat, may be experimentally determined because the temperature of the system or surroundings will change, and this change can be measured. This process is illustrated in Figure 7.1. *Heat flow* is a term that describes the transfer of heat when the direction of transfer is specified. For example, we often use the term *heat flow* to describe the transfer of thermal energy from a hot object to a cold one.

Consider the combustion of methane; that is, the reaction of methane and oxygen to form carbon dioxide and water. If we define the reaction as the system, the temperature of the air surrounding the reaction increases, indicating that some of the potential energy (energy stored in the bonds) is converted to kinetic energy, causing the molecules surrounding the reaction to speed up. This type of kinetic energy is called *thermal energy*. The transfer of thermal energy to the surroundings is known as **heat** and is sometimes called *heat flow*.

Now, an exact temperature measurement of the air before and after the reaction is difficult. However, if we could insulate a portion of the surroundings, to isolate and trap the heat, we could calculate a useful quantity, the heat of the reaction. Experimental strategies for measuring temperature change and calculating heats of reactions, termed *calorimetry*, are discussed in Section 7.2.

## The First Law of Thermodynamics

### Exothermic and Endothermic Reactions

The first law of thermodynamics states that the energy of the universe is constant. It is the law of conservation of energy. The study of energy changes that occur in chemical reactions is a very practical application of the first law. Consider, for example, the generalized reaction:

$$A\text{—}B + C\text{—}D \longrightarrow A\text{—}D + C\text{—}B$$

An **exothermic reaction** releases energy to the surroundings. The surroundings become warmer.

Each chemical bond is stored chemical energy (potential energy). For the reaction to take place, bond *A—B* and bond *C—D* must break; this process *always* requires energy. At the same time, bonds *A—D* and *C—B* must form; this process always releases energy.

If the energy required to break the *A—B* and *C—D* bonds is *less* than the energy given off when the *A—D* and *C—B* bonds form, the reaction will release the excess energy. The energy is a *product*, and the reaction is called an exothermic (Greek *exo*, "out," and Greek *therm*, "heat") reaction.

An example of an exothermic reaction is the combustion of methane, represented by a *thermochemical equation*, a chemical equation that also shows energy as a product or reactant.

$$CH_4(g) + 2O_2(g) \longrightarrow CO_2(g) + 2H_2O(g) + 211 \text{ kilocalories (kcal)}$$
Exothermic reaction

This thermochemical equation reads: the combustion of 1 mole (mol) of methane releases 211 kcal of heat.

An **endothermic reaction** absorbs energy from the surroundings. The surroundings become colder.

If the energy required to break the A—B and C—D bonds is *greater* than the energy released when the A—D and C—B bonds form, the reaction will need an external supply of energy. Insufficient energy is available in the system to initiate the bond-breaking process. Such a reaction is called an endothermic (Greek *endo*, "within," and Greek *therm*, "heat") reaction, and energy is a *reactant*.

The decomposition of ammonia into nitrogen and hydrogen is one example of an endothermic reaction:

$$22 \text{ kcal} + 2NH_3(g) \longrightarrow N_2(g) + 3H_2(g)$$
Endothermic reaction

This thermochemical equation reads: the decomposition of 2 mol of ammonia requires 22 kcal of heat.

The examples used here show the energy absorbed or released as heat energy. Depending on the reaction and the conditions under which the reaction is run, the energy may also take the form of light energy or electrical energy. A firefly releases energy as a soft glow of light on a summer evening. An electrical current results from a chemical reaction in a battery, enabling your car to start.

In an exothermic reaction, heat is released *from the system* to the surroundings. In an endothermic reaction, heat is absorbed *by the system* from the surroundings.

Bond breaking is an endothermic process. Bond formation is an exothermic process.

---

**EXAMPLE 7.1**   **Determining Whether a Process Is Exothermic or Endothermic**

LEARNING GOAL

An ice cube is dropped into a glass of water at room temperature. The ice cube melts. Is the melting of the ice exothermic or endothermic?

**1** Correlate the terms *endothermic* and *exothermic* with heat flow between a *system* and its *surroundings*.

**Solution**

**Step 1.** Consider the ice cube to be the system and the water, the surroundings.

**Step 2.** Recognize that the water (the surroundings) will decrease in temperature. The surroundings are transferring heat to the system, the ice cube. The ice cube uses the heat to overcome hydrogen bonding among molecules, and the ice melts.

**Step 3.** The heat flow is from surroundings to system.

**Step 4.** The system gains energy; hence, the melting process (physical change) is endothermic.

**Practice Problem 7.1**

Are the following processes exothermic or endothermic?

    a. Fuel oil is burned in a furnace.

    b. When solid NaOH is dissolved in water, the solution temperature increases.

▶ For Further Practice: **Questions 7.23 and 7.24.**

### Enthalpy of Reactions

A chemical reaction may involve the breaking and forming of many bonds. Our interest is often focused on the total amount of heat released or absorbed by the overall reaction.

LEARNING GOAL

**2** Explain what is meant by *enthalpy, entropy,* and *free energy* and demonstrate their implications.

# Green Chemistry

## Twenty-First Century Energy

When we purchase gasoline for our automobiles or oil for the furnace, we are certainly buying matter. But that matter is only a storage device; we are really purchasing the energy stored in the chemical bonds. Combustion, burning in oxygen, releases the stored energy (potential energy) in a form suited to its function: mechanical energy to power a vehicle or heat energy to warm a home.

Energy release is a consequence of change. In fuel combustion, this change results in the production of waste products that may be detrimental to our environment. This necessitates the expenditure of time, money, and *more* energy to clean up our surroundings.

If we are paying a considerable price for our energy supply, it would be nice to believe that we are at least getting full value for our expenditure. Even that is not the case. Removal of energy from molecules also extracts a price. For example, a properly tuned automobile engine is perhaps 30% efficient. That means that less than one-third of the available energy actually moves the car. The other two-thirds is released into the atmosphere as wasted energy, mostly heat energy. The law of conservation of energy tells us that the energy is not destroyed, but it is certainly no longer available to us in a useful form.

Can we build a 100%-efficient energy transfer system? Is there such a thing as cost-free energy? The answer to these questions is no, on both counts. It is theoretically impossible, and the laws of thermodynamics tell us why this is so.

Although 100% energy conversion is not possible, there is still room for improvement in our current energy usage. Consuming vast quantities of nonrenewable resources (fossil fuels: coal, oil, and natural gas) and expelling the waste products (carbon dioxide and sulfur oxides) into the atmosphere may not be the best energy generation system that human ingenuity can devise.

The process of generating electricity is simply finding ways to move electrons. Converting water to steam, then using the steam pressure to drive a turbine (a mechanical device to "push" electrons) requires massive quantities of heat to boil the water and produce steam. Nuclear reactions produce heat, which is the basis of a nuclear power plant. Combustion of coal, oil, and natural gas (exothermic reactions) also produces heat. So we see that the essential difference among the various types of power plants lies in the identity and technological complexity of the heat source.

Newer approaches to moving electrons involve wind energy and solar energy. It has been estimated that twenty-first century,

Harvesting energy directly from the sun and converting it to electricity is a safe, nonpolluting strategy to, at least partially, satisfy our growing energy needs.

high-tech windmills erected in unpopulated areas (the shallow waters of the Atlantic Ocean and the plains of the western portion of the United States), coupled with a modern electrical transmission grid, could satisfy the electrical demands of virtually the entire country. Solar energy, collected by photovoltaic cells arranged in solar panels, is converted to electrical energy.

Despite the tremendous progress in the design and development of new technologies, many problems remain. It will take decades to move away from nonrenewable energy sources. Nuclear energy has serious safety questions, raised by the disasters at Three Mile Island, Chernobyl, and Fukushima. Solar energy systems suffer from low efficiencies and cloudy days; they require storage devices that increase the cost of building and maintaining these systems. Wind turbines are perceived by some as unattractive and are most effective in areas with strong prevailing winds. We must remember that electric automobiles replace gasoline with electricity and the electricity (or at least a portion of it) comes from the combustion of fossil fuels.

However, improvement in the design and efficiency of these alternate energy sources holds the promise of reducing dependence on polluting, nonrenewable resources.

### For Further Understanding

▶ Solar and wind power have been mentioned as energy alternatives. Suggest a third alternative.

▶ What do you see as potential advantages (and potential shortcomings) of the alternative you have suggested?

---

**Enthalpy** is the term used to represent heat and is symbolized as H. The *change in enthalpy* is the energy difference between the products and reactants of a chemical reaction and is symbolized as $\Delta H$. By convention, energy released is represented with a negative sign (indicating an exothermic reaction), and energy absorbed is shown with a positive sign (indicating an endothermic reaction). The change in enthalpy is represented by the relationship:

$$\Delta H_{\text{reaction}} = H_{\text{products}} - H_{\text{reactants}}$$

- If $H_{\text{reactants}} > H_{\text{products}}$, $\Delta H$ must be negative and the reaction is exothermic.
- If $H_{\text{reactants}} < H_{\text{products}}$, $\Delta H$ must be positive and the reaction is endothermic.

For the combustion of methane, an exothermic process, energy is a *product* in the thermochemical equation:

$$CH_4(g) + 2O_2(g) \longrightarrow CO_2(g) + 2H_2O(g) + 211 \text{ kcal}$$

and

$$\Delta H = -211 \text{ kcal}$$

For the decomposition of ammonia, an endothermic process, energy is a *reactant* in the thermochemical equation:

$$22 \text{ kcal} + 2NH_3(g) \longrightarrow N_2(g) + 3H_2(g)$$

and

$$\Delta H = +22 \text{ kcal}$$

Diagrams representing changes in enthalpy for exothermic (a) and endothermic (b) reactions are shown in Figure 7.2.

**Question 7.1**    Are the following processes exothermic or endothermic?
 a. $C_6H_{12}O_6(s) \longrightarrow 2C_2H_5OH(l) + 2CO_2(g)$, $\Delta H = -16$ kcal
 b. $N_2O_5(g) + H_2O(l) \longrightarrow 2HNO_3(l) + 18.3$ kcal

**Question 7.2**    Are the following processes exothermic or endothermic?
 a. $S(s) + O_2(g) \longrightarrow SO_2(g)$, $\Delta H = -71$ kcal
 b. $N_2(g) + 2O_2(g) + 16.2 \text{ kcal} \longrightarrow 2NO_2(g)$

## Spontaneous and Nonspontaneous Reactions

It seems that all exothermic reactions should be spontaneous. After all, an external supply of energy does not appear to be necessary; in fact, energy is a product of the reaction. It also seems that all endothermic reactions should be nonspontaneous; energy is a reactant that we must provide. However, these hypotheses are not supported by experimentation.

Experimental measurement has shown that most *but not all* exothermic reactions are spontaneous. Likewise, most *but not all,* endothermic reactions are not spontaneous. There must be some factor in addition to enthalpy that will help us to explain the less obvious cases of nonspontaneous exothermic reactions and spontaneous endothermic reactions. This other factor is entropy.

## The Second Law of Thermodynamics

The first law of thermodynamics considers the enthalpy of chemical reactions. The second law states that the universe spontaneously tends toward increasing disorder or randomness.

## Entropy

A measure of the randomness of a chemical system is its **entropy.** The entropy of a substance is represented by the symbol $S$. A random, or disordered, system is characterized by *high entropy*; a well-organized system has *low entropy*.

What do we mean by disorder in chemical systems? Disorder is simply the absence of a regular repeating pattern. Disorder or randomness increases as we convert from the solid to the liquid to the gaseous state. As we have seen, solids often have an ordered crystalline structure, liquids have, at best, a loose arrangement, and gas particles are virtually random in their distribution. Therefore, gases have high entropy, and crystalline solids have very low entropy. Figures 7.3 and 7.4 illustrate properties of entropy in systems.

In these discussions, we consider the enthalpy change and energy change to be identical. This is true for most common reactions carried out in a lab, with minimal volume change.

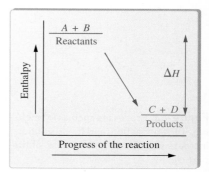

(a)

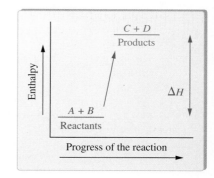

(b)

**Figure 7.2** (a) An exothermic reaction. $\Delta H$ represents the energy released during the progress of the exothermic reaction: $A + B \longrightarrow C + D + \Delta H$. (b) An endothermic reaction. $\Delta H$ represents the energy absorbed during the progress of the endothermic reaction: $\Delta H + A + B \longrightarrow C + D$.

**LEARNING GOAL**

**2**  Explain what is meant by *enthalpy,* *entropy,* and *free energy* and demonstrate their implications.

**Figure 7.3** (a) Gas particles, trapped in the left chamber, spontaneously diffuse into the right chamber, initially under vacuum, when the valve is opened. (b) It is unimaginable that the gas particles will rearrange themselves and reverse the process to create a vacuum. This can only be accomplished using a pump; that is, by doing work on the system.

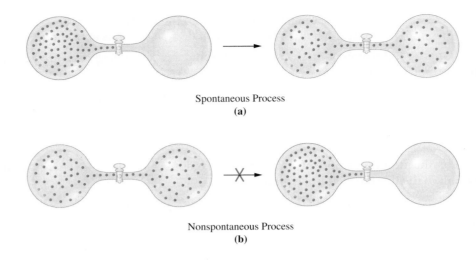

Spontaneous Process
**(a)**

Nonspontaneous Process
**(b)**

The second law describes the entire universe or any isolated system within the universe. On a more personal level, we all fall victim to the law of increasing disorder. Chaos in our room or workplace is certainly not our intent! It happens almost effortlessly. However, reversal of this process requires work and energy. The same is true at the molecular level. The gradual deterioration of our cities'

**Figure 7.4** Processes such as (a) melting, (b) vaporization, and (c) dissolution increase entropy, or randomness, of the particles.

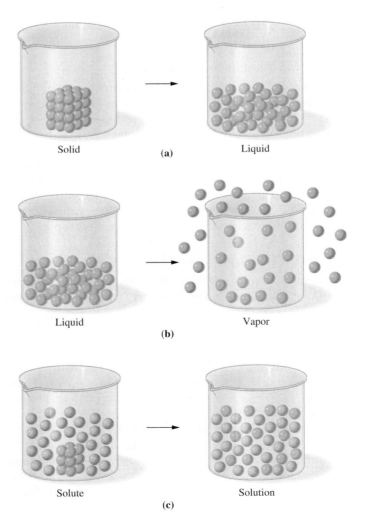

Solid                  **(a)**                  Liquid

Liquid                 **(b)**                  Vapor

Solute                 **(c)**                  Solution

infrastructure (roads, bridges, water mains, and so forth) is an all-too-familiar example. Millions of dollars (translated into energy and work) are needed annually just to try to maintain the status quo.

The entropy of a reaction is measured as a difference, $\Delta S$, between the entropies, $S$, of products and reactants.

The drive toward increased entropy, along with a tendency to achieve a lower potential energy, is responsible for spontaneous chemical reactions. Reactions that are exothermic and whose products are more disordered (higher in entropy) will occur spontaneously, whereas endothermic reactions producing products of lower entropy will not be spontaneous. If they are to take place at all, they will need some energy input.

**Question 7.3** Which substance has the greatest entropy, $He(g)$ or $Na(s)$? Explain your reasoning.

**Question 7.4** Which substance has the greatest entropy, $H_2O(l)$ or $H_2O(g)$? Explain your reasoning.

## Free Energy

The two situations just described are clear-cut and unambiguous. In any other situation, the reaction may or may not be spontaneous. It depends on the relative size of the enthalpy and entropy values.

**Free energy,** symbolized by $\Delta G$, represents the combined contribution of the enthalpy *and* entropy values for a chemical reaction. Thus, free energy is the ultimate predictor of reaction spontaneity and is expressed as

$$\Delta G = \Delta H - T\Delta S$$

$\Delta H$ represents the change in enthalpy between products and reactants, $\Delta S$ represents the change in entropy between products and reactants, and $T$ is the Kelvin temperature of the reaction.

- A reaction with a negative value of $\Delta G$ will *always* be spontaneous.
- A reaction with a positive $\Delta G$ will *always* be nonspontaneous.

We need to know both $\Delta H$ and $\Delta S$ in order to predict the sign of $\Delta G$ and make a definitive statement regarding the spontaneity of the reaction. Additionally, the temperature may determine the direction of spontaneity. Consider the four possible situations:

- $\Delta H$ positive and $\Delta S$ negative: $\Delta G$ is always positive, regardless of the temperature. The reaction is always nonspontaneous.
- $\Delta H$ negative and $\Delta S$ positive: $\Delta G$ is always negative, regardless of the temperature. The reaction is always spontaneous.
- Both $\Delta H$ and $\Delta S$ positive: The sign of $\Delta G$ depends on the temperature.
- Both $\Delta H$ and $\Delta S$ negative: The sign of $\Delta G$ depends on the temperature.

**LEARNING GOAL**

**2** Explain what is meant by *enthalpy*, *entropy*, and *free energy* and demonstrate their implications.

---

**EXAMPLE 7.2** | **Determining the Sign of $\Delta G$**

Determine the sign of $\Delta G$ for the following reaction. Is the reaction spontaneous, nonspontaneous, or temperature dependent?

$$42.5 \text{ kcal} + CaCO_3(s) \longrightarrow CaO(s) + CO_2(g)$$

**Solution**

**Step 1.** Determine the sign of $\Delta H$. Because heat is added as a reactant, the reaction is endothermic. This gives a positive sign for $\Delta H$.

**LEARNING GOAL**

**2** Explain what is meant by *enthalpy*, *entropy*, and *free energy* and demonstrate their implications.

*Continued…*

# A Medical Perspective

## Hot and Cold Packs

Hot packs provide "instant warmth" for hikers and skiers and are used in treatment of injuries such as pulled muscles. Cold packs are in common use today for the treatment of injuries and the reduction of swelling. These useful items are an excellent example of basic science producing a technologically useful product.

Both hot and cold packs depend on large energy changes taking place during a chemical reaction. Cold packs rely on an endothermic reaction, and hot packs generate heat energy from an exothermic reaction.

A cold pack is fabricated as two separate compartments within a single package. One compartment contains $NH_4NO_3$, and the other contains water. When the package is squeezed, the inner boundary between the two compartments ruptures, allowing the components to mix, and the following reaction occurs:

$$6.7 \text{ kcal} + NH_4NO_3(s) \longrightarrow NH_4^+(aq) + NO_3^-(aq)$$

This reaction is endothermic; heat taken from the surroundings produces the cooling effect.

The design of a hot pack is similar. Here, finely divided iron powder is mixed with oxygen. Production of iron oxide results in the creation of heat:

$$4Fe(s) + 3O_2(g) \longrightarrow 2Fe_2O_3(s) + 198 \text{ kcal}$$

This reaction occurs via an oxidation-reduction mechanism (see Chapter 4). The iron atoms are oxidized, and $O_2$ is reduced. Electrons are transferred from the iron atoms to $O_2$, and $Fe_2O_3$

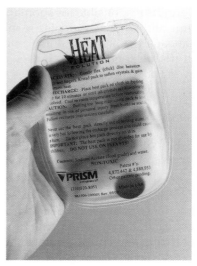

A hot pack

forms exothermically. The rate of the reaction is slow; therefore, the heat is liberated gradually over a period of several hours.

### For Further Understanding

▶ What is the sign of $\Delta H$ for each equation in this story?
▶ Predict whether entropy increases or decreases for each equation in this story.

---

Step 2. Determine the sign of $\Delta S$. This reaction starts with only solid and produces some gas. Therefore, the reaction begins with a small amount of disorder (the solid) and produces a product, $CO_2(g)$, that has a random distribution of molecules. Thus, there is an increase in the disorder and $\Delta S$ is positive.

Step 3. Consider the equation $\Delta G = \Delta H - T\Delta S$. Since $\Delta H$ and $\Delta S$ are both positive, $\Delta G$ is temperature dependent. The reaction is only spontaneous if the $T\Delta S$ term becomes so large that when it is subtracted from $\Delta H$, the value for $\Delta G$ will be negative. Therefore, this reaction is temperature dependent and is spontaneous at high temperature.

### Practice Problem 7.2

Determine the sign of $\Delta G$ for the following reaction. Is the reaction spontaneous, nonspontaneous, or temperature dependent?

$$2H_2(g) + O_2(g) \longrightarrow 2H_2O(l) + 137 \text{ kcal}$$

▶ For Further Practice: **Questions 7.33 and 7.34.**

The introduction to this chapter stated that thermodynamics is used to predict whether or not a reaction will occur. The value of $\Delta G$ determines if a reaction is thermodynamically favorable or unfavorable.

**Question 7.5** Predict whether a reaction with positive $\Delta H$ and negative $\Delta S$ will be spontaneous, nonspontaneous, or temperature dependent. Explain your reasoning.

**Question 7.6** Predict whether a reaction with positive $\Delta H$ and positive $\Delta S$ will be spontaneous, nonspontaneous, or temperature dependent. Explain your reasoning.

## 7.2 Experimental Determination of Energy Change in Reactions

The measurement of heat energy changes in a chemical reaction is **calorimetry.** This technique involves the measurement of the change in the temperature of a quantity of water or solution that is in contact with the reaction of interest and isolated from the surroundings. A device used for these measurements is a *calorimeter,* which measures heat changes in calories (cal) or joules (J).

Think of a calorimeter as a self-contained "universe" where heat can exchange between the system and its surroundings but cannot escape the calorimeter. At the same time, external heat is prevented from entering the calorimeter.

A Styrofoam coffee cup is a simple design for a calorimeter, and it produces surprisingly accurate results. It is a good insulator, and, when filled with solution, it can be used to measure temperature changes taking place as the result of a chemical reaction occurring in that solution (Figure 7.5). The change in the temperature of the solution, caused by the reaction, can be used to calculate the gain or loss of heat energy for the reaction.

For an exothermic reaction, heat released by the reaction is absorbed by the surrounding solution. For an endothermic reaction, the reactants absorb heat from the solution.

The **specific heat** of a substance is defined as the number of calories of heat needed to raise the temperature of 1 gram of the substance 1 degree Celsius (°C). Knowing the specific heat of the water or the aqueous solution along with the total number of g of solution and the temperature increase (measured as the difference between the final and initial temperatures of the solution) enables the experimenter to calculate the heat released during the reaction.

The solution behaves as a "trap" or "sink" for energy released in an exothermic process. The temperature increase indicates a gain in heat energy. Endothermic reactions, on the other hand, take heat energy away from the solution, lowering its temperature.

The quantity of heat absorbed or released by the reaction ($Q$) is the product of the mass of solution in the calorimeter ($m_s$), the specific heat of the solution ($SH_s$), and the change in temperature ($\Delta T_s$) of the solution as the reaction proceeds from the initial to final state.

The heat is calculated by using the following equation:

$$Q = m_s \times \Delta T_s \times SH_s$$

with units

$$\mathrm{cal} = \cancel{g} \times \cancel{°C} \times \frac{\mathrm{cal}}{\cancel{g} \cdot \cancel{°C}}$$

The details of the experimental approach are illustrated in Examples 7.3 and 7.4.

**LEARNING GOAL**

**3** Describe experiments that yield thermochemical information, and use experimental data to calculate the quantity of energy involved in reactions.

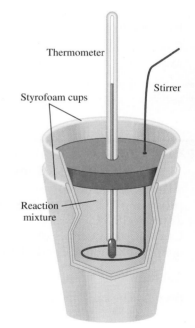

**Figure 7.5** A "coffee cup" calorimeter used for the measurement of heat change in chemical reactions. The concentric Styrofoam cups insulate the solution. Heat released by an exothermic chemical reaction (the system) enters the solution (the surroundings), raising its temperature, which is measured by using a thermometer.

Thermometer

Stirrer

Styrofoam cups

Reaction mixture

## EXAMPLE 7.3 | Calculating Energy Involved in Calorimeter Reactions

LEARNING GOAL

**3** Describe experiments that yield thermochemical information, and use experimental data to calculate the quantity of energy involved in reactions.

When 0.050 mol of hydrochloric acid is mixed with 0.050 mol of sodium hydroxide in a "coffee cup" calorimeter, the temperature of $1.00 \times 10^2$ g of the resulting solution increases from 25.0°C to 31.5°C. If the specific heat of the solution is 1.00 cal/g · °C, calculate the quantity of energy involved in the reaction. Is the reaction endothermic or exothermic?

### Solution

**Step 1.** The calorimetry expression is:

$$Q = m_s \times \Delta T_s \times SH_s$$

The reaction is the system; the solution is the surroundings.

**Step 2.** The change in temperature is

$$\Delta T_s = T_{s\,final} - T_{s\,initial}$$
$$= 31.5°C - 25.0°C = 6.5°C$$

The temperature of the solution has increased by 6.5°C; therefore, the reaction is exothermic.

**Step 3.** Substituting these values into the calorimetry expression:

$$Q = 1.00 \times 10^2 \text{ g solution} \times 6.5°C \times \frac{1.00 \text{ cal}}{\text{g solution} \cdot °C}$$

$$= 6.5 \times 10^2 \text{ cal}$$

$6.5 \times 10^2$ cal (or 0.65 kcal) of heat energy were released by this acid-base reaction to the surroundings, the solution; the reaction is exothermic.

### Practice Problem 7.3

Calculate the temperature change that would have been observed if 50.0 g of solution were in the calorimeter instead of $1.00 \times 10^2$ g of solution.

▶ For Further Practice: **Question 7.43.**

## EXAMPLE 7.4 | Calculating Energy Involved in Calorimeter Reactions

LEARNING GOAL

**3** Describe experiments that yield thermochemical information, and use experimental data to calculate the quantity of energy involved in reactions.

When 0.10 mol of ammonium chloride ($NH_4Cl$) is dissolved in water producing $1.00 \times 10^2$ g solution, the water temperature decreases from 25.0°C to 18.0°C. The specific heat of the resulting solution is 1.00 cal/g · °C. Calculate the quantity of energy involved in the process. Is the dissolution of ammonium chloride endothermic or exothermic?

### Solution

**Step 1.** The calorimetry expression is:

$$Q = m_s \times \Delta T_s \times SH_s$$

The reaction is the system; the solution is the surroundings.

**Step 2.** The change in temperature is

$$\Delta T = T_{s\,final} - T_{s\,initial}$$
$$= 18.0°C - 25.0°C = -7.0°C$$

The temperature of the solution has decreased by 7.0°C; therefore, the dissolution is endothermic.

**Step 3.** Substituting these values into the calorimetry expression:

$$Q = 1.00 \times 10^2 \text{ g solution} \times (-7.0°C) \times \frac{1.00 \text{ cal}}{\text{g solution} \cdot °C}$$

$$= -7.0 \times 10^2 \text{ cal}$$

$7.0 \times 10^2$ cal (or 0.70 kcal) of heat energy were absorbed by the dissolution process because the solution lost $7.0 \times 10^2$ cal of heat energy to the system. The dissolution of ammonium chloride is endothermic.

### Practice Problem 7.4

Calculate the temperature change that would have been observed if $1.00 \times 10^2$ g of another liquid, producing a solution with a specific heat of 0.800 cal/g · °C, were substituted for the water in the calorimeter.

▶ For Further Practice: **Question 7.44.**

**Question 7.7** Using the conversion factor in Chapter 1, convert the energy released in Example 7.3 to joules (J).

**Question 7.8** Using the conversion factor in Chapter 1, convert the energy absorbed in Example 7.4 to joules (J).

Many chemical reactions that produce heat are combustion reactions. In our bodies, many food substances (carbohydrates, proteins, and fats; Chapters 21–23) are oxidized to release energy. **Fuel value** is the amount of energy per g of food.

The fuel value of food is an important concept in nutrition science. The fuel value is generally reported in units of *nutritional Calories*. One **nutritional Calorie (Cal)** is equivalent to one kilocalorie (1000 cal). It is also known as the *large Calorie* (uppercase C).

Energy necessary for our daily activity and bodily function comes largely from the reaction of oxygen with carbohydrates. Chemical energy from foods that is not used to maintain normal body temperature or in muscular activity is stored in the bonds of chemical compounds known collectively as fat. Thus, consumption of "high-calorie" foods is implicated in the problem of obesity.

A special type of calorimeter, a *bomb calorimeter*, is useful for the measurement of the fuel value (Cal) of foods. Such a device is illustrated in Figure 7.6. Its design

*Note: Refer to A Human Perspective: Food Calories, Section 1.6.*

### LEARNING GOAL

**3** Describe experiments that yield thermochemical information, and use experimental data to calculate the quantity of energy involved in reactions.

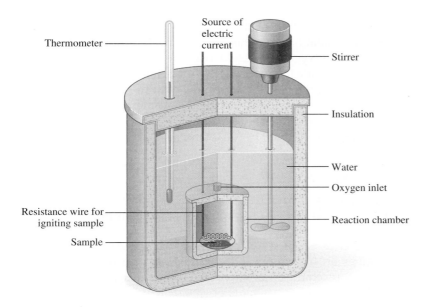

**Figure 7.6** A bomb calorimeter that may be used to measure heat released upon combustion of a sample. This device is commonly used to determine the fuel value of foods. The bomb calorimeter is similar to the "coffee cup" calorimeter. However, note the electrical component necessary to initiate the combustion reaction.

Thermometer

Source of electric current

Stirrer

Insulation

Water

Oxygen inlet

Reaction chamber

Resistance wire for igniting sample

Sample

## EXAMPLE 7.5    Calculating the Fuel Value of Foods

LEARNING GOAL

**3**    Describe experiments that yield thermochemical information, and use experimental data to calculate the quantity of energy involved in reactions.

A 1-g sample of glucose (a common sugar or carbohydrate) was burned in a bomb calorimeter. The temperature of $1.00 \times 10^3$ g $H_2O$ was raised from $25.0°C$ to $28.8°C$ ($\Delta T_s = 3.8°C$). Calculate the fuel value of glucose.

### Solution

**Step 1.** Recall that the fuel value is the number of nutritional Cal liberated by the combustion of 1 g of material, and 1 g of material was burned in the calorimeter.

**Step 2.** Then, the fuel value may be equated with the calorimetry expression:

$$\text{Fuel value} = Q = m_s \times \Delta T_s \times SH_s$$

**Step 3.** Water is the surroundings in the calorimeter; it has a specific heat capacity equal to 1.00 cal/g $H_2O \cdot °C$. Substituting the values provided in the problem into our expression for fuel value:

$$\text{Fuel value} = \text{g } H_2O \times °C \times \frac{1.00 \text{ cal}}{\text{g } H_2O \cdot °C}$$

$$= 1.00 \times 10^3 \text{ g } H_2O \times 3.8 °C \times \frac{1.00 \text{ cal}}{\text{g } H_2O \cdot °C}$$

$$= 3.8 \times 10^3 \text{ cal}$$

**Step 4.** Converting from cal to nutritional Cal:

$$3.8 \times 10^3 \text{ cal} \times \frac{1 \text{ nutritional Cal}}{10^3 \text{ cal}} = 3.8 \text{ Cal (nutritional Calories, or kcal)}$$

Since the quantity of glucose burned in the calorimeter is 1 g, the fuel value of glucose is 3.8 kcal/g.

### Practice Problem 7.5

A 1.0-g sample of a candy bar (which contains lots of sugar and fats!) was burned in a bomb calorimeter. A 3.0°C temperature increase was observed for $1.00 \times 10^3$ g of water. The entire candy bar weighed 2.5 ounces (oz). Calculate the fuel value (in Cal) of the sample and the total caloric content of the candy bar.

▶ For Further Practice: **Questions 7.45 and 7.46.**

is similar, in principle, to that of the "coffee cup" calorimeter discussed earlier. It incorporates the insulation from the surroundings, solution pool, reaction chamber, and thermometer. Oxygen gas is added as one of the reactants, and an electrical igniter is inserted to initiate the reaction. However, it is not open to the atmosphere. In the sealed container, the reaction continues until the sample is completely oxidized. All of the heat energy released during the reaction is captured in the water.

LEARNING GOAL

**4**    Describe the concept of reaction rate and the role of kinetics in chemical and physical change.

## 7.3    Kinetics

### Chemical Kinetics

Thermodynamics helps us to decide whether a chemical reaction is spontaneous. Knowing that a reaction can occur spontaneously tells us nothing about the time it may take.

Chemical **kinetics** is the study of the **rate** (or speed) of chemical reactions. Kinetics also gives an indication of the *mechanism* of a reaction, a step-by-step description of how reactants become products. Kinetic information may be represented as the *disappearance* of reactants or *appearance* of product over time. A typical graph of number of molecules versus time is shown in Figure 7.7.

Information about the rate at which various chemical processes occur is useful. For example, what is the "shelf life" of processed foods? When will slow changes in composition make food unappealing or even unsafe? Many drugs lose their potency with time because the active ingredient decomposes into other substances. The rate of hardening of dental filling material (via a chemical reaction) influences the dentist's technique. Our very lives depend on the efficient transport of oxygen to each of our cells and the rapid use of the oxygen for energy-harvesting reactions.

The diagram in Figure 7.8 is a useful way of depicting the kinetics of a reaction at the molecular level.

Often a color change, over time, can be measured. Such changes are useful in assessing the rate of a chemical reaction (Figure 7.9).

Let's see what actually happens when two chemical compounds react and what experimental conditions affect the rate of a reaction.

## Activation Energy and the Activated Complex

Consider the exothermic reaction we discussed in Section 7.1:

$$CH_4(g) + 2O_2(g) \longrightarrow CO_2(g) + 2H_2O(g) + 211 \text{ kcal}$$

For the reaction to proceed, four C—H and two O=O bonds must be broken, and two C=O and four H—O bonds must be formed. Sufficient energy must be available to cause the bonds to break if the reaction is to take place. This energy is provided by the collision of molecules. If sufficient energy is available at the temperature of the reaction, one or more bonds will break, and the atoms will recombine in a lower energy arrangement, in this case as carbon dioxide and water. A collision producing product molecules is termed an *effective collision*. An effective collision requires sufficient energy and, in the case of complex molecules, the proper orientation of reacting molecules. Only effective collisions lead to chemical reaction.

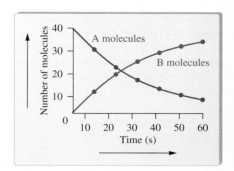

**Figure 7.7** For a hypothetical reaction $A \longrightarrow B$ the number of $A$ molecules (reactant molecules) decreases over time and $B$ molecules (product molecules) increase in number over time.

LEARNING GOAL

**5** Describe the importance of *activation energy* and the *activated complex* in determining reaction rate.

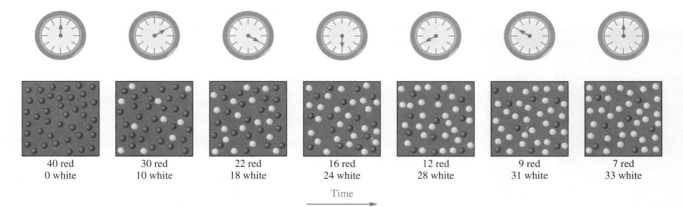

| 40 red | 30 red | 22 red | 16 red | 12 red | 9 red | 7 red |
| 0 white | 10 white | 18 white | 24 white | 28 white | 31 white | 33 white |

Time

**Figure 7.8** An alternate way of representing the information contained in Figure 7.7.

Time

**Figure 7.9** The conversion of reddish brown $Br_2$ in solution to colorless $Br^-$ over time. Figure 7.8 represents this reaction, $A \longrightarrow B$, on a molecular level.

**Figure 7.10** (a) The change in potential energy as a function of reaction time for an exothermic reaction. (b) The change in potential energy as a function of reaction time for an endothermic reaction.

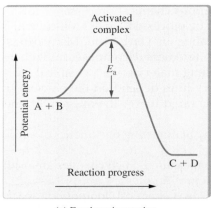

**(a)** Exothermic reaction

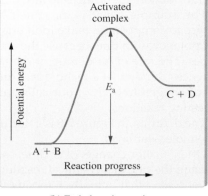

**(b)** Endothermic reaction

The minimum amount of energy required to initiate a chemical reaction is called the **activation energy,** $E_a$, for the reaction.

We can picture the chemical reaction in terms of the changes in potential energy that occur during the reaction. Figure 7.10a graphically shows these changes for an exothermic reaction, and Figure 7.10b shows these changes for an endothermic reaction. Important characteristics of these graphs include the following:

- The reaction proceeds from reactants to products through an extremely unstable state that we call the **activated complex.** The activated complex cannot be isolated from the reaction mixture but may be thought of as a short-lived group of atoms structured in such a way that it quickly and easily breaks apart into the products of the reaction.
- Formation of the activated complex requires energy. The difference between the energy of reactants and that of the activated complex is the activation energy. This energy must be provided by the collision of the reacting molecules or atoms at the temperature of the reaction.

Note the difference in activation energy between an exothermic reaction (Figure 7.10a) and an endothermic reaction (Figure 7.10b).

- The endothermic reaction takes place slowly because of the large activation energy required for the conversion of reactants into products.

Another difference between an exothermic reaction and endothermic reaction is the net energy.

- In an exothermic reaction, the overall energy change must be a *net* release of energy. The *net* release of energy is the difference in energy between products and reactants.

**Question 7.9**    The act of striking a match illustrates the role of activation energy in a chemical reaction. Explain.

**Question 7.10**    Distinguish between the terms *net energy* and *activation energy*.

## Factors that Affect Reaction Rate

The following six factors influence reaction rate:

### • Structure of the Reacting Species

Reactions among ions in solution are usually very rapid. Ionic compounds in solution are dissociated; consequently, their bonds are already broken, and the activation energy for their reaction should be very low. On the other hand,

How does a match illustrate the concept of activation energy?

LEARNING GOAL

**6**  Predict the way reactant structure, concentration, temperature, and catalysis affect the rate of a chemical reaction.

reactions involving covalently bonded compounds may proceed more slowly. Covalent bonds must be broken and new bonds formed. The activation energy for this process would be significantly higher than that for the reaction of free ions. Bond strengths certainly play a role in determining reaction rates because the magnitude of the activation energy, or energy barrier, is related to bond strength.

## • Molecular Shape and Orientation

The size and shape of reactant molecules influence the rate of the reaction. Large molecules, containing bulky groups of atoms, may block the reactive part of the molecule from interacting with another reactive substance, causing the reaction to proceed slowly. Only molecular collisions that have the correct collision orientation, as well as sufficient energy, lead to product formation. These collisions are termed *effective collisions*.

## • The Concentration of Reactants

The rate of a chemical reaction is often a complex function of the concentration of one or more of the reacting substances. The rate will generally *increase* as concentration *increases* simply because a higher concentration means more reactant molecules in a given volume and therefore a greater number of collisions per unit time. If we assume that other variables are held constant, a larger number of collisions leads to a larger number of effective collisions. For example, the rate at which a fire burns depends on the concentration of oxygen in the atmosphere surrounding the fire, as well as the concentration of the fuel (perhaps methane or propane). A common fire-fighting strategy is the use of fire extinguishers filled with carbon dioxide. The carbon dioxide dilutes the oxygen to a level where the combustion process can no longer be sustained.

## • The Temperature of Reactants

The rate of a reaction increases as the temperature increases, because the average kinetic energy of the reacting particles is directly proportional to the Kelvin temperature. Increasing the speed of particles increases the likelihood of collision, and the higher kinetic energy means that a higher percentage of these collisions will result in product formation (effective collisions). A 10°C rise in temperature has often been found to double the reaction rate.

## • The Physical State of Reactants

The rate of a reaction depends on the physical state of the reactants: solid, liquid, or gas. For a reaction to occur, the reactants must collide frequently and have sufficient energy to react. In the solid state, the atoms, ions, or molecules are restricted in their motion. In the gaseous and liquid states, the particles have both free motion and proximity to each other. Hence, reactions tend to be fastest in the gaseous and liquid states and slowest in the solid state.

## • The Presence of a Catalyst

A **catalyst** is a substance that *increases* the reaction rate. If added to a reaction mixture, the catalytic substance undergoes no net change, nor does it alter the outcome of the reaction. However, the catalyst interacts with the reactants to create an alternative pathway for production of products. This alternative path has a lower activation energy. This makes it easier for the reaction to take place and thus increases the rate. This effect is illustrated in Figure 7.11.

Catalysis is important industrially; it may often make the difference between profit and loss in the sale of a product. For example, catalysis is useful in converting double bonds to single bonds. An important application of this principle involves the process of hydrogenation. Hydrogenation converts one or more of

*Concentration is introduced in Section 1.6, and units and calculations are discussed in Sections 6.2 and 6.3.*

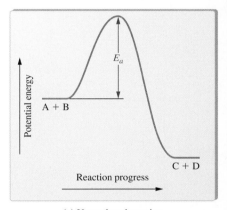

**(a)** Uncatalyzed reaction

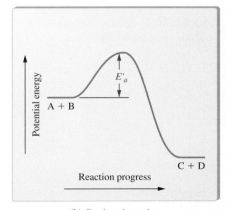

**(b)** Catalyzed reaction

**Figure 7.11** The effect of a catalyst on the magnitude of the activation energy of a chemical reaction: (a) uncatalyzed reaction, (b) catalyzed reaction. Note that the presence of a catalyst decreases the activation energy ($E'_a < E_a$), thus increasing the rate of the reaction.

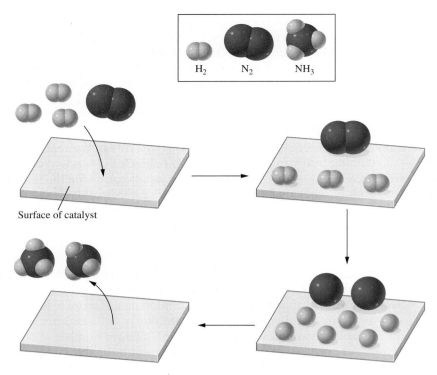

**Figure 7.12** The synthesis of ammonia, an important industrial product, is facilitated by a solid-phase catalyst (the Haber process). $H_2$ and $N_2$ bind to the surface, their bonds are weakened, dissociation and reformation as ammonia occur, and the newly formed ammonia molecules leave the surface. This process is repeated over and over, with no change in the catalyst.

the carbon-carbon double bonds of unsaturated fats (e.g., corn oil, olive oil) to single bonds characteristic of saturated fats (such as margarine). The use of a metal catalyst, such as nickel, in contact with the reaction mixture dramatically increases the rate of the reaction.

*For a detailed discussion of enzyme catalysis, see Chapter 19.*

Thousands of essential biochemical reactions in our bodies are controlled and speeded up by biological catalysts called *enzymes*.

A molecular-level view of the action of a solid catalyst widely used in industrial synthesis of ammonia is presented in Figure 7.12.

**Question 7.11**  Would you imagine that a substance might act as a poison if it interfered with the function of an enzyme? Explain your reasoning.

**Question 7.12**  Bacterial growth decreases markedly in a refrigerator. Why?

## Mathematical Representation of Reaction Rate

Consider the decomposition reaction of $N_2O_5$ (dinitrogen pentoxide) in the gas phase. When heated, $N_2O_5$ decomposes and forms two products: $NO_2$ (nitrogen dioxide) and $O_2$ (diatomic oxygen). The balanced chemical equation for the reaction is

$$2N_2O_5(g) \xrightarrow{\Delta} 4NO_2(g) + O_2(g)$$

When all of the factors that affect the rate of the reaction (except concentration) are held constant (that is, the nature of the reactant, temperature and physical

## Too Fast or Too Slow?

Kinetics plays a vital role in the development of a wide range of commercial products. We will consider a few of these applications that contribute to our health, our enjoyment, and the preservation of our environment.

### Refrigeration

Throughout history, few technologies have had a more profound benefit to human health than the development of inexpensive and efficient refrigeration, allowing food to be stored for long periods without spoiling. At room temperature, unwanted chemical reactions, with the help of bacteria, rapidly decompose many foods, especially meats and fish, making them unsuitable for human consumption. Storing food at low temperatures slows the rate of decomposition by slowing the rate of bacterial reproduction and the rate of the destructive chemical reactions. Refrigeration is a straightforward application of kinetics: Rates are halved for each 10°C decrease in temperature.

### Dentistry

The most widely used strategy for whitening teeth is bleaching with hydrogen peroxide ($H_2O_2$). Because the reaction is slow, manufacturers of home-use products use devices to trap the $H_2O_2$ and hold it in contact with the teeth. A better strategy involves higher concentrations of $H_2O_2$. (Remember, the rate of a reaction is proportional to the reactant concentration.) However, these treatments must be administered by a dentist; used incorrectly, high concentrations of $H_2O_2$ can damage sensitive tissues, such as the gums and the interior of the mouth.

### Artwork and Photography

Old paintings and photographs are very susceptible to the effects of ultraviolet (UV) light. Chemical reactions that produce discoloration are energized by UV light. More molecules achieve the necessary activation energy, and the quality and value of the artwork degrade more rapidly. Glass that absorbs UV radiation (conservation glass) robs these reactions of needed energy, and the lifetime of these valuable materials is extended.

### The Environment

An essential requirement for herbicides and pesticides is biodegradability. Ideally, these materials enter soil or vegetation, quickly complete their task of killing weeds or bugs, and rapidly decompose, often with the help of bacteria. Most people are aware of the problems caused by earlier, nonbiodegradable pesticides, most famously DDT (dichlorodiphenyltrichloroethane). DDT degrades very slowly in the environment. It is fat-soluble, bioaccumulates in animal tissue, and is responsible for many detrimental environmental effects, most notably its interference with bird reproduction. Even though it has been banned in the United States for decades, DDT can still be found in the environment. It has been replaced with compounds that exhibit more favorable decay kinetics.

### Automobiles

The catalytic converter in modern automobiles helps to speed up the rate of conversion of harmful emissions (CO and NO,

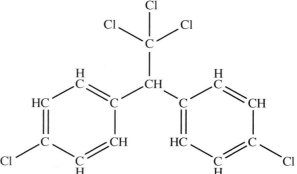

Egg shell thinning is one of the chronic impacts that DDT has had on the environment.

for example) to less harmful products ($CO_2$ and $N_2$ gas). The converter contains the metals platinum and palladium, which serve as solid catalysts, enabling the almost complete conversion of the auto emissions before they leave the tailpipe.

### Nuclear Waste

Conversion of nuclear waste to harmless products is *not* a chemical process. We wish that chemical kinetics applied to radioactive waste. Perhaps we could heat the waste and it would convert to harmless products. Not so! Radioactive decay (Chapter 9) is a nuclear process and is immune to all of the strategies routinely used to accelerate the rate of chemical reactions. That leaves us with a serious radioactive waste disposal problem. For more details, refer to Green Chemistry: Nuclear Waste Disposal in Chapter 9.

### For Further Understanding

▶ Provide another example of a process that has a less-than-optimal rate. What changes in conditions would improve the rate of this process?

▶ Use the Internet to find the current market values of platinum and palladium. How does this help to explain the high cost of a replacement catalytic converter?

state of the reactant, and the presence or absence of a catalyst), the rate of the reaction is proportional to the concentration of $N_2O_5$, the reactant.

$$Rate \propto concentration\ N_2O_5$$

We will represent the concentration of $N_2O_5$ in units of molarity and represent molar concentration using brackets.

$$Concentration\ N_2O_5 = [N_2O_5]$$

Then,

$$Rate \propto [N_2O_5]$$

Laboratory measurement shows that the rate of the reaction depends on the molar concentration raised to an experimentally determined exponent, which we will symbolize as $n$, the *reaction order*. The **reaction order** represents the number of molecules that are involved in the formation of product.

$$Rate \propto [N_2O_5]^n$$

In expressions such as the one shown, the proportionality symbol, $\alpha$, may be replaced by an equality sign and a proportionality constant that we represent as $k$, the **rate constant.**

$$Rate = k[N_2O_5]^n$$

Equations that follow this format, the rate being equal to the rate constant multiplied by the reactant concentration raised to an exponent that is the reaction order, are termed **rate laws.**

For the reaction described here, $n$ has been experimentally determined and is equal to 1; hence, the reaction is first order in $N_2O_5$ and the rate law for the reaction is:

$$Rate = k[N_2O_5]$$

In general, the rate of reaction for an equation of the general form:

$$A \longrightarrow product$$

is represented by the rate law

$$Rate = k[A]^n$$

in which

$$n = the\ reaction\ order$$
$$k = the\ rate\ constant\ of\ the\ reaction$$
$$[A] = the\ molar\ concentration\ of\ the\ reactant$$

An equation involving two reactants

$$A + B \longrightarrow products$$

has a rate law of the form

$$Rate = k[A]^n[B]^{n'}$$

Both the value of the rate constant and the reaction order are deduced from a series of experiments. We cannot predict them by simply looking at the chemical equation.

Knowledge of the form of the rate law, coupled with the experimental determination of the value of the rate constant, $k$, and the order, $n$, are valuable in a number of ways. Industrial chemists use this information to establish optimum conditions for preparing a product in the shortest practical time. The design of an entire manufacturing facility may, in part, depend on the rates of the critical reactions.

Note that the exponent, $n$, in the rate law is not the same as the coefficient of $N_2O_5$ in the balanced equation. However, in some reactions the coefficient in the balanced equation and the exponent $n$ (the order of the reaction) are numerically the same.

*In Section 7.4, we will see how the rate law forms the basis for describing equilibrium reactions.*

| EXAMPLE 7.6 | Writing Rate Laws |
|---|---|

Write the rate law for the oxidation of ethanol ($C_2H_5OH$). The reaction has been experimentally determined to be first order in ethanol and third order in oxygen ($O_2$). The chemical reaction for this process is:

$$C_2H_5OH(l) + 3O_2(g) \longrightarrow 2CO_2(g) + 3H_2O(l)$$

**Solution**

**Step 1.** The rate law involves only the reactants, $C_2H_5OH$ and $O_2$. Depict their concentrations as

$$[C_2H_5OH][O_2]$$

**Step 2.** Now raise each to an exponent corresponding to its experimentally determined order

$$[C_2H_5OH][O_2]^3$$

**Step 3.** This is proportional to the rate:

$$\text{Rate} \propto [C_2H_5OH][O_2]^3$$

**Step 4.** Proportionality ($\alpha$) is incorporated into an equation using a proportionality constant, $k$.

$$\text{Rate} = k[C_2H_5OH][O_2]^3$$

*Helpful Hint:* Remember that 1 is understood as an exponent; $[C_2H_5OH]$ is correct and $[C_2H_5OH]^1$ is not.

**Practice Problem 7.6**

Write the general form of the rate law for each of the following processes. Represent the order as $n$, $n'$, and so forth.

    a. $N_2(g) + O_2(g) \longrightarrow 2NO(g)$      c. $CH_4(g) + 2O_2(g) \longrightarrow CO_2(g) + 2H_2O(g)$

    b. $2C_4H_6(g) \longrightarrow C_8H_{12}(g)$      d. $2NO_2(g) \longrightarrow 2NO(g) + O_2(g)$

▶ For Further Practice: **Questions 7.63 and 7.64.**

## 7.4 Equilibrium

### Physical Equilibrium

Recall from Chapter 1 that change can be described as physical or chemical. While a chemical change is a consequence of chemical reactions, a physical change produces a recognizable difference in the appearance of a substance without causing any change in the composition or identity of the substance. Consequently, a **physical equilibrium** is one that occurs between two phases of the same substance. Examples of physical equilibria include:

- Liquid water in equilibrium with either ice or water vapor
- A saturated solution (Section 6.1) consisting of an ionic solid, such as silver chloride, in equilibrium with a solution of silver ions and chloride ions
- A saturated solution consisting of a covalent solid, such as glucose, in equilibrium with a solution of glucose molecules.

Dissolution of sugar in water, producing a saturated solution, is a convenient illustration of a state of *dynamic equilibrium.*

A **dynamic equilibrium** is a situation in which the rate of the forward process in a reversible reaction is exactly balanced by the rate of the reverse process.

A physical equilibrium, such as sugar dissolving in water, is a reversible reaction. A **reversible reaction** is a process that can occur in both directions. It is indicated by using the equilibrium arrows (⇌) symbol.

### Sugar in Water

Imagine that you mix a small amount of sugar (2 or 3 g) in 100 milliliters (mL) of water. After you stir it for a short time, all of the sugar dissolves; there is no residual solid sugar because the sugar has dissolved *completely*. The reaction clearly has converted all solid sugar to its dissolved state, an aqueous solution of sugar, or

$$\text{sugar}(s) \longrightarrow \text{sugar}(aq)$$

Now, suppose that you add a very large amount of sugar (100 g), more than can possibly dissolve, to the same volume of water. As you stir the mixture, you observe more and more sugar dissolving. After some time, the amount of solid sugar remaining in contact with the solution appears constant. Over time, you observe no further decrease in the amount of undissolved sugar. Although nothing further appears to be happening, in reality a great deal of activity is taking place!

An equilibrium situation has been established. Over time, the amount of sugar dissolved in the measured volume of water (the concentration of sugar in water) does not change. Hence, the amount of undissolved sugar remains the same. However, if you could look at the individual sugar molecules, you would see something quite amazing. Rather than sugar molecules in the solid simply staying in place, you would see them continuing to leave the solid state and go into solution. At the same time, a like number of dissolved sugar molecules would leave the water and form more solid. This active process is described as a *dynamic equilibrium*. The reaction is proceeding in a forward (left to right) and a reverse (right to left) direction at the same time, making it a reversible reaction:

$$\text{sugar}(s) \rightleftharpoons \text{sugar}(aq)$$

The rates of the forward and reverse reactions are identical, and the amount of sugar present as solid and in solution is constant. The system is at equilibrium. The equilibrium arrows serve as

- an indicator of a reversible process,
- an indicator of an equilibrium process, and
- a reminder of the dynamic nature of the process.

Examples of physical equilibria abound in nature. Many environmental systems depend on fragile equilibria. The amount of oxygen dissolved in a certain volume of lake water (the oxygen concentration) is governed by the principles of equilibrium because solubility equilibria are temperature dependent (Henry's law, Section 6.1). The lives of plants and animals within this system are critically related to the levels of dissolved oxygen in the water.

Dynamic equilibrium may be dangerous for living cells in certain situations because it represents a process in which nothing is getting done. There is no gain. Let's consider an exothermic reaction designed to produce a net gain of energy for the cell. In a dynamic equilibrium, the rate of the forward (energy-releasing) reaction is equal to the rate of the backward (energy-requiring) reaction. Thus, there is no net gain of energy to fuel cellular activity, and the cell will die.

**Question 7.13**   Correlate a busy restaurant at lunchtime to dynamic equilibrium.

**Question 7.14**   A certain change in reaction conditions for an equilibrium process was found to increase the rate of the forward reaction much more than that of the reverse reaction. Did the amount of product increase, decrease, or remain the same? Explain your reasoning.

## Chemical Equilibrium

We have assumed that most chemical reactions considered thus far proceed to completion. A complete reaction is one in which all reactants have been converted to products. However, many important chemical reactions do not go to completion. As a result, after no further obvious change is taking place, measurable quantities of reactants and products remain. Reactions of this type (incomplete reactions) are called *equilibrium reactions*. **Chemical equilibrium** is the state of a reaction in which the rates of the forward and reverse reactions are equal.

## The Reaction of $N_2$ and $H_2$

When we mix nitrogen gas ($N_2$) and hydrogen gas ($H_2$) at an elevated temperature (perhaps 500°C), some of the molecules will collide with sufficient energy and proper orientation to break N≡N and H—H bonds. Rearrangement of the atoms will produce the product ($NH_3$):

$$N_2(g) + 3H_2(g) \rightleftharpoons 2NH_3(g)$$

Beginning with a mixture of hydrogen and nitrogen, the rate of the reaction is initially rapid, because the reactant concentration is high; as the reaction proceeds, the concentration of reactants decreases. At the same time, the concentration of the product, ammonia, is increasing. At equilibrium, the *rate of depletion* of hydrogen and nitrogen *is equal to* the *rate of depletion* of ammonia. In other words, *the rates of the forward and reverse reactions are equal.*

The concentration of the various species is fixed at equilibrium because product is being *consumed and formed at the same rate.* In other words, the reaction continues indefinitely (dynamic), but the concentration of products and reactants is fixed (equilibrium). This is a *dynamic equilibrium.* The rate of this reaction as a function of time is depicted in Figure 7.13.

For systems at equilibrium, an **equilibrium constant** expression can be written; it summarizes the relationship between the concentration of reactants and products in an equilibrium reaction.

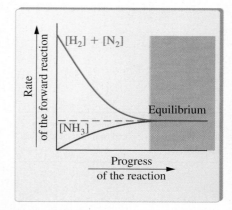

**Figure 7.13** The change of the rate of reaction of $H_2$ and $N_2$ as a function of time. The rate of reaction, initially rapid, decreases as the concentration of reactants decreases and product increases. The rate approaches a limiting value at equilibrium.

## The Generalized Equilibrium Constant Expression for a Chemical Reaction

We write the general form of an equilibrium chemical reaction as

$$aA + bB \rightleftharpoons cC + dD$$

in which $A$ and $B$ represent reactants, $C$ and $D$ represent products, and $a$, $b$, $c$, and $d$ are the coefficients of the balanced equation. The equilibrium constant expression for this general case is

$$K_{eq} = \frac{[C]^c[D]^d}{[A]^a[B]^b}$$

For the ammonia system, it follows that the appropriate equilibrium expression is:

$$K_{eq} = \frac{[NH_3]^2}{[N_2][H_2]^3}$$

It does not matter what initial amounts (concentrations) of reactants or products we choose. When the system reaches equilibrium, the calculated value of $K_{eq}$ will not change. The magnitude of $K_{eq}$ can be altered only by changing the temperature. Thus, $K_{eq}$ is temperature dependent. The chemical industry uses this fact to its advantage by choosing a reaction temperature that will maximize the yield of a desired product.

**Question 7.15** How could we determine when a reaction has reached equilibrium?

**Question 7.16** Does the attainment of equilibrium imply that no further change is taking place in the system?

## Writing Equilibrium Constant Expressions

An equilibrium constant expression can be written only after a correct, balanced chemical equation that describes the equilibrium system has been developed.

LEARNING GOAL

9 Write equilibrium constant expressions, and use these expressions to calculate equilibrium constants or equilibrium concentrations.

A balanced equation is essential because the *coefficients* in the equation become the *exponents* in the equilibrium constant expression.

Each chemical reaction has a unique equilibrium constant value at a specified temperature. Equilibrium constants listed in the chemical literature are often reported at 25°C, to allow comparison of one system with any other. For any equilibrium reaction, the value of the equilibrium constant changes with temperature.

---

*Products* of the overall equilibrium reaction are in the numerator, and *reactants* are in the denominator.

---

The brackets represent molar concentration or molarity; recall that molarity has units of moles per liter (mol/L). In our discussion of equilibrium, all equilibrium constants are shown as *unitless*.

A properly written equilibrium constant expression may not include all of the terms in the chemical equation upon which it is based. Only the concentrations of gases and substances in solution are shown, because their concentrations can change. Concentration terms for liquids and solids are *not* shown. The concentration of a liquid is constant. Most often, the liquid is the solvent for the reaction under consideration. A solid also has a fixed concentration and, for solution reactions, is not really a part of the solution. When a solid is formed, it exists as a solid phase in contact with a liquid phase (the solution).

---

## EXAMPLE 7.7    Writing an Equilibrium Constant Expression

Write an equilibrium constant expression for the reversible reaction:

$$H_2(g) + F_2(g) \rightleftharpoons 2HF(g)$$

**LEARNING GOAL**

**9** Write equilibrium constant expressions, and use these expressions to calculate equilibrium constants or equilibrium concentrations.

### Solution

**Step 1.** Inspection of the chemical equation reveals that no solids or liquids are present. Hence, all reactants and products appear in the equilibrium constant expression.

**Step 2.** The numerator term is the product term $[HF]^2$. The exponent for [HF] is identical to the coefficient of HF in the balanced equation.

**Step 3.** The denominator terms are the reactants $[H_2]$ and $[F_2]$. Note that each term contains an exponent identical to the corresponding coefficient in the balanced equation.

**Step 4.** Arranging the numerator and denominator terms as a fraction and setting the fraction equal to $K_{eq}$ yields

$$K_{eq} = \frac{[HF]^2}{[H_2][F_2]}$$

### Practice Problem 7.7

Write an equilibrium constant expression for each of the following reversible reactions.

a. $2NO_2(g) \rightleftharpoons N_2(g) + 2O_2(g)$    b. $2H_2O(l) \rightleftharpoons 2H_2(g) + O_2(g)$

▶ For Further Practice: **Questions 7.83 and 7.84.**

## Interpreting Equilibrium Constants

What utility does the equilibrium constant have? The reversible arrow in the chemical equation alerts us to the fact that an equilibrium exists. Some measurable quantity of the product and reactant remain. However, there is no indication whether products predominate, reactants predominate, or significant concentrations of both products and reactants are present at equilibrium.

| EXAMPLE 7.8 | Writing an Equilibrium Constant Expression |
|---|---|

**LEARNING GOAL**

Write an equilibrium constant expression for the reversible reaction:

$$MnO_2(s) + 4H^+(aq) + 2Cl^-(aq) \rightleftharpoons Mn^{2+}(aq) + Cl_2(g) + 2H_2O(l)$$

**9** Write equilibrium constant expressions, and use these expressions to calculate equilibrium constants or equilibrium concentrations.

**Solution**

**Step 1.** $MnO_2$ is a solid and $H_2O$ is a liquid. Thus, they are not written in the equilibrium constant expression.

$$MnO_2(s) + 4H^+(aq) + 2Cl^-(aq) \rightleftharpoons Mn^{2+}(aq) + Cl_2(g) + 2H_2O(l)$$

Not a part of the $K_{eq}$ expression

**Step 2.** The numerator term includes the remaining products:

$$[Mn^{2+}] \quad and \quad [Cl_2]$$

**Step 3.** The denominator term includes the remaining reactants:

$$[H^+]^4 \quad and \quad [Cl^-]^2$$

Note that each exponent is identical to the corresponding coefficient in the chemical equation.

**Step 4.** Arranging the numerator and denominator terms as a ratio and setting the ratio equal to $K_{eq}$ yields

$$K_{eq} = \frac{[Mn^{2+}][Cl_2]}{[H^+]^4[Cl^-]^2}$$

**Practice Problem 7.8**

Write an equilibrium constant expression for each of the following reversible reactions.

a. $AgCl(s) \rightleftharpoons Ag^+(aq) + Cl^-(aq)$    b. $PCl_5(s) \rightleftharpoons PCl_3(g) + Cl_2(g)$

▶ For Further Practice: **Questions 7.85 and 7.87.**

The numerical value of the equilibrium constant provides this additional information. It tells us the extent to which reactants have converted to products. This is important information for anyone who wants to manufacture and sell the product. It also is important to anyone who studies the effect of equilibrium reactions on environmental systems and living organisms.

Although an absolute interpretation of the numerical value of the equilibrium constant depends on the form of the equilibrium constant expression, the following generalizations are useful:

- $K_{eq}$ greater than $1 \times 10^3$. A large numerical value of $K_{eq}$ indicates that the numerator (product term) is much larger than the denominator (reactant term) and that at equilibrium mostly product is present.
- $K_{eq}$ less than $1 \times 10^{-3}$. A small numerical value of $K_{eq}$ indicates that the numerator (product term) is much smaller than the denominator (reactant term) and that at equilibrium mostly reactant is present.
- $K_{eq}$ between $1 \times 10^{-3}$ and $1 \times 10^3$. In this case, the equilibrium mixture contains significant concentrations of both reactants and products.

**Question 7.17** At a given temperature, the equilibrium constant for a certain reaction is $1 \times 10^{20}$. Does this equilibrium favor products or reactants? Why?

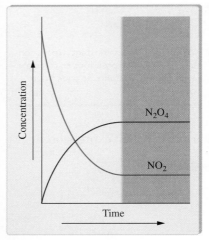

**Figure 7.14** For the reaction $2NO_2(g) \rightleftharpoons N_2O_4(g)$, the concentration of reactant ($NO_2$) diminishes rapidly while the $N_2O_4$ concentration builds. Eventually, the concentrations of both reactant and product become constant over time (blue area). The equilibrium condition has been attained.

## LEARNING GOAL

**9**   Write equilibrium constant expressions, and use these expressions to calculate equilibrium constants or equilibrium concentrations.

**Question 7.18**   At a given temperature, the equilibrium constant for a certain reaction is $1 \times 10^{-18}$. Does this equilibrium favor products or reactants? Why?

## Calculating Equilibrium Constants

The magnitude of the equilibrium constant for a chemical reaction is determined experimentally. The reaction under study is allowed to proceed until the concentration of products and reactants no longer changes (Figure 7.14). This may be a matter of seconds, minutes, hours, or even months or years, depending on the rate of the reaction. The reaction mixture is then analyzed to determine the molar concentration of each of the products and reactants. These concentrations are substituted in the equilibrium constant expression, and the equilibrium constant is calculated. The following example illustrates this process.

---

**EXAMPLE 7.9**    **Calculating an Equilibrium Constant**

Hydrogen iodide is placed in a sealed container and allowed to come to equilibrium. The equilibrium reaction is:

$$2HI(g) \rightleftharpoons H_2(g) + I_2(g)$$

and the equilibrium concentrations are:

$$[HI] = 0.54 \ M$$
$$[H_2] = 1.72 \ M$$
$$[I_2] = 1.72 \ M$$

Calculate the equilibrium constant.

**Solution**

**Step 1.** Write the equilibrium constant expression:

$$K_{eq} = \frac{[H_2][I_2]}{[HI]^2}$$

**Step 2.** Substitute the equilibrium concentrations of products and reactants to obtain

$$K_{eq} = \frac{[1.72][1.72]}{[0.54]^2} = \frac{2.96}{0.29}$$
$$= 10.1 \text{ or } 1.0 \times 10^1 \text{ (two significant figures)}$$

---

**Practice Problem 7.9**

A container holds the following mixture at equilibrium:

$$[NH_3] = 0.25 \ M$$
$$[N_2] = 0.11 \ M$$
$$[H_2] = 1.91 \ M$$

If the reaction is:

$$N_2(g) + 3H_2(g) \rightleftharpoons 2NH_3(g)$$

calculate the equilibrium constant.

▶ For Further Practice: **Questions 7.88.**

## Using Equilibrium Constants

We have seen that the equilibrium constant for a reaction can be calculated if we know the equilibrium concentrations of all of the reactants and products. Once known, the equilibrium constant can be used to obtain equilibrium concentrations of one or more reactants or products for a variety of different situations. These calculations can be quite complex. Let's look at one straightforward but useful case, one where the equilibrium concentration of reactants is known and we wish to calculate the product concentration.

---

**EXAMPLE 7.10**    **Using an Equilibrium Constant**

LEARNING GOAL

Given the equilibrium reaction studied in Example 7.9:

$$2HI(g) \rightleftharpoons H_2(g) + I_2(g)$$

**9** Write equilibrium constant expressions, and use these expressions to calculate equilibrium constants or equilibrium concentrations.

A sample mixture of HI, $H_2$, and $I_2$, at equilibrium, was found to have $[H_2] = 1.0 \times 10^{-2}\ M$ and $[HI] = 4.0 \times 10^{-2}\ M$. Calculate the molar concentration of $I_2$ in the equilibrium mixture.

**Solution**

**Step 1.** From Example 7.9, the equilibrium expression and equilibrium constant are:

$$K_{eq} = \frac{[H_2][I_2]}{[HI]^2}; \quad K_{eq} = 1.0 \times 10^1$$

**Step 2.** To solve the equilibrium expression for $[I_2]$, first multiply both sides of the equation by $[HI]^2$:

$$[H_2][I_2] = K_{eq}[HI]^2$$

Then, divide both sides by $[H_2]$:

$$[I_2] = \frac{K_{eq}[HI]^2}{[H_2]}$$

**Step 3.** Substitute the values:

$$K_{eq} = 1.0 \times 10^1$$
$$[H_2] = 1.0 \times 10^{-2}\ M$$
$$[HI] = 4.0 \times 10^{-2}\ M$$

**Step 4.** Solve:

$$[I_2] = \frac{[1.0 \times 10^1][4.0 \times 10^{-2}]^2}{[1.0 \times 10^{-2}]}$$
$$= 1.6\ M$$

---

**Practice Problem 7.10**

Using the reaction given above, calculate the $[I_2]$ if both $[H_2]$ and $[HI]$ were $1.0 \times 10^{-4}\ M$.

▶ For Further Practice: **Questions 7.89 and 7.90.**

**10** Use LeChatelier's principle to predict changes in equilibrium position.

Addition of products or reactants may have a profound effect on the composition of a reaction mixture but *does not* affect the value of the equilibrium constant.

## LeChatelier's Principle

In the nineteenth century, the French chemist H. L. LeChatelier discovered that changes in equilibrium depend on the amount of "stress" applied to the system. The stress may take the form of an increase or decrease of the temperature of the system at equilibrium, or perhaps a change in the amount of reactant or product present in a fixed volume (the concentration of reactant or product).

**LeChatelier's principle** states that if a stress is placed on a system at equilibrium, the system will respond by altering the equilibrium composition in such a way as to minimize the stress.

Consider the equilibrium situation discussed earlier:

$$N_2(g) + 3H_2(g) \rightleftharpoons 2NH_3(g)$$

If the reactants and products are present in a fixed volume, such as 1 liter (L), and more $NH_3$ (the *product*) is introduced into the container, the system will be stressed—the equilibrium will be disturbed. The system will try to alleviate the stress (as we all do) by *removing* as much of the added material as possible. How can it accomplish this? By converting some $NH_3$ to $H_2$ and $N_2$. The position of the equilibrium shifts to the left, and a new dynamic equilibrium is soon established.

Adding extra $H_2$ or $N_2$ would apply the stress to the reactant side of the equilibrium. To minimize the stress, the system would "use up" some of the excess $H_2$ or $N_2$ to make product, $NH_3$. The position of the equilibrium would shift to the right.

In summary,

$$N_2(g) + 3H_2(g) \rightleftharpoons 2NH_3(g)$$

Product introduced:      position of the equilibrium shifted left

Reactant introduced:      position of the equilibrium shifted right

What would happen if some of the ammonia molecules were *removed* from the system? The loss of ammonia represents a stress on the system; to relieve that stress, the ammonia would be replenished by the reaction of hydrogen and nitrogen. The position of the equilibrium would shift to the right.

Product removed:      position of the equilibrium shifted right

Reactant removed:      position of the equilibrium shifted left

### Effect of Concentration

Addition of extra product or reactant to a fixed reaction volume is just another way of saying that we have increased the concentration of product or reactant. Removal of material from a fixed volume decreases the concentration. Therefore, changing the concentration of one or more components of a reaction mixture is a way to alter the equilibrium composition of an equilibrium mixture (Figure 7.15). Let's look at some additional experimental variables that may change the equilibrium composition.

(a)        (b)        (c)

**Figure 7.15** The effect of concentration on the equilibrium composition of the reaction:

$$FeSCN^{2+}(aq) \rightleftharpoons Fe^{3+}(aq) + SCN^-(aq)$$
  (red)          (yellow)      (colorless)

Solution (a) represents this reaction at equilibrium; (b) addition of $SCN^-$ shifts the position of the equilibrium to the left, intensifying the red color. (c) Removal of $SCN^-$ shifts the position of the equilibrium to the right, shown by the disappearance of the red color.

### Effect of Heat

The change in equilibrium composition caused by the addition or removal of heat from an equilibrium mixture can be explained by treating heat as a product or reactant. The reaction of nitrogen and hydrogen is an exothermic reaction:

$$N_2(g) + 3H_2(g) \rightleftharpoons 2NH_3(g) + 22 \text{ kcal}$$

Adding heat by raising the temperature is similar to increasing the amount of product. The position of the equilibrium will shift to the left, increasing the amounts of $N_2$ and $H_2$ and decreasing the amount of $NH_3$. If the reaction takes place in a fixed volume, the concentrations of $N_2$ and $H_2$ increase and the $NH_3$ concentration decreases.

Removal of heat by lowering the temperature produces the reverse effect. More ammonia is produced from $N_2$ and $H_2$, and the concentrations of these reactants must decrease.

In the case of an endothermic reaction, such as

$$39 \text{ kcal} + 2N_2(g) + O_2(g) \rightleftharpoons 2N_2O(g)$$

addition of heat is analogous to the addition of reactant, and the position of the equilibrium shifts to the right. Removal of heat would shift the reaction to the left, favoring the formation of reactants.

The dramatic effect of heat on the position of equilibrium is shown in Figure 7.16.

### Effect of Pressure

Only gases are affected significantly by changes in pressure because gases are free to expand and compress in accordance with Boyle's law. However, liquids and solids are not compressible, so their volumes are unaffected by pressure.

Therefore, pressure changes will alter equilibrium composition only in reactions that involve a gas or variety of gases as products and/or reactants. Again, consider the ammonia example,

$$N_2(g) + 3H_2(g) \rightleftharpoons 2NH_3(g)$$

One mole of $N_2$ and three moles of $H_2$ (total of 4 mol of reactants) react to form two moles of $NH_3$ (2 mol of product). The equilibrium mixture (perhaps at 25°C) contains $N_2$, $H_2$, and $NH_3$. An increase in pressure will cause a stress to the system because the pressure is greater than the equilibrium pressure. To relieve the stress, the system will shift toward the side of the reaction that has fewer mol of gas. As the number of mol decreases, the pressure will decrease. In the example of ammonia, an increase in pressure will shift the position of the equilibrium to the right, producing more $NH_3$ at the expense of $N_2$ and $H_2$.

A decrease in pressure will be countered by the reaction shifting toward the side that contains more mol of gas because the pressure is less than the equilibrium pressure. As the number of mol of gas increases, the pressure will increase. Therefore, in the equilibrium reaction of ammonia, a decrease in pressure will cause the position of the equilibrium to shift to the left, and ammonia decomposes to form more nitrogen and hydrogen.

In contrast, the decomposition of hydrogen iodide,

$$2HI(g) \rightleftharpoons H_2(g) + I_2(g)$$

is unaffected by pressure. The number of mol of gaseous product and reactant are identical. No volume advantage is gained by a shift in equilibrium composition. In summary:

- Pressure affects the equilibrium composition only of reactions that involve at least one gaseous substance.
- Additionally, the relative number of mol of gaseous products and reactants must differ.
- The equilibrium composition will shift to increase the number of mol of gas when the pressure decreases; it will shift to decrease the number of mol of gas when the pressure increases.

**Figure 7.16** The effect of heat on the equilibrium position. For the reaction:

$$CoCl_4{}^{2-}(aq) + 6H_2O(l) \rightleftharpoons$$
(blue)
$$Co(H_2O)_6{}^{2+}(aq) + 4Cl^-(aq)$$
(pink)

heating the solution favors the blue $CoCl_4{}^{2-}$ species; cooling favors the pink $Co(H_2O)_6{}^{2+}$ species.

*Expansion and compression of gases and Boyle's law are discussed in Section 5.1.*

The industrial process for preparing ammonia, the Haber process, uses pressures of several hundred atmospheres (atm) to increase the yield.

### Effect of a Catalyst

A catalyst has no effect on the equilibrium composition. A catalyst increases the rates of both forward and reverse reactions to the same extent. The equilibrium composition *and* equilibrium concentration do not change when a catalyst is used, but the equilibrium composition is achieved in a shorter time. The role of a solid-phase catalyst in the synthesis of ammonia is shown in Figure 7.12.

---

**EXAMPLE 7.11**    **Predicting Changes in Equilibrium Composition**

**LEARNING GOAL**

A geologically important reaction, shown below, is critical for the formation of the stalactites and stalagmites in caves.

**10** Use LeChatelier's principle to predict changes in equilibrium position.

$$4.67 \text{ kcal} + Ca^{2+}(aq) + 2HCO_3^-(aq) \rightleftharpoons CaCO_3(s) + CO_2(aq) + H_2O(l)$$

Predict the effect on the equilibrium composition for each of the following changes.
  a. The concentration of $Ca^{2+}$ is increased by addition of some $CaCl_2$.
  b. Some solid $CaCO_3$ is removed from the mixture.
  c. The concentration of $HCO_3^-$ is decreased.
  d. The temperature of the system is increased.
  e. A catalyst is added.

**Solution**
  a. The addition of $Ca^{2+}$ ions will cause the position of the equilibrium to shift to the right, and more products will form.
  b. Because $CaCO_3$ is a solid, addition or removal of the substance will have no effect on the equilibrium composition.
  c. If $HCO_3^-(aq)$ is removed from the system, the position of the equilibrium will shift to the left to produce more $HCO_3^-$ and other reactants.
  d. The reaction is endothermic. The addition of heat by the raising of the temperature will shift the position of the equilibrium to the right, and more products will form.
  e. The addition of a catalyst has no effect on the equilibrium composition.

---

**Practice Problem 7.11**

The reaction

$$382 \text{ cal} + Pb(s) + 2H^+(aq) \rightleftharpoons Pb^{2+}(aq) + H_2(g)$$

is carried out at constant pressure. Predict whether the volume of hydrogen gas would increase, decrease, or remain the same for each of the following changes.

  a. Addition of $Pb(s)$.
  b. Addition of $Pb^{2+}$ ions by adding some $Pb(NO_3)_2$ to the solution.
  c. Removal of $H^+$ ions.
  d. Lowering of the temperature.
  e. Addition of a catalyst.

▶ For Further Practice: **Questions 7.91 and 7.92.**

# A Human Perspective

## An Extraordinary Molecule

Think for a moment: What is the only common molecule that exists in all three physical states of matter (solid, liquid, and gas) under natural conditions on earth? This molecule is absolutely essential for life; in fact, life probably arose in this substance. It is the most abundant molecule in the cells of living organisms (70–95%) and covers 75% of the earth's surface. Without it, cells quickly die, and without it the earth would not be a fit environment in which to live. By now, you have guessed that we are talking about the water molecule. It is so abundant on earth that we take this deceptively simple molecule for granted.

As we finish our discussion of thermodynamics, kinetics, and equilibrium, it is fitting that we take a further look at water and its unique properties. Enormous quantities of water continuously convert from solid $\rightleftharpoons$ liquid $\rightleftharpoons$ gas in our environment; equally large energy changes (storage and release) are essential to these processes. This is thermodynamics in action! One of our best examples of physical equilibrium is change of state (ice $\rightleftharpoons$ liquid $\rightleftharpoons$ vapor). This equilibrium process can have a profound influence on our weather.

Life can exist only within a fairly narrow range of temperatures. Above or below that range, the chemical reactions necessary for life, and thus life itself, will cease. Water can moderate temperature fluctuation and maintain the range necessary for life, and one property that allows it to do so is its unusually high specific heat, $1 \text{ cal/g} \cdot {}^{\circ}\text{C}$. This means that water can absorb or lose more heat energy than many other substances without a significant temperature change. This is because in the liquid state, every water molecule is hydrogen bonded to other water molecules. Because a temperature increase is really just a measure of increased (more rapid) molecular movement, we must get the water molecules moving more rapidly, independent of one another, to register a temperature increase. Before we can achieve this independent, increased activity, the hydrogen bonds between molecules must be broken. Much of the heat energy that water absorbs is involved in breaking hydrogen bonds and is *not* used to increase molecular movement. Thus, a great deal of heat is needed to raise the temperature of water even a little bit.

Water also has a very high heat of vaporization. It takes 540 calories (cal) to change 1 g of liquid water at 100°C to a gas, and even more, 603 cal/g, when the water is at 37°C, human body temperature. That is about twice the heat of vaporization of alcohol. As water molecules evaporate, the surface of the liquid cools because only the highest-energy (or "hottest") molecules leave as a gas. Only the "hottest" molecules have enough energy to break the hydrogen bonds that bind them to other water molecules. Indeed, evaporation of water molecules from the surfaces of lakes and oceans helps to maintain stable temperatures in those bodies of water. Similarly, evaporation of

Beauty is also a property of water.

perspiration from body surfaces helps to prevent overheating on a hot day or during strenuous exercise.

Even the process of freezing helps stabilize and moderate temperatures. This is especially true in the fall. Water releases heat when hydrogen bonds are formed. This is an example of an exothermic process. Thus, when water freezes, solidifying into ice, additional hydrogen bonds are formed, and heat is released into the environment. As a result, the temperature change between summer and winter is more gradual, allowing organisms to adjust to the change.

One last feature that we take for granted is the fact that when we put ice in our iced tea on a hot summer day, the ice floats. This means that the solid state of water is actually *less* dense than the liquid state! In fact, it is about 10% less dense, having an open lattice structure with each molecule hydrogen bonded to the maximum of four other water molecules. What would happen if ice did sink? All bodies of water, including the mighty oceans would eventually freeze solid, killing all aquatic and marine plant and animal life. Even in the heat of summer, only a few inches of ice at the surface would thaw. Instead, the ice forms at the surface and provides a layer of insulation that prevents the water below from freezing.

As we continue our study of chemistry, we will refer again and again to this amazing molecule. In other Human Perspective features, we will examine properties of water that make it essential to life.

### For Further Understanding

▶ Why is the high heat of vaporization of water important to our bodies?

▶ Why is it cooler at the ocean shore than in the desert during summer?

# CHAPTER MAP

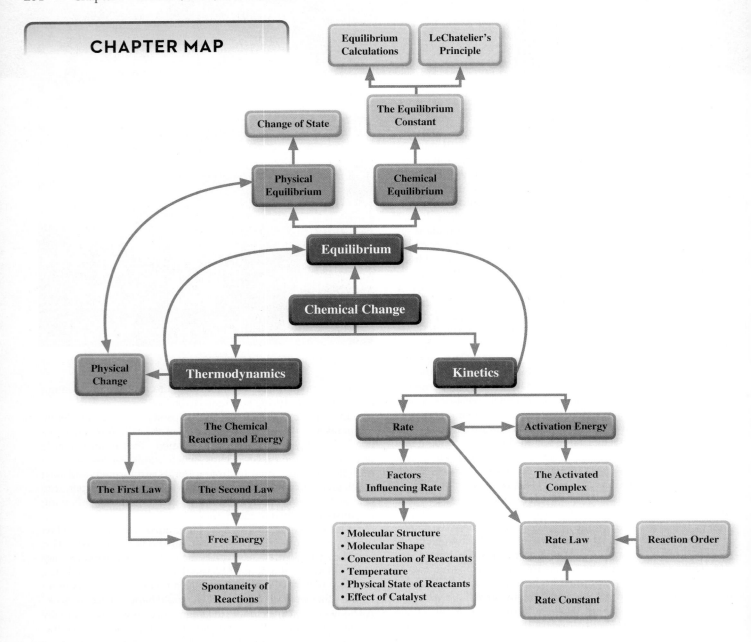

# SUMMARY

## 7.1  Thermodynamics

▶ **Thermodynamics** is the study of energy, work, and **heat,** and is useful in predicting the spontaneity of chemical change.

▶ Thermodynamics can be applied to the study of chemical reactions because we can determine the quantity of heat flow (by measuring the temperature change) between the **system** and the **surroundings.**

▶ **Exothermic reactions** release energy and produce products that are lower in energy than the reactants.

▶ **Endothermic reactions** require energy input. Heat energy is represented as **enthalpy,** $H$.

▶ The energy gain or loss is the change in enthalpy, $\Delta H$, and is one factor that is useful in predicting whether a reaction is spontaneous or nonspontaneous.

▶ **Entropy,** $S$, is a measure of the randomness of a system. A random or disordered system has high entropy; a well-ordered system has low entropy. The change in entropy in a chemical reaction, $\Delta S$, is also a factor in predicting reaction spontaneity.

▶ **Free energy,** $\Delta G$, incorporates both factors, enthalpy and entropy; as such, it is an absolute predictor of the spontaneity of a chemical reaction.

## 7.2 Experimental Determination of Energy Change in Reactions

▶ A **calorimeter** measures heat changes (in cal or J) that occur in chemical reactions.

▶ The **specific heat** of a substance is the number of cal of heat needed to raise the temperature of 1 g of the substance 1°C.

▶ The amount of energy per g of food is referred to as its **fuel value.** Fuel values are commonly reported in units of **nutritional Calories** (1 nutritional Cal = 1 kcal). A bomb calorimeter is useful for measurement of the fuel value of foods.

## 7.3 Kinetics

▶ Chemical **kinetics** is the study of the **rate** or speed of a chemical reaction. Energy for reactions is provided by molecular collisions. If this energy is sufficient, bonds may break, and atoms may recombine in a different arrangement to produce product. A collision producing one or more product molecules is termed an *effective collision.*

▶ The minimum amount of energy needed for a reaction is the **activation energy.** The reaction proceeds from reactants to products through an intermediate state, the **activated complex.**

▶ Experimental conditions influencing the reaction rate include the structure and shape of the reacting species, the concentration of reactants, the temperature of reactants, the physical state of reactants, and the presence or absence of a catalyst.

▶ A **catalyst** increases the rate of a reaction. The catalytic substance undergoes no net change in the reaction, nor does it alter the outcome of the reaction.

▶ The **rate law** relates the rate of a reaction to the **rate constant** multiplied by the concentration of the reactants raised to a power that is the **reaction order.**

## 7.4 Equilibrium

▶ Incomplete reactions are *equilibrium reactions.*

▶ Physical changes are often **reversible reactions.** A **physical equilibrium** occurs between two phases of the same substance.

▶ Many chemical reactions do not completely convert reactants to products. A mixture of products and reactants exists, and its composition will remain constant until the experimental conditions are changed. This mixture is in a state of **chemical equilibrium.**

▶ The position of the equilibrium is indicated by the **equilibrium constant.**

▶ An equilibrium reaction continues indefinitely (dynamic), but the concentrations of products and reactants are fixed (equilibrium) because the rates of the forward and reverse reactions are equal. This is a **dynamic equilibrium.**

▶ **LeChatelier's principle** states that if a stress is placed on an equilibrium system, the system will respond by altering the equilibrium in such a way as to minimize the stress.

## ANSWERS TO PRACTICE PROBLEMS

**7.1**  **a.** Exothermic
  **b.** Exothermic

**7.2**  $\Delta G$ is temperature dependent.

**7.3**  13°C

**7.4**  $-8.8$°C

**7.5**  3.0 nutritional Cal in 1.0 g of candy and

$$\frac{2.1 \times 10^2 \text{ nutritional Cal}}{\text{candy bar}}$$

**7.6**  **a.**  rate $= k[N_2]^n[O_2]^{n'}$
  **b.**  rate $= k[C_4H_6]^n$
  **c.**  rate $= k[CH_4]^n[O_2]^{n'}$
  **d.**  rate $= k[NO_2]^n$

**7.7**  **a.**  $K_{eq} = \dfrac{[N_2][O_2]^2}{[NO_2]^2}$

  **b.**  $K_{eq} = [H_2]^2[O_2]$

**7.8**  **a.**  $K_{eq} = [Ag^+][Cl^-]$
  **b.**  $K_{eq} = [PCl_3][Cl_2]$

**7.9**  $K_{eq} = 8.2 \times 10^{-2}$

**7.10**  $1 \times 10^{-3} M$

**7.11**  **a.**  The addition of Pb(s) would have no effect on the volume of hydrogen gas. This is because the substance is a solid, and addition of a solid has no effect on the equilibrium composition.
  **b.**  The addition of $Pb^{2+}$ (aq) would result in a decrease in the volume of hydrogen gas.
  **c.**  The removal of $H^+$ would result in a decrease in the volume of hydrogen gas.
  **d.**  Lowering the temperature would result in a decrease in the volume of hydrogen gas.
  **e.**  Addition of a catalyst would have no effect on the volume of hydrogen gas.

## QUESTIONS AND PROBLEMS

### Thermodynamics

**Foundations**

**7.19**  State the first law of thermodynamics.
**7.20**  State the second law of thermodynamics.
**7.21**  Describe what is meant by an exothermic reaction.
**7.22**  Describe what is meant by an endothermic reaction.

**7.23** The combustion of fuels (coal, oil, gasoline) are exothermic reactions. Why?

**7.24** Provide an explanation for the fact that most decomposition reactions are endothermic but most combination reactions are exothermic.

**7.25** Explain what is meant by the term *free energy*. When free energy is a positive value, what does it indicate about the spontaneity of the reaction?

**7.26** Write the expression for free energy. When $\Delta G$ is a negative value, what does it indicate about the spontaneity of the reaction?

**7.27** Explain what is meant by the term *enthalpy*.

**7.28** Explain what is meant by the term *entropy*.

### Applications

**7.29** Predict whether each of the following processes increases or decreases entropy, and explain your reasoning.
 **a.** melting of a solid metal
 **b.** boiling of water

**7.30** Predict whether each of the following processes increases or decreases entropy, and explain your reasoning.
 **a.** burning a log in a fireplace
 **b.** condensing of water vapor on a cold surface

**7.31** Isopropyl alcohol, commonly known as rubbing alcohol, feels cool when applied to the skin. Explain why.

**7.32** Energy is required to break chemical bonds during the course of a reaction. When is energy released?

**7.33** Predict whether a reaction with a negative $\Delta H$ and a positive $\Delta S$ will be spontaneous, nonspontaneous, or temperature dependent. Explain your reasoning.

**7.34** Predict whether a reaction with a negative $\Delta H$ and a negative $\Delta S$ will be spontaneous, nonspontaneous, or temperature dependent. Explain your reasoning.

### Experimental Determination of Energy Change in Reactions

#### Foundations

**7.35** Explain what is meant by fuel value.

**7.36** Explain what is meant by the term *specific heat*.

**7.37** Describe how a calorimeter is used to distinguish between exothermic and endothermic reactions.

**7.38** Construct a diagram of a coffee-cup calorimeter.

**7.39** What are the energy units most commonly employed in chemistry?

**7.40** What energy unit is commonly employed in nutrition science?

**7.41** Why does a calorimeter have a "double-walled" container?

**7.42** Explain why the fuel value of foods is an important factor in nutrition science.

### Applications

**7.43** A 5.00-g sample of octane is burned in a bomb calorimeter containing $2.00 \times 10^2$ g $H_2O$. How much energy, in cal, is released if the water temperature increases 6.00°C?

**7.44** A 0.325-mol sample of ammonium nitrate was dissolved in water producing a $4.00 \times 10^2$ g solution. The temperature decreased from 25.0°C to 15.7°C. If the specific heat of the resulting solution is 1.00 cal/g · °C, calculate the quantity of energy absorbed in the process. Is the dissolution of ammonium nitrate endothermic or exothermic?

**7.45** A 30-g sample of chips is burned in a bomb calorimeter containing $2.50 \times 10^2$ g $H_2O$. What is the fuel value (in nutritional Cal) if the temperature of the water increased from 25.0°C to 34.6°C?

**7.46** A 0.0500-mol sample of a nutrient substance is burned in a bomb calorimeter containing $2.00 \times 10^2$ g $H_2O$. If the formula weight of this nutrient substance is 114 g/mol, what is the fuel value (in nutritional Cal) if the temperature of the water increased 5.70°C?

## Kinetics

### Foundations

**7.47** Provide an example of a reaction that is extremely slow, taking days, weeks, or years to complete.

**7.48** Provide an example of a reaction that is extremely fast, perhaps quicker than the eye can perceive.

**7.49** Define the term *activated complex* and explain its significance in a chemical reaction.

**7.50** Define and explain the term *activation energy* as it applies to chemical reactions.

**7.51** Distinguish among the terms *rate, rate constant*, and *reaction order*.

**7.52** Distinguish between the terms *kinetics* and *thermodynamics*.

**7.53** Describe the general characteristics of a catalyst.

**7.54** Select one enzyme from a later chapter in this book and describe its biochemical importance.

**7.55** Describe how an increase in the concentration of reactants increases the rate of a reaction.

**7.56** Describe how an increase in the temperature of reactants increases the rate of a reaction.

**7.57** Describe how a catalyst speeds up a chemical reaction.

**7.58** Explain how a catalyst can be involved in a chemical reaction without being consumed in the process.

**7.59** Sketch a potential energy diagram for a reaction that shows the effect of a catalyst on an exothermic reaction.

**7.60** Sketch a potential energy diagram for a reaction that shows the effect of a catalyst on an endothermic reaction.

### Applications

**7.61** Write the rate law for:

$$CH_4(g) + 2O_2(g) \longrightarrow 2H_2O(l) + CO_2(g)$$

if the order of all reactants is one.
Will the rate of the reaction increase, decrease, or remain the same if the rate constant doubles?

**7.62** Will the rate of the reaction in Question 7.61 increase, decrease, or remain the same if the concentration of methane increases?

**7.63** Write the rate law for the reaction:

$$N_2O_4(g) \rightleftharpoons 2NO_2(g)$$

Represent the order as $n, n'$, and so forth.

**7.64** Write the rate law for the reaction:

$$H_2S(aq) + Cl_2(aq) \rightleftharpoons S(s) + 2HCl(aq)$$

Represent the order as $n, n'$, and so forth.

**7.65** For the equilibrium

$$2I(g) \rightleftharpoons I_2(g)$$

the rate law is:

$$\text{rate} = k[I]^2$$

at 23°C, $k = 7.0 \times 10^9$ $M^{-1}$ $s^{-1}$. What effect will doubling the [I] have on the rate?

**7.66**   For the reaction

$$2H_2O_2(aq) \longrightarrow 2H_2O(l) + O_2(g)$$

the rate law is:

$$rate = k[H_2O_2]$$

at 25°C, $k = 3.1 \times 10^{-3} s^{-1}$. What effect would doubling the $[H_2O_2]$ have on the rate?

## Equilibrium

### Foundations

**7.67**   Explain LeChatelier's principle.

**7.68**   How can LeChatelier's principle help us to increase yields of chemical reactions?

**7.69**   Distinguish between a physical equilibrium and a chemical equilibrium.

**7.70**   Distinguish between the rate constant and the equilibrium constant for a reaction.

**7.71**   Does a large equilibrium constant mean that products or reactants are favored?

**7.72**   Does a large equilibrium constant mean that the reaction must be rapid?

**7.73**   Label each of the following statements as true or false and explain why.
   a. A slow reaction is an incomplete reaction.
   b. The rates of forward and reverse reactions are never the same.

**7.74**   Label each of the following statements as true or false and explain why.
   a. A reaction is at equilibrium when no reactants remain.
   b. A reaction at equilibrium is undergoing continual change.

**7.75**   The following diagram represents the reversible reaction $A(g) \rightleftharpoons 2B(g)$ at equilibrium with a total pressure of $P$.

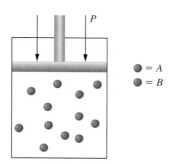

The pressure is increased to $P'$. Which of the following diagrams would represent the system once equilibrium is reestablished?

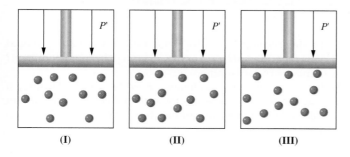

(I)            (II)            (III)

**7.76**   The following diagram represents the endothermic reaction at equilibrium at 25°C: heat $+ A(g) \rightleftharpoons 2B(g)$.

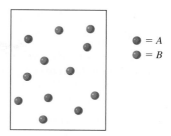

a. The temperature is increased to 50°C. Which of the following diagrams would represent the system once equilibrium is reestablished?

b. The temperature is decreased to 15°C. Which of the following diagrams would represent the system once equilibrium is reestablished?

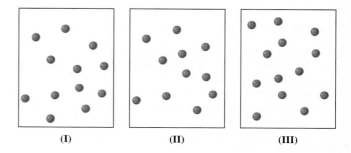

(I)            (II)            (III)

**7.77**   Describe the meaning of the term *dynamic equilibrium*.

**7.78**   What is the relationship between the forward and reverse rates for a reaction at equilibrium?

**7.79**   Describe the meaning of the term *position of the equilibrium*.

**7.80**   Can a catalyst alter the position of the equilibrium?

**7.81**   Name three factors that can shift the position of an equilibrium.

**7.82**   A change in pressure could have the greatest effect on which type of equilibria: gaseous, liquid, or solid?

### Applications

**7.83**   Write a valid equilibrium constant expression for the reaction shown in Question 7.63.

**7.84**   Write a valid equilibrium constant expression for the reaction shown in Question 7.64.

**7.85**   Write the equilibrium constant expression for the reaction:

$$N_2(g) + 3H_2(g) \rightleftharpoons 2NH_3(g)$$

**7.86**   Using the equilibrium constant expression in Question 7.85, calculate the equilibrium constant if:

$$[N_2] = 0.071\ M$$
$$[H_2] = 9.2 \times 10^{-3}\ M$$
$$[NH_3] = 1.8 \times 10^{-4}\ M$$

**7.87**   Write the equilibrium constant expression for the reaction:

$$2H_2(g) + S_2(g) \rightleftharpoons 2H_2S(g)$$

**7.88** Using the equilibrium constant expression in Question 7.87, calculate the equilibrium constant if:

$$[H_2] = 2.1 \times 10^{-1} M$$
$$[S_2] = 1.1 \times 10^{-6} M$$
$$[H_2S] = 7.3 \times 10^{-1} M$$

**7.89** Use the equilibrium constant expression you wrote in Question 7.85 and the equilibrium constant you calculated in Question 7.86 to determine the equilibrium concentration of $NH_3$ if:

$$[N_2] = 8.0 \times 10^{-2} M$$
$$[H_2] = 5.0 \times 10^{-3} M$$

**7.90** Use the equilibrium constant expression you wrote in Question 7.87 and the equilibrium constant you calculated in Question 7.88 to determine the equilibrium concentration of $H_2S$ if:

$$[H_2] = 1.0 \times 10^{-1} M$$
$$[S_2] = 1.0 \times 10^{-5} M$$

**7.91** For the reaction

$$CH_4(g) + Cl_2(g) \rightleftharpoons CH_3Cl(g) + HCl(g) + 26.4 \text{ kcal}$$

predict the effect on the position of the equilibrium (will it shift to the left or to the right, or will there be no change?) for each of the following changes.
**a.** The temperature is increased.
**b.** The pressure is increased by decreasing the volume of the container.
**c.** A catalyst is added.

**7.92** For the reaction

$$47 \text{ kcal} + 2SO_3(g) \rightleftharpoons 2SO_2(g) + O_2(g)$$

predict the effect on the position of the equilibrium (will it shift to the left or to the right, or will there be no change?) for each of the following changes.
**a.** The temperature is increased.
**b.** The pressure is increased by decreasing the volume of the container.
**c.** A catalyst is added.

**7.93** Use LeChatelier's principle to predict whether the amount of $PCl_3$ in a 1.00-L container is increased, is decreased, or remains the same for the equilibrium

$$PCl_3(g) + Cl_2(g) \rightleftharpoons PCl_5(g) + \text{heat}$$

when each of the following changes is made.
**a.** $PCl_5$ is added.
**b.** $Cl_2$ is added.
**c.** $PCl_5$ is removed.
**d.** The temperature is decreased.
**e.** A catalyst is added.

**7.94** Use LeChatelier's principle to predict the effects, if any, of each of the following changes on the equilibrium system, described below, in a closed container.

$$C(s) + 2H_2(g) \rightleftharpoons CH_4(g) + 18 \text{ kcal}$$

**a.** C is added.
**b.** $H_2$ is added.
**c.** $CH_4$ is removed.

**d.** The temperature is increased.
**e.** A catalyst is added.

**7.95** Will an increase in pressure increase, decrease, or have no effect on the concentration of $H_2(g)$ in the reaction:

$$C(s) + H_2O(g) \rightleftharpoons CO(g) + H_2(g)$$

**7.96** Will an increase in pressure increase, decrease, or have no effect on the concentration of $NO(g)$ in the reaction:

$$N_2(g) + O_2(g) \rightleftharpoons 2NO(g)$$

**7.97** Write the equilibrium constant expression for the reaction described in Question 7.95.

**7.98** Write the equilibrium constant expression for the reaction described in Question 7.96.

**7.99** True or false: The position of the equilibrium will shift to the right when a catalyst is added to the mixture described in Question 7.95. Explain your reasoning.

**7.100** True or false: The position of the equilibrium for an endothermic reaction will shift to the right when the reaction mixture is heated. Explain your reasoning.

**7.101** Why is it dangerous to heat an unopened bottle of cola?

**7.102** Carbonated beverages quickly go flat (lose $CO_2$) when heated. Explain, using LeChatelier's principle.

**7.103** **a.** Write the equilibrium constant expression for the reaction:

$$2SO_2(g) + O_2(g) \rightleftharpoons 2 SO_3(g)$$

**b.** Calculate the equilibrium constant if

$$[SO_2] = 0.10 \, M$$
$$[O_2] = 0.12 \, M$$
$$[SO_3] = 0.60 \, M$$

**7.104** **a.** Write the equilibrium constant expression for the reaction:

$$C(s) + H_2O(g) \rightleftharpoons CO(g) + H_2(g)$$

**b.** Calculate the equilibrium constant if

$$[H_2O] = 0.40 \, M$$
$$[CO] = 0.40 \, M$$
$$[H_2] = 0.20 \, M$$

**7.105** Suggest a change in experimental conditions that would increase the yield of $SO_3$ in the reaction in Question 7.103.

**7.106** Suggest a change in experimental conditions that would increase the yield of $H_2$ in the reaction in Question 7.104.

## CHALLENGE PROBLEMS

**1.** Predict the sign of $\Delta G$ for perspiration evaporating. Would you expect the $\Delta H$ term or the $\Delta S$ term to be more dominant? Explain your reasoning.

**2.** Can the following statement ever be true? "Heating a reaction mixture increases the rate of a certain reaction but decreases the yield of product from the reaction." Explain why or why not.

3. Molecules must collide for a reaction to take place. Sketch a model of the orientation and interaction of HI and Cl that is most favorable for the reaction:

$$HI(g) + Cl(g) \longrightarrow HCl(g) + I(g)$$

4. Refer to Question 7.92. Choose the statements that are correct.
   a. $K_{eq}$ (at 25°C) > $K_{eq}$ (at 50°C)
   b. $K_{eq}$ (at 25°C) < $K_{eq}$ (at 50°C)
   c. $K_{eq}$ (at 25°C) = $K_{eq}$ (at 50°C)
   d. $K_{eq}$ (at 25°C) > $K_{eq}$ (at 15°C)
   e. $K_{eq}$ (at 25°C) < $K_{eq}$ (at 15°C)
   f. $K_{eq}$ (at 25°C) = $K_{eq}$ (at 15°C)

5. Silver ion reacts with chloride ion to form the precipitate silver chloride:

$$Ag^+(aq) + Cl^-(aq) \rightleftharpoons AgCl(s)$$

After the reaction reached equilibrium, the chemist filtered 99% of the solid silver chloride from the solution, hoping to shift the equilibrium to the right, to form more product. Critique the chemist's experiment.

6. Human behavior often follows LeChatelier's principle. Provide one example and explain in terms of LeChatelier's principle.

7. A clever device found in some homes is a figurine that is blue on dry, sunny days and pink on damp, rainy days. These figurines are coated with substances containing chemical species that undergo the following equilibrium reaction:

$$Co(H_2O)_6^{2+}(aq) + 4Cl^-(aq) \rightleftharpoons CoCl_4^{2-}(aq) + 6H_2O(l)$$

   a. Which substance is blue?
   b. Which substance is pink?
   c. How is LeChatelier's principle applied here?

8. You have spent the entire morning in a 20°C classroom. As you ride the elevator to the cafeteria, six persons enter the elevator after being outside on a subfreezing day. You suddenly feel chilled. Explain the heat flow situation in the elevator in thermodynamic terms.

# 8

# Acids and Bases

Solution properties, including clarity and bacteria levels, are often pH dependent.

## OUTLINE

## LEARNING GOALS

1 Classify compounds with acid-base properties as acids, bases, or amphiprotic.

2 Write equations illustrating the role of water in acid-base reactions.

3 Identify conjugate acid-base pairs.

4 Describe the relationship between acid and base strength and dissociation.

5 Use the ion product constant for water to solve for hydronium and hydroxide ion concentrations.

6 Calculate pH from solution concentration data.

7 Calculate hydronium and/or hydroxide ion concentration from pH data.

8 Describe the meaning and utility of neutralization reactions.

9 Use titration data to determine the molar concentration of an unknown solution.

10 Demonstrate the reactions and dissociation of polyprotic substances.

11 Describe the effects of adding acid or base to a buffer system.

12 Calculate the pH of buffer solutions.

13 Explain the role of buffers in the control of blood pH under various conditions.

# INTRODUCTION

Acids and bases include some of the most important compounds in nature. Historically, it was recognized that certain compounds, acids, had a sour taste, were able to dissolve some metals, and caused vegetable dyes to change color. Bases have long been recognized by their bitter taste, slippery feel, and corrosive nature. Bases react strongly with acids and cause many metal ions in solution to form a solid precipitate.

Digestion of proteins is aided by stomach acid (hydrochloric acid), and many biochemical processes such as enzyme catalysis depend on the proper level of acidity. Indeed, a wide variety of chemical reactions critically depend on the acid-base composition of the solution. This is especially true of the biochemical reactions occurring in the cells of our bodies. For this reason, the level of acidity must be very carefully regulated. This is done with substances called buffers.

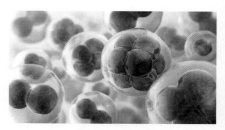

Various processes that occur within our cells are pH dependent.

## 8.1 Acids and Bases

Properties specific to acids and bases are due to unique characteristics of their chemical structures. Two important theories help us to understand the behavior of these classes of compounds in aqueous solution.

### Acid and Base Theories

#### Arrhenius Theory

The Arrhenius theory was proposed in the late 1800s to describe general characteristics of acids and bases. According to this early theory, when an **Arrhenius acid** dissolves in water, it dissociates to form *hydrogen ions* or *protons* **(H⁺)**, and when an **Arrhenius base** dissolves in water, it dissociates to form *hydroxide ions* **(OH⁻)**. For example, hydrochloric acid dissociates in aqueous solution according to the reaction:

$$HCl(aq) \longrightarrow H^+(aq) + Cl^-(aq)$$

Sodium hydroxide, a base, produces hydroxide ions in aqueous solution:

$$NaOH(aq) \longrightarrow Na^+(aq) + OH^-(aq)$$

The Arrhenius theory also explains neutralization of acids and bases. When an acid and base react, a *salt* (an ionic compound) and water form. The water is formed from the proton generated by the acid and the hydroxide ion generated by the base.

Although the Arrhenius theory explains the behavior of many acids and bases, it does not explain substances with basic properties that do not contain OH⁻. For example, a substance such as ammonia ($NH_3$) has basic properties that cannot be explained as an Arrhenius base because it does not contain OH⁻. Another observation not explained by the Arrhenius theory is that protons do not exist as H⁺ in aqueous solutions. Rather, they interact with water and form **hydronium ions, $H_3O^+$.**

#### Brønsted-Lowry Theory

The Brønsted-Lowry theory was developed in the 1920s from the Arrhenius theory, and it explains the acid-base chemistry that could not be explained by the Arrhenius theory. The expanded nature of the Brønsted-Lowry theory considers the central role of the solvent water in the dissociation process.

According to this inclusive theory, a **Brønsted-Lowry acid** is defined as a proton donor, and a **Brønsted-Lowry base** is defined as a proton acceptor.

As a Brønsted-Lowry acid, hydrochloric acid in aqueous solution donates a proton to the solvent, water, which results in the formation of the hydronium ion, $H_3O^+$. A single arrow in the following equation is used because this acid-base reaction is essentially an irreversible process.

$$HCl(aq) + H_2O(l) \longrightarrow H_3O^+(aq) + Cl^-(aq)$$

**LEARNING GOAL**

**1** Classify compounds with acid-base properties as acids, bases, or amphiprotic.

**LEARNING GOAL**

**2** Write equations illustrating the role of water in acid-base reactions.

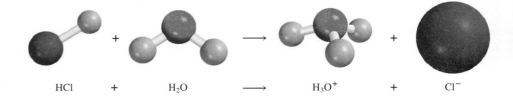

HCl    +    H₂O    ⟶    H₃O⁺    +    Cl⁻

Only this hydrogen can be donated as a proton, H⁺.

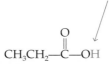

**Figure 8.1** This organic acid contributes to the flavor of Swiss cheese.

Organic acids (those principally comprised of carbon, hydrogen, and oxygen) are classified as Brønsted-Lowry acids. Although most organic acids contain several hydrogen atoms, only a specific hydrogen can be donated as a proton. When evaluating the structures of these organic acids, it is essential to examine the bonds. There are often hydrogen atoms directly attached to carbon atoms along with a carbon atom that shares a double bond with one oxygen atom and is also bonded to an OH. Only the hydrogen that is directly bonded to this electronegative oxygen can be donated as a proton (Figure 8.1). Below, you can see how such an organic acid donates its proton to water.

$$CH_3CH_2COOH(aq) + H_2O(l) \rightleftharpoons H_3O^+(aq) + CH_3CH_2COO^-(aq)$$

The double arrows in the above equation are used because this acid-base reaction is seen as a reversible equilibrium process. In this dynamic equilibrium (see Section 7.4), a mixture of $CH_3CH_2COOH$, $H_2O$, $H_3O^+$, and $CH_3CH_2COO^-$ results.

The basic properties of ammonia are also accounted for by this expanded theory. As a Brønsted-Lowry base, ammonia accepts a proton from the solvent water and produces the hydroxide ion, $OH^-$.

$$NH_3(aq) + H_2O(l) \rightleftharpoons NH_4^+(aq) + OH^-(aq)$$

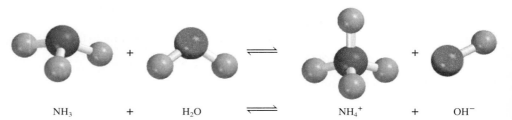

NH₃    +    H₂O    ⇌    NH₄⁺    +    OH⁻

Many organic bases are derivatives of ammonia. When the nitrogen atom in these molecules has only three bonds and a lone pair of electrons, it can function as a Brønsted-Lowry base and form a fourth bond upon accepting a proton.

---

**EXAMPLE 8.1** | **Classifying a Compound as an Acid or Base**

Classify $NH_4^+$ as a Brønsted-Lowry acid or base, and write the reaction of $NH_4^+$ with water.

**Solution**

**Step 1.** The central atom, nitrogen, contains four bonds. Nitrogen cannot accept an additional proton because it cannot form a fifth bond. Since the nitrogen in this molecule is directly attached to four hydrogens and carries a positive charge, it can donate a proton. Therefore, $NH_4^+$ is a Brønsted-Lowry acid.

**Step 2.** Since $NH_4^+$ is a Brønsted-Lowry acid, it donates a proton when it reacts with water.

$$NH_4^+ + H_2O \rightleftharpoons NH_3 + H_3O^+$$

*Helpful Hint:* When the ammonium ion, $NH_4^+$, donates a proton, the $H^+$ is transferred to water to form a hydronium ion. In this reaction, water serves as a Brønsted-Lowry base because it accepts the proton.

**LEARNING GOALS**

**1** Classify compounds with acid-base properties as acids, bases, or amphiprotic.

**2** Write equations illustrating the role of water in acid-base reactions.

**Practice Problem 8.1**

Classify $CH_3COO^-$ as a Brønsted-Lowry acid or base, and write the reaction of $CH_3COO^-$ with water.

▶ For Further Practice: **Questions 8.23 and 8.24.**

**Question 8.1** Classify each of the following compounds as a Brønsted-Lowry acid or base.
   a. $HClO_4$     b. $HCOOH$     c. $ClO_4^-$     d. $C_6H_5COO^-$

**Question 8.2** Classify each of the following compounds as a Brønsted-Lowry acid or base.
   a. $PO_4^{3-}$     b. $CH_3NH_3^+$     c. $HI$     d. $H_3PO_4$

## Amphiprotic Nature of Water

**LEARNING GOAL**

**2** Write equations illustrating the role of water in acid-base reactions.

The role that the solvent, water, plays in acid-base reactions is noteworthy. As shown in a previous example, the water molecule accepts a proton from the HCl molecule. The water is behaving as a proton acceptor, a Brønsted-Lowry base.

However, when water is a solvent for ammonia ($NH_3$), a Brønsted-Lowry base, the water molecule donates a proton to the ammonia molecule. The water, in this situation, is acting as a proton donor, a Brønsted-Lowry acid.

Water, owing to the fact that it possesses *both* acidic and basic properties, is termed **amphiprotic.** Water is the most commonly used solvent for acids and bases. In addition to its amphiprotic properties, the solute-solvent interactions between water with acids (or bases) promote both the solubility and the dissociation of acids and bases.

The bicarbonate ion, $HCO_3^-$, is an example of another amphiprotic compound. It can serve as a proton donor and a proton acceptor.

**Question 8.3** Write an equation for the reversible reactions of each of the following with water.
   a. $HF$     b. $C_6H_5COO^-$

**Question 8.4** Write an equation for the reversible reactions of each of the following with water.
   a. $H_3PO_4$     b. $CH_3NH_2$

## Conjugate Acid-Base Pairs

**LEARNING GOAL**

**3** Identify conjugate acid-base pairs.

When a Brønsted-Lowry acid donates a proton to a Brønsted-Lowry base, the base that accepts the proton becomes a **conjugate acid.** Alternatively, the acid that donated the proton becomes a **conjugate base.** The product acids and bases are termed conjugate acids and bases.

Consider the model equation below in which HX is an acid and Y is a base. In the forward reaction, the acid (HX) donates a proton to the base (Y) leading to the formation of a conjugate acid ($HY^+$) and a conjugate base ($X^-$).

$$HX \; + \; Y \; \rightleftharpoons \; HY^+ \; + \; X^-$$

Acid     Base     Conjugate acid     Conjugate base

**Conjugate acid-base pairs**

In the reverse reaction, it is the conjugate acid ($HY^+$) that behaves as an acid; it donates its proton to $X^-$. Therefore, $X^-$ is a base in its own right because it accepts the proton. An acid and base on the opposite sides of the equation are collectively termed a **conjugate acid-base pair.** The two conjugate acid-base pairs in the above equation are $HX/X^-$ and $HY^+/Y$.

When hydrogen sulfide, $H_2S$, reacts with water, $H_2S$ donates a proton to water and forms the conjugate base $HS^-$. Water accepts the proton and forms the conjugate acid, $H_3O^+$.

$$H_2S(aq) \quad + \quad H_2O(l) \quad \rightleftharpoons \quad H_3O^+(aq) \quad + \quad HS^-(aq)$$

Acid          Base        Conjugate acid    Conjugate base

**Conjugate acid-base pairs**

The two conjugate acid-base pairs in this reaction are $H_2S/HS^-$ and $H_3O^+/H_2O$.

> **Question 8.5**   Identify the conjugate acid-base pairs for the reversible reactions in Question 8.3.

> **Question 8.6**   Identify the conjugate acid-base pairs for the reversible reactions in Question 8.4.

## Acid and Base Strength

Acids and bases are electrolytes. When dissolved in water, the dissociation of the acid (or base) produces ions that can conduct an electrical current. The strength of an acid (or base) is measured by the degree of dissociation of the acid (or base) in solution. As a result of the differences in the degree of dissociation, *strong acids and bases are strong electrolytes while weak acids and bases are weak electrolytes.* It is important to note that acid (or base) strength is independent of acid (or base) concentration. Recall that concentration refers to the amount of solute (in this case, the quantity of acid or base) per quantity of solution.

The strength of an acid (or base) in an aqueous solution depends on the extent to which it reacts with the solvent, water. Although in several reactions, we show the forward and reverse arrows to indicate the reversibility of the reaction, seldom are the two processes "equal but opposite." One reaction, either forward or reverse, is usually favored. Consider the reaction of hydrochloric acid in water:

Significant

$$HCl(aq) \quad + \quad H_2O(l) \quad \rightleftharpoons \quad H_3O^+(aq) \quad + \quad Cl^-(aq)$$

Insignificant

In this reaction, the forward reaction predominates, the reverse reaction is inconsequential, and hydrochloric acid is termed a strong acid.

Acids and bases are classified as *strong* when the reaction with water is virtually 100% complete and as *weak* when the reaction with water is much less than 100% complete. Since strong acids and bases are 100% dissociated in water, we use only a single forward arrow to represent its behavior.

Important strong acids include:

| | |
|---|---|
| Hydrochloric acid | $HCl(aq) + H_2O(l) \longrightarrow H_3O^+(aq) + Cl^-(aq)$ |
| Nitric acid | $HNO_3(aq) + H_2O(l) \longrightarrow H_3O^+(aq) + NO_3^-(aq)$ |
| Sulfuric acid | $H_2SO_4(aq) + H_2O(l) \longrightarrow H_3O^+(aq) + HSO_4^-(aq)$ |

Note that the equation for the dissociation of each of these acids is written with a single forward arrow to represent their behavior. This indicates that the reaction has little or no tendency to proceed in the reverse direction to establish equilibrium. Each of these acids is virtually completely dissociated in water, forming ions.

All common strong bases are *metal hydroxides.* Strong bases completely dissociate in aqueous solution to produce hydroxide ions and metal cations. Of the common metal hydroxides, only NaOH and KOH are soluble in water.

Sodium hydroxide     $NaOH(aq) \longrightarrow Na^+(aq) + OH^-(aq)$
Potassium hydroxide   $KOH(aq) \longrightarrow K^+(aq) + OH^-(aq)$

Both NaOH and KOH are used in the production of soap from animal fats and vegetable oils.

Weak acids and weak bases dissolve in water principally in the molecular form. Only a small percentage of the molecules dissociate to form the hydronium or hydroxide ion. All organic acids are weak acids.

Two important weak acids are:

Acetic acid     $CH_3COOH(aq) + H_2O(l) \rightleftharpoons H_3O^+(aq) + CH_3COO^-(aq)$
Carbonic acid   $HOCOOH(aq) + H_2O(l) \rightleftharpoons H_3O^+(aq) + HOCOO^-(aq)$

Diluted acetic acid is in vinegar, and carbonic acid is used in make bubbly beverages like soda.

We have already mentioned the most common weak base, ammonia. Many organic derivatives of ammonia function as weak bases. Two examples of weak bases are:

Aniline       $C_6H_5NH_2(aq) + H_2O(l) \rightleftharpoons C_6H_5NH_3^+(aq) + OH^-(aq)$
Methylamine   $CH_3NH_2(aq) + H_2O(l) \rightleftharpoons CH_3NH_3^+(aq) + OH^-(aq)$

The chemistry of organic acids will be discussed in Chapter 14, and the chemistry of organic bases will be discussed in Chapter 15.

The fundamental chemical difference between strong and weak acids (or bases) is their equilibrium ion concentration. A strong acid in aqueous solution, such as HCl, does not exist to any measurable degree in equilibrium with its ions, $H_3O^+$ and $Cl^-$. On the other hand, a weak acid in aqueous solution, such as acetic acid, establishes a dynamic equilibrium with its ions, $H_3O^+$ and $CH_3COO^-$, as illustrated in Figure 8.2.

This explains the inverse correlation that exists between conjugate acid-base pairs. The strongest acids and bases have the weakest conjugate bases and acids. Conjugate acid-base pairs are listed in the middle columns of Figure 8.3.

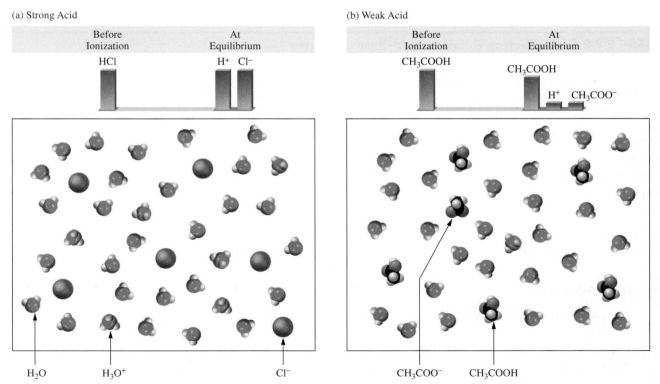

**Figure 8.2** Initially, there were six HCl and six $CH_3COOH$ molecules present. (a) The strong acid is completely dissociated in aqueous solution, whereas (b) the weak acid exists in equilibrium with its ions.

**Figure 8.3** Conjugate acid-base pairs. Strong acids have weak conjugate bases; strong bases have weak conjugate acids. Note the complementary nature of the conjugate acid-base pairs. In every case, the conjugate base has one fewer $H^+$ than the corresponding conjugate acid.

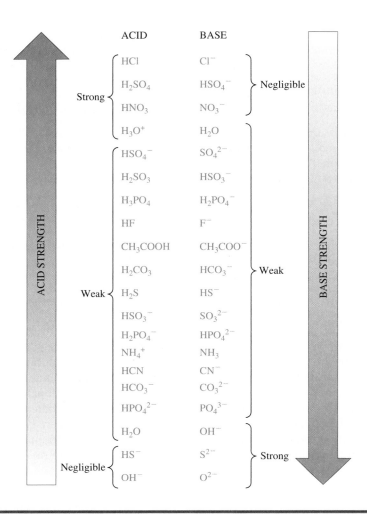

---

### EXAMPLE 8.2 | Predicting Relative Acid-Base Strengths

a. Write the conjugate acid of $HS^-$.
b. Using Figure 8.3, identify the stronger base, $HS^-$ or $F^-$.
c. Using Figure 8.3, identify the stronger acid, $H_2S$ or $HF$.

#### Solution

**For part a,**
The conjugate acid may be constructed by adding a proton ($H^+$) to the base structure, consequently, $H_2S$.

**For part b,**
$HS^-$ is the stronger base because it is located farther down the right-hand column.

**For part c,**
$HF$ is the stronger acid because its conjugate base is weaker *and* because it is located farther up the left-hand column.

---

#### Practice Problem 8.2

a. In each pair, write the conjugate base of each acid and identify the stronger acid.
$H_2O$ or $NH_4^+$            $H_2SO_4$ or $H_2SO_3$

b. In each pair, write the conjugate acid of each base and identify the stronger base.
$CO_3^{2-}$ or $PO_4^{3-}$            $HCO_3^-$ or $HPO_4^{2-}$

▶ For Further Practice: **Questions 8.37–8.40.**

As illustrated, the strongest acids (top left) are directly adjacent to the weakest bases (top right), and the weakest acids (bottom left) are directly adjacent to the strongest bases (bottom right).

## Self-Ionization of Water and $K_w$

Although pure water is virtually 100% molecular, a small number of water molecules do ionize. This process, called **self-ionization,** occurs by the transfer of a proton from one water molecule to another, producing a hydronium ion and a hydroxide ion:

$$H_2O(l) + H_2O(l) \rightleftharpoons H_3O^+(aq) + OH^-(aq)$$

Based on the self-ionization reaction, the generalized equilibrium constant expression is:

$$K_{eq} = [H_3O^+][OH^-]$$

The water term is not included in the equilibrium concentration expression because water is a liquid and its concentration does not change (see Equilibrium, Section 7.4). As a result, the equilibrium constant for water is the product of the hydronium and hydroxide ion concentrations and is called the **ion product constant for water,** symbolized by $K_w$ (the subscript $w$ refers to water).

$$K_w = [H_3O^+][OH^-]$$

It has been determined that at 25°C, pure water has a hydronium ion concentration of $1.0 \times 10^{-7}$ M. When two water molecules react, one hydroxide ion is produced for each hydronium ion. Therefore, the hydroxide ion concentration is also $1.0 \times 10^{-7}$ M. As we saw in Chapter 7, the molar equilibrium concentration is conveniently indicated by brackets around the species whose concentration is represented:

$$[H_3O^+] = [OH^-] = 1.0 \times 10^{-7}\,M \quad \text{(at 25°C)}$$

These molar equilibrium concentrations can be used to solve for $K_w$.

$$K_w = [H_3O^+][OH^-] = (1.0 \times 10^{-7}\,M)(1.0 \times 10^{-7}\,M) = 1.0 \times 10^{-14}\,M$$

The ion product constant for water is a temperature-dependent quantity but it does not depend on the identity or concentration of the solute. When solutes are added to water, they alter the relative concentrations of the hydronium and hydroxide ions, but not the product $[H_3O^+][OH^-]$. *The product, $[H_3O^+][OH^-]$, always equals $1.0 \times 10^{-14}$ M (at 25°C).* This product relationship is the basis for the pH scale which is useful in the measurement of the level of acidity (or basicity) of solutions.

**LEARNING GOAL**

**5** Use the ion product constant for water to solve for hydronium and hydroxide ion concentrations.

Since the ion product, $[H_3O^+][OH^-]$, is constant, increasing the concentration of one results in a decreased concentration of the other.

---

**EXAMPLE 8.3** | **Using the Ion Product Constant for Water to Calculate an Unknown Hydroxide Ion Concentration**

A solution of green tea has a hydronium ion concentration of $4.0 \times 10^{-4}$ M (at 25°C). What is the concentration of hydroxide ions in this solution?

**Solution**

**Step 1.** Write the expression for the ion product constant for water.

$$K_w = [H_3O^+][OH^-] = 1.0 \times 10^{-14}\,M$$

**LEARNING GOAL**

**5** Use the ion product constant for water to solve for hydronium and hydroxide ion concentrations.

*Continued…*

**Step 2.** To solve the expression for $[OH^-]$, divide both sides of the equation by $[H_3O^+]$.

$$\frac{K_w}{[H_3O^+]} = [OH^-]$$

**Step 3.** Substitute the values:

$$\frac{1.0 \times 10^{-14}\,M}{4.0 \times 10^{-4}\,M} = [OH^-]$$

**Step 4.** Solve:

$$[OH^-] = 2.5 \times 10^{-11}\,M$$

### Practice Problem 8.3

Analysis of a patient's blood sample indicated that the hydroxide ion concentration was $3.0 \times 10^{-7}\,M$ (at 25°C). What was the hydronium ion concentration in the blood sample?

▶ For Further Practice: **Questions 8.51 and 8.52.**

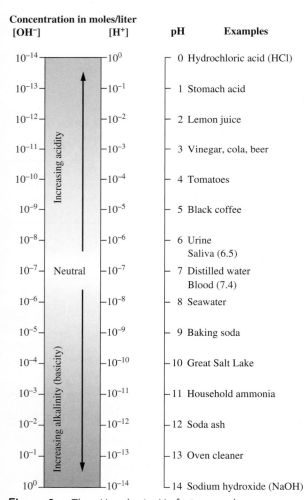

**Figure 8.4** The pH scale. A pH of 7 is neutral ($[H_3O^+] = [OH^-]$). Values less than 7 are acidic ($H_3O^+$ predominates), and values greater than 7 are basic ($OH^-$ predominates).

**Question 8.7** Calculate the hydroxide ion concentration in an aqueous solution of lemon juice that has a hydronium ion concentration of 0.025 $M$.

**Question 8.8** The hydroxide ion concentration in a sample of urine was determined to be of $1.0 \times 10^{-8}\,M$ (at 25°C). Calculate the hydronium ion concentration of this aqueous solution.

## 8.2  pH: A Measurement Scale for Acids and Bases

### A Definition of pH

The **pH scale** gauges the hydronium ion concentration and reflects the degree of acidity or basicity of a solution. The pH scale is somewhat analogous to the temperature scale used for assignment of relative levels of hot or cold. The temperature scale was developed to allow us to indicate how cold or how hot an object is. The pH scale specifies how acidic or how basic a solution is. The pH scale has values that range from 0 (very acidic) to 14 (very basic). A pH of 7, the middle of the scale, is neutral, neither acidic nor basic. Figure 8.4 provides a convenient overview of solution pH.

To help us develop a concept of pH, let's consider the following:

- Addition of an acid (proton donor) to water *increases* the $[H_3O^+]$ and decreases the $[OH^-]$.
- Addition of a base (proton acceptor) to water *decreases* the $[H_3O^+]$ by increasing the $[OH^-]$.
- $[H_3O^+] = [OH^-]$ when *equal* amounts of acid and base are present.

In all three cases, $[H_3O^+][OH^-] = 1.0 \times 10^{-14}$ = the ion product for water at 25°C.

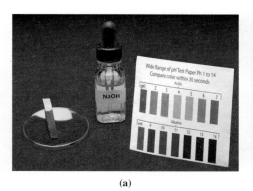

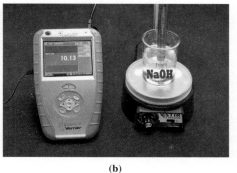

**Figure 8.5** The measurement of pH.
(a) A strip of test paper impregnated with indicator (a material that changes color as the acidity of the surroundings changes) is put in contact with the solution of interest. The resulting color is matched with a standard color chart (colors shown as a function of pH) to obtain the approximate pH. (b) A pH meter uses a sensor (a pH electrode) that develops an electrical potential that is proportional to the pH of the solution.

## Measuring pH

The pH of a solution can be calculated if the concentration of either $H_3O^+$ or $OH^-$ is known. Alternatively, measurement of pH allows the calculation of the $H_3O^+$ or $OH^-$ concentration. The pH of aqueous solutions may be approximated by using indicating paper (pH paper) that develops a color related to the solution pH. Alternatively, a pH meter can give us a much more exact pH measurement. A sensor measures an electrical property of a solution that is proportional to pH (Figure 8.5).

pH values greater than 14 and less than zero are possible, but largely meaningless, due to ion association characteristics of very concentrated solutions.

## Calculating pH

One of our objectives in this chapter is to calculate the pH of a solution when the hydronium or hydroxide ion concentration is known, and to calculate $[H_3O^+]$ or $[OH^-]$ from the measured pH.

The pH of a solution is defined as the negative logarithm of the molar concentration of the hydronium ion:

$$pH = -\log [H_3O^+]$$

The proper use of the logarithm function often appears to contradict our understanding of significant figures. This is because the logarithm is an exponent that contains two kinds of information: the information in the measurement and the position of the decimal point.

The operative rule is that the number of decimal places in the logarithm is equal to the number of significant figures in the original number. In Examples 8.4 and 8.5, two significant figures in concentration correspond to two decimal places in pH (the logarithm).

**LEARNING GOAL**

**6**  Calculate pH from solution concentration data.

---

**EXAMPLE 8.4**    **Calculating pH from Acid Molarity**

Calculate the pH of a $1.0 \times 10^{-3}$ $M$ solution of HCl.

**LEARNING GOAL**

**6**  Calculate pH from solution concentration data.

**Solution**

**Step 1.**  Recognize that HCl is a strong acid; consequently, it is 100% dissociated.

**Step 2.**  One $H_3O^+$ is produced for each HCl. Therefore, a $1.0 \times 10^{-3}$ $M$ HCl solution has $[H_3O^+] = 1.0 \times 10^{-3}$ $M$.

**Step 3.**  Using the expression for pH:

$$pH = -\log [H_3O^+]$$

*Continued...*

**Step 4.** Substituting for $[H_3O^+]$:

$$pH = -\log(1.0 \times 10^{-3})$$
$$= -(-3.00) = 3.00$$

**Practice Problem 8.4**

Calculate the pH of a $1.0 \times 10^{-4}\ M$ solution of $HNO_3$.

▶ For Further Practice: **Questions 8.55 and 8.56.**

---

**EXAMPLE 8.5**  **Calculating $[H_3O^+]$ from pH**

LEARNING GOAL

**7** Calculate hydronium and/or hydroxide ion concentration from pH data.

Calculate the $[H_3O^+]$ of a solution of hydrochloric acid with pH = 4.00.

**Solution**

**Step 1.** Based on the pH expression:

$$pH = -\log[H_3O^+]$$

an alternative mathematical form of this equation is:

$$[H_3O^+] = 10^{-pH}$$

**Step 2.** Substituting for pH:

$$[H_3O^+] = 10^{-4.00}$$
$$= 1.0 \times 10^{-4}\ M$$

**Practice Problem 8.5**

Calculate the $[H_3O^+]$ of a solution of $HNO_3$ that has a pH = 5.00.

▶ For Further Practice: **Questions 8.57 and 8.58.**

It is important to remember that in the case of a base you must convert the $[OH^-]$ to $[H_3O^+]$, using the expression for the ion product for the solvent, water. It is useful to be aware that, because pH is a base 10 logarithmic function, each tenfold change in concentration changes the pH by one unit. A tenfold change in concentration is equivalent to moving the decimal point one place.

---

**EXAMPLE 8.6**  **Calculating the pH of a Base**

LEARNING GOAL

**6** Calculate pH from solution concentration data.

Calculate the pH of a $1.0 \times 10^{-5}\ M$ solution of NaOH.

**Solution**

**Step 1.** Recognize that NaOH is a strong base; consequently, it is 100% dissociated.

**Step 2.** One $[OH^-]$ is produced for each NaOH. Therefore, a $1.0 \times 10^{-5}\ M$ NaOH solution has $[OH^-] = 1.0 \times 10^{-5}\ M$.

**Step 3.** To calculate pH, we need $[H_3O^+]$. Recall that

$$[H_3O^+][OH^-] = 1.0 \times 10^{-14}$$

**Step 4.** Solving this equation for $[H_3O^+]$,

$$[H_3O^+] = \frac{1.0 \times 10^{-14}}{[OH^-]}$$

**Step 5.** Substituting the information provided in the problem,

$$[H_3O^+] = \frac{1.0 \times 10^{-14}}{1.0 \times 10^{-5}} = 1.0 \times 10^{-9}\,M$$

**Step 6.** The solution is now similar to that in Example 8.4:

$$\begin{aligned} pH &= -\log [H_3O^+] \\ &= -\log (1.0 \times 10^{-9}) \\ &= 9.00 \end{aligned}$$

**Practice Problem 8.6**

a. Calculate the pH corresponding to a $1.0 \times 10^{-2}\,M$ solution of sodium hydroxide.
b. Calculate the pH corresponding to a $1.0 \times 10^{-6}\,M$ solution of sodium hydroxide.

▶ For Further Practice: **Questions 8.59 and 8.60.**

**EXAMPLE 8.7** **Calculating Both Hydronium and Hydroxide Ion Concentrations from pH**

LEARNING GOAL

**7** Calculate hydronium and/or hydroxide ion concentration from pH data.

Calculate the $[H_3O^+]$ and $[OH^-]$ of a sodium hydroxide solution with a pH = 10.00.

**Solution**

**Step 1.** First, calculate $[H_3O^+]$ using our expression for pH:

$$\begin{aligned} pH &= -\log [H_3O^+] \\ [H_3O^+] &= 10^{-pH} \\ &= 10^{-10}\,M \end{aligned}$$

**Step 2.** To calculate the $[OH^-]$, we need to solve for $[OH^-]$ by using the following expression:

$$K_w = [H_3O^+][OH^-] = 1.0 \times 10^{-14}$$

$$[OH^-] = \frac{1.0 \times 10^{-14}}{[H_3O^+]}$$

**Step 3.** Substituting the $[H_3O^+]$ from the first step, we have

$$[OH^-] = \frac{1.0 \times 10^{-14}}{1.0 \times 10^{-10}} = 1.0 \times 10^{-4}\,M$$

**Practice Problem 8.7**

Calculate the $[H_3O^+]$ and $[OH^-]$ of a potassium hydroxide solution with a pH = 8.00.

▶ For Further Practice: **Questions 8.61 and 8.62.**

Often, the pH or $[H_3O^+]$ will not be a whole number (pH = 1.5, pH = 5.3, $[H_3O^+]$ = 1.5 × $10^{-3}$ and so forth) as shown in Examples 8.4–8.7. Consider Examples 8.8 and 8.9.

---

**EXAMPLE 8.8**    **Calculating pH with Noninteger Numbers**

**LEARNING GOAL**

Calculate the pH of a sample of lake water that has a $[H_3O^+]$ = 6.5 × $10^{-5}$ M.

**6**   Calculate pH from solution concentration data.

**Solution**

**Step 1.** Use the expression for pH:

$$pH = -\log[H_3O^+]$$

**Step 2.** Substituting the hydronium ion concentration provided into the problem,

$$pH = -\log(6.5 \times 10^{-5})$$
$$= 4.19$$

Note: The pH, 4.19, is low enough to suspect acid rain. (See Green Chemistry: Acid Rain in this chapter.)

**Practice Problem 8.8**

Calculate the pH of a sample of blood that has a $[H_3O^+]$ = 3.3 × $10^{-8}$ M.

▶ For Further Practice: **Questions 8.73 and 8.74.**

---

**EXAMPLE 8.9**    **Calculating $[H_3O^+]$ from pH**

**LEARNING GOAL**

The measured pH of a sample of stream water is 6.40. Calculate $[H_3O^+]$.

**7**   Calculate hydronium and/or hydroxide ion concentration from pH data.

**Solution**

**Step 1.** An alternative mathematical form of

$$pH = -\log[H_3O^+]$$

is the expression

$$[H_3O^+] = 10^{-pH}$$

**Step 2.** Substituting the pH provided into this expression to solve for $[H_3O^+]$:

$$[H_3O^+] = 10^{-6.40}$$
$$= 3.98 \times 10^{-7} \quad \text{or} \quad 4.0 \times 10^{-7} M$$

**Practice Problem 8.9**

a. Calculate the $[H_3O^+]$ corresponding to pH = 8.50.
b. Calculate the $[H_3O^+]$ corresponding to pH = 4.50.

▶ For Further Practice: **Questions 8.69 and 8.70.**

# A Medical Perspective

## Drug Delivery

When a doctor prescribes medicine to treat a disease or relieve its symptoms, the medication may be administered in a variety of ways. Drugs may be taken orally, injected into a muscle or a vein, or absorbed through the skin. Specific instructions are often provided to regulate the particular combination of drugs that can or cannot be taken. The diet, both before and during the drug therapy, may be of special importance.

To appreciate why drugs are administered in a specific way, it is necessary to understand a few basic facts about medications and how they interact with the body.

Drugs function by undergoing one or more chemical reactions in the body. Few compounds react in only one way, to produce a limited set of products, even in the simple environment of a beaker or flask. Imagine the number of possible reactions that a drug can undergo in a complex chemical factory like the human body. In many cases, a drug can react in a variety of ways other than its intended path. These alternative paths are side reactions, sometimes producing *side effects* such as nausea, vomiting, insomnia, or drowsiness. Side effects may be unpleasant and may actually interfere with the primary function of the drug.

The development of safe, effective medication, with minimal side effects, is a slow and painstaking process, and determining the best drug delivery system is a critical step. For example, a drug that undergoes an unwanted side reaction in an acidic solution would not be very effective if administered orally. The acidic digestive fluids in the stomach could prevent the drug from even reaching the intended organ, let alone retaining its potency. The drug could be administered through a vein into the blood; blood is not acidic, in contrast to digestive fluids. In this way, the drug may be delivered intact to the intended site in the body, where it is free to undergo its primary reaction.

Drug delivery has become a science in its own right. Pharmacology, the study of drugs and their uses in the treatment of disease, has a goal of creating drugs that are highly

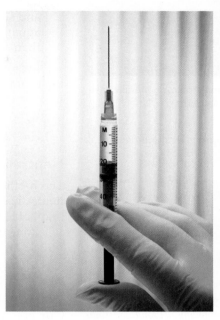

selective. In other words, they will undergo only one reaction, the intended reaction. Encapsulation of drugs, enclosing them within larger molecules or collections of molecules, may protect them from unwanted reactions as they are transported to their intended site.

### For Further Understanding

▶ Certain drugs lose potency when consumed with grapefruit juice. Can you propose a possible reason?
▶ Would you expect that the drugs referred to (above) are basic, acidic, or neutral? Explain your reasoning.

---

**Question 8.9** Calculate the $[OH^-]$ of a $1.0 \times 10^{-3}\,M$ solution of HCl.

**Question 8.10** Calculate the $[OH^-]$ of a solution of hydrochloric acid with pH = 4.00.

## The Importance of pH and pH Control

Solution pH and pH control play a major role in many facets of our lives. Consider a few examples:

- *Agriculture:* Crops grow best in a soil of proper pH. Proper fertilization involves the maintenance of a suitable pH.
- *Physiology:* If the pH of our blood were to shift by one unit, we would die. Many biochemical reactions in living organisms are extremely pH dependent.

Healthy lakes and streams generally have a pH between 6.5 and 7.5.

*See Green Chemistry: Acid Rain in this chapter.*

*Equation balancing and net ionic equations are discussed in Chapter 4.*

• *Industry:* From the manufacture of processed foods to the manufacture of automobiles, industrial processes often require rigorous pH control.
• *Municipal services:* Purification of drinking water and treatment of sewage must be carried out at their optimum pH.
• *Acid rain:* Nitric acid and sulfuric acid, resulting largely from reactions of components of vehicle emissions and electric power generation (nitrogen and sulfur oxides) with water, are carried down by precipitation and enter aquatic systems (lakes and streams), lowering the pH of the water. A less than optimum pH poses serious problems for native fish populations.

In summary, any change that takes place in aqueous solution generally has at least some pH dependence.

## 8.3    Reactions between Acids and Bases

### Neutralization

The reaction of an acid with a base to produce a salt and water is referred to as **neutralization.** In the strictest sense, neutralization requires equal numbers of moles (mol) of $H_3O^+$ and $OH^-$ to produce a neutral solution (no excess acid or base).

Consider the reaction of a solution of hydrochloric acid and sodium hydroxide:

$$\underset{\text{Acid}}{HCl(aq)} + \underset{\text{Base}}{NaOH(aq)} \longrightarrow \underset{\text{Salt}}{NaCl(aq)} + \underset{\text{Water}}{H_2O(l)}$$

Our objective is to make the balanced equation represent the process actually occurring. We recognize that HCl, NaOH, and NaCl are dissociated in solution:

$$H^+(aq) + Cl^-(aq) + Na^+(aq) + OH^-(aq) \longrightarrow Na^+(aq) + Cl^-(aq) + H_2O(l)$$

We also know that $Na^+$ and $Cl^-$ are unchanged in the reaction; they are termed *spectator ions.* If we write only those components that actually change, ignoring the spectator ions, we produce a *net ionic equation:*

$$H^+(aq) + OH^-(aq) \longrightarrow H_2O(l)$$

If we realize that the $H^+$ occurs in aqueous solution as the hydronium ion, $H_3O^+$, the most correct form of the net ionic equation is

$$H_3O^+(aq) + OH^-(aq) \longrightarrow 2H_2O(l)$$

The equation for any strong acid/strong base neutralization reaction is the same as this equation.

A neutralization reaction may be used to determine the concentration of an unknown acid or base solution. The technique of **titration** involves the addition of measured amounts of a **standard solution** (one whose concentration is known with certainty) to neutralize the second, unknown solution. From the volumes of the two solutions and the concentration of the standard solution, the concentration of the unknown solution may be determined.

A strategy for carrying out an acid-base titration is summarized in Table 8.1. The calculations involved in an acid-base titration are illustrated in Example 8.10.

### Polyprotic Substances

Not all acid-base reactions occur in a 1:1 combining ratio (as hydrochloric acid and sodium hydroxide in Example 8.10). Acid-base reactions with other than 1:1

## TABLE 8.1 Conducting an Acid-Base Titration

1. A known volume, perhaps 25.00 milliliters (mL), of the unknown acid of unknown concentration is measured into a flask using a pipet.

2. An **indicator,** a substance that changes color as the solution reaches a certain pH, is added to the unknown solution. We must know, from prior experience, the expected pH at the equivalence point (see step 4). For this titration, two indicators, phenol red or phenolphthalein, would be suitable choices.

3. A solution of sodium hydroxide, perhaps 0.1000 M, is carefully added to the unknown solution using a **buret** (Figure 8.6), which is a long glass tube calibrated in mL. A stopcock at the bottom of the buret regulates the amount of liquid dispensed. The standard solution is added until the indicator changes color.

4. At this point, the **equivalence point,** the number of mol of hydroxide ion added is equal to the number of mol of hydronium ion present in the unknown acid. The solution is neutral, with a pH equal to 7.

5. The volume dispensed by the buret, perhaps 35.00 mL, is measured.

6. Using the data from the experiment (volume of the unknown, volume of the titrant, and molarity of the titrant), the molar concentration of the unknown substance is calculated.

Phenol red, a commonly used indicator, is yellow in acid solution and turns red after all acid is neutralized. Phenolphthalein is colorless in acid solution and turns pink after all acid is neutralized. Phenolphthalein is often the indicator of choice because it is easier to discern a change of colorless to a color, rather than one color to another.

(a)                                (b)

**Figure 8.6** An acid-base titration. (a) An exact volume of a standard solution (in this example, a base) is added to a solution of unknown concentration (in this example, an acid). (b) From the volume (read from the buret) and concentration of the standard solution, coupled with the mass or volume of the unknown, the molar concentration of the unknown may be calculated.

---

**EXAMPLE 8.10**   ### Determining the Concentration of a Solution of Hydrochloric Acid

LEARNING GOAL

**9** Use titration data to determine the molar concentration of an unknown solution.

A 25.00-mL sample of a hydrochloric acid solution of unknown concentration was transferred to a flask. A few drops of the indicator phenolphthalein were added, and the resulting solution was titrated with 0.1000 $M$ sodium hydroxide solution. After 35.00 mL of sodium hydroxide solution were added, the indicator turned pink, signaling that the unknown and titrant had reached their equivalence point. Calculate the $M$ of the HCl solution.

*Continued…*

## Solution

**Step 1.** Pertinent information for this titration includes:

Volume of the unknown HCl solution, 25.00 mL

Volume of the NaOH solution added, 35.00 mL

Concentration of the NaOH solution, 0.1000 $M$

**Step 2.** From the balanced equation, we know that 1 mol of HCl will react with 1 mol of NaOH:

$$HCl(aq) + NaOH(aq) \longrightarrow NaCl(aq) + H_2O(l)$$

Note: The net ionic equation for this reaction provides the same information; 1 mol of $H_3O^+$ reacts with 1 mol of $OH^-$.

$$H_3O^+(aq) + OH^-(aq) \longrightarrow 2H_2O(l)$$

**Step 3.** The number of mol NaOH can be calculated from the volume of NaOH using conversion factors (1000 mL = 1 L and $M$ = mol/L):

$$35.00 \text{ mL NaOH} \times \frac{1 \text{ L NaOH}}{10^3 \text{ mL NaOH}} \times \frac{0.1000 \text{ mol NaOH}}{1 \text{ L NaOH}} = 3.500 \times 10^{-3} \text{ mol NaOH}$$

    Data Given       Conversion Factor   Conversion Factor      Relating Unit

**Step 4.** Knowing that HCl and NaOH undergo a 1:1 reaction, the number of mol HCl in the unknown solution can be calculated from the number of mol NaOH added.

$$3.500 \times 10^{-3} \text{ mol NaOH} \times \frac{1 \text{ mol HCl}}{1 \text{ mol NaOH}} = 3.500 \times 10^{-3} \text{ mol HCl}$$

      Relating Unit        Conversion Factor    Initial Data Result

**Step 5.** The concentration of HCl can be calculated from the number of mol HCl in 25.00 mL.

$$\frac{3.500 \times 10^{-3} \text{ mol HCl}}{25.00 \text{ mL HCl soln}} \times \frac{10^3 \text{ mL HCl soln}}{1 \text{ L HCl soln}} = 1.400 \times 10^{-1} \text{ mol HCl/L HCl soln} = 0.1400 \ M$$

   Initial Data Result     Conversion Factor          Desired Result

### Practice Problem 8.10

  a. Calculate the molar concentration of a sodium hydroxide solution if 40.00 mL of this solution were required to neutralize 20.00 mL of a 0.2000 M solution of hydrochloric acid.

  b. Calculate the molar concentration of a sodium hydroxide solution if 36.00 mL of this solution were required to neutralize 25.00 mL of a 0.2000 M solution of hydrochloric acid.

▶ For Further Practice: **Questions 8.87 and 8.88.**

combining ratios occur between what are termed *polyprotic substances*. **Polyprotic substances** donate (as acids) or accept (as bases) more than one proton per formula unit.

### Reactions of Polyprotic Substances

HCl dissociates to produce one $H^+$ ion for each HCl. For this reason, it is termed a *monoprotic acid*. Its reaction with sodium hydroxide is:

$$HCl(aq) + NaOH(aq) \longrightarrow H_2O(l) + Na^+(aq) + Cl^-(aq)$$

Sulfuric acid, in contrast, is a *diprotic acid*. Each unit of $H_2SO_4$ produces two $H^+$ ions (the prefix *di*- indicating two). Its reaction with sodium hydroxide is:

$$H_2SO_4(aq) + 2NaOH(aq) \longrightarrow 2H_2O(l) + 2Na^+(aq) + SO_4^{2-}(aq)$$

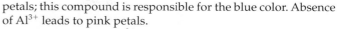

## Hydrangea, pH, and Soil Chemistry

It is difficult to pass a group of hydrangea in a park or garden without stopping, at least briefly, to take note of their beauty. Most are blue or pink; occasionally, one flower shows a mixture of two colors. They are usually the variety *Hydrangea macrophylla,* a plant native to Japan.

It was originally believed that the pink and blue-flowered plants were different species. It was subsequently determined that they were, in fact, the same species, and the color that developed was a function of the type of soil used. Shortly thereafter, soil pH was implicated; low pH favored blue coloration, and high pH favored pink. The mechanism was probably protonation and deprotonation of one or more molecules whose color depended on the extent of protonation.

We learned in Chapter 1 that theories are subject to further investigation and this investigation may lead to revised theories. This is certainly true with the hydrangea. Recent studies have shown that a compound containing $Al^{3+}$ must form in the petals; this compound is responsible for the blue color. Absence of $Al^{3+}$ leads to pink petals.

Where must the $Al^{3+}$ originate? Certainly, it must be found in the soil. Aluminum in soil is present as compounds, such as $Al_2O_3$ or $Al(OH)_3$. Aluminum compounds are notoriously insoluble in neutral or slightly basic soils, but their solubility increases markedly in acidic soils.

So, low pH indicates high acid concentration, increased solubility of aluminum-containing soil compounds, higher concentration of $Al^{3+}(aq)$ transported from the soil to the petals, and, as a final consequence, beautiful blue hydrangea.

### For Further Understanding

▶ Explain how a hydrangea can function as an indicator of soil pH.

▶ The petals of some hydrangea appear purple. Construct a possible explanation for this phenomenon.

Phosphoric acid is a *triprotic acid.* Each unit of $H_3PO_4$ produces three $H^+$ ions. Its reaction with sodium hydroxide is:

$$H_3PO_4(aq) + 3NaOH(aq) \longrightarrow 3H_2O(l) + 3Na^+(aq) + PO_4^{3-}(aq)$$

## Dissociation of Polyprotic Substances

Sulfuric acid, and other diprotic acids, dissociate in two steps:

**Step 1.** $H_2SO_4(aq) + H_2O(l) \longrightarrow H_3O^+(aq) + HSO_4^-(aq)$

**Step 2.** $HSO_4^-(aq) + H_2O(l) \rightleftharpoons H_3O^+(aq) + SO_4^{2-}(aq)$

Notice that $H_2SO_4$ behaves as a strong acid (step 1) and $HSO_4^-$ behaves as a weak acid, indicated by a double arrow (step 2).

Phosphoric acid dissociates in three steps, all forms behaving as weak acids.

**Step 1.** $H_3PO_4(aq) + H_2O(l) \rightleftharpoons H_3O^+(aq) + H_2PO_4^-(aq)$

**Step 2.** $H_2PO_4^+(aq) + H_2O(l) \rightleftharpoons H_3O^+(aq) + HPO_4^{2-}(aq)$

**Step 3.** $HPO_4^{2-}(aq) + H_2O(l) \rightleftharpoons H_3O^+(aq) + PO_4^{3-}(aq)$

Bases exhibit this property as well.

NaOH produces one $OH^-$ ion per formula unit:

$$NaOH(aq) \longrightarrow Na^+(aq) + OH^-(aq)$$

$Ba(OH)_2$, barium hydroxide, produces two $OH^-$ ions per formula unit:

$$Ba(OH)_2(aq) \longrightarrow Ba(OH)^+(aq) + OH^-(aq)$$

and

$$Ba(OH)^+(aq) \longrightarrow Ba^{2+}(aq) + OH^-(aq)$$

## 8.4   Acid-Base Buffers

A **buffer solution** contains components that enable the solution to resist large changes in pH when either acids or bases are added. Buffer solutions may be prepared in the laboratory to maintain optimum conditions for a chemical reaction. Buffers are routinely used in commercial products to maintain optimum conditions for product behavior.

Buffer solutions also occur naturally. Blood, for example, is a complex natural buffer solution maintaining a pH of approximately 7.4, optimum for oxygen transport. The major buffering agent in blood is the mixture of carbonic acid ($H_2CO_3$) and bicarbonate ions ($HCO_3^-$).

### The Buffer Process

The basis of buffer action is the establishment of an equilibrium between either a weak acid and its conjugate base or a weak base and its conjugate acid. Let's consider the case of a weak acid and its conjugate base.

A common buffer solution may be prepared from acetic acid ($CH_3COOH$) and sodium acetate ($CH_3COONa$). Sodium acetate is a salt that is the source of the conjugate base $CH_3COO^-$. An *equilibrium* is established in solution between the weak acid and the conjugate base.

$$\underset{\substack{\text{Acetic acid} \\ \text{(weak acid)}}}{CH_3COOH(aq)} + \underset{\text{Water}}{H_2O(l)} \rightleftharpoons \underset{\text{Hydronium ion}}{H_3O^+(aq)} + \underset{\substack{\text{Acetate ion} \\ \text{(conjugate base)}}}{CH_3COO^-(aq)}$$

A buffer solution functions in accordance with LeChatelier's principle, which states that an equilibrium system, when stressed, will shift its equilibrium position to relieve that stress. This principle is illustrated by the following examples.

### Addition of Base or Acid to a Buffer Solution

Addition of a basic substance to our buffer solution causes the following changes.

- $OH^-$ from the base reacts with $H_3O^+$, producing water.
- Molecular acetic acid *dissociates* to replace the $H_3O^+$ consumed by the base, maintaining the pH close to the initial level.

This is an example of LeChatelier's principle, because the loss of $H_3O^+$ (the *stress*) is compensated for by the dissociation of acetic acid to produce more $H_3O^+$.

Addition of an acidic solution to the buffer results in the following changes.

- $H_3O^+$ from the acid increases the overall $[H_3O^+]$.
- The system reacts to this stress, in accordance with LeChatelier's principle, to form more molecular acetic acid; the acetate ion combines with $H_3O^+$. Thus, the $H_3O^+$ concentration and the pH remain close to the initial level.

This follows LeChatelier's principle because the added $H_3O^+$ (the *stress*) is consumed by the acetate ion (conjugate base) to produce more undissociated acetic acid.

We ignore $Na^+$ in the description of the buffer. $Na^+$ does not actively participate in the reaction and is termed a *spectator ion*.

The acetate ion is the conjugate base of acetic acid.

*See Section 7.4 for a discussion of LeChatelier's principle.*

**LEARNING GOAL**

**11**   Describe the effects of adding acid or base to a buffer system.

These effects may be summarized as follows:

$$CH_3COOH(aq) + H_2O(l) \rightleftharpoons H_3O^+(aq) + CH_3COO^-(aq)$$

OH⁻ added, equilibrium position shifts to the right

H₃O⁺ added, equilibrium position shifts to the left

The weak acid is the key component in buffering against excess $OH^-$, and the salt of the weak acid (the conjugate base) is key to buffering against excess $H_3O^+$.

## Buffer Capacity

**Buffer capacity** is a measure of the ability of a solution to resist large changes in pH when a strong acid or strong base is added. More specifically, buffer capacity is described as the amount of strong acid or strong base that can be added to a buffer solution without significantly changing its pH. Buffering capacity against base is a function of the concentration of the weak acid (in this case, $CH_3COOH$). Buffering capacity against acid is dependent on the concentration of the anion of the salt, the conjugate base ($CH_3COO^-$ in this example). Buffer solutions are often designed to have an identical buffer capacity for both acids and bases. This is achieved when, in the above example, $[CH_3COO^-]/[CH_3COOH] = 1$. As an added bonus, making the $[CH_3COO^-]$ and $[CH_3COOH]$ as large as is practical ensures a high buffer capacity for both added acid and added base.

## Determining Buffer Solution pH

It is useful to understand how to determine the pH of a buffer solution. Many chemical reactions produce the largest amount of product only when they are run at an optimal, constant pH. The study of biologically important processes in the laboratory often requires conditions that approximate the composition of biological fluids. A constant pH would certainly be essential.

The buffer process is an equilibrium reaction and is described by an equilibrium constant expression. For acids, the equilibrium constant is represented as $K_a$ (the subscript $a$ implying an acid equilibrium). For example, the acetic acid/acetate ion system is described by

$$CH_3COOH(aq) + H_2O(l) \rightleftharpoons H_3O^+(aq) + CH_3COO^-(aq)$$

and

$$K_a = \frac{[H_3O^+][CH_3COO^-]}{[CH_3COOH]}$$

Using a few mathematical maneuvers, we can turn this equilibrium constant expression into one that will allow us to calculate the pH of the buffer if we know how much acid (acetic acid) and conjugate base (acetate ion) are present in a known volume of the solution.

First, multiply both sides of the equation by the concentration of acetic acid, $[CH_3COOH]$. This will eliminate the denominator on the right side of the equation.

$$[CH_3COOH]K_a = \frac{[H_3O^+][CH_3COO^-][CH_3COOH]}{[CH_3COOH]}$$

or

$$[CH_3COOH]K_a = [H_3O^+][CH_3COO^-]$$

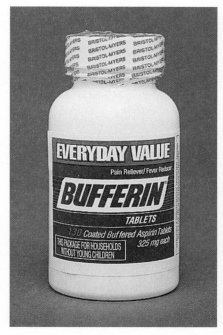

Some commercial products claim improved function owing to their ability to control pH. This product contains antacids (calcium carbonate and magnesium oxide) in addition to aspirin, an acid. Can you name other products whose performance is pH dependent?

**LEARNING GOAL**

**12** Calculate the pH of buffer solutions.

Now, dividing both sides of the equation by the acetate ion concentration $[CH_3COO^-]$ will give us an expression for the hydronium ion concentration $[H_3O^+]$:

$$\frac{[CH_3COOH]K_a}{[CH_3COO^-]} = [H_3O^+]$$

*The calculation of pH from $[H_3O^+]$ is discussed in Section 8.2.*

Once we know the value for $[H_3O^+]$, we can easily find the pH. To use this equation:

- assume that $[CH_3COOH]$ represents the concentration of the acid component of the buffer.
- assume that $[CH_3COO^-]$ represents the concentration of the conjugate base (principally from the dissociation of the salt, sodium acetate) component of the buffer.

$$\frac{[CH_3COOH]K_a}{[CH_3COO^-]} = [H_3O^+]$$

$$\frac{[acid]K_a}{[conjugate\ base]} = [H_3O^+]$$

Let's look at examples of practical applications of this equation.

---

**EXAMPLE 8.11**    **Calculating the pH of a Buffer Solution**

LEARNING GOAL

Calculate the pH of a buffer solution in which both the acetic acid and sodium acetate concentrations are $1.0 \times 10^{-1}\ M$. The equilibrium constant, $K_a$, for acetic acid is $1.8 \times 10^{-5}$.

**12**  Calculate the pH of buffer solutions.

**Solution**

**Step 1.**  Acetic acid is the acid; $[acid] = 1.0 \times 10^{-1}\ M$.
Sodium acetate is the salt, furnishing the conjugate base; $[conjugate\ base] = 1.0 \times 10^{-1}\ M$.

**Step 2.**  The equilibrium equation is

$$CH_3COOH(aq) + H_2O(l) \rightleftharpoons H_3O^+(aq) + CH_3COO^-(aq)$$
$$\text{Acid} \qquad\qquad\qquad\qquad\qquad \text{Conjugate base}$$

**Step 3.**  The hydronium ion concentration is expressed as

$$[H_3O^+] = \frac{[acid]K_a}{[conjugate\ base]}$$

**Step 4.**  Substituting the values given in the problem:

$$[H_3O^+] = \frac{(1.0 \times 10^{-1})(1.8 \times 10^{-5})}{1.0 \times 10^{-1}}$$
$$= 1.8 \times 10^{-5}$$

**Step 5.**  This hydronium ion concentration is substituted into the expression for pH:

$$pH = -\log[H_3O^+]$$
$$= -\log(1.8 \times 10^{-5})$$
$$= 4.74$$

The pH of the buffer solution is 4.74.

## Practice Problem 8.11

A buffer solution is prepared in such a way that the concentrations of propanoic acid and sodium propanoate are each $2.00 \times 10^{-1} M$. If the buffer equilibrium is described by

$$C_2H_5COOH(aq) + H_2O(l) \rightleftharpoons H_3O^+(aq) + C_2H_5COO^-(aq)$$

Propanoic acid                                    Propanoate anion

with $K_a = 1.34 \times 10^{-5}$, calculate the pH of the solution.

▶ For Further Practice: **Questions 8.101 and 8.102.**

---

**EXAMPLE 8.12** | **Calculating the pH of a Buffer Solution**

LEARNING GOAL

Calculate the pH of a buffer solution similar to that described in Example 8.11, except that the acid concentration is doubled, while the salt concentration remains the same.

**12** Calculate the pH of buffer solutions.

### Solution

**Step 1.** Acetic acid is the acid; [acid] = $2.0 \times 10^{-1} M$ (remember, the acid concentration is twice that of Example 8.11; $2 \times [1.0 \times 10^{-1}] = 2.0 \times 10^{-1} M$).

Sodium acetate is the salt, furnishing the conjugate base; [conjugate base] = $1.0 \times 10^{-1} M$.

$K_a$ for acetic acid is $1.8 \times 10^{-5}$.

**Step 2.** The equilibrium equation is

$$CH_3COOH(aq) + H_2O(l) \rightleftharpoons H_3O^+(aq) + CH_3COO^-(aq)$$

Acid                                    Conjugate base

**Step 3.** The hydronium ion concentration is expressed as,

$$[H_3O^+] = \frac{[acid]K_a}{[conjugate\ base]}$$

**Step 4.** Substituting the values from step 1:

$$[H_3O^+] = \frac{(2.0 \times 10^{-1})(1.8 \times 10^{-5})}{1.00 \times 10^{-1}}$$

$$= 3.60 \times 10^{-5}$$

**Step 5.** This hydronium ion concentration is substituted into the expression for pH:

$$pH = -\log [H_3O^+]$$

$$= -\log (3.60 \times 10^{-5})$$

$$= 4.44$$

The pH of the buffer solution is 4.44.

---

## Practice Problem 8.12

A buffer solution is prepared in such a way that the concentration of propanoic acid is $2.00 \times 10^{-1} M$ and the concentration of sodium propanoate is $4.00 \times 10^{-1} M$. If the buffer equilibrium is described by

$$C_2H_5COOH(aq) + H_2O(l) \rightleftharpoons H_3O^+(aq) + C_2H_5COO^-(aq)$$

Propanoic acid                                    Propanoate anion

with $K_a = 1.34 \times 10^{-5}$, calculate the pH of the solution.

▶ For Further Practice: **Questions 8.105 and 8.106.**

A comparison of the two solutions described in Examples 8.11 and 8.12 demonstrates a buffer solution's most significant attribute: the ability to stabilize pH. Although the acid concentration of these solutions differs by a factor of two, the difference in their pH is only 0.30 units.

### The Henderson-Hasselbalch Equation

**LEARNING GOAL**

**12**  Calculate the pH of buffer solutions.

The solution of the equilibrium constant expression and the pH are sometimes combined into one operation. The combined expression is termed the **Henderson-Hasselbalch equation.**

For the acetic acid/sodium acetate buffer system,

$$CH_3COOH(aq) + H_2O(l) \rightleftharpoons H_3O^+(aq) + CH_3COO^-(aq)$$

$$K_a = \frac{[H_3O^+][CH_3COO^-]}{[CH_3COOH]}$$

Taking the $-\log$ of both sides of the equation:

$$-\log K_a = -\log [H_3O^+] - \log \frac{[CH_3COO^-]}{[CH_3COOH]}$$

$$pK_a = pH - \log \frac{[CH_3COO^-]}{[CH_3COOH]}$$

---

$pK_a = -\log K_a$, which is analogous to $pH = -\log[H_3O^+]$.

---

the Henderson-Hasselbalch expression is:

$$pH = pK_a + \log \frac{[CH_3COO^-]}{[CH_3COOH]}$$

The form of this equation is especially amenable to buffer problem calculations. In this expression, $[CH_3COOH]$ represents the molar concentration of the weak acid and $[CH_3COO^-]$ is the molar concentration of the conjugate base of the weak acid. The generalized expression is:

$$pH = pK_a + \log \frac{[\text{conjugate base}]}{[\text{acid}]}$$

Substituting concentrations along with the value for the $pK_a$ of the acid allows the calculation of the pH of the buffer solution in problems such as those shown in Examples 8.11 and 8.12.

**Question 8.11**   Use the Henderson-Hasselbalch equation to calculate the pH of a buffer solution in which both the acetic acid and the sodium acetate concentrations are $1.0 \times 10^{-1}$ M. The equilibrium constant, $K_a$, for acetic acid is $1.8 \times 10^{-5}$.

**Question 8.12**   Use the Henderson-Hasselbalch equation to calculate the pH of a buffer solution in which the acetic acid concentration is $2.0 \times 10^{-1}$ M and the sodium acetate concentration is $1.0 \times 10^{-1}$ M. The equilibrium constant, $K_a$, for acetic acid is $1.8 \times 10^{-5}$.

**Question 8.13**   A buffer solution is prepared in such a way that the concentrations of propanoic acid and sodium propanoate are each $2.00 \times 10^{-1}$ M. If the buffer equilibrium is described by

$$C_2H_5COOH(aq) + H_2O(l) \rightleftharpoons H_3O^+(aq) + C_2H_5COO^-(aq)$$
Propanoic acid                                              Propanoate anion

$$K_a = 1.34 \times 10^{-5}$$

use the Henderson-Hasselbalch equation to calculate the pH of the solution.

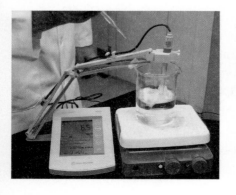

**Question 8.14** A buffer solution is prepared in such a way that the concentration of propanoic acid is $2.00 \times 10^{-1}$ M and the concentration of sodium propanoate is $4.00 \times 10^{-1}$ M. If the buffer equilibrium is described by

$$C_2H_5COOH(aq) + H_2O(l) \rightleftharpoons H_3O^+(aq) + C_2H_5COO^-(aq)$$

Propanoic acid                                                              Propanoate anion

$$K_a = 1.34 \times 10^{-5}$$

use the Henderson-Hasselbalch equation to calculate the pH of the solution.

## Control of Blood pH

A pH of 7.4 is maintained in blood partly by a carbonic acid–bicarbonate buffer system based on the following equilibrium:

$$H_2CO_3(aq) + H_2O(l) \rightleftharpoons H_3O^+(aq) + HCO_3^-(aq)$$

Carbonic acid                                              Bicarbonate ion
(weak acid)                                                 (conjugate base)

LEARNING GOAL

**13** Explain the role of buffers in the control of blood pH under various conditions.

The regulation process based on LeChatelier's principle is similar to the acetic acid–sodium acetate buffer equilibrium, which we have already discussed.

Red blood cells transport $O_2$, bound to hemoglobin, to the cells of body tissue. The metabolic waste product, $CO_2$, is picked up by the blood and delivered to the lungs.

The $CO_2$ in the blood also participates in the carbonic acid–bicarbonate buffer equilibrium. Carbon dioxide reacts with water in the blood to form carbonic acid:

$$CO_2(aq) + H_2O(l) \rightleftharpoons H_2CO_3(aq)$$

As a result, the buffer equilibrium becomes more complex:

$$CO_2(aq) + 2H_2O(l) \rightleftharpoons H_2CO_3(aq) + H_2O(l) \rightleftharpoons H_3O^+(aq) + HCO_3^-(aq)$$

Through this sequence of relationships, the concentration of $CO_2$ in the blood affects the blood pH.

Higher than normal $CO_2$ concentrations shift the above equilibrium to the right (LeChatelier's principle), increasing $[H_3O^+]$ and lowering the pH. The blood becomes too acidic, leading to numerous medical problems. A situation of high blood $CO_2$ levels and low pH is termed *acidosis*. Respiratory acidosis results from various diseases (emphysema, pneumonia) that restrict the breathing process, causing the buildup of waste $CO_2$ in the blood.

Lower than normal $CO_2$ levels, on the other hand, shift the equilibrium to the left, decreasing $[H_3O^+]$ and making the pH more basic. This condition is termed *alkalosis* (from "alkali," implying basic). Hyperventilation, or rapid breathing, is a common cause of respiratory alkalosis.

**Question 8.15** Explain how the molar concentration of $H_2CO_3$ in the blood would change if the partial pressure of $CO_2$ in the lungs were to increase.

**Question 8.16** Explain how the molar concentration of $H_2CO_3$ in the blood would change if the partial pressure of $CO_2$ in the lungs were to decrease.

**Question 8.17** Explain how the molar concentration of hydronium ions in the blood would change under each of the conditions described in Questions 8.15 and 8.16.

**Question 8.18** Explain how the pH of blood would change under each of the conditions described in Questions 8.15 and 8.16.

**Question 8.19** Write the Henderson-Hasselbalch expression for the equilibrium between carbonic acid and the bicarbonate ion.

**Question 8.20** Calculate the $[HCO_3^-]/[H_2CO_3]$ that corresponds to a pH of 7.4. The $K_a$ for carbonic acid is $4.2 \times 10^{-7}$.

# Green Chemistry

## Acid Rain

Acid rain is a global environmental problem, caused by our industrial society, that has raised public awareness of the chemicals polluting the air. Normal rain has a pH of about 5.6 as a result of the chemical reaction between carbon dioxide gas and water in the atmosphere. The following equation shows this reaction:

$$CO_2(g) \; + \; H_2O(l) \rightleftharpoons H_2CO_3(aq)$$
$$\text{Carbon dioxide} \quad \text{Water} \quad \text{Carbonic acid}$$

Acid rain refers to conditions that are much more acidic than this. In upstate New York, the rain has as much as twenty-five times the acidity of normal rainfall. One rainstorm, recorded in West Virginia, produced rainfall that measured 1.5 on the pH scale. This is approximately the pH of stomach acid or about ten thousand times more acidic than "normal rain" (remember that the pH scale is logarithmic; a 1 pH unit decrease represents a tenfold increase in hydronium ion concentration).

Acid rain is destroying life in streams and lakes. More than half the highland lakes in the western Adirondack Mountains now have no native game fish. In addition to these 300 lakes, 140 lakes in Ontario have suffered a similar fate. It is estimated that 48,000 other lakes in Ontario and countless others in the northeastern and central United States are threatened. Our forests are endangered as well. The acid rain decreases soil pH, which in turn alters the solubility of minerals needed by plants. Studies have shown that about 40% of the red spruce and maple trees in New England have died. Increased acidity of rainfall appears to be the major culprit.

What is the cause of this acid rain? The combustion of fossil fuels (gas, oil, and coal) by power plants produces oxides of sulfur and nitrogen. Nitrogen oxides, in excess of normal levels, arise mainly from conversion of atmospheric nitrogen to nitrogen oxides in the engines of gasoline and diesel-powered vehicles. Sulfur oxides result from the oxidation of sulfur in fossil fuels. The sulfur atoms were originally a part of the amino acids and proteins of plants and animals that became, over the millennia, our fuel. These react with water, as does the $CO_2$ in normal rain, but the products are strong acids: sulfuric and nitric acids. Let's look at the equations for these processes.

In the atmosphere, nitric oxide (NO) can react with oxygen to produce nitrogen dioxide as shown:

$$2NO(g) + O_2(g) \longrightarrow 2NO_2(g)$$
$$\text{Nitric oxide} \quad \text{Oxygen} \quad \text{Nitrogen dioxide}$$

Nitrogen dioxide (which causes the brown color of smog) then reacts with water to form nitric acid:

$$3NO_2(g) + H_2O(l) \longrightarrow 2HNO_3(aq) + NO(g)$$

A similar chemistry is seen with the sulfur oxides. Coal may contain as much as 3% sulfur. When the coal is burned, the sulfur also burns. This produces choking, acrid sulfur dioxide gas:

$$S(s) + O_2(g) \longrightarrow SO_2(g)$$

By itself, sulfur dioxide can cause serious respiratory problems for people with asthma or other lung diseases, but matters are worsened by the reaction of $SO_2$ with atmospheric oxygen:

$$2SO_2(g) + O_2(g) \longrightarrow 2SO_3(g)$$

Sulfur trioxide will react with water in the atmosphere:

$$SO_3(g) + H_2O(l) \longrightarrow H_2SO_4(aq)$$

The product, sulfuric acid, is even more irritating to the respiratory tract. When the acid rain created by the reactions shown above falls to earth, the biological impact is significant, as we have already noted.

It is easy to balance these chemical equations, but decades could be required to balance the ecological systems that we have disrupted by our massive consumption of fossil fuels. A sudden decrease of even 25% in the use of fossil fuels would lead to worldwide financial chaos. Development of alternative fuel sources, such as solar energy and safe nuclear power, are helping to reduce our dependence on fossil fuels and helping us to balance the global equation.

### For Further Understanding

▶ Criticize this statement: "Passing and enforcing strong legislation against sulfur and nitrogen oxide emission will solve the problem of acid rain in the United States."

▶ Use the Internet to determine the percentage of electricity that is produced from coal in your state of residence.

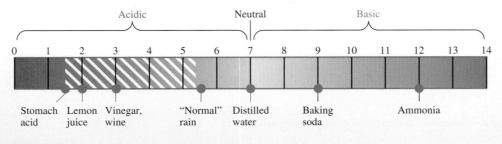

**pH Values for a Variety of Substances Compared with the pH of Acid Rain**

Acidic — Neutral — Basic

0 1 2 3 4 5 6 7 8 9 10 11 12 13 14

Stomach acid — Lemon juice — Vinegar, wine — "Normal" rain — Distilled water — Baking soda — Ammonia

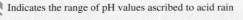 Indicates the range of pH values ascribed to acid rain

Damage caused by acid rain.

# CHAPTER MAP

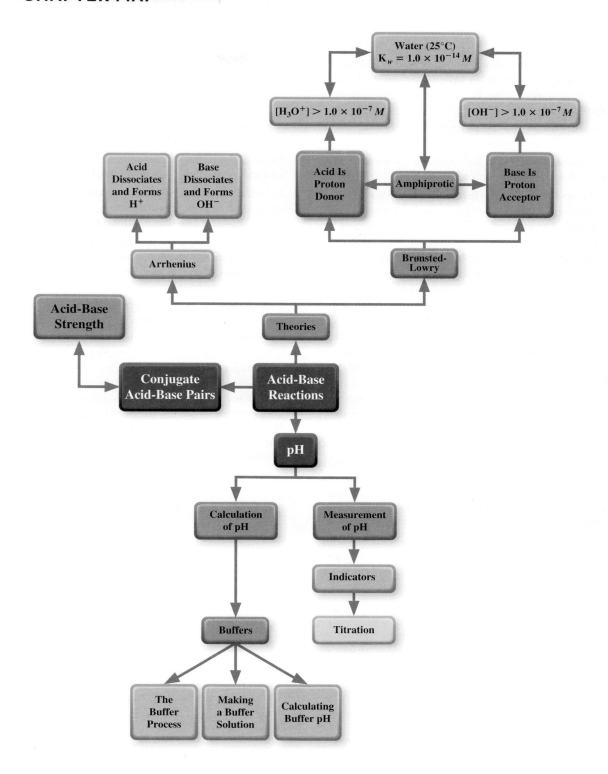

# SUMMARY

## 8.1 Acids and Bases

▶ One of the earliest definitions of acids and bases is the **Arrhenius theory.** According to this theory, an acid dissociates to form hydrogen ions, **H⁺**, and a base dissociates to form hydroxide ions, **OH⁻**.

▶ The **Brønsted-Lowry theory** defines an acid as a proton (H⁺) donor and a base as a proton acceptor.

▶ Water, the solvent in many acid-base reactions, is **amphiprotic.** It has both acid and base properties.

▶ A **conjugate acid** is the species formed when a base accepts a proton. A **conjugate base** is the species formed when an acid donates a proton. The acid and base on the opposite sides of the equation are collectively termed a **conjugate acid-base pair.**

▶ The strength of acids and bases in water depends on their degree of dissociation, the extent to which they react with the solvent, water. Acids and bases are strong when their reaction with water is virtually 100% complete and are weak when their reaction with water is much less than 100% complete.

▶ Weak acids and weak bases dissolve in water principally in the molecular form. Only a small percentage of the molecules dissociate to form the **hydronium ion ($H_3O^+$)** or hydroxide ion ($OH^-$).

▶ Aqueous solutions of acids and bases are electrolytes. The dissociation of the acid or base produces ions, which conduct an electrical current. Strong acids and bases are strong electrolytes. Weak acids and bases are weak electrolytes.

▶ Although pure water is virtually 100% molecular, a small number of water molecules do ionize. This process occurs by the transfer of a proton from one water molecule to another, producing a *hydronium ion* and a *hydroxide ion*. This process is the **self-ionization** of water.

▶ Pure water at 25°C has a hydronium ion concentration of $1.0 \times 10^{-7}\ M$. The hydroxide ion concentration is also $1.0 \times 10^{-7}\ M$. The product of hydronium and hydroxide ion concentration ($1.0 \times 10^{-14}\ M$) is the **ion product for water,** $K_w$.

## 8.2 pH: A Measurement Scale for Acids and Bases

▶ The **pH scale** correlates the hydronium ion concentration with a number, the pH, that serves as a useful indicator of the degree of acidity or basicity of a solution. The pH of a solution is defined as the negative logarithm of the molar concentration of the hydronium ion (pH $= -\log[H_3O^+]$).

## 8.3 Reactions between Acids and Bases

▶ The reaction of an acid with a base to produce a salt and water is referred to as **neutralization.**

▶ Neutralization requires equal numbers of mol of $H_3O^+$ and $OH^-$ to produce a neutral solution (no excess acid or base).

▶ A neutralization reaction may be used to determine the concentration of an unknown acid or base solution. The technique of **titration** involves the addition of measured amounts of a **standard solution** (one whose concentration is known) from a **buret** to neutralize the second, unknown solution. The **equivalence point** is signaled by an **indicator.** This signal is termed the *end point.*

▶ **Polyprotic substances** donate (as acids) or accept (as bases) more than one proton per formula unit.

## 8.4 Acid-Base Buffers

▶ A **buffer solution** contains components that enable the solution to resist large changes in pH when acids or bases are added.

▶ Buffer action relies on the equilibrium between either a weak acid and its conjugate base or a weak base and its conjugate acid.

▶ A buffer solution follows LeChatelier's principle, which states that an equilibrium system, when stressed, will shift its equilibrium position to alleviate that stress.

▶ Buffering against base is a function of the concentration of the weak acid for an acidic buffer, whereas buffering against acid is dependent on the concentration of the anion of the salt (conjugate base).

▶ **Buffer capacity** is a measure of the ability of a solution to resist large changes in pH when a strong acid or strong base is added.

▶ A buffer solution can be described by an equilibrium constant expression. The equilibrium constant expression for an acidic system can be rearranged and solved for $[H_3O^+]$. In that way, the pH of a buffer solution can be obtained, if the composition of the solution is known. Alternatively, the **Henderson-Hasselbalch equation,** derived from the equilibrium constant expression, may be used to calculate the pH of a buffer solution.

# ANSWERS TO PRACTICE PROBLEMS

8.1   Brønsted-Lowry base with water.

$$CH_3COO^- + H_2O \rightleftharpoons CH_3COOH + OH^-$$

8.2   **a.** Conjugate base:      $OH^-$    and   $NH_3$
                                  $HSO_4^-$   and   $HSO_3^-$
      Stronger acid of each pair: $NH_4^+$ and $H_2SO_4$

      **b.** Conjugate acid:      $HCO_3^-$   and   $HPO_4^{2-}$
                                  $H_2CO_3$   and   $H_2PO_4^-$
      Stronger base of each pair: $PO_4^{3-}$ and $HPO_4^{2-}$

8.3   $3.3 \times 10^{-8}\ M$

8.4   pH $= 4.00$

8.5   $[H_3O^+] = 1.0 \times 10^{-5}\ M$

8.6   **a.** pH $= 12.00$
      **b.** pH $= 8.00$

**8.7**  $[H_3O^+] = 1.0 \times 10^{-8}\,M$
$[OH^-] = 1.0 \times 10^{-6}\,M$

**8.8**  pH = 7.48

**8.9**  **a.** $[H_3O^+] = 3.2 \times 10^{-9}\,M$
**b.** $[H_3O^+] = 3.2 \times 10^{-5}\,M$

**8.10**  **a.** $0.1000\,M$
**b.** $0.1389\,M$

**8.11**  pH = 4.87

**8.12**  pH = 5.17

# QUESTIONS AND PROBLEMS

## Acids and Bases

### Foundations

**8.21**  **a.** Define an acid according to the Arrhenius theory.
**b.** Define an acid according to the Brønsted-Lowry theory.

**8.22**  **a.** Define a base according to the Arrhenius theory.
**b.** Define a base according to the Brønsted-Lowry theory.

**8.23**  What are the essential differences between the Arrhenius and Brønsted-Lowry theories?

**8.24**  Why is ammonia described as a Brønsted-Lowry base and not an Arrhenius base?

**8.25**  Classify each of the following as either a Brønsted-Lowry acid, base, or as amphiprotic.
**a.** $H_3O^+$     **b.** $OH^-$     **c.** $H_2O$

**8.26**  Classify each of the following as either a Brønsted-Lowry acid, base, or as amphiprotic.
**a.** $NH_4^+$     **b.** $NH_3$     **c.** $CH_3CH_2CH_2NH_3^+$

**8.27**  Classify each of the following as either a Brønsted-Lowry acid, base, or as amphiprotic.
**a.** $HOCOOH$   **b.** $HCO_3^-$     **c.** $CO_3^{2-}$

**8.28**  Classify each of the following as either a Brønsted-Lowry acid, base, or as amphiprotic.
**a.** $H_2SO_4$     **b.** $HSO_4^-$     **c.** $SO_4^{2-}$

### Applications

**8.29**  Write an equation for the reaction of each of the following with water:
**a.** $HNO_2$     **b.** $HCN$     **c.** $CH_3CH_2CH_2COO^-$

**8.30**  Write an equation for the reaction of each of the following with water:
**a.** $HNO_3$     **b.** $HCOOH$     **c.** $CH_3CH_2CH_2NH_2$

**8.31**  Write the formula of the conjugate acid of $CN^-$.

**8.32**  Write the formula of the conjugate acid of $Br^-$.

**8.33**  Write the formula of the conjugate base of $HI$.

**8.34**  Write the formula of the conjugate base of $HCOOH$.

**8.35**  Write the formula of the conjugate acid of $NO_3^-$.

**8.36**  Write the formula of the conjugate acid of $F^-$.

If necessary, consult Figure 8.3 when solving Questions 8.37–8.40.

**8.37**  Which is the stronger base, $NO_3^-$ or $CN^-$?

**8.38**  Which is the stronger acid, $HNO_3$ or $HCN$?

**8.39**  Which is the stronger acid, HF or $CH_3COOH$?

**8.40**  Which is the stronger base, $F^-$ or $CH_3COO^-$?

**8.41**  Identify the conjugate acid-base pairs in each of the following chemical equations:
**a.** $NH_4^+(aq) + CN^-(aq) \rightleftharpoons NH_3(aq) + HCN(aq)$
**b.** $CO_3^{2-}(aq) + HCl(aq) \rightleftharpoons HCO_3^-(aq) + Cl^-(aq)$

**8.42**  Identify the conjugate acid-base pairs in each of the following chemical equations:
**a.** $HCOOH(aq) + NH_3(aq) \rightleftharpoons HCOO^-(aq) + NH_4^+(aq)$
**b.** $HCl(aq) + OH^-(aq) \rightleftharpoons H_2O(l) + Cl^-(aq)$

**8.43**  Distinguish between the terms acid-base *strength* and acid-base *concentration*.

**8.44**  Of the following diagrams, which one represents:
**a.** a concentrated strong acid
**b.** a dilute strong acid
**c.** a concentrated weak acid
**d.** a dilute weak acid

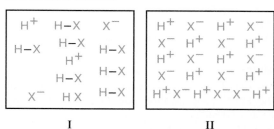

I                    II

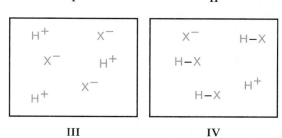

III                    IV

**8.45**  Label each of the following as a strong or weak acid:
**a.** $H_2SO_3$     **b.** $H_2CO_3$     **c.** $H_3PO_4$

**8.46**  Label each of the following as a strong or weak base:
**a.** $KOH$     **b.** $CN^-$     **c.** $SO_4^{2-}$

**8.47**  Calculate the $[H_3O^+]$ of an aqueous solution that is:
**a.** $1.0 \times 10^{-7}\,M$ in $OH^-$     **b.** $1.0 \times 10^{-3}\,M$ in $OH^-$

**8.48**  Calculate the $[H_3O^+]$ of an aqueous solution that is:
**a.** $1.0 \times 10^{-9}\,M$ in $OH^-$     **b.** $1.0 \times 10^{-5}\,M$ in $OH^-$

**8.49**  Calculate the $[OH^-]$ of an aqueous solution that is:
**a.** $1.0 \times 10^{-4}\,M$ in $H_3O^+$     **b.** $1.0 \times 10^{-2}\,M$ in $H_3O^+$

**8.50**  Calculate the $[OH^-]$ of an aqueous solution that is:
**a.** $1.0 \times 10^{-6}\,M$ in $H_3O^+$     **b.** $1.0 \times 10^{-8}\,M$ in $H_3O^+$

**8.51**  The concentration of hydronium ions in a sample of pomegranate juice is $6.0 \times 10^{-4}\,M$. What is the concentration of hydroxide ions in the juice sample?

**8.52**  What is the concentration of hydronium ions in an aqueous solution of acetaminophen if the concentration of hydroxide ions is $2.5 \times 10^{-9}\,M$?

## pH: A Measurement Scale for Acids and Bases

### Foundations

**8.53**  Consider two beakers, one containing 0.10 $M$ HCl and the other, 0.10 $M$ $CH_3COOH$. Which solution has the greater pH? Why?

**8.54** Consider two beakers, one containing 0.10 $M$ NaOH and the other, 0.10 $M$ NH$_3$. Which solution has the greater pH? Why?

**8.55** Calculate the pH of a solution that is:
a. $1.0 \times 10^{-2}$ $M$ in HCl    b. $1.0 \times 10^{-4}$ $M$ in HNO$_3$

**8.56** Calculate the pH of a solution that is:
a. $1.0 \times 10^{-1}$ $M$ in HCl    b. $1.0 \times 10^{-5}$ $M$ in HNO$_3$

**8.57** Calculate [H$_3$O$^+$] for a solution of nitric acid for which:
a. pH = 1.00    b. pH = 5.00

**8.58** Calculate [H$_3$O$^+$] for a solution of hydrochloric acid for which:
a. pH = 2.00    b. pH = 3.00

**8.59** Calculate the pH of a $1.0 \times 10^{-3}$ $M$ solution of KOH.

**8.60** Calculate the pH of a $1.0 \times 10^{-5}$ $M$ solution of NaOH.

**8.61** Calculate *both* [H$_3$O$^+$] and [OH$^-$] for a solution for which:
a. pH = 1.30    b. pH = 9.70

**8.62** Calculate *both* [H$_3$O$^+$] and [OH$^-$] for a solution for which:
a. pH = 5.50    b. pH = 7.00

**8.63** What is a neutralization reaction?

**8.64** Describe the purpose of a titration.

## Applications

**8.65** The pH of urine may vary between 4.5 and 8.2. Determine the H$_3$O$^+$ concentration and OH$^-$ concentration if the measured pH is:
a. 6.00    b. 5.20    c. 7.80

**8.66** The hydronium ion concentration in the blood of three different patients was:

| Patient | [H$_3$O$^+$] |
|---------|--------------|
| A | $5.0 \times 10^{-8}$ |
| B | $3.1 \times 10^{-8}$ |
| C | $3.2 \times 10^{-8}$ |

What is the pH of each patient's blood? If the normal range is 7.30–7.50, which, if any, of these patients has an abnormal blood pH?

**8.67** Criticize the following statement: A lakewater sample of pH = 3.0 is twice as acidic as a lakewater sample of pH = 6.0.

**8.68** Can a dilute solution of a strong acid ever have a higher pH than a more concentrated solution of a weak acid? Why or why not?

**8.69** What is the H$_3$O$^+$ concentration of a solution with a pH of:
a. 5.00    b. 12.00    c. 5.50

**8.70** What is the H$_3$O$^+$ concentration of a solution with a pH of:
a. 6.80    b. 4.60    c. 2.70

**8.71** Calculate the pH of a solution with a H$_3$O$^+$ concentration of:
a. $1.0 \times 10^{-6}$ $M$    b. $1.0 \times 10^{-8}$ $M$    c. $5.6 \times 10^{-4}$ $M$

**8.72** What is the OH$^-$ concentration of each solution in Question 8.71?

**8.73** Calculate the pH of a solution that has [H$_3$O$^+$] = $7.5 \times 10^{-4}$ $M$.

**8.74** Calculate the pH of a solution that has [H$_3$O$^+$] = $6.6 \times 10^{-5}$ $M$.

**8.75** Calculate the pH of a solution that has [OH$^-$] = $5.5 \times 10^{-4}$ $M$.

**8.76** Calculate the pH of a solution that has [OH$^-$] = $6.7 \times 10^{-9}$ $M$.

## Reactions between Acids and Bases

### Foundations

**8.77** In a neutralization reaction, how many mol of HCl are needed to react with 4 mol of NaOH?

**8.78** In a neutralization reaction, how many mol of NaOH are needed to react with 3 mol of HCl?

**8.79** What function does an indicator perform?

**8.80** What are the products of a neutralization reaction?

**8.81** Write an equation to represent the neutralization of an aqueous solution of HNO$_3$ with an aqueous solution of NaOH.

**8.82** Write an equation to represent the neutralization of an aqueous solution of HCl with an aqueous solution of KOH.

**8.83** Rewrite the equation in Question 8.81 as a net, balanced ionic equation.

**8.84** Rewrite the equation in Question 8.82 as a net, balanced ionic equation.

**8.85** Carbonic acid, H$_2$CO$_3$, is a polyprotic acid. How many protons can it donate?

**8.86** Chromic acid, H$_2$CrO$_4$, is a polyprotic acid. How many protons can it donate?

## Applications

**8.87** Titration of 15.00 mL of HCl solution requires 22.50 mL of 0.1200 $M$ NaOH solution. What is the molarity of the HCl solution?

**8.88** Titration of 17.85 mL of HNO$_3$ solution requires 16.00 mL of 0.1600 $M$ KOH solution. What is the molarity of the HNO$_3$ solution?

**8.89** What volume of 0.1500 $M$ NaOH is required to titrate 20.00 mL of 0.1000 $M$ HCl?

**8.90** What volume of 0.2000 $M$ KOH is required to titrate 25.00 mL of 0.1500 $M$ HNO$_3$?

**8.91** Write out each step of the dissociation of carbonic acid, H$_2$CO$_3$.

**8.92** Write out each step of the dissociation of chromic acid, H$_2$CrO$_4$.

## Acid-Base Buffers

### Foundations

**8.93** Which of the following are capable of forming a buffer solution?
a. NH$_3$ and NH$_4$Cl    b. HNO$_3$ and KNO$_3$

**8.94** Which of the following are capable of forming a buffer solution?
a. HBr and MgCl$_2$    b. H$_2$CO$_3$ and NaHCO$_3$

**8.95** Consider two beakers, one containing a mixture of HCl and NaCl (each solute is 0.10 $M$) and the other containing a mixture of CH$_3$COOH and CH$_3$COONa (each solute is also 0.10 $M$). If we add 0.10 $M$ NaOH (10.0 mL) to each beaker, which solution will have the greater change in pH? Why?

**8.96** Consider two beakers, one containing a mixture of NaOH and NaCl (each solute is 0.10 $M$) and the other containing a mixture of NH$_3$ and NH$_4$Cl (each solute is also 0.10 $M$). If we add 0.10 $M$ HNO$_3$ (10.0 mL) to each beaker, which solution will have the greater change in pH? Why?

**8.97** Explain how the molar concentration of carbonic acid in the blood would be changed during a situation of acidosis.

**8.98** Explain how the molar concentration of carbonic acid in the blood would be changed during a situation of alkalosis.

## Applications

**8.99**   For the equilibrium situation involving acetic acid, $CH_3COOH(aq) + H_2O(l) \rightleftharpoons CH_3COO^-(aq) + H_3O^+(aq)$, explain the equilibrium shift occurring for the following changes:

    **a.** A strong acid is added to the solution.

    **b.** The solution is diluted with water.

**8.100**   For the equilibrium situation involving acetic acid, $CH_3COOH(aq) + H_2O(l) \rightleftharpoons CH_3COO^-(aq) + H_3O^+(aq)$, explain the equilibrium shift occurring for the following changes:

    **a.** A strong base is added to the solution.

    **b.** More acetic acid is added to the solution.

**8.101**   What is $[H_3O^+]$ for a buffer solution that is 0.200 $M$ in acid and 0.500 $M$ in the corresponding salt if the weak acid $K_a = 5.80 \times 10^{-7}$?

**8.102**   What is the pH of the solution described in Question 8.101?

**8.103**   For the buffer system described in Question 8.99, which substance is responsible for buffering capacity against added hydrochloric acid? Explain.

**8.104**   For the buffer system described in Question 8.99, which substance is responsible for buffering capacity against added sodium hydroxide? Explain.

**8.105**   Calculate the pH of a buffer system containing 1.0 $M$ $CH_3COOH$ and 1.0 $M$ $CH_3COONa$. ($K_a$ of acetic acid, $CH_3COOH$, is $1.8 \times 10^{-5}$.)

**8.106**   Calculate the pH of a buffer system containing 1.0 $M$ $NH_3$ and 1.0 $M$ $NH_4Cl$. ($K_a$ of $NH_4^+$, the acid in this system, is $5.6 \times 10^{-10}$.)

**8.107**   The pH of blood plasma is 7.40. The principal buffer system is $HCO_3^-/H_2CO_3$. Calculate the ratio $[HCO_3^-]/[H_2CO_3]$ in blood plasma. ($K_a$ of $H_2CO_3$, carbonic acid, is $4.5 \times 10^{-7}$.)

**8.108**   The pH of blood plasma from a patient was found to be 7.6, a life-threatening situation. Calculate the ratio $[HCO_3^-]/[H_2CO_3]$ in this sample of blood plasma. ($K_a$ of $H_2CO_3$, carbonic acid, is $4.5 \times 10^{-7}$.)

# CHALLENGE PROBLEMS

1.   Acid rain is a threat to our environment because it can increase the concentration of toxic metal ions, such as $Cd^{2+}$ and $Cr^{3+}$, in rivers and streams. If cadmium and chromium are present in sediment as $Cd(OH)_2$ and $Cr(OH)_3$, write reactions that demonstrate the effect of acid rain. Use the Internet to find the properties of cadmium and chromium responsible for their environmental impact.

2.   Aluminum carbonate is soluble in acidic solution, forming aluminum cations. Write a reaction (or series of reactions) that explains this observation.

3.   Carbon dioxide reacts with the hydroxide ion to produce the bicarbonate anion. Write the Lewis structure for each reactant and product. Label each as a Brønsted acid or base. Explain the reaction using the Brønsted theory. Why would the Arrhenius theory provide an inadequate description of this reaction?

4.   Maalox is an antacid composed of $Mg(OH)_2$ and $Al(OH)_3$. Explain the origin of the trade name Maalox. Write chemical reactions that demonstrate the antacid activity of Maalox.

5.   Acid rain has been described as a regional problem, whereas the greenhouse effect is a global problem. Do you agree with this statement? Why or why not?

# 9

# The Nucleus, Radioactivity, and Nuclear Medicine

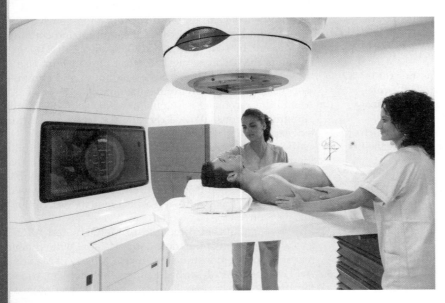

Nuclear technology has revolutionized the practice of medicine.

## OUTLINE

## LEARNING GOALS

1 Use nuclear symbols to represent isotopes and nuclides.

2 Enumerate characteristics of alpha, beta, positron, and gamma radiation.

3 Write balanced equations for nuclear processes.

4 Calculate the amount of radioactive substance remaining after a specified time has elapsed.

5 Explain the process of radiocarbon dating.

6 Describe how nuclear energy can generate electricity: fission, fusion, and the breeder reactor.

7 Cite examples of the use of radioactive isotopes in medicine.

8 Describe the use of ionizing radiation in cancer therapy.

9 Discuss the preparation and use of radioisotopes in diagnostic imaging studies.

10 Explain the difference between natural and artificial radioactivity.

11 Describe characteristics of radioactive materials that relate to radiation exposure and safety.

12 Be familiar with common techniques for the detection of radioactivity.

13 Interpret common units of radiation intensity and discuss their biological implications.

# INTRODUCTION

Our discussion of the atom and atomic structure in Chapter 2 revealed a nucleus containing protons and neutrons surrounded by electrons. Until now, we have treated the nucleus as simply a region of positive charge in the center of the atom. The focus of our interest has been the electrons and their arrangement around the nucleus. Electron arrangement is an essential part of a discussion of bonding or chemical change.

In this chapter, we consider the nucleus and nuclear properties. The behavior of nuclei may have as great an effect on our everyday lives as any of the thousands of synthetic compounds developed over the past several decades. Examples of nuclear technology range from everyday items (smoke detectors) to sophisticated instruments for medical diagnosis and treatment and electric power generation (nuclear power plants).

Beginning in 1896 with Becquerel's discovery of radiation emitted from uranium ore, the technology arising from this and related findings has produced both risks and benefits. Although early discoveries of radioactivity and its properties expanded our fundamental knowledge and brought fame to the investigators, it was not accomplished without a price. Several early investigators died prematurely of cancer and other diseases caused by the radiation they studied.

Even today, the existence of nuclear energy and its associated technology is a mixed blessing. On one side, the horrors of Nagasaki and Hiroshima, the fear of nuclear war, and potential contamination of populated areas resulting from the peaceful application of nuclear energy are critical problems facing society. Conversely, hundreds of thousands of lives have been saved because of the early detection of disease such as cancer by diagnosis based on the interaction of radiation and the body. The use of techniques such as cobalt-60 therapy is considered a routine part of comprehensive treatment for a variety of tumors. Furthermore, nuclear energy is an alternative energy source, providing an opportunity for us to compensate for the depletion of nonrenewable oil reserves.

High energy radiation is used to target cancer cells.

## 9.1   Natural Radioactivity

**Radioactivity** is the process by which some atoms emit energy and particles. The energy and particles are termed *radiation*. Nuclear radiation occurs as a result of an alteration in nuclear composition or structure. This process occurs in a nucleus that is unstable and hence radioactive. Radioactivity is a nuclear event: *matter and energy released during this process come from the nucleus.*

We shall designate the nucleus using *nuclear symbols*, analogous to the *atomic symbols* that were discussed in Chapter 2. The nuclear symbols consist of the *symbol* of the element, the *atomic number* (the number of protons in the nucleus), and the *mass number*, which is defined as the sum of neutrons and protons in the nucleus.

With the use of nuclear symbols, the fluorine nucleus is represented as

$$\text{Mass number} \longrightarrow {}^{19}_{9}\text{F} \longleftarrow \text{Element symbol}$$
$$\text{Atomic number} \longrightarrow$$
$$\text{(or nuclear charge)}$$

This symbol is equivalent to writing fluorine-19. This alternative representation is frequently used to denote specific isotopes of elements.

Not all nuclei are unstable. Only unstable nuclei undergo change and produce radioactivity, the process of *radioactive decay*. Recall that *isotopes* can exist when atoms of the same element have different masses. One isotope of an element may be radioactive, whereas others of the same element may be quite stable. It is important to distinguish between the terms *isotope* and *nuclide*. The term *isotope* refers to any atoms that have the same atomic number but different mass

Be careful not to confuse the mass number (a simple count of the neutrons and protons) with the atomic mass, which includes the contribution of electrons and is a true *mass* figure.

### LEARNING GOAL

**1**   Use nuclear symbols to represent isotopes and nuclides.

*Isotopes are introduced in Section 2.1.*

**Figure 9.1** Three isotopes of carbon. Each nucleus contains the same number of protons (depicted in blue). Only the number of neutrons (depicted in red) is different; hence, each isotope has a different mass.

Carbon-12 has
six protons and
six neutrons

Carbon-13 has
six protons and
seven neutrons

Carbon-14 has
six protons and
eight neutrons

numbers. The term **nuclide** refers to any atom characterized by an atomic number and a mass number.

Many elements in the periodic table occur in nature as mixtures of isotopes. Two common examples include carbon (Figure 9.1),

$$^{12}_{6}\text{C} \qquad ^{13}_{6}\text{C} \qquad ^{14}_{6}\text{C}$$

Carbon-12       Carbon-13       Carbon-14

and hydrogen,

$$^{1}_{1}\text{H} \qquad ^{2}_{1}\text{H} \qquad ^{3}_{1}\text{H}$$

Hydrogen-1       Hydrogen-2       Hydrogen-3
Protium          Deuterium        Tritium

Carbon has three isotopes, three distinct nuclides, C-12, C-13, and C-14.

Hydrogen has three isotopes, three distinct nuclides, H-1, H-2, and H-3.

Protium is a stable isotope and makes up more than 99.9% of naturally occurring hydrogen. Deuterium (D) can be isolated from hydrogen; it can form compounds such as "heavy water," $D_2O$. Tritium (T) is rare and unstable, and hence radioactive.

In writing the symbols for a nuclear process, it is essential to indicate the particular isotope involved. This is why the mass number and atomic number are used. These values tell us the number of neutrons in the species, and hence the isotope's identity.

Natural radiation emitted by unstable nuclei includes *alpha particles, beta particles, positrons,* and *gamma rays.*

Other radiation particles, such as neutrinos and deuterons, will not be discussed here.

## Alpha Particles

An **alpha particle** (α) contains two protons and two neutrons. An alpha particle is identical to the nucleus of the helium atom (He) or a *helium ion* (He$^{2+}$), which also contains two protons (atomic number = 2) and two neutrons (mass number − atomic number = 2). Having no electrons to counterbalance the nuclear charge, the alpha particle may be symbolized as

$$^{4}_{2}\text{He}^{2+} \qquad \text{or} \qquad ^{4}_{2}\text{He} \qquad \text{or} \qquad \alpha$$

Alpha particles have a relatively large mass compared to other nuclear particles. Consequently, alpha particles emitted by radioisotopes are relatively slow-moving particles (approximately 10% of the speed of light), and they are stopped by barriers as thin as a few pages of this book.

## Beta Particles and Positrons

The **beta particle** (β), in contrast, is a fast-moving electron traveling at approximately 90% of the speed of light as it leaves the nucleus. It is formed in the nucleus by the conversion of a neutron into a proton. The beta particle is represented as

$$^{0}_{-1}\text{e} \qquad \text{or} \qquad ^{0}_{-1}\beta \qquad \text{or} \qquad \beta$$

**LEARNING GOAL**

**2** Enumerate characteristics of alpha, beta, positron, and gamma radiation.

The subscript −1 is written in the same position as the atomic number and, like the atomic number (number of protons), indicates the charge of the particle.

Beta particles are smaller and faster than alpha particles. They are more penetrating and are stopped only by denser materials such as wood, metal, or several layers of clothing.

A **positron** has the same mass as a beta particle but carries a positive charge and is symbolized as

$$_{+1}^{0}e \quad \text{or} \quad _{+1}^{0}\beta$$

Positrons are produced by the conversion of a proton to a neutron in the nucleus of the isotope. The proton, in effect, loses its positive charge, as well as a tiny bit of mass. This positively charged mass that is released is the positron.

## Gamma Rays

**Gamma rays** ($\gamma$) are the most energetic part of the electromagnetic spectrum (see Section 2.3) and result from nuclear processes; in contrast, alpha radiation and beta radiation are matter. Because electromagnetic radiation has no protons, neutrons, or electrons, the symbol for a gamma ray is simply

$$\gamma$$

Gamma radiation is highly energetic and is the most penetrating form of nuclear radiation. Barriers of lead, concrete, or, more often, a combination of the two are required for protection from this type of radiation.

## Properties of Alpha, Beta, Positron, and Gamma Radiation

Important properties of alpha, beta, positron, and gamma radiation are summarized in Table 9.1.

Alpha, beta, positron, and gamma radiation are collectively termed *ionizing radiation*. **Ionizing radiation** produces a trail of ions throughout the material that it penetrates. The ionization process changes the chemical composition of the material. When the material is living tissue, radiation-induced illness may result (Section 9.6).

The penetrating power of alpha radiation is very low. Damage to internal organs from this form of radiation is negligible except when an alpha particle emitter is actually ingested. Beta particles and positrons have much higher velocities than alpha particles; still, they have limited penetrating power. They cause skin and eye damage and, to a lesser extent, damage to internal organs. The great penetrating power and high energy of gamma radiation can damage internal organs.

Anyone working with any type of radiation must take precautions. Radiation safety is required, monitored, and enforced in the United States by the Occupational Safety and Health Administration (OSHA).

**Question 9.1** Gamma radiation is a form of *electromagnetic radiation*. Provide examples of other forms of electromagnetic radiation.

**Question 9.2** How does the energy of gamma radiation compare with that of other regions of the electromagnetic spectrum?

**LEARNING GOAL**

**2** Enumerate characteristics of alpha, beta, positron, and gamma radiation.

**TABLE 9.1 A Summary of the Major Properties of Alpha, Beta, Positron, and Gamma Radiation**

| Name and Symbol | Identity | Charge | Mass (amu) | Velocity | Penetration |
|---|---|---|---|---|---|
| Alpha ($\alpha$) | Helium nucleus | +2 | 4.0026 | 5–10% of the speed of light | Low |
| Beta ($_{-1}^{0}\beta$) | Electron | −1 | 0.000549 | Up to 90% of the speed of light | Medium |
| Positron ($_{+1}^{0}\beta$) | Electron | +1 | 0.000549 | Up to 90% of the speed of light | Medium |
| Gamma ($\gamma$) | Radiant energy | 0 | 0 | Speed of light | High |

## Origin of the Elements

The current, most widely held theory of the origin of the universe is the "big bang" theory. An explosion of very dense matter was followed by expansion into space of the fragments resulting from this explosion. This is one of the scenarios that have been created by scientists fascinated by the origins of matter, the stars and planets, and life as we know it today.

The first fragments, or particles, were protons and neutrons moving with tremendous velocity and possessing large amounts of energy. Collisions involving these high-energy protons and neutrons formed deuterium atoms ($_1^2H$), which are isotopes of hydrogen. As the universe expanded and cooled, tritium ($_1^3H$), another hydrogen isotope, formed as a result of collisions of neutrons with deuterium atoms. Subsequent capture of a proton produced helium (He). Scientists theorize that a universe that was principally composed of hydrogen atoms and helium atoms persisted for perhaps 100,000 years until the temperature decreased sufficiently to allow the formation of a simple unit, diatomic hydrogen, two atoms of hydrogen bonded together ($H_2$).

Many millions of years later, the effect of gravity caused these small units to coalesce, first into clouds and eventually into stars, with temperatures of millions of degrees. In this setting, these small collections of protons and neutrons combined to form larger atoms such as carbon (C) and oxygen (O), then sodium (Na), neon (Ne), magnesium (Mg), silicon (Si), and so forth. Subsequent explosions of stars provided the conditions that formed many larger atoms. These fragments, gathered together by the force of gravity, are the most probable origin of the planets in our own solar system.

The reactions that formed the elements as we know them today were a result of a series of *fusion reactions,* the joining of nuclei to produce larger atoms at very high temperatures (millions of degrees Celsius). These fusion reactions are similar to processes that are currently being studied as a possible alternative source of nuclear power.

Nuclear reactions of this type do not naturally occur on the earth today. The temperature is simply too low. As a result we have, for the most part, a collection of stable elements existing as chemical compounds, atoms joined together by chemical bonds while retaining their identity even in the combined state.

New stars are forming by fusion reactions within the clouds of dust and gas of the Orion nebula.

Silicon exists all around us as sand and soil in a combined form, silicon dioxide; most metals exist as a part of a chemical compound, such as iron ore.

The wonder and complexity of our universe is a legacy of events that happened a long time ago. As our understanding of bonding, molecular structure, and structure-property relationships has developed, our ability to design and synthesize useful new compounds has dramatically increased.

### For Further Understanding

▶ How does tritium differ from "normal" hydrogen?
▶ Would you expect to find similar atoms on other planets? Explain your reasoning.

## 9.2 Writing a Balanced Nuclear Equation

### LEARNING GOAL

**3** Write balanced equations for nuclear processes.

Nuclear equations represent nuclear change in much the same way as chemical equations represent chemical change.

A **nuclear equation** can be used to represent the process of radioactive decay. In radioactive decay, a *nuclide* breaks down, producing a *new nuclide, smaller particles, and/or energy.* The concept of mass balance, required when writing chemical equations, is also essential for nuclear equations. When writing a balanced equation, remember that:

- the total mass on each side of the reaction arrow must be identical, and
- the sum of the atomic numbers on each side of the reaction arrow must be identical.

## Alpha Decay

Consider the decay of one isotope of uranium, $^{238}_{92}U$, into thorium and an alpha particle. Because an alpha particle is lost in this process, this decay is called *alpha decay*.

Examine the balanced equation for this nuclear reaction:

$$^{238}_{92}U \longrightarrow \quad ^{234}_{90}Th \quad + \quad ^{4}_{2}He$$
$$\text{Uranium-238} \qquad \text{Thorium-234} \qquad \text{Helium-4}$$

The sum of the mass numbers on the right ($234 + 4 = 238$) is equal to the mass number on the left. The sum of atomic numbers on the right ($90 + 2 = 92$) is equal to the atomic number on the left.

## Beta Decay

*Beta decay* is illustrated by the decay of one of the less-abundant nitrogen isotopes, $^{16}_{7}N$. Upon decomposition, nitrogen-16 produces oxygen-16 and a beta particle. Conceptually, a neutron = proton + electron. In beta decay, one neutron in nitrogen-16 is converted to a proton, and the electron, the beta particle, is released. The reaction is represented as

$$^{16}_{7}N \longrightarrow {}^{16}_{8}O + {}^{0}_{-1}e$$

or

$$^{16}_{7}N \longrightarrow {}^{16}_{8}O + \beta$$

Beta decay *increases the atomic number of the nuclide by one unit.*

Note that the mass number of the beta particle is zero, because the electron has no protons or neutrons. Sixteen nuclear particles are accounted for on both sides of the reaction arrow. Note also that the product nuclide has the same mass number as the parent nuclide but the atomic number has *increased* by one unit.

The atomic number on the left (7) is counterbalanced by [8 + (−1)] or (7) on the right. Therefore, the equation is correctly balanced.

## Positron Emission

The decay of carbon-11 to a stable isotope, boron-11, is one example of *positron emission*.

$$^{11}_{6}C \longrightarrow {}^{11}_{5}B + {}^{0}_{+1}e$$

or

$$^{11}_{6}C \longrightarrow {}^{11}_{5}B + {}^{0}_{+1}\beta$$

Positron emission *decreases the atomic number of the nuclide by one unit.*

A positron has the same mass as an electron, or beta particle, but opposite (+1) charge. In contrast to beta emission, the product nuclide has the same mass number as the parent nuclide, but the atomic number has *decreased* by one unit.

The atomic number on the left (6) is counterbalanced by [5 + (+1)] or (6) on the right. Therefore, the equation is correctly balanced.

## Gamma Production

If *gamma radiation* were the only product of nuclear decay, there would be no measurable change in the mass or identity of the radioactive nuclei. This is so because the gamma emitter has simply gone to a lower energy state. An example of an isotope that decays in this way is technetium-99m. It is described as a *metastable isotope,* meaning that it is unstable and increases its stability through gamma decay without change in the mass or charge of the isotope. The letter $m$ is used to denote a metastable isotope. The decay equation for $^{99m}_{43}\text{Tc}$ is

$$^{99m}_{43}\text{Tc} \longrightarrow \; ^{99}_{43}\text{Tc} + \gamma$$

---

Gamma production produces *no change* in the atomic number of the nuclide.

---

More often, gamma radiation is produced along with other products. For example, iodine-131 decays as follows:

$$^{131}_{53}\text{I} \longrightarrow \; ^{131}_{54}\text{Xe} + \; ^{0}_{-1}\text{e} + \; \gamma$$

Iodine-131    Xenon-131    Beta    Gamma
                                      particle    ray

This reaction may also be represented as

$$^{131}_{53}\text{I} \longrightarrow \; ^{131}_{54}\text{Xe} + \; ^{0}_{-1}\beta + \gamma$$

An isotope of xenon, a beta particle, and gamma radiation are produced.

## Predicting Products of Nuclear Decay

It is possible to use a nuclear equation to predict one of the products of a nuclear reaction if the others are known. Consider the following example, in which we represent the unknown product as ?:

$$^{40}_{19}\text{K} \longrightarrow ? + \; ^{0}_{-1}\text{e}$$

**Step 1.** The mass number of this isotope of potassium is 40. Therefore, the sum of the mass number of the products must also be 40. Since the mass number of the beta particle is 0, the unknown mass number must be 40, because [40 + 0 = 40].

**Step 2.** Likewise, the atomic number on the left is 19, and the sum of the unknown atomic number plus the charge of the beta particle (−1) must equal 19.

Therefore, the unknown atomic number must be 20, because [20 + (−1) = 19].

**Step 3.** If we consult the periodic table, the element that has atomic number 20 is calcium; therefore, the unknown product, ?, is $^{40}_{20}\text{Ca}$.

**Step 4.** Verify the result. Use the complete equation

$$^{40}_{19}\text{K} \longrightarrow \; ^{40}_{20}\text{Ca} + \; ^{0}_{-1}\text{e}$$

to confirm that the mass number of the reactant is equal to the mass number of the products (40). In addition, the atomic number of the reactant must be equal to the atomic number of the products (19).

Mass number of reactants = 40
Mass number of products = 40 + 0 = 40

and

Atomic number of reactants = 19
Atomic number of products = 20 + (−1) = 19

| EXAMPLE 9.1 | Predicting the Product of Alpha Decay | LEARNING GOAL |

Determine the identity of the unknown product of the alpha decay of curium-245:

**3** Write balanced equations for nuclear processes.

$$^{245}_{96}Cm \longrightarrow {}^{4}_{2}He + ?$$

**Solution**

**Step 1.** The mass number of the curium isotope is 245. The sum of the mass numbers of the products must also be 245. Since the mass number of the alpha particle is 4, the unknown mass number must be 241, because [241 + 4 = 245].

**Step 2.** Likewise, the atomic number on the left is 96, and the sum of the unknown atomic number plus the atomic number of the alpha particle (2) must equal 96. Therefore, the unknown atomic number must be 94, because [94 + 2 = 96].

**Step 3.** Referring to the periodic table, we find that the element that has atomic number 94 is plutonium; therefore, the unknown product, ?, is $^{241}_{94}Pu$.

**Step 4.** Verify the result. The complete equation is:

$$^{245}_{96}Cm \longrightarrow {}^{4}_{2}He + {}^{241}_{94}Pu$$

Mass number of reactants = 245
Mass number of products = 4 + 241 = 245

and

Atomic number of reactant = 96
Atomic number of products = 2 + 94 = 96

**Practice Problem 9.1**

Complete each of the following nuclear equations:

a. $? \longrightarrow {}^{4}_{2}He + {}^{222}_{86}Rn$

b. $^{11}_{5}B \longrightarrow {}^{7}_{3}Li + ?$

▶ For Further Practice: **Questions 9.44 and 9.46.**

**Question 9.3**   Neodymium-144 is a rare earth isotope that undergoes alpha decay. Write a balanced nuclear equation for this process.

**Question 9.4**   Samarium-147 is one of many rare earth isotopes that undergo alpha decay. Write a balanced nuclear equation for this process.

| EXAMPLE 9.2 | Predicting the Product of Beta Decay | LEARNING GOAL |

Determine the identity of the unknown product of the beta decay of chromium-55.

**3** Write balanced equations for nuclear processes.

$$^{55}_{24}Cr \longrightarrow {}^{0}_{-1}e + ?$$

**Solution**

**Step 1.** The mass number of the chromium isotope is 55. Therefore, the sum of the mass numbers of the products must also be 55. Since the mass number of the beta particle is 0, the unknown mass number must be 55, because [55 + 0 = 55].

**Step 2.** Likewise, the atomic number on the left is 24, and the sum of the unknown atomic number plus (−1), representing the beta particle, equals the atomic number of the chromium isotope.

Unknown atomic number + (−1) = 24
Unknown atomic number = 24 + 1 = 25

*Continued…*

**Step 3.** Referring to the periodic table, we find that the element having atomic number 25 is manganese; therefore, the unknown product, ?, is $^{55}_{25}\text{Mn}$.

**Step 4.** Verify the result. The complete equation is:

$$^{55}_{24}\text{Cr} \longrightarrow {}^{0}_{-1}\text{e} + {}^{55}_{25}\text{Mn}$$

Mass number of reactants = 55
Mass number of products = 0 + 55 = 55

and

Atomic number of reactants = 24
Atomic number of products = (−1) + 25 = 24

---

### Practice Problem 9.2

Complete each of the following nuclear equations:

a. $^{85}_{36}\text{Kr} \longrightarrow ? + {}^{0}_{-1}\text{e}$
b. $^{239}_{92}\text{U} \longrightarrow ? + {}^{0}_{-1}\text{e}$

▶ For Further Practice: **Questions 9.43 and 9.45.**

**Question 9.5**  Iodine-131, useful in the treatment of certain kinds of thyroid disease, decays by beta emission. Write a balanced nuclear equation for this process.

**Question 9.6**  Phosphorus-31, known to bioaccumulate in the liver, decays by beta emission. Write a balanced nuclear equation for this process.

---

**EXAMPLE 9.3**   **Predicting the Product of Positron Emission**

LEARNING GOAL

**3**  Write balanced equations for nuclear processes.

Determine the identity of the unknown product of positron emission from xenon-118.

$$^{118}_{54}\text{Xe} \longrightarrow {}^{0}_{+1}\text{e} + ?$$

**Solution**

**Step 1.** The mass number of the xenon isotope is 118. Therefore, the sum of the mass numbers of the products must also be 118. Since the mass number of the positron is 0, the unknown mass number must be 118, because [118 + 0 = 118].

**Step 2.** Likewise, the atomic number on the left is 54, and the sum of the unknown atomic number plus (+1), representing the positron, equals the atomic number of the xenon isotope.

Unknown atomic number + (+1) = 54
Unknown atomic number = 54 − 1 = 53

**Step 3.** Referring to the periodic table, we find that the element having atomic number 53 is iodine; therefore, the unknown product, ?, is $^{118}_{53}\text{I}$.

**Step 4.** Verify the result. The complete equation is:

$$^{118}_{54}\text{Xe} \longrightarrow {}^{0}_{+1}\text{e} + {}^{118}_{53}\text{I}$$

Mass number of reactants = 118
Mass number of products = 118 + 0 = 118

and

Atomic number of reactant = 54
Atomic number of products = (+1) + 53 = 54

**Practice Problem 9.3**

Complete each of the following nuclear equations:

a. $^{79}_{37}Rb \longrightarrow ? + {}^{0}_{+1}e$

b. $^{38}_{20}Ca \longrightarrow ? + {}^{0}_{+1}e$

▶ For Further Practice: **Questions 9.51 and 9.52.**

**Question 9.7**   In what way do beta particles and positrons differ?

**Question 9.8**   In what way are beta particles and positrons similar?

# 9.3   Properties of Radioisotopes

Why are some isotopes radioactive but others are not? Do all radioactive isotopes decay at the same rate? Are all radioactive materials equally hazardous? We address these and other questions in this section.

## Nuclear Structure and Stability

A measure of nuclear stability is the **binding energy** of the nucleus. The binding energy of the nucleus is the energy required to break up a nucleus into its component protons and neutrons. This must be very large, because identically charged protons in the nucleus exert extreme repulsive forces on one another. These forces must be overcome if the nucleus is to be stable. When a nuclide decays, some energy is released because the products are more stable than the parent nuclide. The energy released serves as the basis for much of our nuclear technology.

Why are some isotopes more stable than others? The answer to this question is not completely clear. Evidence obtained so far points to several important factors that describe stable nuclei:

- Nuclear stability correlates with the ratio of neutrons to protons in the isotope. For example, for light atoms a neutron:proton ratio of 1:1 characterizes a stable atom.
- All isotopes (except hydrogen-1) with more protons than neutrons are unstable. However, the reverse is not true.
- Nuclei with large numbers of protons (84 or more) tend to be unstable.
- Naturally occurring isotopes containing 2, 8, 20, 50, 82, or 126 protons or neutrons are stable. These *magic numbers* seem to indicate the presence of energy levels in the nucleus, analogous to electronic energy levels in the atom.
- Isotopes with even numbers of protons or neutrons are generally more stable than those with odd numbers of protons or neutrons.

## Half-Life

The **half-life** ($t_{1/2}$) of an isotope is the time required for one-half of a given quantity of the radioactive isotope to undergo change. Half-life is symbolized as $t_{1/2}$. Not all radioactive isotopes decay at the same rate. The rate of nuclear decay is generally represented in terms of the half-life of the isotope. Each isotope has its own characteristic half-life that may be as short as a few millionths of a second or as long as billions of years. Half-lives of some naturally occurring and synthetic isotopes are given in Table 9.2.

The stability of an isotope is indicated by the isotope's half-life. Isotopes with short half-lives decay rapidly; they are very unstable. This is not meant to imply that substances with long half-lives are less hazardous. Often, just the reverse is true.

**LEARNING GOAL**

**4**  Calculate the amount of radioactive substance remaining after a specified time has elapsed.

*Refer to the discussion of radiation exposure and safety in Sections 9.6 and 9.7.*

**TABLE 9.2 Half-Lives of Selected Radioisotopes**

| Name | Symbol | Half-Life |
|---|---|---|
| Carbon-14 | $^{14}_{6}C$ | 5730 years |
| Cobalt-60 | $^{60}_{27}Co$ | 5.3 years |
| Hydrogen-3 | $^{3}_{1}H$ | 12.3 years |
| Iodine-131 | $^{131}_{53}I$ | 8.1 days |
| Iron-59 | $^{59}_{26}Fe$ | 45 days |
| Molybdenum-99 | $^{99}_{42}Mo$ | 67 hours |
| Sodium-24 | $^{24}_{11}Na$ | 15 hours |
| Strontium-90 | $^{90}_{38}Sr$ | 28 years |
| Technetium-99m | $^{99m}_{43}Tc$ | 6 hours |
| Uranium-235 | $^{235}_{92}U$ | 710 million years |

**Figure 9.2** The decay curve for the medically useful radioisotope technetium-99m. Note that the number of radioactive atoms remaining—hence the radioactivity—approaches zero.

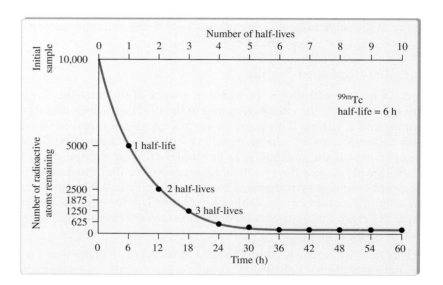

Imagine that we begin with 100 milligrams (mg) of a radioactive isotope that has a half-life of 24 hours (h). After one half-life, or 24 h, 1/2 of 100 mg will have decayed to other products, and 50 mg remain. After two half-lives (48 h), 1/2 of the remaining material has decayed, leaving 25 mg, and so forth:

$$100 \text{ mg} \xrightarrow[\substack{\text{Half-life} \\ (24 \text{ h})}]{\text{First}} 50 \text{ mg} \xrightarrow[\substack{\text{Half-life} \\ (48 \text{ h total})}]{\text{Second}} 25 \text{ mg} \longrightarrow \text{etc.}$$

Decay of a radioisotope that has a reasonably short $t_{1/2}$ is experimentally determined by following its activity as a function of time. Graphing the results produces a radioactive decay curve, as shown in Figure 9.2.

The mass of any radioactive substance remaining after a period may be calculated with a knowledge of the initial mass and the half-life of the isotope, following the scheme just outlined. The general equation for this process is:

$$m_f = m_i (0.5)^n$$

where  $m_f$ = final or remaining mass
  $m_i$ = initial mass
  $n$ = number of half-lives

| EXAMPLE 9.4 | Predicting the Extent of Radioactive Decay |
|---|---|

A 50.0-mg supply of iodine-131, used in hospitals in the treatment of hyperthyroidism, was stored for 32.4 days (d). If the half-life of iodine-131 is 8.1 d, how many mg remain?

**Solution**

**Step 1.**   The general equation for calculating remaining mass is:

$$m_f = m_i (0.5)^n$$

**Step 2.**   The number of half-lives elapsed, $n$, is calculated using the half-life as a conversion factor:

$$n = 32.4 \, \cancel{d} \times \frac{1 \text{ half-life}}{8.1 \, \cancel{d}} = 4.0 \text{ half-lives}$$

**Step 3.**   Substituting the initial mass, $m_i$, provided in the problem and the number of half-lives, $n$, calculated into the equation:

$$m_f = (50.0 \text{ mg})(0.5)^4$$
$$m_f = 3.13 \text{ mg of iodine-131 remain after 32.4 d}$$

*Helpful Hint:* Alternatively, the calculated number of half-lives can be used to determine the final mass stepwise by using an illustration.

| | First | | Second | | Third | | Fourth | |
|---|---|---|---|---|---|---|---|---|
| 50.0 mg | $\longrightarrow$ | 25.0 mg | $\longrightarrow$ | 12.5 mg | $\longrightarrow$ | 6.25 mg | $\longrightarrow$ | 3.13 mg |
| | Half-life | | Half-life | | Half-life | | Half-life | |

**Practice Problem 9.4**

a. A 100.0 nanogram (ng) sample of sodium-24 was stored in a lead-lined cabinet for 2.5 d. How much sodium-24 remained? See Table 9.2 for the half-life of sodium-24.

b. If a patient is administered 10 ng of technetium-99m, how much will remain 1 day later, assuming that no technetium has been eliminated by any other process? See Table 9.2 for the half-life of technetium-99m.

▶ For Further Practice: **Questions 9.63 and 9.64.**

**Question 9.9**   The half-life of molybdenum-99 is 67 h. A 200 microgram (µg) quantity decays, over time, to 25 µg. How much time has elapsed?

**Question 9.10**   The half-life of strontium-87 is 2.8 h. What percentage of this isotope will remain after 8 h and 24 minutes (min)?

## Radiocarbon Dating

Natural radioactivity is useful in establishing the approximate age of objects of archaeological, anthropological, or historical interest. **Radiocarbon dating** is the estimation of the age of objects through measurement of isotopic ratios of carbon.

Radiocarbon dating is based on the measurement of the relative amounts (or ratio) of $^{14}_{6}C$ and $^{12}_{6}C$ present in an object. The $^{14}_{6}C$ is formed in the upper atmosphere by the bombardment of $^{14}_{7}N$ by high-speed neutrons (cosmic radiation):

$$^{14}_{7}N + ^{1}_{0}n \longrightarrow ^{14}_{6}C + ^{1}_{1}H$$

The carbon-14, along with the more abundant carbon-12, is converted into living plant material by the process of photosynthesis. Carbon proceeds up the

# A Human Perspective

## An Extraordinary Woman in Science

The path to a successful career in science, or any other field for that matter, is seldom smooth or straight. That was certainly true for Madame Marie Sklodowska Curie. Her lifelong ambition was to raise a family and do something interesting for a career. This was a lofty goal for a nineteenth-century woman.

The political climate in Poland, coupled with the prevailing attitudes toward women and careers, especially careers in science, certainly did not make it any easier for Mme. Curie. To support herself and her sister, she toiled at menial jobs until moving to Paris to resume her studies.

It was in Paris that she met her future husband and fellow researcher, Pierre Curie. Working with crude equipment in a laboratory that was primitive, even by the standards of the time, she and Pierre made a most revolutionary discovery only 2 years after Henri Becquerel discovered radioactivity. Radioactivity, the emission of energy from certain substances, was released from *inside* the atom and was independent of the molecular form of the substance. The absolute proof of this assertion came only after the Curies processed over 1 *ton* (t) of a material (pitchblende) to isolate less than a gram (g) of pure radium. The difficult conditions under which this feat was accomplished are perhaps best stated by Sharon Bertsch McGrayne in her book *Nobel Prize Women in Science* (Birch Lane Press, New York, 2001):

> The only space large enough at the school was an abandoned dissection shed. The shack was stifling hot in summer and freezing cold in winter. It had no ventilation system for removing poisonous fumes, and its roof leaked. A chemist accustomed to Germany's modern laboratories called it "a cross between a stable and a potato cellar and, if I had not seen the work table with the chemical apparatus, I would have thought it a practical joke." This ramshackle shed became the symbol of the Marie Curie legend.

The pale green glow emanating from the radium was beautiful to behold. Mme. Curie would go to the shed in the middle of the night to bask in the light of her accomplishment. She did not realize that this wonderful accomplishment would, in time, be responsible for her death.

Mme. Curie received not one, but two Nobel Prizes, one in physics and one in chemistry. She was the first woman in France to earn the rank of professor.

Mme. Curie (left) standing beside her daughter, Irene.

### For Further Understanding

► Paradoxically, radiation can both cause and cure cancer. Use the Internet to develop an explanation for this paradox.

► What is the message that you, personally, can take away from this story?

food chain as the plants are consumed by animals, including humans. When a plant or animal dies, the uptake of both carbon-14 and carbon-12 ceases. However, the amount of carbon-14 slowly decreases because carbon-14 is radioactive ($t_{1/2}$ = 5730 years). Consequently, the ratio of $^{14}_{6}C/^{12}_{6}C$ decreases over time in a predictable way.

Carbon-14 decay produces nitrogen and a beta particle:

$$^{14}_{6}C \longrightarrow {}^{14}_{7}N + {}^{0}_{-1}e$$

**TABLE 9.3 Isotopes Useful in Radioactive Dating**

| Isotope | Half-Life (years) | Upper Limit (years) | Dating Applications |
|---------|-------------------|---------------------|---------------------|
| Carbon-14 | 5730 | $5 \times 10^4$ | Charcoal, organic material, artwork |
| Hydrogen-3 | 12.3 | $1 \times 10^2$ | Aged wines, artwork |
| Potassium-40 | $1.3 \times 10^9$ | Age of earth ($4 \times 10^9$) | Rocks, planetary material |
| Rhenium-187 | $4.3 \times 10^{10}$ | Age of earth ($4 \times 10^9$) | Meteorites |
| Uranium-238 | $4.5 \times 10^9$ | Age of earth ($4 \times 10^9$) | Rocks, earth's crust |

When an artifact is found and studied, the relative amounts of carbon-14 and carbon-12 are determined. By using suitable equations involving the $t_{1/2}$ of carbon-14, it is possible to approximate the age of the artifact.

This technique has been widely used to increase our knowledge about the history of the earth, to establish the age of objects (Figure 9.3), and even to detect art forgeries. Early paintings were made with inks fabricated from vegetable dyes (plant material that, while alive, metabolized carbon).

The carbon-14 dating technique is limited to objects that are less than fifty thousand years old, or approximately nine half-lives, which is a practical upper limit. Older objects that have geological or archaeological significance may be dated using naturally occurring isotopes having much longer half-lives.

Examples of isotopes that are useful in radioactive dating are listed in Table 9.3.

**Figure 9.3** Radiocarbon dating was used in the authentication study of the Shroud of Turin. It is a minimally destructive technique and is valuable in estimating the age of historical artifacts. It was found that the Shroud is approximately 700 years old, negating the claim that it was used to wrap the body of Jesus.

## 9.4 Nuclear Power

### Energy Production

Einstein predicted that a small amount of nuclear mass corresponds to a very large amount of energy that is released when the nucleus breaks apart. Einstein's equation is

$$E = mc^2$$

in which

$$E = \text{energy}$$
$$m = \text{mass}$$
$$c = \text{speed of light}$$

This energy, when rapidly released, is the basis for the greatest instruments of destruction developed by humankind, nuclear bombs. However, when nuclear energy is released in a controlled fashion, as in a nuclear power plant, the heat from the nuclear reaction converts liquid water into steam. The steam, in turn, drives an electrical generator, which produces electricity. The entire process takes place within a **nuclear reactor.**

### Nuclear Fission

**Fission** (splitting) occurs when a heavy nuclear particle is split into lighter nuclei by collision with a smaller nuclear particle (such as a neutron). This splitting process is accompanied by the release of large amounts of energy.

A nuclear power plant uses a fissionable material (capable of undergoing fission), such as uranium-235, as fuel. The energy released by the fission process in the nuclear core heats water in an adjoining chamber, producing steam. The high pressure of the steam drives a turbine, which converts this heat energy into

LEARNING GOAL

**6** Describe how nuclear energy can generate electricity: fission, fusion, and the breeder reactor.

The Sequoyah Nuclear Power Plant in Tennessee uses water to transform nuclear energy into electrical energy.

electricity using an electric power generator. The energy transformation may be summarized as follows:

$$\begin{array}{ccccccc}
\text{Nuclear} & \longrightarrow & \text{heat} & \longrightarrow & \text{mechanical} & \longrightarrow & \text{electrical} \\
\text{energy} & & \text{energy} & & \text{energy} & & \text{energy} \\
\text{Reactor} & & \text{Steam} & & \text{Turbine} & & \text{Electricity} \\
\text{core} & & & & & &
\end{array}$$

The fission reaction, once initiated, is self-perpetuating. For example, neutrons are used to initiate the reaction:

$$\underset{\text{Fuel}}{{}^{1}_{0}\text{n} + {}^{235}_{92}\text{U}} \longrightarrow \underset{\text{Unstable}}{{}^{236}_{92}\text{U}} \longrightarrow \underset{\text{Products of reaction}}{{}^{92}_{36}\text{Kr} + {}^{141}_{56}\text{Ba} + 3{}^{1}_{0}\text{n} + \text{energy}}$$

Note that three neutrons are released as product for each single reacting neutron. Each of the three neutrons produced is available to initiate another fission process. Nine neutrons are released from this process. These, in turn, react with other nuclei. The fission process continues and intensifies, producing very large amounts of energy (Figure 9.4). This process of intensification is referred to as a **chain reaction.**

To maintain control over the process and to prevent dangerous overheating, rods fabricated from cadmium or boron are inserted into the core. These rods, which are controlled by the reactor's main operating system, absorb free neutrons as needed, thereby moderating the reaction.

A nuclear fission reactor may be represented as a series of energy transfer zones, as depicted in Figure 9.5. The head of a fission reactor is shown in Figure 9.6.

## Nuclear Fusion

**Fusion** (meaning *to join together*) results from the combination of two small nuclei to form a larger nucleus with the concurrent release of large amounts of energy. The best example of a fusion reactor is the sun. Continuous fusion processes furnish our solar system with light and heat.

An example of a fusion reaction is the combination of two isotopes of hydrogen, deuterium (${}^{2}_{1}\text{H}$) and tritium (${}^{3}_{1}\text{H}$), to produce helium, a neutron, and energy:

$${}^{2}_{1}\text{H} + {}^{3}_{1}\text{H} \longrightarrow {}^{4}_{2}\text{He} + {}^{1}_{0}\text{n} + \text{energy}$$

Although fusion is capable of producing tremendous amounts of energy, no commercially successful fusion plant exists in the United States. Safety concerns relating to problems of containment of the reaction, resulting directly from the technological problems associated with containing high temperatures (millions of degrees) and pressures required to sustain a fusion process, have slowed the development of fusion reactors.

## Breeder Reactors

A **breeder reactor** is a variation of a fission reactor that literally manufactures its own fuel. A perceived shortage of fissionable isotopes makes the breeder an attractive alternative to conventional fission reactors. A breeder reactor uses ${}^{238}_{92}\text{U}$, which is abundant but nonfissionable. In a series of steps, the uranium-238 is converted to plutonium-239, which *is* fissionable and undergoes a fission chain reaction, producing energy. The attractiveness of a reactor that makes its own fuel from abundant starting materials is offset by the high cost of the system, potential environmental damage, and fear of plutonium proliferation. Plutonium can be readily used to manufacture nuclear bombs. Currently, only a few countries operate breeder reactors for electrical power generation.

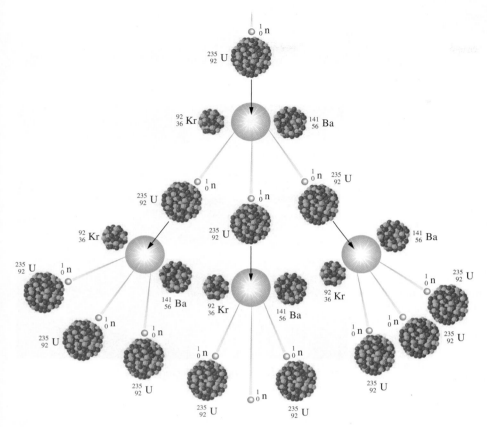

**Figure 9.4** The fission of uranium-235 producing a chain reaction. Note that the number of available neutrons, which "trigger" the decomposition of the fissionable nuclei to release energy, increases at each step in the "chain." In this way, the reaction builds in intensity. Control rods stabilize (or limit) the extent of the chain reaction to a safe level.

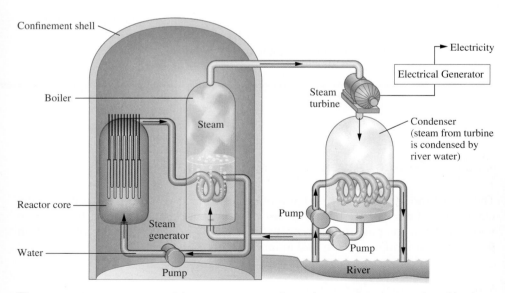

**Figure 9.5** A representation of the "energy zones" of a nuclear reactor. Heat produced by the reactor core (red zone) is carried by water to a boiler (blue zone). Water in the boiler is converted to steam, which drives a turbine to convert heat energy to electrical energy. The isolation of these zones from each other allows heat energy transfer without actual physical mixing. This minimizes the transport of radioactive material into the environment (green zone).

**Figure 9.6** The nuclear reactor vessel contains coolant and the reactor core.

# Green Chemistry

## Nuclear Waste Disposal

Nuclear waste arises from a variety of sources. A major source is the spent fuel from nuclear power plants. Medical laboratories generate significant amounts of low-level waste from tracers and therapy. Even household items with limited lifetimes, such as certain types of smoke detectors, use a tiny amount of radioactive material, americium-241.

Virtually everyone is aware, through news reports and the Internet, of the problems of solid waste (nonnuclear) disposal that our society faces. For the most part, this material will degrade in some reasonable amount of time. Still, we are disposing of trash and garbage at a rate that far exceeds nature's ability to recycle it.

Now imagine the problem with nuclear waste. We cannot alter the rate at which it decays. This is defined by the half-life. We can't heat it, stir it, or add a catalyst to speed up the process as we can with chemical reactions. Furthermore, the half-lives of many nuclear waste products are very long: plutonium, for example, has a half-life in excess of 24,000 years. Ten half-lives represents the approximate time required for the radioactivity of a substance to reach background levels. So we are talking about a *very* long storage time, on the order of 250,000 years!

Where on earth can something so very hazardous be contained and stored with reasonable assurance that it will lie undisturbed for a quarter of a million years? Perhaps this is a rhetorical question. Scientists, engineers, and politicians have debated this question for almost 50 years. As yet, no permanent disposal site has been agreed upon. Most agree that the best solution is burial in a stable rock formation, but there is no firm agreement on the location. Fear of earthquakes, which may release large quantities of radioactive materials into the underground water system, is the most serious consideration. Such a disaster could render large sections of the country unfit for habitation.

Many argue for the continuation of temporary storage sites with the hope that the progress of science and technology will,

Spent nuclear fuel is temporarily stored in a storage pond.

in the years ahead, provide a safer and more satisfactory long-term solution.

The nuclear waste problem, important for its own sake, also affects the development of future societal uses of nuclear chemistry. Before we can fully enjoy its benefits, we must learn to use and dispose of its waste products safely.

### For Further Understanding

▸ Summarize the major arguments supporting expanded use of nuclear power for electrical energy.

▸ Enumerate the characteristics of an "ideal" solution to the nuclear waste problem.

---

## LEARNING GOAL

**7** Cite examples of the use of radioactive isotopes in medicine.

## 9.5 Medical Applications of Radioactivity

The use of radiation in the treatment of various forms of cancer, as well as in the newer area of **nuclear medicine,** the use of radioisotopes in diagnosis, has become widespread in the past quarter century. Let's look at the properties of radiation that make it an indispensable tool in modern medical care.

## Cancer Therapy Using Radiation

## LEARNING GOAL

**8** Describe the use of ionizing radiation in cancer therapy.

When high-energy radiation, such as gamma radiation, passes through a cell, it may collide with one of the molecules in the cell and cause it to lose one or more electrons, causing a series of events that result in the production of ion pairs. For this reason, such radiation is termed *ionizing radiation* (Section 9.1).

Ions produced in this way are highly energetic. Consequently, they may damage biological molecules and cause changes in cellular biochemical processes. Interaction of ionizing radiation with intracellular water produces free electrons and other particles that can damage DNA. This may result in diminished or altered cell function or, in extreme cases, the death of the cell.

An organ that is cancerous is composed of both healthy cells and malignant cells. Tumor cells are more susceptible to the effects of gamma radiation than normal cells because they are undergoing cell division more frequently. Consequently, exposure of the tumor area to carefully targeted and controlled dosages of high-energy gamma radiation from cobalt-60 (a high-energy gamma ray source) will kill a higher percentage of abnormal cells than normal cells. If the dosage is administered correctly, a sufficient number of malignant cells will die, destroying the tumor, and enough normal cells will survive to maintain the function of the affected organ.

Gamma radiation can cure cancer. Paradoxically, the exposure of healthy cells to gamma radiation can actually cause cancer. For this reason, radiation therapy for cancer is a treatment that requires unusual care and sophistication.

## Nuclear Medicine

The diagnosis of a host of biochemical irregularities or diseases of the human body has been made routine through the use of radioactive tracers. Medical **tracers** are small amounts of radioactive substances used as probes to study internal organs. Medical techniques involving tracers are **nuclear imaging** procedures.

A small amount of the tracer, an isotope of an element that is known to be attracted to the organ of interest, is administered to the patient. For a variety of reasons, such as ease of administration of the isotope to the patient and targeting the organ of interest, the isotope is often a part of a larger molecule or ion. Because the isotope is radioactive, its path may be followed by using suitable detection devices. A radioimage, or "picture," of the organ is obtained, often far more detailed than is possible with conventional X-rays. Such techniques are noninvasive; that is, surgery is not required to investigate the condition of the internal organ, eliminating the risk associated with an operation.

The radioactive isotope of an element chosen for tracer studies has a chemical behavior similar to any other isotope of the same element. For example, iodine-127, the most abundant nonradioactive isotope of iodine, is used by the body in the synthesis of thyroid hormones and tends to concentrate in the thyroid gland. Both iodine-127 and radioactive iodine-131 behave in the same way, making it possible to use iodine-131 to study the thyroid. The rate of uptake of the radioactive isotope gives valuable information regarding underactivity or overactivity (hypoactive or hyperactive thyroid).

Isotopes with short half-lives are preferred for tracer studies. These isotopes emit their radiation in a more concentrated burst (short half-life materials have greater activity), facilitating their detection. If the radioactive decay is easily detected, the method is more sensitive and thus capable of providing more information. Furthermore, an isotope with a short half-life decays to background more rapidly. This is a mechanism for removal of the radioactivity from the body. If the radioactive element is also rapidly metabolized and excreted, this is beneficial as well.

The following examples illustrate the use of imaging procedures for diagnosis of disease.

- *Bone disease and injury.* The most widely used isotope for bone studies is technetium-99m, which is incorporated into a variety of ions and molecules that direct the isotope to the tissue being investigated. Technetium compounds containing phosphate are preferentially adsorbed on the surface of bone. New bone formation (common to virtually all bone injuries) increases the incorporation of the technetium compound. As a result, an enhanced image appears at the site of the injury. Bone tumors behave in a similar fashion.

LEARNING GOAL

**9**  Discuss the preparation and use of radioisotopes in diagnostic imaging studies.

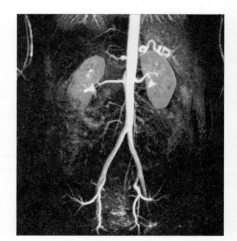

A radioimage of human kidneys (in light blue)

- *Cardiovascular disease.* Thallium-201 is used in the diagnosis of coronary artery disease. The isotope is administered intravenously and delivered to the heart muscle in proportion to the blood flow. Areas of restricted flow are observed as having lower levels of radioactivity, indicating some type of blockage.
- *Pulmonary disease.* Xenon is one of the noble gases. Radioactive xenon-133 may be inhaled by the patient. The radioactive isotope will be transported from the lungs and distributed through the circulatory system. Monitoring the distribution, as well as the reverse process, the removal of the isotope from the body (exhalation), can provide evidence of obstructive pulmonary disease, such as cancer or emphysema.

Examples of useful isotopes and the area(s) of the body in which they tend to concentrate are summarized in Table 9.4.

For many years, imaging with radioactive tracers was used exclusively for diagnosis. Recent applications have expanded to other areas of medicine. Imaging is now used extensively to guide surgery, assist in planning radiation therapy, and support the technique of angioplasty.

**Question 9.11**   Technetium-99m is used in diagnostic imaging studies involving the brain. What fraction of the radioisotope remains after 12 h have elapsed? See Table 9.2 for the half-life of technetium-99m.

**Question 9.12**   Barium-131 is a radioisotope used to study bone formation. A patient ingested barium-131. How much time will elapse until only one-fourth of the barium-131 remains, assuming that none of the isotope is eliminated from the body through normal processes? The half-life of barium-131 is 11.6 min.

## Making Isotopes for Medical Applications

In early experiments with radioactivity, the radioactive isotopes were naturally occurring. For this reason, the radioactivity produced by these unstable isotopes is described as **natural radioactivity.** If, on the other hand, a normally stable, nonradioactive nucleus is made radioactive, the resulting radioactivity is termed **artificial radioactivity.** The stable nucleus is made unstable by the introduction of "extra" protons, neutrons, or both.

The process of forming radioactive substances is often accomplished in the core of a *nuclear reactor,* in which an abundance of small nuclear particles,

**LEARNING GOAL**

**10**   Explain the difference between natural and artificial radioactivity.

### TABLE 9.4 Isotopes Commonly Used in Nuclear Medicine

| Area of Body | Isotope | Use |
|---|---|---|
| Blood | Chromium-51 | Determine blood volume in body |
| Bone | *Technetium-99m, barium-131, strontium-87 | Allow early detection of the extent of bone tumors and active sites of rheumatoid arthritis |
| Brain | *Technetium-99m | Detect and locate brain tumors and stroke |
| Coronary artery | Thallium-201 | Determine the presence and location of obstructions in coronary arteries |
| Heart | *Technetium-99m | Determine cardiac output, size, and shape |
| Kidney | *Technetium-99m | Determine renal function and location of cysts; a common follow-up procedure for kidney transplant patients |
| Liver-spleen | *Technetium-99m | Determine size and shape of liver and spleen; location of tumors |
| Lung | Xenon-133 | Determine whether lung fills properly; locate region of reduced ventilation and tumors |
| Thyroid | Iodine-131 | Determine rate of iodine uptake by thyroid |

*The destination of this isotope is determined by the identity of the compound in which it is incorporated.

particularly neutrons, is available. Alternatively, extremely high velocity charged particles (such as alpha and beta particles) may be produced in *particle accelerators*, such as a cyclotron. Accelerators are extremely large and use magnetic and electric fields to "push and pull" charged particles toward their target at very high speeds. A portion of the accelerator at the Brookhaven National Laboratory is shown in Figure 9.7.

Many isotopes that are useful in medicine are produced by particle bombardment. A few examples include the following:

- Gold-198, used as a tracer in the liver, is prepared by neutron bombardment.

$$^{197}_{79}\text{Au} + {}^{1}_{0}\text{n} \longrightarrow {}^{198}_{79}\text{Au}$$

- Gallium-67, used in the diagnosis of Hodgkin's disease, is prepared by proton bombardment.

$$^{66}_{30}\text{Zn} + {}^{1}_{1}\text{p} \longrightarrow {}^{67}_{31}\text{Ga}$$

Some medically useful isotopes with short half-lives must be prepared near the site of the clinical test. Preparation and shipment from a reactor site would waste time and result in an isotopic solution that had already undergone significant decay, resulting in diminished activity.

A common example is technetium-99m. It has a half-life of only 6 h. It is prepared in a small generator, often housed in a hospital's radiology laboratory (Figure 9.8). The generator contains radioactive molybdate ion ($\text{MoO}_4^{2-}$). Molybdenum-99 is more stable than technetium-99m; it has a half-life of 67 h.

The molybdenum in molybdate ion decays according to the following nuclear equation:

$$^{99}_{42}\text{Mo} \longrightarrow {}^{99\text{m}}_{43}\text{Tc} + {}^{0}_{-1}\text{e}$$

The *m* in technetium-99m means that the isotope is *metastable*, indicating that, over time, the isotope decays to a more stable form of the same isotope. In this case:
$$^{99\text{m}}_{43}\text{Tc} \longrightarrow {}^{99}_{43}\text{Tc} + \gamma$$

**Figure 9.7** A portion of a linear accelerator located at Brookhaven National Laboratory in New York. Particles can be accelerated at velocities close to the speed of light and accurately strike small "target" nuclei. At such facilities, rare isotopes can be synthesized and their properties studied.

# A Medical Perspective

## Magnetic Resonance Imaging

The Nobel Prize in physics was awarded to Otto Stern in 1943 and to Isidor Rabi in 1944. They discovered that certain atomic nuclei have a property known as spin, analogous to the spin associated with electrons, which we discussed in Chapter 2. The spin of electrons is responsible for the magnetic properties of atoms. Spinning nuclei behave as tiny magnets, producing magnetic fields as well.

One very important aspect of this phenomenon is the fact that the atoms in close proximity to the spinning nucleus (its chemical environment) exert an effect on the nuclear spin. In effect, measurable differences in spin are indicators of their surroundings. This relationship has been exhaustively studied for one atom in particular, hydrogen, and magnetic resonance techniques have become useful tools for the study of molecules containing hydrogen.

Human organs and tissues are made up of compounds containing hydrogen atoms. In the 1970s and 1980s, the experimental technique was extended beyond tiny laboratory samples of pure compounds to the most complex sample possible—the human body. The result of these experiments is termed *magnetic resonance imaging (MRI)*.

MRI is noninvasive to the body, requires no use of radioactive substances, and is quick, safe, and painless. A person is placed in a cavity surrounded by a magnetic field, and an image (based on the extent of radio frequency energy absorption) is generated, stored, and sorted in a computer. Differences between normal and malignant tissue, atherosclerotic thickening of an aortal wall, and a host of other problems may be seen clearly in the final image.

Advances in MRI technology have provided medical practitioners with a powerful tool in diagnostic medicine. This is

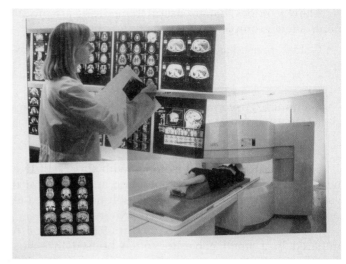

A patient is in an MRI scanner while a doctor studies brain scan images.

but one more example of basic science leading to technological advancement.

### For Further Understanding

▶ Why is hydrogen a useful atom to study in biological systems?
▶ Why would MRI provide minimal information about bone tissue?

---

**Figure 9.8** Preparation of technetium-99m. (a) A diagram depicting the conversion of $^{99}MoO_4^{2-}$ to $^{99m}TcO_4^-$ through radioactive decay. The radioactive pertechnetate ion is periodically removed from the generator in saline solution and used in tracer studies. (b) A photograph of a commercially available technetium-99m generator suitable for use in a hospital laboratory.

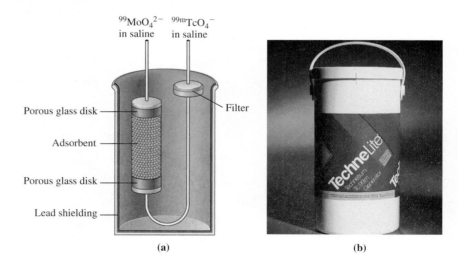

Chemically, radioactive molybdate $MoO_4^{2-}$ converts to radioactive pertechnetate ion ($TcO_4^-$). The radioactive $TcO_4^-$ is removed from the generator when needed. It is administered to the patient as an aqueous salt solution that has an osmotic pressure identical to that of human blood.

## 9.6 Biological Effects of Radiation

It is necessary to use suitable precautions in working with radioactive substances. The chosen protocol is based on an understanding of the effects of radiation, dosage levels and "tolerable levels," the way in which radiation is detected and measured, and the basic precepts of radiation safety.

### Radiation Exposure and Safety

In working with radioactive materials, the following factors must be considered.

LEARNING GOAL

11 Describe characteristics of radioactive materials that relate to radiation exposure and safety.

#### The Magnitude of the Half-Life

Short-half-life radioisotopes produce a larger amount of radioactivity per unit time than a long-half-life substance. For example, consider equal amounts of hypothetical isotopes that produce alpha particles. One has a half-life of 10 days; the other has a half-life of 100 days. In one half-life, each substance will produce exactly the same number of alpha particles. However, the first substance generates the alpha particles in only one-tenth of the time, and hence emits ten times as much radiation per unit time. Equal exposure times will result in higher levels of radiation exposure for substances with short half-lives, and lower levels for substances with long half-lives.

On the other hand, materials with short half-lives (weeks, days, or less) may be safer to work with, especially if an accident occurs. Over time (depending on the magnitude of the half-life), radioactive isotopes will decay to **background radiation** levels. This is the level of radiation attributable to our surroundings on a day-to-day basis.

Virtually all matter is composed of both radioactive and nonradioactive isotopes. Small amounts of radioactive material in the air, water, soil, and so forth make up a part of the background levels. Cosmic rays from outer space continually bombard us with radiation, contributing to the total background. Owing to the inevitability of background radiation, there can be no situation on earth where we observe zero radiation levels.

An isotope with a short half-life, for example 5.0 min, may decay to background in less than 1 h:

$$10 \text{ half-lives} \times \frac{5.0 \text{ min}}{1 \text{ half-life}} = 50 \text{ min}$$

A spill of such material could be treated by evacuating the area and waiting ten half-lives, perhaps by going to lunch. When you return to the laboratory, the material that was spilled will be no more radioactive than the floor itself. An accident with plutonium-239, which has a half-life of 24,000 years, would be quite a different matter! After 50 min, virtually all of the plutonium-239 would still remain. Long-half-life isotopes, by-products of nuclear technology, pose the greatest problems for safe disposal. Finding a site that will remain undisturbed "forever" is quite a formidable task.

*See Green Chemistry: Nuclear Waste Disposal.*

**Question 9.13** Describe the advantage of using isotopes with short half-lives for tracer applications in a medical laboratory.

**Question 9.14** Can you think of any disadvantage associated with the use of isotopes described in Question 9.13? Explain.

#### Shielding

Alpha and beta particles, being relatively low in penetrating power, require low-level *shielding*. **Shielding** is protection from harmful radiation. A lab coat and gloves are generally sufficient protection from this low-penetration radiation. On the other hand, shielding made of lead, concrete, or both is required for gamma

**Figure 9.9** Photograph of the construction of one-million-gallon (gal) capacity storage tanks for radioactive waste. Located in Hanford, Washington, they are now covered with 6–8 feet (ft) of earth.

rays (and X-rays, which are also high-energy radiation). Extensive manipulation of gamma emitters is often accomplished in laboratory and industrial settings by using robotic control: computer-controlled mechanical devices that can be programmed to perform virtually all manipulations normally carried out by humans.

### Distance from the Radioactive Source

Radiation intensity varies *inversely* with the *square* of the distance from the source. Doubling the distance from the source *decreases* the intensity by a factor of four ($2^2$). Again, the use of robot manipulators is advantageous, allowing a greater distance between the operator and the radioactive source.

### Time of Exposure

The effects of radiation are cumulative. Generally, potential damage is directly proportional to the time of exposure. Workers exposed to moderately high levels of radiation on the job may be limited in the time that they can perform that task. For example, workers involved in the cleanup of the Fukushima Daiichi nuclear plant, incapacitated in 2011, observed strict limits on the amount of time that they could be involved in the cleanup activities.

### Types of Radiation Emitted

Alpha and beta emitters are generally less hazardous than gamma emitters, owing to differences in energy and penetrating power that require less shielding. However, ingestion or inhalation of an alpha emitter or beta emitter can, over time, cause serious tissue damage; the radioactive substance is in direct contact with sensitive tissue. Green Chemistry: Radon and Indoor Air Pollution expands on this problem.

### Waste Disposal

Virtually all applications of nuclear chemistry create radioactive waste and, along with it, the problems of safe handling and disposal. Most disposal sites, at present, are considered temporary, until a long-term safe solution can be found. Figure 9.9 conveys a sense of the enormity of the problem. Green Chemistry: Nuclear Waste Disposal examines this problem in more detail.

## 9.7   Measurement of Radiation

The changes that take place when radiation interacts with matter (such as photographic film) provide the basis of operation for various radiation detection devices.

The principal detection methods involve the use of either photographic film to create an image of the location of the radioactive substance or a counter that allows the measurement of intensity of radiation emitted from some source by converting the radiation energy to an electrical signal.

### Photographic Imaging

This approach is often used in nuclear medicine. An isotope, perhaps iodine-131, is administered to a patient to study the thyroid gland, and the isotope begins to concentrate in the organ of interest. Nuclear images (photographs) of that region of the body are taken at periodic intervals using a special type of film. The emission of radiation from the radioactive substance creates the image, in much the same way as light causes the formation of images on conventional film in a camera. Upon development of the series of photographs, a record of the organ's uptake of the isotope over time enables the radiologist to assess the condition of the organ.

## Computer Imaging

The coupling of rapid developments in the technology of television and computers, resulting in the marriage of these two devices, has brought about a versatile alternative to photographic imaging.

A specialized television camera, sensitive to emitted radiation from a radioactive substance administered to a patient, develops a continuous and instantaneous record of the voyage of the isotope throughout the body. The signal, transmitted to the computer, is stored, sorted, and portrayed on a monitor. Advantages include increased sensitivity, allowing a lower dose of the isotope, speed through elimination of the developing step, and versatility of application, limited perhaps only by the creativity of the medical practitioners.

A particular type of computer imaging, useful in diagnostic medicine, is the CT scanner. The CT scanner measures the interaction of X-rays with biological tissue, gathering huge amounts of data and processing the data to produce detailed information, all in a relatively short time. Such a device may be less hazardous than conventional X-ray techniques because it generates more useful information per unit of radiation. It often produces a superior image. Images of the human brain taken by a CT scanner are shown in Figure 9.10.

CT represents *computerized tomography*: the computer reconstructs a series of measured images of tissue density (tomography). Small differences in tissue density may indicate the presence of a tumor.

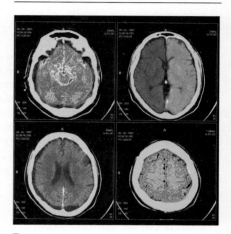

**Figure 9.10** CT scanned images of the human brain can allow for detection of disease.

## The Geiger Counter

A Geiger counter is an instrument that detects ionizing radiation (Figure 9.11). Ions, produced by radiation passing through a tube filled with an ionizable gas, can conduct an electrical current between two electrodes. This current flow can be measured and is proportional to the level of radiation (Figure 9.12). Such devices, which were routinely used in laboratory and industrial monitoring, have been largely replaced by more sophisticated devices, often used in conjunction with a computer.

## Film Badges

A common sight in any hospital or medical laboratory or any laboratory that routinely uses radioisotopes is the film badge worn by all staff members exposed in any way to low-level radioactivity.

A film badge is merely a piece of photographic film that is sensitive to energies corresponding to radioactive emissions. It is shielded from light, which would interfere, and mounted in a clip-on plastic holder that can be worn throughout the workday. The badges are periodically collected and developed. The degree of darkening is proportional to the amount of radiation to which the worker has been exposed, just as a conventional camera produces images on film in proportion to the amount of light that it "sees."

Proper record keeping thus allows the laboratory using radioactive substances to maintain an ongoing history of each individual's exposure and, at the same time, promptly pinpoint any hazards that might otherwise go unnoticed.

**Figure 9.11** A worker in a protective suit is measuring the ground using a Geiger counter.

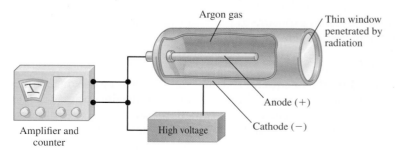

**Figure 9.12** The design of a Geiger counter used for the measurement of radioactivity.

# Green Chemistry

## Radon and Indoor Air Pollution

Marie and Pierre Curie first discovered that air in contact with radium compounds became radioactive. Later experiments by Ernest Rutherford and others isolated the radioactive substance from the air. This substance was an isotope of the noble gas radon (Rn).

We now know that radium (Ra) produces radon by spontaneous decay:

$$^{226}_{88}Ra \longrightarrow {}^{4}_{2}He + {}^{222}_{86}Rn$$

Radium in trace quantities is found in soil and rock and is unequally distributed in the soil. The decay product, radon, is emitted from the soil to the surrounding atmosphere. Radon is also found in higher concentrations where uranium is found in the soil. This is not surprising, because radium is formed as a part of the stepwise decay of uranium.

If someone constructs a building over soil or rock that has a high radium content (or uses stone with a high radium content to build the foundation!), the radon gas can percolate through the basement and accumulate in the house. Couple this with the need to build more energy-efficient, well-insulated dwellings, and the radon levels in buildings in some regions of the country can become quite high.

Radon itself is radioactive; however, its radiation is not the major problem. Because it is a gas and chemically inert, it is rapidly exhaled after breathing. However, radon decays to polonium:

$$^{222}_{86}Rn \longrightarrow {}^{4}_{2}He + {}^{218}_{84}Po$$

This polonium isotope is radioactive and is a nonvolatile heavy metal that can attach itself to bronchial or lung tissue, emitting hazardous radiation and producing other isotopes that are also radioactive.

In the United States, homes are now being tested and monitored for radon. In many states, proof of acceptable levels of radon is a condition of sale of the property. Studies continue to

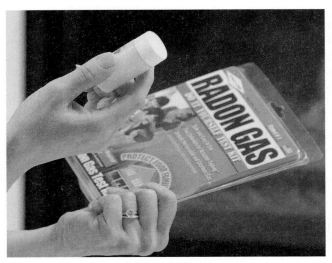

A radon gas detector can be used by a homeowner to quickly determine the level of radon present in a home. However, the collection kit must be sent to a laboratory for analysis.

attempt to find reasonable solutions to the radon problem. Current recommendations include sealing cracks and openings in basements, increasing ventilation, and evaluating sites before construction of buildings. Debate continues within the scientific community regarding a safe and attainable indoor air quality standard for radon.

### For Further Understanding

▶ Why is indoor radon more hazardous than outdoor radon?
▶ Polonium-218 has a very long half-life. Explain why this constitutes a potential health problem.

---

## Units of Radiation Measurement

The amount of radiation emitted by a source or received by an individual is reported in a variety of ways, using units that describe different aspects of radiation. The *curie* and the *becquerel* describe the intensity of the emitted radiation, the *roentgen* describes exposure to radiation, and the *rad, gray, rem*, and the *sievert* describe the biological effects of radiation.

### Radioactivity

The **curie** (Ci) and the **becquerel** (Bq) are units describing the measurement of the amount of radioactivity in a radioactive source. Both the curie and the becquerel are independent of the nature of the radiation and its effect on biological tissue. A curie is defined as the amount of radioactive material that produces $3.7 \times 10^{10}$ atomic disintegrations per second (s). A becquerel is the amount of radioactive material that produces 1 atomic disintegration per second. Therefore, one Ci is equivalent to $3.7 \times 10^{10}$ Bq.

## Exposure

The **roentgen** is a measure of very high energy ionizing radiation (X-ray and gamma ray) only. The roentgen is defined as the amount of radiation needed to produce $2 \times 10^9$ ion pairs when passing through 1 cubic centimeter ($cm^3$) of air at 0°C. The roentgen is a measure of radiation's interaction with air and gives no information about the effect on biological tissue. Since the measurement is based on air ionization, it can be used to determine exposure. Generally, it would be lethal if a human were exposed to 500 roentgens in 5 hours.

## Absorbed Dosage

The **rad,** or *radiation absorbed dosage,* provides more meaningful information than either of the previous units of measure. It takes into account the nature of the absorbing material. It is defined as the dosage of radiation able to transfer $2.4 \times 10^{-3}$ calories (cal) of energy to 1 kilogram (kg) of matter. The **gray** (Gy) is also used to measure an absorbed dosage. The Gy is commonly used in radiation therapy. It is defined as the absorption of 1 joule (J) of energy by 1 kg of matter.

## Dose Equivalent

The **rem,** or *roentgen equivalent for man,* describes the biological damage caused by the absorption of different kinds of radiation by the human body. The *rem* is obtained by multiplication of the *rad* by a factor called the *relative biological effect (RBE).* The RBE is a function of the type of radiation. Although a beta particle is more penetrating than an alpha particle, an alpha particle is approximately ten times more damaging to biological tissue. As a result, the RBE is ten for alpha particles and one for beta particles. The **sievert,** Sv, describes the biological effect that results when one Gy of radiation energy is absorbed by human tissue. One Sv is equivalent to 100 rem.

The **lethal dose (LD$_{50}$)** of radiation is defined as the acute dosage of radiation that would be fatal for 50% of the exposed population within 30 days. An estimated lethal dose is 500 rems, or 5 Sv. Some biological effects, however, may be detectable at a level as low as 25 rems, or 0.25 Sv. Relative yearly background radiation dosages received by Americans are shown in Figure 9.13.

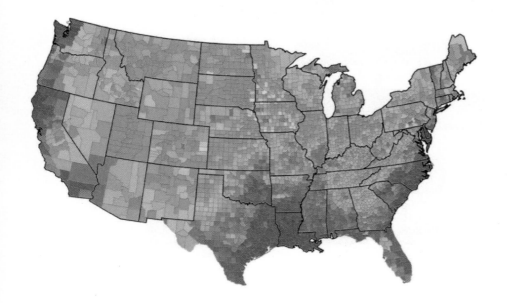

**Figure 9.13**  Relative yearly radiation dosages for individuals in the continental United States. Red, yellow, and green shading indicates higher levels of background radiation. Blue shading indicates regions of lower background exposure.

**Question 9.15** From a clinical standpoint, what advantages does expressing radiation in rems have over the use of other radiation units?

**Question 9.16** Is the roentgen unit used in the measurement of alpha particle radiation? Why or why not?

# CHAPTER MAP

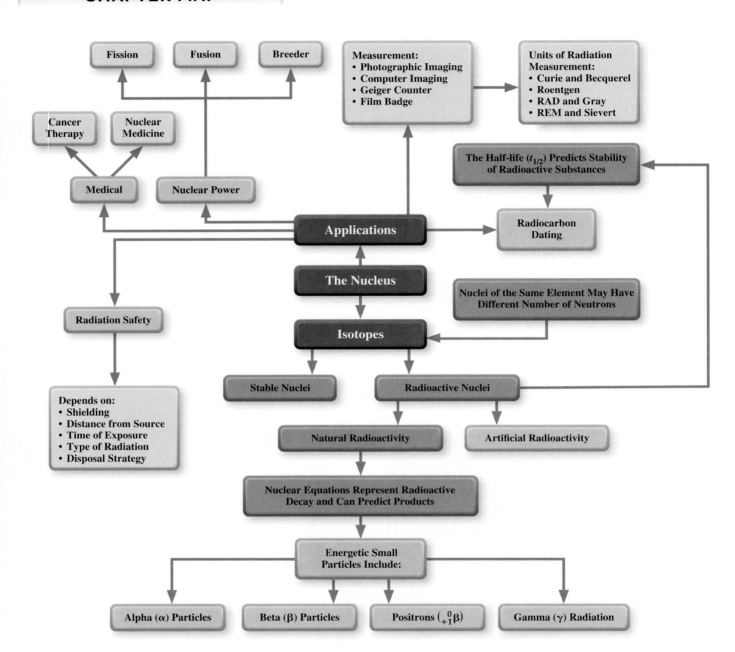

# SUMMARY

## 9.1 Natural Radioactivity

▶ **Radioactivity** is the process by which atoms emit energetic, ionizing particles or rays. These particles or rays are termed radiation.

▶ Nuclear radiation occurs because the nucleus is unstable, hence radioactive.

▶ Nuclear symbols consist of the elemental symbol, the atomic number, and the mass number.

▶ Not all **nuclides** are unstable. Only unstable nuclides undergo change and produce radioactivity in the process of radioactive decay.

▶ Natural radiation emitted by unstable nuclei includes **alpha particles ($\alpha$), beta particles ($\beta$), positrons ($_{+1}^{0}\beta$),** and **gamma rays ($\gamma$).**

▶ This radiation is collectively termed **ionizing radiation.**

## 9.2 Writing a Balanced Nuclear Equation

▶ A **nuclear equation** represents a nuclear process such as radioactive decay.

▶ In a nuclear equation, the total of the mass numbers on each side of the reaction arrow must be identical, and the sum of the atomic numbers of the reactants must equal the sum of the atomic numbers of the products.

▶ Nuclear equations can be used to predict products of nuclear reactions.

## 9.3 Properties of Radioisotopes

▶ The **binding energy** of the nucleus is a measure of nuclear stability. When an isotope decays, energy is released.

▶ Nuclear stability correlates with the ratio of neutrons to protons in the isotope. Isotopes (except hydrogen-1) with more protons than neutrons are unstable. Nuclei with large numbers of protons tend to be unstable, and isotopes containing 2, 8, 20, 50, 82, or 126 protons or neutrons (magic numbers) are stable. Also, isotopes with even numbers of protons or neutrons are generally more stable than those with odd numbers of protons or neutrons.

▶ The **half-life,** $t_{1/2}$, is the time required for one-half of a given quantity of a substance to undergo change. Each isotope has its own characteristic half-life. The degree of stability of an isotope is indicated by the isotope's half-life. Isotopes with short half-lives decay rapidly; they are very unstable.

▶ **Radiocarbon dating** is based on the measurement of the relative amounts of carbon-12 and carbon-14 present in an object. The ratio of the masses of these isotopes changes slowly over time, making it useful in determining the age of objects containing carbon.

## 9.4 Nuclear Power

▶ Einstein predicted that a small amount of nuclear mass would convert to a very large amount of energy when the nucleus breaks apart. His prediction formed the basis for the modern **nuclear reactor.**

▶ **Fission** reactors, relying on a **chain reaction,** are used to generate electrical power. Technological problems with **fusion** and **breeder reactors** have prevented their commercialization in the United States.

## 9.5 Medical Applications of Radioactivity

▶ The use of radiation in the treatment of various forms of cancer, and in the newer area of **nuclear medicine,** has become widespread in the past quarter century.

▶ **Ionizing radiation** causes changes in cellular biochemical processes that may damage or kill the cell.

▶ A cancerous organ is composed of both healthy and malignant cells. Exposure of the tumor area to controlled dosages of high-energy gamma radiation from cobalt-60 will kill a higher percentage of abnormal cells than normal cells and is a valuable cancer therapy.

▶ The diagnosis of a host of biochemical irregularities or diseases of the human body has been made routine through the use of radioactive tracers.

▶ **Tracers** are small amounts of radioactive substances used as probes to study internal organs. Because the isotope is radioactive, its path may be followed by using suitable detection devices. An image of the organ is obtained, far more detailed than is possible with conventional X-rays. Medical techniques involving tracers are **nuclear imaging** procedures.

▶ The radioactivity produced by unstable isotopes is described as **natural radioactivity.** A normally stable, nonradioactive nucleus can be made radioactive, and this is termed **artificial radioactivity** (the process produces synthetic isotopes).

▶ Synthetic isotopes are often used in clinical situations. Isotopic synthesis may be carried out in the core of a nuclear reactor or in a *particle accelerator.* Short-lived isotopes, such as technetium-99m, are often produced directly at the site of the clinical testing.

## 9.6 Biological Effects of Radiation

▶ Safety considerations are based on the magnitude of the **half-life, shielding,** distance from the radioactive source, time of exposure, and type of radiation emitted.

▶ We are never entirely free of the effects of radioactivity. **Background radiation** is normal radiation attributable to our surroundings.

▶ Virtually all applications of nuclear chemistry create radioactive waste and, along with it, the problems of safe handling and disposal. Most disposal sites are considered temporary, until a long-term safe solution can be found.

## 9.7 Measurement of Radiation

▶ The changes that take place when radiation interacts with matter provide the basis for various radiation detection devices. Photographic imaging, computer imaging, the

Geiger counter, and film badges represent the most frequently used devices for detecting and measuring radiation.

▶ Commonly used radiation units include the **curie** and **becquerel**, measurements of the amount of radioactivity in a radioactive source; the **roentgen**, a measurement of high-energy radiation (X-ray and gamma ray); the **rad** (radiation absorbed dosage) and **gray**, which take into account the nature of the absorbing material; and the **rem** (roentgen equivalent for man) and **sievert**, which describe the biological damage caused by the absorption of different kinds of radiation by the human body.

▶ The **lethal dose** of radiation, $LD_{50}$, is defined as the dose that would be fatal for 50% of the exposed population within 30 days.

## ANSWERS TO PRACTICE PROBLEMS

**9.1**   **a.** $^{226}_{88}\text{Ra} \longrightarrow {}^{4}_{2}\text{He} + {}^{222}_{86}\text{Rn}$   **b.** $^{11}_{5}\text{B} \longrightarrow {}^{7}_{3}\text{Li} + {}^{4}_{2}\text{He}$

**9.2**   **a.** $^{85}_{36}\text{Kr} \longrightarrow {}^{85}_{37}\text{Rb} + {}^{0}_{-1}\text{e}$   **b.** $^{239}_{92}\text{U} \longrightarrow {}^{239}_{93}\text{Np} + {}^{0}_{-1}\text{e}$

**9.3**   **a.** $^{79}_{37}\text{Rb} \longrightarrow {}^{79}_{36}\text{Kr} + {}^{0}_{+1}\text{e}$   **b.** $^{38}_{20}\text{Ca} \longrightarrow {}^{38}_{19}\text{K} + {}^{0}_{+1}\text{e}$

**9.4**   **a.** 6.3 ng of sodium-24 remains after 2.5 days
**b.** 0.6 ng of technetium-99m remains after 1 day

## QUESTIONS AND PROBLEMS

### Natural Radioactivity

#### Foundations

**9.17**   Describe the meaning of the term *natural radioactivity*.
**9.18**   Describe what is meant by the term *nuclide*.
**9.19**   What is the composition of an alpha particle?
**9.20**   What is alpha decay?
**9.21**   What is the composition of a beta particle?
**9.22**   What is the composition of a positron?
**9.23**   What are the major differences between alpha and beta particles?
**9.24**   What are the major differences between alpha particles and gamma radiation?
**9.25**   How do nuclear reactions and chemical reactions differ?
**9.26**   We can control the rate of chemical reactions. Can we control the rate of natural radiation?
**9.27**   Write the nuclear symbol for an alpha particle.
**9.28**   Write the nuclear symbol for a beta particle.
**9.29**   How does an alpha particle differ from a helium atom?
**9.30**   What is the major difference between beta and gamma radiation?

**9.31**   Compare and contrast the four major types of radiation produced by nuclear decay.
**9.32**   Rank the four major types of radiation in order of size, speed, and penetrating power.

#### Applications

**9.33**   Write the nuclear symbol for nitrogen-15.
**9.34**   Write the nuclear symbol for carbon-14.
**9.35**   Write the nuclear symbol for uranium-235.
**9.36**   How many protons and neutrons are contained in the nucleus of uranium-235?
**9.37**   How many protons and neutrons are contained in each of the three isotopes of hydrogen?
**9.38**   How many protons and neutrons are contained in each of the three isotopes of carbon?

### Writing a Balanced Nuclear Equation

#### Foundations

**9.39**   Write a nuclear equation to represent cobalt-60 decaying to nickel-60 plus a beta particle plus a gamma ray.
**9.40**   Write a nuclear equation to represent radium-226 decaying to radon-222 plus an alpha particle.
**9.41**   Complete the following nuclear equation:

$$^{23}_{11}\text{Na} + {}^{2}_{1}\text{H} \longrightarrow ? + {}^{1}_{1}\text{H}$$

**9.42**   Complete the following nuclear equation:

$$^{238}_{92}\text{U} + {}^{14}_{7}\text{N} \longrightarrow ? + 6\,{}^{1}_{0}\text{n}$$

**9.43**   Complete the following nuclear equation:

$$^{24}_{10}\text{Ne} \longrightarrow \beta + ?$$

**9.44**   Complete the following nuclear equation:

$$^{190}_{78}\text{Pt} \longrightarrow \alpha + ?$$

**9.45**   Complete the following nuclear equation:

$$? \longrightarrow {}^{140}_{56}\text{Ba} + {}^{0}_{-1}\text{e}$$

**9.46**   Complete the following nuclear equation:

$$? \longrightarrow {}^{214}_{90}\text{Th} + {}^{4}_{2}\text{He}$$

#### Applications

**9.47**   Element 107 was synthesized by bombarding bismuth-209 with chromium-54. Write the equation for this process if one product is a neutron.
**9.48**   Element 109 was synthesized by bombarding bismuth-209 with iron-58. Write the equation for this process if one product is a neutron.
**9.49**   Write a balanced nuclear equation for beta emission by magnesium-27.
**9.50**   Write a balanced nuclear equation for alpha decay of bismuth-212.
**9.51**   Write a balanced nuclear equation for positron emission by nitrogen-12.

**9.52** Write a balanced nuclear equation for positron emission by manganese-52.

**9.53** Americium-241, found in many home smoke detectors, decays by alpha emission. The alpha particle ionizes surrounding air molecules, and ions produced conduct an electric current. Smoke particles block this process and the change in current triggers an alarm. Write the balanced nuclear equation for the decay of americium-241.

**9.54** Element 106 was named seaborgium (Sg) in honor of Glenn T. Seaborg, a pioneer in the discovery of lanthanide and actinide elements. Seaborgium-263 decays by alpha emission. Write a balanced nuclear equation for this process.

## Properties of Radioisotopes

### Foundations

**9.55** Summarize the major characteristics of nuclei for which we predict a high degree of stability.

**9.56** Explain why the binding energy of a nucleus is expected to be large.

**9.57** Sodium-24 has a half-life of 15 h. How many half-lives occur after 225 h?

**9.58** Cobalt-60 has a half-life of 5.3 years. How many half-lives occur after 21.2 years?

### Applications

**9.59** Would you predict oxygen-20 to be stable? Explain your reasoning.

**9.60** Would you predict cobalt-59 to be stable? Explain your reasoning.

**9.61** Would you predict chromium-48 to be stable? Explain your reasoning.

**9.62** Would you predict lithium-9 to be stable? Explain your reasoning.

**9.63** If 3.2 mg of the radioisotope iodine-131 is administered to a patient, how much will remain in the body after 24 days, assuming that no iodine has been eliminated from the body by any other process? (See Table 9.2 for the half-life of iodine-131.)

**9.64** A patient receives 9.0 ng of a radioisotope with a half-life of 12 h. How much will remain in the body after 2.0 days, assuming that radioactive decay is the only path for removal of the isotope from the body?

**9.65** A sample containing $1.00 \times 10^2$ mg of iron-59 is stored for 135 days. What mass of iron-59 will remain at the end of the storage period? (See Table 9.2 for the half-life of iron-59.)

**9.66** An instrument for cancer treatment containing a cobalt-60 source was manufactured in 1988. In 1995, it was removed from service and, in error, was buried in a landfill with the source still in place. What percentage of its initial radioactivity will remain in the year 2020? (See Table 9.2 for the half-life of cobalt-60.)

**9.67** Describe the process used to determine the age of the wooden coffin of King Tut.

**9.68** What property of carbon enables us to assess the age of a painting?

## Nuclear Power

### Foundations

**9.69** Which type of nuclear process splits nuclei to release energy?

**9.70** Which type of nuclear process combines small nuclei to release energy?

**9.71** **a.** Describe the process of fission.
**b.** How is this reaction useful as the basis for the production of electrical energy?

**9.72** **a.** Describe the process of fusion.
**b.** How could this process be used for the production of electrical energy?

### Applications

**9.73** Write a balanced nuclear equation for a fusion reaction.

**9.74** What are the major disadvantages of a fission reactor for electrical energy production?

**9.75** What is meant by the term *breeder reactor?*

**9.76** What are the potential advantages and disadvantages of breeder reactors?

**9.77** Describe what is meant by the term *chain reaction.*

**9.78** Why are cadmium rods used in a fission reactor?

**9.79** What is the greatest barrier to development of fusion reactors?

**9.80** What type of nuclear reaction fuels our solar system?

## Medical Applications of Radioactivity

### Foundations

**9.81** Why is radiation therapy an effective treatment for certain types of cancer?

**9.82** Describe how radioactive tracers are used in the diagnosis of disease.

**9.83** What is the difference between natural radioactivity and artificial radioactivity?

**9.84** Describe how medically useful isotopes may be prepared.

### Applications

**9.85** Describe an application of each of the following isotopes:
**a.** technetium-99m
**b.** xenon-133

**9.86** Describe an application of each of the following isotopes:
**a.** iodine-131
**b.** thallium-201

**9.87** The isotope indium-111 is used in medical laboratories as a label for blood platelets. To prepare indium-111, silver-108 is bombarded with an alpha particle, forming an intermediate isotope of indium. Write a nuclear equation for the process, and identify the intermediate isotope of indium.

**9.88** Radioactive molybdenum-99 is used to produce the tracer isotope, technetium-99m. Write a nuclear equation for the formation of molybdenum-99 from stable molybdenum-98 bombarded with neutrons.

## Biological Effects of Radiation

### Foundations

**9.89** What is the source of background radiation?

**9.90** Why do high-altitude jet flights increase a person's exposure to background radiation?

## Applications

Answer Questions 9.91 through 9.98 based on the assumption that you are employed by a clinical laboratory that prepares radioactive isotopes for medical diagnostic tests. Consider alpha, beta, positron, and gamma emission.

**9.91** What would be the effect on your level of radiation exposure if you increase your average distance from a radioactive source?

**9.92** Would wearing gloves have any significant effect? Why?

**9.93** Would limiting your time of exposure have a positive effect? Why?

**9.94** Would wearing a lab apron lined with thin sheets of lead have a positive effect? Why?

**9.95** Would the use of robotic manipulation of samples have an effect? Why?

**9.96** Would the use of concrete rather than wood paneling help to protect workers in other parts of the clinic? Why?

**9.97** Would the thickness of the concrete in Question 9.96 be an important consideration? Why?

**9.98** Suggest a protocol for radioactive waste disposal.

## Measurement of Radiation

### Foundations

**9.99** What is meant by the term *relative biological effect?*

**9.100** What is meant by the term *lethal dose* of radiation?

**9.101** Define each of the following units:
a. curie
b. roentgen
c. becquerel

**9.102** Define each of the following radiation units:
a. rad
b. rem
c. gray

### Applications

**9.103** X-ray technicians often wear badges containing photographic film. How is this film used to indicate exposure to X-rays?

**9.104** Why would a Geiger counter be preferred to film for assessing the immediate danger resulting from a spill of some solution containing a radioisotope?

# CHALLENGE PROBLEMS

1. Isotopes used as radioactive tracers have chemical properties that are similar to those of a nonradioactive isotope of the same element. Explain why this is a critical consideration in their use.

2. A chemist proposes a research project to discover a catalyst that will speed up the decay of radioactive isotopes that are waste products of a medical laboratory. Such a discovery would be a potential solution to the problem of nuclear waste disposal. Critique this proposal.

3. A controversial solution to the disposal of nuclear waste involves burial in sealed chambers far below the earth's surface. Describe the potential pros and cons of this approach.

4. What type of radioactive decay is favored if the number of protons in the nucleus is much greater than the number of neutrons? Explain your reasoning.

5. If the proton-to-neutron ratio in Problem 4 (above) were reversed, what radioactive decay process would be favored? Explain.

6. Radioactive isotopes are often used as "tracers" to follow an atom through a chemical reaction, and the following is an example. Acetic acid reacts with methanol by eliminating a molecule of water to form methyl acetate. Explain how you would use the radioactive isotope oxygen-18 to show whether the oxygen atom in the water product comes from the —OH of acetic acid or the —OH of methanol.

$$H_3C\overset{\overset{O}{\|}}{C}—OH + HO—CH_3 \longrightarrow H_3C\overset{\overset{O}{\|}}{C}—O—CH_3 + H_2O$$

Acetic acid        Methanol        Methyl acetate

7. Chromium-51, used as a tracer to study red blood cells, decays by electron capture. In this process, a proton in the chromium nucleus is, in effect, converted to a neutron by combining with (capturing) an electron. Write a balanced equation for this process. What is the identity of the product?

# Glossary

## A

**absolute specificity** (19.5) the property of an enzyme that allows it to bind and catalyze the reaction of only one substrate

**accuracy** (1.4) the nearness of an experimental value to the true value

**acetal** (13.4) the family of organic compounds formed via the reaction of two molecules of alcohol with an aldehyde or a ketone in the presence of an acid catalyst

**acetyl coenzyme A (acetyl CoA)** (14.4, 22.2) a molecule composed of coenzyme A and an acetyl group; the intermediate that provides acetyl groups for complete oxidation by aerobic respiration

**acid anhydride** (14.3) the product formed by the combination of an acid chloride and a carboxylate ion; structurally they are two carboxylic acids with a water molecule removed:

$$(Ar)R-\overset{\overset{\displaystyle O}{\|}}{C}-O-\overset{\overset{\displaystyle O}{\|}}{C}-R(Ar)$$

**acid-base reaction** (4.7) reaction that involves the transfer of a hydrogen ion ($H^+$) from one reactant to another

**acid chloride** (14.3) member of the family of organic compounds with the general formula

$$(Ar)R-\overset{\overset{\displaystyle O}{\|}}{C}-Cl$$

**activated complex** (7.3) the arrangement of atoms at the top of the potential energy barrier as a reaction proceeds

**activation energy** (7.3) the threshold energy that must be overcome to produce a chemical reaction

**active site** (19.4) the cleft in the surface of an enzyme that is the site of substrate binding

**acyl carrier protein (ACP)** (23.4) the protein that forms a thioester linkage with fatty acids during fatty acid synthesis

**acyl group** (14.3, 15.3) the functional group found in carboxylic acid derivatives that contains the carbonyl group attached to one alkyl or aryl group:

$$(Ar)R-\overset{\overset{\displaystyle O}{\|}}{C}-$$

**addition polymer** (11.5) polymers prepared by the sequential addition of a monomer

**addition reaction** (11.5, 13.4) a reaction in which two molecules add together to form a new molecule; often involves the addition of one molecule to a double or triple bond in an unsaturated molecule;

e.g., the addition of alcohol to an aldehyde or ketone to form a hemiacetal

**adenosine triphosphate (ATP)** (14.4, 21.1) a nucleotide composed of the purine adenine, the sugar ribose, and three phosphoryl groups; the primary energy storage and transport molecule used by the cells in cellular metabolism

**adipocyte** (23.1) a fat cell

**adipose tissue** (23.1) fatty tissue that stores most of the body lipids

**aerobic respiration** (22.3) the oxygen-requiring degradation of food molecules and production of ATP

**alcohol** (12.1) an organic compound that contains a hydroxyl group (—OH) attached to an alkyl group

**aldehyde** (13.1) a class of organic molecules characterized by a carbonyl group; the carbonyl carbon is bonded to a hydrogen atom and to another hydrogen or an alkyl or aryl group. Aldehydes have the following general structure:

$$(Ar)-\overset{\overset{\displaystyle O}{\|}}{C}-H \qquad R-\overset{\overset{\displaystyle O}{\|}}{C}-H$$

**aldose** (16.2) a sugar that contains an aldehyde (carbonyl) group

**aliphatic hydrocarbon** (10.1) any member of the alkanes, alkenes, and alkynes or the substituted alkanes, alkenes, and alkynes

**alkali metal** (2.4) an element within Group IA (1) of the periodic table

**alkaline earth metal** (2.4) an element within Group IIA (2) of the periodic table

**alkaloid** (15.2) a class of naturally occurring compounds that contain one or more nitrogen heterocyclic rings; many of the alkaloids have medicinal and other physiological effects

**alkane** (10.2) a hydrocarbon that contains only carbon and hydrogen and is bonded together through carbon-hydrogen and carbon-carbon single bonds; a saturated hydrocarbon with the general molecular formula $C_nH_{2n+2}$

**alkene** (11.1) a hydrocarbon that contains one or more carbon-carbon double bond; an unsaturated hydrocarbon with the general formula $C_nH_{2n}$

**alkyl group** (10.2) a hydrocarbon group that results from the removal of one hydrogen from the original hydrocarbon (e.g., methyl, —$CH_3$; ethyl, —$CH_2CH_3$)

**alkyl halide** (10.5) a substituted hydrocarbon with the general structure R—X, in which R— represents any alkyl group and X = a halogen (F—, Cl—, Br—, or I—)

**alkylammonium ion** (15.1) the ion formed when the lone pair of electrons of the

nitrogen atom of an amine is shared with a proton ($H^+$) from a water molecule

**alkyne** (11.1) a hydrocarbon that contains one or more carbon-carbon triple bond; an unsaturated hydrocarbon with the general formula $C_nH_{2n-2}$

**allosteric enzyme** (19.9) an enzyme that has an effector binding site and an active site; effector binding changes the shape of the active site, rendering it either active or inactive

**alpha particle** (9.1) a particle consisting of two protons and two neutrons; the alpha particle is identical to a helium nucleus

**amide bond** (15.3) the bond between the carbonyl carbon of a carboxylic acid and the amino nitrogen of an amine

**amides** (15.3) the family of organic compounds formed by the reaction between a carboxylic acid derivative and an amine and characterized by the amide group

**amines** (15.1) the family of organic molecules with the general formula $RNH_2$, $R_2NH$, or $R_3N$ (R— can represent either an alkyl or aryl group); they may be viewed as substituted ammonia molecules in which one or more of the ammonia hydrogens has been substituted by a more complex organic group

**α-amino acid** (15.4, 18.1) the subunits of proteins composed of an α-carbon bonded to a carboxylate group, a protonated amino group, a hydrogen atom, and a variable R group

**aminoacyl group** (15.4) the functional group that is characteristic of an amino acid; the aminoacyl group has the following general structure:

$$H_3\overset{+}{N}-\overset{\overset{\displaystyle H}{|}}{\underset{\underset{\displaystyle R}{|}}{C}}-\overset{\overset{\displaystyle O}{\|}}{C}-$$

**aminoacyl tRNA** (20.6) the transfer RNA covalently linked to the correct amino acid

**aminoacyl tRNA binding site of ribosome (A-site)** (20.6) a pocket on the surface of a ribosome that holds the aminoacyl tRNA during translation

**aminoacyl tRNA synthetase** (20.6) an enzyme that recognizes one tRNA and covalently links the appropriate amino acid to it

**amorphous solid** (5.3) a solid with no organized, regular structure

**amphibolic pathway** (22.9) a metabolic pathway that functions in both anabolism and catabolism

**amphiprotic** (8.1) a substance that can behave either as a Brønsted acid or a Brønsted base

**amylopectin** (16.6)   a highly branched form of amylose; the branches are attached to the C-6 hydroxyl by α(1 ⟶ 6) glycosidic linkage; a component of starch

**amylose** (16.6)   a linear polymer of α-D-glucose molecules bonded in α(1 ⟶ 4) glycosidic linkage that is a component of starch; a polysaccharide storage form

**anabolism** (21.1, 22.9)   all of the cellular energy-requiring biosynthetic pathways

**anaerobic threshold** (21.4)   the point at which the level of lactate in the exercising muscle inhibits glycolysis, and the muscle, deprived of energy, ceases to function

**analgesic** (15.2)   any drug that acts as a painkiller, e.g., aspirin, acetaminophen

**anaplerotic reaction** (22.9)   a reaction that replenishes a substrate needed for a biochemical pathway

**anesthetic** (15.2)   a drug that causes a lack of sensation in part of the body (local anesthetic) or causes unconsciousness (general anesthetic)

**anion** (2.6)   a negatively charged atom or group of atoms

**anode** (4.8)   the positively charged electrode in an electrical cell

**anomers** (16.4)   isomers of cyclic monosaccharides that differ from one another in the arrangement of bonds around the hemiacetal carbon

**antibodies** (18: Intro)   immunoglobulins; specific glycoproteins produced by cells of the immune system in response to invasion by infectious agents

**anticodon** (20.6)   a sequence of three ribonucleotides on a tRNA that are complementary to a codon on the mRNA; codon-anticodon binding results in delivery of the correct amino acid to the site of protein synthesis

**antigen** (18: Intro)   any substance that is able to stimulate the immune system; generally a protein or large carbohydrate

**antiparallel strands** (20.2)   a term describing the polarities of the two strands of the DNA double helix; on one strand, the sugar-phosphate backbone advances in the 5′ ⟶ 3′ direction; on the opposite, complementary strand, the sugar-phosphate backbone advances in the 3′ ⟶ 5′ direction

**apoenzyme** (19.7)   the protein portion of an enzyme that requires a cofactor to function in catalysis

**aqueous solution** (6.1)   any solution in which the solvent is water

**arachidonic acid** (17.2)   a fatty acid derived from linoleic acid; the precursor of the prostaglandins

**aromatic hydrocarbon** (10.1, 11.6)   an organic compound that contains the benzene ring or a derivative of the benzene ring

**Arrhenius acid** (8.1)   a substance that dissociates to produce $H^+$

**Arrhenius base** (8.1)   a substance that dissociates to produce $OH^-$

**Arrhenius theory** (8.1)   a theory that describes an acid as a substance that dissociates to produce $H^+$, and a base as a substance that dissociates to produce $OH^-$

**artificial radioactivity** (9.5)   radiation that results from the conversion of a stable nucleus to another, unstable nucleus

**atherosclerosis** (17.4)   deposition of excess plasma cholesterol and other lipids and proteins on the walls of arteries, resulting in decreased artery diameter and increased blood pressure

**atom** (2.1)   the smallest unit of an element that retains the properties of that element

**atomic mass** (2.1, 4.1)   the mass of an atom expressed in atomic mass units

**atomic mass unit** (4.1)   1/12 of the mass of a $^{12}C$ atom, equivalent to $1.661 \times 10^{-24}$ g

**atomic number** (2.1)   the number of protons in the nucleus of an atom; it is a characteristic identifier of an element

**atomic orbital** (2.3, 2.5)   a specific region of space where an electron may be found

**ATP synthase** (22.6)   a multiprotein complex within the inner mitochondrial membrane that uses the energy of the proton ($H^+$) gradient to produce ATP

**autoionization** (8.1)   also known as *self-ionization*, the reaction of a substance, such as water, with itself to produce a positive and a negative ion

**Avogadro's law** (5.1)   a law that states that the volume is directly proportional to the number of moles of gas particles, assuming that the pressure and temperature are constant

**Avogadro's number** (4.1)   $6.022 \times 10^{23}$ particles of matter contained in 1 mol of a substance

## B

**background radiation** (9.6)   the radiation that emanates from natural sources

**barometer** (5.1)   a device for measuring pressure

**base pair** (20.2)   a hydrogen-bonded pair of nitrogenous bases within the DNA double helix; the standard base pairs always involve a purine and a pyrimidine; in particular, adenine always base pairs with thymine and cytosine with guanine

**Becquerel** (9.7)   amount of radioactive material that produces 1 atomic disintegration per second

**Benedict's reagent** (16.4)   a buffered solution of $Cu^{2+}$ ions that can be used to test for reducing sugars or to distinguish between aldehydes and ketones

**Benedict's test** (13.4)   a test used to determine the presence of reducing sugars or to distinguish between aldehydes and ketones; it requires a buffered solution of $Cu^{2+}$ ions that are reduced to $Cu^+$, which precipitates as brick-red $Cu_2O$

**bent** (3.4)   a planar molecule with bond angles other than 180°

**beta particle** (9.1)   an electron formed in the nucleus by the conversion of a neutron into a proton

**bile** (23.1)   micelles of lecithin, cholesterol, bile salts, protein, inorganic ions, and bile pigments that aid in lipid digestion by emulsifying fat droplets

**binding energy** (9.3)   the energy required to break down the nucleus into its component parts

**bioinformatics** (20.10)   an interdisciplinary field that uses computer information sciences and DNA technology to devise methods for understanding, analyzing, and applying DNA sequence information

**boat conformation** (10.4)   a form of a six-member cycloalkane that resembles a rowboat. It is less stable than the chair conformation because the hydrogen atoms are not perfectly staggered

**boiling point** (3.3)   the temperature at which the vapor pressure of a liquid is equal to the atmospheric pressure

**bond energy** (3.4)   the amount of energy necessary to break a chemical bond

**Boyle's law** (5.1)   a law stating that the volume of a gas varies inversely with the pressure exerted if the temperature and number of moles of gas are constant

**breeder reactor** (9.4)   a nuclear reactor that produces its own fuel in the process of providing electrical energy

**Brønsted-Lowry acid** (8.1)   a proton donor

**Brønsted-Lowry base** (8.1)   a proton acceptor

**buffer capacity** (8.4)   a measure of the ability of a solution to resist large changes in pH when a strong acid or strong base is added

**buffer solution** (8.4)   a solution containing a weak acid or base and its salt (the conjugate base or acid) that is resistant to large changes in pH upon addition of strong acids or bases

**buret** (8.3)   a device calibrated to deliver accurately known volumes of liquid, as in a titration

## C

**C-terminal amino acid** (18.2)   the amino acid in a peptide that has a free α-$CO_2^-$ group; the last amino acid in a peptide

**calorimetry** (7.2)   the measurement of heat energy changes during a chemical reaction

**cap structure** (20.4)   a 7-methylguanosine unit covalently bonded to the 5′ end of a mRNA by a 5′-5′ triphosphate bridge

**carbinol carbon** (12.1)   that carbon in an alcohol to which the hydroxyl group is attached

**carbohydrate** (16.1)   generally sugars and polymers of sugars; the primary source of energy for the cell

**carbonyl group** (13: Intro)   the functional group that contains a carbon-oxygen double bond: —C═O; the functional group found in aldehydes and ketones

**carboxyl group** (14.1)   the —COOH functional group; the functional group found in carboxylic acids

**carboxylic acid** (14.1)   a member of the family of organic compounds that contain the —COOH functional group

**carboxylic acid derivative** (14.2)   any of several families of organic compounds, including the esters and amides, that are derived from carboxylic acids and have the general formula

$$(Ar) - \overset{\overset{\text{O}}{\|}}{C} - Z \qquad R - \overset{\overset{\text{O}}{\|}}{C} - Z$$

$Z =$ —OR or OAr for the esters, and $Z =$ —$NH_2$ for the amides

**carcinogen** (20.7)   any chemical or physical agent that causes mutations in the DNA that lead to uncontrolled cell growth or cancer

**catabolism** (21.1, 22.9)   the degradation of fuel molecules and production of ATP for cellular functions

**catalyst** (7.3)   any substance that increases the rate of a chemical reaction (by lowering the activation energy of the reaction) and that is not destroyed in the course of the reaction

**cathode** (4.8)   the negatively charged electrode in an electrical cell

**cation** (2.6)   a positively charged atom or group of atoms

**cellulose** (16.6)   a polymer of β-D-glucose linked by $\beta(1 \longrightarrow 4)$ glycosidic bonds

**central dogma** (20.4)   a statement of the directional transfer of the genetic information in cells: DNA $\longrightarrow$ RNA $\longrightarrow$ Protein

**chain reaction** (9.4)   the process in a fission reactor that involves neutron production and causes subsequent reactions accompanied by the production of more neutrons in a continuing process

**chair conformation** (10.4)   the most stable conformation for a six-member cycloalkane; so-called for its resemblance to a lawn chair

**Charles's law** (5.1)   a law stating that the volume of a gas is directly proportional to the temperature of the gas, assuming that the pressure and number of moles of the gas are constant

**chemical bond** (3.1)   the attractive force holding two atomic nuclei together in a chemical compound

**chemical change** (1.2)   a process in which one or more atoms of a substance is rearranged, removed, replaced, or added to produce a new substance

**chemical equation** (4.3)   a record of chemical change, showing the conversion of reactants to products

**chemical equilibrium** (7.4)   the state of a reaction in which the rates of the forward and reverse reactions are equal

**chemical formula** (4.2)   the representation of a compound or ion in which elemental symbols represent types of atoms, and subscripts show the relative numbers of atoms

**chemical properties** (1.2)   characteristics of a substance that relate to the substance's participation in a chemical reaction

**chemical reaction** (1.2)   a process in which atoms are rearranged to produce new combinations

**chemistry** (1.1)   the study of matter, its chemical and physical properties, the chemical and physical changes it undergoes, and the energy changes that accompany these processes

**chiral carbon** (16.3)   a carbon atom bonded to four different atoms or groups of atoms

**chiral molecule** (16.3)   molecule capable of existing in mirror-image forms

**cholesterol** (17.4)   a twenty-seven-carbon steroid ring structure that serves as the precursor of the steroid hormones

**chromosome** (20.2)   a piece of DNA that carries the genetic instructions, or genes, of an organism

**chylomicron** (17.5, 23.1)   a plasma lipoprotein (aggregate of protein and triglycerides) that carries triglycerides from the intestine to all body tissues via the bloodstream

**cis-trans isomers** (10.3)   isomers that differ from one another in the placement of substituents on a double bond or ring

**citric acid cycle** (22.4)   a cyclic biochemical pathway that is the final stage of degradation of carbohydrates, fats, and amino acids. It results in the complete oxidation of acetyl groups derived from these dietary fuels

**cloning vector** (20.8)   a DNA molecule that can carry a cloned DNA fragment into a cell and that has a replication origin that allows the DNA to be replicated abundantly within the host cell

**coagulation** (18.10)   the process by which proteins in solution are denatured and aggregate with one another to produce a solid

**codon** (20.5)   a group of three ribonucleotides on the mRNA that specifies the addition of a specific amino acid onto the growing peptide chain

**coenzyme** (19.7)   an organic group required by some enzymes; it generally serves as a donor or acceptor of electrons or a functional group in a reaction

**coenzyme A** (22.2)   a molecule derived from ATP and the vitamin pantothenic acid; coenzyme A functions in the transfer of acetyl groups in lipid and carbohydrate metabolism

**cofactor** (19.7)   an inorganic group, usually a metal ion, that must be bound to an apoenzyme to maintain the correct configuration of the active site

**colipase** (23.1)   a protein that aids in lipid digestion by binding to the surface of lipid droplets and facilitating binding of pancreatic lipase

**colligative property** (6.4)   property of a solution that is dependent only on the concentration of solute particles

**colloidal suspension** (6.1)   a heterogeneous mixture of solute particles in a solvent; distribution of solute particles is not uniform because of the size of the particles

**combination reaction** (4.3)   a reaction in which two substances join to form another substance

**combined gas law** (5.1)   an equation that describes the behavior of a gas when volume, pressure, and temperature may change simultaneously

**combustion** (4.8)   the oxidation of hydrocarbons by burning in the presence of air to produce carbon dioxide and water

**competitive inhibitor** (19.10)   a structural analog; a molecule that has a structure very similar to the natural substrate of an enzyme, competes with the natural substrate for binding to the enzyme active site, and inhibits the reaction

**complementary strands** (20.2)   the opposite strands of the double helix which are hydrogen-bonded to one another such that adenine and thymine or guanine and cytosine are always paired

**complete protein** (18.11)   a protein source that contains all the essential and nonessential amino acids

**complex lipid** (17.5)   a lipid bonded to other types of molecules

**compound** (1.2)   a substance that is characterized by constant composition and that can be chemically broken down into elements

**concentration** (1.6, 6.2)   a measure of the quantity of a substance contained in a specified volume of solution

**concentration gradient** (6.4)   region where concentration decreases over distance

**condensation** (5.2)   the conversion of a gas to a liquid

**condensation polymer** (14.2)   a polymer, which is a large molecule formed by the combination of many small molecules (monomers) that results from the joining of monomers in a reaction that forms a small molecule, such as water or an alcohol

**condensed formula** (10.2)   a structural formula showing all of the atoms in a molecule and placing them in a sequential arrangement that details which atoms are bonded to each other; the bonds themselves are not shown

**conformations, conformers** (10.4)   discrete, distinct isomeric structures that may be converted, one to the other, by rotation about the bonds in the molecule

**conjugate acid** (8.1)   substance that has one more proton than the base from which it is derived

**conjugate acid-base pair** (8.1)   two species related to each other through the gain or loss of a proton

**conjugate base** (8.1)   substance that has one fewer proton than the acid from which it is derived

**constitutional isomers** (10.2)   two molecules having the same molecular formulas, but different chemical structures

**Cori Cycle** (21.6)   a metabolic pathway in which the lactate produced by working muscle is taken up by cells in the liver and converted back to glucose by gluconeogenesis

**corrosion** (4.8)   the unwanted oxidation of a metal

**covalent bonding** (3.1)   a pair of electrons shared between two atoms

**covalent solid** (5.3)   a collection of atoms held together by covalent bonds

**cristae** (22.1)   the folds of the inner membrane of the mitochondria

**crystal lattice** (3.1)   a unit of a solid characterized by a regular arrangement of components

**crystalline solid** (5.3)   a solid having a regular repeating atomic structure

**curie** (9.7)   the quantity of radioactive material that produces $3.7 \times 10^{10}$ nuclear disintegrations per second

**cycloalkane** (10.3)   a cyclic alkane; a saturated hydrocarbon that has the general formula $C_nH_{2n}$

## D

**Dalton's law** (5.1)   also called the law of partial pressures; states that the total pressure exerted by a gas mixture is the sum of the partial pressures of the component gases

**data** (1.1)   facts resulting from an experiment

**decomposition reaction** (4.3)   the breakdown of a substance into two or more substances

**defense proteins** (18: Intro)   proteins that defend the body against infectious diseases; antibodies are defense proteins

**degenerate code** (20.5)   a term used to describe the fact that several triplet codons may be used to specify a single amino acid in the genetic code

**dehydration (of alcohols)** (12.4)   a reaction that involves the loss of a water molecule, in this case the loss of water from an alcohol and the simultaneous formation of an alkene

**deletion mutation** (20.7)   a mutation that results in the loss of one or more nucleotides from a DNA sequence

**denaturation** (18.10)   the process by which the organized structure of a protein is disrupted, resulting in a completely disorganized, nonfunctional form of the protein

**density** (1.6)   mass per unit volume of a substance

**deoxyribonucleic acid (DNA)** (20.1)   the nucleic acid molecule that carries all of the genetic information of an organism; the DNA molecule is a double helix composed of two strands, each of which is composed of phosphate groups, deoxyribose, and the nitrogenous bases thymine, cytosine, adenine, and guanine

**deoxyribonucleotide** (20.1)   a nucleoside phosphate or nucleotide composed of a nitrogenous base in β-N-glycosidic linkage to the 1′ carbon of the sugar 2′-deoxyribose and with one, two, or three phosphoryl groups esterified at the hydroxyl of the 5′ carbon

**deviation** (1.4)   the amount of variation present in a set of replicate measurements

**diabetes mellitus** (23.3)   a disease caused by the production of insufficient levels of insulin and characterized by the appearance of very high levels of glucose in the blood and urine

**dialysis** (6.5)   the removal of waste material via transport across a membrane

**diastereomers** (16.3)   stereoisomers with at least two chiral carbons that are not mirror images of one another

**diffusion** (6.4)   net movement of solute or solvent molecules from a region of high concentration to a region of low concentration

**diglyceride** (17.3)   the product of esterification of glycerol at two positions

**dipole-dipole interactions** (5.2)   attractive forces between polar molecules

**disaccharide** (16.1)   a sugar composed of two monosaccharides joined through an oxygen atom bridge

**dissociation** (3.3)   production of positive and negative ions when an ionic compound dissolves in water

**disulfide** (12.8)   an organic compound that contains a disulfide group (—S—S—)

**DNA polymerase III** (20.3)   the enzyme that catalyzes the polymerization of daughter DNA strands using the parental strand as a template

**double bond** (3.4)   a bond in which two pairs of electrons are shared by two atoms

**double helix** (20.2)   the spiral staircase–like structure of the DNA molecule characterized by two sugar-phosphate backbones wound around the outside and nitrogenous bases extending into the center

**double-replacement reaction** (4.3)   a chemical change in which cations and anions "exchange partners"

**dynamic equilibrium** (7.4)   the state that exists when the rate of change in the concentration of products and reactants is equal, resulting in no net concentration change

## E

**eicosanoid** (17.2)   any of the derivatives of twenty-carbon fatty acids, including the prostaglandins, leukotrienes, and thromboxanes

**electrolysis** (4.8)   an electrochemical process that uses electrical energy to cause nonspontaneous oxidation-reduction reactions to occur

**electrolyte** (3.3, 6.1)   a material that dissolves in water to produce a solution that conducts an electrical current

**electromagnetic radiation** (2.3)   energy that is propagated as waves at the speed of light

**electron** (2.1)   a negatively charged particle outside of the nucleus of an atom

**electron affinity** (2.7)   the energy released when an electron is added to an isolated atom

**electron configuration** (2.5)   the arrangement of electrons around the nucleus of an atom, an ion, or a collection of nuclei of a molecule

**electron density** (2.3)   the probability of finding the electron in a particular location

**electron transport system** (22.6)   the series of electron transport proteins embedded in the inner mitochondrial membrane that accept high-energy electrons from NADH and $FADH_2$ and transfer them in stepwise fashion to molecular oxygen ($O_2$)

**electronegativity** (3.1)   a measure of the tendency of an atom in a molecule to attract shared electrons

**element** (1.2)   a substance that cannot be decomposed into simpler substances by chemical or physical means

**elimination reaction** (12.4)   a reaction in which a molecule loses atoms or ions from its structure

**elongation factor** (20.6)   proteins that facilitate the elongation phase of translation

**emulsifying agent** (17.3)   a bipolar molecule that aids in the suspension of fats in water

**enantiomers** (16.3)   stereoisomers that are nonsuperimposable mirror images of one another

**endothermic reaction** (7.1)   a chemical or physical change in which energy is absorbed

**energy** (1.1)   the ability to do work

**energy level** (2.3)   one of numerous atomic regions where electrons may be found

**enol** (13.4)   a tautomer containing a carbon-carbon double bond and a hydroxyl group

**enthalpy** (7.1)   a term that represents heat energy

**entropy** (7.1)   a measure of randomness or disorder

**enzyme** (18: Intro, 19: Intro)   a protein that serves as a biological catalyst

**enzyme specificity** (19.5)   the ability of an enzyme to bind to only one, or a very few, substrates and thus catalyze only a single reaction

**enzyme-substrate complex** (19.4)   a molecular aggregate formed when the substrate binds to the active site of the enzyme

**equilibrium constant** (7.4)   number equal to the ratio of the equilibrium concentrations of products to the equilibrium concentrations of reactants, each raised to the power corresponding to its coefficient in the balanced equation

**equivalence point** (8.3)   the situation in which reactants have been mixed in the molar ratio corresponding to the balanced equation

**error** (1.4)   the difference between the true value and the experimental value for data or results

**essential amino acid** (18.11)   an amino acid that cannot be synthesized by the body and must therefore be supplied by the diet

**essential fatty acids** (17.2)   the fatty acids linolenic and linoleic acids that must be supplied in the diet because they cannot be synthesized by the body

**ester** (14.2)   a carboxylic acid derivative formed by the reaction of a carboxylic acid and an alcohol. Esters have the following general formula:

$$(Ar)R\overset{\overset{\displaystyle O}{\|}}{-}C-OR(Ar)$$

**esterification** (17.2)   the formation of an ester in the reaction of a carboxylic acid and an alcohol

**ether** (12.7)   an organic compound that contains two alkyl and/or aryl groups attached to an oxygen atom; R—O—R, Ar—O—R, and Ar—O—Ar

**eukaryote** (20.2)   an organism having cells containing a true nucleus enclosed by a nuclear membrane and having a variety of membrane-bound organelles that segregate different cellular functions into different compartments

**evaporation** (5.2)   the conversion of a liquid to a gas below the boiling point of the liquid

**excited state** (2.3)   an electronic state of an atom when energy has been adsorbed by the ground state atom and one or more electrons are promoted into a higher energy level

**exon** (20.4)   protein-coding sequences of a gene found on the final mature mRNA

**exothermic reaction** (7.1)   a chemical or physical change that releases energy

**extensive property** (1.2)   a property of a substance that depends on the quantity of the substance

## F

**$F_0 F_1$ complex** (22.6)   an alternative term for ATP synthase, the multiprotein complex in the inner mitochondrial membrane that uses the energy of the proton gradient to produce ATP

**fatty acid** (14.1, 17.2)   any member of the family of continuous-chain carboxylic acids that generally contain four to twenty carbon atoms; the most concentrated source of energy used by the cell

**feedback inhibition** (19.9)   the process whereby excess product of a biosynthetic pathway turns off the entire pathway for its own synthesis

**fermentation** (12.3, 21.4)   anaerobic (in the absence of oxygen) catabolic reactions that occur with no net oxidation. Pyruvate or an organic product produced from pyruvate is reduced as NADH is oxidized

**fibrous protein** (18.4)   a protein composed of peptides arranged in long sheets or fibers

**Fischer Projection** (16.3)   a two-dimensional drawing of a molecule that shows a chiral carbon at the intersection of two lines and horizontal lines representing bonds projecting out of the page, and vertical lines representing bonds that project into the page

**fission** (9.4)   the splitting of heavy nuclei into lighter nuclei accompanied by the release of large quantities of energy

**fluid mosaic model** (17.6)   the model of membrane structure that describes the fluid nature of the lipid bilayer and the presence of numerous proteins embedded within the membrane

**formula** (3.2)   the representation of the fundamental compound unit using chemical symbols and numerical subscripts

**formula mass** (4.2)   the mass of a formula unit of a compound relative to a standard (carbon-12)

**formula unit** (4.2)   the smallest collection of atoms from which the formula of a compound can be established

**free energy** (7.1)   the combined contribution of entropy and enthalpy for a chemical reaction

**fructose** (16.4)   a ketohexose that is also called levulose and fruit sugar; the sweetest of all sugars, abundant in honey and fruits

**fuel value** (7.2)   the amount of energy derived from a given mass of material

**functional group** (10.1)   an atom (or group of atoms and their bonds) that imparts specific chemical and physical properties to a molecule

**fusion** (9.4)   the joining of light nuclei to form heavier nuclei, accompanied by the release of large amounts of energy

## G

**galactose** (16.4)   an aldohexose that is a component of lactose (milk sugar)

**galactosemia** (16.5)   a human genetic disease caused by the inability to convert galactose to a phosphorylated form of glucose (glucose-1-phosphate) that can be used in cellular metabolic reactions

**gamma ray** (9.1)   a high-energy emission from nuclear processes, traveling at the speed of light; the high-energy region of the electromagnetic spectrum

**gaseous state** (1.2)   a physical state of matter characterized by a lack of fixed shape or volume and ease of compressibility

**genome** (20.2)   the complete set of genetic information in all the chromosomes of an organism

**geometric isomer** (10.3, 11.3)   an isomer that differs from another isomer in the placement of substituents on a double bond or a ring

**globular protein** (18.5)   a protein composed of polypeptide chains that are tightly folded into a compact spherical shape

**glucagon** (21.7, 23.6)   a peptide hormone synthesized by the α-cells of the islets of Langerhans in the pancreas and secreted in response to low blood glucose levels; glucagon promotes glycogenolysis and gluconeogenesis and thereby increases the concentration of blood glucose

**gluconeogenesis** (21.6)   the synthesis of glucose from noncarbohydrate precursors

**glucose** (16.4)   an aldohexose, the most abundant monosaccharide; it is a component of many disaccharides, such as lactose and sucrose, and of polysaccharides, such as cellulose, starch, and glycogen

**glyceraldehyde** (16.4)   an aldotriose that is the simplest carbohydrate; phosphorylated forms of glyceraldehyde are important intermediates in cellular metabolic reactions

**glyceride** (17.3)   a lipid that contains glycerol

**glycogen** (16.6, 21.7)   a long, branched polymer of glucose stored in liver and muscles of animals; it consists of a linear backbone of α-D-glucose in $\alpha(1 \longrightarrow 4)$ linkage, with numerous short branches attached to the C-6 hydroxyl group by $\alpha(1 \longrightarrow 6)$ linkage

**glycogenesis** (21.7)   the metabolic pathway that results in the addition of glucose to growing glycogen polymers when blood glucose levels are high

**glycogen granule** (21.7)   a core of glycogen surrounded by enzymes responsible for glycogen synthesis and degradation

**glycogenolysis** (21.7)   the biochemical pathway that results in the removal of glucose molecules from glycogen polymers when blood glucose levels are low

**glycolysis** (21.3)   the enzymatic pathway that converts a glucose molecule into two molecules of pyruvate; this anaerobic process generates a net energy yield of two molecules of ATP and two molecules of NADH

**glycoprotein** (18.6)   a protein bonded to sugar groups

**glycosidic bond** (16.1)   the bond between the hydroxyl group of the C-1 carbon of one sugar and a hydroxyl group of another sugar

**gray** (9.7)   the absorption of 1 joule of energy by 1 kg of matter

**ground state** (2.3)   the electronic state of an atom in which all of the electrons are in the lowest possible energy levels

**group** (2.4)   any one of eighteen vertical columns of elements; often referred to as a *family*

**group specificity** (19.5)   an enzyme that catalyzes reactions involving similar substrate molecules having the same functional groups

**guanosine triphosphate (GTP)** (21.6)   a nucleotide composed of the purine guanine, the sugar ribose, and three phosphoryl groups

## H

**half-life ( $t_{1/2}$ )** (9.3, 9.6)   the length of time required for one-half of the initial mass of an isotope to decay to products

**halogen** (2.4)   an element found in Group VIIA (17) of the periodic table

**halogenation** (10.5, 11.5)   a reaction in which one of the C—H bonds of a hydrocarbon is replaced with a C—X bond (X = Br or Cl generally)

**Haworth projection** (16.4)   a means of representing the orientation of substituent groups around a cyclic sugar molecule

**heat** (7.1)   energy transferred between a system and its surroundings due to a temperature difference between system and surroundings

**α-helix** (18.4)   a right-handed coiled secondary structure maintained by hydrogen bonds between the amide hydrogen of one amino acid and the carbonyl oxygen of an amino acid four residues away

**heme group** (18.8)   the chemical group found in hemoglobin and myoglobin that is responsible for the ability to carry oxygen

**hemiacetal** (13.4, 16.4)   the family of organic compounds formed via the reaction of one molecule of alcohol with an aldehyde or a ketone in the presence of an acid catalyst

**hemoglobin** (18.8)   the major protein component of red blood cells; the function of this red, iron-containing protein is transport of oxygen

**Henderson-Hasselbalch equation** (8.4)   an equation for calculating the pH of a buffer system:

$$pH = pK_a + \log \frac{[\text{conjugate base}]}{[\text{weak acid}]}$$

**Henry's law** (6.1)   a law stating that the number of moles of a gas dissolved in a liquid at a given temperature is proportional to the partial pressure of the gas

**heterocyclic amine** (15.2)   a heterocyclic compound that contains nitrogen in at least one position in the ring skeleton

**heterocyclic aromatic compound** (11.7)   cyclic aromatic compound having at least one atom other than carbon in the structure of the aromatic ring

**heterogeneous mixture** (1.2)   a mixture of two or more substances characterized by nonuniform composition

**heteropolysaccharide** (16.6)   a polysaccharide composed of two or more different monosaccharides

**hexose** (16.2)   a six-carbon monosaccharide

**high-density lipoprotein (HDL)** (17.5)   a plasma lipoprotein that transports cholesterol from peripheral tissue to the liver

**holoenzyme** (19.7)   an active enzyme consisting of an apoenzyme bound to a cofactor

**homogeneous mixture** (1.2)   a mixture of two or more substances characterized by uniform composition

**homopolysaccharide** (16.6)   a polysaccharide composed of identical monosaccharides

**hybridization** (20.8)   a technique for identifying DNA or RNA sequences that is based on specific hydrogen bonding between a radioactive probe and complementary DNA or RNA sequences

**hydrate** (4.2)   any substance that has water molecules incorporated in its structure

**hydration** (11.5, 12.4)   a reaction in which water is added to a molecule, e.g., the addition of water to an alkene to form an alcohol

**hydrocarbon** (10.1)   a compound composed solely of the elements carbon and hydrogen

**hydrogen bonding** (5.2)   the attractive force between a hydrogen atom covalently bonded to a small, highly electronegative atom and another atom containing an unshared pair of electrons

**hydrogenation** (11.5, 13.4, 17.2)   a reaction in which hydrogen ($H_2$) is added to a double or a triple bond

**hydrohalogenation** (11.5)   the addition of a hydrohalogen (HCl, HBr, or HI) to an unsaturated bond

**hydrolase** (19.1)   an enzyme that catalyzes hydrolysis reactions

**hydrolysis** (14.2)   a chemical change that involves the reaction of a molecule with water; the process by which molecules are broken into their constituents by addition of water

**hydronium ion** (8.1)   a protonated water molecule, $H_3O^+$

**hydrophilic amino acid** (18.1)   "water loving"; a polar or ionic amino acid that has a high affinity for water

**hydrophobic amino acid** (18.1)   "water fearing"; a nonpolar amino acid that prefers contact with other nonpolar molecules over contact with water

**hydroxide ion** (8.1)   the anion consisting of one oxygen atom and one hydrogen atom ($—OH^-$)

**hydroxyl group** (12.1)   the —OH functional group that is characteristic of alcohols

**hyperammonemia** (22.8)   a genetic defect in one of the enzymes of the urea cycle that results in toxic or even fatal elevation of the concentration of ammonium ions in the body

**hyperglycemia** (21.7)   blood glucose levels that are higher than normal

**hypertonic solution** (6.4)   the more concentrated solution of two separated by a semipermeable membrane

**hypoglycemia** (21.7)   blood glucose levels that are lower than normal

**hypothesis** (1.1)   an attempt to explain observations in a commonsense way

**hypotonic solution** (6.4)   the more dilute solution of two separated by a semipermeable membrane

# I

**ideal gas** (5.1)   a gas in which the particles do not interact and the volume of the individual gas particles is assumed to be negligible

**ideal gas law** (5.1)   a law stating that for an ideal gas the product of pressure and volume is proportional to the product of the number of moles of the gas and its temperature; the proportionality constant for an ideal gas is symbolized $R$

**incomplete protein** (18.11)   a protein source that does not contain all the essential and nonessential amino acids

**indicator** (8.3)   a solute that shows some condition of a solution (such as acidity or basicity) by its color

**induced fit model** (19.4)   the theory of enzyme-substrate binding that assumes that the enzyme is a flexible molecule and that both the substrate and the enzyme change their shapes to accommodate one another as the enzyme-substrate complex forms

**initiation factors** (20.6)   proteins that are required for formation of the translation initiation complex, which is composed of the large and small ribosomal subunits, the mRNA, and the initiator tRNA, methionyl tRNA

**inner mitochondrial membrane** (22.1)   the highly folded, impermeable membrane within the mitochondrion that is the location of the electron transport system and ATP synthase

**insertion mutation** (20.7)   a mutation that results in the addition of one or more nucleotides to a DNA sequence

**insulin** (21.7, 23.6)   a hormone released from the pancreas in response to high blood glucose levels; insulin stimulates glycogenesis, fat storage, and cellular uptake and storage of glucose from the blood

**intensive property** (1.2)   a property of a substance that is independent of the quantity of the substance

**intermembrane space** (22.1)   the region between the outer and inner mitochondrial membranes, which is the location of the proton ($H^+$) reservoir that drives ATP synthesis

**intermolecular force** (3.5)   any attractive force that occurs between molecules

**intramolecular force** (3.5)   any attractive force that occurs within molecules

**intron** (20.4)   a noncoding sequence within a eukaryotic gene that must be removed from the primary transcript to produce a functional mRNA

**ion** (2.6)   an electrically charged particle formed by the gain or loss of electrons

**ionic bonding** (3.1)   an electrostatic attractive force between ions resulting from electron transfer

**ionic solid** (5.3)   a solid composed of positive and negative ions in a regular three-dimensional crystalline arrangement

**ionization energy** (2.7)   the energy needed to remove an electron from an atom in the gas phase

**ionizing radiation** (9.1, 9.5)   radiation that is sufficiently high in energy to cause ion formation upon impact with an atom

**ion product constant for water** (8.1)   the product of the hydronium and hydroxide ion concentrations in pure water at a specified temperature; at 25°C, it has a value of $1.0 \times 10^{-14}$

**irreversible enzyme inhibitor** (19.10)   a chemical that binds strongly to the R groups of an amino acid in the active site and eliminates enzyme activity

**isoelectronic** (2.6)   atoms, ions, and molecules containing the same number of electrons

**isomerase** (19.1)   an enzyme that catalyzes the conversion of one isomer to another

**isomers** (3.4)   molecules having the same molecular formula but different chemical structures

**isotonic solution** (6.4)   a solution that has the same solute concentration as another solution with which it is being compared; a solution that has the same osmotic pressure as a solution existing within a cell

**isotope** (2.1) atom of the same element that differs in mass because it contains different numbers of neutrons

**IUPAC Nomenclature System** (10.2) the International Union of Pure and Applied Chemistry (IUPAC) standard, universal system for the nomenclature of organic compounds

# K

**α-keratin** (18.4) a member of the family of fibrous proteins that form the covering of most land animals; major components of fur, skin, beaks, and nails

**ketoacidosis** (23.3) a drop in the pH of the blood caused by elevated levels of ketone bodies

**ketone** (13.1) a family of organic molecules characterized by a carbonyl group; the carbonyl carbon is bonded to two alkyl groups, two aryl groups, or one alkyl and one aryl group; ketones have the following general structures:

$$\underset{R-C-R}{\overset{O}{\parallel}} \quad \underset{R-C-(Ar)}{\overset{O}{\parallel}} \quad \underset{(Ar)-C-(Ar)}{\overset{O}{\parallel}}$$

**ketone bodies** (23.3) acetone, acetoacetone, and β-hydroxybutyrate produced from fatty acids in the liver via acetyl CoA

**ketose** (16.2) a sugar that contains a ketone (carbonyl) group

**ketosis** (23.3) an abnormal rise in the level of ketone bodies in the blood

**kinetic energy** (1.6) the energy resulting from motion of an object [kinetic energy = $1/2$(mass)(velocity)$^2$]

**kinetic molecular theory** (5.1) the fundamental model of particle behavior in the gas phase

**kinetics** (7.3) the study of rates of chemical reactions

# L

**lactose** (16.5) a disaccharide composed of β-D-galactose and either α- or β-D-glucose in β(1 ⟶ 4) glycosidic linkage; milk sugar

**lactose intolerance** (16.5) the inability to produce the digestive enzyme lactase, which degrades lactose to galactose and glucose

**lagging strand** (20.3) in DNA replication, the strand that is synthesized discontinuously from numerous RNA primers

**law of conservation of mass** (4.3) a law stating that, in chemical change, matter cannot be created or destroyed

**leading strand** (20.3) in DNA replication, the strand that is synthesized continuously from a single RNA primer

**LeChatelier's principle** (7.4) a law stating that when a system at equilibrium is disturbed, the equilibrium shifts in the direction that minimizes the disturbance

**lethal dose (LD$_{50}$)** (9.7) the quantity of toxic material (such as radiation) that causes the death of 50% of a population of an organism

**Lewis structure** (3.1) representation of a molecule (or polyatomic ion) that shows valence electron arrangement among the atoms in a molecule (or polyatomic ion)

**Lewis symbol** (3.1) representation of an atom (or ion) using the atomic symbol (for the nucleus and core electrons) and dots to represent valence electrons

**ligase** (19.1) an enzyme that catalyzes the joining of two molecules

**linear** (3.4) the structure of a molecule in which the bond angle(s) about the central atom(s) is (are) 180°

**line formula** (10.2) the simplest representation of a molecule, in which it is assumed that there is a carbon atom at any location where two or more lines intersect, there is a carbon at the end of any line, and each carbon is bonded to the correct number of hydrogen atoms

**linkage specificity** (19.5) the property of an enzyme that allows it to catalyze reactions involving only one kind of bond in the substrate molecule

**lipase** (23.1) an enzyme that hydrolyzes the ester linkage between glycerol and the fatty acids of triglycerides

**lipid** (17.1) a member of the group of biological molecules of varying composition that are classified together on the basis of their solubility in nonpolar solvents

**liquid state** (1.2) a physical state of matter characterized by a fixed volume and the absence of a fixed shape

**lock-and-key model** (19.4) the theory of enzyme-substrate binding that depicts enzymes as inflexible molecules; the substrate fits into the rigid active site in the same way a key fits into a lock

**London dispersion forces** (5.2) weak attractive forces between molecules that result from short-lived dipoles that occur because of the continuous movement of electrons in the molecules

**lone pair** (3.1) an electron pair that is not involved in bonding

**low-density lipoprotein (LDL)** (17.5) a plasma lipoprotein that carries cholesterol to peripheral tissues and helps to regulate cholesterol levels in those tissues

**lyase** (19.1) an enzyme that catalyzes a reaction involving double bonds

# M

**maltose** (16.5) a disaccharide composed of α-D-glucose and a second glucose molecule in α(1 ⟶ 4) glycosidic linkage

**Markovnikov's rule** (11.5) the rule stating that a hydrogen atom, adding to a carbon-carbon double bond, will add to the carbon having the larger number of hydrogens attached to it

**mass** (1.3) a quantity of matter

**mass/mass percent [% (m/m)]** (6.2) the concentration of a solution expressed as a ratio of mass of solute to mass of solution multiplied by 100%

**mass number** (2.1) the sum of the number of protons and neutrons in an atom

**mass/volume percent [% (m/V)]** (6.2) the concentration of a solution expressed as a ratio of grams of solute to milliliters of solution multiplied by 100%

**matrix space** (22.1) the region of the mitochondrion within the inner membrane; the location of the enzymes that carry out the reactions of the citric acid cycle and β-oxidation of fatty acids

**matter** (1.1) anything that has mass and occupies space

**melting point** (3.3, 5.2) the temperature at which a solid converts to a liquid

**meso compound** (16.3) a special case of stereoisomers that occurs when a molecule has two chiral carbons and an internal plane of symmetry; these molecules are achiral because they have a plane of symmetry within the molecule

**messenger RNA** (20.4) an RNA species produced by transcription and that specifies the amino acid sequence for a protein

**metal** (2.4) an element located on the left side of the periodic table (left of the "staircase" boundary)

**metallic solid** (5.3) a solid composed of metal atoms held together by metallic bonds

**metalloid** (2.4) an element along the "staircase" boundary between metals and nonmetals; metalloids exhibit both metallic and nonmetallic properties

**metastable isotope** (9.3) an isotope that will give up some energy to produce a more stable form of the same isotope

**micelle** (23.1) an aggregation of molecules having nonpolar and polar regions; the nonpolar regions of the molecules aggregate, leaving the polar regions facing the surrounding water

**mitochondria** (22.1) the cellular "power plants" in which the reactions of the citric acid cycle, β-oxidation of fatty acids, the electron transport system, and ATP synthase function to produce ATP

**mixture** (1.2) a material composed of two or more substances

**molality** (6.4) the number of moles of solute per kilogram of solvent

**molarity** (6.3) the number of moles of solute per liter of solution

**molar mass** (4.1, 4.2) the mass in grams of 1 mol of a substance

**molar volume** (5.1) the volume occupied by 1 mol of a substance

**mole** (4.1) the amount of substance containing Avogadro's number of particles

**molecular formula** (10.2) a formula that provides the atoms and number of each type of atom in a molecule but gives no information regarding the bonding pattern involved in the structure of the molecule

**molecular solid** (5.3)   a solid in which the molecules are held together by dipole-dipole and London dispersion forces (van der Waals forces)

**molecule** (3.1)   a unit in which the atoms of two or more elements are held together by chemical bonds

**monatomic ion** (3.2)   an ion formed by electron gain or loss from a single atom

**monoglyceride** (17.3)   the product of the esterification of glycerol at one position

**monomer** (11.5)   the individual molecules from which a polymer is formed

**monosaccharide** (16.1)   the simplest type of carbohydrate consisting of a single saccharide unit

**movement protein** (18: Intro)   a protein involved in any aspect of movement in an organism, for instance, actin and myosin in muscle tissue and flagellin that composes bacterial flagella

**mutagen** (20.7)   any chemical or physical agent that causes changes in the nucleotide sequence of a gene

**mutation** (20.7)   any change in the nucleotide sequence of a gene

**myoglobin** (18.8)   the oxygen storage protein found in muscle

# N

**N-terminal amino acid** (18.2)   the amino acid in a peptide that has a free $\alpha$-N$^+$H$_3$ group; the first amino acid of a peptide

**natural radioactivity** (9.5)   the spontaneous decay of a nucleus to produce high-energy particles or rays

**negative allosterism** (19.9)   effector binding inactivates the active site of an allosteric enzyme

**neurotransmitter** (15.5)   a chemical that carries a message, or signal, from a nerve cell to a target cell

**neutral glyceride** (17.3)   the product of the esterification of glycerol at one, two, or three positions

**neutralization** (4.7, 8.3)   the reaction between an acid and a base

**neutron** (2.1)   an uncharged particle, with the same mass as the proton, in the nucleus of an atom

**nicotinamide adenine dinucleotide (NAD$^+$)** (21.3)   a molecule synthesized from the vitamin niacin and the nucleotide ATP and that serves as a carrier of hydride anions; a coenzyme that is an oxidizing agent used in a variety of metabolic processes

**noble gas** (2.4)   elements in Group VIIIA (18) of the periodic table

**nomenclature** (3.2)   a system for naming chemical compounds

**nonelectrolyte** (3.3, 6.1)   a substance that, when dissolved in water, produces a solution that does not conduct an electrical current

**nonessential amino acid** (18.11)   any amino acid that can be synthesized by the body

**nonmetal** (2.4)   an element located on the right side of the periodic table (right of the "staircase" boundary)

**nonreducing sugar** (16.5)   a sugar that cannot be oxidized by Benedict's or Tollens' reagent

**normal boiling point** (5.2)   the temperature at which a substance will boil at 1 atm of pressure

**nuclear equation** (9.2)   a balanced equation accounting for the products and reactants in a nuclear reaction

**nuclear imaging** (9.5)   the generation of images of components of the body (organs, tissues) using techniques based on the measurement of radiation

**nuclear medicine** (9.5)   a field of medicine that uses radioisotopes for diagnostic and therapeutic purposes

**nuclear reactor** (9.4)   a device for conversion of nuclear energy into electrical energy

**nucleoside** (20.1)   a molecule composed of a nitrogenous base and a five-carbon sugar

**nucleosome** (20.2)   the first level of chromosome structure consisting of a strand of DNA wrapped around a small disk of histone proteins

**nucleotide** (20.1, 21.1)   a molecule composed of a nitrogenous base, a five-carbon sugar, and one, two, or three phosphoryl groups

**nucleus** (2.1)   the small, dense center of positive charge in the atom

**nuclide** (9.1)   any atom characterized by an atomic number and a mass number

**nutrient protein** (18: Intro)   a protein that serves as a source of amino acids for embryos or infants

**nutritional Calorie** (7.2)   equivalent to 1 kilocalorie (1000 calories); also known as a large Calorie

# O

**octet rule** (2.6)   a rule predicting that atoms form the most stable molecules or ions when they are surrounded by eight electrons in their highest occupied energy level

**oligosaccharide** (16.1)   an intermediate-sized carbohydrate composed of from three to ten monosaccharides

**osmolarity** (6.4)   the molarity of particles in solution

**osmosis** (6.4)   net flow of a solvent across a semipermeable membrane in response to a concentration gradient

**osmotic pressure** (6.4)   the net force with which water enters a solution through a semipermeable membrane; alternatively, the pressure required to stop net transfer of solvent across a semipermeable membrane

**outer mitochondrial membrane** (22.1)   the membrane that surrounds the mitochondrion and separates it from the contents of the cytoplasm; it is highly permeable to small "food" molecules

**β-oxidation** (23.2)   the biochemical pathway that results in the oxidation of fatty acids and the production of acetyl CoA

**oxidation** (4.8, 12.4, 13.4, 14.1)   a loss of electrons; in organic compounds, it may be recognized as a loss of hydrogen atoms or the gain of oxygen

**oxidation-reduction reaction** (4.8)   also called *redox reaction,* a reaction involving the transfer of one or more electrons from one reactant to another

**oxidative deamination** (22.7)   an oxidation-reduction reaction in which NAD$^+$ is reduced and the amino acid is deaminated

**oxidative phosphorylation** (21.3, 22.6)   production of ATP using the energy of electrons harvested during biological oxidation-reduction reactions

**oxidizing agent** (4.8)   a substance that oxidizes, or removes electrons from, another substance; the oxidizing agent is reduced in the process

**oxidoreductase** (19.1)   an enzyme that catalyzes an oxidation-reduction reaction

# P

**pancreatic serine proteases** (19.11)   a family of proteolytic enzymes, including trypsin, chymotrypsin, and elastase, that arose by divergent evolution

**parent compound or parent chain** (10.2)   in the IUPAC Nomenclature System, the parent compound is the longest carbon-carbon chain containing the principal functional group in the molecule that is being named

**partial pressure** (5.1)   the pressure exerted by one component of a gas mixture

**parts per million** (6.2)   number of parts of solute in one million parts of solvent

**parts per thousand** (6.2)   number of parts of solute per thousand parts of solvent

**pentose** (16.2)   a five-carbon monosaccharide

**pentose phosphate pathway** (21.5)   an alternative pathway for glucose degradation that provides the cell with reducing power in the form of NADPH

**peptide bond** (15.4, 18.2)   the amide bond between two amino acids in a peptide chain

**peptidyl tRNA binding site of ribosome (P-site)** (20.6)   a pocket on the surface of the ribosome that holds the tRNA bound to the growing peptide chain

**percent yield** (4.9)   the ratio of the actual and theoretical yields of a chemical reaction multiplied by 100%

**period** (2.4)   any one of seven horizontal rows of elements in the periodic table

**periodic law** (2.4)   a law stating that properties of elements are periodic functions of their atomic numbers (Note that Mendeleev's original statement was based on atomic masses.)

**peripheral membrane protein** (17.6)   a protein bound to either the inner or the outer surface of a membrane

**phenol** (12.6)   an organic compound that contains a hydroxyl group (—OH) attached to a benzene ring

**phenyl group** (11.6)   a benzene ring that has had a hydrogen atom removed, $C_6H_5$—

**pH optimum** (19.8)   the pH at which an enzyme catalyzes the reaction at maximum efficiency

**phosphatidate** (17.3)   a molecule of glycerol with fatty acids esterified to C-1 and C-2 of glycerol and a free phosphoryl group esterified at C-3

**phosphoanhydride** (14.4)   the bond formed when two phosphate groups react with one another and a water molecule is lost

**phosphoester** (14.4)   the product of the reaction between phosphoric acid and an alcohol

**phosphoglyceride** (17.3)   a molecule with fatty acids esterified at the C-1 and C-2 positions of glycerol and a phosphoryl group esterified at the C-3 position

**phospholipid** (17.3)   a lipid containing a phosphoryl group

**phosphopantetheine** (23.4)   the portion of coenzyme A and the acyl carrier protein that is derived from the vitamin pantothenic acid

**photon** (2.3)   a particle of light

**pH scale** (8.2)   a numerical representation of acidity or basicity of a solution; pH $= -\log[H_3O^+]$

**physical change** (1.2)   a change in the form of a substance but not in its chemical composition; no chemical bonds are broken in a physical change

**physical equilibrium** (7.4)   occurs between two phases of the same substance

**physical property** (1.2)   a characteristic of a substance that can be observed without the substance undergoing change (examples include color, density, melting and boiling points)

**plane-polarized light** (16.3)   light in which all of the light waves are vibrating in the same, parallel direction

**plasma lipoprotein** (17.5)   a complex composed of lipid and protein that is responsible for the transport of lipids throughout the body

**β-pleated sheet** (18.4)   a common secondary structure of a peptide chain that resembles the pleats of an Oriental fan

**point mutation** (20.7)   the substitution of one nucleotide pair for another within a gene

**polar covalent bond** (3.1)   a covalent bond in which the electrons are not equally shared

**poly(A) tail** (20.4)   a tract of 100–200 adenosine monophosphate units covalently attached to the 3′ end of eukaryotic messenger RNA molecules

**polyatomic ion** (3.2)   an ion containing a number of atoms

**polymer** (11.5)   a very large molecule formed by the combination of many small molecules (called *monomers*) (e.g., polyamides, nylons)

**polyprotic substance** (8.3)   a substance that can accept or donate more than one proton per molecule

**polysaccharide** (16.1)   a large, complex carbohydrate composed of long chains of monosaccharides

**polysome** (20.6)   complexes of many ribosomes all simultaneously translating a single mRNA

**positive allosterism** (19.9)   effector binding activates the active site of an allosteric enzyme

**positron** (9.1)   particle that has the same mass as an electron but opposite (+) charge

**post-transcriptional modification** (20.4)   alterations of the primary transcripts produced in eukaryotic cells; these include addition of a poly(A) tail to the 3′ end of the mRNA, addition of the cap structure to the 5′ end of the mRNA, and RNA splicing

**potential energy** (1.6)   stored energy or energy caused by position or composition

**precipitate** (4.5, 6.1)   an insoluble substance formed and separated from a solution

**precision** (1.4)   the degree of agreement among replicate measurements of the same quantity

**pressure** (5.1)   a force per unit area

**primary (1°) alcohol** (12.1)   an alcohol with the general formula $RCH_2OH$

**primary (1°) amide** (15.3)   an amide produced in a reaction between a carboxylic acid and ammonia and having only one carbon, the carbonyl carbon, bonded to the nitrogen. They have the following general structure:

**primary (1°) amine** (15.1)   an amine with the general formula $RNH_2$

**primary (1°) carbon** (10.2)   a carbon atom that is bonded to only one other carbon atom

**primary structure (of a protein)** (18.3)   the linear sequence of amino acids in a protein chain determined by the genetic information of the gene for each protein

**primary transcript** (20.4)   the RNA product of transcription in eukaryotic cells, before post-transcriptional modifications are carried out

**principal energy level** (2.5)   a region where electrons may be found; has integral values $n = 1, n = 2$, and so forth

**product** (4.3, 19.1)   the chemical species that results from a chemical reaction and that appears on the right side of a chemical equation

**proenzyme** (19.9)   the inactive form of a proteolytic enzyme

**prokaryote** (20.2)   an organism with simple cellular structure in which there is no true nucleus enclosed by a nuclear membrane and there are no true membrane-bound organelles in the cytoplasm

**promoter** (20.4)   the sequence of nucleotides immediately before a gene that is recognized by the RNA polymerase and signals the start point and direction of transcription

**properties** (1.2)   characteristics of matter

**prostaglandins** (17.2)   a family of hormonelike substances derived from the twenty-carbon fatty acid, arachidonic acid; produced by many cells of the body, they regulate many body functions

**prosthetic group** (18.6)   the nonprotein portion of a protein that is essential to the biological activity of the protein; often a complex organic compound

**protein** (18: Intro)   a macromolecule whose primary structure is a linear sequence of α-amino acids and whose final structure results from folding of the chain into a specific three-dimensional structure; proteins serve as catalysts, structural components, and nutritional elements for the cell

**protein modification** (19.9)   a means of enzyme regulation in which a chemical group is covalently added to or removed from a protein. The chemical modification either turns the enzyme on or turns it off

**proteolytic enzyme** (19.11)   an enzyme that hydrolyzes the peptide bonds between amino acids in a protein chain

**proton** (2.1)   a positively charged particle in the nucleus of an atom

**pure substance** (1.2)   a substance with constant composition

**purine** (20.1)   a family of nitrogenous bases (heterocyclic amines) that are components of DNA and RNA and consist of a six-sided ring fused to a five-sided ring; the common purines in nucleic acids are adenine and guanine

**pyridoxal phosphate** (22.7)   a coenzyme derived from vitamin $B_6$ that is required for all transamination reactions

**pyrimidine** (20.1)   a family of nitrogenous bases (heterocyclic amines) that are components of nucleic acids and consist of a single six-sided ring; the common pyrimidines of DNA are cytosine and thymine; the common pyrimidines of RNA are cytosine and uracil

**pyrimidine dimer** (20.7)   UV light–induced covalent bonding of two adjacent pyrimidine bases in a strand of DNA

**pyruvate dehydrogenase complex** (22.2)   a complex of all the enzymes and coenzymes required for the synthesis of $CO_2$ and acetyl CoA from pyruvate

## Q

**quaternary ammonium salt** (15.1)   an amine salt with the general formula $R_4N^+A^-$ (in which R— can be an alkyl or aryl group or a hydrogen atom and $A^-$ can be any anion)

**quaternary (4°) carbon** (10.2)   a carbon atom that is bonded to four other carbon atoms

**quaternary structure (of a protein)** (18.6)   aggregation of more than one folded peptide chain to yield a functional protein

## R

**racemic mixture** (16.3)   a mixture of equal amounts of a pair of enantiomers

**rad** (9.7)   abbreviation for *radiation absorbed dose*, the absorption of $2.4 \times 10^{-3}$ calories of energy per kilogram of absorbing tissue

**radioactivity** (9.1)   the process by which atoms emit high-energy particles or rays; the spontaneous decomposition of a nucleus to produce a different nucleus

**radiocarbon dating** (9.3)   the estimation of the age of objects through measurement of isotopic ratios of carbon

**Raoult's law** (6.4)   a law stating that the vapor pressure of a component is equal to its mole fraction times the vapor pressure of the pure component

**rate constant** (7.3)   the proportionality constant that relates the rate of a reaction and the concentration of reactants

**rate law** (7.3)   expresses the rate of a reaction in terms of reactant concentration and a rate constant

**rate (of chemical reaction)** (7.3)   the change in concentration of a reactant or product per unit time

**reactant** (4.3)   starting material for a chemical reaction, appearing on the left side of a chemical equation

**reaction order** (7.3)   the exponent of each concentration term in the rate equation

**reducing agent** (4.8)   a substance that reduces, or donates electrons to, another substance; the reducing agent is itself oxidized in the process

**reducing sugar** (16.4)   a sugar that can be oxidized by Benedict's or Tollens' reagents; includes all monosaccharides and most disaccharides

**reduction** (4.8, 12.4)   the gain of electrons; in organic compounds it may be recognized by a gain of hydrogen or loss of oxygen

**regulatory proteins** (18: Intro)   proteins that control cell functions such as metabolism and reproduction

**release factor** (20.6)   a protein that binds to the termination codon in the empty A-site of the ribosome and causes the peptidyl transferase to hydrolyze the bond between the peptide and the peptidyl tRNA

**rem** (9.7)   abbreviation for *roentgen equivalent for man,* the product of rad and RBE

**replication fork** (20.3)   the point at which new nucleotides are added to the growing daughter DNA strand

**replication origin** (20.3)   the region of a DNA molecule where DNA replication always begins

**representative element** (2.4)   member of the groups of the periodic table designated as A

**resonance** (3.4)   a condition that occurs when more than one valid Lewis structure can be written for a particular molecule

**restriction enzyme** (20.8)   a bacterial enzyme that recognizes specific nucleotide sequences on a DNA molecule and cuts the sugar-phosphate backbone of the DNA at or near that site

**result** (1.1)   the outcome of a designed experiment, often determined from individual bits of data

**reversible, competitive enzyme inhibitor** (19.10)   a chemical that resembles the structure and charge distribution of the natural substrate and competes with it for the active site of an enzyme

**reversible reaction** (7.4)   a reaction that will proceed in either direction, reactants to products or products to reactants

**ribonucleic acid (RNA)** (20.1)   single-stranded nucleic acid molecules that are composed of phosphoryl groups, ribose, and the nitrogenous bases uracil, cytosine, adenine, and guanine

**ribonucleotide** (20.1)   a ribonucleoside phosphate or nucleotide composed of a nitrogenous base in $\beta$-$N$-glycosidic linkage to the 1' carbon of the sugar ribose and with one, two, or three phosphoryl groups esterified at the hydroxyl of the 5' carbon of the ribose

**ribose** (16.4)   a five-carbon monosaccharide that is a component of RNA and many coenzymes

**ribosomal RNA (rRNA)** (20.4)   the RNA species that are structural and functional components of the small and large ribosomal subunits

**ribosome** (20.6)   an organelle composed of a large and a small subunit, each of which is made up of ribosomal RNA and proteins; the platform on which translation occurs and that carries the enzymatic activity that forms peptide bonds

**RNA polymerase** (20.4)   the enzyme that catalyzes the synthesis of RNA molecules using DNA as the template

**RNA splicing** (20.4)   removal of portions of the primary transcript that do not encode protein sequences

**roentgen** (9.7)   the dose of radiation producing $2.1 \times 10^9$ ions in $1 \text{ cm}^3$ of air at $0°C$ and 1 atm of pressure

## S

**saccharide** (16.1)   a sugar molecule

**saponification** (14.2, 17.3)   a reaction in which a soap is produced; more generally, the hydrolysis of an ester by an aqueous base

**saturated fatty acid** (17.2)   a long-chain monocarboxylic acid in which each carbon of the chain is bonded to the maximum number of hydrogen atoms

**saturated hydrocarbon** (10.1)   an alkane; a hydrocarbon that contains only carbon and hydrogen bonded together through carbon-hydrogen and carbon-carbon single bonds

**saturated solution** (6.1)   one in which undissolved solute is in equilibrium with the solution

**scientific law** (1.1)   a summary of a large quantity of information

**scientific method** (1.1)   the process of studying our surroundings that is based on experimentation

**scientific notation** (1.4)   a system used to represent numbers as powers of ten

**secondary (2°) alcohol** (12.1)   an alcohol with the general formula $R_2CHOH$

**secondary (2°) amide** (15.3)   an amide produced in a reaction between an acid chloride and a primary amine and having the following general structure:

**secondary (2°) amine** (15.1)   an amine with the general formula $R_2NH$

**secondary (2°) carbon** (10.2)   a carbon atom that is bonded to two other carbon atoms

**secondary structure (of a protein)** (18.4)   folding of the primary structure of a protein into an $\alpha$-helix or a $\beta$-pleated sheet; folding is maintained by hydrogen bonds between the amide hydrogen and the carbonyl oxygen of the peptide bond

**selectively permeable membrane** (6.4)   a membrane that restricts diffusion of some ions and molecules (based on size and charge) across the membrane

**self-ionization** (8.1)   transfer of a proton from one water molecule to another

**semiconservative DNA replication** (20.3)   DNA polymerase "reads" each parental strand of DNA and produces a complementary daughter strand; thus, all newly synthesized DNA molecules consist of one parental and one daughter strand

**semipermeable membrane** (6.4)   a membrane permeable to the solvent but not the solute; a material that allows the transport of certain substances from one side of the membrane to the other

**shielding** (9.6)   material used to provide protection from radiation

**sickle cell anemia** (18.8)   a human genetic disorder resulting from inheriting mutant hemoglobin genes from both parents

**sievert** (9.7)   the biological effect that results when 1 Gy of radiation energy is absorbed by human tissue

**significant figures** (1.4)   all digits in a number known with certainty and the first uncertain digit

**silent mutation** (20.7)   a mutation that changes the sequence of the DNA but does not alter the amino acid sequence of the protein encoded by the DNA

**single bond** (3.4)   a bond in which one pair of electrons is shared by two atoms

**single-replacement reaction** (4.3)   also called *substitution reaction,* one in which one atom in a molecule is displaced by another

**soap** (14.1)   any of a variety of the alkali metal salts of fatty acids

**solid state** (1.2)   a physical state of matter characterized by its rigidity and fixed volume and shape

**solubility** (3.5, 6.1)   the amount of a substance that will dissolve in a given volume of solvent at a specified temperature

**solute** (6.1) a component of a solution that is present in lesser quantity than the solvent

**solution** (6.1) a homogeneous (uniform) mixture of two or more substances

**solvent** (6.1) the solution component that is present in the largest quantity

**specific gravity** (1.6) the ratio of the density of a substance to the density of water at 4°C or any specified temperature

**specific heat** (7.2) the quantity of heat (calories) required to raise the temperature of 1 g of a substance 1 degree Celsius

**spectroscopy** (2.3) the measurement of intensity and energy of electromagnetic radiation

**speed of light** (2.3) $2.99 \times 10^8$ m/s in a vacuum

**sphingolipid** (17.4) a phospholipid that is derived from the amino alcohol sphingosine rather than from glycerol

**sphingomyelin** (17.4) a sphingolipid found in abundance in the myelin sheath that surrounds and insulates cells of the central nervous system

**standard solution** (8.3) a solution whose concentration is accurately known

**standard temperature and pressure (STP)** (5.1) defined as 273 K and 1 atm

**stereochemical specificity** (19.5) the property of an enzyme that allows it to catalyze reactions involving only one enantiomer of the substrate

**stereochemistry** (16.3) the study of the spatial arrangement of atoms in a molecule

**stereoisomers** (10.3, 16.3) a pair of molecules having the same structural formula and bonding pattern but differing in the arrangement of the atoms in space

**steroid** (17.4) a lipid derived from cholesterol and composed of one five-sided ring and three six-sided rings; the steroids include sex hormones and anti-inflammatory compounds

**structural analog** (19.10) a chemical having a structure and charge distribution very similar to those of a natural enzyme substrate

**structural formula** (10.2) a formula showing all of the atoms in a molecule and exhibiting all bonds as lines

**structural isomers** (10.2) molecules having the same molecular formula but different chemical structures

**structural protein** (18: Intro) a protein that provides mechanical support for large plants and animals

**sublevel** (2.5) a set of equal-energy orbitals within a principal energy level

**sublimation** (5.3) a process whereby some molecules in the solid state convert directly to the gaseous state

**substituted hydrocarbon** (10.1) a hydrocarbon in which one or more hydrogen atoms is replaced by another atom or group of atoms

**substitution reaction** (10.5, 11.6) a reaction that results in the replacement of one group for another

**substrate** (19.1) the reactant in a chemical reaction that binds to an enzyme active site and is converted to product

**substrate-level phosphorylation** (21.3) the production of ATP by the transfer of a phosphoryl group from the substrate of a reaction to ADP

**sucrose** (16.5) a disaccharide composed of α-D-glucose and β-D-fructose in (α1 ⟶ β2) glycosidic linkage; table sugar

**supersaturated solution** (6.1) a solution that is more concentrated than a saturated solution (Note that such a solution is not at equilibrium.)

**surface tension** (5.2) a measure of the strength of the attractive forces at the surface of a liquid

**surfactant** (5.2) a substance that decreases the surface tension of a liquid

**surroundings** (7.1) the universe outside of the system

**suspension** (6.1) a heterogeneous mixture of particles; the suspended particles are larger than those found in a colloidal suspension

**system** (7.1) the process under study

## T

**tautomers** (13.4) structural isomers that differ from one another in the placement of a hydrogen atom and a double bond

**temperature** (1.6) a measure of the relative "hotness" or "coldness" of an object

**temperature optimum** (19.8) the temperature at which an enzyme functions optimally and the rate of reaction is maximal

**terminal electron acceptor** (22.6) the final electron acceptor in an electron transport system that removes the low-energy electrons from the system; in aerobic organisms, the terminal electron acceptor is molecular oxygen

**termination codon** (20.6) a triplet of ribonucleotides with no corresponding anticodon on a tRNA; as a result, translation will end because there is no amino acid to transfer to the peptide chain

**terpene** (17.4) the general term for lipids that are synthesized from isoprene units; the terpenes include steroids, bile salts, lipid-soluble vitamins, and chlorophyll

**tertiary (3°) alcohol** (12.1) an alcohol with the general formula $R_3COH$

**tertiary (3°) amide** (15.3) an amide produced in a reaction between a secondary amine and an acid chloride and having the following general structure:

$$R^1 \overset{\overset{\displaystyle O}{\|}}{C} \underset{\underset{\displaystyle R^3}{|}}{N} R^2$$

**tertiary (3°) amine** (15.1) an amine with the general formula $R_3N$

**tertiary (3°) carbon** (10.2) a carbon atom that is bonded to three other carbon atoms

**tertiary structure (of a protein)** (18.5) the globular, three-dimensional structure of a protein that results from folding

the regions of secondary structure; this folding occurs spontaneously as a result of interactions of the side chains or R groups of the amino acids

**tetrahedral structure** (3.4) a molecule consisting of four groups attached to a central atom that occupy the four corners of an imagined regular tetrahedron

**tetrose** (16.2) a four-carbon monosaccharide

**theoretical yield** (4.9) the maximum amount of product that can be produced from a given amount of reactant

**theory** (1.1) a hypothesis supported by extensive testing that explains and predicts facts

**thermodynamics** (7.1) the branch of science that deals with the relationship between energies of systems, work, and heat

**thioester** (14.4) the product of a reaction between a thiol and a carboxylic acid

**thiol** (12.8) an organic compound that contains a thiol group (—SH)

**titration** (8.3) the process of adding a solution from a buret to a sample until a reaction is complete, at which time the volume is accurately measured and the concentration of the sample is calculated

**Tollens' test** (13.4) a test reagent (silver nitrate in ammonium hydroxide) used to distinguish aldehydes and ketones; also called the Tollens' silver mirror test

**tracer** (9.5) a radioisotope that is rapidly and selectively transmitted to the part of the body for which diagnosis is desired

**transaminase** (22.7) an enzyme that catalyzes the transfer of an amino group from one molecule to another

**transamination** (22.7) a reaction in which an amino group is transferred from one molecule to another

**transcription** (20.4) the synthesis of RNA from a DNA template

**transferase** (19.1) an enzyme that catalyzes the transfer of a functional group from one molecule to another

**transfer RNA (tRNA)** (15.4, 20.4) small RNAs that bind to a specific amino acid at the 3′ end and mediate its addition at the appropriate site in a growing peptide chain; accomplished by recognition of the correct codon on the mRNA by the complementary anticodon on the tRNA

**transition element** (2.4) any element located between Groups IIA (2) and IIIA (13) in the long periods of the periodic table

**transition state** (19.6) the unstable intermediate in catalysis in which the enzyme has altered the form of the substrate so that it now shares properties of both the substrate and the product

**translation** (20.6) the synthesis of a protein from the genetic code carried on the mRNA

**translocation** (20.6) movement of the ribosome along the mRNA during translation

**transmembrane protein** (17.6) a protein that is embedded within a membrane and crosses the lipid bilayer, protruding from the membrane both inside and outside the cell

**transport protein** (18: Intro)   a protein that transports materials across the cell membrane or throughout the body

**triglyceride** (17.3, 23.1)   triacylglycerol; a molecule composed of glycerol esterified to three fatty acids

**trigonal planar** (3.4)   a molecular geometry in which a central atom is bonded to three atoms that lie at the vertices of an equilateral triangle. All atoms lie within one plane and all bond angles are 120°

**trigonal pyramidal** (3.4)   a nonplanar structure involving three groups bonded to a central atom in which each group is equidistant from the central atom

**triose** (16.2)   a three-carbon monosaccharide

**triple bond** (3.4)   a bond in which three pairs of electrons are shared by two atoms

**true solution** (6.1)   a homogeneous mixture with uniform properties throughout

## U

**unit** (1.3)   a determinate quantity (of length, time, etc.) that has been adopted as a standard of measurement

**unsaturated fatty acid** (17.2)   a long-chain monocarboxylic acid having at least one carbon-to-carbon double bond

**unsaturated hydrocarbon** (10.1, 11: Intro)   a hydrocarbon containing at least one multiple (double or triple) bond

**urea cycle** (22.8)   a cyclic series of reactions that detoxifies ammonium ions by incorporating them into urea, which is excreted from the body

**uridine triphosphate (UTP)** (21.7)   a nucleotide composed of the pyrimidine uracil, the sugar ribose, and three phosphoryl groups and that serves as a carrier of glucose-1-phosphate in glycogenesis

## V

**valence electron** (2.6)   electron in the outermost shell (principal quantum level) of an atom

**valence-shell electron-pair repulsion (VSEPR) theory** (3.4)   a model that predicts molecular geometry using the premise that electron pairs will arrange themselves as far apart as possible, to minimize electron repulsion

**van der Waals forces** (5.2)   a general term for intermolecular forces that include dipole-dipole and London dispersion forces

**vapor pressure lowering** (6.4)   the decrease in the tendency of a liquid to become a gas when a solute is added

**vapor pressure of a liquid** (5.2)   the pressure exerted by the vapor at the surface of a liquid at equilibrium

**very low density lipoprotein (VLDL)** (17.5)   a plasma lipoprotein that binds triglycerides synthesized by the liver and carries them to adipose tissue for storage

**viscosity** (5.2)   a measure of the resistance to flow of a substance at constant temperature

**vitamin** (19.7)   an organic substance that is required in the diet in small amounts; water-soluble vitamins are used in the synthesis of coenzymes required for the function of cellular enzymes; lipid-soluble vitamins are involved in calcium metabolism, vision, and blood clotting

**voltaic cell** (4.8)   an electrochemical cell that converts chemical energy into electrical energy

## W

**wax** (17.4)   a collection of lipids that are generally considered to be esters of long-chain alcohols

**weight** (1.3)   the force exerted on an object by gravity

## Z

**Zaitsev's rule** (12.4)   states that in an elimination reaction, the alkene with the greatest number of alkyl groups on the double-bonded carbon (the more highly substituted alkene) is the major product of the reaction

# Answers to Odd-Numbered Questions and Problems

## Chapter 1

**1.1** Homogeneous mixture

**1.3** a. Physical property
b. Chemical property
c. Physical property

**1.5** a. Extensive property
b. Intensive property

**1.7** a. Three       d. Two
b. Three       e. Three
c. Four        f. Two

**1.9** a. $2.4 \times 10^{-3}$    d. $6.73 \times 10^{5}$
b. $1.80 \times 10^{-2}$   e. $7.2420 \times 10^{1}$
c. $2.24 \times 10^{2}$    f. $8.3 \times 10^{-1}$

**1.11** a. 61.4         d. 63.7
b. 6.17         e. 8.77
c. $6.65 \times 10^{-2}$

**1.13** a. 8.09
b. 5.9
c. 20.19

**1.15** $8.84 \times 10^{-4}$

**1.17** a. 51          d. $8.6 \times 10^{-1}$
b. $8.0 \times 10^{1}$    e. $4.63 \times 10^{8}$
c. $5.80 \times 10^{1}$   f. $2.0 \times 10^{-3}$

**1.19** $2.49 \times 10^{3}$ J

**1.21** Chemistry is the study of matter, its chemical and physical properties, the chemical and physical changes it undergoes, and the energy changes that accompany those processes.
When wood is burned, energy is released while its matter undergoes chemical and physical changes.

**1.23** Experiments are necessary to test hypotheses and theories. Experimental results that are derived from measured or observed data may or may not support the hypotheses and theories.

**1.25** You need the cost per gallon, the average miles per gallon, and the distance between New York City and Washington, D.C.

**1.27** According to the model, methane has one carbon atom and four hydrogen atoms per molecule. The model also provides the spatial relationship of the atoms, and the location and number of bonds that hold the unit together.

**1.29** A hypothesis is essentially an "educated guess." A theory is a hypothesis supported by extensive experimentation; it can explain and predict new facts.

**1.31** Many examples exist; one could involve the time it takes to get to work: hypothesis—taking the "back roads" is faster than choosing the crowded interstate highway. The experiment would involve driving each path several times, starting at the same time, timing each trip, and calculating an average time for each path.

**1.33** A theory. The word "potential" indicates the scientific status of the statement.

**1.35** Freeze the contents of two beakers, one containing pure water, and the other containing salt dissolved in water. Slowly warm each container and measure the temperature of each as they convert from the solid to the liquid state. This temperature is the melting point; hence, the freezing point. Note that the melting and freezing point of a solution are the same temperature.

**1.37** The gaseous state, the liquid state, and the solid state are the three states of matter.

**1.39** A pure substance has constant composition with only a single substance, whereas a mixture is composed of two or more substances.

**1.41** An intensive property is a property of matter that is independent of the quantity of the substance. A substance's boiling point is an example of an intensive property.

**1.43** Mixtures are composed of two or more substances. A homogeneous mixture has uniform composition, while a heterogeneous mixture has non-uniform composition.

**1.45** Physical properties are characteristics of a substance that can be observed without the substance undergoing a change in chemical composition. Chemical properties can be observed only through chemical reactions that result in a change in chemical composition of the substance.

**1.47** a. Gas
b. Solid
c. Solid

**1.49**

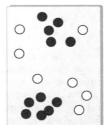

**1.51** a. Chemical reaction
b. Physical change
c. Physical change

**1.53** a. Physical property
b. Chemical property

**1.55** a. Mixture       c. Mixture
b. Pure substance  d. Pure substance

**1.57** a. Heterogeneous  c. Homogeneous
b. Homogeneous   d. Homogeneous

**1.59** The state of matter represented in the diagram is the gaseous state. The diagram represents a homogeneous mixture.

**1.61** a. Surface area and mass
b. Color and shape

**1.63** Mass describes the quantity of matter in an object.

**1.65** Length is the distance between two points.

**1.67** A liter (L) is the volume occupied by 1000 g of water at 4°C.

**1.69** mm < m < km

**1.71** 23.92

**1.73** **a.** Precision is a measure of the agreement of replicate results.

**b.** Accuracy is the degree of agreement between the true value and measured value.

**1.75** **a.** 3          **d.** 4

**b.** 3          **e.** 4

**c.** 3          **f.** 3

**1.77** **a.** $3.87 \times 10^{-3}$          **d.** 24.3

**b.** $5.20 \times 10^{-2}$          **e.** $2.40 \times 10^2$

**c.** $2.62 \times 10^{-3}$          **f.** 2.41

**1.79** **a.** $1.5 \times 10^4$          **d.** 1139.42

**b.** $2.41 \times 10^{-1}$          **e.** $7.21 \times 10^3$

**c.** 5.99

**1.81** **a.** $1.23 \times 10^1$          **e.** $9.2 \times 10^7$

**b.** $5.69 \times 10^{-2}$          **f.** $5.280 \times 10^{-3}$

**c.** $-1.527 \times 10^3$          **g.** $1.279 \times 10^0$

**d.** $7.89 \times 10^{-7}$          **h.** $-5.3177 \times 10^2$

**1.83** These measurements have high levels of precision and accuracy.

**1.85** Unlike the English system, the metric system is systematic. Since it is composed of a set of units that are related to each other decimally, it is simpler to convert one unit to another.

**1.87** **a.** k, $10^3$          **c.** μ, $10^{-6}$

**b.** c, $10^{-2}$

**1.89** $\dfrac{1 \text{ ft}}{12 \text{ in}}$ and $\dfrac{12 \text{ in}}{1 \text{ ft}}$

**1.91** **a.** 32 oz          **d.** $9.1 \times 10^5$ mg

**b.** $1.0 \times 10^{-3}$ t          **e.** $9.1 \times 10^1$ dag

**c.** $9.1 \times 10^2$ g

**1.93** **a.** $6.6 \times 10^{-3}$ lb          **d.** $3.0 \times 10^2$ cg

**b.** $1.1 \times 10^{-1}$ oz          **e.** $3.0 \times 10^3$ mg

**c.** $3.0 \times 10^{-3}$ kg

**1.95** 15.0 mg

**1.97** 13.4 m$^2$

**1.99** 4 L

**1.101** 101°F

**1.103** 5 cm is shorter than 5 in.

**1.105** 5.0 μg is smaller than 5.0 mg.

**1.107** **a.** First, the boundary measurements that are in feet should be converted to kilometers. Using the unit relationships provided in the textbook, feet can first be converted to yards. Then, yards can be converted to meters, and meters can be converted to kilometers. The boundary measurements that are in meters also need to be converted to kilometers. Finally, after all of the lengths have the same units (km), they can be added together to determine the circumference of the property.

**b.** 0.470 km

**1.109** Celsius, Fahrenheit, and Kelvin

**1.111** Energy may be categorized as either kinetic energy, the energy of motion, or potential energy, the energy of position.

**1.113** **a.** Extensive property          **c.** Intensive property

**b.** Extensive property

**1.115** **a.** 10.0°C          **b.** 283.2 K

**1.117** **a.** 293.2 K          **b.** 68.0°F

**1.119** $3 \times 10^4$ J

**1.121** 6.00 g/mL

**1.123** $6.20 \times 10^2$ L

**1.125** $1.08 \times 10^3$ g

**1.127** 5110 g salt

**1.129** Lead has the lowest density and platinum has the greatest density.

**1.131** 12.6 mL

**1.133** 1.03 g/mL

**1.135** 0.789

**1.137** 1.05

## Chapter 2

**2.1** **a.** 35 protons, 35 electrons, 44 neutrons

**b.** 35 protons, 35 electrons, 46 neutrons

**c.** 26 protons, 26 electrons, 30 neutrons

**2.3** Electron density is the probability that an electron will be found in a particular region of an atomic orbital.

**2.5** **a.** Na, metal          **c.** Mn, metal

**b.** Ra, metal          **d.** Mg, metal

**2.7** **a.** Zr (zirconium)          **c.** Cr (chromium)

**b.** 22.99 amu          **d.** At (astatine)

**2.9** a. Helium, atomic number = 2, mass = 4.009 amu

**b.** Fluorine, atomic number = 9, mass = 19.00 amu

**c.** Manganese, atomic number = 25, mass = 54.94 amu

**2.11** a. 8 protons, 10 electrons

**b.** 12 protons, 10 electrons

**c.** 26 protons, 23 electrons

**2.13** **a.** $1s^2\, 2s^2\, 2p^6\, 3s^2\, 3p^6$          [Ar]

**b.** $1s^2\, 2s^2\, 2p^6\, 3s^2\, 3p^6$          [Ar]

**c.** $1s^2\, 2s^2\, 2p^6\, 3s^2\, 3p^6\, 4s^2\, 3d^{10}\, 4p^6$          [Kr]

**d.** $1s^2\, 2s^2\, 2p^6\, 3s^2\, 3p^6\, 4s^2\, 3d^{10}\, 4p^6$          [Kr]

**2.15** **a.** $K^+$ and Ar are isoelectronic.

**b.** $Sr^{2+}$ and Kr are isoelectronic.

**c.** $S^{2-}$ and Ar are isoelectronic.

**d.** $Mg^{2+}$ and Ne are isoelectronic.

**e.** $P^{3-}$ and Ar are isoelectronic.

**f.** $Be^{2+}$ and He are isoelectronic.

**2.17** **a.** (Smallest) F, N, Be (largest)

**b.** (Lowest) Be, N, F (highest)

**c.** (Lowest) Be, N, F, (highest)

**2.19** The mass number is equal to the sum of the number of protons and neutrons in an atom.

The atomic mass is the weighted average of the masses of isotopes of an element in amu.

**2.21** **a.** Neutrons          **c.** Protons, neutrons

**b.** Protons          **d.** Nucleus, negative

**2.23** Isotopes of an element have different numbers of neutrons. They have similar chemical behavior.

**2.25** **a.** True          **c.** True

**b.** True

**2.27** **a.** 56 protons, 80 neutrons, 56 electrons

**b.** 84 protons, 125 neutrons, 84 electrons

**c.** 48 protons, 65 neutrons, 48 electrons

**2.29** $^{19}_{9}\text{F}$

**2.31** **a.** All isotopes of Rn have 86 protons.

**b.** 134 neutrons

**2.33** **a.** 34          **b.** 46

**2.35** **a.** $^1_1\text{H}$          **b.** $^{14}_{6}\text{C}$

**2.37** 63.55 amu

**2.39** • All matter consists of tiny particles called atoms.

• Atoms cannot be created, divided, destroyed, or converted to any other type of atom.

• All atoms of a particular element have identical properties.

• Atoms of different elements have different properties.

- Atoms combine in simple whole-number ratios.
- Chemical change involves joining, separating, or rearranging atoms.

**2.41** Our understanding of the nucleus is based on the gold foil experiment performed by Geiger and interpreted by Rutherford. In this experiment, Geiger bombarded a piece of gold foil with alpha particles, and observed that some alpha particles passed straight through the foil, others were deflected and some simply bounced back. This led Rutherford to propose that the atom consisted of a small, dense nucleus (alpha particles bounced back), surrounded by a cloud of electrons (some alpha particles were deflected). The size of the nucleus is small when compared to the volume of the atom (alpha particles were able to pass through the foil).

**2.43** **a.** Dalton—developed the law of multiple proportions; determined the relative atomic weights of the elements known at that time; developed the first scientific atomic theory.

**b.** Crookes—developed the cathode ray tube and discovered "cathode rays"; characterized electron properties.

**c.** Chadwick—demonstrated the existence of the neutron.

**d.** Goldstein—identified positive charge in the atom.

**2.45** A cathode ray is the negatively charged particle formed in a cathode ray tube. It was characterized as an electron, with a mass of nearly zero and a charge of $1^-$.

**2.47** Electrons surround the nucleus in a diffuse region. Electrons are negatively charged, and electrons are very low in mass in contrast to protons and neutrons.

**2.49** It was believed that protons and electrons were uniformly distributed throughout the atom.

**2.51** Spectroscopy is the measurement of intensity and energy of electromagnetic radiation.

**2.53** Electromagnetic radiation, or light, travels in waves from its source. Each wavelength of light has its own characteristic energy.

**2.55** False.

**2.57** Infrared radiation has greater energy than microwave radiation. Energy is inversely proportional to the wavelength. Since infrared radiation has shorter wavelengths than microwave radiation, it has more energy than microwave radiation.

**2.59** When electrical energy is applied to a sample of hydrogen gas, the electrons in lower orbits are "excited" to higher orbits. As they fall back down into lower orbits, they release an amount of energy equal to the amount of energy they absorbed to jump to the higher orbit. This energy may be released in the form of light, and the wavelength is proportional to the energy difference. This produces a line spectrum that is characteristic of hydrogen.

**2.61** According to Bohr, Planck, and others, electrons exist only in certain allowed regions, quantum levels, outside of the nucleus.

**2.63** • Electrons are found in orbits at discrete distances from the nucleus.
- The orbits are quantized—they are of discrete energies.
- Electrons can only be found in these orbits, never in between (they are able to jump instantaneously from orbit to orbit).
- Electrons can undergo transitions—if an electron absorbs energy, it will jump to a higher orbit; when the electron falls back to a lower orbit, it will release energy.

**2.65** Bohr's atomic model was the first to successfully account for electronic properties of atoms—specifically, the interaction of atoms and light (spectroscopy).

**2.67** **a.** atomic number 11, atomic mass 22.99, sodium

**b.** atomic number 19, atomic mass 39.10, potassium

**c.** atomic number 12, atomic mass 24.31, magnesium

**d.** atomic number 5, atomic mass 10.81, boron

**2.69** Group IA (or 1) is known collectively as the alkali metals and consists of Li, Na, K, Rb, Cs, and Fr.

**2.71** Group VIIA (or 17) is known collectively as the halogens and consists of fluorine, chlorine, bromine, iodine, and astatine.

**2.73** **a.** Na, Ni, Al          **c.** Ar

**b.** Na, Al

**2.75**

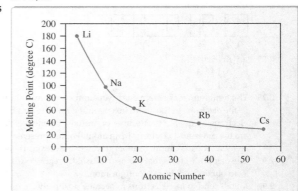

According to periodic law, the physical and chemical properties of the elements are periodic functions of their atomic numbers. As atomic number increases, the melting point decreases.

**2.77** A principal energy level is designated $n = 1, 2, 3$, and so forth. It is similar to Bohr's orbit in concept. A sublevel is a part of a principal energy level and is designated $s, p, d$, and $f$.

**2.79** See Figure 2.11 for a sketch of the $s$ atomic orbital. The $s$ orbital represents the probability of finding an electron in a region of space surrounding the nucleus.

**2.81** $2\,e^-$ for $n = 1$
$8\,e^-$ for $n = 2$
$18\,e^-$ for $n = 3$

**2.83** According to the Pauli exclusion principle, each orbital can hold up to two electrons with the electrons spinning in opposite directions (paired). Therefore, since the $d$ sublevel has five orbitals, it can contain a maximum of ten electrons.

**2.85** **a.** $1s^2\,2s^2\,2p^6\,3s^2\,3p^1$

**b.** $1s^2\,2s^2\,2p^6\,3s^1$

**c.** $1s^2\,2s^2\,2p^6\,3s^2\,3p^6\,4s^2\,3d^1$

**2.87** **a.** $1s^2\,2s^2\,2p^1$

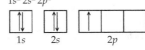

**b.** $1s^2\,2s^2\,2p^6\,3s^2\,3p^4$

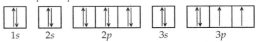

**c.** $1s^2\,2s^2\,2p^6\,3s^2\,3p^6$

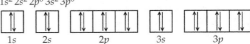

**2.89**  **a.** Not possible; $n = 1$ level can have only $s$-level orbitals.
  **b.** Possible; the electron configuration that is shown represents the carbon atom.
  **c.** Not possible; cannot have two identical orbitals ($2s^2$).
  **d.** Not possible; cannot have three electrons in an $s$ orbital ($2s^3$).

**2.91**  Diagram A is incorrect.

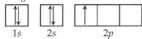

  Diagram B is correct.
  Diagram C is incorrect.

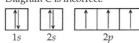

**2.93**  **a.** [Kr] $5s^2 4d^2$
  **b.** [Ar] $4s^2 3d^{10} 4p^5$
  **c.** [Ar] $4s^1$

**2.95**  The total number of electrons in an atom would include all of the electrons in the atom. In a neutral atom, the number of electrons is equal to the number of protons. Valence electrons are the outermost electrons in an atom. For a representative element, the maximum number of valence electrons is eight.

**2.97**  The octet rule states that atoms will usually react in such a way as to obtain a noble gas configuration.

**2.99**  Metals tend to lose electrons to become positively charged cations.

**2.101**

| Atom | Total electrons | Valence electrons | Principal energy level number |
|---|---|---|---|
| **a.** H | 1 | 1 | 1 |
| **b.** Na | 11 | 1 | 3 |
| **c.** B | 5 | 3 | 2 |
| **d.** F | 9 | 7 | 2 |
| **e.** Ne | 10 | 8 | 2 |
| **f.** He | 2 | 2 | 1 |

**2.103**  **a.** 17 protons, 18 electrons
  **b.** 20 protons, 18 electrons
  **c.** 26 protons, 24 electrons

**2.105**  **a.** Two    **c.** One
  **b.** One    **d.** Two

**2.107**  **a.** $Li^+$    **c.** $S^{2-}$
  **b.** $Ca^{2+}$

**2.109**  **a.** Isoelectronic
  **b.** Isoelectronic

**2.111**  **a.** $1s^2 2s^2 2p^6 3s^2 3p^6 4s^2 3d^{10} 4p^6 5s^2 4d^{10} 5p^6$    [Xe]
  **b.** $1s^2 2s^2 2p^6 3s^2 3p^6 4s^2 3d^{10} 4p^6 5s^2 4d^{10} 5p^6$    [Xe]
  **c.** $1s^2 2s^2 2p^6 3s^2 3p^6 4s^2 3d^{10} 4p^6$    [Kr]
  **d.** $1s^2 2s^2 2p^6$    [Ne]

**2.113**  Atomic size decreases from left to right across a period in the periodic table.

**2.115**  Ionization energy is the energy required to remove an electron from an isolated atom.

**2.117**  $Na + \text{ionization energy} \longrightarrow Na^+ + e^-$

**2.119**  **a.** (Smallest) F, O, N (Largest)
  **b.** (Smallest) Li, K, Cs (Largest)
  **c.** (Smallest) Cl, Br, I (Largest)
  **d.** (Smallest) Be, Mg, Ra (Largest)

**2.121**  **a.** (Smallest) N, O, F (Largest)
  **b.** (Smallest) Cs, K, Li (Largest)

**2.123**  **a.** (Largest) Li, Na, K (Smallest)
  **b.** (Largest) Te, Sn, Sr (Smallest)

**2.125**  **a.** A positive ion is always smaller than its parent atom because the positive charge of the nucleus is shared among fewer electrons in the ion. As a result, each electron is pulled closer to the nucleus and the volume of the ion decreases.
  **b.** The fluoride ion has a completed octet of electrons and an electron configuration resembling its nearest noble gas. The electron affinity of fluorine is very high; therefore, it is energetically favorable for the fluorine atom to gain the electron.

**2.127**  $Cl^-$ is larger because it has a smaller nuclear (positive) charge.

## Chapter 3

**3.1**  **a.** Potassium cyanide
  **b.** Magnesium sulfide
  **c.** Magnesium acetate

**3.3**  **a.** The bonded nuclei are closer together when a double bond exists, in comparison to a single bond.
  **b.** The bond strength increases as the bond order increases. Therefore, a double bond is stronger than a single bond. The distance of separation and bond strength are inversely related.

**3.5**  **a.** H—P—H, with H below; trigonal pyramidal
  **b.** H—Si—H, with H above and below; tetrahedral

**3.7**  **a.** The bond is polar.    **c.** The bond is nonpolar.
    $S \longrightarrow O$
  **b.** The bond is polar.    **d.** The bond is polar.
    $C \equiv N$          $I \longrightarrow Cl$

**3.9**  **a.** Nonpolar    **c.** Polar
  **b.** Polar    **d.** Nonpolar

**3.11**  **a.** $H_2O$    **c.** $NH_3$
  **b.** $CO$    **d.** $ICl$

**3.13**  **a.** H·    **c.** ·S̈i·
  **b.** He:    **d.** ·N̈·

**3.15**  **a.** $Li^+$    **b.** $Mg^{2+}$    **c.** $\left[:\ddot{Cl}:\right]^-$    **d.** $\left[:\ddot{P}:\right]^{3-}$

**3.17**  Covalent bonding involves a sharing of electrons between atoms to complete the octet of electrons for each atom participating in the bond. Ionic bonding involves a transfer of one or more electrons from one atom to another. An ionic bond is the electrostatic force between the resulting anion and a cation.

**3.19**  Electronegativity values increase as we proceed left to right and bottom to top of the table. The most electronegative elements are located in the upper right corner of the periodic table.

**3.21**  **a.** Ionic    **c.** Nonpolar covalent
  **b.** Polar covalent    **d.** Polar covalent

**3.23**  **a.** $Li\cdot + :\ddot{Br}\cdot \longrightarrow Li^+ + \left[:\ddot{Br}:\right]^-$
  **b.** $\cdot Mg \cdot + 2:\ddot{Cl}\cdot \longrightarrow Mg^{2+} + 2\left[:\ddot{Cl}:\right]^-$
  **c.** $\cdot\ddot{P}\cdot + 3H\cdot \longrightarrow$ H—P—H, with H below

**3.25** He has two valence electrons (electron configuration $1s^2$) and a complete N = 1 level. It has a stable electron configuration, with no tendency to gain or lose electrons, and satisfies the octet rule (2 e⁻ for period 1). Hence, it is nonreactive.
He:

**3.27** MgS

**3.29** **a.** Sodium ion
**b.** Copper(I) ion (or cuprous ion)
**c.** Magnesium ion

**3.31** **a.** Bicarbonate ion
**b.** Hydronium ion
**c.** Carbonate ion

**3.33** **a.** $K^+$  **b.** $Ni^{2+}$

**3.35** **a.** $SO_4^{2-}$  **b.** $NO_3^-$

**3.37** **a.** $Al_2O_3$  **b.** $Li_2S$

**3.39** **a.** Magnesium chloride
**b.** Aluminum chloride
**c.** Copper (II) nitrate

**3.41** **a.** NaCl  **b.** $MgBr_2$

**3.43** **a.** AgCN  **b.** $NH_4Cl$

**3.45** **a.** CuO  **b.** $Fe_2O_3$

**3.47** **a.** $NaNO_3$  **b.** $Mg(NO_3)_2$

**3.49** **a.** $NH_4I$  **b.** $(NH_4)_2SO_4$

**3.51** **a.** Nitrogen dioxide  **c.** Sulfur trioxide
**b.** Selenium trioxide

**3.53** **a.** $SiO_2$  **b.** $SO_2$

**3.55** Ionic solid-state compounds exist in regular, repeating, three-dimensional structures; the crystal lattice. The crystal lattice is made up of positive and negative ions. Solid-state covalent compounds are made up of molecules that may be arranged in a regular crystalline pattern or in an irregular (amorphous) structure.

**3.57** The boiling points of ionic solids are generally much higher than those of covalent solids.

**3.59** KCl would be expected to exist as a solid at room temperature; it is an ionic compound, and ionic compounds are characterized by high melting points.

**3.61** Water will have a higher boiling point. Water is a polar molecule with strong intermolecular attractive forces, whereas carbon tetrachloride is a nonpolar molecule with weak intermolecular attractive forces. More energy—hence, a higher temperature is required to overcome the attractive forces among the water molecules.

**3.63** Yes, $MgCl_2$ in water forms an electrolytic solution. $MgCl_2$ is an ionic solid that dissociates in water, and the resulting solution is capable of conducting a current of electricity.

**3.65** The least electronegative atom will usually be the central atom. The central atom is often the element in the compound for which there is only one atom.

**3.67** For polyatomic cations, subtract one electron for each unit of positive charge.

**3.69** Single bond < double bond < triple bond
(Lowest energy)    (Highest energy)

**3.71** $C_5H_{12}$. As the size of the hydrocarbon increases, the number of possible isomers increases.

**3.73** Resonance can occur when more than one valid Lewis structure can be written for a molecule. Each individual structure which can be drawn is a resonance form. The true nature of the structure for the molecule is the resonance hybrid, which consists of the "average" of the resonance forms.

**3.75** 120°

**3.77** True. A molecule containing only nonpolar bonds must be a nonpolar molecule.

**3.79** **a.** Cl—N—Cl, Cl   **c.** S=C=S

**b.** H—C—O—H, H   **d.** Cl—C—H, H

**3.81** H—C—C(=O)(H), H (H on C)

**3.83** H—C—C—C—H with O on middle C, H's on outer C's

**3.85** $[:N{\equiv}O:]^+$

**3.87** $[:\ddot{O}{-}H]^-$

**3.89** $\left[ H{-}C({-}H){=}C({=}O)(O:) \right]^- \rightleftharpoons \left[ H{-}C({-}H){-}C({=}O)(O) \right]^-$

**3.91** **a.** $:C{\equiv}O:$  **b.** H—O—H  **c.** $O{=}C{=}O$

**3.93** $:Cl{-}Be{-}Cl:$

**3.95**

**3.97** **a.** Bent  **b.** Trigonal planar

O—S—O

**3.99** **a.** Polar  **b.** Nonpolar

**3.101** Both a. $CO_2$ and c. $CF_4$

**3.103** A molecule containing no polar bonds *must* be nonpolar. A molecule containing polar bonds may or may not itself be polar. It depends upon the number and arrangement of the bonds.

**3.105** **a.** Cl—N—Cl, Cl
Trigonal pyramidal
polar
water soluble

**c.** $S{=}C{=}S$
Linear
nonpolar
not water soluble

**b.** H—C—O, H, H
Tetrahedral around C
bent around O
polar, water soluble

**d.** H—C—Cl, Cl
Tetrahedral
polar
water soluble

**3.107** Polar compounds have strong intermolecular attractive forces. Higher temperatures are needed to overcome these forces and convert the solid to a liquid; hence, we predict higher melting points for polar compounds when compared to nonpolar compounds.

**3.109** Yes

**3.111** a. $NH_3$        b. $CF_4$        c. NaCl

# Chapter 4

**4.1** $3.33 \times 10^{-10}$ g Hg

**4.3** Formula mass = 194.20 amu
Molar mass = 194.20 g/mol

**4.5** a. DR        c. DR
b. SR        d. D

**4.7** The black precipitate is CuS. $Cu^{2+}(aq) + S^{2-}(aq) \longrightarrow CuS(s)$

**4.9** $Ca \rightarrow Ca^{2+} + 2e^-$ (oxidation ½ reaction)
$S + 2e^- \rightarrow S^{2-}$ (reduction ½ reaction)
$Ca + S \rightarrow CaS$ (complete reaction)

**4.11** Oxidizing agent: S
Reducing agent: Ca
Substance oxidized: Ca
Substance reduced: S

**4.13** a. In order for $Cr^{3+}(aq)$ to form $Cr(s)$ and the electrode to be electro-plated, $Cr^{3+}$ must gain 3 electrons and undergo reduction. Therefore, the electrode must have a negative charge.
b. Cathode
c. $Cr^{3+}(aq) + 3e^- \rightarrow Cr(s)$

**4.15** a. 47.9 g $NO_2$        b. 52.2%

**4.17** a. 200.6 amu        c. 24.31 amu
b. 83.80 amu

**4.19** a. 28.09 g/mol        c. 74.92 g/mol
b. 107.9 g/mol

**4.21** 39.95 g

**4.23** $6.0 \times 10^{19}$ carbon atoms

**4.25** $1.7 \times 10^{-22}$ mol As

**4.27** 40.36 g Ne

**4.29** 4.00 g/mol

**4.31** a. 5.00 mol He        c. $4.2 \times 10^{-2}$ mol $Cl_2$
b. 1.7 mol Na

**4.33** $1.62 \times 10^3$ g Ag

**4.35** $8.37 \times 10^{22}$ Ag atoms

**4.37** A molecule is a single unit composed of atoms joined by covalent bonds. An ion pair is composed of positive and negatively charged ions joined by electrostatic attraction, the ionic bond. The ion pairs, unlike the molecule, do not form single units; the electrostatic charge is directed to other ions in a crystal lattice as well.

**4.39** a. 58.44 amu and 58.44 g/mol
b. 142.04 amu and 142.04 g/mol
c. 357.49 amu and 357.49 g/mol

**4.41** 32.00 amu and 32.00 g/mol

**4.43** 249.70 amu and 249.70 g/mol

**4.45** a. 0.257 mol NaCl        b. 0.106 mol $Na_2SO_4$

**4.47** a. 18.02 g $H_2O$        c. 40.0 g He
b. 116.9 g NaCl        d. $2.02 \times 10^2$ g $H_2$

**4.49** a. 1.60 g $CH_4$        c. 4.00 g NaOH
b. 10.0 g $CaCO_3$        d. 9.81 g $H_2SO_4$

**4.51** a. 0.420 mol KBr        c. $6.57 \times 10^{-1}$ mol $CS_2$
b. 0.415 mol $MgSO_4$        d. $2.14 \times 10^{-1}$ mol $Al_2(CO_3)_3$

**4.53** The ultimate basis for a balanced chemical equation is the law of conservation of mass. No mass may be gained or lost in a chemical reaction, and the chemical equation must reflect this fact.

**4.55** A reactant is the starting material for a chemical reaction. Reactants are found on the left side of the reaction arrow.

**4.57** Heat is necessary for the reaction to occur.

**4.59** a. D        c. C
b. DR        d. SR

**4.61** The subscript tells us the number of atoms or ions contained in one unit of the compound.

**4.63** If we change the subscript, we change the identity of the compound.

**4.65** a. $2C_2H_6(g) + 7O_2(g) \rightarrow 4CO_2(g) + 6H_2O(g)$
b. $6K_2O(s) + P_4O_{10}(s) \rightarrow 4K_3PO_4(s)$
c. $MgBr_2(aq) + H_2SO_4(aq) \rightarrow 2HBr(g) + MgSO_4(aq)$
d. $C_2H_5OH(l) + 3O_2(g) \rightarrow 2CO_2(g) + 3H_2O(g)$

**4.67** a. $Ca(s) + F_2(g) \rightarrow CaF_2(s)$
b. $2Mg(s) + O_2(g) \rightarrow 2MgO(s)$
c. $3H_2(g) + N_2(g) \rightarrow 2NH_3(g)$

**4.69** a. $2C_4H_{10}(g) + 13O_2(g) \rightarrow 10H_2O(g) + 8CO_2(g)$
b. $Au_2S_3(s) + 3H_2(g) \rightarrow 2Au(s) + 3H_2S(g)$
c. $Al(OH)_3(s) + 3HCl(aq) \rightarrow AlCl_3(aq) + 3H_2O(l)$
d. $(NH_4)_2Cr_2O_7(s) \rightarrow Cr_2O_3(s) + N_2(g) + 4H_2O(g)$

**4.71** a. $N_2(g) + 3H_2(g) \rightarrow 2NH_3(g)$
b. $HCl(aq) + NaOH(aq) \rightarrow NaCl(aq) + H_2O(l)$
c. $C_6H_{12}O_6(s) + 6O_2(g) \rightarrow 6H_2O(l) + 6CO_2(g)$
d. $Na_2CO_3(s) \rightarrow Na_2O(s) + CO_2(g)$

**4.73** a. $Na_2SO_4$ will not form a precipitate.
b. $BaSO_4$ will form a precipitate.
c. $BaCO_3$ will form a precipitate.
d. $K_2CO_3$ will not form a precipitate.

**4.75** Yes. $PbI_2$

**4.77** Yes. $CaCO_3$

**4.79** An ionic equation shows all reactants and products as free ions unless they are precipitates. Ions that appear on both sides of the equation do not appear in the net ionic equation. The net ionic equation only shows the chemical species that actually undergo change.

**4.81** $Ag^+(aq) + Br^-(aq) \rightarrow AgBr(s)$

**4.83** An acid loses a hydrogen cation.

**4.85** HCN is the acid, and KOH is the base.

**4.87** The species oxidized *loses* electrons.

**4.89** During an oxidation-reduction reaction the species *oxidized* is the reducing agent.

**4.91**     $Cl_2$      +      2KI      $\rightarrow$ 2KCl + $I_2$
substance reduced   substance oxidized
oxidizing agent       reducing agent

**4.93** $2I^- \rightarrow I_2 + 2e^-$ (oxidation ½ reaction)
$Cl_2 + 2e^- \rightarrow 2Cl^-$ (reduction ½ reaction)

**4.95** An oxidation-reduction reaction must take place to produce electron flow in a voltaic cell.

**4.97** Storage battery

**4.99** The coefficients represent the relative number of moles of product(s) and reactant(s).

**4.101** 27.7 g $B_2H_6$

**4.103** 0.658 mol $CrCl_3$

**4.105** a. $N_2(g) + 3H_2(g) \rightarrow 2NH_3(g)$
b. Three moles of $H_2$ will react with one mole of $N_2$.
c. One mole of $N_2$ will produce two moles of the product $NH_3$.
d. 1.50 mol $H_2$
e. 17.0 g $NH_3$

**4.107** **a.** 149.21 g/mol        **c.** 32.00 g O
        **b.** $1.20 \times 10^{24}$ O atoms    **d.** 10.7 g O
**4.109** 7.39 g $O_2$
**4.111** $6.77 \times 10^4$ g $CO_2$
**4.113** 70.6 g $C_{10}H_{22}$
**4.115** $9.13 \times 10^2$ g $N_2$
**4.117** 92.6%
**4.119** $6.85 \times 10^2$ g $N_2$

## Chapter 5

**5.1** **a.** 0.954 atm        **c.** 0.730 atm
      **b.** 0.382 atm        **d.** 6.5 atm
**5.3** 2.91 atm
**5.5** Radon (Rn) is a collection of atoms (recall that all atoms are inherently nonpolar), and nitrogen dioxide ($NO_2$) molecules are polar. Since nonpolar molecules are only weakly attracted to each other, they exhibit more ideal gas behavior.
**5.7** Molecules with complex structures, which do not "slide" smoothly past each other, and polar molecules tend to have higher viscosities.
**5.9** Evaporation is the conversion of a liquid to a gas at a temperature lower than the boiling point of the liquid. Condensation is the conversion of a gas to a liquid at a temperature lower than the boiling point of the liquid.
**5.11** $CO_2 < CH_3Cl < CH_3OH$. Only $CH_3OH$ exhibits London dispersion forces, dipole-dipole interactions, and hydrogen bonding. Hence, $CH_3OH$ has the strongest intermolecular forces and, therefore, the highest boiling point.
**5.13** **a.** Ionic solids generally have high melting points and a tendency to be hard and brittle.
      **b.** Table salt (NaCl) and calcium chloride ($CaCl_2$)
**5.15** A monometer can be used to measure $O_2$ gas pressure in terms of the height of a column of liquid (mercury, for example) that is supported by the force exerted on the surface of the liquid by the $O_2$ gas being measured.
**5.17** **a.** 1.24 atm        **c.** 0.197 atm
      **b.** 0.0954 atm      **d.** 1.23 kPa
**5.19** **a.** 10.4 psi        **c.** 15 psi
      **b.** 3.00 psi        **d.** 22.1 psi
**5.21** In all cases, gas particles are much farther apart than similar particles in the liquid or solid state. In most cases, particles in the liquid state are, on average, farther apart than those in the solid state. Water is the exception; liquid water's molecules are closer together than they are in the solid state.
**5.23** Gases are easily compressed simply because there is a great deal of space between particles; they can be pushed closer together (compressed) because the space is available.
**5.25** Gas particles are in continuous, random motion. They are free (minimal attractive forces between particles) to roam, up to the boundary of their container.
**5.27** Gases exhibit more ideal behavior at low pressures. At low pressures, gas particles are more widely separated and therefore the attractive forces between particles are less. The ideal gas model assumes negligible attractive forces between gas particles.
**5.29** The kinetic molecular theory states that the average kinetic energy of the gas particles increases as the temperature increases. Kinetic energy is proportional to (velocity)$^2$. Therefore, as the temperature increases, the gas particle velocity increases and the rate of mixing increases as well.

**5.31** Boyle's law states that the volume of a gas varies inversely with the gas pressure if the temperature and the number of moles of gas are held constant.
**5.33** Volume will decrease according to Boyle's law. Volume is inversely proportional to the pressure exerted on the gas.
**5.35** 1 atm
**5.37** 5 L·atm
**5.39** 5.23 atm
**5.41** Charles's law states that the volume of a gas varies directly with the absolute temperature if pressure and number of moles of gas are constant.
**5.43** The Kelvin scale is the only scale that is directly proportional to molecular motion, and it is this motion that determines the physical properties of gases.
**5.45** No. The volume is proportional to the temperature in K, not Celsius.
**5.47** 0.96 L
**5.49** 1.51 L
**5.51** 120°F
**5.53** • Volume and temperature are *directly* proportional; increasing $T$ increases $V$.
       • Volume and pressure are *inversely* proportional; decreasing $P$ increases $V$.
       Therefore, both variables work together to *increase* the volume.
**5.55** $V_f = \dfrac{P_i V_i T_f}{P_f T_i}$
**5.57** $1.82 \times 10^{-2}$ L
**5.59** 1.5 atm
**5.61** Avogadro's law states that equal volumes of any ideal gas contain the same number of moles if measured at constant temperature and pressure.
**5.63** 6.00 L
**5.65** No. One mole of an ideal gas will occupy exactly 22.4 L; however, there is no completely ideal gas, and careful measurement will show different volumes for gases exhibiting varying degrees of ideality.
**5.67** Standard temperature is 273 K.
**5.69** 0.80 mol
**5.71** 35.2 L
**5.73** 1.25 g/L
**5.75** 0.276 mol
**5.77** $5.94 \times 10^{-2}$ L
**5.79** 172°C
**5.81** $9.08 \times 10^3$ L
**5.83** Dalton's law states that the total pressure of a mixture of gases is the sum of the partial pressures of the component gases.
**5.85** 0.74 atm
**5.87** 0.29 atm
**5.89** Limitations to the ideal gas model arise from interactive forces that are present between the individual atoms or molecules of a gas. These interactive forces are present in gases composed of polar molecules. The forces increase as the temperature of the gas decreases or the pressure of the gas increases.
**5.91** When temperature increases, the attractive forces present in gases decrease. CO behaves more ideally at 50 K than at 5 K.
**5.93** Intermolecular forces in liquids are considerably stronger than intermolecular forces in gases. Particles are, on average, much closer together in liquids and the strength of attraction decreases as the distance of separation increases.
**5.95** The vapor pressure of a liquid increases as the temperature of the liquid increases.

**5.97** Viscosity is the resistance to flow caused by intermolecular attractive forces. Complex molecules may become entangled and not slide smoothly across one another.

**5.99** All molecules exhibit London dispersion forces. This is because electrons are in constant motion in all molecules.

**5.101** Only methanol exhibits hydrogen bonding. Methanol has an oxygen atom bonded to a hydrogen atom, a necessary condition for hydrogen bonding.

**5.103** Propylene glycol

**5.105** Solids are essentially incompressible because the average distance of separation among particles in the solid state is small. There is literally no space for the particles to crowd closer together.

**5.107** **a.** High melting temperature, brittle
**b.** High melting temperature, hard

**5.109** Beryllium. Metallic solids are good electrical conductors. Carbon forms covalent solids that are poor electrical conductors.

**5.111** Mercury. Mercury is a liquid at room temperature, whereas chromium is a solid at room temperature. Liquids have higher vapor pressures than solids.

## Chapter 6

**6.1** A chemical analysis must be performed in order to determine the identity of all components, a qualitative analysis. If only one component is found, it is a pure substance; two or more components indicates a true solution.

**6.3** After the container of soft drink is opened, $CO_2$ diffuses into the surrounding atmosphere; consequently, the partial pressure of $CO_2$ over the soft drink decreases and the equilibrium

$$CO_2(g) \rightleftharpoons CO_2(aq)$$

shifts to the left, lowering the concentration of $CO_2$ in the soft drink.

**6.5** $0.19\ M$

**6.7** $0.125$ mol HCl

**6.9** Pure water

**6.11** $4.0 \times 10^{-2}$ mol particles/L KCl, $3 \times 10^{-1}$ mol particles/L glucose

**6.13** $0.110$ mol/L

**6.15** A solution is described as clear if it efficiently transmits light, showing no evidence of suspended particles. The solution does not have to be colorless to meet these conditions.

**6.17** **a.** Electrolyte    **b.** Nonelectrolyte    **c.** Electrolyte

**6.19** A true solution contains more than one substance, with the particles having a diameter less than $1 \times 10^{-9}$ m. Particles with diameters of $1 \times 10^{-9}$ m to $2 \times 10^{-7}$ m are colloids. A suspension contains particles much larger than $2 \times 10^{-7}$ m.

**6.21** A saturated solution is one in which undissolved solute is in equilibrium with the solution. A supersaturated solution is a solution that is more concentrated than a saturated solution.

**6.23** A colloidal dispersion of albumin is not completely homogenous. The colloid particles scatter light (Tyndall effect). Saline solution is completely homogenous, and the dissolved NaCl ions do not scatter light.

**6.25** $CCl_4$ is more likely to form a solution in benzene ($C_6H_6$). The rule "like dissolves like" suggests that $CCl_4$ is soluble in benzene because both $CCl_4$ and benzene are nonpolar.

**6.27** Stream temperature is much lower in early spring than mid-August. Henry's law predicts that the concentration of dissolved oxygen in the stream is greater at lower water temperatures. Trout require oxygen and thrive in early spring.

**6.29** $0.033$ mol/L

**6.31** **a.** $6.60\%\ C_6H_{12}O_6$    **b.** $2.00\%$ NaCl

**6.33** **a.** $10.0\%$ ethanol    **b.** $5.00\%$ ethanol

**6.35** **a.** $21.0\%$ NaCl    **b.** $3.75\%$ NaCl

**6.37** $19.5\%\ KNO_3$

**6.39** $1.00$ g sugar

**6.41** **a.** $2.25$ g NaCl    **b.** $3.13$ g $NaC_2H_3O_2$

**6.43** $2.0 \times 10^{-3}$ ppt

**6.45** $0.04\%$ (m/m) solution is more concentrated

**6.47** $0.50\ M$

**6.49** $0.900\ M$

**6.51** Laboratory managers often purchase concentrated solutions for practical reasons such as economy and conservation of storage space.

**6.53** **a.** $1.46$ g NaCl    **b.** $9.00$ g $C_6H_{12}O_6$

**6.55** $158$ g glucose

**6.57** $0.266$ L

**6.59** $50.0$ mL

**6.61** $20.0\ M$

**6.63** $5.00 \times 10^{-2}\ M$

**6.65** A colligative property is a solution property that depends on the concentration of solute particles rather than the identity of the particles.

**6.67** Salt is an ionic substance that dissociates in water to produce positive and negative ions. These ions (or particles) lower the freezing point of water. If the concentration of salt particles is large, the freezing point may be depressed below the surrounding temperature, and the ice would melt.

**6.69** Raoult's law states that when a solute is added to a solvent, the vapor pressure of the solvent decreases in proportion to the concentration of the solute.

**6.71** One mole of $CaCl_2$ produces three moles of particles in solution, whereas one mole of NaCl produces two moles of particles in solution. Therefore, a one molar $CaCl_2$ solution contains a greater number of particles than a one molar NaCl solution and will produce a greater freezing-point depression.

**6.73** **a.** $-2.79°C$    **b.** $-5.58°C$

**6.75** Freezing Temperature for NaCl Solution $= -1.86°C$
Freezing Temperature for Sucrose Solution $= -0.93°C$

**6.77** Sucrose

**6.79** $A \rightarrow B$

**6.81** No net flow

**6.83** $1.0 \times 10^{-3}$ mol particles/L

**6.85** $24$ atm

**6.87** Hypertonic

**6.89** Hypotonic

**6.91** Water is often termed the "universal solvent" because it is a polar molecule and will dissolve, at least to some extent, most ionic and polar covalent compounds. The majority of our body mass is water and this water is an important part of the nutrient transport system due to its solvent properties. This is true in other animals and plants as well. Because of its ability to hydrogen bond, water has a high boiling point and a low vapor pressure. Also, water is abundant and easily purified.

**6.93**

**6.95** The number of particles in solution is dependent on the degree of dissociation.

**6.97** In dialysis, sodium ions move from a region of high concentration to a region of low concentration. If we wish to remove (transport) sodium ions from the blood, they can move to a region of lower concentration, the dialysis solution.

**6.99** The shelf life is a function of the stability of the ammonia-water solution. The ammonia can react with the water to convert to the extremely soluble and stable ammonium ion. Also, ammonia and water are polar molecules. Polar interactions, particularly hydrogen bonding, are strong and contribute to the long-term solution stability.

**6.101**

$$\delta^+ H$$
$$\searrow$$
$$O \; \delta^- \; Na^+$$
$$\delta^+ \; ^H \nearrow$$

**6.103** Polar; like dissolves like ($H_2O$ is polar)

**6.105** Elevated concentrations of sodium ion in the blood may cause confusion, stupor, or coma.

**6.107** Elevated concentrations of sodium ion in the blood may occur whenever large amounts of water are lost. Diarrhea, diabetes, and certain high-protein diets are particularly problematic.

**6.109** 0.10 eq/L

**6.111** **a.** 0.154 mol/L    **b.** 0.154 mol/L

**6.113** $4.0 \times 10^{-2}$ mol/L

# Chapter 7

**7.1** **a.** Exothermic
**b.** Exothermic

**7.3** He(g). Gases have a greater degree of disorder than solids.

**7.5** $\Delta G = (+) - T(-)$
$\Delta G$ must always be positive. A positive value for $\Delta G$ indicates a nonspontaneous process.

**7.7** $2.7 \times 10^3$ J

**7.9** Heat energy produced by the friction of striking the match provides the activation energy necessary for this combustion process.

**7.11** If the enzyme catalyzed a process needed to sustain life, the substance interfering with that enzyme would be classified as a poison.

**7.13** At a busy restaurant during lunchtime, approximately the same number of people will enter and exit the restaurant at any given moment. Throughout lunchtime, the number of people in the restaurant may be essentially unchanged, but the identity of the individuals in the restaurant is continually changing.

**7.15** Measure the concentrations of products and reactants at a series of times until no further concentration change is observed.

**7.17** Product formation

**7.19** The first law of thermodynamics, the law of conservation of energy, states that the energy of the universe is constant.

**7.21** An exothermic reaction is one in which energy is released during chemical change.

**7.23** A fuel must release heat in the combustion (oxidation) process.

**7.25** Free energy is the combined contribution of entropy and enthalpy for a chemical reaction.

**7.27** Enthalpy is a measure of heat energy.

**7.29** **a.** Entropy increases. Conversion of a solid to a liquid results in an increase in disorder of the substance. Solids retain their shape while liquids will flow and their shapes are determined by their container.
**b.** Entropy increases. Conversion of a liquid to a gas results in an increase in disorder of the substance. Gas particles

move randomly with very weak interactions between particles, much weaker than those interactions in the liquid state.

**7.31** Isopropyl alcohol quickly evaporates (liquid ⟶ gas) after being applied to the skin. Conversion of a liquid to a gas requires heat energy. The heat energy is supplied by the skin. When this heat is lost, the skin temperature drops.

**7.33** $\Delta G = (-) - T(+)$
$\Delta G$ must always be negative; the process is spontaneous.

**7.35** Fuel value is the amount of energy per gram of food.

**7.37** The temperature of the water (or solution) is measured in a calorimeter. If the reaction being studied is exothermic, released energy heats the water and the temperature increases. In an endothermic reaction, heat flows from the water to the reaction and the water temperature decreases.

**7.39** Joule

**7.41** Double-walled containers, used in calorimeters, provide a small airspace between the part of the calorimeter (inside wall) containing the sample solution and the outside wall contacting the surroundings. This gap makes heat transfer more difficult.

**7.43** $1.20 \times 10^3$ cal

**7.45** $8 \times 10^{-2}$ nutritional Calories/g substance

**7.47** Decomposition of leaves and twigs to produce soil.

**7.49** The activated complex is the arrangement of reactants in an unstable transition state as a chemical reaction proceeds. The activated complex must form in order to convert reactants to products.

**7.51** The rate of a reaction is the change in concentration of a reactant or product per unit time. The rate constant is the proportionality constant that relates rate and concentration. The order is the exponent of each concentration term in the rate equation.

**7.53** A catalyst increases the rate of a reaction without itself undergoing change.

**7.55** An increase in concentration of reactants means that there are more molecules in a certain volume. The probability of collision is enhanced because they travel a shorter distance before meeting another molecule. The rate is proportional to the number of collisions per unit time.

**7.57** A catalyst speeds up a chemical reaction by facilitating the formation of the activated complex, thus lowering the activation energy, the energy barrier for the reaction.

**7.59** See textbook Figure 7.11.

**7.61** Rate = $k[CH_4][O_2]$   Increase

**7.63** Rate = $k[N_2O_4]^n$   Note: $n$ must be experimentally determined.

**7.65** The rate of the reaction increases four-fold.

**7.67** LeChatelier's principle states that when a system at equilibrium is disturbed, the equilibrium shifts in the direction that minimizes the disturbance.

**7.69** A physical equilibrium occurs between two phases of the same substance. A chemical equilibrium is a state of a chemical reaction in which the rates of the forward and reverse reactions are equal.

**7.71** Products

**7.73** **a.** False. A slow reaction may go to completion, but take a longer period of time.
**b.** False. The rate of forward and reverse reactions is equal in a dynamic equilibrium situation.

**7.75** (I)

**7.77** A dynamic equilibrium has fixed concentrations of all reactants and products—these concentrations do not change with time. However, the process is dynamic because products and reactants are continuously being formed and consumed. The concentrations do not change because the rates of production and consumption are equal.

**7.79** The position of the equilibrium addresses the question of whether products or reactants are favored. In a hypothetical equilibrium, if the equilibrium position shifts to the left, that means more reactants are formed. If the equilibrium position shifts to the right, that means more products are formed.

**7.81** 1. Concentration
2. Heat
3. Pressure

**7.83** $K_{eq} = \dfrac{[NO_2]^2}{[N_2O_4]}$

**7.85** $K_{eq} = \dfrac{[NH_3]^2}{[N_2][H_2]^3}$

**7.87** $K_{eq} = \dfrac{[H_2S]^2}{[H_2]^2[S_2]}$

**7.89** $7.7 \times 10^{-5} M$

**7.91** **a.** Equilibrium shifts to the left.   **c.** No change
**b.** No change

**7.93** **a.** $PCl_3$ increases   **d.** $PCl_3$ decreases
**b.** $PCl_3$ decreases   **e.** $PCl_3$ remains the same
**c.** $PCl_3$ decreases

**7.95** Decrease

**7.97** $K_{eq} = \dfrac{[CO][H_2]}{[H_2O]}$

**7.99** False. The position of equilibrium is not affected by a catalyst, only the rate at which equilibrium is attained.

**7.101** Carbon dioxide is dissolved in cola. Heating shifts the equilibrium to the right.

$$CO_2(l) \rightleftharpoons CO_2(g)$$

Since gases are less soluble at elevated temperatures, the pressure buildup from the carbon dioxide gas in the sealed bottle can lead to an explosion.

**7.103** **a.** $K_{eq} = \dfrac{[SO_3]^2}{[SO_2]^2[O_2]}$   **b.** $3.0 \times 10^2$

**7.105** Adding $SO_2(g)$ or $O_2(g)$ or increasing the pressure

## Chapter 8

**8.1** **a.** Brønsted-Lowry acid
**b.** Brønsted-Lowry acid
**c.** Brønsted-Lowry base
**d.** Brønsted-Lowry base

**8.3** **a.** $HF(aq) + H_2O(l) \rightleftharpoons F^-(aq) + H_3O^+(aq)$
**b.** $C_6H_5COO^-(aq) + H_2O(l) \rightleftharpoons C_6H_5COOH(aq) + OH^-(aq)$

**8.5** **a.** $HF/F^-$ and $H_3O^+/H_2O$
**b.** $H_2O/OH^-$ and $C_6H_5COOH/C_6H_5COO^-$

**8.7** $4.0 \times 10^{-13} M$

**8.9** $1.0 \times 10^{-11} M$

**8.11** pH = 4.74

**8.13** pH = 4.87

**8.15** $CO_2 + H_2O \rightleftharpoons H_2CO_3 \rightleftharpoons H_3O^+ + HCO_3^-$
An increase in the partial pressure of $CO_2$ is a stress on the left side of the equilibrium. The equilibrium will shift to the right in an effort to decrease the concentration of $CO_2$. This will cause the molar concentration of $H_2CO_3$ to increase.

**8.17** In Question 8.15, the equilibrium shifts to the right. Therefore, the molar concentration of $H_3O^+$ should increase.
In Question 8.16, the equilibrium shifts to the left. Therefore, the molar concentration of $H_3O^+$ should decrease.

**8.19** $pH = pK_a + \log\dfrac{[HCO_3^-]}{[H_2CO_3]}$

**8.21** **a.** An Arrhenius acid is a substance that dissociates, producing hydrogen ions.
**b.** A Brønsted-Lowry acid is a substance that behaves as a proton donor.

**8.23** The Brønsted-Lowry theory provides a broader view of acid-base theory than does the Arrhenius theory. Brønsted-Lowry emphasizes the role of the solvent in the dissociation process.

**8.25** **a.** Brønsted-Lowry acid   **c.** Amphiprotic
**b.** Brønsted-Lowry base

**8.27** **a.** Brønsted-Lowry acid
**b.** Amphiprotic
**c.** Brønsted-Lowry base

**8.29** **a.** $HNO_2(aq) + H_2O(l) \rightleftharpoons H_3O^+(aq) + NO_2^-(aq)$
**b.** $HCN(aq) + H_2O(l) \rightleftharpoons H_3O^+(aq) + CN^-(aq)$
**c.** $CH_3CH_2CH_2COO^-(aq) + H_2O(l) \longrightarrow CH_3CH_2CH_2COOH(aq) + OH^-(aq)$

**8.31** HCN

**8.33** $I^-$

**8.35** $HNO_3$

**8.37** $CN^-$

**8.39** HF

**8.41** **a.** $HCN/CN^-$ and $NH_4^+/NH_3$
**b.** $HCO_3^-/CO_3^{2-}$ and $HCl/Cl^-$

**8.43** Concentration refers to the quantity of acid or base contained in a specified volume of solvent. Strength refers to the degree of dissociation of the acid or base.

**8.45** **a.** Weak   **b.** Weak   **c.** Weak

**8.47** **a.** $1.0 \times 10^{-7} M$   **b.** $1.0 \times 10^{-11} M$

**8.49** **a.** $1.0 \times 10^{-10} M$   **b.** $1.0 \times 10^{-12} M$

**8.51** $1.7 \times 10^{-11} M$

**8.53** The beaker containing $0.10 M$ $CH_3COOH$. $CH_3COOH$ is a weaker acid than HCl. Thus, it has a higher pH than HCl.

**8.55** **a.** pH = 2.00   **b.** pH = 4.00

**8.57** **a.** $[H_3O^+] = 1.0 \times 10^{-1} M$
**b.** $[H_3O^+] = 1.0 \times 10^{-5} M$

**8.59** pH = 11.00

**8.61** **a.** $[H_3O^+] = 5.0 \times 10^{-2} M$
$[OH^-] = 2.0 \times 10^{-13} M$
**b.** $[H_3O^+] = 2.0 \times 10^{-10} M$
$[OH^-] = 5.0 \times 10^{-5} M$

**8.63** A neutralization reaction is one in which an acid and a base react to produce water and a salt (a "neutral" solution).

**8.65** **a.** $[H_3O^+] = 1.0 \times 10^{-6} M$
$[OH^-] = 1.0 \times 10^{-8} M$
**b.** $[H_3O^+] = 6.3 \times 10^{-6} M$
$[OH^-] = 1.6 \times 10^{-9} M$
**c.** $[H_3O^+] = 1.6 \times 10^{-8} M$
$[OH^-] = 6.3 \times 10^{-7} M$

**8.67** The statement is incorrect. The pH = 3 solution is 1000 times as acidic as the pH = 6 solution because pH is a logarithmic function.

**8.69** **a.** $[H_3O^+] = 1.0 \times 10^{-5} M$
**b.** $[H_3O^+] = 1.0 \times 10^{-12} M$
**c.** $[H_3O^+] = 3.2 \times 10^{-6} M$

**8.71** a. pH = 6.00    b. pH = 8.00    c. pH = 3.25

**8.73** pH = 3.12

**8.75** pH = 10.74

**8.77** 4 mol HCl

**8.79** An indicator is a substance that is added to a solution and changes color as the solution reaches a certain pH. It is often used in the technique of titration to determine the equivalence point.

**8.81** $HNO_3(aq) + NaOH(aq) \longrightarrow H_2O(l) + NaNO_3(aq)$

**8.83** $H^+(aq) + OH^-(aq) \longrightarrow H_2O(l)$ or
$H_3O^+(aq) + OH^-(aq) \longrightarrow 2H_2O(l)$

**8.85** Two protons

**8.87** $0.1800\ M$

**8.89** 13.33 mL

**8.91** Step 1. $H_2CO_3(aq) + H_2O(l) \rightleftharpoons H_3O^+(aq) + HCO_3^-(aq)$
Step 2. $HCO_3^-(aq) + H_2O(l) \rightleftharpoons H_3O^+(aq) + CO_3^{2-}(aq)$

**8.93** a. $NH_3$ and $NH_4Cl$ can form a buffer solution.
b. $HNO_3$ and $KNO_3$ cannot form a buffer solution.

**8.95** HCl/NaCl is not a buffer solution. It is a strong acid and a salt. The NaOH would produce a significant pH change. On the other hand, $CH_3COOH/CH_3COONa$ is a buffer solution because it is a weak acid and its salt. Therefore, it would resist significant pH change upon addition of a strong base.

**8.97** The equilibrium reaction is:
$CO_2 + H_2O \rightleftharpoons H_2CO_3 \rightleftharpoons H_3O^+ + HCO_3^-$
A situation of high blood $CO_2$ levels and low pH is termed acidosis. A high concentration of $CO_2$ is a stress on the left side of the equilibrium. The equilibrium will shift to the right in an effort to decrease the concentration of $CO_2$. This will cause the molar concentration of carbonic acid ($H_2CO_3$) to increase.

**8.99** a. Addition of strong acid is equivalent to adding $H_3O^+$. This is a stress on the right side of the equilibrium, and the equilibrium will shift to the left. Consequently, the [$CH_3COOH$] increases.
b. Water, in this case, is a solvent and does not appear in the equilibrium expression. Hence, it does not alter the position of the equilibrium.

**8.101** $[H_3O^+] = 2.32 \times 10^{-7}\ M$

**8.103** $CH_3COO^-$, a conjugate base, reacts with added $H_3O^+$ to maintain pH.

**8.105** pH = 4.74

**8.107** $11.2 = \dfrac{[HCO_3^-]}{[H_2CO_3]}$

## Chapter 9

**9.1** X-ray, ultraviolet, visible, infrared, microwave, and radiowave

**9.3** $^{144}_{60}Nd \longrightarrow {}^{140}_{58}Ce + {}^{4}_{2}He$

**9.5** $^{131}_{53}I \longrightarrow {}^{131}_{54}Xe + {}^{0}_{-1}e$

**9.7** A positron has a positive charge, and a beta particle has a negative charge.

**9.9** 201 hours

**9.11** 1/4 of the radioisotope remains after two half-lives.

**9.13** Isotopes with short half-lives release their radiation rapidly. There is much more radiation per unit time observed with short half-life substances; hence, the signal is stronger and the sensitivity of the procedure is enhanced.

**9.15** The rem takes into account the relative biological effect of the radiation in addition to the quantity of radiation. This provides a more meaningful estimate of potential radiation damage to human tissue.

**9.17** Natural radioactivity is the spontaneous decay of a nucleus to produce high-energy particles or rays.

**9.19** Two protons and two neutrons

**9.21** An electron with a $-1$ charge.

**9.23** • charge, $\alpha = +2$, $\beta = -1$
• mass, $\alpha = 4$ amu, $\beta = 0.000549$ amu
• velocity, $\alpha = 10\%$ of the speed of light, $\beta = 90\%$ of the speed of light

**9.25** Chemical reactions involve joining, separating, and rearranging atoms; valence electrons are critically involved. Nuclear reactions only involve changes in nuclear composition.

**9.27** $^{4}_{2}He$

**9.29** A helium atom has two electrons; an alpha particle has no electrons.

**9.31** Alpha particles, beta particles, and positrons are matter; gamma radiation is pure energy. Alpha particles are large and relatively slow moving. They are the least energetic and least penetrating. Beta particles and positrons are smaller, faster, and more penetrating than alpha particles. Gamma radiation moves at the speed of light, is highly energetic, and is most penetrating.

**9.33** $^{15}_{7}N$

**9.35** $^{235}_{92}U$

**9.37** $^{1}_{1}H = 0$ neutrons and 1 proton
$^{2}_{1}H = 1$ neutron and 1 proton
$^{3}_{1}H = 2$ neutrons and 1 proton

**9.39** $^{60}_{27}Co \longrightarrow {}^{60}_{28}Ni + {}^{0}_{-1}\beta + \gamma$

**9.41** $^{23}_{11}Na + {}^{2}_{1}H \longrightarrow {}^{24}_{11}Na + {}^{1}_{1}H$

**9.43** $^{24}_{10}Ne \longrightarrow {}^{0}_{-1}\beta + {}^{24}_{11}Na$

**9.45** $^{140}_{55}Cs \longrightarrow {}^{140}_{56}Ba + {}^{0}_{-1}e$

**9.47** $^{209}_{83}Bi + {}^{54}_{24}Cr \longrightarrow {}^{262}_{107}Bh + {}^{1}_{0}n$

**9.49** $^{27}_{12}Mg \longrightarrow {}^{0}_{-1}e + {}^{27}_{13}Al$

**9.51** $^{12}_{7}N \longrightarrow {}^{12}_{6}C + {}^{0}_{+1}e$

**9.53** $^{241}_{95}Am \longrightarrow {}^{4}_{2}\alpha + {}^{237}_{93}Np$

**9.55** • Nuclei for light atoms tend to be most stable if their neutron/proton ratio is close to 1.
• Nuclei with more than 84 protons tend to be unstable.
• Isotopes with a "magic number" of protons or neutrons (2, 8, 20, 50, 82, or 126 protons or neutrons) tend to be stable.
• Isotopes with even numbers of protons or neutrons tend to be more stable.

**9.57** 15 half-lives

**9.59** $^{20}_{8}O$; Oxygen-20 has $20 - 8 = 12$ neutrons, an n/p of 12/8, or 1.5. The n/p is probably too high for stability even though it does have a "magic number" of protons and an even number of protons and neutrons.

**9.61** Chromium-48 has $48 - 24 = 24$ neutrons, an n/p of 24/24, or 1.0. It also has an even number of protons and neutrons. It would probably be stable.

**9.63** 0.40 mg of iodine-131 remains

**9.65** 13 mg of iron-59 remains

**9.67** Radiocarbon dating is a process used to determine the age of objects. The ratio of the masses of the stable isotope, carbon-12, and unstable isotope, carbon-14, is measured. Using this value and the half-life of carbon-14, the age of the coffin may be calculated.

**9.69** Fission

**9.71** **a.** The fission process involves the breaking down of large, unstable nuclei into smaller, more stable nuclei. This process releases some of the binding energy in the form of heat and/or light.

**b.** The heat generated during the fission process could be used to generate steam, which is then used to drive a turbine to create electricity.

**9.73** $_1^3H + _1^1H \rightarrow _2^4He + energy$

**9.75** A "breeder" reactor creates the fuel that can be used by a conventional fission reactor during its fission process.

**9.77** The reaction in a fission reactor that involves neutron production and causes subsequent reactions accompanied by the production of more neutrons in a continuing process.

**9.79** High operating temperatures

**9.81** Radiation therapy provides sufficient energy to destroy molecules critical to the reproduction of cancer cells.

**9.83** Natural radioactivity is a spontaneous process; artificial radioactivity is nonspontaneous and results from a nuclear reaction that produces an unstable nucleus.

**9.85** **a.** Technetium-99 m is used to study the heart (cardiac output, size, and shape), kidney (follow-up procedure for kidney transplant), and liver and spleen (size, shape, presence of tumors).

**b.** Xenon-133 is used to locate regions of reduced ventilation and presence of tumors in the lung.

**9.87** $_{47}^{108}Ag + _2^4He \rightarrow _{49}^{112}In$

**9.89** Background radiation, radiation from natural sources, is emitted by the sun as cosmic radiation, and from naturally radioactive isotopes found throughout our environment.

**9.91** Level decreases

**9.93** Yes, it would lead to a positive effect. Potential damage is often directly proportional to the time of exposure.

**9.95** Yes, it would lead to a positive effect. The operator of the robotic device could be located far from the source, no physical contact with the source is necessary, and barriers of lead or other shielding can isolate the control and the robot.

**9.97** Yes. Concrete has a higher density than wood and thus serves as a better radiation shield.

**9.99** Relative biological effect is a measure of the damage to biological tissue caused by different forms of radiation.

**9.101** **a.** The curie is the amount of radioactive material needed to produce $3.7 \times 10^{10}$ atomic disintegrations per second.

**b.** The roentgen is the amount of radioactive material needed to produce $2 \times 10^9$ ion-pairs when passing through 1 cc of air at 0°C.

**c.** The becquerel is the amount of radioactive material needed to produce 1 atomic disintegration per second.

**9.103** A film badge detects gamma radiation by darkening photographic film in proportion to the amount of radiation exposure over time. Badges are periodically collected and evaluated for their level of exposure. This mirrors the level of exposure of the personnel wearing the badges.

## Chapter 10

**10.1** The student could test the solubility of the substance in water and in an organic solvent, such as hexane. Solubility in hexane would suggest an organic substance; whereas solubility in water would indicate an inorganic compound. The student could also determine the melting and boiling points of the substance. If the melting and boiling points are very high, an inorganic substance would be suspected.

**10.3** **a.**

**b.**

**c.**

**10.5** **a.** The monobromination of propane will produce two products, as shown in the following two equations:

$$CH_3CH_2CH_3 + Br_2 \xrightarrow{Light\ or\ heat} CH_3CH_2CH_2Br + HBr$$

$$CH_3CH_2CH_3 + Br_2 \xrightarrow{Light\ or\ heat} CH_3CHBrCH_3 + HBr$$

**b.** The monochlorination of butane will produce two products, as shown in the following two equations:

$$CH_3CH_2CH_2CH_3 + Cl_2 \xrightarrow{Light\ or\ heat} CH_3CH_2CH_2CH_2Cl + HCl$$

$$CH_3CH_2CH_2CH_3 + Cl_2 \xrightarrow{Light\ or\ heat} CH_3CH_2CHClCH_3 + HCl$$

**c.** The monochlorination of cyclobutane:

**d.** The monobromination of pentane will produce three products as shown in the following equations:

$$CH_3CH_2CH_2CH_2CH_3 + Br_2 \xrightarrow{Light\ or\ heat} CH_3CH_2CH_2CH_2CH_2Br + HBr$$

$$CH_3CH_2CH_2CH_2CH_3 + Br_2 \xrightarrow{Light\ or\ heat} CH_3CH_2CH_2CHBrCH_3 + HBr$$

$$CH_3CH_2CH_2CH_2CH_3 + Br_2 \xrightarrow{Light\ or\ heat} CH_3CH_2CHBrCH_2CH_3 + HBr$$

**10.7** The number of organic compounds is nearly limitless because carbon forms stable covalent bonds with other carbon atoms in a variety of different patterns. In addition, carbon can form stable bonds with other elements and functional groups. Finally, carbon can form double or triple bonds with other carbon atoms to produce organic molecules with different properties.

**10.9** Because ionic substances often form three-dimensional crystals made up of many positive and negative ions, they generally have much higher melting and boiling points than covalent compounds.

**10.11** **a.** $LiCl > H_2O > CH_4$

**b.** $NaCl > C_3H_8 > C_2H_6$

**10.13** **a.** LiCl would be a solid; $H_2O$ would be a liquid; and $CH_4$ would be a gas.

**b.** NaCl would be a solid; both $C_3H_8$ and $C_2H_6$ would be gases.

**10.15** **a.** Water-soluble inorganic compounds

**b.** Inorganic compounds

**c.** Organic compounds

**d.** Inorganic compounds

**e.** Organic compounds

**10.17  a.** $C_{19}H_{40}$

**b.**

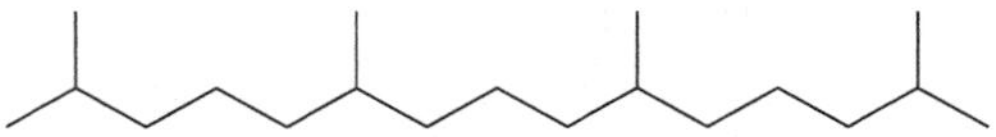

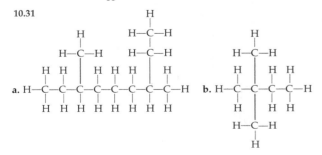

$CH(CH_3)_2(CH_2)_3CH(CH_3)(CH_2)_3CH(CH_3)(CH_2)_3CH(CH_3)_2$

**c.** 268.51 g/mol

**10.19  a.** $CH_3CH_2CH(CH_3)_2$
**b.** $CH_3CH_2C(CH_3)_2(CH_2)_2CH(CH_3)_2$
**c.** $CH_3CH_2C(CH_3)_2(CH_2)_3CH(CH_3)CH(CH_3)_2$

**10.21  a.**          **b.** 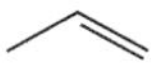          **c.**

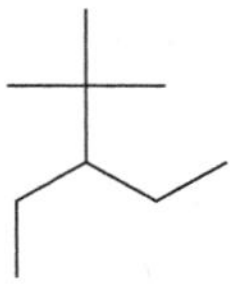

**10.23  a.** $(CH_3)_3CCH(CH_2CH_3)_2$
**b.** $CH_3CHCH_2$
**c.** $CH_3CH_2CH_3$

**10.25**

**a.**          **b.**

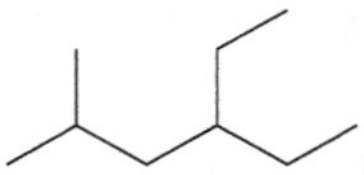

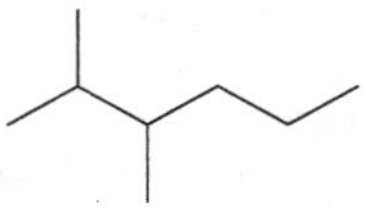

**c.**           **d.**

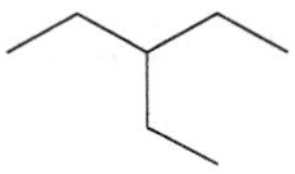

**10.27 a.**  Tricosane:

Pentacosane:

Heptacosane:

**b.** Tricosane: 324.61 g/mol
Pentacosane: 352.67 g/mol
Heptacosane: 380.72 g/mol

**10.29**

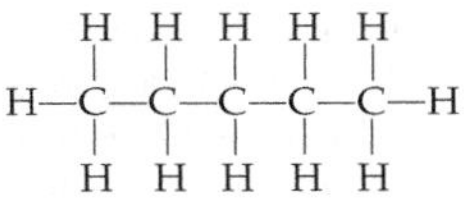

**10.31**

**10.33  a.** Hydroxyl group      **e.** Ester group
**b.** Amino group          **f.** Ether group
**c.** Carbonyl group        **g.** Halide
**d.** Carboxyl group

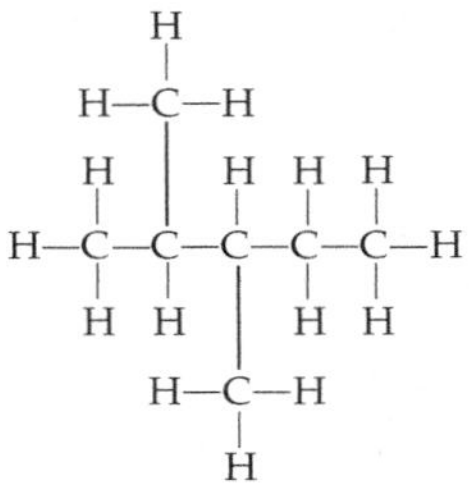

**10.35  a.** $C_nH_{2n+2}$          **d.** $C_nH_{2n}$
**b.** $C_nH_{2n-2}$          **e.** $C_nH_{2n-2}$
**c.** $C_nH_{2n}$

**10.37** Alkanes have only carbon-to-carbon and carbon-to-hydrogen single bonds, as in the molecule ethane:

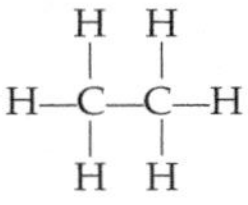

Alkenes have at least one carbon-to-carbon double bond, as in the molecule ethene:

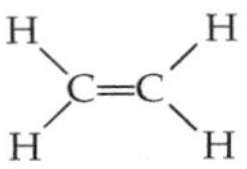

Alkynes have at least one carbon-to-carbon triple bond, as in the molecule ethyne:

$$H-C\equiv C-H$$

**10.39**

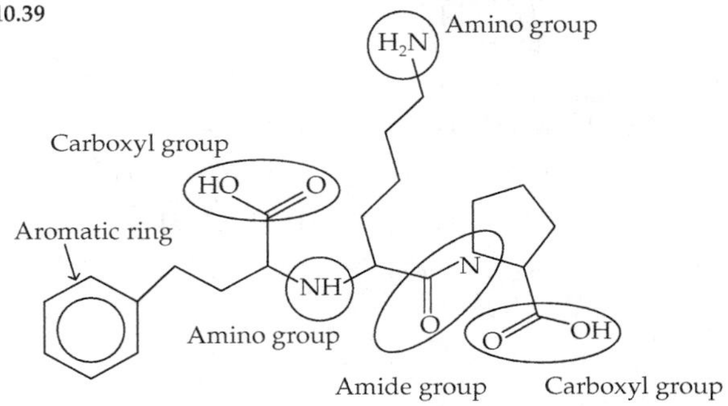

Amino group
Carboxyl group
Aromatic ring
Amino group
Amide group      Carboxyl group

**10.41**

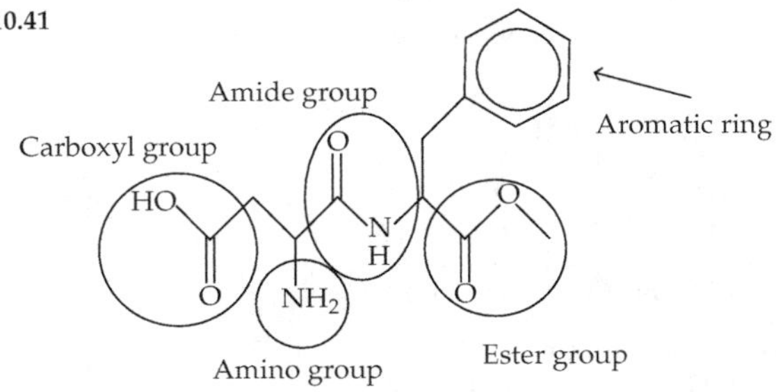

Amide group
Aromatic ring
Carboxyl group
Amino group      Ester group

**10.43** van der Waals forces are the attractive forces between neutral molecules. They include dipole-dipole attractions and London dispersion forces.

**10.45** London dispersion forces result from the attraction of two molecules that experience short-lived dipoles as a result of transient shifts in the electron cloud. Larger molecules with more electrons exhibit a stronger attraction. As a result, they will have higher melting and boiling points.

**10.47** Hydrocarbons are nonpolar molecules, and hence are not soluble in water.

**10.49  a.** Heptane > Hexane > Butane > Ethane
**b.** $CH_3CH_2CH_2CH_2CH_2CH_2CH_2CH_2CH_3 >$
$CH_3CH_2CH_2CH_2CH_3 > CH_3CH_2CH_3$

**10.51**  **a.** Heptane and hexane would be liquid at room temperature; butane and ethane would be gases.

**b.** $CH_3CH_2CH_2CH_2CH_2CH_2CH_2CH_3$ and $CH_3CH_2CH_2CH_2CH_3$ would be liquids at room temperature; $CH_3CH_2CH_3$ would be a gas.

**10.53**  Nonane: $CH_3CH_2CH_2CH_2CH_2CH_2CH_2CH_2CH_3$
Pentane: $CH_3CH_2CH_2CH_2CH_3$
Propane: $CH_3CH_2CH_3$

**10.55**  **a.**

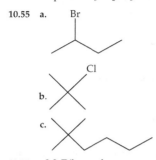

**b.**

**c.**

**10.57**  **a.** 2,2-Dibromobutane:

```
    H  Br H  H
    |  |  |  |
H—C—C—C—C—H
    |  |  |  |
    H  Br H  H
```

**b.** 2-Iododecane:

```
    H  I  H  H  H  H  H  H  H  H
    |  |  |  |  |  |  |  |  |  |
H—C—C—C—C—C—C—C—C—C—C—H
    |  |  |  |  |  |  |  |  |  |
    H  H  H  H  H  H  H  H  H  H
```

**c.** 1,2-Dichloropentane:

```
     H  Cl H  H  H
     |  |  |  |  |
Cl—C—C—C—C—C—H
     |  |  |  |  |
     H  H  H  H  H
```

**d.** 1-Bromo-2-methylpentane:

```
         H
         |
     H—C—H
     H  |  H  H  H
     |  |  |  |  |
 H—C—C—C—C—C—H
     |  |  |  |  |
     Br H  H  H  H
```

**10.59**  **a.** 3-Methylpentane
**b.** 2,5-Dimethylhexane
**c.** 1-Bromoheptane
**d.** 1-Chloro-3-methylbutane

**10.61**  **a.** 2-Chloropropane
**b.** 2-Iodobutane
**c.** 2,2-Dibromopropane
**d.** 1-Chloro-2-methylpropane
**e.** 2-Iodo-2-methylpropane

**10.63**  **a.** The straight chain isomers of molecular formula $C_4H_9Br$:

```
    H  H  H  H            H  H  Br H
    |  |  |  |            |  |  |  |
H—C—C—C—C—Br      H—C—C—C—C—H
    |  |  |  |            |  |  |  |
    H  H  H  H            H  H  H  H
```

**b.** The straight chain isomers of molecular formula $C_4H_8Br_2$:

```
    H  H  H  Br            H  H  Br H
    |  |  |  |             |  |  |  |
H—C—C—C—C—Br      H—C—C—C—C—Br
    |  |  |  |             |  |  |  |
    H  H  H  H             H  H  H  H

    H  Br H  H            H  H  H  H
    |  |  |  |            |  |  |  |
H—C—C—C—C—Br      Br—C—C—C—C—Br
    |  |  |  |            |  |  |  |
    H  H  H  H            H  H  H  H

    H  H  Br H            H  Br Br H
    |  |  |  |            |  |  |  |
H—C—C—C—C—H       H—C—C—C—C—H
    |  |  |  |            |  |  |  |
    H  H  Br H            H  H  H  H
```

**10.65**  **a.** 2-Chlorohexane      **c.** 3-Chloropentane
**b.** 1,4-Dibromobutane   **d.** 2-Methylheptane

**10.67**  **a.** The first pair of molecules are constitutional isomers: hexane and 2-methylpentane.
**b.** The second pair of molecules are identical. Both are heptane.

**10.69**  Structures "a" and "c"

**10.71**  **a.** Incorrect: 3-Methylhexane   **c.** Incorrect: 3-Methylheptane
**b.** Incorrect: 2-Methylbutane   **d.** Correct

**10.73**  **a.**

$$CH_3CHCH_2CHCH_3$$

with CH$_3$ above first CH and CH$_3$ below second CH — The name given in the problem is correct.

**b.**

$$CH_3CH_2CH_2CHCH_2CH_2CH_3$$

with CH$_3$ above — The correct name is 4-methylheptane.

**c.** $I—CH_2CH_2CH_2CH_2CH_2—I$   The name given in the problem is correct.

**d.** $CH_3CH_2CH_2CH_2CH_2CHCH_2CH_2CH_3$   The correct name is 4-ethylnonane.

with CH$_2$CH$_3$ below

**e.** $CH_2CH_2CH_2CH_2CH_2CCH_2CH_3$   The name given in the problem is correct.

with Br above the first CH$_2$, and Br above and CH$_3$ below the C

**10.75**  Cycloalkanes are a family of molecules having carbon-to-carbon bonds in a ring structure.

**10.77**  The general formula for a cycloalkane is $C_nH_{2n}$.

**10.79**  **a.** Chlorocyclopropane
**b.** *cis*-1,2-Dichlorocyclopropane
**c.** *trans*-1,2-Dichlorocyclopropane
**d.** Bromocyclopropane

**10.81**  **a.**            **c.**

**10.83** There are three structural isomers of dichlorocyclopropane. Two of these isomers are geometric isomers.

**10.85**  **a.** Incorrect—1,2-Dibromocyclobutane
**b.** Incorrect—1,2-Diethylcyclobutane
**c.** Correct
**d.** Incorrect—1,2,3-Trichlorocyclohexane

**10.87**  **a.** *cis*-l,3-Dibromocyclopentane

**b.** *trans-1,2-Dimethylcyclobutane*

**c.** *cis*-1,2-Dichlorocyclopropane

**d.** *trans-1,4-Diethylcyclohexane*

**10.89**  **a.** *cis*-1,2-Dibromocyclopentane
**b.** *trans*-1,3-Dibromocyclopentane
**c.** *cis*-1,2-Dimethylcyclohexane
**d.** *cis*-1,2-Dimethylcyclopropane

**10.91** Conformational isomers are distinct isomeric structures that may be converted into one another by rotation about the bonds in the molecule.

**10.93** In the chair conformation, the hydrogen atoms, and thus the electron pairs of the C—H bonds, are farther from one another. As a result, there is less electron repulsion and the structure is more stable. In the boat conformation, the electron pairs are more crowded. This causes greater electron repulsion, producing a less stable conformation.

**10.95** Combustion is the oxidation of hydrocarbons by burning in the presence of air to produce carbon dioxide and water.

**10.97**  **a.** $C_3H_8 + 5O_2 \longrightarrow 4H_2O + 3CO_2$
**b.** $C_7H_{16} + 11O_2 \longrightarrow 8H_2O + 7CO_2$
**c.** $C_9H_{20} + 14O_2 \longrightarrow 10H_2O + 9CO_2$
**d.** $2C_{10}H_{22} + 31O_2 \longrightarrow 22H_2O + 20CO_2$

**10.99** $2C_{16}H_{34} + 49O_2 \longrightarrow 32CO_2 + 34H_2O$

**10.101**  **a.** $8CO_2 + 10H_2O$
**b.**

$$Br{-}\underset{\underset{CH_3}{|}}{\overset{\overset{CH_3}{|}}{C}}{-}CH_3 + CH_3CHCH_2Br + 2HBr$$

**c.** $Cl_2$ and light

**10.103** The following molecules are all isomers of $C_6H_{14}$.

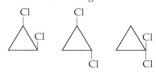

$CH_3CH_2CH_2CH_2CH_2CH_3$

Hexane

$CH_3CHCH_2CH_2CH_3$ (with $CH_3$ above)

2-Methylpentane

$CH_3CH_2CHCH_2CH_3$ (with $CH_3$ above)

3-Methylpentane

$CH_3CHCHCH_3$ (with $CH_3$ above and $CH_3$ below)

2,3-Dimethylbutane

$CH_3CCH_2CH_3$ (with $CH_3$ above and $CH_3$ below)

2,2-Dimethylbutane

**a.** 2,3-Dimethylbutane produces only two monobrominated derivatives: 1-bromo-2,3-dimethylbutane and 2-bromo-2, 3-dimethylbutane.
**b.** Hexane produces three monobrominated products: 1-bromohexane, 2-bromohexane, and 3-bromohexane. 2,2-Dimethylbutane also produces three monobrominated products: 1-bromo-2,2-dimethylbutane, 2-bromo-3, 3-dimethylbutane, and 1-bromo-3,3-dimethylbutane.
**c.** 3-Methylpentane produces four monobrominated products: 1-bromo-3-methylpentane, 2-bromo-3-methylpentane, 3-bromo-3-methylpentane, and 1-bromo-2-ethylbutane.

**10.105** The hydrocarbon is cyclooctane, and it has the molecular formula $C_8H_{16}$.

$$\text{(octagon)} \quad + 12\,O_2 \longrightarrow 8\,CO_2 + 8\,HO_2 + \text{heat energy}$$

## Chapter 11

**11.1 a.** $CH_2BrCH_2C{\equiv}CCH_2CH_3$

**b.** $CH_3C{\equiv}CCH_3$

**c.** $ClC{\equiv}CCl$      $Cl{-}\!{=\!=}\!{-}Cl$

**d.** $HC{\equiv}C(CH_2)_7I$

**11.3 a.** *cis*-3-Hexene      *trans*-3-Hexene

**b.** *trans*-2,3-Dibromo-2-butene      *cis*-2,3-Dibromo-2-butene

**11.5**   Molecule "c" can exist as *cis*- and *trans*-isomers because there are two different groups on each of the carbon atoms attached by the double bond.

**11.7**   **a.**

$$CH_3CH_2 \quad CH_2CH_2CH_2CH_3$$
$$C=C$$
$$H \qquad H$$

**b.**

$$CH_3 \qquad H$$
$$C=C$$
$$H \qquad CH_2CHCH_3$$
$$\qquad\qquad Cl$$

**c.**

$$CH_3 \qquad Cl$$
$$C=C$$
$$Cl \qquad CH_3$$

**11.9**   The hydrogenation of the *cis* and *trans* isomers of 2-pentene would produce the same product, pentane.

**11.11**   **a.**

$$H_3C-C\equiv C-CH_3 + 2\,H_2 \xrightarrow{\text{Ni}} H-\overset{\underset{\displaystyle H}{|}}{\underset{\underset{\displaystyle H}{|}}{C}}-\overset{\underset{\displaystyle H}{|}}{\underset{\underset{\displaystyle H}{|}}{C}}-\overset{\underset{\displaystyle H}{|}}{\underset{\underset{\displaystyle H}{|}}{C}}-\overset{\underset{\displaystyle H}{|}}{\underset{\underset{\displaystyle H}{|}}{C}}-H$$

2-Butyne                Butane

**b.**

$$H_3C-C\equiv C-CH_2CH_3 + 2\,H_2 \xrightarrow{\text{Ni}} H-C-C-C-C-C-H$$

2-Pentyne              Pentane

**11.13**

**a.** $CH_3CH=CH_2 + Br_2 \longrightarrow$

$$H-\overset{\underset{\displaystyle H}{|}}{\underset{\underset{\displaystyle H}{|}}{C}}-\overset{\underset{\displaystyle Br}{|}}{\underset{\underset{\displaystyle H}{|}}{C}}-\overset{\underset{\displaystyle H}{|}}{\underset{\underset{\displaystyle Br}{|}}{C}}-H$$

**b.** $CH_3CH=CHCH_3 + Br_2 \longrightarrow$

$$H-C-C-C-C-H$$

**11.15**

**a.** $CH_3C\equiv CCH_3 + 2\,Cl_2 \longrightarrow$

$$H-C-C-C-C-H$$

**b.** $CH_3C\equiv CCH_2CH_3 + 2\,Cl_2 \longrightarrow$

$$H-C-C-C-C-C-H$$

**11.17**   **a.** $CH_3CH=CHCH_3 + H_2O \xrightarrow{H+} CH_3CHOHCH_2CH_3$

**b.** $H_2C=CHCH_2CH_2CH(CH_3)_2 + H_2O \xrightarrow{H+}$
$$CH_3CHOHCH_2CH_2CH(CH_3)_2$$
(Major product)

$H_2C=CHCH_2CH_2CH(CH_3)_2 + H_2O \xrightarrow{H+}$
$$CH_2OHCH_2CH_2CH_2CH(CH_3)_2$$
(Minor product)

**c.** $CH_3CH_2CH_2CH=CHCH_2CH_3 + H_2O \xrightarrow{H+}$
$$CH_3CH_2CH_2CHOHCH_2CH_2CH_3$$

$CH_3CH_2CH_2CH=CHCH_2CH_3 + H_2O \xrightarrow{H+}$
$$CH_3CH_2CH_2CH_2CHOHCH_2CH_3$$

**d.** $CH_3CHClCH=CHCHClCH_3 + H_2O \xrightarrow{H+}$
$$CH_3CHClCHOHCH_2CHClCH_3$$
Only product

**11.19**   **a.** $H_3CC\equiv CH + H_2O \xrightarrow{H^+}$

$$H-C-C=C-H$$

$$\longrightarrow H-C-C-C-H$$

Or

$H_3CC\equiv CH + H_2O \xrightarrow{H^+}$

$$H-C-C=C-H$$

$$\longrightarrow H-C-C-C-H$$

**b.** $H_3CC\equiv CCH_2CH_3 + H_2O \xrightarrow{H^+}$

$$H-C-C=C-C-C-H$$

$$\longrightarrow H-C-C-C-C-C-H$$

Or

$H_3CC\equiv CCH_2CH_3 + H_2O \xrightarrow{H^+}$

$$H-C-C=C-C-C-H$$

$$\longrightarrow H-C-C-C-C-C-H$$

**11.21**   **a.**

**b.**

**c.**

**d.**

**e.**

**f.**

**11.23**   As the length of the hydrocarbon chain increases, the London dispersion forces between the molecules increase. The stronger these attractive forces between molecules are, the higher the boiling point will be.

**11.25**   The general formula for an alkane is $C_nH_{2n+2}$.
The general formula for an alkene is $C_nH_{2n}$.
The general formula for an alkyne is $C_nH_{2n-2}$.

**11.27** Ethene is a planar molecule. All of the bond angles are 120°.

**11.29** In alkanes, such as ethane, the four bonds around each carbon atom have tetrahedral geometry. The bond angles are 109.5°. In alkenes, such as ethene, each carbon is bonded by two single bonds and one double bond. The molecule is planar and each bond angle is approximately 120°.

**11.31** Ethyne is a linear molecule. All of the bond angles are 180°.

**11.33** In alkanes, such as ethane, the four bonds around each carbon atom have tetrahedral geometry. The bond angles are 109.5°. In alkenes, such as ethene, each carbon is bonded by two single bonds and one double bond. The molecule is planar and each bond angle is approximately 120°. In alkynes, such as ethyne, each carbon is bonded by one single bond and one triple bond. The molecule is linear and the bond angles are 180°.

**11.35** **a.** 2-Pentyne > Propyne > Ethyne
**b.** 3-Decene > 2-Butene > Ethene

**11.37** Identify the longest carbon chain containing the carbon-to-carbon double or triple bond. Replace the –ane suffix of the alkane name with –ene for an alkene or -yne for an alkyne. Number the chain to give the lowest number to the first of the two carbons involved in the double or triple bond. Determine the name and carbon number of each substituent group and place that information as a prefix in front of the name of the parent compound.

**11.39** Geometric isomers of alkenes differ from one another in the placement of substituents attached to each of the carbon atoms of the double bond. Of the pair of geometric isomers, the cis-isomer is the one in which identical groups are on the same side of the double bond.

**11.41** **a.**

$H_3C$, $CH_2CH_2CH_3$, $H_3C$, $H$ — $C=C$

**b.** $CH_3CH_2$, $H$, $H$, $CH_2CH_2CH_3$ — $C=C$

**c.** $ClCH_2$, $CH_2CH_3$, $H$, $H$ — $C=C$

**d.** $(H_3C)_2CCl$, $CH_2CH_2CH_3$, $H$, $H$ — $C=C$

**e.** $(H_3C)_2CH$, $H$, $H$, $CHBrCH(CH_3)CH_2CH_3$ — $C=C$

**11.43** **a.** 3-Methyl-1-pentene
**b.** 7-Bromo-1-heptene
**c.** 5-Bromo-3-heptene
**d.** 1-t-Butyl-4-methylcyclohexene

**11.45** **a.** $CH_2FCH_2CHFCH_2CH_2F$
**b.**

$H$, $H$, $H_3C$, $CH_2CH_2CH_2CH_2CH_3$ — $C=C$

**c.** $CH_3CH_2CH_2C≡CCH_2CH_2CH_3$

**11.47** **a.** 1-Heptene can only be drawn one way. Therefore, a cis-trans isomer does not exist.
**b.** 2-Heptene can be drawn two ways. Therefore, cis-trans isomers do exist.
**c.** 3-Heptene can be drawn two ways. Therefore, cis-trans isomers do exist.
**d.** 2-Methyl-2-hexene can only be drawn one way. Therefore, cis-trans isomers do not exist.
**e.** 3-Methyl-2-hexene can be drawn two ways. Therefore, cis-trans isomers do exist.

**11.49** Alkenes b and c would not exhibit cis-trans isomerism.

**11.51** Alkenes b and d can exist as both cis- and trans- isomers.

**11.53** **a.** 1,5-Nonadiene    **c.** 2,5-Octadiene
**b.** 1,4,7-Nonatriene    **d.** 4-Methyl-2,5-heptadiene

**11.55**

$$\begin{array}{c} R\diagdown \quad \diagup R \\ C=C \\ R \diagup \quad \diagdown R \end{array} + H_2 \xrightarrow[\text{heat or pressure}]{Pt, Pd, or Ni} \begin{array}{c} H \quad R \\ | \quad | \\ R-C-C-R \\ | \quad | \\ R \quad H \end{array}$$

**11.57**

$$\begin{array}{c} R\diagdown \quad \diagup R \\ C=C \\ R \diagup \quad \diagdown R \end{array} + X_2 \longrightarrow \begin{array}{c} X \quad R \\ | \quad | \\ R-C-C-R \\ | \quad | \\ R \quad X \end{array}$$

**11.59**

$$\begin{array}{c} R\diagdown \quad \diagup R \\ C=C \\ R \diagup \quad \diagdown R \end{array} + H_2O \xrightarrow{H^+} \begin{array}{c} H \quad R \\ | \quad | \\ R-C-C-R \\ | \quad | \\ R \quad OH \end{array}$$

**11.61** The primary difference between complete hydrogenation of an alkene and an alkyne is that 2 moles of $H_2$ are required for the complete hydrogenation of an alkyne.

**11.63**

**a.** $CH_2=CH(CH_2)_4CH_3 + H_2O \xrightarrow{H^+}$ $CH_3CHOH(CH_2)_4CH_3$ Major Product + $CH_2OH(CH_2)_5CH_3$ Minor Product

**b.** $CH_3CH=CH(CH_2)_3CH_3 + HBr \longrightarrow$ $CH_3CH_2CHBr(CH_2)_3CH_3$ + $CH_3CHBr(CH_2)_4CH_3$

**c.** $CH_3CH_2CH=CH(CH_2)_2CH_3 + H_2 \xrightarrow[\text{heat or pressure}]{Pt, Pd, or Ni}$ $CH_3(CH_2)_5CH_3$

**d.** $CH_3C≡CHCH_2CH_2CH_3$ with $CH_3$ $+ HCl \longrightarrow$

$$CH_3\overset{Cl}{\underset{CH_3}{C}}(CH_2)_3CH_3$$ Major Product

+

$$CH_3\underset{Cl}{CH}CH(CH_2)_2CH_3$$ with $CH_3$ Minor Product

**11.65** **a.** $H_2$    **d.** $19O_2 \rightarrow 12CO_2 + 14H_2O$
**b.** $H_2O$    **e.** $Cl_2$
**c.** HBr    **f.**

**11.67  a.**

$H_3CC{\equiv}CCH_3 + 2H_2 \xrightarrow[\text{heat or pressure}]{\text{Pt, Pd, or Ni}}$ H$_3$C–C–C–CH$_3$ (with H H / H H substituents)

2-Butyne

**b.**

$CH_3CH_2C{\equiv}CCH_3 + 2X_2 \longrightarrow$ CH$_3$CH$_2$–C–C–CH$_3$ (with X X / X X substituents)

2-Pentyne

**11.69  a.** Reactant—*cis*-2-butene; Only product—butane
**b.** Reactant—1-butene; Major product—2-butanol
**c.** Reactant—2-butene; Only product—2,3-dichlorobutane
**d.** Reactant—1-pentene; Major product— 2-bromopentane

**11.71  a.** Hydrogenation of 4-chlorocyclooctene

(cyclooctene with Cl) $+ H_2 \xrightarrow[\text{heat}]{\text{Pt}}$ (cyclooctane with Cl)

**b.** Halogenation of 1,3-cyclooctadiene

(1,3-cyclooctadiene) $+2\,Cl_2 \longrightarrow$ (cyclooctane with Cl Cl Cl Cl)

**c.** Hydration of 3-methylcyclobutene

(methylcyclobutene) $+H_2O \xrightarrow{H^+}$ (cyclobutane with OH and CH$_3$) and (cyclobutane with HO and CH$_3$)

**d.** Hydrohalogenation of cyclopentene

(cyclopentene) $+HBr \longrightarrow$ (cyclopentane with Br)

**11.73** CH$_2$=CHCH$_2$CH$_2$CH$_3$,  CH$_3$CH=CHCH$_2$CH$_3$,

CH$_3$C=CHCH$_3$,  CH$_2$=CCH$_2$CH$_3$,  CH$_2$=CHCHCH$_3$
(with CH$_3$)     (with CH$_3$)        (with CH$_3$)

**11.75  a.**  CH$_3$CHCH$_2$CH$_3$ (with Br)

**b.**

CH$_3$CH$_2$–C–CH$_2$CH$_2$CH$_3$ (with CH$_3$ and I) + CH$_3$CHCHCH$_2$CH$_2$CH$_3$ (with I CH$_3$)

(Major product)                (Minor product)

**c.** (cyclopentane with Cl)

**11.77** A polymer is a macromolecule composed of repeating structural units called *monomers*.

**11.79** Polyvinyl chloride (PVC) is used in pipes, detergent bottles, and cleanser bottles.

$n$ (H,Cl)C=C(H,H) $\xrightarrow[\text{Pressure}]{\text{Catalyst Heat}}$ —[C–C]$_n$— (with H H / Cl H)

**11.81** The IUPAC name for (a) is 2-pentene, for (b) is 3-bromo-1-propene, and for (c) is 3,4-dimethylcyclohexene.
**a.** These products will be formed in approximately equal amounts.

$CH_3CH{=}CHCH_2CH_3 + H_2O \xrightarrow{H^+}$
$CH_3CHOHCH_2CH_3CH_3$

$CH_3CH{=}CHCH_2CH_3 + H_2O \xrightarrow{H^+}$
$CH_3CH_2CHOHCH_2CH_3$

**b.** $CH_3BrCH{=}CH_2 + H_2O \xrightarrow{H^+}$

$CH_2BrCH_2CH_2OH + CH_2BrCHOHCH_3$
Minor product        Major product

**c.** These products will be formed in approximately equal amounts.

(cyclohexene with CH$_3$, CH$_3$) $+ H_2O \xrightarrow{H^+}$ (cyclohexane with OH, CH$_3$, CH$_3$)

(cyclohexene with CH$_3$, CH$_3$) $+ H_2O \xrightarrow{H^+}$ (cyclohexane with HO, CH$_3$, CH$_3$)

**11.83  a.** This is the minor product of this reaction.

$H_2C{=}CHCH_2CH(CH_3)_2 + H_2O \xrightarrow{H^+}$
$CH_2OHCH_2CH_2CH(CH_3)_2$

**b.** $CH_3CH{=}CHCH_2CH_2CH_3 + HBr \xrightarrow{H^+}$
$CH_3CH_2CHBrCH_2CH_2CH_3$

or

$CH_3CH_2CH{=}CHCH_2CH_3 + HBr \longrightarrow$
$CH_3CH_2CHBrCH_2CH_2CH_3$

**c.**

(cyclohexene with CH$_3$) $+ HBr \longrightarrow$ (cyclohexane with Br and CH$_3$)

**d.**

(cyclopentene with CH$_2$CH$_3$) $+ H_2O \xrightarrow{H^+}$ (cyclopentane with CH$_2$CH$_3$ and OH)

**11.85  a.**
$CH_2{=}CHCH_2CH{=}CHCH_3 + 2H_2 \xrightarrow[\text{heat}]{\text{Pt}} CH_3(CH_2)_4CH_3$
1,4-Hexadiene                        Hexane

**b.**
$CH_3CH{=}CHCH{=}CHCH{=}CHCH_3 + 3H_2$
2,4,6-Octatriene   $\xrightarrow[\text{heat}]{\text{Ni}}$  $CH_3(CH_2)_6CH_3$
Octane

**c.**

(1,3-cyclohexadiene) $+ 2H_2 \xrightarrow[\text{Pressure}]{\text{Pd}}$ (cyclohexane)

1,3-Cyclohexadiene                Cyclohexane

**d.**

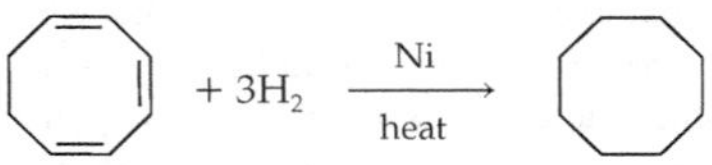

1,3,5-Cyclooctatriene          Cyclooctane

**11.87** The term aromatic hydrocarbon was first used as a term to describe the pleasant-smelling resins of tropical trees.

**11.89** Resonance hybrids are molecules for which more than one valid Lewis structure can be written.

**11.91 a.**

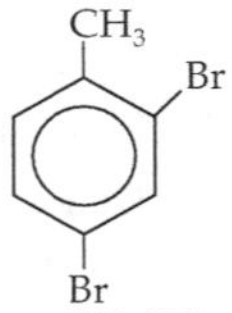

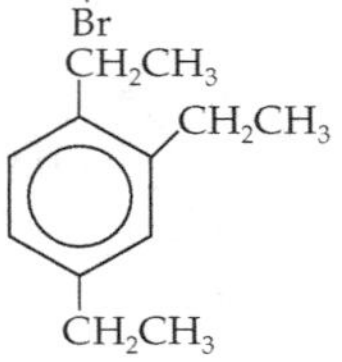

**c.** CH₃CHCH₃

**b.**

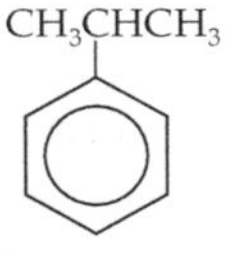

**d.**

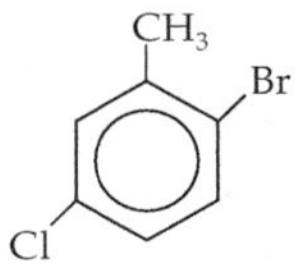

**11.93 a.**

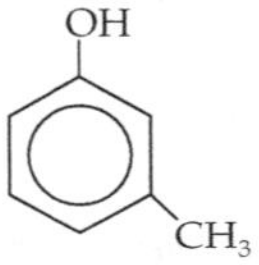

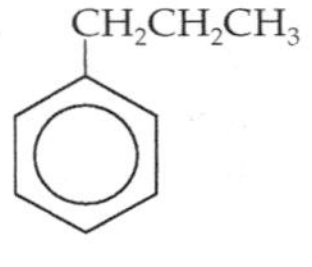

**c.**

**b.** CH₂CH₂CH₃

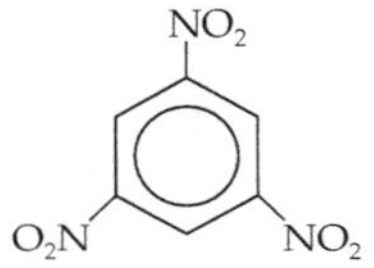

**d.**

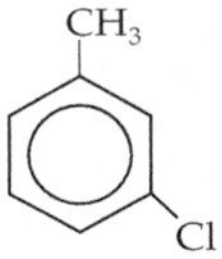

**11.95** Kekulé proposed that single and double carbon-carbon bonds alternate around the benzene ring. To explain why benzene does not react like other unsaturated compounds, he proposed that the double and single bonds shift positions rapidly.

**11.97** An addition reaction involves addition of a molecule to a double or triple bond in an unsaturated molecule. In a substitution reaction, one chemical group replaces another.

**11.99 a.**

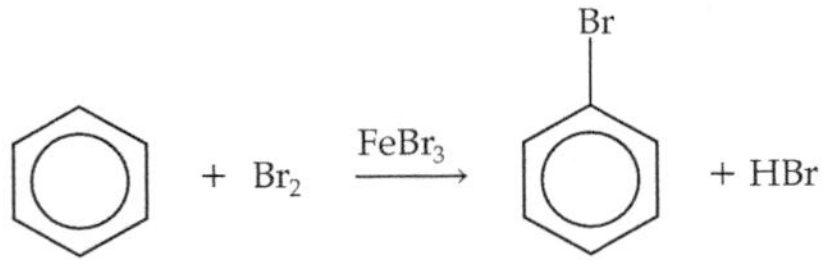

**b.**

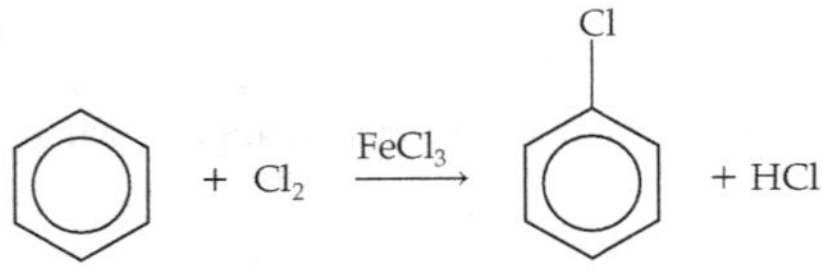

**c.**

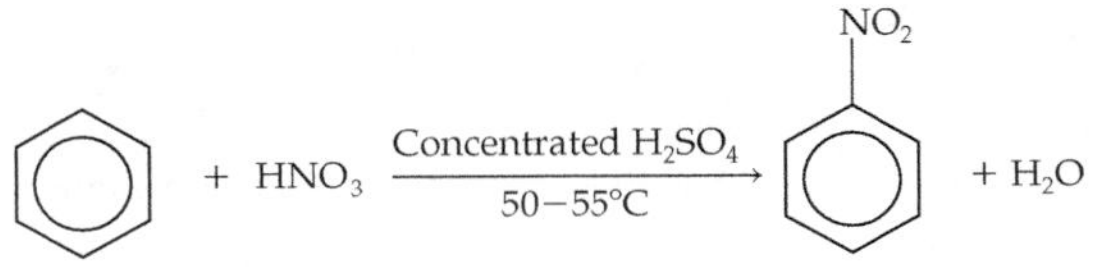

**11.101**

Pyrimidine

**11.103**

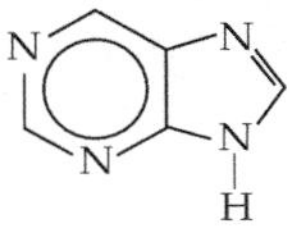

Purine

## Chapter 12

**12.1 a.** 2-Methyl-1-propanol

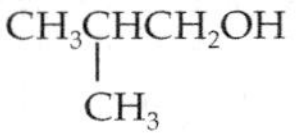

**b.** 2-Chlorocyclopentanol

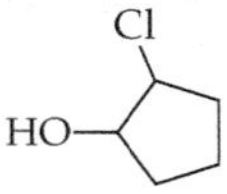

**c.** 2,4-Dimethylcyclohexanol

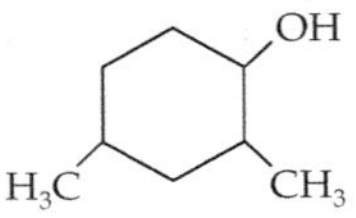

**d.** 2,3-Dichloro-3-hexanol

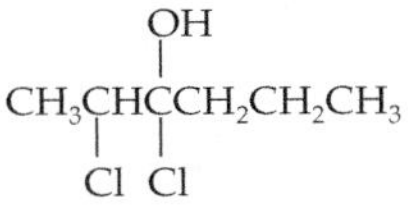

**12.3** IUPAC name: 1-Butanol
Common name: Butyl alcohol
Primary alcohol

**12.5 a.** Ethanol is a primary alcohol. The product is ethene.
**b.** 2-Propanol is a secondary alcohol. The product is propene.
**c.** 4-Methyl-3-hexanol is a secondary alcohol. The products are 3-methyl-3-hexene and 4-methyl-2-hexene.
**d.** 2-Methyl-2-propanol is a tertiary alcohol. The product is 2-methyl-1-propene.

**12.7 a.** The reactant is 2-butanol and the product is butanone.
**b.** The reactant is 2-pentanol and the product is 2-pentanone.

**12.9** Simple phenols are somewhat soluble in water because they have the polar hydroxyl group.

**12.11** Ethers have much lower boiling points than alcohols because ether molecules cannot hydrogen bond to one another.

**12.13** The longer the hydrocarbon tail of an alcohol becomes, the less water soluble it will be.

**12.15** The carbinol carbon is the one to which the hydroxyl group is bonded.

**12.17 a.** Primary alcohol        **d.** Tertiary alcohol
**b.** Secondary alcohol       **e.** Tertiary alcohol
**c.** Tertiary alcohol

**12.19 a.** Primary alcohol        **d.** Primary alcohol
**b.** Secondary alcohol       **e.** Secondary alcohol
**c.** Primary alcohol

**12.21** **a.** 2-Nonanol is a secondary alcohol:
$CH_3CHOHCH_2CH_2CH_2CH_2CH_2CH_2CH_3$
**b.** 2-Heptanol is a secondary alcohol:
$CH_3CHOHCH_2CH_2CH_2CH_2CH_3$
**c.** 2-Undecanol is a secondary alcohol:
$CH_3CHOHCH_2CH_2CH_2CH_2CH_2CH_2CH_2CH_2CH_3$

**12.23** a < d < c < b

**12.25** **a.** $CH_3CH_2OH$
**b.** $CH_3CH_2CH_2CH_2OH$
**c.** $CH_3CHCH_3$
        |
        OH

**12.27** The IUPAC rules for the nomenclature of alcohols require you to name the parent compound, that is the longest continuous carbon chain bonded to the —OH group. Replace the –*e* ending of the parent alkane with –*ol* of the alcohol. Number the parent chain so that the carbon bearing the hydroxyl group has the lowest possible number. Name and number all other substituents. If there is more than one hydroxyl group, the –*ol* ending will be modified to reflect the number. If there are two —OH groups, the suffix –*diol* is used; if it has three —OH groups, the suffix –*triol* is used, etc.

**12.29** **a.** 1,4-Hexanediol
**b.** 2,3-Pentanediol
**c.** 2-Methyl-3-pentanol

**12.31** **a.**

**b.**

**c.**

**12.33** **a.** Cyclopentanol    **c.** 3-Methylcyclohexanol
**b.** Cycloheptanol

**12.35** **a.** Methyl alcohol    **c.** Ethylene glycol
**b.** Ethyl alcohol    **d.** Propyl alcohol

**12.37** **a.** $CH_3CHOHCH_2CH(CH_3)CH_2CH_3$    **d.** $CH_3CHOH(CH_2)_6CH_3$
**b.** $CH(CH_3)_2CH_2OH$    **e.**
**c.** $CH_2OH(CH_2)_3CH_2OH$

**12.39** Denatured alcohol is 100% ethanol to which benzene or methanol is added. The additive makes the ethanol unfit to drink and prevents illegal use of pure ethanol.

**12.41** Fermentation is the anaerobic degradation of sugar that involves no net oxidation. The alcohol fermentation, carried out by yeast, produces ethanol and carbon dioxide.

**12.43** When the ethanol concentration in a fermentation reaches 12–13%, the yeast producing the ethanol are killed by it. To produce a liquor of higher alcohol concentration, the product of the original fermentation must be distilled.

**12.45**

Alkene                          Alcohol

**12.47**

Alcohol                         Alkene

**12.49**

Secondary alcohol               Ketone

**12.51** **a.** The predicted products are 1-hexanol (minor) and 2-hexanol (major).
**b.** The predicted products are 2-hexanol and 3-hexanol. These products will be formed in approximately equal amounts.
**c.** The predicted products are 5-methyl-3-hexanol and 2-methyl-3-hexanol. These products will be formed in approximately equal amounts.
**d.** The predicted products are 2,2-dimethyl-4-heptanol and 2,2-dimethyl-3-heptanol. These products will be formed in approximately equal amounts.

**12.53** **a.**

2-Hexene

$CH_3CHCH_2CH_2CH_2CH_3$
        |
        OH
2-Hexanol
and
$CH_3CH_2CHCH_2CH_2CH_3$
        |
        OH
3-Hexanol

These products will be formed in approximately equal amounts.

**b.**

Cyclopentene                    Cyclopentanol

**c.** $CH_2$=$CHCH_2CH_2CH_2CH_2CH_2CH_3$ + $H_2O$ $\xrightarrow{H^+}$

1-Octene

$CH_3CHCH_2CH_2CH_2CH_2CH_2CH_3$
|
OH

2-Octanol
(Major product)
and

$CH_2CH_2CH_2CH_2CH_2CH_2CH_2CH_3$
|
OH

1-Octanol
(Minor product)

**d.**

1-Methylcyclohexene + $H_2O$ $\xrightarrow{H^+}$

and

1-Methylcyclohexanol        2-Methylcyclohexanol
(Major product)              (Minor product)

**12.55 a.** Butanone
**b.** N.R.
**c.** Cyclohexanone
**d.** N.R.

**12.57 a.** 3-Pentanol; 3-Pentanone
**b.** 1-Propanol; Propanal (Upon further oxidation, propanoic acid would be formed.)
**c.** 4-Methyl-2-pentanol; 4-Methyl-2-pentanone
**d.** 2-Methyl-2-butanol; N.R.
**e.** 3-Phenyl-1-propanol; 3-Phenylpropanal (Upon further oxidation, 3-phenylpropanoic acid will be formed.)

**12.59**

$CH_3CH_2OH$ $\xrightarrow{\text{liver enzymes}}$ $CH_3$–$\overset{\displaystyle O}{\overset{\|}{C}}$–H

Ethanol                          Ethanal

The product, ethanal, is responsible for the symptoms of a hangover.

**12.61** The reaction in which a water molecule is added to 1-butene is a hydration reaction.

$CH_3CH_2CH$=$CH_2$ + $H_2O$ $\xrightarrow{H^+}$ $CH_3CH_2\overset{\displaystyle OH}{\overset{|}{C}}HCH_3$

1-Butene                        2-Butanol

**12.63**

$CH_3CH$=$CH_2$ $\xrightarrow{H_2O, H^+}$ $CH_3\overset{\displaystyle OH}{\overset{|}{C}}HCH_3$ $\xrightarrow{[O]}$ $CH_3\overset{\displaystyle O}{\overset{\|}{C}}CH_3$

Propene          2-Propanol          Propanone
(propylene)      (isopropanol)       (acetone)

**12.65 a.** [structure] + $H_2$ $\xrightarrow{\text{catalyst}}$ [structure]
**b.** [structure] + $H_2$ $\xrightarrow{\text{catalyst}}$ [structure]
**c.** [structure] + $H_2$ $\xrightarrow{\text{catalyst}}$ [structure]
**d.** [structure] + $H_2$ $\xrightarrow{\text{catalyst}}$ [structure]

**12.67** Oxidation is a loss of electrons, whereas reduction is a gain of electrons.

**12.69**

$CH_3CH_2CH_3 < CH_3CH_2CH_2OH < CH_3CH_2\overset{\displaystyle O}{\overset{\|}{C}}-H < CH_3CH_2\overset{\displaystyle O}{\overset{\|}{C}}-OH$

**12.71** Phenols are compounds with an —OH attached to a benzene ring.

**12.73**   Picric acid:              2,4,6,-Trinitrotoluene:

Picric acid is water-soluble because of the polar hydroxyl group that can form hydrogen bonds with water.

**12.75** Hexachlorophene, hexylresorcinol, and o-phenylphenol are phenol compounds used as antiseptics or disinfectants.

**12.77** Ethers have much lower boiling points than alcohols of similar molar mass, but higher boiling points than alkanes of similar molar mass. The boiling points are higher than alkanes because the R—O—R bond is polar. However, there is no —OH group, so ether molecules cannot hydrogen bond to one another. This is the reason that the boiling points are lower than alcohols of similar molar mass.

**12.79** Alcohols of molecular formula $C_4H_{10}O$

$CH_3CH_2CH_2CH_2OH$,        $CH_3\overset{\displaystyle OH}{\overset{|}{C}}HCH_2CH_3$,

$CH_3\overset{\displaystyle }{\underset{\displaystyle CH_3}{\overset{|}{C}}}HCH_2OH$,        $CH_3\overset{\displaystyle OH}{\overset{|}{\underset{\displaystyle CH_3}{\underset{|}{C}}}}CH_3$

Ethers of molecular formula $C_4H_{10}O$
$CH_3$—O—$CH_2CH_2CH_3$        $CH_3CH_2$—O—$CH_2CH_3$
$CH_3$—O—$\overset{\displaystyle }{\underset{\displaystyle CH_3}{\underset{|}{C}}}HCH_3$

**12.81 a.** $CH_3CH_2—O—CH_2CH_3 + H_2O$
**b.** $CH_3CH_2—O—CH_2CH_3 + CH_3—O—CH_3 +$
$CH_3—O—CH_2CH_3 + H_2O$
**c.** $CH_3—O—CH_3 + CH_3—O—\overset{\overset{\displaystyle |}{}}{C}HCH_3 +$
$\phantom{CH_3—O—CH_3 + CH_3—O—}\underset{\displaystyle CH_3}{}$

$CH_3\overset{\overset{\displaystyle |}{}}{C}H—O—\overset{\overset{\displaystyle |}{}}{C}HCH_3 + H_2O$
$\underset{\displaystyle CH_3}{}\phantom{H—O—}\underset{\displaystyle CH_3}{}$

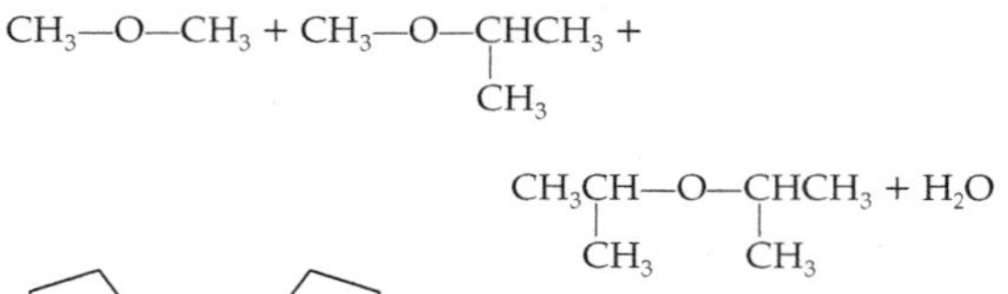

**d.**

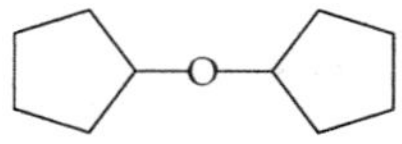

$+ H_2O$

**12.83 a.** 2-Ethoxypentane
**b.** 2-Methoxybutane
**c.** 1-Ethoxybutane
**d.** Methoxycyclopentane

**12.85 a.**

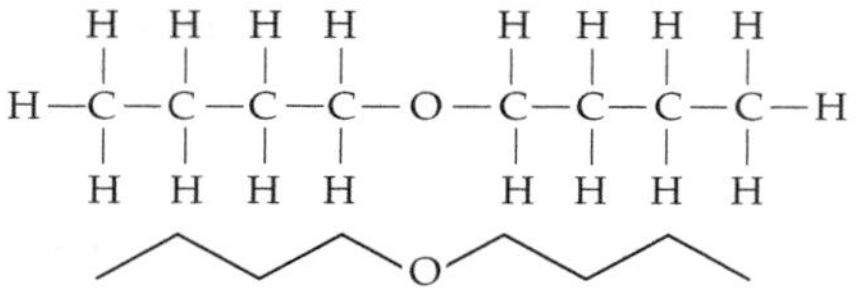

**b.**

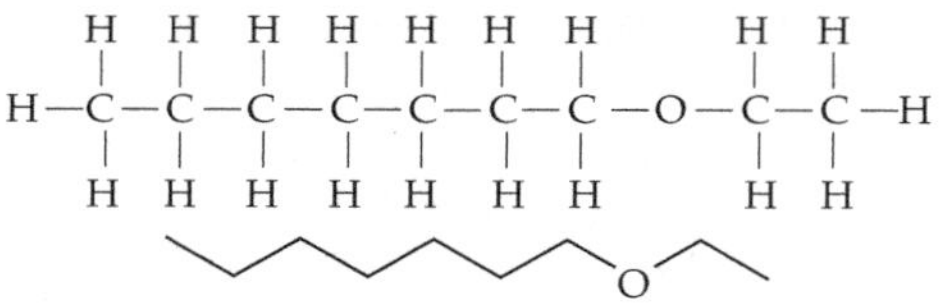

**c.**

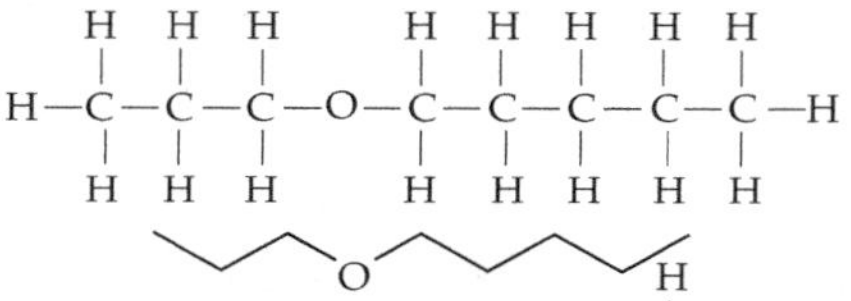

**d.**

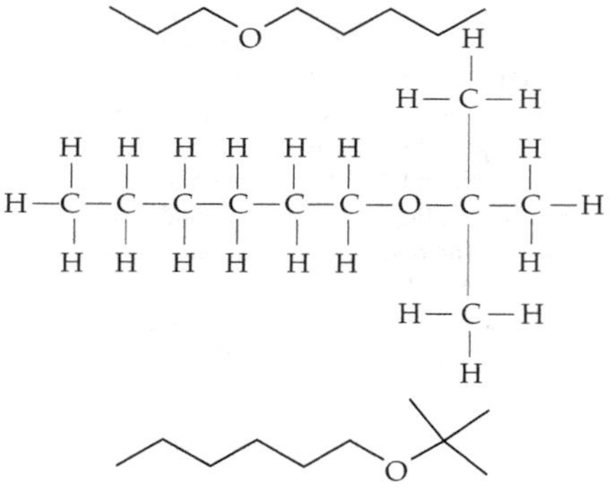

**12.87** Thiols contain the sulfhydryl group (—SH). The sulfhydryl group is similar to the hydroxyl group (—OH) of alcohols, except that a sulfur atom replaces the oxygen atom.

**12.89** Cystine:

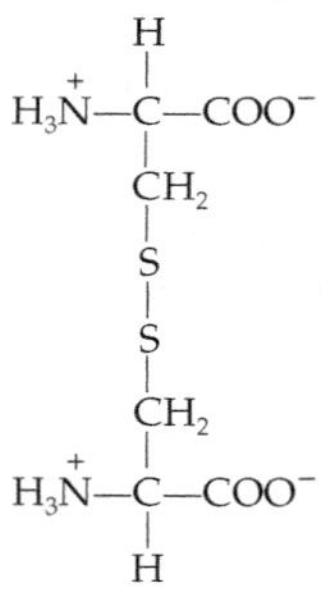

**12.91 a.** 1-Propanethiol  **c.** 2-Methyl-2-butanethiol
**b.** 2-Butanethiol  **d.** 1,4-Cyclohexanedithiol

# Chapter 13

**13.1 a.**

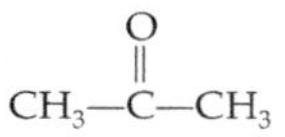

**b.**

**13.3 a.**

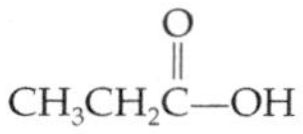

**b.**

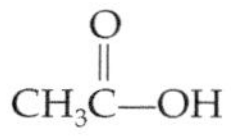

**13.5 a.** 2,3-Dichloropentanal  **d.** Butanal

$CH_3CH_2CHClCHClCH \overset{O}{\underset{}{}}$   $CH_3CH_2CH_2CH \overset{O}{\underset{}{}}$

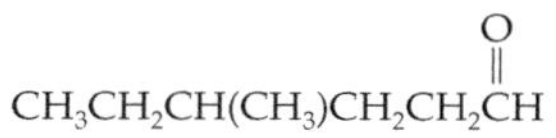

**b.** 2-Bromobutanal  **e.** 2,4-Dimethylpentanal

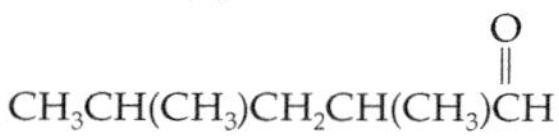

$CH_3CH_2CHBrCH \overset{O}{\underset{}{}}$   $CH_3CH(CH_3)CH_2CH(CH_3)CH \overset{O}{\underset{}{}}$

**c.** 4-Methylhexanal

$CH_3CH_2CH(CH_3)CH_2CH_2CH \overset{O}{\underset{}{}}$

**13.7 a.** 3-Iodobutanone  **d.** 2-Methyl-3-pentanone
**b.** 4-Methyl-2-octanone  **e.** 2-Fluoro-3-pentanone
**c.** 3-Methylbutanone

**13.9**

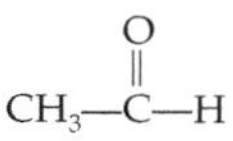

**13.11 a.** Reduction  **d.** Oxidation
**b.** Reduction  **e.** Reduction
**c.** Reduction

**13.13 a.** Hemiacetal  **c.** Acetal
**b.** Acetal  **d.** Hemiacetal

**13.15** As the carbon chain length increases, the compounds become less polar and more hydrocarbon-like. As a result, their solubility in water decreases.

**13.17** A good solvent should dissolve a wide range of compounds. Simple ketones are considered to be universal solvents because they have both a polar carbonyl group and nonpolar side chains. As a result, they dissolve organic compounds and are also miscible in water.

**13.19**

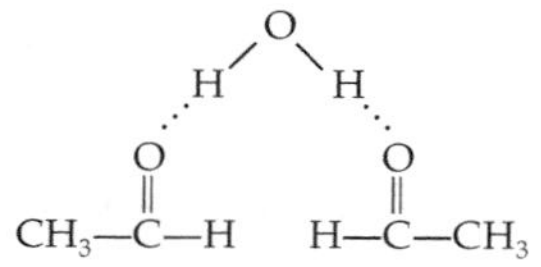

**13.21** Alcohols have higher boiling points than aldehydes or ketones of comparable molar mass because alcohol molecules can form intermolecular hydrogen bonds with one another. Aldehydes and ketones cannot form intermolecular hydrogen bonds.

**13.23 a.**

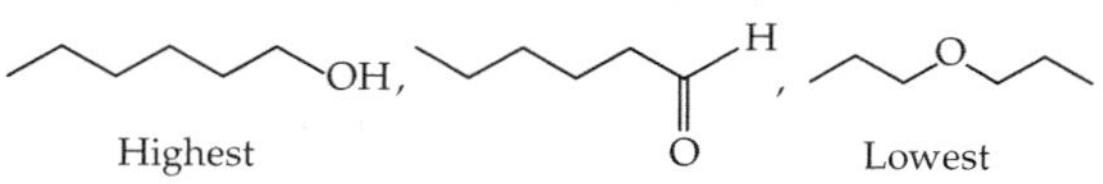

**b.**

**13.25** To name an aldehyde using the IUPAC Nomenclature System, identify and name the longest carbon chain containing the carbonyl group. Replace the final -*e* of the alkane name with -*al*. Number and name all substituents as usual. Remember that the carbonyl carbon is always carbon-1 and does not need to be numbered in the name of the compound.

**13.27** The common names of aldehydes are derived from the same Latin roots as the corresponding carboxylic acids. For instance, methanal is formaldehyde; ethanal is acetaldehyde; propanal is propionaldehyde, *etc.*

Substituted aldehydes are named as derivatives of the straight-chain parent compound. Greek letters are used to indicate the position of substituents. The carbon nearest the carbonyl group is the α-carbon, the next is the β-carbon, and so on.

**13.29** **a.**

**b.** $(CH_3)_2CHCH(CH_3)CH_2CH$

**c.** $CH_3(CH_2)_4CH(CH_2CH_3)CH$

**d.** $CH_2ClCH_2CHCl(CH_2)_3CH$

**13.31 a.** $CH_3CH(CH_3)CCH_2CH_3$

**b.** $CH_3(CH_2)_2CCH_2CH_3$

**c.** $CH_3(CH_2)_3C(CH_2)_3CH_3$

**d.** $CH_3(CH_2)_5C(CH_2)_6CH_3$

**13.33** **a.** Butanone  **b.** 2-Ethylhexanal
**13.35** **a.** 3-Nitrobenzaldehyde  **b.** 3,4-Dihydroxycyclopentanone
**13.37** 7-Hydroxy-3,7-dimethyloctanal
**13.39** **a.** 4,6-Dimethyl-3-heptanone  **b.** 3,3-Dimethylcyclopentanone
**13.41** **a.** Acetone  **d.** Propionaldehyde
  **b.** Ethyl methyl ketone  **e.** Methyl isopropyl ketone
  **c.** Acetaldehyde
**13.43** **a.** 3-Hydroxybutanal  **b.** 2-Methylpentanal

$CH_3CHOHCH_2CH$  $CH_3(CH_2)_2CH(CH_3)CH$

**c.** 4-Bromohexanal  **d.** 3-Iodopentanal

$CH_3CH_2CHBr(CH_2)_2CH$  $CH_3CH_2CHICH_2CH$

**e.** 2-Hydroxy-3-methylheptanal

$CH_3(CH_2)_3CH(CH_3)CHOHCH$

**13.45** Acetone is a good solvent because it can dissolve a wide range of compounds. It has both a polar carbonyl group and nonpolar side chains. As a result, it dissolves organic compounds and is also miscible in water.
**13.47** The liver
**13.49** In organic molecules, oxidation may be recognized as a gain of oxygen or a loss of hydrogen. An aldehyde may be oxidized to form a carboxylic acid as in the following example in which ethanal is oxidized to produce ethanoic acid.

$$H_3C-\overset{O}{\overset{\|}{C}}-H \xrightarrow{[O]} H_3C-\overset{O}{\overset{\|}{C}}-OH$$

Ethanal          Ethanoic acid

**13.51** Addition reactions of aldehydes or ketones are those in which a second molecule is added to the double bond of the carbonyl group.
**13.53** The following equation represents the oxidation of an aldehyde. The product is a carboxylic acid.

$$R-\overset{O}{\overset{\|}{C}}-H \xrightarrow{[O]} R-\overset{O}{\overset{\|}{C}}-OH$$

Aldehyde          Carboxylic acid

**13.55** The following general equation represents the addition of one alcohol molecule to an aldehyde:

$$R-\overset{O}{\overset{\|}{C}}-H + R'OH \xrightarrow{H^+} R-\overset{OH}{\underset{H}{\overset{|}{\underset{|}{C}}}}-OR'$$

Aldehyde          Hemiacetal

The following general equation represents the addition of one alcohol molecule to a ketone:

$$R-\overset{O}{\overset{\|}{C}}-R + R'OH \xrightarrow{H^+} R-\overset{OH}{\underset{R}{\overset{|}{\underset{|}{C}}}}-OR'$$

Ketone          Hemiacetal

**13.57** **a.**         13.57

4-Methyl-2-heptanol $\xrightarrow{[O]}$ 4-Methyl-2-heptanone

**b.**

3,4-Dimethyl-1-pentanol $\xrightarrow{[O]}$ 3,4-Dimethylpentanal

**c.**

4-Ethyl-2-heptanol $\xrightarrow{[O]}$ 4-Ethyl-2-heptanone

**d.**

5,7-Dichloro-3-heptanol $\xrightarrow{[O]}$ 5,7-Dichloro-3-heptanone

**13.59** $R-CH_2OH \xrightarrow{[O]} R-\overset{O}{\overset{\|}{C}}-H \xrightarrow{[O]} R-\overset{O}{\overset{\|}{C}}-OH$

Primary          Aldehyde          Carboxylic
alcohol                                  acid

**13.61  a.** Reduction reaction

$$CH_3-\overset{\overset{\displaystyle O}{\|}}{C}-H + H_2 \xrightarrow{Pt} CH_3CH_2OH$$

Ethanal                Ethanol

**b.** Reduction reaction

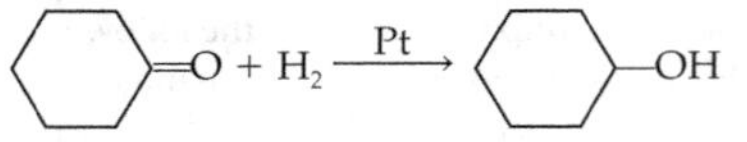

Cyclohexanone            Cyclohexanol

**c.** Oxidation reaction

$$CH_3\overset{\overset{\displaystyle OH}{|}}{C}HCH_3 \xrightarrow{[O]} CH_3-\overset{\overset{\displaystyle O}{\|}}{C}-CH_3$$

2-Propanol            Propanone

**13.63  a.**

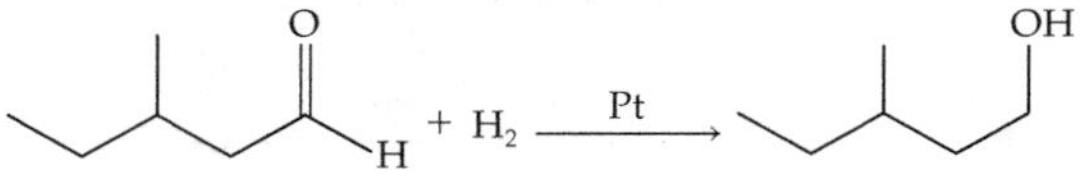

**b.**

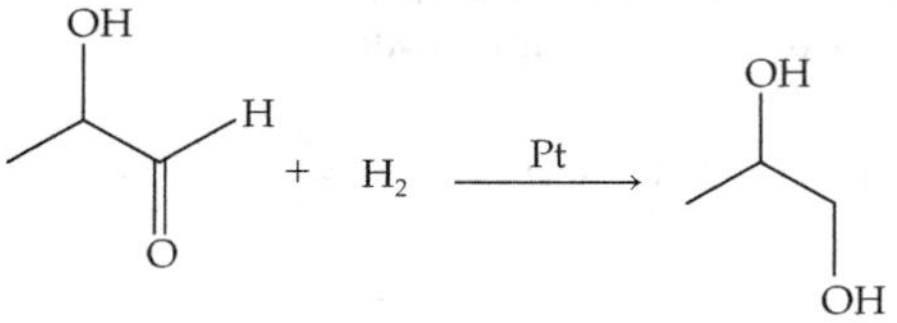

**c.**

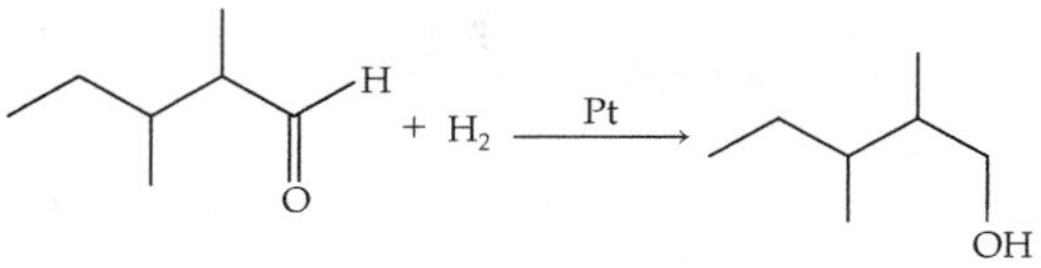

**d.**

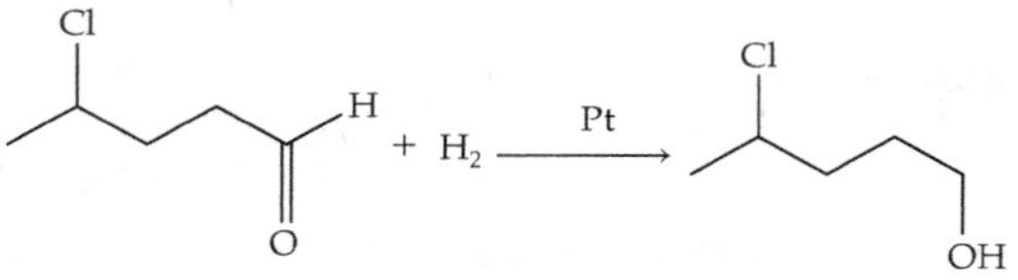

**13.65  a.**

$$CH_3CH_2CH_2\overset{\overset{\displaystyle O}{\|}}{C}H + H_2 \xrightarrow{Pt} CH_3CH_2CH_2CH_2OH$$

Butanal                1-Butanol

**b.**

$$CH_3CH_2\overset{\overset{\displaystyle}{|}}{C}HCH_2\overset{\overset{\displaystyle O}{\|}}{C}H + H_2 \xrightarrow{Pt} CH_3CH_2\overset{\overset{\displaystyle}{|}}{C}HCH_2CH_2OH$$
$$\quad\quad CH_3 \quad\quad\quad\quad\quad\quad\quad\quad CH_3$$

3-Methylpentanal        3-Methyl-1-pentanol

**c.**

$$CH_3\overset{\overset{\displaystyle}{|}}{C}H\overset{\overset{\displaystyle O}{\|}}{C}H + H_2 \xrightarrow{Pt} CH_3\overset{\overset{\displaystyle}{|}}{C}HCH_2OH$$
$$\quad CH_3 \quad\quad\quad\quad\quad\quad CH_3$$

2-Methylpropanal        2-Methyl-1-propanol

**13.67**  Only (c) 3-methylbutanal and (f) acetaldehyde would give a positive Tollens' test.

**13.69  a.**

$$CH_3CH_2\overset{\overset{\displaystyle O}{\|}}{C}H + CH_3CH_2OH \xrightarrow{H^+} CH_3CH_2-\overset{\overset{\displaystyle OH}{|}}{\underset{\underset{\displaystyle OCH_2CH_3}{|}}{C}}-H$$

**b.**

$$CH_3\overset{\overset{\displaystyle O}{\|}}{C}H + CH_3CH_2OH \xrightarrow{H^+} CH_3-\overset{\overset{\displaystyle OH}{|}}{\underset{\underset{\displaystyle OCH_2CH_3}{|}}{C}}-H$$

**13.71  a.**

$$CH_3CH_2\overset{\overset{\displaystyle O}{\|}}{C}H + 2\ CH_3OH \xrightarrow{H^+} CH_3CH_2-\overset{\overset{\displaystyle OCH_3}{|}}{\underset{\underset{\displaystyle OCH_3}{|}}{C}}-H + H_2O$$

**b.**

$$CH_3\overset{\overset{\displaystyle O}{\|}}{C}H + 2\ CH_3OH \xrightarrow{H^+} CH_3-\overset{\overset{\displaystyle OCH_3}{|}}{\underset{\underset{\displaystyle OCH_3}{|}}{C}}-H + H_2O$$

**13.73  a.**

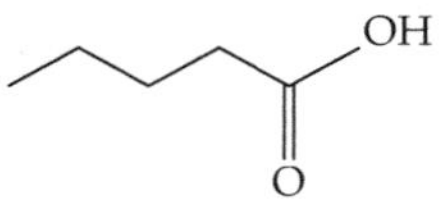

**b.**

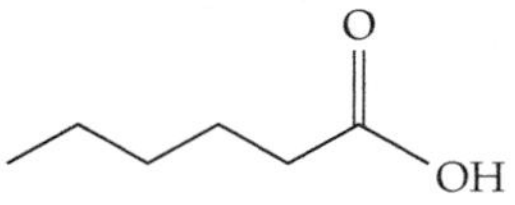

**c.**

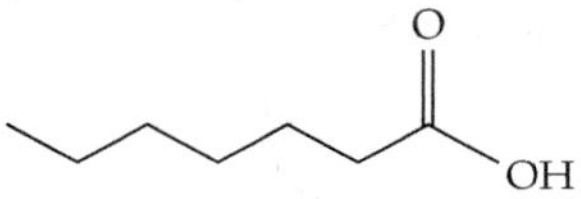

**d.**

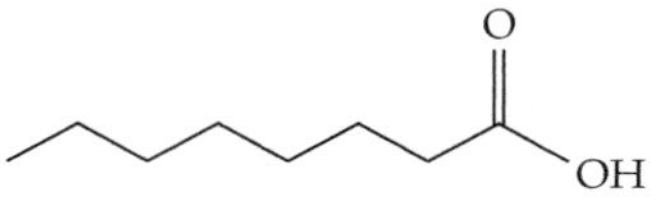

**13.75  a.** Methanal
**b.** Propanal

**13.77  a.** False
**b.** True
**c.** False
**d.** False

**13.79**

$$\overset{\overset{\displaystyle O}{\|}}{CH_3CCH_3}$$

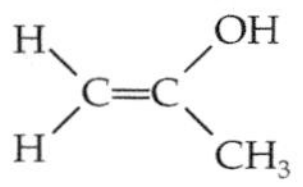

Keto form of            Enol form of
Propanone            Propanone

**13.81  a.**

$$CH_3CH_2CH_2-\overset{\overset{\displaystyle OH}{|}}{\underset{\underset{\displaystyle OCH_2CH_3}{|}}{C}}-CH_3$$

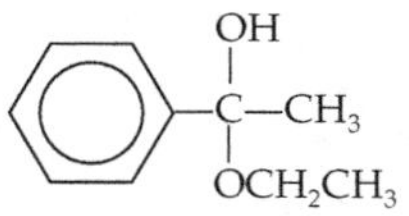

**c.**

**b.**

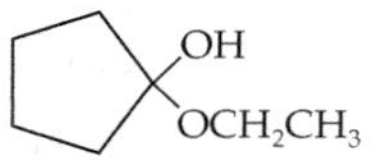

**13.83** (1) $2CH_3CH_2OH$

(2) $KMnO_4/OH^-$

(3) $CH_3CH=CH_2$

# Chapter 14

**14.1** a. Ketone

b. Ketone

c. Alkane

**14.3** The carboxyl group consists of two very polar groups, the carbonyl group and the hydroxyl group. Thus, carboxylic acids are very polar, in addition to which, they can hydrogen bond to one another. Aldehydes are polar, as a result of the carbonyl group, but cannot hydrogen bond to one another. As a result, carboxylic acids have higher boiling points than aldehydes of the same carbon chain length.

**14.5** a. 3-Methylcyclohexanecarboxylic acid

b. 2-Ethylcyclopentanecarboxylic acid

**14.7** a. $CH_3COOH + CH_3CH_2CH_2OH$
Ethanoic acid    1-Propanol

b. $CH_3CH_2CH_2CH_2CH_2COO^-K^+ + CH_3CH_2CH_2OH$
Potassium hexanoate           1-Propanol

c. $CH_3CH_2CH_2CH_2COO^-Na^+ + CH_3OH$
Sodium pentanoate    Methanol

d. $CH_3CH_2CH_2CH_2CH_2COOH + CH_3CHCH_2CH_2CH_3$
                                                    |
                                                    OH
Hexanoic acid                    2-Pentanol

**14.9** a.

3-Methylbutanoyl chloride

3-Methylbutanoic anhydride

b.

Methanoyl chloride

Ethanoic methanoic anhydride

**14.11** Aldehydes are polar, as a result of the carbonyl group, but cannot hydrogen bond to one another. Alcohols are polar and can hydrogen bond as a result of the polar hydroxyl group. The carboxyl group of the carboxylic acids consists of both of these groups: the carbonyl group and the hydroxyl group. Thus, carboxylic acids are more polar than either aldehydes or alcohols, in addition to which, they can hydrogen bond to one another. As a result, carboxylic acids have higher boiling points than aldehydes or alcohols of comparable molar mass.

**14.13** a. Pentanoic acid

b. 2-Pentanol

c. 2-Pentanol

**14.15**

Propanoic acid        2-Butanol

Butanal        2-Methylbutane

**14.17** a. Heptanoic acid

b. 1-Propanol

c. Pentanoic acid

d. Butanoic acid

**14.19** The smaller carboxylic acids are water-soluble. They have sharp, sour tastes and unpleasant aromas.

**14.21** Citric acid is found naturally in citrus fruits. It is added to foods to give them a tart flavor or to act as a food preservative and antioxidant.

**14.23** Glutaric acid is useful in the synthesis of condensation polymers because it has an odd number of carbons in the chain, which reduces the elasticity of the polymer.

**14.25** Determine the name of the parent compound; that is, the longest carbon chain containing the carboxyl group. Change the -e ending of the alkane name to -oic acid. Number the chain so that the carboxyl carbon is carbon-1. Name and number substituents in the usual way.

**14.27** The IUPAC name for adipic acid is hexanedioic acid. Adipic acid is a natural food additive that reduces spoilage by lowering the pH and thereby inhibiting the growth of bacteria and fungi.

**14.29** a. $CH_3(CH_2)_2CH(CH_3)CH_2COOH$

b. $CH_3(CH_2)_2C(CH_3)(CH_2CH_3)COOH$

c.

**14.31** a. IUPAC name: Methanoic acid
Common name: Formic acid

b. IUPAC name: 3-Methylbutanoic acid
Common name: β-Methylbutyric acid

c. IUPAC name: Cyclopentanecarboxylic acid
Common name: Cyclovalericcarboxylic acid

**14.33**

Butanoic acid

Methylpropanoic acid

**14.35 a.**

$$CH_3CH_2\underset{\underset{CH_3}{|}}{\overset{\overset{CH_3}{|}}{C}}CH_2CH_2COOH$$

**c.**

benzene ring with —COOH, and O₂N, NO₂ substituents

**b.**

$$CH_3\underset{\underset{Br}{|}}{\overset{\overset{CH_3}{|}}{CH}}CHCH_2COOH$$

**d.**

cyclohexane ring with —COOH and H₃C substituents

**14.37 a.** IUPAC name: 2-Hydroxypropanoic acid
Common name: α-Hydroxypropionic acid
**b.** IUPAC name: 3-Hydroxybutanoic acid
Common name: β-Hydroxybutyric acid
**c.** IUPAC name: 4,4-Dimethylpentanoic acid
Common name: γ,γ-Dimethylvaleric acid
**d.** IUPAC name: 3, 3-Dichloropentanoic acid
Common name: β,β-Dichlorovaleric acid

**14.39 a.** 3-Bromobenzoic acid (or *meta*-bromobenzoic acid or
*m*-bromobenzoic acid)
**b.** 2-Ethylbenzoic acid (or *ortho*-ethylbenzoic acid or
*o*-ethylbenzoic acid)
**c.** 4-Hydroxybenzoic acid (or *para*-hydroxybenzoic acid or
*p*-hydroxybenzoic acid)

**14.41** In organic molecules, oxidation may be recognized as a gain
of oxygen or a loss of hydrogen. An aldehyde may be oxidized
to form a carboxylic acid as in the following example in which
ethanal is oxidized to produce ethanoic acid.

$$H_3C-\overset{\overset{O}{\|}}{C}-H \xrightarrow{[O]} H_3C-\overset{\overset{O}{\|}}{C}-OH$$

Ethanal                    Ethanoic acid

**14.43** The following general equation represents the dissociation of a
carboxylic acid.

$$R-\overset{\overset{O}{\|}}{C}-OH \rightleftharpoons R-\overset{\overset{O}{\|}}{C}-O^- + H^+$$

**14.45** When a strong base is added to a carboxylic acid, neutralization
occurs.

**14.47** Soaps are made from water, a strong base, and natural fats or
oils.

**14.49 a.**

**b.**

**c.**

$\xrightarrow{[O]}$ No Reaction

**14.51 a.** $CH_3COOH$
**b.**

$$CH_3CH_2CH_2-\overset{\overset{O}{\|}}{C}-O-CH_3 + H_2O$$

**c.** $CH_3OH$

**14.53 a.** The oxidation of 1-pentanol yields pentanal.
**b.** Continued oxidation of pentanal yields pentanoic acid.

**14.55**

**a.**

+ NaOH ⟶ + H₂O

**b.**

+ KOH ⟶ + H₂O

**c.**

2 ... + Ca(OH)₂ ⟶ ... + 2H₂O

**14.57** The structure of the calcium salt of propionic acid is
$[CH_3CH_2\,COO^-]_2Ca^{2+}$. The common name of this salt is calcium
propionate and the IUPAC name is calcium propanoate.

**14.59** Esters are slightly polar as a result of the polar carbonyl group
within the structure.

**14.61** Esters are formed in the reaction of a carboxylic acid with an
alcohol. The name is derived by using the alkyl or aryl portion
of the alcohol IUPAC name as the first name. The *-ic* acid ending
of the IUPAC name of the carboxylic acid is replaced with *-ate*
and follows the name of the aryl or alkyl group.

**14.63 a.**

benzene ring with C(=O)—OCH₃

**b.**

$$CH_3CH_2CH_2CH_2CH_2CH_2CH_2CH_2CH_2-\overset{\overset{O}{\|}}{C}-O-CH_2CH_2CH_2CH_3$$

**c.**

$$CH_3CH_2-\overset{\overset{O}{\|}}{C}-O-CH_3$$

**d.**

$$CH_3CH_2-\overset{\overset{O}{\|}}{C}-O-CH_2CH_3$$

**14.65 a.** Ethyl ethanoate          **c.** Methyl-3-methylbutanoate
**b.** Methyl propanoate       **d.** Cyclopentyl benzoate

**14.67** The following equation shows the general reaction for the
preparation of an ester:

$$R-\overset{\overset{O}{\|}}{C}-OH + R-OH \underset{}{\overset{H^+, heat}{\rightleftharpoons}} R-\overset{\overset{O}{\|}}{C}-OR + H_2O$$

Carboxylic        Alcohol                      Ester            Water
acid

**14.69** The following equation shows the general reaction for the acid-
catalyzed hydrolysis of an ester:

$$R-\overset{\overset{O}{\|}}{C}-OR + H_2O \underset{}{\overset{H^+, heat}{\rightleftharpoons}} R-\overset{\overset{O}{\|}}{C}-OH + R-OH$$

Ester             Water                    Carboxylic      Alcohol
acid

**14.71** A hydrolysis reaction is the cleavage of any bond by the
addition of a water molecule.

**14.73 a.**

$$CH_3CH_2CH_2-\overset{\overset{\displaystyle O}{\|}}{C}-O-CH_2CH_3$$

**b.**

$$CH_3CH_2-\overset{\overset{\displaystyle O}{\|}}{C}-OH + CH_3CH_2OH$$

**c.** $CH_3CH_2CH_2OH$

**d.**

$$CH_3CH_2\overset{\overset{\displaystyle Br}{|}}{C}HCH_2-\overset{\overset{\displaystyle O}{\|}}{C}-O^- + CH_3CH_2OH$$

**14.75 a.** Isobutyl methanoate is made from isobutyl alcohol (IUPAC name 2-methyl-1-propanol) and methanoic acid.

$$CH_3\overset{\overset{\displaystyle CH_3}{|}}{C}HCH_2OH + HCOOH \rightarrow HCOCH_2\overset{\overset{\displaystyle CH_3}{|}}{C}HCH_3$$

Isobutyl alcohol   Methanoic acid   Isobutyl methanoate

Isobutyl alcohol is an allowed starting material, but methanoic acid is not. However, it can easily be produced by the oxidation of its corresponding alcohol, methanol:

$$CH_3OH \xrightarrow{[O]} HCHO \xrightarrow{[O]} HCOOH$$

Methanol   Methanal   Methanoic acid

**b.** Pentyl butanoate is made from 1-pentanol and butanoic acid.

$$CH_3(CH_2)_3CH_2OH + CH_3CH_2CH_2COOH$$

1-Pentanol   Butanoic acid

$$\rightarrow CH_3CH_2CH_2\overset{\overset{\displaystyle O}{\|}}{C}OCH_2(CH_2)_3CH_3$$

Pentyl butanoate

Pentanol is an allowed starting material but butanoic acid is not. However, it can easily be produced by the oxidation of its corresponding alcohol, 1-butanol:

$$CH_3CH_2CH_2CH_2OH \xrightarrow{[O]} CH_3CH_2CH_2CHO \xrightarrow{[O]} CH_3CH_2CH_2COOH$$

1-Butanol   Butanal   Butanoic acid

**14.77** Saponification is a reaction in which soap is produced. More generally, it is the hydrolysis of an ester in the presence of a base. The following reaction shows the base-catalyzed hydrolysis of an ester:

$$CH_3(CH_2)_{14}-\overset{\overset{\displaystyle O}{\|}}{C}-O-CH_3 + NaOH \longrightarrow$$

$$CH_3(CH_2)_{14}-\overset{\overset{\displaystyle O}{\|}}{C}-O^- Na^+ + CH_3OH$$

**14.79**

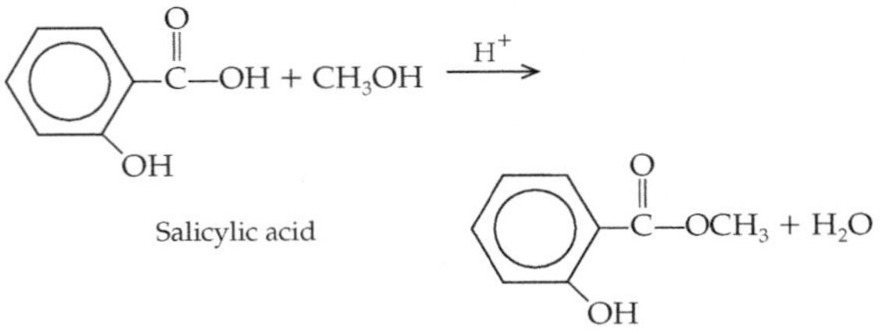

Salicylic acid

Methyl salicylate

**14.81** Compound A is

$$CH_3CH_2CH_2CH_2-\overset{\overset{\displaystyle O}{\|}}{C}-O-CH_3$$

Compound B is

$$CH_3CH_2CH_2CH_2-\overset{\overset{\displaystyle O}{\|}}{C}-OH$$

Compound C is $CH_3OH$

**14.83 a.**

$$CH_3CH_2-\overset{\overset{\displaystyle O}{\|}}{C}-OCH_2CH_2CH_3 \underset{}{\overset{H^+, \text{ heat}}{\rightleftharpoons}} CH_3CH_2-\overset{\overset{\displaystyle O}{\|}}{C}-OH$$

Propyl propanoate   Propanoic acid

$$+ CH_3CH_2CH_2OH$$

1-Propanol

**b.**

$$H-\overset{\overset{\displaystyle O}{\|}}{C}-OCH_2CH_2CH_2CH_3 \underset{}{\overset{H^+, \text{ heat}}{\rightleftharpoons}} H-\overset{\overset{\displaystyle O}{\|}}{C}-OH$$

Butyl methanoate   Methanoic acid

$$+ CH_3CH_2CH_2CH_2OH$$

1-Butanol

**c.**

$$H-\overset{\overset{\displaystyle O}{\|}}{C}-OCH_2CH_3 \underset{}{\overset{H^+, \text{ heat}}{\rightleftharpoons}} H-\overset{\overset{\displaystyle O}{\|}}{C}-OH$$

Ethyl methanoate   Methanoic acid

$$+ CH_3CH_2OH$$

Ethanol

**d.**

$$CH_3CH_2CH_2CH_2-\overset{\overset{\displaystyle O}{\|}}{C}-OCH_3 \underset{}{\overset{H^+, \text{ heat}}{\rightleftharpoons}}$$

Methyl pentanoate

$$CH_3CH_2CH_2CH_2-\overset{\overset{\displaystyle O}{\|}}{C}-OH + CH_3OH$$

Pentanoic acid   Methanol

**14.85** Acid chlorides are noxious, irritating chemicals. They are slightly polar and have boiling points similar to comparable aldehydes or ketones. They cannot be dissolved in water because they react violently with it.

**14.87** Acid anhydrides have much lower boiling points than carboxylic acids of comparable molar mass. They are also less soluble in water, and often react with it.

**14.89 a.**

$$CH_3(CH_2)_8-\overset{\overset{\displaystyle O}{\|}}{C}-O-\overset{\overset{\displaystyle O}{\|}}{C}-(CH_2)_8CH_3$$

**b.**

$$CH_3-\overset{\overset{\displaystyle O}{\|}}{C}-O-\overset{\overset{\displaystyle O}{\|}}{C}-CH_3$$

**14.91 a.**

$$CH_3(CH_2)_6\overset{\overset{\displaystyle O}{\|}}{C}Cl$$

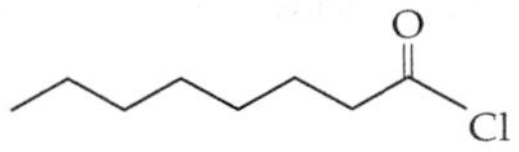

**b.**

$$CH_3(CH_2)_2\overset{\overset{\displaystyle O}{\|}}{C}Cl$$

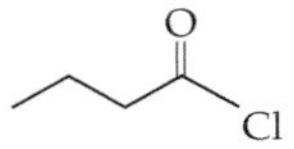

**c.**

$$CH_3(CH_2)_7\overset{\overset{\displaystyle O}{\|}}{C}Cl$$

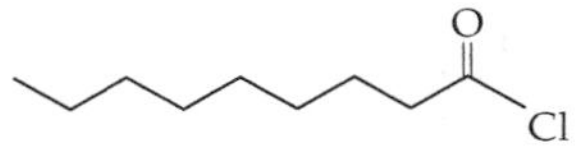

**14.93** The following equation represents the synthesis of methanoic anhydride:

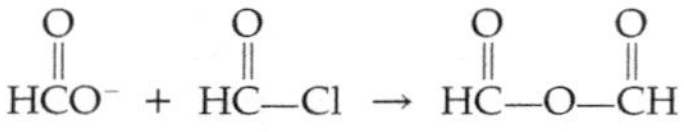

Methanoate   Methanoic   Methanoic
anion        chloride    anhydride

**14.95  a.**

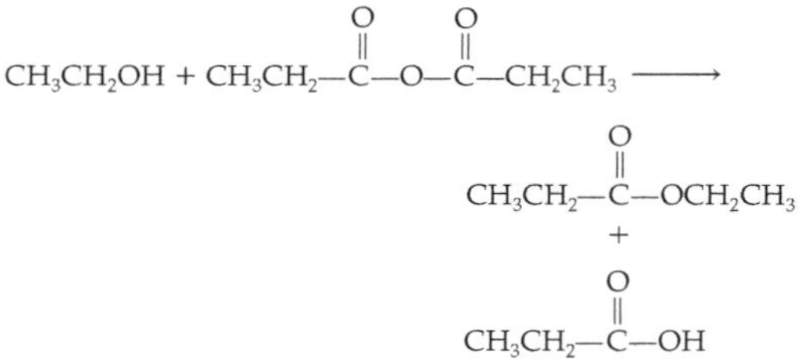

$$CH_3CH_2OH + CH_3CH_2-\overset{O}{\overset{||}{C}}-O-\overset{O}{\overset{||}{C}}-CH_2CH_3 \longrightarrow$$

$$CH_3CH_2-\overset{O}{\overset{||}{C}}-OCH_2CH_3$$
+
$$CH_3CH_2-\overset{O}{\overset{||}{C}}-OH$$

**b.**

$$CH_3CH_2OH + CH_3-\overset{O}{\overset{||}{C}}-O-\overset{O}{\overset{||}{C}}-CH_3 \longrightarrow$$

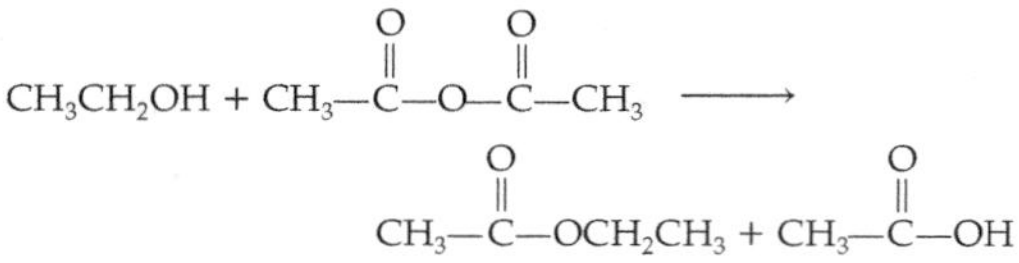

$$CH_3-\overset{O}{\overset{||}{C}}-OCH_2CH_3 + CH_3-\overset{O}{\overset{||}{C}}-OH$$

**c.**

$$CH_3CH_2OH + H-\overset{O}{\overset{||}{C}}-O-\overset{O}{\overset{||}{C}}-H \longrightarrow$$

$$H-\overset{O}{\overset{||}{C}}-OCH_2CH_3 + H-\overset{O}{\overset{||}{C}}-OH$$

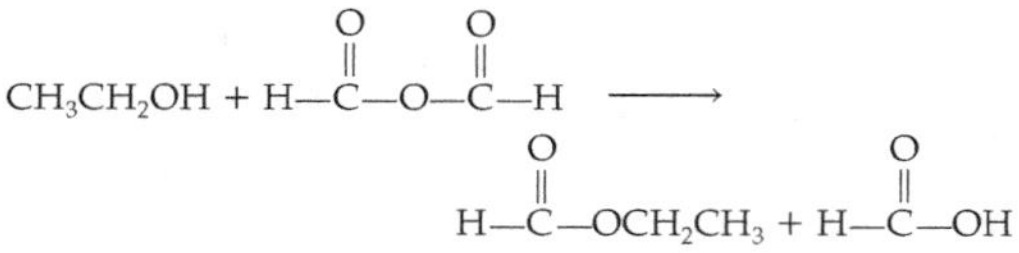

**14.97  a.** Monoester:

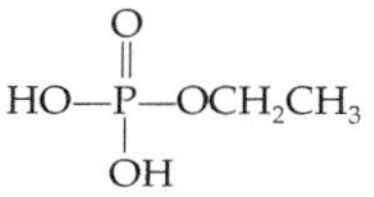

$$HO-\overset{O}{\underset{OH}{\overset{||}{P}}}-OCH_2CH_3$$

**b.** Diester:

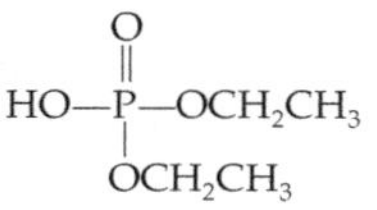

$$HO-\overset{O}{\underset{OCH_2CH_3}{\overset{||}{P}}}-OCH_2CH_3$$

**c.** Triester:

$$CH_3CH_2O-\overset{O}{\underset{OCH_2CH_3}{\overset{||}{P}}}-OCH_2CH_3$$

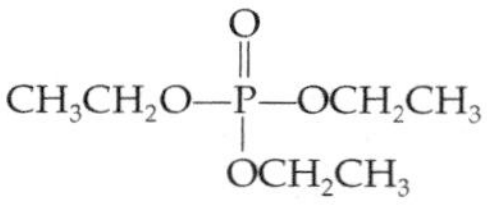

**14.99** ATP is the molecule used to store the energy released in metabolic reactions. The energy is stored in the phosphoanhydride bonds between two phosphoryl groups. The energy is released when the bond is hydrolyzed. A portion of the energy can be transferred to another molecule if the phosphoryl group is transferred from ATP to the other molecule.

**14.101**

$$CH_3-\overset{O}{\overset{||}{C}}\sim S-COENZYME\ A$$

The squiggle denotes a high-energy bond.

**14.103**

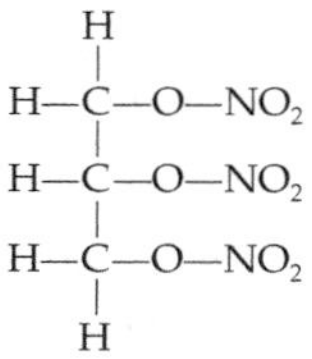

# Chapter 15

**15.1**

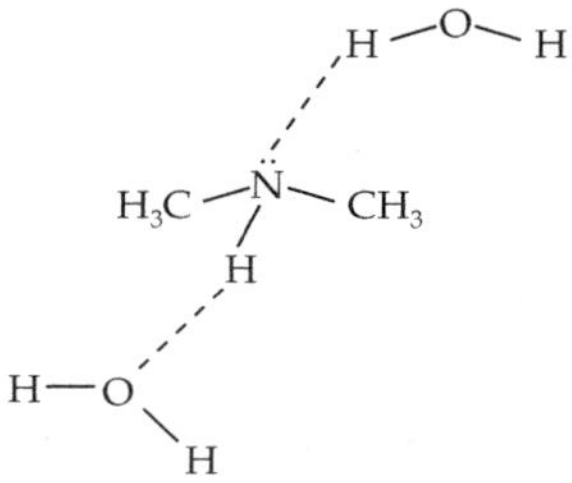

**15.3  a.**

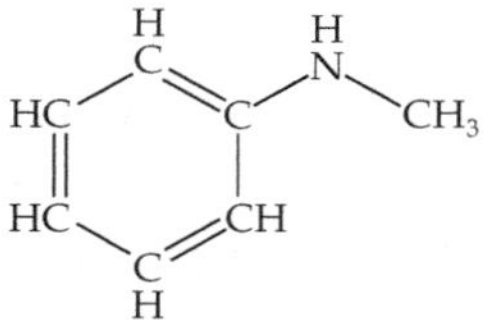

**b.**

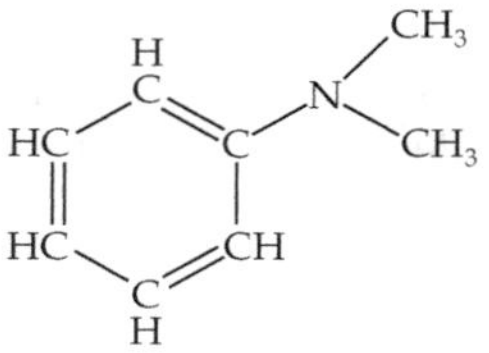

**c.**

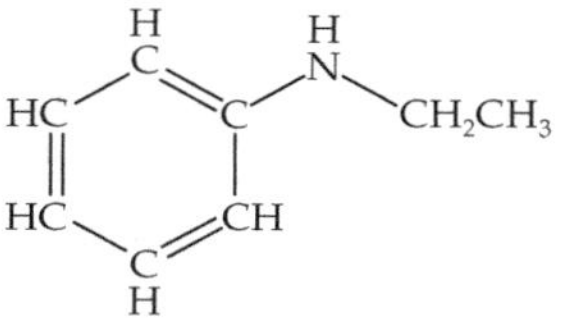

**d.**

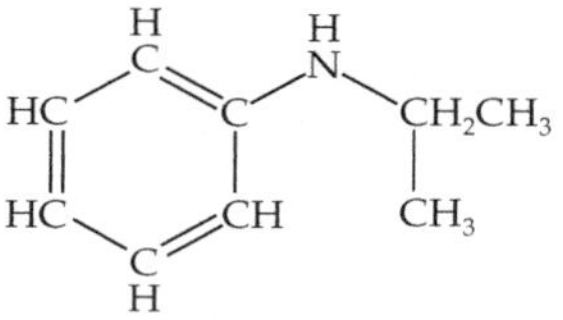

**15.5  a.**

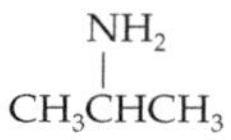

$$\underset{CH_3CHCH_3}{\overset{NH_2}{|}}$$

**b.**

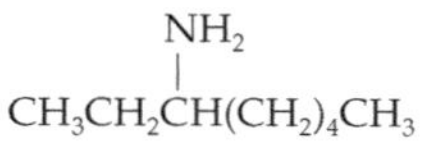

$$\underset{CH_3CH_2CH(CH_2)_4CH_3}{\overset{NH_2}{|}}$$

**c.**

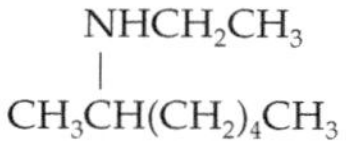

$$\underset{CH_3CH(CH_2)_4CH_3}{\overset{NHCH_2CH_3}{|}}$$

**d.** $NH_2C(CH_3)_2(CH_2)_2CH_3$

**e.** $NH_2(CH_2)_3\underset{Cl\ \ I}{\overset{|\ \ |}{CHCH}}(CH_2)_3CH_3$

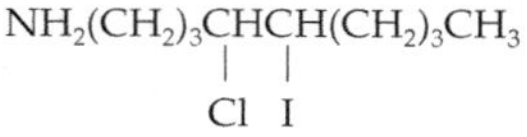

**f.** $(CH_3CH_2)_2N(CH_2)_4CH_3$

**15.7** **a.**

**b.**

$$CH_3CH_2-\overset{\overset{\displaystyle H}{|}}{\underset{\underset{\displaystyle H}{|}}{N^+}}-CH_3 + OH^-$$

**c.** $CH_3-N^+H_3 + OH^-$

**15.9** **a.** $CH_3-NH_2$

**b.** $CH_3-\overset{\overset{\displaystyle CH_3}{|}}{NH}$

**15.11** The nitrogen atom is more electronegative than the hydrogen atom in amines; thus, the N—H bond is polar and hydrogen bonding can occur between primary or secondary amine molecules. Thus, amines have a higher boiling point than alkanes, which are nonpolar. Because nitrogen is not as electronegative as oxygen, the N—H bond is not as polar as the O—H. As a result, intermolecular hydrogen bonds between primary and secondary amine molecules are not as strong as the hydrogen bonds between alcohol molecules. Thus, alcohols have a higher boiling point.

**15.13** In systematic nomenclature, primary amines are named by determining the name of the parent compound, the longest continuous carbon chain containing the amine group. The -e ending of the alkane chain is replaced with -amine. Thus, an alkane becomes an alkanamine. The parent chain is then numbered to give the carbon bearing the amine group the lowest possible number. Finally, all substituents are named and numbered and added as prefixes to the "alkanamine" name.

**15.15** Amphetamines elevate blood pressure and pulse rate. They also decrease the appetite.

**15.17** **a.** 1-Pentamine would be more soluble in water because it has a polar amine group that can form hydrogen bonds with water molecules.
**b.** 2-Butamine would be more soluble in water because it has a polar amine group that can form hydrogen bonds with water molecules.

**15.19** Triethylamine molecules cannot form hydrogen bonds with one another, but 1-hexanamine molecules are able to do so.

**15.21** **a.** 2-Butanamine
**b.** 3-Hexanamine
**c.** Cyclopentanamine
**d.** 2-Methyl-2-propanamine

**15.23** **a.** $CH_3CH_2NHCH_2CH_3$

**b.** $CH_3(CH_2)_3NH_2$

**c.**

$$CH_3(CH_2)_6\overset{\overset{\displaystyle NH_2}{|}}{CH}CH_2CH_3$$

**d.**

$$CH_3\overset{\overset{\displaystyle NH_2}{|}}{CH}CHCH_2CH_3 \qquad$$
$$\underset{\underset{\displaystyle Br}{|}}{}$$

**e.**

**15.25** **a.** $CH_3CH_2CH(NH_2)(CH_2)_2CH_3$

**b.** $CH_3(CH_2)_5NH(CH_2)_4CH_3$

**c.** $\underset{\underset{\displaystyle H_2C-CH_2}{|\qquad|}}{H_2C-\overset{\overset{\displaystyle NH_2}{|}}{CH}}$

**d.**

**e.**

$$\underset{\underset{\displaystyle CH_2CH_3}{|}}{CH_3CH_2\overset{\overset{\displaystyle \qquad Cl^-}{}}{N^+}HCH_2CH_3}$$

**15.27** $CH_3CH_2CH_2CH_2NH_2$

1-Butanamine
(Primary amine)

$CH_3CH_2\overset{\overset{\displaystyle}{}}{\underset{\underset{\displaystyle NH_2}{|}}{CH}}CH_3$

2-Butanamine
(Primary amine)

$CH_3\overset{\overset{\displaystyle}{}}{\underset{\underset{\displaystyle CH_3}{|}}{CH}}CH_2NH_2$

2-Methyl-1-propanamine
(Primary amine)

$CH_3-\overset{\overset{\displaystyle CH_3}{|}}{\underset{\underset{\displaystyle NH_2}{|}}{C}}-CH_3$

2-Methyl-2-propanamine
(Primary amine)

$CH_3CH_2-\overset{\overset{\displaystyle CH_3}{|}}{N}-CH_3$

N,N-Dimethylethanamine
(Tertiary amine)

$CH_3CH_2-NH-CH_2CH_3$

N-Ethylethanamine
(Secondary amine)

$\underset{\underset{\displaystyle NH-CH_3}{|}}{CH_3\overset{\overset{\displaystyle}{}}{CH}CH_3}$

N-Methyl-2-propanamine
(Secondary amine)

$CH_3CH_2CH_2-NH-CH_3$

N-Methyl-1-propanamine
(Secondary amine)

**15.29** **a.** Primary     **c.** Primary
**b.** Secondary     **d.** Tertiary

**15.31** **a.**

**b.**

**c.**

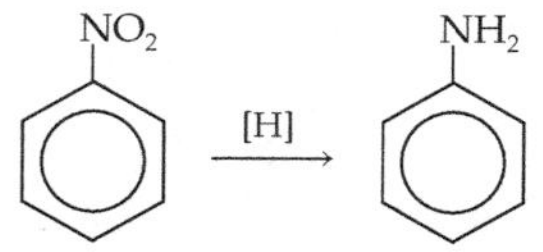

$$NO_2 \xrightarrow{[H]} NH_2$$

**d.**

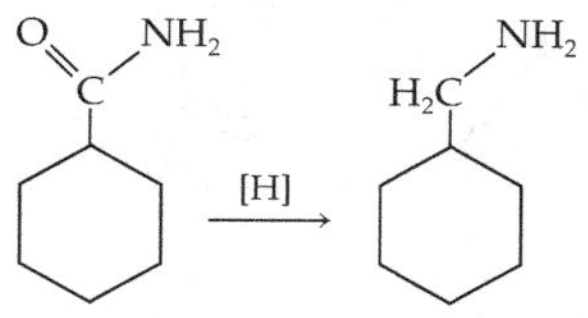

**15.33 a.** $H_2O$
**b.** HBr
**c.** $CH_3CH_2CH_2-N^+H_3$
**d.** $CH_3CH_2-N^+H_2Cl^-$
      | 
      $CH_2CH_3$

**15.35 a.**

$$CH_3(CH_2)_4\overset{O}{\overset{||}{C}}NH_2 \xrightarrow{[H]} CH_3(CH_2)_5NH_2$$

**b.**

$$CH_3(CH_2)_2\overset{O}{\overset{||}{C}}NHCH_3 \xrightarrow{[H]} CH_3(CH_2)_3NHCH_3$$

**c.**

$$CH_3CH_2\overset{O}{\overset{||}{C}}NCH_3 \xrightarrow{[H]} CH_3(CH_2)_2NCH_3$$
$$\qquad\qquad | \qquad\qquad\qquad\qquad\qquad |$$
$$\qquad\qquad CH_3 \qquad\qquad\qquad\qquad\quad CH_3$$

**15.37** Lower molar mass amines are soluble in water because the N—H bond is polar and can form hydrogen bonds with water molecules.

**15.39** Drugs containing amine groups are generally administered as ammonium salts because the salt is more soluble in water and, hence, in body fluids.

**15.41** Putrescine (1,4-Butanediamine):

$$CH_2CH_2CH_2CH_2$$
$$\ |\qquad\qquad\quad|$$
$$NH_2\qquad\qquad NH_2$$

Cadaverine (1,5-Pentanediamine):

$$CH_2CH_2CH_2CH_2CH_2$$
$$\ |\qquad\qquad\qquad\quad|$$
$$NH_2\qquad\qquad\quad NH_2$$

**15.43 a.**

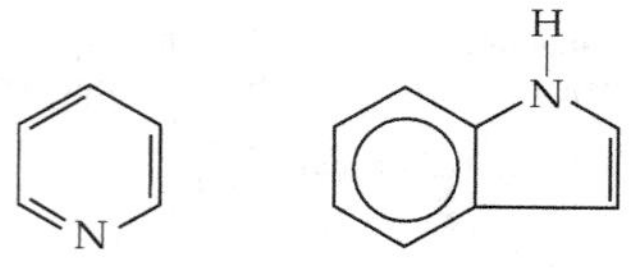

Pyridine                Indole

**b.** The indole ring is found in lysergic acid diethylamide, which is a hallucinogenic drug. The pyridine ring is found in vitamin $B_6$, an essential water-soluble vitamin.

**15.45** Morphine, codeine, quinine, and vitamin $B_6$

**15.47** Amides have very high boiling points because the amide group consists of two very polar functional groups, the carbonyl group and the amino group. Strong intermolecular hydrogen bonding between the N—H bond of one amide and the C=O group of a second amide results in very high boiling points.

**15.49** The IUPAC names of amides are derived from the IUPAC names of the carboxylic acids from which they are derived. The *-oic acid* ending of the carboxylic acid is replaced with the *-amide* ending.

**15.51** Barbiturates are often called "downers" because they act as sedatives. They are sometimes used as anticonvulsants for epileptics and people suffering from other disorders that manifest as neurosis, anxiety, or tension.

**15.53 a.** IUPAC name: Propanamide
        Common name: Propionamide
**b.** IUPAC name: Pentanamide
        Common name: Valeramide
**c.** IUPAC name: *N,N*-Dimethylethanamide
        Common name: *N,N*-Dimethylacetamide

**15.55 a.**

$$CH_3CH_2\overset{O}{\overset{||}{C}}NH_2$$

**b.**

$$CH_3(CH_2)_2\overset{O}{\overset{||}{C}}N(CH_2CH_3)_2$$

**c.**

$$(CH_3CH_2)_2CHCH(CH_2CH_3)\overset{O}{\overset{||}{C}}NH_2$$

**d.**

$$CH_3(CH_2)_4\overset{O}{\overset{||}{C}}NHCH_3$$

**15.57 a.**

$$CH_3-\overset{O}{\overset{||}{C}}-NH_2,$$

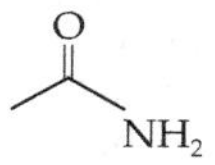

**b.**

$$CH_3CH_2-\overset{O}{\overset{||}{C}}-NHCH_3,$$

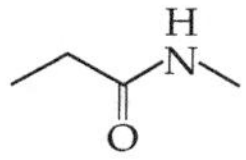

**c.**

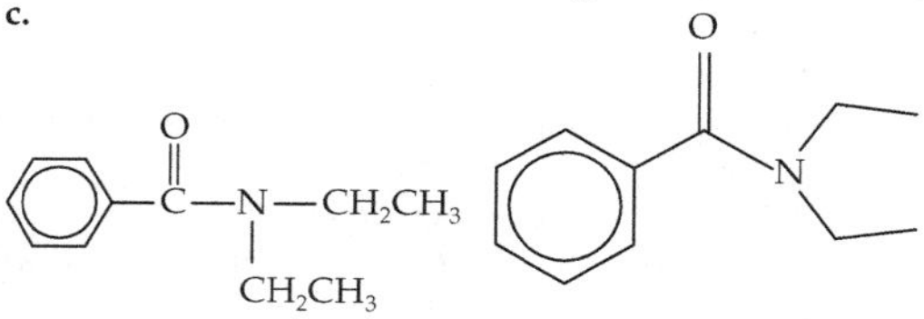

**d.**

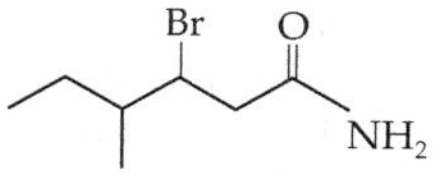

**e.** $CH_3-\overset{O}{\overset{||}{C}}-\overset{}{\underset{|}{N}}-CH_3,$
$$\qquad\qquad\quad CH_3$$

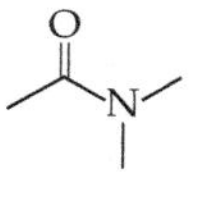

**15.59** *N,N*-Diethyl-*m*-toluamide:

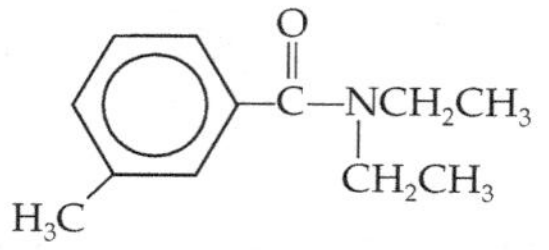

Hydrolysis of this compound would release the carboxylic acid *m*-toluic acid and the amine *N*-ethylethanamine (diethylamine).

**15.61** Amides are not proton acceptors (bases) because the highly electronegative carbonyl oxygen has a strong attraction for the nitrogen lone pair of electrons. As a result, they cannot "hold" a proton.

**15.63**

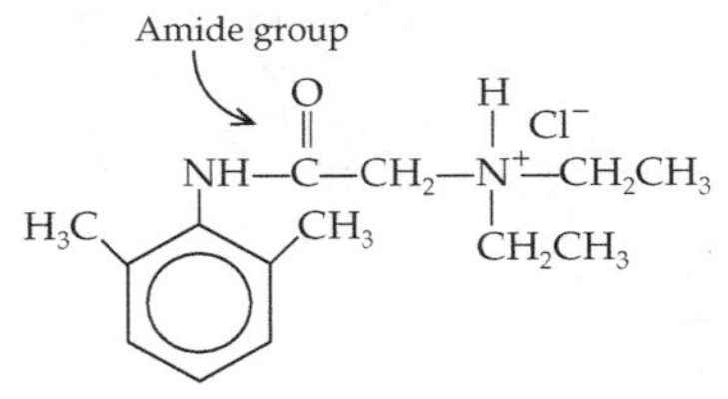

Amide group

Lidocaine hydrochloride

**15.65**

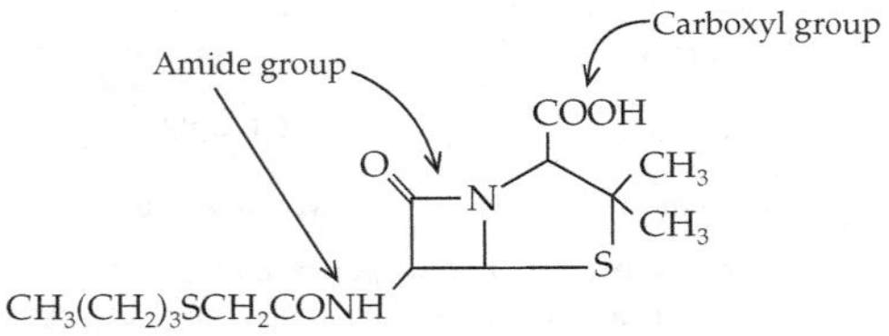

Amide group — Carboxyl group

$CH_3(CH_2)_3SCH_2CONH$

Penicillin BT

**15.67**

**a.**

$$CH_3-\overset{O}{\underset{\|}{C}}-NHCH_3 + H_3O^+ \longrightarrow$$

*N*-Methylethanamide

$$CH_3COOH + CH_3N^+H_3$$

Ethanoic acid    Methylammonium ion

**b.**

$$CH_3CH_2CH_2-\overset{O}{\underset{\|}{C}}-NH-CH_3 + H_3O^+ \longrightarrow$$

*N*-Methylbutanamide

$$CH_3CH_2CH_2COOH + CH_3N^+H_3$$

Butanoic acid    Methylammonium ion

**c.**

$$CH_3\overset{CH_3}{\underset{|}{C}}HCH_2-\overset{O}{\underset{\|}{C}}-NH-CH_2CH_3 + H_3O^+ \longrightarrow$$

*N*-Ethyl-3-methylbutanamide

$$CH_3\overset{|}{\underset{CH_3}{C}}HCH_2COOH + CH_3CH_2N^+H_3$$

3-Methylbutanoic acid    Ethylammonium ion

**15.69  a.**

$$CH_3CH_2-\overset{O}{\underset{\|}{C}}-O-\overset{O}{\underset{\|}{C}}-CH_2CH_3$$

**b.**

$$CH_3CH_2-\overset{O}{\underset{\|}{C}}-NH_2 + NH_4^+Cl^-$$

**c.**

$$CH_3CH_2CH_2-\overset{O}{\underset{\|}{C}}-Cl + 2CH_3CH_2NH_2$$

**15.71** A primary (1°) amide is the product of the reaction between ammonia and an acid chloride. A primary amide has only one carbon, the carbonyl carbon, bonded to the nitrogen and has the following general structure:

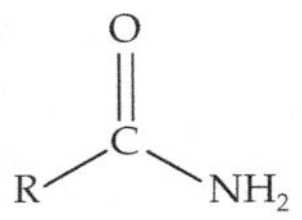

$$R-\overset{O}{\underset{\|}{C}}-NH_2$$

**15.73** A tertiary (3°) amide is the product of a reaction between a secondary amine and an acid chloride. A tertiary amide has three carbon atoms bonded to the nitrogen. One is the carbonyl carbon from the acid chloride and the other two are from the secondary amine reactant. The following is the general structure:

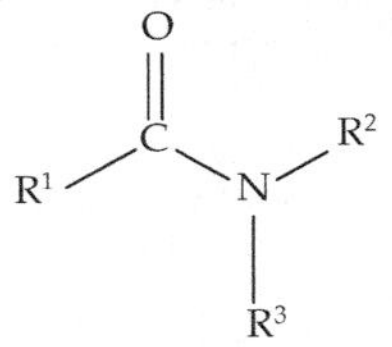

$$R^1-\overset{O}{\underset{\|}{C}}-N\overset{R^2}{\underset{R^3}{<}}$$

**15.75**

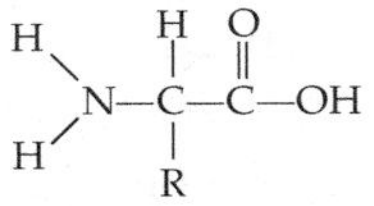

**15.77** Glycine:

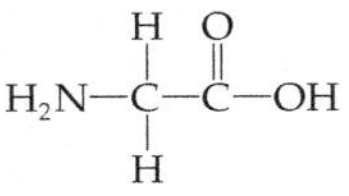

Alanine:

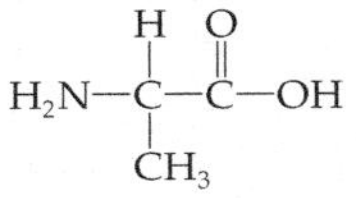

**15.79**

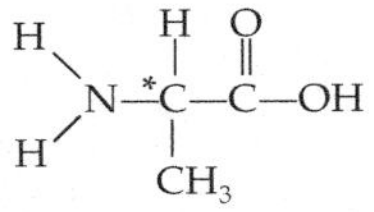

**15.81** In an acyl group transfer reaction, the acyl group of an acid chloride is transferred from the Cl of the acid chloride to the N of an amine or ammonia. The product is an amide.

**15.83** A chemical that carries messages or signals from a nerve to a target cell

**15.85  a.** Tremors, monotonous speech, loss of memory and problem-solving ability, and loss of motor function
**b.** Parkinson's disease
**c.** Schizophrenia, intense satiety sensations

**15.87** In proper amounts, dopamine causes a pleasant, satisfied feeling. This feeling becomes intense as the amount of dopamine increases. Several drugs, including cocaine, heroin, amphetamines, alcohol, and nicotine increase the levels of dopamine. It is thought that the intense satiety response this brings about may contribute to addiction to these substances.

**15.89** Epinephrine is a component of the flight or fight response. It stimulates glycogen breakdown to provide the body with glucose to supply the needed energy for this stress response.

**15.91** The amino acid tryptophan

**15.93** Perception of pain, thermoregulation, and sleep

**15.95** Promotes the itchy skin rash associated with poison ivy and insect bites; the respiratory symptoms characteristic of hay fever; secretion of stomach acid

**15.97** Inhibitory neurotransmitters

**15.99** When acetylcholine is released from a nerve cell, it binds to receptors on the surface of muscle cells. This binding stimulates the muscle cell to contract. To stop the contraction, the acetylcholine is then broken down to choline and acetate ion. This is catalyzed by the enzyme acetylcholinesterase.

**15.101** Organophosphates inactivate acetylcholinesterase by binding covalently to it. Since acetylcholine is not broken down, nerve transmission continues, resulting in muscle spasm. Pyridine aldoxime methiodide (PAM) is an antidote to organophosphate poisoning because it displaces the organophosphate, thereby allowing acetycholinesterase to function.

# Chapter 16

**16.1** It is currently recommended that 45–55% of the calories in the diet should be carbohydrates. Of that amount, the World Health Organization recommends that no more than 5% should be simple sugars.

**16.3** An aldose is a sugar with an aldehyde functional group. A ketose is a sugar with a ketone functional group.

**16.5** **a.**

**b.**

**c.**

**16.7** **a.** D-
   **b.** L-
   **c.** D-

**16.9**

D-Galactose

**16.11** α-Amylase and β-amylase are digestive enzymes that break down the starch amylose. α-Amylase cleaves glycosidic bonds of the amylose chain at random, producing shorter polysaccharide chains. β-Amylase sequentially cleaves maltose (a disaccharide of glucose) from the reducing end of the polysaccharide chain.

**16.13** A monosaccharide is the simplest sugar and consists of a single saccharide unit. A disaccharide is made up of two monosaccharides joined covalently by a glycosidic bond.

**16.15** Mashed potato flakes, rice, and corn starch contain amylose and amylopectin, both of which are polysaccharides. A candy bar contains sucrose, a disaccharide. Orange juice contains fructose, a monosaccharide. It may also contain sucrose if the label indicates that sugar has been added.

**16.17** Four

**16.19**

D-Galactose          D-Fructose
(An aldohexose)      (A ketohexose)

**16.21** An aldose is a sugar that contains an aldehyde (carbonyl) group.

**16.23** A tetrose is a sugar with a four-carbon backbone.

**16.25** A ketopentose is a sugar with a five-carbon backbone and containing a ketone (carbonyl) group.

**16.27** **a.** β-D-Glucose
   **b.** β-D-Fructose
   **c.** α-D-Galactose

**16.29**

D-Glyceraldehyde          L-Glyceraldehyde

**16.31** Stereoisomers are a pair of molecules that have the same structural formula and bonding pattern but that differ in the arrangement of the atoms in space.

**16.33** A chiral carbon is one that is bonded to four different chemical groups.

**16.35** A polarimeter converts monochromatic light into monochromatic plane-polarized light. This plane-polarized light is passed through a sample and into an analyzer. If the sample is optically active, it will rotate the plane of the light. The degree and angle of rotation are measured by the analyzer.

**16.37** A Fischer Projection is a two-dimensional drawing of a molecule that shows a chiral carbon at the intersection of two lines. Horizontal lines at the intersection represent bonds projecting out of the page, and vertical lines represent bonds that project into the page.

**16.39** Diastereomers are a pair of stereoisomers that are not enantiomers.

**16.41**

Sorbitol          Mannitol

**16.43** Dextrose is a common name used for D-glucose.

**16.45** D- and L-Glyceraldehyde are a pair of enantiomers; that is, they are nonsuperimposable mirror images of one another.

**16.47** **a.**          **b.**          **c.**

**16.49 a.**

The stereoisomers are A, C, and D. Compounds A and B are identical and they are meso compounds because they have an internal plane of symmetry. Compounds C and D are enantiomers. Compound A is a diastereomer to both compounds C and D.

**b.**

There are four possible stereoisomers. The two pairs of enantiomers are A with B and C with D. Compounds A and B are both diastereomers to compounds C and D.

**16.51 a.**

The stereoisomers are A, C, and D. Compounds A and B are identical and they are meso compounds because they have an internal plane of symmetry. Compounds C and D are enantiomers. Compound A is a diastereomer to both compounds C and D.

**b.**

There are four possible stereoisomers. Compounds A and B are enantiomers, and compounds C and D are enantiomers. Compounds A and B are diastereomers to both compounds C and D.

**16.53** Anomers are isomers that differ in the arrangement of bonds around the hemiacetal carbon.

**16.55** A hemiacetal is a member of the family of organic compounds formed in the reaction of one molecule of alcohol with an aldehyde or a ketone.

**16.57** When the carbonyl group at C-1 of D-glucose reacts with the C-5 hydroxyl group, a new chiral carbon is created (C-1). In the α-isomer of the cyclic sugar, the C-1 hydroxyl group is below the ring; and in the β-isomer, the C-1 hydroxyl group is above the ring.

**16.59** β-Maltose and α-lactose would give positive Benedict's tests. Glycogen would give only a weak reaction because there are fewer reducing ends for a given mass of the carbohydrate.

**16.61** Enantiomers are stereoisomers that are nonsuperimposable mirror images of one another. For instance:

D-Glyceraldehyde          L-Glyceraldehyde

**16.63** An aldehyde sugar forms an intramolecular hemiacetal when the carbonyl group of the monosaccharide reacts with a hydroxyl group on one of the other carbon atoms.

**16.65** A disaccharide is a simple carbohydrate composed of two monosaccharides.

**16.67** A glycosidic bond is the bond formed between the hydroxyl group of the C-1 carbon of one sugar and a hydroxyl group of another sugar.

**16.69**

β-Maltose

**16.71** Milk

**16.73** Eliminating milk and milk products from the diet

**16.75** Lactose intolerance is the inability to produce the enzyme lactase that hydrolyzes the milk sugar lactose into its component monosaccharides: glucose and galactose.

**16.77** A polymer is a very large molecule formed by the combination of many small molecules, called monomers.

**16.79** Starch

**16.81** Homopolysaccharides are a class of polysaccharides that are composed of a single monosaccharide.

**16.83** Starch, glycogen, and cellulose are examples of homopolysaccharides. These homopolysaccharides are all made up of glucose.

**16.85** The glucose units of amylose are joined by α $(1 \rightarrow 4)$ glycosidic bonds and those of cellulose are bonded together by β $(1 \rightarrow 4)$ glycosidic bonds.

**16.87** Glycogen serves as a storage molecule for glucose.

**16.89** The salivary glands and the pancreas

## Chapter 17

**17.1  a.** $CH_3(CH_2)_7CH = CH(CH_2)_7COOH$
   **b.** $CH_3(CH_2)_{10}COOH$
   **c.** $CH_3(CH_2)_4CH = CH—CH_2—CH = CH(CH_2)_7COOH$
   **d.** $CH_3(CH_2)_{16}COOH$

**17.3**

Tetradecanoic acid    Ethanol    Ethyl tetradecanoate

**17.5**

Pentyl butanoate

Butanoic acid    1-Pentanol

**17.7**

$$CH_3\overset{O}{\overset{\|}{C}}-O-CH_2(CH_2)_2CH_3 \ + \ KOH \ \rightarrow$$

Butyl acetate

$$CH_3\overset{O}{\overset{\|}{C}}-O^- K^+ \ + \ CH_3(CH_2)_2CH_2OH$$

Potassium          1-Butanol
acetate

**17.9**

$$CH_3CH_2CH=CHCH_2CH=CHCH_2CH=CH(CH_2)_7COOH \ + \ 3H_2$$

All *cis*-9,12,15-Octadecatrienoic acid

$$\downarrow Ni$$

$$CH_3(CH_2)_{16}COOH$$

Octadecanoic acid

**17.11**    **a.** $CH_3(CH_2)_7CH=CH(CH_2)_7-\overset{}{C}-O-CH_2$
$\overset{\|}{O}$

$CH-OH$

$CH_2-OH$

$CH_3(CH_2)_7CH=CH(CH_2)_7-\overset{}{C}-O-CH_2$
$\overset{\|}{O}$

$CH_3(CH_2)_7CH=CH(CH_2)_7-\overset{}{C}-O-CH$
$\overset{\|}{O}$

$CH_2-OH$

$CH_3(CH_2)_7CH=CH(CH_2)_7-\overset{}{C}-O-CH_2$
$\overset{\|}{O}$

$CH_3(CH_2)_7CH=CH(CH_2)_7-\overset{}{C}-O-CH$
$\overset{\|}{O}$

$CH_3(CH_2)_7CH=CH(CH_2)_7-\overset{}{C}-O-CH_2$
$\overset{\|}{O}$

**b.** $CH_3(CH_2)_8-\overset{}{C}-O-CH_2$
$\overset{\|}{O}$

$CH-OH$

$CH_2-OH$

$CH_3(CH_2)_8-\overset{}{C}-O-CH_2$
$\overset{\|}{O}$

$CH_3(CH_2)_8-\overset{}{C}-O-CH$
$\overset{\|}{O}$

$CH_2-OH$

$CH_3(CH_2)_8-\overset{}{C}-O-CH_2$
$\overset{\|}{O}$

$CH_3(CH_2)_8-\overset{}{C}-O-CH$
$\overset{\|}{O}$

$CH_3(CH_2)_8-\overset{}{C}-O-CH_2$
$\overset{\|}{O}$

**17.13**

Steroid nucleus

**17.15**  Receptor-mediated endocytosis

**17.17**  Fatty acids, glycerides, nonglyceride lipids, and complex lipids

**17.19**  Lipid-soluble vitamins are transported into cells of the small intestine in association with dietary fat molecules. Thus, a diet low in fat reduces the amount of vitamins A, D, E, and K that enters the body.

**17.21**  A saturated fatty acid is one in which the hydrocarbon tail has only carbon-to-carbon single bonds. An unsaturated fatty acid has at least one carbon-to-carbon double bond.

**17.23**  The melting points increase.

**17.25**  The melting points of fatty acids increase as the length of the hydrocarbon chains increase. This is because the intermolecular attractive forces, including London dispersion forces, increase as the length of the hydrocarbon chain increases.

**17.27**  **a.** Decanoic acid $CH_3(CH_2)_8COOH$
**b.** Stearic acid    $CH_3(CH_2)_{16}COOH$

**17.29**  **a.** IUPAC name: Hexadecanoic acid
Common name: Palmitic acid
**b.** IUPAC name: Dodecanoic acid
Common name: Lauric acid

**17.31**  Esterification of glycerol with three molecules of myristic acid:

$$\begin{array}{l} CH_2OH \\ CHOH \\ CH_2OH \end{array} + 3\ CH_3(CH_2)_{12}-\overset{O}{\overset{\|}{C}}-OH \longrightarrow$$

$$CH_3(CH_2)_{12}-\overset{O}{\overset{\|}{C}}-O-CH_2$$
$$CH_3(CH_2)_{12}-\overset{O}{\overset{\|}{C}}-O-CH \ + 3H_2O$$
$$CH_3(CH_2)_{12}-\overset{O}{\overset{\|}{C}}-O-CH_2$$

**17.33**

$$H-\overset{H}{\underset{}{C}}-O-\overset{O}{\overset{\|}{C}}-(CH_2)_7CH=CH(CH_2)_7CH_3$$
$$H-\overset{}{\underset{}{C}}-O-\overset{O}{\overset{\|}{C}}-(CH_2)_7CH=CH(CH_2)_7CH_3 \ + 3H_2O$$
$$H-\overset{}{\underset{H}{C}}-O-\overset{O}{\overset{\|}{C}}-(CH_2)_7CH=CH(CH_2)_7CH_3$$

$$\downarrow H^+, heat$$

$$H-\overset{H}{\underset{}{C}}-OH \ + \ HO-\overset{O}{\overset{\|}{C}}-(CH_2)_7CH=CH(CH_2)_7CH_3$$
$$H-\overset{}{\underset{}{C}}-OH \ + \ HO-\overset{O}{\overset{\|}{C}}-(CH_2)_7CH=CH(CH_2)_7CH_3$$
$$H-\overset{}{\underset{H}{C}}-OH \ + \ HO-\overset{O}{\overset{\|}{C}}-(CH_2)_7CH=CH(CH_2)_7CH_3$$

Glycerol          3 Oleic acid molecules

**17.35**

$HO-\overset{O}{\overset{\|}{C}}-(CH_2)_6CH_3$ $\xrightarrow{KOH}$ $K^+\ ^-O-\overset{O}{\overset{\|}{C}}-(CH_2)_6CH_3$

Octanoic acid                    Potassium octanoate

$HO-\overset{O}{\overset{\|}{C}}-(CH_2)_{16}CH_3$ $\xrightarrow{KOH}$ $K^+\ ^-O-\overset{O}{\overset{\|}{C}}-(CH_2)_{16}CH_3$

Stearic acid                    Potassium stearate

**17.37**  This line drawing of EPA shows the bends or "kinks" introduced into the molecule by the double bonds.

All *cis*-5,8,11,14,17-Eicosapentaenoic acid (EPA)

$+ 5H_2 \Big| Ni$

Eicosanoic acid

**17.39**

$H-\overset{H}{\underset{|}{C}}-O-\overset{O}{\overset{\|}{C}}-(CH_2)_{10}CH_3$   Lauric acid

$H-\overset{|}{\underset{|}{C}}-O-\overset{O}{\overset{\|}{C}}-(CH_2)_{16}CH_3$   Stearic acid

$H-\overset{|}{\underset{|}{\underset{H}{C}}}-O-\overset{O}{\overset{\|}{C}}-(CH_2)_8CH_3$   Capric acid

$\Big| NaOH$

$H-\overset{H}{\underset{|}{C}}-OH\ +\ Na^+\ ^-O-\overset{O}{\overset{\|}{C}}-(CH_2)_{10}CH_3$

$H-\overset{|}{\underset{|}{C}}-OH\ +\ Na^+\ ^-O-\overset{O}{\overset{\|}{C}}-(CH_2)_{16}CH_3$

$H-\overset{|}{\underset{H}{\underset{|}{C}}}-OH\ +\ Na^+\ ^-O-\overset{O}{\overset{\|}{C}}-(CH_2)_8CH_3$

**17.41**

$H-\overset{H}{\underset{|}{C}}-OH\ +\ HO-\overset{O}{\overset{\|}{C}}-(CH_2)_8CH_3$   Decanoic acid

$H-\overset{|}{\underset{|}{C}}-OH\ +\ HO-\overset{O}{\overset{\|}{C}}-(CH_2)_{10}CH_3$   Dodecanoic acid

$H-\overset{|}{\underset{H}{\underset{|}{C}}}-OH\ +\ HO-\overset{O}{\overset{\|}{C}}-(CH_2)_{14}CH_3$   Hexadecanoic acid

Glycerol

$\Big\downarrow H^+, heat$

$H-\overset{H}{\underset{|}{C}}-O-\overset{O}{\overset{\|}{C}}-(CH_2)_8CH_3$

$H-\overset{|}{\underset{|}{C}}-O-\overset{O}{\overset{\|}{C}}-(CH_2)_{10}CH_3\ +\ 3H_2O$

$H-\overset{|}{\underset{|}{C}}-O-\overset{O}{\overset{\|}{C}}-(CH_2)_{14}CH_3$

$\overset{|}{H}$

**17.43**  The essential fatty acid linoleic acid is required for the synthesis of arachidonic acid, a precursor for the synthesis of the prostaglandins, a group of hormonelike molecules.

**17.45**  Aspirin effectively decreases the inflammatory response by inhibiting the synthesis of all prostaglandins. Aspirin works by inhibiting cyclooxygenase, the first enzyme in prostaglandin biosynthesis. This inhibition results from the transfer of an acetyl group from aspirin to the enzyme. Because cyclooxygenase is found in all cells, synthesis of all prostaglandins is inhibited.

**17.47**  Smooth muscle contraction, enhancement of fever and swelling associated with the inflammatory response, bronchial dilation, inhibition of secretion of acid into the stomach

**17.49**  The name of these fatty acids arises from the position of the double bond nearest the terminal *methyl group* of the molecule. The terminal methyl group is designated omega ($\omega$). In $\omega$-3 fatty acids, the double bond nearest the $\omega$ methyl group is three carbons along the chain. In $\omega$-6 fatty acids, the nearest double bond is six carbons from the end.

**17.51**  Omega-3 fatty acids reduce the risk of cardiovascular disease by decreasing blood clot formation, blood triglyceride levels, and growth of atherosclerotic plaque.

**17.53**  The decrease in blood clot formation, along with the reduced blood triglyceride levels and decreased atherosclerotic plaque result in improved arterial health. This, in turn, results in lower blood pressure and a decreased risk of sudden death and heart arrhythmias.

**17.55**  Omega-3 fatty acids are precursors of prostaglandins that exhibit anti-inflammatory effects. On the other hand, omega-6 fatty acids are precursors to prostaglandins that have inflammatory effects. To reduce the inflammatory response contribution to cardiovascular disease, it is logical to increase the amount of omega-3 fatty acids in the diet and to decrease the amount of omega-6 fatty acids.

**17.57**  A glyceride is a lipid ester that contains the glycerol molecule and from one to three fatty acids.

**17.59**  An emulsifying agent is a molecule that aids in the suspension of triglycerides in water. They are amphipathic molecules, such as lecithin, that serve as bridges holding together the highly polar water molecules and the nonpolar triglycerides.

**17.61**  A triglyceride with three saturated fatty acid tails would be a solid at room temperature. The long, straight fatty acid tails would stack with one another because of strong intermolecular and intramolecular London dispersion force attractions.

**17.63**

$$CH_3(CH_2)_{14}-\overset{O}{\overset{\|}{C}}-O-\underset{1}{CH_2}$$

$$\underset{CH_3(CH_2)_4CH_2}{\overset{H}{\diagdown}}C=C\overset{CH_2(CH_2)_6-\overset{O}{\overset{\|}{C}}-O-\underset{2}{CH}}{\diagup}$$

$$\underset{CH_3(CH_2)_4CH_2}{\diagdown}C=C\underset{H}{\overset{CH_2(CH_2)_6-\overset{O}{\overset{\|}{C}}-O-\underset{3}{CH_2}}{\diagup}}$$

**17.65**

$$CH_3CH_2CH_2CH_2CH_2CH_2CH_2CH_2CH_2-\overset{O}{\overset{\|}{C}}-O-\underset{1}{CH_2}$$

$$CH_3CH_2CH_2CH_2CH_2CH_2CH_2CH_2CH_2CH_2-\underset{\overset{\|}{O}}{\overset{}{C}}-O-\underset{2}{CH}$$

$$\underset{3}{CH_2}-O-\overset{O}{\underset{O^-}{\overset{\|}{P}}}-O^-$$

**17.67** Triglycerides consist of three fatty acids esterified to the three hydroxyl groups of glycerol. In phospholipids, there are only two fatty acids esterified to glycerol. A phosphoryl group is esterified (phosphoester linkage) to the third hydroxyl group.

**17.69** A sphingolipid is a lipid that is not derived from glycerol, but rather from sphingosine, a long-chain, nitrogen-containing (amino) alcohol. Like phospholipids, sphingolipids are amphipathic.

**17.71** A glycosphingolipid or glycolipid is a lipid that is built on a ceramide backbone structure. Ceramide is a fatty acid derivative of sphingosine.

**17.73** Sphingomyelins are important structural lipid components of nerve cell membranes. They are found in the myelin sheath that surrounds and insulates cells of the central nervous system.

**17.75** Cholesterol is readily soluble in the hydrophobic region of biological membranes. It is involved in regulating the fluidity of the membrane.

**17.77** Progesterone is the most important hormone associated with pregnancy. Testosterone is needed for development of male secondary sexual characteristics. Estrone is required for proper development of female secondary sexual characteristics.

**17.79** Cortisone is used to treat rheumatoid arthritis, asthma, gastrointestinal disorders, and many skin conditions.

**17.81** Myricyl palmitate (beeswax) is made up of the fatty acid palmitic acid and the alcohol myricyl alcohol—$CH_3(CH_2)_{28}CH_2OH$.

**17.83** Isoprenoids are a large, diverse collection of lipids that are synthesized from the isoprene unit:

$$CH_2=\overset{\overset{CH_3}{|}}{C}-CH=CH_2$$

**17.85** Steroids and bile salts, lipid-soluble vitamins, certain plant hormones, and chlorophyll

**17.87** Chylomicrons, high-density lipoproteins, low-density lipoproteins, and very low density lipoproteins

**17.89** The terms "good" and "bad" cholesterol refer to two classes of lipoprotein complexes. The high-density lipoproteins, or HDL, are considered to be "good" cholesterol because a correlation has been made between elevated levels of HDL and a reduced incidence of atherosclerosis. Low-density lipoproteins, or LDL, are considered

to be "bad" cholesterol because evidence suggests that a high level of LDL is associated with increased risk of atherosclerosis.

**17.91** Atherosclerosis results when cholesterol and other substances coat the arteries, causing a narrowing of the passageways. As the passageways become narrower, greater pressure is required to provide adequate blood flow. This results in higher blood pressure (hypertension).

**17.93** If the LDL receptor is defective, it cannot function to remove cholesterol-bearing LDL particles from the blood. The excess cholesterol, along with other substances, will accumulate along the walls of the arteries, causing atherosclerosis.

**17.95** The basic structure of a biological membrane is a bilayer of phospholipid molecules arranged so that the hydrophobic hydrocarbon tails are packed in the center and the hydrophilic head groups are exposed on the inner and outer surfaces.

**17.97** A peripheral membrane protein is bound to only one surface of the membrane, either inside or outside the cell.

**17.99** Cholesterol is freely soluble in the hydrophobic layer of a biological membrane. It moderates the fluidity of the membrane by disrupting the stacking of the fatty acid tails of membrane phospholipids.

**17.101** Specific membrane proteins on human and mouse cells were labeled with red and green fluorescent dyes, respectively. The human and mouse cells were fused into single-celled hybrids and were observed using a microscope with an ultraviolet light source. The ultraviolet light caused the dyes to fluoresce. Initially, the dyes were localized in regions of the membrane representing the original human or mouse cell. Within an hour, the proteins were evenly distributed throughout the membrane of the fused cell.

**17.103** If the fatty acid tails of the membrane phospholipids are converted from saturated to unsaturated, the fluidity of the membrane will increase.

## Chapter 18

**18.1** **a.** Glycine (gly or G):

$$H_3^+N-\overset{\overset{COO^-}{|}}{\underset{\underset{H}{|}}{C}}-H$$

**b.** Proline (pro or P):

$$H_2^+N\overset{\overset{COO^-}{|}}{-}\overset{|}{\underset{\underset{H_2}{H_2C}\diagdown_C\diagup CH_2}{CH}}$$

**c.** Threonine (thr or T):

$$H_3^+N-\overset{\overset{COO^-}{|}}{\underset{\underset{\underset{CH_3}{|}}{H-C-OH}}{C}}-H$$

**d.** Aspartate (asp or D):

$$H_3^+N-\overset{\overset{COO^-}{|}}{\underset{\underset{\underset{COO^-}{|}}{H-C-H}}{C}}-H$$

**e.** Lysine (lys or K):

$$
\begin{array}{c}
COO^- \\
| \\
H_3^+N-C-H \\
| \\
H-C-H \\
| \\
H-C-H \\
| \\
H-C-H \\
| \\
H-C-H \\
| \\
N^+H_3
\end{array}
$$

**18.3**   **a.** Alanyl-phenylalanine:

$$
H_3^+N-\overset{\overset{\displaystyle H}{|}}{C}-\overset{\overset{\displaystyle O}{||}}{C}-\overset{\overset{\displaystyle H}{|}}{N}-\overset{\overset{\displaystyle H}{|}}{C}-COO^-
$$

with $CH_3$ on first $C$ and $CH_2$ (attached to a benzene ring) on the second $C$.

**b.** Lysyl-alanine:

$$
H_3^+N-\overset{\overset{\displaystyle H}{|}}{C}-\overset{\overset{\displaystyle O}{||}}{C}-\overset{\overset{\displaystyle H}{|}}{N}-\overset{\overset{\displaystyle H}{|}}{C}-COO^-
$$

with side chains $CH_2CH_2CH_2CH_2N^+H_3$ and $CH_3$.

**c.** Phenylalanyl-tyrosyl-leucine:

$$
H_3^+N-\overset{H}{\underset{CH_2}{C}}-\overset{O}{C}-N-\overset{H}{\underset{CH_2}{C}}-\overset{O}{C}-N-\overset{H}{\underset{CH_2}{C}}-COO^-
$$

first $CH_2$ attached to a benzene ring; second $CH_2$ attached to a benzene ring with $OH$; third side chain $CH_2CHCH_3$ with $CH_3$.

**18.5**   The primary structure of a protein is the amino acid sequence of the protein chain. Regular, repeating folding of the peptide chain caused by hydrogen bonding between the amide nitrogens and carbonyl oxygens of the peptide bond is the secondary structure of a protein. The two most common types of secondary structure are the α-helix and the β-pleated sheet. Tertiary structure is the further folding of the regions of the α-helix and β-pleated sheet into a compact, spherical structure. Formation and maintenance of the tertiary structure results from weak attractions between amino acid R groups. The binding of two or more peptides to produce a functional protein defines the quaternary structure.

**18.7**   Oxygen is efficiently transferred from hemoglobin to myoglobin in the muscle because myoglobin has a greater affinity for oxygen.

**18.9**   High temperature disrupts the hydrogen bonds and other weak interactions that maintain protein structure.

**18.11**   Vegetables vary in amino acid composition. Most vegetables do not provide all of the amino acid requirements of the body. By eating a variety of different vegetables, all the amino acid requirements of the human body can be met.

**18.13**   An enzyme is a protein that serves as a biological catalyst, speeding up biological reactions.

**18.15**   A transport protein is a protein that transports materials across the cell membrane or throughout the body.

**18.17**   Enzymes speed up reactions that might take days or weeks to occur on their own. They also catalyze reactions that might require very high temperatures or harsh conditions if carried out in the laboratory. In the body, these reactions occur quickly under physiological conditions.

**18.19**   Transferrin is a transport protein that carries iron from the liver to the bone marrow, where it is used to produce the heme group for hemoglobin and myoglobin. Hemoglobin transports oxygen in the blood.

**18.21**   Egg albumin is a nutrient protein that serves as a source of protein for the developing chick. Casein is the nutrient storage protein in milk, providing protein, a source of amino acids, for mammals.

**18.23**   The general structure of an L-α-amino acid has a carbon in the center that is referred to as the alpha carbon. Bonded to the alpha carbon are a protonated amino group, a carboxylate group, a hydrogen atom, and a side chain, R.

$$
\begin{array}{c}
COO^- \\
| \\
H_3^+N-C-H \\
| \\
R
\end{array}
$$

**18.25**   A zwitterion is a neutral molecule with equal numbers of positive and negative charges. Under physiological conditions, amino acids are zwitterions.

**18.27**   A chiral carbon is one that has four different atoms or groups of atoms attached to it.

**18.29**   Interactions between the R groups of the amino acids in a polypeptide chain are important for the formation and maintenance of the tertiary and quaternary structures of proteins.

**18.31**

$$
\begin{array}{c}
COO^- \\
| \\
H_3^+N-C-H \\
| \\
CH_2 \\
| \\
OH
\end{array}
$$

L-Serine

$$
\begin{array}{c}
COO^- \\
| \\
H_3^+N-C-H \\
| \\
H-C-OH \\
| \\
CH_3
\end{array}
$$

L-Threonine

$$
\begin{array}{c}
COO^- \\
| \\
H_3^+N-C-H \\
| \\
CH_2 \\
| \\
SH
\end{array}
$$

L-Cysteine

$$
\begin{array}{c}
COO^- \\
| \\
H_3^+N-C-H \\
| \\
CH_2
\end{array}
$$
(attached to benzene ring with OH)

L-Tyrosine

$$
\begin{array}{c}
COO^- \\
| \\
H_3^+N-C-H \\
| \\
CH_2 \\
| \\
C(=O)NH_2
\end{array}
$$

L-Asparagine

$$
\begin{array}{c}
COO^- \\
| \\
H_3^+N-C-H \\
| \\
CH_2 \\
| \\
CH_2 \\
| \\
C(=O)NH_2
\end{array}
$$

L-Glutamine

**18.33**   A peptide bond is an amide bond between two amino acids in a peptide chain.

**18.35**   Linus Pauling and his colleagues carried out X-ray diffraction studies of protein. Interpretation of the pattern formed when X-rays were diffracted by a crystal of pure protein led Pauling to conclude that peptide bonds are both planar (flat) and rigid and that the N—C bonds are shorter than expected. In other words, they deduced that the peptide bond has a partial double bond character because it exhibits resonance. There is no free rotation about the amide bond because the carbonyl group of the amide bond has a strong attraction for the amide nitrogen lone pair of electrons.

**18.37**

a. $H_3^+N$—CH—C(=O)—N(H)—CH—C(=O)—N(H)—CH—C(=O)—O$^-$

with CH$_2$ (benzene ring), CH—CH$_3$ / CH$_3$, CH$_2$ (benzene ring with OH)

b. $H_3^+N$—CH—C(=O)—N(H)—CH—C(=O)—N(H)—CH—C(=O)—O$^-$

with CH$_3$; CH$_2$—CH$_2$—C(=O)—O$^-$; CH$_2$—SH

c. $H_3^+N$—CH—C(=O)—N(H)—CH—C(=O)—N(H)—CH—C(=O)—O$^-$

with CH$_2$—C(=O)—NH$_2$; CH$_2$—CH—CH$_3$/CH$_3$; H

**18.39** The primary structure of a protein is the sequence of amino acids bonded to one another by peptide bonds.

**18.41** The primary structure of a protein determines its three-dimensional shape and biological function because the location of R groups along the protein chain is determined by the primary structure. The interactions among the R groups, based on their location in the chain, will govern how the protein folds. This, in turn, dictates its three-dimensional structure and biological function.

**18.43**

$H_3^+N$—CH—C(=O)—O$^-$ (CH$_2$, CH—CH$_3$, CH$_3$) + $H_3^+N$—CH—C(=O)—O$^-$ (CH$_2$, CH$_2$, CH$_2$, NH, C=NH$_2^+$, NH$_2$) ⟶ $H_3^+N$—CH—C(=O)—N(H)—CH—C(=O)—O$^-$ (CH$_2$, CH—CH$_3$, CH$_3$; CH$_2$, CH$_2$, CH$_2$, NH, C=NH$_2^+$, NH$_2$) + $H_2O$

**18.45** The secondary structure of a protein is the folding of the primary structure into an α-helix or β-pleated sheet.

**18.47** a. α-Helix
b. β-Pleated sheet

**18.49** A fibrous protein is one that is composed of peptides arranged in long sheets or fibers.

**18.51** A parallel β-pleated sheet is one in which the hydrogen bonded peptide chains have their amino-termini aligned head-to-head.

**18.53** The tertiary structure of a protein is the globular, three-dimensional structure of a protein that results from folding the regions of secondary structure.

**18.55**

COO$^-$
|
$H_3^+N$—C—H
|
CH$_2$
|
S
|
S
|
CH$_2$
|
$H_3^+N$—C—H
|
COO$^-$

**18.57** The tertiary structure is a level of folding of a protein chain that has already undergone secondary folding. The regions of α-helix and β-pleated sheet are folded into a globular structure.

**18.59** Quaternary protein structure is the aggregation of two or more folded peptide chains to produce a functional protein.

**18.61** A glycoprotein is a protein with covalently attached sugars.

**18.63** Hydrogen bonding maintains the secondary structure of a protein and contributes to the stability of the tertiary and quaternary levels of structure.

**18.65** The peptide bond exhibits resonance, which results in a partially double bonded character. This causes the rigidity of the peptide bond.

[ R—C(=Ö)—N(H)—R′  ⟷  R—C(=Ö:$^-$)—N$^+$(H)—R′ ]

**18.67** The code for the primary structure of a protein is carried in the genetic information (DNA).

**18.69** The function of hemoglobin is to carry oxygen from the lungs to oxygen-demanding tissues throughout the body. Hemoglobin is found in red blood cells.

**18.71** Hemoglobin is a protein composed of four subunits—two α-globin and two β-globin subunits. Each subunit holds a heme group, which in turn carries an $Fe^{2+}$ ion.

**18.73** The function of the heme group in hemoglobin and myoglobin is to bind to molecular oxygen.

**18.75** Because carbon monoxide binds tightly to the heme groups of hemoglobin, it is not easily removed or replaced by oxygen. As a result, the effects of oxygen deprivation (suffocation) occur.

**18.77** When sickle cell hemoglobin (HbS) is deoxygenated, the amino acid valine fits into a hydrophobic pocket on the surface of another HbS molecule. Many such sickle cell hemoglobin molecules polymerize into long rods that cause the red blood cell to sickle. In normal hemoglobin, glutamic acid is found in the place of the valine. This negatively charged amino acid will not "fit" into the hydrophobic pocket.

**18.79** When individuals have one copy of the sickle cell gene and one copy of the normal gene, they are said to carry the sickle cell trait. These individuals will not suffer serious side effects, but may pass the trait to their offspring. Individuals with two copies of the sickle cell globin gene exhibit all the symptoms of the disease and are said to have sickle cell anemia.

**18.81** Albumin

**18.83** Albumin in the blood can serve as a carrier for $Ca^{2+}$ because it contains acidic amino acids. The negative charges in the acidic amino acids can form salt bridges (or ionic bonds) with $Ca^{2+}$. Albumin can also serve as a carrier for fatty acids because it contains basic amino acids. The positive charges in the basic amino acids can form salt bridges with the anionic fatty acids.

**18.85** Denaturation is the process by which the organized structure of a protein is disrupted, resulting in a completely disorganized, nonfunctional form of the protein.

**18.87** Heat is an effective means of sterilization because it destroys the proteins of microbial life-forms, including fungi, bacteria, and viruses.

**18.89** The low pH of the yogurt denatures the proteins of microbial contaminants, inhibiting their growth.

**18.91** An essential amino acid is one that must be provided in the diet because it cannot be synthesized in the body.

**18.93** A complete protein is one that contains all of the essential and nonessential amino acids.

**18.95** Chymotrypsin catalyzes the hydrolysis of peptide bonds on the carbonyl side of aromatic amino acids.

Site of chymotrypsin-catalyzed hydrolysis

Phenylalanyl-alanine + $H_2O$ ⟶

⟶ Phenylalanine + Alanine

**18.97** In a vegetarian diet, vegetables are the only source of dietary protein. Because most individual vegetable sources do not provide all the needed amino acids, vegetables must be mixed to provide all the essential and nonessential amino acids in the amounts required for biosynthesis.

**18.99** Synthesis of digestive enzymes must be carefully controlled because the active enzyme would digest, and thus destroy, the cell that produces it.

# Chapter 19

**19.1  a.** Pyruvate kinase catalyzes the transfer of a phosphoryl group from phosphoenolpyruvate to adenosine diphosphate.

Phosphoenolpyruvate ⟶ (ADP, ATP, Pyruvate kinase) ⟶ Pyruvate

**b.** Alanine transaminase catalyzes the transfer of an amino group from alanine to α-ketoglutarate, producing pyruvate and glutamate.

Alanine + α-Ketoglutarate ⟶ (Alanine transaminase) ⟶ Pyruvate + Glutamate

**c.** Triose phosphate isomerase catalyzes the isomerization of the ketone dihydroxyacetone phosphate to the aldehyde glyceraldehyde-3-phosphate.

Dihydroxyacetone phosphate ⟶ (Triose phosphate isomerase) ⟶ Glyceraldehyde-3-phosphate

**d.** Pyruvate dehydrogenase catalyzes the oxidation and decarboxylation of pyruvate, producing acetyl coenzyme A and $CO_2$.

Pyruvate + H-S-CoA ⟶ (Pyruvate dehydrogenase) ⟶ $H_3C-C-S\text{~}CoA + CO_2$ (Acetyl coenzyme A)

**19.3  a.** Sucrose

 **b.** Pyruvate

 **c.** Succinate

**19.5** The induced fit model assumes that the enzyme is flexible. Both the enzyme and the substrate are able to change shape to form the enzyme-substrate complex. The lock-and-key model assumes that the enzyme is inflexible (the lock) and the substrate (the key) fits into a specific rigid site (the active site) on the enzyme to form the enzyme-substrate complex.

**19.7** An enzyme might distort a bond, thereby catalyzing bond breakage. An enzyme could bring two reactants into close proximity and in the proper orientation for the reaction to occur. Finally, an enzyme could alter the pH of the microenvironment of the active site, thereby serving as a transient donor or acceptor of $H^+$.

**19.9** Water-soluble vitamins are required by the body for the synthesis of coenzymes that are required for the function of a variety of enzymes.

**19.11** A decrease in pH will change the degree of ionization of the R groups within a peptide chain. This disturbs the weak interactions that maintain the structure of an enzyme, which may denature the enzyme. Less drastic alterations in the charge of R groups in the active site of the enzyme can inhibit enzyme-substrate binding or destroy the catalytic ability of the active site.

**19.13** Irreversible inhibitors bind very tightly, sometimes even covalently, to an R group in enzyme active sites. They generally inhibit many different enzymes. The loss of enzyme activity impairs normal cellular metabolism, resulting in the death of the cell or the individual.

**19.15** A structural analog is a molecule that has a structure and charge distribution very similar to that of the natural substrate of an enzyme. Generally, they are able to bind to the enzyme active site. This inhibits enzyme activity because the normal substrate must compete with the structural analog to form an enzyme-substrate complex.

**19.17 a.**

Bond cleaved by chymotrypsin

$H_3N^+$—C—C—N—C—C—N—C—COO$^-$

ala-phe-ala

**b.**

Bond cleaved by chymotrypsin

$H_3N^+$—C—C—N—C—C—N—C—COO$^-$

tyr-ala-tyr

**19.19**

Chymotrypsin   Elastase   Elastase

$H_3^+N$—C—C—N—C—C—N—C—C—N—C—C—N—C—COO$^-$

**19.21** The common name of an enzyme is often derived from the name of the substrate and/or the type of reaction that it catalyzes.

**19.23** 1. Urease
2. Peroxidase
3. Lipase
4. Aspartase
5. Glucose-6-phosphatase
6. Sucrase

**19.25 a.** Citrate decarboxylase catalyzes the cleavage of a carboxyl group from citrate.
**b.** Adenosine diphosphate phosphorylase catalyzes the addition of a phosphate group to ADP.
**c.** Oxalate reductase catalyzes the reduction of oxalate.
**d.** Nitrite oxidase catalyzes the oxidation of nitrite.
**e.** *cis-trans* Isomerase catalyzes interconversion of *cis* and *trans* isomers.

**19.27** A substrate is the reactant in an enzyme-catalyzed reaction that binds to the active site of the enzyme and is converted into product.

**19.29** The activation energy of a reaction is the energy required for the reaction to occur.

**19.31** The equilibrium constant for a chemical reaction is a reflection of the difference in energy of the reactants and products. Consider the following reaction:

$$aA + bB \longrightarrow cC + dD$$

The equilibrium constant for this reaction is:

$$K_{eq} = [D]^d[C]^c/[A]^a[B]^b = [products]/[reactants]$$

Because the difference in energy between reactants and products is the same regardless of what path the reaction takes, an enzyme does not alter the equilibrium constant of a reaction.

**19.33** The rate of an uncatalyzed chemical reaction typically doubles every time the substrate concentration is doubled.

**19.35** The rate-limiting step is that step in an enzyme-catalyzed reaction that is the slowest, and hence limits the speed with which the substrate can be converted into product.

**19.37**

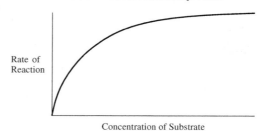

Rate of Reaction

Concentration of Substrate

**19.39** The enzyme-substrate complex is the molecular aggregate formed when the substrate binds to the active site of an enzyme.

**19.41** The catalytic groups of an enzyme active site are those functional groups that are involved in carrying out catalysis.

**19.43** Enzyme active sites are pockets in the surface of an enzyme that include R groups involved in binding and R groups involved in catalysis. The shape of the active site is complementary to the shape of the substrate. Thus, the conformation of the active site determines the specificity of the enzyme. Enzyme-substrate binding involves weak, noncovalent interactions.

**19.45** The lock-and-key model of enzyme-substrate binding was proposed by Emil Fischer in 1894. He thought that the active site was a rigid region of the enzyme into which the substrate fit perfectly. Thus, the model purports that the substrate simply snaps into place within the active site, like two pieces of a jigsaw puzzle fitting together.

**19.47** Enzyme specificity is the ability of an enzyme to bind to only one, or a very few, substrates and thus catalyze only a single reaction.

**19.49** Group specificity means that an enzyme catalyzes reactions involving similar molecules having the same functional group.

**19.51** Absolute specificity means that an enzyme catalyzes the reaction of only one substrate.

**19.53** Hexokinase has group specificity. The advantage is that the cell does not need to encode many enzymes to carry out the phosphorylation of six-carbon sugars. Hexokinase can carry out many of these reactions.

**19.55** Methionyl tRNA synthetase has absolute specificity. This is the enzyme that attaches the amino acid methionine to the transfer RNA (tRNA) that will carry the amino acid to the site of protein synthesis. If the wrong amino acid were attached to the tRNA, it could be incorporated into the protein, destroying its correct three-dimensional structure and biological function.

**19.57** The first step of an enzyme-catalyzed reaction is the formation of the enzyme-substrate complex. In the second step, the transition state is formed. This is the state in which the substrate assumes a form intermediate between the original substrate and the product. In step 3, the substrate is converted to product and the enzyme-product complex is formed. Step 4 involves the release of the product and regeneration of the enzyme in its original form.

**19.59** In a reaction involving bond breaking, the enzyme might distort a bond, producing a transition state in which the bond is stressed. An enzyme could bring two reactants into close proximity and in the proper orientation for the reaction to occur, producing a transition state in which the proximity of the reactants facilitates bond formation. Finally, an enzyme could alter the pH of the microenvironment of the active site, thereby serving as a transient donor or acceptor of $H^+$.

**19.61** A cofactor helps maintain the shape of the active site of an enzyme.

**19.63** Thiamine ($B_1$) is found in the coenzyme thiamine pyrophosphate. Riboflavin ($B_2$) is found in both flavin mononucleotide and flavin adenine dinucleotide. Niacin ($B_3$) is found in both nicotinamide adenine dinucleotide and nicotinamide adenine dinucleotide phosphate. Pyridoxine ($B_6$) is found in both pyridoxal phosphate and pyridoxamine phosphate. Cyanocobalamin ($B_{12}$) is found in deoxyadenosyl cobalamin. Folic acid is found in tetrahydrofolic acid. Pantothenic acid is found in coenzyme A. Biotin is found in biocytin.

**19.65** At the temperature optimum, the enzyme is functioning optimally and the rate of the reaction is maximal. Above the temperature optimum, increasing temperature begins to denature the enzyme and stop the reaction.

**19.67** Each of the following answers assumes that the enzyme was purified from an organism with optimal conditions for life near 37°C, pH 7.
  **a.** Decreasing the temperature from 37°C to 10°C will cause the rate of an enzyme-catalyzed reaction to decrease because the frequency of collisions between enzyme and substrate will decrease as the rate of molecular movement decreases.
  **b.** Increasing the pH from 7 to 11 will generally cause a decrease in the rate of an enzyme-catalyzed reaction. In fact, most enzymes would be denatured by a pH of 11 and enzyme activity would cease.
  **c.** Heating an enzyme from 37°C to 100°C will destroy enzyme activity because the enzyme would be denatured by the extreme heat.

**19.69** High temperature denatures bacterial enzymes and structural proteins. Because the life of the cell is dependent on the function of these proteins, the cell dies.

**19.71** A lysosome is a membrane-bound vesicle in the cytoplasm of cells that contains approximately fifty hydrolytic enzymes. Some of the enzymes in the lysosomes can degrade proteins to amino acids, others hydrolyze polysaccharides into monosaccharides, and some degrade lipids and nucleic acids. The lysosome contains these enzymes to prevent degradation of large biological molecules that are important to maintain cell integrity.

**19.73** Enzymes used for clinical assays in hospitals are typically stored at refrigerator temperatures to ensure that they are not denatured by heat. In this way, they retain their activity for long periods.

**19.75** **a.** Cells regulate the level of enzyme activity to conserve energy. It is a waste of cellular energy to produce an enzyme if its substrate is not present or if its product is in excess.
  **b.** Production of proteolytic digestive enzymes must be carefully controlled because the active enzyme could destroy the cell that produces it. Thus, they are produced in an inactive form in the cell and are only activated at the site where they carry out digestion.

**19.77** In positive allosterism, binding of the effector molecule turns the enzyme on. In negative allosterism, binding of the effector molecule turns the enzyme off.

**19.79** A proenzyme is the inactive form of an enzyme that is converted to the active form at the site of its activity.

**19.81** Blood clotting is a critical protective mechanism in the body, preventing excessive loss of blood following an injury. However, it can be a dangerous mechanism if it is triggered inappropriately. The resulting clot could cause a heart attack or stroke. By having a cascade of proteolytic reactions leading to the final formation of the clot, there are many steps at which the process can be regulated. This ensures that it will only be activated under the appropriate conditions.

**19.83** Competitive enzyme inhibition occurs when a structural analog of the normal substrate occupies the enzyme active site so that the reaction cannot occur. The structural analog and the normal substrate compete for the active site. Thus, the rate of the reaction will depend on the relative concentrations of the two molecules.

**19.85** A structural analog has a shape and charge distribution that are very similar to those of the normal substrate for an enzyme.

**19.87** Irreversible inhibitors bind tightly to and block the active site of an enzyme and eliminate catalysis at the site.

**19.89** The compound would be a competitive inhibitor of the enzyme.

**19.91** A proteolytic enzyme catalyzes the cleavage of the peptide bond that maintains the primary protein structure.

**19.93** The structural similarities among chymotrypsin, trypsin, and elastase suggest that these enzymes evolved from a single ancestral gene that was duplicated. Each copy then evolved independently.

**19.95**

tyr-lys-ala-phe

**19.97** Elastase will cleave the peptide bonds on the carbonyl side of alanine and glycine. Trypsin will cleave the peptide bonds on the carbonyl side of lysine and arginine. Chymotrypsin will cleave the peptide bonds on the carbonyl side of tryptophan and phenylalanine.

**19.99** Analysis of blood serum for levels of certain enzymes can confirm a preliminary diagnosis that was made based on disease symptoms or a clinical picture. When cells die, they release their enzymes into the bloodstream. Enzyme assays can measure amounts of certain enzymes in the blood.

**19.101** Creatine kinase-MB and aspartate aminotransferase (AST/SGOT)

**19.103** Urease is used in the clinical analysis of urea in blood. In a test called the blood urea nitrogen test (BUN), urea is converted to ammonia using the enzyme urease; the ammonia becomes an indicator of urea. This allows for the levels of urea to be measured. This measurement is useful in the diagnosis of kidney malfunction.

## Chapter 20

**20.1 a.** Adenosine diphosphate:

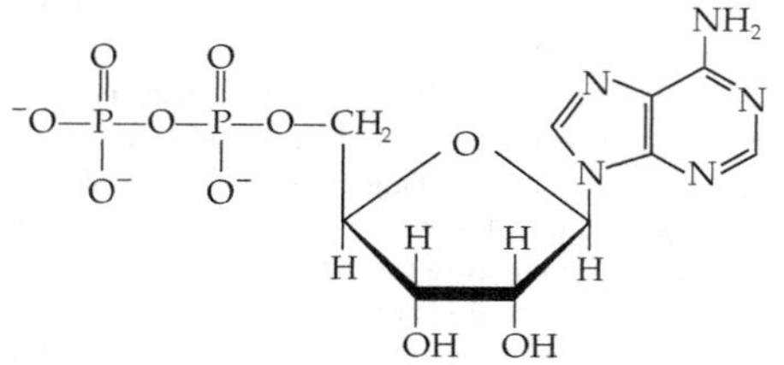

**b.** Deoxyguanosine triphosphate:

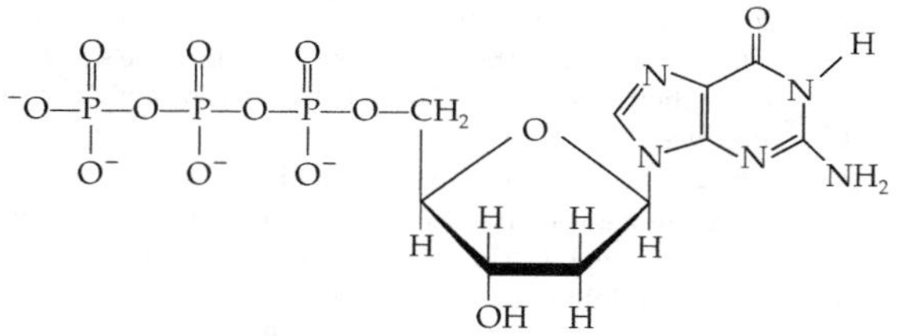

**20.3** The RNA polymerase recognizes the promoter site for a gene, separates the strands of DNA, and catalyzes the polymerization of an RNA strand complementary to the DNA strand that carries the genetic code for a protein. It recognizes a termination site at the end of the gene and releases the RNA molecule.

**20.5** The genetic code is said to be degenerate because several different triplet codons may serve as code words for a single amino acid.

**20.7** The nitrogenous bases of the codons are complementary to those of the anticodons. As a result, they are able to hydrogen bond to one another according to the base pairing rules.

**20.9** The ribosomal P-site holds the peptidyl tRNA during protein synthesis. The peptidyl tRNA is the tRNA carrying the growing peptide chain. The only exception to this is during initiation of translation when the P-site holds the initiator tRNA.

**20.11** The normal mRNA sequence, AUG-CCC-GAC-UUU, would encode the peptide sequence methionine-proline-aspartate-phenylalanine. The mutant mRNA sequence, AUG-CGC-GAC-UUU, would encode the mutant peptide sequence methionine-arginine-aspartate-phenylalanine. This would not be a silent mutation because a hydrophobic amino acid (proline) has been replaced by a positively charged amino acid (arginine).

**20.13** A heterocyclic amine is a compound that contains nitrogen in at least one position of the ring skeleton.

**20.15** It is the N-9 of the purine that forms the N-glycosidic bond with C-1 of the five-carbon sugar. The general structure of the purine ring is shown below:

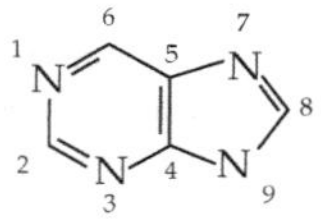

**20.17** The ATP nucleotide is composed of the five-carbon sugar ribose, the purine adenine, and a triphosphate group.

**20.19** The two strands of DNA in the double helix are said to be antiparallel because they run in opposite directions. One strand progresses in the $5' \rightarrow 3'$ direction, and the opposite strand progresses in the $3' \rightarrow 5'$ direction.

**20.21** The DNA double helix is 2 nm in width. The nitrogenous bases are stacked at a distance of 0.34 nm from one another. One complete turn of the helix is 3.4 nm, or 10 base pairs.

**20.23**

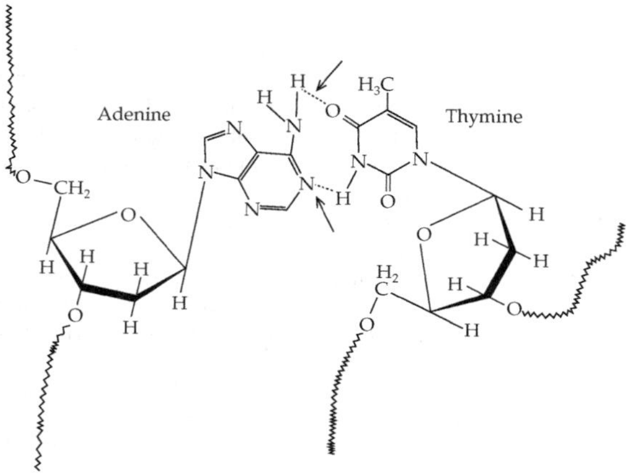

**20.25**

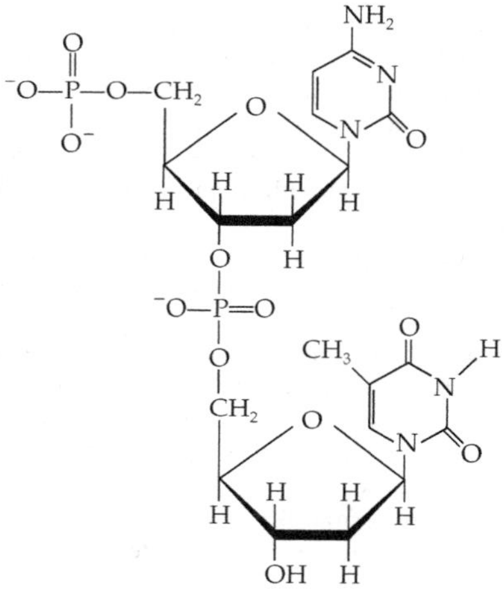

**20.27** The prokaryotic chromosome is a circular DNA molecule that is supercoiled; that is, the helix is coiled on itself.

**20.29** The term semiconservative DNA replication refers to the fact that each parental DNA strand serves as the template for the synthesis of a daughter strand. As a result, each of the daughter DNA molecules is made up of one strand of the original parental DNA and one strand of newly synthesized DNA.

**20.31** The two primary functions of DNA polymerase III are to read a template DNA strand and catalyze the polymerization of a new daughter strand, and to proofread the newly synthesized strand and correct any errors by removing the incorrectly inserted nucleotide and adding the proper one.

**20.33** 3'-TACGGGCTCGACTAACTAGTCT-5'

**20.35** The replication origin of a DNA molecule is the unique sequence on the DNA molecule where DNA replication begins.

**20.37** The enzyme helicase separates the strands of DNA at the origin of DNA replication so that the proteins involved in replication can interact with the nitrogenous base pairs.

**20.39** The RNA primer "primes" DNA replication by providing a 3'—OH which can be used by DNA polymerase III for the addition of the next nucleotide in the growing DNA chain.

**20.41** DNA → RNA → Protein

**20.43** Anticodons are found on transfer RNA molecules.

**20.45** 3'-AUGCCCGUAUCCGGAAUUUCGAUCGAA-5'

**20.47** RNA splicing is the process by which the noncoding sequences (introns) of the primary transcript of a eukaryotic mRNA are removed and the protein coding sequences (exons) are spliced together.

**20.49** Messenger RNA, transfer RNA, and ribosomal RNA

**20.51** Spliceosomes are small ribonucleoprotein complexes that carry out RNA splicing.

**20.53** The poly(A) tail is a stretch of 100–200 adenosine nucleotides polymerized onto the 3' end of a mRNA by the enzyme poly(A) polymerase.

**20.55** The cap structure is made up of the nucleotide 7-methylguanosine attached to the 5' end of a mRNA by a 5'-5' triphosphate bridge. Generally, the first two nucleotides of the mRNA are also methylated.

**20.57** Sixty-four

**20.59** The reading frame of a gene is the sequential set of triplet codons that carries the genetic code for the primary structure of a protein.

**20.61** Methionine and tryptophan

**20.63** The codon 5'-UUU-3' encodes the amino acid phenylalanine. The mutant codon 5'-UUA-3' encodes the amino acid leucine. Both leucine and phenylalanine are hydrophobic amino acids; however, leucine has a smaller R group. It is possible that the smaller R group would disrupt the structure of the protein.

**20.65** The ribosomes serve as a platform on which protein synthesis can occur. They also carry the enzymatic activity that forms peptide bonds.

**20.67** 5'-AUG GCU GGG CUU UGU AUG UGG UAU UCU AUU GGG UAA-3'

**20.69** The sequence of DNA nucleotides in a gene is transcribed to produce a complementary sequence of RNA nucleotides in a messenger RNA (mRNA). In the process of translation, the sequence of the mRNA is read sequentially in words of three nucleotides (codons) to produce a protein. Each codon calls for the addition of a particular amino acid to the growing peptide chain. If one of those codons has been altered by mutation, it may now call for the addition of the wrong amino acid to the growing peptide chain. This could result in improper folding of the protein and in loss of biological function.

**20.71** An ester bond

**20.73** A point mutation is the substitution of one nucleotide pair for another in a gene.

**20.75** Some mutations are silent because the change in the nucleotide sequence does not alter the amino acid sequence of the protein. This can happen because there are many amino acids encoded by multiple codons.

**20.77** UV light causes the formation of pyrimidine dimers, the covalent bonding of two adjacent pyrimidine bases. Mutations occur when the UV damage repair system makes an error during the repair process. This causes a change in the nucleotide sequence of the DNA.

**20.79** **a.** A carcinogen is a compound that causes cancer. Cancers are caused by mutations in the genes responsible for controlling cell division.
**b.** Carcinogens cause DNA damage that results in changes in the nucleotide sequence of the gene. Thus, carcinogens are also mutagens.

**20.81** A restriction enzyme is a bacterial enzyme that "cuts" the sugar–phosphate backbone of DNA molecules at a specific nucleotide sequence.

**20.83** A selectable marker is a genetic trait that can be used to detect the presence of a plasmid in a bacterium. Many plasmids have antibiotic resistance genes as selectable markers. Bacteria containing the plasmid will be able to grow in the presence of the antibiotic; those without the plasmid will be killed.

**20.85** Human insulin, interferon, human growth hormone, and human blood clotting factor VIII

**20.87** 4096 copies

**20.89** The goals of the Human Genome Project were to identify and map all of the genes of the human genome and to determine the DNA sequences of the complete three billion nucleotide pairs.

**20.91** A genome library is a set of clones that represents all of the DNA sequences in the genome of an organism.

**20.93** A dideoxynucleotide is one that has hydrogen atoms rather than hydroxyl groups bonded to both the 2' and 3' carbons of the five-carbon sugar.

**20.95** Sequences that these DNA sequences have in common are highlighted in bold.
**a.** 5'-**AGCTCCT**GATTTCATACAGTTTCTACT**ACCTACTA**-3'
**b.** 5'-AGACATTCTATCTACCTAGACTATG**TTCAGAA**-3'
**c.** 5'-**TTCAGAA**CTCATTCAGACCTACTACTATACCTTGG **GAGCTCCT**-3'
**d.** 5'-**ACCTACTA**GACTATACTACTACTAAGGGGACTATT CCAGACTT-3'
The 5' end of sequence (a) is identical to the 3' end of sequence (c). The 3' end of sequence (a) is identical to the 5' end of sequence (d). The 3' end of sequence (b) is identical to the 5' end of sequence (c). From 5' to 3', the sequences would form the following map:

```
      b
  _____
                _____c_____
                          _____a_____
                                    _____d_____
```

## Chapter 21

**21.1** ATP is called the universal energy currency because it is the major molecule used by all organisms to store energy.

**21.3** The first stage of catabolism is the digestion (hydrolysis) of dietary macromolecules in the stomach and intestine.

In the second stage of catabolism, monosaccharides, amino acids, fatty acids, and glycerol are converted by metabolic reactions into molecules that can be completely oxidized.

In the third stage of catabolism, the two-carbon acetyl group of acetyl CoA is completely oxidized by the reactions of the citric acid cycle. The energy of the electrons harvested in these oxidation reactions is used to make ATP.

**21.5**  Substrate level phosphorylation is one way the cell can make ATP. In this reaction, a high-energy phosphoryl group of a substrate in the reaction is transferred to ADP to produce ATP.

**21.7**  Glycolysis is a pathway involving ten reactions. In reactions 1–3, energy is invested in the beginning substrate, glucose. This is done by transferring high-energy phosphoryl groups from ATP to the intermediates in the pathway. The product is fructose-1, 6-bisphosphate. In the energy-harvesting reactions of glycolysis, fructose-1,6-bisphosphate is split into two three-carbon molecules that begin a series of rearrangement, oxidation-reduction, and substrate-level phosphorylation reactions that produce four ATP, two NADH, and two pyruvate molecules. Because of the investment of two ATP in the early steps of glycolysis, the net yield of ATP is two.

**21.9**  Both the alcohol and lactate fermentations are anaerobic reactions that use the pyruvate and re-oxidize the NADH produced in glycolysis.

**21.11**  Gluconeogenesis (synthesis of glucose from noncarbohydrate sources) appears to be the reverse of glycolysis (the first stage of carbohydrate degradation) because the intermediates in the two pathways are the same. However, reactions 1, 3, and 10 of glycolysis are not reversible reactions. Thus, the reverse reactions must be carried out by different enzymes.

**21.13**  The enzyme glycogen phosphorylase catalyzes the phosphorolysis of a glucose unit at one end of a glycogen molecule. The reaction involves the displacement of the glucose by a phosphate group. The products are glucose-1-phosphate and a glycogen molecule that is one glucose unit shorter.

**21.15**  Glucokinase traps glucose within the liver cell by phosphorylating it. Because the product, glucose-6-phosphate, is charged, it cannot be exported from the cell.

**21.17**  Glucagon indirectly stimulates glycogen phosphorylase, the first enzyme of glycogenolysis. This speeds up glycogen degradation. Glucagon also inhibits glycogen synthase, the first enzyme in glycogenesis. This inhibits glycogen synthesis.

**21.19**  ATP

**21.21**

Adenosine triphosphate

Adenosine diphosphate

**21.23**  A coupled reaction is one that can be thought of as a two-step process. In a coupled reaction, two reactions occur simultaneously. Frequently, one of the reactions releases the energy that drives the second, energy-requiring reaction.

**21.25**  Carbohydrates

**21.27**  The following equation represents the hydrolysis of maltose:

β-Maltose

β-D-Glucose

**21.29**

**21.31**  The hydrolysis of a triglyceride containing oleic acid, stearic acid, and linoleic acid is represented in the following equation:

Glycerol

Oleic acid

Stearic acid

Linoleic acid

**21.33** The hydrolysis of the dipeptide alanyl leucine is represented in the following equation:

Alanyl leucine

Alanine          Leucine

**21.35** Glycolysis is the enzymatic pathway that converts a glucose molecule into two molecules of pyruvate. The pathway generates a net energy yield of two ATP and two NADH. Glycolysis is the first stage of carbohydrate catabolism.

**21.37** Glycolysis requires $NAD^+$ for reaction 6 in which glyceraldehyde-3-phosphate dehydrogenase catalyzes the oxidation of glyceraldehyde-3-phosphate. $NAD^+$ is reduced.

**21.39** Two ATP per glucose

**21.41** Although muscle cells have enough ATP stored for only a few seconds of activity, glycolysis speeds up dramatically when there is a demand for more energy. If the cells have a sufficient supply of oxygen, aerobic respiration (the citric acid cycle and oxidative phosphorylation) will contribute large amounts of ATP. If oxygen is limited, the lactate fermentation will speed up. This will use up the pyruvate and re-oxidize the NADH produced by glycolysis and allow continued synthesis of ATP for muscle contraction.

**21.43** $C_6H_{12}O_6$ + 2ADP + 2$P_i$ + 2NAD+ $\longrightarrow$
Glucose          2$C_3H_3O_3$ + 2ATP + 2NADH + 2$H_2O$
          Pyruvate

**21.45**  **a.** 7          **f.** 9
          **b.** 2          **g.** 5
          **c.** 6          **h.** 10
          **d.** 4          **i.** 3
          **e.** 1          **j.** 8

**21.47** Myopathy and hemolytic anemia are symptoms associated with a genetic defect in some of the enzymes of glycolysis. Myopathy can lead to exercise intolerance, muscle breakdown, and blood

in the urine. Tarui's disease is also caused by a deficiency in one of the enzymes of glycolysis. Its symptoms include muscle pain, exercise intolerance, respiratory failure, heart muscle disease, seizures, and blindness.

**21.49** If a person is deficient in some of the enzymes of glycolysis, muscle cells may begin to die, which can lead to the release of myoglobin into the blood and the urine. This condition is called myoglobinuria, and it results in urine that is the color of cola soft drinks.

**21.51** Isomerase

**21.53** Enediol

**21.55** A kinase transfers a phosphoryl group from one molecule to another.

**21.57** $NAD^+$ is reduced, accepting a hydride anion.

**21.59** To optimize efficiency and minimize waste, it is important that energy-harvesting pathways, such as glycolysis, respond to the energy demands of the cell. If energy in the form of ATP is abundant, there is no need for the pathway to continue at a rapid rate. When this is the case, allosteric enzymes that catalyze the reactions of the pathway are inhibited by binding to their negative effectors. Similarly, when there is a great demand for ATP, the pathway speeds up as a result of the action of allosteric enzymes binding to positive effectors.

**21.61** ATP and citrate are allosteric inhibitors of phosphofructokinase, whereas AMP and ADP are allosteric activators.

**21.63** Citrate, which is the first intermediate in the citric acid cycle, is an allosteric inhibitor of phosphofructokinase. The citric acid cycle is a pathway that results in the complete oxidation of the pyruvate produced by glycolysis. A high concentration of citrate signals that sufficient substrate is entering the citric acid cycle. The inhibition of phosphofructokinase by citrate is an example of feedback inhibition: the product, citrate, allosterically inhibits the activity of an enzyme early in the pathway.

**21.65**

Acetaldehyde          Ethanol

**21.67** Lactate fermentation

**21.69** Yogurt and some cheeses

**21.71** Lactate dehydrogenase

**21.73** This child must have the enzymes to carry out the alcohol fermentation. When the child exercised hard, there was not enough oxygen in the cells to maintain aerobic respiration. As a result, glycolysis and the alcohol fermentation were responsible for the majority of the ATP production by the child. The accumulation of alcohol (ethanol) in the child caused the symptoms of drunkenness.

**21.75** The ribose-5-phosphate is used for the biosynthesis of nucleotides. The erythrose-4-phosphate is used for the biosynthesis of aromatic amino acids.

**21.77** Gluconeogenesis is production of glucose from noncarbohydrate starting materials. This pathway can provide glucose when starvation or strenuous exercise leads to a depletion of glucose from the body.

**21.79** The liver

**21.81** Lactate is first converted to pyruvate.

**21.83** Because steps 1, 3, and 10 of glycolysis are irreversible, gluconeogenesis is not simply the reverse of glycolysis. The reverse reactions must be carried out by different enzymes.

**21.85**  Steps 1, 3, and 10 of glycolysis are irreversible. Step 1 is the transfer of a phosphoryl group from ATP to carbon-6 of glucose and is catalyzed by hexokinase. Step 3 is the transfer of a phosphoryl group from ATP to carbon-1 of fructose-6-phosphate and is catalyzed by phosphofructokinase. Step 10 is the substrate-level phosphorylation in which a phosphoryl group is transferred from phosphoenolpyruvate to ADP and is catalyzed by pyruvate kinase.

**21.87**  The liver and pancreas

**21.89**  Hypoglycemia is the condition in which blood glucose levels are too low.

**21.91**  **a.** Insulin stimulates glycogen synthase, the first enzyme in glycogen synthesis. It also stimulates uptake of glucose from the bloodstream into cells and phosphorylation of glucose by the enzyme glucokinase.
**b.** This traps glucose within liver cells and increases the storage of glucose in the form of glycogen.
**c.** These processes decrease blood glucose levels.

**21.93**  Any defect in the enzymes required to degrade glycogen or export glucose from liver cells will result in a reduced ability of the liver to provide glucose at times when blood glucose levels are low. This will cause hypoglycemia.

**21.95**  Glycogen phosphorylase catalyzes phosphorolysis of a glucose at one end of a glycogen polymer. The reaction involves the displacement of a glucose unit of glycogen by a phosphate group. As a result, glucose-1-phosphate is produced.

$$\text{Glycogen(glucose)}_x + n\text{HPO}_4^{2-} \longrightarrow \text{Glycogen(glucose)}_{n-x} + n\text{glucose-1-phosphate}$$

**21.97**  In glycogen degradation, phosphoglucomutase converts glucose-1-phosphate to glucose-6-phosphate. In glycogen synthesis, phosphoglucomutase converts glucose-6-phosphate to glucose-1-phosphate.

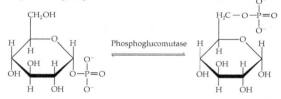

**21.99**  Glucokinase converts glucose to glucose-6-phosphate as the first reaction of glycogen synthesis.

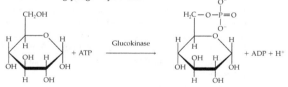

## Chapter 22

**22.1**  Mitochondria are the organelles responsible for aerobic respiration.

**22.3**

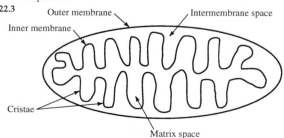

**22.5**  Pyruvate is converted to acetyl CoA by the pyruvate dehydrogenase complex. This huge enzyme complex requires four coenzymes, each of which is made from a different vitamin. The four coenzymes are thiamine pyrophosphate (made from thiamine), FAD (made from riboflavin), $NAD^+$ (made from niacin), and coenzyme A (made from the vitamin pantothenic acid). The coenzyme lipoamide is also involved in this reaction.

**22.7**  Oxidative phosphorylation is the process by which the energy of electrons harvested from oxidation of a fuel molecule is used to phosphorylate ADP to produce ATP.

**22.9**  $NAD^+ + H:^- \longrightarrow NADH$

**22.11**  During transamination reactions, the α-amino group is transferred to the coenzyme pyridoxal phosphate. In the last part of the reaction, the α-amino group is transferred from pyridoxal phosphate to an α-keto acid.

**22.13**  The purpose of the urea cycle is to convert toxic ammonium ions to urea, which is excreted in the urine of land animals.

**22.15**  An amphibolic pathway is a metabolic pathway that functions both in anabolism and catabolism. The citric acid cycle is amphibolic because it has a catabolic function—it completely oxidizes the acetyl group carried by acetyl CoA to provide electrons for ATP synthesis. Because citric acid cycle intermediates are precursors for the biosynthesis of many other molecules, it also serves a function in anabolism.

**22.17**  The mitochondrion is an organelle that serves as the cellular power plant. The reactions of the citric acid cycle, the electron transport system, and ATP synthase function together within the mitochondrion to harvest ATP energy for the cell.

**22.19**  The intermembrane compartment is the location of the high-energy proton ($H^+$) reservoir produced by the electron transport system. The energy of this $H^+$ reservoir is used to make ATP.

**22.21**  The outer mitochondrial membrane is freely permeable to substances of molar mass less than 10,000 g/mol. The inner mitochondrial membrane is highly impermeable. Embedded within the inner mitochondrial membrane are the electron carriers of the electron transport system, and ATP synthase, the multisubunit enzyme that makes ATP.

**22.23**  Coenzyme A is a molecule derived from ATP and the vitamin pantothenic acid. It functions in the transfer of acetyl groups in lipid and carbohydrate metabolism.

**22.25**  Decarboxylation is a chemical reaction in which a carboxyl group is removed from a molecule.

**22.27**  Under aerobic conditions pyruvate is converted to acetyl CoA.

**22.29**  The coenzymes $NAD^+$, FAD, thiamine pyrophosphate, and coenzyme A are required by the pyruvate dehydrogenase complex for the conversion of pyruvate to acetyl CoA. These coenzymes are synthesized from the vitamins niacin, riboflavin, thiamine, and pantothenic acid, respectively. If the vitamins are not available, the coenzymes will not be available and pyruvate cannot be converted to acetyl CoA. Because the complete oxidation of the acetyl group of acetyl CoA produces the vast majority of the ATP for the body, ATP production would be severely inhibited by a deficiency of any of these vitamins.

**22.31**  A condensation is a reaction in which aldehydes or ketones react to form larger molecules.

**22.33**  Oxidation reduction

**22.35**  A dehydrogenation reaction is an oxidation reaction in which protons and electrons are removed from a molecule.

**22.37**  **a.** 1          **e.** 4
       **b.** 6          **f.** 2
       **c.** 2          **g.** 5
       **d.** 2          **h.** 2

**22.39** True

**22.41** Three

**22.43** Two ATP per glucose

**22.45** The function of acetyl CoA in the citric acid cycle is to bring the two-carbon remnant (acetyl group) of pyruvate from glycolysis and transfer it to oxaloacetate. In this way, the acetyl group enters the citric acid cycle for the final stages of oxidation.

**22.47** The high-energy phosphoryl group of the GTP is transferred to ADP to produce ATP. This reaction is catalyzed by the enzyme dinucleotide diphosphokinase.

**22.49** Fumarate contains an alkene carbon-carbon double bond. Addition of water to the double bond of fumarate gives malate. The enzyme fumarase catalyzes this reaction. When water is added to the alkene double bond, one of the carbons forms a new bond to —OH, and the other carbon forms a new bond to —H. As a result, the alkene becomes an alcohol.

**22.51** First, pyruvate is converted to acetyl CoA:

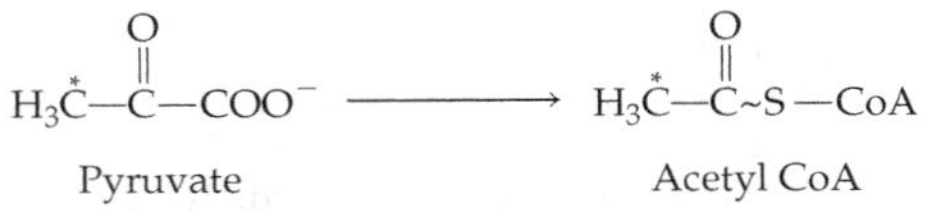

$$H_3\overset{*}{C}-\underset{\underset{Pyruvate}{}}{\overset{\overset{O}{\parallel}}{C}}-COO^- \longrightarrow H_3\overset{*}{C}-\underset{\underset{Acetyl\ CoA}{}}{\overset{\overset{O}{\parallel}}{C}}-S-CoA$$

Then, citrate is formed from oxaloacetate and the radiolabeled acetyl CoA.

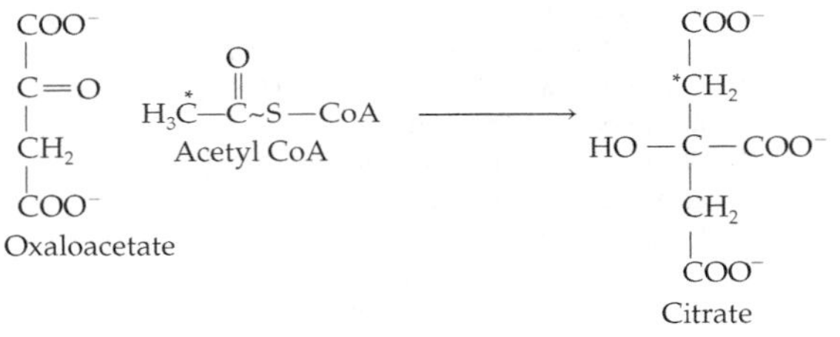

The following structures are the intermediates of the citric acid cycle. An asterisk is on the radiolabeled carbon, and circles are on the —COO⁻ groups that are released as $CO_2$.

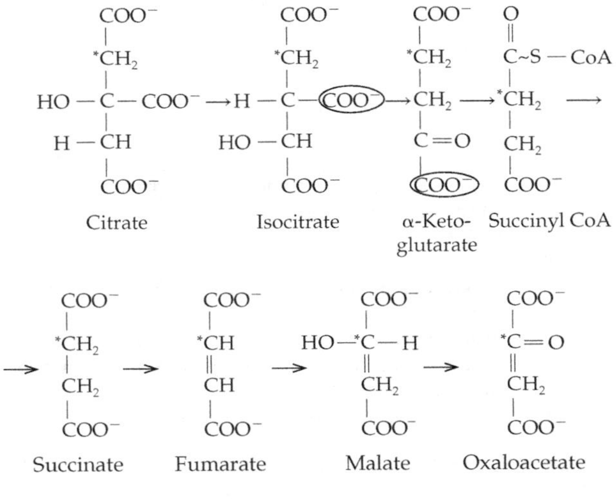

Citrate   Isocitrate   α-Keto-glutarate   Succinyl CoA

Succinate   Fumarate   Malate   Oxaloacetate

**22.53** This reaction is an example of the oxidation of a secondary alcohol to a ketone. The two functional groups are the hydroxyl group of the alcohol and the carbonyl group of the ketone.

**22.55** It is a kinase because it transfers a phosphoryl group from one molecule to another. Kinases are a specific type of transferase.

**22.57** Mutations of the citric acid cycle enzymes frequently appear first in the central nervous system because of the high energy (ATP) demands of this tissue.

**22.59** Deficiencies of citric acid cycle enzymes cause hypotonia because there is insufficient ATP.

**22.61** An allosteric enzyme is one that has an effector binding site and an active site. Effector binding can change the shape of the active site, causing it to be active or inactive.

**22.63** Allosteric enzymes are an efficient means to regulate a biochemical pathway because they bind to effectors, such as ATP or ADP, that alter the shape of the enzyme active site, either stimulating the rate of the reaction or inhibiting the reaction.

**22.65** The citric acid cycle is regulated by the following four enzymes or enzyme complexes: pyruvate dehydrogenase complex, citrate synthase, isocitrate dehydrogenase, and the α-ketoglutarate dehydrogenase complex.

**22.67** Energy-harvesting pathways, such as the citric acid cycle, must be responsive to the energy needs of the cell. If the energy requirements are high, as during exercise, the reactions must speed up. If energy demands are low and ATP is in excess, the reactions of the pathway slow down.

**22.69** ADP

**22.71** The electron transport system is a series of electron transport proteins embedded in the inner mitochondrial membrane that accept high-energy electrons from NADH and $FADH_2$ and transfer them in stepwise fashion to molecular oxygen ($O_2$).

**22.73** Three ATP

**22.75** The oxidation of a variety of fuel molecules, including carbohydrates, the carbon skeletons of amino acids, and fatty acids provides the electrons. The energy of these electrons is used to produce an $H^+$ reservoir. The energy of this proton reservoir is used for ATP synthesis.

**22.77** The electron transport system passes electrons harvested during oxidation of fuel molecules to molecular oxygen. At three sites, protons are pumped from the mitochondrial matrix into the intermembrane compartment. Thus, the electron transport system builds the high-energy $H^+$ reservoir that provides energy for ATP synthesis.

**22.79** a. Two ATP per glucose (net yield) are produced in glycolysis, whereas the complete oxidation of glucose in aerobic respiration (glycolysis, the citric acid cycle, and oxidative phosphorylation) results in the production of 36 ATP per glucose.

 b. Thus, aerobic respiration harvests nearly 40% of the potential energy of glucose, and anaerobic glycolysis harvests only about 2% of the potential energy of glucose.

**22.81** Transaminases transfer amino groups from amino acids to ketoacids.

**22.83** The glutamate family of transaminases is very important because the ketoacid corresponding to glutamate is α-ketoglutarate, one of the citric acid cycle intermediates. This provides a link between the citric acid cycle and amino acid metabolism. These transaminases provide amino groups for amino acid synthesis and collect amino groups during catabolism of amino acids.

**22.85** a. Pyruvate        d. Acetyl CoA
 b. α-Ketoglutarate    e. Succinate
 c. Oxaloacetate      f. α-Ketoglutarate

**22.87** Transaminase binds to the amino acid in its active site. Then, the α-amino group is transferred to pyridoxal phosphate, producing pyridoxamine phosphate. The amino group is then transferred to an α-keto acid.

**22.89** Hyperammonemia

**22.91** **a.** The source of one amino group of urea is the ammonium ion, and the source of the other is the α-amino group of the amino acid aspartate.

   **b.** The carbonyl group of urea is derived from $CO_2$.

**22.93** Anabolism is a term used to describe all of the cellular energy-requiring biosynthetic pathways.

**22.95** α-Ketoglutarate

**22.97** Citric acid cycle intermediates are the starting materials for the biosynthesis of many biological molecules.

**22.99** An essential amino acid is one that cannot be synthesized by the body and must be provided in the diet.

**22.101**

   Pyruvate          Oxaloacetate

## Chapter 23

**23.1** Because dietary lipids are hydrophobic, they arrive in the small intestine as large fat globules. The bile salts emulsify these fat globules into tiny fat droplets. This greatly increases the surface area of the lipids, allowing them to be more accessible to pancreatic lipases and thus more easily digested.

**23.3** Starvation, a diet low in carbohydrates, and diabetes mellitus are conditions that lead to the production of ketone bodies.

**23.5** **(1)** Fatty acid biosynthesis occurs in the cytoplasm, whereas β-oxidation occurs in the mitochondria.

   **(2)** The acyl group carrier in fatty acid biosynthesis is acyl carrier protein, while the acyl group carrier in β-oxidation is coenzyme A.

   **(3)** The seven enzymes of fatty acid biosynthesis are associated as a multienzyme complex called fatty acid synthase. The enzymes involved in β-oxidation are not physically associated with one another.

   **(4)** NADPH is the reducing agent used in fatty acid biosynthesis. NADH and $FADH_2$ are produced by β-oxidation.

**23.7** When excess fuel is available, the liver synthesizes fatty acids and triglycerides.

**23.9** Insulin stimulates uptake of glucose and amino acids by cells, glycogen and protein synthesis, and storage of lipids. It inhibits glycogenolysis, gluconeogenesis, breakdown of stored triglycerides, and ketogenesis.

**23.11**

Cholate

Chenodeoxycholate

**23.13** A micelle is an aggregation of molecules having nonpolar and polar regions; the nonpolar regions of the molecules aggregate, leaving the polar regions facing the surrounding water.

**23.15** A triglyceride is a molecule composed of glycerol esterified to three fatty acids.

**23.17** Triglycerides, cholesterol, and phospholipids are packaged into a protein-coated shell to produce the class of plasma lipoproteins called chylomicrons.

**23.19** Triglycerides

**23.21** The large fat globule that takes up nearly the entire cytoplasm

**23.23** Lipases catalyze the hydrolysis of the ester bonds of triglycerides.

**23.25** Acetyl CoA is the precursor for fatty acids, several amino acids, cholesterol, and other steroids.

**23.27** Chylomicrons carry dietary triglycerides from the intestine to all tissues via the bloodstream.

**23.29** Bile salts are detergents that emulsify the lipids, increasing their surface area and making them more accessible to digestive enzymes (pancreatic lipases).

**23.31** When dietary lipids in the form of fat globules reach the duodenum, they are emulsified by bile salts. The triglycerides in the resulting tiny fat droplets are hydrolyzed into monoglycerides and fatty acids by the action of pancreatic lipases, assisted by colipase. The monoglycerides and fatty acids are absorbed by cells lining the intestine.

**23.33** The hydrolysis of ATP into AMP and $PP_i$

**23.35** Carnitine is a carrier molecule that brings fatty acyl groups into the mitochondrial matrix.

**23.37** The following equation represents the reaction catalyzed by acyl-CoA dehydrogenase. Notice that the reaction involves the loss of two hydrogen atoms. Thus, this is an oxidation reaction.

**23.39** An alcohol is the product of the hydration of an alkene.

**23.41** Six acetyl CoA, one phenyl acetate, six NADH, and six $FADH_2$

**23.43** 112 ATP

**23.45** 95 ATP

**23.47** The acetyl CoA produced by β-oxidation will enter the citric acid cycle.

**23.49** Ketone bodies include the compounds acetone, acetoacetone, and β-hydroxybutyrate, which are produced from fatty acids in the liver via acetyl CoA.

**23.51** Ketosis is an abnormal rise in the level of ketone bodies in the blood.

**23.53** Matrix of the mitochondrion

**23.55**

Acetoacetate                    β-Hydroxybutyrate

**23.57** In those suffering from uncontrolled diabetes, the glucose in the blood cannot get into the cells of the body. The excess glucose is excreted in the urine. Body cells degrade fatty acids because glucose is not available. β-oxidation of fatty acids yields enormous quantities of acetyl CoA, so much acetyl CoA, in fact, that it cannot all enter the citric acid cycle because there is not enough oxaloacetate available. Excess acetyl CoA is used for ketogenesis.

**23.59** Ketone bodies are the preferred energy source of the heart.

**23.61** Cytoplasm

**23.63**

**23.65** **a.** The phosphopantetheine group allows formation of a high-energy thioester bond with a fatty acid.
**b.** It is derived from the vitamin pantothenic acid.

**23.67** Fatty acid synthase is a huge multienzyme complex consisting of the seven enzymes involved in fatty acid synthesis. It is found in the cell cytoplasm. The enzymes involved in β-oxidation are not physically associated with one another. They are free in the mitochondrial matrix space.

**23.69** The liver produces ketone bodies under conditions of starvation or fasting.

**23.71** Working muscle obtains most of its energy from the degradation of its supply of glycogen.

**23.73** β-oxidation of fatty acids

**23.75** Because ketone bodies have a free carboxylate group and are soluble in the blood, they can enter the brain and be used as an energy source.

**23.77** Ketone bodies are the major fuel for the heart. Glucose is the major energy source of the brain, and the liver obtains most of its energy from the oxidation of amino acid carbon skeletons.

**23.79** Fatty acids are absorbed from the bloodstream by adipocytes. Using glycerol-3-phosphate, produced as a by-product of glycolysis, triglycerides are synthesized. Triglycerides are constantly being hydrolyzed and resynthesized in adipocytes. The rates of hydrolysis and synthesis are determined by lipases that are under hormonal control.

**23.81** In general, insulin stimulates anabolic processes and inhibits catabolic processes.

**23.83** A target cell is one that has a receptor for a particular hormone.

**23.85** Decreased blood glucose levels

**23.87** In the β-cells of the islets of Langerhans in the pancreas.

**23.89** Insulin stimulates the uptake of glucose from the blood into cells. It enhances glucose storage by stimulating glycogenesis and inhibiting glycogen degradation and gluconeogenesis.

**23.91** Insulin stimulates synthesis and storage of triglycerides.

**23.93** Insulin is secreted when blood glucose levels are high. It facilitates the uptake and storage of glucose by target cells to restore normal blood glucose levels. Glucagon is secreted when blood glucose levels are too low. It stimulates release of glucose into the blood to restore normal levels.

# Credits

## Photo Credits

### Design Elements

A Human Perspective: © kristiansekulic/ Vetta/Getty Images RF; Chemistry at the Crime Scene: © McGraw-Hill Education; A Medical Perspective: © Martin Barraud/ OJOImages/Age Fotostock RF; Green Chemistry: © ViewStock/Getty Images RF, © Tetra Images/Alamy RF; Kitchen Chemistry: © Stockbrokerxtra Images/Photolibrary RF.

### Front Matter

Table of Contents 1: © Purestock/SuperStock RF; 2: Image Science and Analysis Laboratory, 3: © Javier Trueba/MSF/Science Source; 4: © ImageSource/Veer RF; 5: © Royalty-Free/ DigitalStock/Corbis RF; 6: © John Gillmoure/ Spirit/Corbis RF; 7: © Jorg Greuel/Getty Images RF; 8: © Richard Carey/Getty Images RF; 9: © Javier Larrea/Pixtal/Age Fotostock RF; 10: © Digital Vision/PunchStock RF; 11: © Digital Vision/Getty Images RF; 12: © Photodisc/Getty Images RF; 13: © Iconotec RF; 14: © Stockbyte/Corbis RF; 15: © Parvinder Sethi; 16: © Phanie/Science Source; 17: © Steve Satushek/Getty Images; 18: © Fotohunter/ Getty Images; 19: Courtesy Dr. Robert E. Shoemaker; 20: © Barbara Penoyar/Photodisc/ Getty Images RF; 21: © Chris Falkenstein/ Photodisc/Getty Images RF; 22: © Chris Falkenstein/Photodisc/Getty Images RF; 23: © Emilio Simion/Getty Images RF.

### Chapter 1

Opener: © Purestock/SuperStock RF; Page 3 (top right): © Digital Vision/Getty Images RF; Page 5 (top right): © Graham Bell/ Cardinal/Corbis; 1.2d: © David M. Dennis/ Age Fotostock; 1.2c: © David Parker/Segate Microelectronics/SPL/Science Source; 1.2b: © Patrik Stollarz/AFP/Getty Images; 1.2a: © Adam Gault/OJO Images/Getty Images RF; 1.4c: © Danaè R. QuirkDorr, Ph.D.; 1.4a: © ImageSource RF; 1.4b: © ImageSource RF; 1.5b: © McGraw-Hill Education/Jeff Topping, photographer; 1.5c: © McGraw-Hill Education/ Louis Rosenstock, photographer; 1.5a: © Corey Hochachka/DesignPics RF; 1.6a: © McGraw-Hill Education/Ken Karp, photographer; 1.6b: © McGraw-Hill Education/Ken Karp, photographer; Page 11: © McGraw-Hill Education/John Thoeming, photographer; 1.7a-c: © McGraw-Hill Education/ Louis Rosenstock, photographer; 1.9a-d: © McGraw-Hill Education/Louis Rosenstock, photographer; Page 21: © Adam Gault/ Getty Images RF; Page 25 (top center): © Fred Hutchinson Cancer Research Center/Susan M. Parkhurst, Ph.D., photographer; Page 25 (top right): © Maximilian Weinzierl/Alamy; Page 30: © ImageSource/Corbis RF; 1.12: © McGraw-Hill Education/Louis Rosenstock, photographer; Page 35: © Photolink/Getty Images RF.

### Chapter 2

Opener: Image Science and Analysis Laboratory, NASA-Johnson Space Center; 2.1: © IBM Corporation, Almaden Research Center; 2.6: © Yoav Levy/Phototakeusa.com; 2.7a: © McGraw-Hill Education; Page 54: (top right) © Scott Camazine/Science Source; Page 54 (bottom left): © Earth Satellite Corp./ SPL/Science Source; Page 56: © Photodisc/ Getty Images RF; Page 59: © McGraw-Hill Education/Stephen Frisch, photographer; 2.14: © McGraw-Hill Education/Jacques Cornell, photographer.

### Chapter 3

Opener: © Javier Trueba/MSF/Science Source; 3.1c: © McGraw-Hill Education/Dennis Strete, photographer; Page 99: © Comstock/ PictureQuest RF; Page 102: © Pixtal/ Age Fotostock RF; 3.14: © David A. Tietz/ EditorialImage, LLC.

### Chapter 4

Opener: © ImageSource/Veer RF; Page 129: © Royalty-Free/Corbis RF; 4.1: © McGraw-Hill Education/Louis Rosenstock, photographer; 4.3: © McGraw-Hill Education/Louis Rosenstock, photographer; Page 145: © McGraw-Hill Education/Charles D. Winters, photographer; Page 148: © McGraw-Hill Education/Stephen Frisch, photographer; Page 149: © McGraw-Hill Education/Louis Rosenstock, photographer; 4.6a-b: © McGraw-Hill Education/Stephen Frisch, photographer; Page 157: © David R .Frazier Photolibrary, Inc RF; Page 160: © Keith Eng, 2008 RF; Page 163: © Radius Images/Getty Images RF; 4.10a: © Stockbyte/ Getty Images RF; 4.10b: © Dynamic Graphics Group/Getty Images RF.

### Chapter 5

Opener: © Royalty-Free/DigitalStock/ Corbis RF; Page 173: © Javier Larrea/Age Fotostock RF; Page 175: © Archive Holdings Inc/The Image Bank/Getty Images; 5.2a-b: © McGraw-Hill Education/Louis Rosenstock, photographer; 5.5: © Open Door/Alamy RF; Page 189: © Keith Thomas Productions/ Brand X Pictures/PictureQuest RF; Page 192: © Mikael Karlsson RF; Page 195: © Photodisc/ Getty Images RF.

### Chapter 6

Opener: © John Gillmoure/Spirit/Corbis RF; Page 201: © Keith Eng; 6.1: © McGraw-Hill Education; Page 205: © Martin Strmiska/ Alamy RF; Page 206: © Don Farrall/Photodisc/ Getty Images RF; 6.4: © McGraw-Hill Education/Louis Rosenstock, photographer; Page 219: © Ingram Publishing/SuperStock RF; 6.6a: © David M. Phillips/Science Source; 6.6b: © David M. Phillips/Science Source; 6.6c: © David M. Phillips/Science Source;

6.7: © Sean Justice/Corbis RF; Page 222 (top right): Courtesy of Rita Colwell, National Science Foundation; 6.8a-b: © McGraw-Hill Education/Louis Rosenstock, photographer; Page 228: © AJ Photo/Science Source.

### Chapter 7

Opener: © Jorg Greuel/Getty Images RF; Page 235: U.S. Coast Guard; Page 238: Warren Gretz/National Renewable Energy Laboratory/U.S. Department of Energy; Page 242: © McGraw-Hill Education/Jill Braaten, photographer; 7.9: © McGraw-Hill Education/Ken Karp, photographer; Page 248: © Alan Marsh/DesignPics/PunchStock RF; Page 251: © mykidsmom/Getty Images RF; 7.15: © McGraw-Hill Education/Ken Karp, photographer; 7.16: © McGraw-Hill Education/Ken Karp, photographer; Page 263: © McGraw-Hill Education/Louis Rosenstock, photographer.

### Chapter 8

Opener: © Richard Carey/Getty Images RF; Page 271: © Evgeny Terentev/Getty Images RF; 8.1: © ballyscanlon/Photodisc/Getty Images RF; 8.5a: © McGraw-Hill Education/ Charles D. Winters, photographer; 8.5b: © McGraw-Hill Education; Page 283: © Steve Cole/Vetta/Getty Images RF; Page 284: © Danita Delimont/Alamy RF; Page 285 (center left): © McGraw-Hill Education/ Stephen Frisch, photographer; Page 285 (center): © McGraw-Hill Education/Stephen Frisch, photographer; Page 287 (center right): © McGraw-Hill Education/Louis Rosenstock, photographer; Page 287 (center left): © McGraw-Hill Education/Louis Rosenstock, photographer; Page 289: © Terry Wild Studio/McGraw-Hill Education; Page 292: © McGraw-Hill Higher Education/Auburn University Photographic Services; Page 294: © McGraw-Hill Education/Louis Rosenstock, photographer.

### Chapter 9

Opener: © Javier Larrea/Pixtal/Age Fotostock RF; Page 302: © Mark Kostich/Vetta/Getty Images RF; Page 305: Space Telescope Science Institute (STScI)/NASA; Page 313: © Ingram Publishing RF; 9.3: © Gianni Tortoli/Science Source; Page 315: © Brand X Pictures/ Alamy RF; 9.6: NRC File Photo/U.S. Nuclear Regulatory Commission (NRC); Page 317: © Steve Allen/Brand X Pictures/Alamy RF; Page 318: © Science Photo Library- MIRIAMMASLO/Brand X Pictures/Getty Images; 9.7: © Blair Seitz/Science Source; Page 321 (top right): © Don Carstens/Artville RF; 9.8: © Bristol-Myers Squibb Medical Imaging; 9.9: © U.S. DoE/Mark Marten/ Science Source; 9.1: © Stockbyte/Punchstock RF; 9.11: © Arthur S Aubry/Photodisc/Getty Images RF; Page 325: © Keith Eng.

## Chapter 10

Opener: © Digital Vision/PunchStock RF; Page 336: IODP/NOAA/John W. Beck, Marine Laboratory Specialist (Photographer); Page 356: © Digital Stock/Corbis RF; Page 357 (center right): © Digital Stock/Corbis RF; Page 357 (top right): © C Squared Studios/Photodisc/Getty Images RF; Page 358: © Ingram Publishing/Fotosearch RF; Page 360: © Royalty-Free/DigitalStock/Corbis RF.

## Chapter 11

Opener: © Digital Vision/Getty Images RF; Page 371: © Photolink/Photodisc/Getty Images RF; Page 372: (center left) © F. Schussler/PhotoLink/Getty Images RF; Page 372 (bottom left): © BananaStock/PunchStock RF; Page 377: © Martia lColomb/Photodisc/Getty Images RF; Page 378: © Steven P. Lynch; Page 384: (center right) © Andrew Dernie/Photodisc/Getty Images RF; Page 384: (top right) © Ingram Publishing/SuperStock RF; Page 384 (bottom right): © Steven P. Lynch; Page 385: © Akira Kaede/Digital Vision/Getty Images RF; Page 387: © Photodisc/Getty Images RF; 11.4: © McGraw-Hill Education/Ken Karp, photographer; Page 397: © moodboard/Corbis RF.

## Chapter 12

Opener: © C Squared Studios/Photodisc/Getty Images RF; Page 416: © Barry Gregg/Corbis RF; 12.3: © PhotoLink/Getty Images RF; Page 424: © C. Sherburne/PhotoLink/Getty Images RF; 12.4: © Stan Fellerman/DigitalStock/Corbis RF; Page 435: © Food Collection/StockFood RF; 12.8: © Glow Wellness/Getty Images; 12.9: © Photodisc/Getty Images RF; Page 442: © Photodisc Collection/Getty Images RF.

## Chapter 13

Opener: © Iconotec RF; Page 454 (top right): © Andrew Syred/Science Source; Page 454: (bottom left) © Víctor Suárez/Age Fotostock; Page 457: © Photodisc/Getty Images RF; Page 460: © IZA Stock/Getty Images RF; Page 460: (center left) © PhotoLink/Photodisc/Getty Images RF; Page 461: (center right) © IT Stock/Punch Stock RF; Page 461: (center left) © Goodshoot/PunchStock RF; Page 461: (bottom center) © Dynamic Graphics Group/Punch Stock RF; Page 461: (bottom right) © John Foxx Images/Imagestate Media RF; Page 461: (center) © Eisenhut and Mayer Wien/Photolibrary/Getty Images; 13.4a-c: © McGraw-Hill Education/Charles D. Winters, photographer; 13.5: © Andrew Lambert Photography/Science Source; Page 469: © Michael Grayson/Flickr RF/Getty Images RF.

## Chapter 14

Opener: © Stockbyte/Corbis RF; Page 484: © peng wu/Getty Images; Page 487: © Digital Stock/Corbis RF; Page 490: © Reuters/Corbis; Page 502 (center right): © Digital Stock/Corbis RF; Page 502 (center left): © S. Alden/PhotoLink/Getty Images RF; Page 502 (center): © C Squared Studios/Photodisc/Getty Images RF; Page 502 (center): © John A. Rizzo/Photodisc/Getty Images RF; Page 502 (bottom center): © Digital Stock/Corbis RF; Page 502 (bottom left): © Digital Stock/Corbis RF; Page 502 (bottom right): © Digital Stock/Corbis RF.

## Chapter 15

Opener: © Parvinder Sethi; Page 525: © Spike Mafford/Photodisc/Getty Images RF; Page 531: © Duncan Smith/SPL/Science Source; Page 532: © Creatas/PunchStock RF; Page 539 (top left): © Digital Stock/Corbis RF; Page 539 (top center): © Digital Stock/Corbis RF; Page 539 (top right): © Hobbs/PhotoLink/Getty Images RF; Page 540: © Steven P. Lynch; Page 552 (top right): © Photodisc/PhotoLink/Getty Images RF; Page 552 (top right): © Phil Larkin, CSIRO Plant Industry.

## Chapter 16

Opener: © Phanie/Science Source; 16.1: Scott Bauer/U.S. Department of Agriculture; 16.2: © Mitch Hrdlicka/Photodisc/Getty Images RF; Page 567: © Steve Gschmeissner/SPL/Getty Images RF; 16.3: © Royalty-Free/Corbis; Page 576: © Digital Stock/Corbis RF; Page 580 (top left): Keith Weller/U.S. Department of Agriculture; Page 580 (center left): © McGraw-Hill Education/Jill Braaten, photographer; Page 581: © M. Freeman/Photodisc/PhotoLink/Getty Images RF; Page 582 (center): © Food Collection/SuperStock RF; Page 582 (center left): © Food and Drink Photos/Alamy; Page 586: © JGI/Blend Images/Getty Images RF; Page 587: © Pixtal/SuperStock RF; Page 589: © John A. Rizzo/Photodisc/Getty Images RF; Page 591: © Digital Stock/Corbis RF.

## Chapter 17

Opener: © Steve Satushek/Getty Images; Page 603 (center right): © Chris Shorten/Cole Group/Photodisc/Getty Image RF; Page 603 (center): © Cole Group/Photodisc/Getty Images RF; Page 604: © Michael Lamotte/Cole Group/Photodisc/Getty Images RF; Page 617: © Photodisc/Photo Link/Getty Images RF; Page 618: © Photodisc/Getty Images RF; Page 619: © Steven P .Lynch; 17.1: © James Dennis/Phototake; Page 626: © Royalty-Free/Corbis.

## Chapter 18

Opener: © Fotohunter/Getty Images; Page 642: © Pat Hastings/Getty Images; Page 644: © SW Productions/Photodisc/Getty Images RF; 18.14: © Meckes/Ottawa/Science Source; Page 653 (bottom center): © C. Sherburne/Photo Link/Getty Images RF; Page 655 (top right): © Burke/Triolo Productions/Brand X Pictures/Getty Images RF; Page 655 (top right): © Michael Lamotte/Cole Group/Photodisc/Getty Images RF; Page 655 (center right): © McGraw-Hill Education/Bob Coyle, photographer; Page 656: © Laszlo Selly/Getty Images; Page 657: © Vibe Images/Getty Images.

## Chapter 19

Opener: Courtesy Dr. Robert E. Shoemaker; Page 667: © Comstock Images/Alamy RF; Page 672: Courtesy of Adam Melonas/www .madridlab.net/melonas/adam-melonas; Page 678: © Laguna Design/Getty Images.

## Chapter 20

Opener: © Barbara Penoyar/Photodisc/Getty Images RF; Page 706: © Randy Allbritton/Photodisc/Getty Images RF; Page 726: © Photodisc Collection/Getty Images RF; Page 731 (bottom left): Dr. Charles S. Helling/USDA; Page 731 (top right): © Courtesy of Orchid Cellmark, Germantown, Maryland.

## Chapter 21

Opener: © Chris Falkenstein/Photodisc/Getty Images RF; Page 744: © Barry Gregg/Spirit/Corbis RF; Page 755: © Karl Weatherly/Photodisc/Getty Images RF; Page 757: © McGraw-Hill Education/Louis Rosenstock, photographer; Page 761: Tech. Sgt. Tracy L. DeMarc/U.S. Air Force.

## Chapter 22

Opener: © Chris Falkenstein/Photodisc/Getty Images RF; 22.1a: © CNRI/Phototake; Page 778 (top left): © Digital Vision/Getty Images RF; Page 778 (top right): © Photodisc/Photo Link/Getty Images RF.

## Chapter 23

Opener: © Emilio Simion/Getty Images RF; Page 819: © Ryan McVay/Photodisc/Getty Images RF.

# Text Credits

## Chapter 1

Page 8, Figure 1.5: Janice Smith, *General, Organic, & Biological Chemistry*, 3e, 2015, pg. 4, figure 1.3. Copyright © 2015 by McGraw-Hill Education. All rights reserved. Used with permission.

## Chapter 2

Page 53, Figure 2.7: Raymond Chang & Kenneth Goldsby, *General Chemistry The Essential Concepts*, 7e, 2013, p. 216, figure 7.3. Copyright © 2013 by McGraw-Hill Education. All rights reserved. Used with permission.

## Chapter 5

Page 189, Figure 5.8: Rich Bauer, James Birk & Pamela Marks, *Introduction to Chemistry*, 2e, p. 388, figure 10.15. Copyright © 2009 by McGraw-Hill Education. All rights reserved. Used with permission.

## Chapter 10

Page 354: Francis Carey & Robert Giuliano, *Organic Chemistry* 9e, 2013, p. 97. Copyright © 2013 by McGraw-Hill Education. All rights reserved. Used with permission.

## Chapter 12

Page 417: Francis Carey & Robert Giuliano, Organic Chemistry 9e, 2013, p. 138. Copyright © 2013 by McGraw-Hill Education. All rights reserved. Used with permission.

# Index

REPRESENTATIVE ELEMENTS

**Key**

| 1 | — Atomic number |
|---|---|
| **H** | — Symbol |
| Hydrogen | |
| 1.008 | — Atomic mass |

**Legend**
- Metals (main group)
- Metals (transition)
- Metals (inner transition)
- Metalloids
- Nonmetals
- Unknown

── TRANSITION ELEMENTS ──

| Period | IA (1) | IIA (2) | IIIB (3) | IVB (4) | VB (5) | VIB (6) | VIIB (7) | VIIIB (8) | VIIIB (9) | VIIIB (10) | IB (11) | IIB (12) | IIIA (13) | IVA (14) | VA (15) | VIA (16) | VIIA (17) | VIIIA (18) |
|---|---|---|---|---|---|---|---|---|---|---|---|---|---|---|---|---|---|---|
| 1 | 1 **H** Hydrogen 1.008 | | | | | | | | | | | | | | | | | 2 **He** Helium 4.003 |
| 2 | 3 **Li** Lithium 6.941 | 4 **Be** Beryllium 9.012 | | | | | | | | | | | 5 **B** Boron 10.81 | 6 **C** Carbon 12.01 | 7 **N** Nitrogen 14.01 | 8 **O** Oxygen 16.00 | 9 **F** Fluorine 19.00 | 10 **Ne** Neon 20.18 |
| 3 | 11 **Na** Sodium 22.99 | 12 **Mg** Magnesium 24.31 | | | | | | | | | | | 13 **Al** Aluminum 26.98 | 14 **Si** Silicon 28.09 | 15 **P** Phosphorus 30.97 | 16 **S** Sulfur 32.07 | 17 **Cl** Chlorine 35.45 | 18 **Ar** Argon 39.95 |
| 4 | 19 **K** Potassium 39.10 | 20 **Ca** Calcium 40.08 | 21 **Sc** Scandium 44.96 | 22 **Ti** Titanium 47.88 | 23 **V** Vanadium 50.94 | 24 **Cr** Chromium 52.00 | 25 **Mn** Manganese 54.94 | 26 **Fe** Iron 55.85 | 27 **Co** Cobalt 58.93 | 28 **Ni** Nickel 58.69 | 29 **Cu** Copper 63.55 | 30 **Zn** Zinc 65.39 | 31 **Ga** Gallium 69.72 | 32 **Ge** Germanium 72.61 | 33 **As** Arsenic 74.92 | 34 **Se** Selenium 78.96 | 35 **Br** Bromine 79.90 | 36 **Kr** Krypton 83.80 |
| 5 | 37 **Rb** Rubidium 85.47 | 38 **Sr** Strontium 87.62 | 39 **Y** Yttrium 88.91 | 40 **Zr** Zirconium 91.22 | 41 **Nb** Niobium 92.91 | 42 **Mo** Molybdenum 95.94 | 43 **Tc** Technetium (98) | 44 **Ru** Ruthenium 101.1 | 45 **Rh** Rhodium 102.9 | 46 **Pd** Palladium 106.4 | 47 **Ag** Silver 107.9 | 48 **Cd** Cadmium 112.4 | 49 **In** Indium 114.8 | 50 **Sn** Tin 118.7 | 51 **Sb** Antimony 121.8 | 52 **Te** Tellurium 127.6 | 53 **I** Iodine 126.9 | 54 **Xe** Xenon 131.3 |
| 6 | 55 **Cs** Cesium 132.9 | 56 **Ba** Barium 137.3 | 57 **La** Lanthanum 138.9 | 72 **Hf** Hafnium 178.5 | 73 **Ta** Tantalum 180.9 | 74 **W** Tungsten 183.9 | 75 **Re** Rhenium 186.2 | 76 **Os** Osmium 190.2 | 77 **Ir** Iridium 192.2 | 78 **Pt** Platinum 195.1 | 79 **Au** Gold 197.0 | 80 **Hg** Mercury 200.6 | 81 **Tl** Thallium 204.4 | 82 **Pb** Lead 207.2 | 83 **Bi** Bismuth 209.0 | 84 **Po** Polonium (209) | 85 **At** Astatine (210) | 86 **Rn** Radon (222) |
| 7 | 87 **Fr** Francium (223) | 88 **Ra** Radium (226) | 89 **Ac** Actinium (227) | 104 **Rf** Rutherfordium (261) | 105 **Db** Dubnium (262) | 106 **Sg** Seaborgium (266) | 107 **Bh** Bohrium (262) | 108 **Hs** Hassium (265) | 109 **Mt** Meitnerium (266) | 110 **Ds** Darmstadtium (281) | 111 **Rg** Roentgenium (272) | 112 **Cn** Copernicium (277) | 113 **Uut** Ununtrium (284) | 114 **Fl** Flerovium (285) | 115 **Uup** Ununpentium (288) | 116 **Lv** Livermorium (289) | 117 **Uus** Ununseptium (294) | 118 **Uuo** Ununoctium (294) |

── INNER TRANSITION ELEMENTS ──

| 6 Lanthanides | 58 **Ce** Cerium 140.1 | 59 **Pr** Praseodymium 140.9 | 60 **Nd** Neodymium 144.2 | 61 **Pm** Promethium (147) | 62 **Sm** Samarium 150.4 | 63 **Eu** Europium 152.0 | 64 **Gd** Gadolinium 157.3 | 65 **Tb** Terbium 158.9 | 66 **Dy** Dysprosium 162.5 | 67 **Ho** Holmium 164.9 | 68 **Er** Erbium 167.3 | 69 **Tm** Thulium 168.9 | 70 **Yb** Ytterbium 173.0 | 71 **Lu** Lutetium 175.0 |
|---|---|---|---|---|---|---|---|---|---|---|---|---|---|---|
| 7 Actinides | 90 **Th** Thorium 232.0 | 91 **Pa** Protactinium (231) | 92 **U** Uranium 238.0 | 93 **Np** Neptunium (237) | 94 **Pu** Plutonium (242) | 95 **Am** Americium (243) | 96 **Cm** Curium (247) | 97 **Bk** Berkelium (247) | 98 **Cf** Californium (251) | 99 **Es** Einsteinium (252) | 100 **Fm** Fermium (257) | 101 **Md** Mendelevium (258) | 102 **No** Nobelium (259) | 103 **Lr** Lawrencium (260) |

The 1–18 group designation is recommended (International Union of Pure and Applied Chemistry) but not widely used. This text also uses standard U.S. notation for groups (IA–VIIIA and IB–VIIIB).

# List of the Elements with Their Symbols and Atomic Masses*

| Element | Symbol | Atomic Number | Atomic Mass | Element | Symbol | Atomic Number | Atomic Mass |
|---------|--------|---------------|-------------|---------|--------|---------------|-------------|
| Actinium | Ac | 89 | (227) | Mendelevium | Md | 101 | (256) |
| Aluminum | Al | 13 | 26.98 | Mercury | Hg | 80 | 200.6 |
| Americium | Am | 95 | (243) | Molybdenum | Mo | 42 | 95.94 |
| Antimony | Sb | 51 | 121.8 | Neodymium | Nd | 60 | 144.2 |
| Argon | Ar | 18 | 39.95 | Neon | Ne | 10 | 20.18 |
| Arsenic | As | 33 | 74.92 | Neptunium | Np | 93 | (237) |
| Astatine | At | 85 | (210) | Nickel | Ni | 28 | 58.69 |
| Barium | Ba | 56 | 137.3 | Niobium | Nb | 41 | 92.91 |
| Berkelium | Bk | 97 | (247) | Nitrogen | N | 7 | 14.01 |
| Beryllium | Be | 4 | 9.012 | Nobelium | No | 102 | (253) |
| Bismuth | Bi | 83 | 209.0 | Osmium | Os | 76 | 190.2 |
| Bohrium | Bh | 107 | (262) | Oxygen | O | 8 | 16.00 |
| Boron | B | 5 | 10.81 | Palladium | Pd | 46 | 106.4 |
| Bromine | Br | 35 | 79.90 | Phosphorus | P | 15 | 30.97 |
| Cadmium | Cd | 48 | 112.4 | Platinum | Pt | 78 | 195.1 |
| Calcium | Ca | 20 | 40.08 | Plutonium | Pu | 94 | (242) |
| Californium | Cf | 98 | (249) | Polonium | Po | 84 | (210) |
| Carbon | C | 6 | 12.01 | Potassium | K | 19 | 39.10 |
| Cerium | Ce | 58 | 140.1 | Praseodymium | Pr | 59 | 140.9 |
| Cesium | Cs | 55 | 132.9 | Promethium | Pm | 61 | (147) |
| Chlorine | Cl | 17 | 35.45 | Protactinium | Pa | 91 | (231) |
| Chromium | Cr | 24 | 52.00 | Radium | Ra | 88 | (226) |
| Cobalt | Co | 27 | 58.93 | Radon | Rn | 86 | (222) |
| Copernicium | Cn | 112 | (227) | Rhenium | Re | 75 | 186.2 |
| Copper | Cu | 29 | 63.55 | Rhodium | Rh | 45 | 102.9 |
| Curium | Cm | 96 | (247) | Roentgenium | Rg | 111 | (272) |
| Darmstadtium | Ds | 110 | (281) | Rubidium | Rb | 37 | 85.47 |
| Dubnium | Db | 105 | (262) | Ruthenium | Ru | 44 | 101.1 |
| Dysprosium | Dy | 66 | 162.5 | Rutherfordium | Rf | 104 | (257) |
| Einsteinium | Es | 99 | (254) | Samarium | Sm | 62 | 150.4 |
| Erbium | Er | 68 | 167.3 | Scandium | Sc | 21 | 44.96 |
| Europium | Eu | 63 | 152.0 | Seaborgium | Sg | 106 | (263) |
| Fermium | Fm | 100 | (253) | Selenium | Se | 34 | 78.96 |
| Flerovium | Fl | 114 | (285) | Silicon | Si | 14 | 28.09 |
| Fluorine | F | 9 | 19.00 | Silver | Ag | 47 | 107.9 |
| Francium | Fr | 87 | (223) | Sodium | Na | 11 | 22.99 |
| Gadolinium | Gd | 64 | 157.3 | Strontium | Sr | 38 | 87.62 |
| Gallium | Ga | 31 | 69.72 | Sulfur | S | 16 | 32.07 |
| Germanium | Ge | 32 | 72.59 | Tantalum | Ta | 73 | 180.9 |
| Gold | Au | 79 | 197.0 | Technetium | Tc | 43 | (99) |
| Hafnium | Hf | 72 | 178.5 | Tellurium | Te | 52 | 127.6 |
| Hassium | Hs | 108 | (265) | Terbium | Tb | 65 | 158.9 |
| Helium | He | 2 | 4.003 | Thallium | Tl | 81 | 204.4 |
| Holmium | Ho | 67 | 164.9 | Thorium | Th | 90 | 232.0 |
| Hydrogen | H | 1 | 1.008 | Thulium | Tm | 69 | 168.9 |
| Indium | In | 49 | 114.8 | Tin | Sn | 50 | 118.7 |
| Iodine | I | 53 | 126.9 | Titanium | Ti | 22 | 47.88 |
| Iridium | Ir | 77 | 192.2 | Tungsten | W | 74 | 183.9 |
| Iron | Fe | 26 | 55.85 | Ununoctium | Uuo | 118 | (294) |
| Krypton | Kr | 36 | 83.80 | Ununpentium | Uup | 115 | (288) |
| Lanthanum | La | 57 | 138.9 | Ununseptium | Uus | 117 | (294) |
| Lawrencium | Lr | 103 | (257) | Ununtrium | Uut | 113 | (284) |
| Lead | Pb | 82 | 207.2 | Uranium | U | 92 | 238.0 |
| Lithium | Li | 3 | 6.941 | Vanadium | V | 23 | 50.94 |
| Livermorium | Lv | 116 | (289) | Xenon | Xe | 54 | 131.3 |
| Lutetium | Lu | 71 | 175.0 | Ytterbium | Yb | 70 | 173.0 |
| Magnesium | Mg | 12 | 24.31 | Yttrium | Y | 39 | 88.91 |
| Manganese | Mn | 25 | 54.94 | Zinc | Zn | 30 | 65.39 |
| Meitnerium | Mt | 109 | (266) | Zirconium | Zr | 40 | 91.22 |

*All atomic masses have four significant figures except radioactive elements that have no stable isotope. For these elements, masses of the longest-lived isotope are given in parentheses. These values are recommended by the Committee on Teaching of Chemistry, International Union of Pure and Applied Chemistry.

## PRINCIPAL FUNCTIONAL GROUPS IN ORGANIC COMPOUNDS

| Type of Compound | Structural Formula | Condensed Formula | Chapter Reference | Example Structural Formula | Example IUPAC Name | Example Common Name |
|---|---|---|---|---|---|---|
| Alcohol | R—O—H | ROH | 12 | $CH_3CH_2$—O—H | Ethanol | Ethyl alcohol |
| Aldehyde | R—C(=O)—H | RCHO | 13 | $CH_3$C(=O)—H | Ethanal | Acetaldehyde |
| Amide | R—C(=O)—N(H)—H | $RCONH_2$ | 15 | $CH_3$C(=O)—N(H)—H | Ethanamide | Acetamide |
| Amine | R—N(H)—H | $RNH_2$ | 15 | $CH_3CH_2$N(H)—H | Ethanamine | Ethylamine |
| Carboxylic acid | R—C(=O)—O—H | RCOOH | 14 | $CH_3$C(=O)—O—H | Ethanoic acid | Acetic acid |
| Ester | R—C(=O)—O—R' | RCOOR' | 14 | $CH_3$C(=O)—$OCH_3$ | Methyl ethanoate | Methyl acetate |
| Ether | R—O—R' | ROR' | 12 | $CH_3OCH_3$ | Methoxymethane | Dimethyl ether |
| Halide | —Cl (or —Br, —F, —I) | RCl | 10 | $CH_3CH_2Cl$ | Chloroethane | Ethyl chloride |
| Ketone | R—C(=O)—R' | RCOR' | 13 | $CH_3$C(=O)$CH_3$ | Propanone | Acetone |

## METRIC PREFIXES

| Multiple | Prefix | Symbol | Submultiple | Prefix | Symbol |
|----------|--------|--------|-------------|--------|--------|
| $10^{12}$ | tera | T | $10^{-1}$ | deci | d |
| $10^9$ | giga | G | $10^{-2}$ | centi | c |
| $10^6$ | mega | M | $10^{-3}$ | milli | m |
| $10^3$ | kilo | k | $10^{-6}$ | micro | μ |
| $10^2$ | hecto | h | $10^{-9}$ | nano | n |
| $10^1$ | deka | da | $10^{-12}$ | pico | p |

## CONVERSION FACTORS

**Length:**
1 meter (m) = 39.4 inches (in)
1 inch (in) = 2.54 centimeters (cm)
1 Ångstrom (Å) = $10^{-10}$ meter (m)

**Mass:**
1 kilogram (kg) = 2.20 pounds (lb)
1 pound (lb) = 454 grams (g)
1 atomic mass unit (amu)
   = $1.6605 \times 10^{-24}$ grams (g)

**Volume:**
1 liter (L) = 1000 milliliters (mL)
   = 1000 cm$^3$
1 liter (L) = 1.06 quarts (qt)

**Energy:**
1 calorie (cal) = 4.18 joules (J)

**Temperature:**
$T_{°F} = (1.8 \times T_{°C}) + 32$
$T_{°C} = \dfrac{(T_{°F} - 32)}{1.8}$
$T_K = T_{°C} + 273.15$

**Pressure:**
1 atmosphere (atm) = 14.7 lbs/in$^2$ (psi)
1 atm = 760 millimeters of mercury
   (760 mm Hg = 760 torr)

## PHYSICAL CONSTANTS

**Avogadro's number:** $6.022 \times 10^{23}$ units/mol

**Speed of light:** $3.0 \times 10^8$ m/sec

**Gas constant (R):** $0.0821$ L · atm · K$^{-1}$ · mol$^{-1}$

**Mass of an electron:** $9.1094 \times 10^{-28}$ g
   or
$5.486 \times 10^{-4}$ amu

**Mass of a proton:** $1.6726 \times 10^{-24}$ g
   or
1.007 amu

**Mass of a neutron:** $1.6750 \times 10^{-24}$ g
   or
1.009 amu

**Volume of one mole
   of ideal gas:** 22.4 L (@ 273 K and 1 atm)